Dear Adam
What a happy
resolved to write
that you ?

...fault; and an emb...
...sifts if...
him? W...

...Recto...
...lcot
Oxon OX 11
3 OCT 1994

CHURCH,
...ORD.

OXFORD
7 15 PM
8 JNE
1953
A

ITHE

Lady Alexandra Howard
Birchfield
Melrose
Scotland

Oriel College,
Oxford.

11/10/59

just tled from Sunday
Oriel : I wish that
diners were less dull or
ore drinkable!
rave at any rate
to write you a
do hope you are
wish you were
...on are better in
...wood is th...
there.

HUGH TREVOR-ROPER

Also by Adam Sisman

A.J.P. Taylor: A Biography
Boswell's Presumptuous Task: Writing the Life of Dr Johnson
The Friendship: Wordsworth and Coleridge

Michael Wardle
2010

HUGH
TREVOR-ROPER

The Biography

ADAM SISMAN

Adam Sisman

Weidenfeld & Nicolson
LONDON

First published in Great Britain in 2010
by Weidenfeld & Nicolson

1 3 5 7 9 10 8 6 4 2

© Adam Sisman 2010

A CIP catalogue record for this book
is available from the British Library.

ISBN: 978 0 297 85214 8

Typeset by Input Data Services Ltd,
Bridgwater, Somerset

Printed and bound in the UK by
CPI Mackays, Chatham, Kent

The Orion Publishing Group's policy is to use papers that
are natural, renewable and recyclable products and made
from wood grown in sustainable forests. The logging and
manufacturing processes are expected to conform to
environmental regulations of the country of origin.

Weidenfeld & Nicolson

Orion Publishing Group Ltd
Orion House
5 Upper Saint Martin's Lane
London, WC2H 9EA
An Hachette UK Company

www.orionbooks.co.uk

Contents

List of Illustrations	vii
Acknowledgements	ix
Foreword	xv

1	Boy	1
2	Carthusian	17
3	Undergraduate	25
4	Researcher	43
5	Cadet	66
6	Soldier	77
7	Major	92
8	Sleuth	122
9	Student	143
10	Traveller	164
11	Historian	183
12	Destroyer	202
13	Lover	223
14	Husband	257
15	Professor	278
16	Scholar	298
17	Controversialist	328
18	Essayist	359
19	Ghostwriter	383
20	Spy	409
21	Lord	430
22	Master	454
23	Expert	475
24	Stoic	507

Books by Hugh Trevor-Roper	541
Notes	542
Index	575

List of Illustrations

Unless credited otherwise, all pictures are reproduced courtesy of the Estate of Hugh Trevor-Roper. While every effort has been made to trace copyright holders, if any have been inadvertently overlooked the publishers will be happy to acknowledge them in future editions.

FIRST SECTION

In nursery clothes, *c.* 1917
With his sister Sheila and his brother Patrick
Bertie Trevor-Roper in the garden of Alnwick
Kathleen Trevor-Roper
On the Northumberland shoreline
Belhaven Hill preparatory school, *c.* 1927 (*Belhaven Hill*)
Rowing on Ullswater
Daviesites, Charterhouse, *c.* 1932 (*Charterhouse*)
The three Trevor-Roper siblings, 1931
With 'Hazel', mid 1930s
Relaxing during a country walk
On Mont St Victoire, spring 1934
On horseback
Logan Pearsall Smith, portrait by Ethel Sands (*National Portrait Gallery, London*)
J.C. Masterman (*Senior Common Room, Christ Church, Oxford*)
Father Martin D'Arcy, portrait by Wyndham Lewis (© Wyndham Lewis and the estate of the late Mrs G.A. Wyndham Lewis by kind permission of the Wyndham Lewis Memorial Trust)
Lieutenant Trevor-Roper, *c.* 1939.
Hitler's ruined bunker, May 1945 (*Getty*)

SECOND SECTION

Photograph of the newly elected Student taken for the Senior Common Room album (*Senior Common Room, Christ Church, Oxford*)
The young historian in his Peckwater Quad rooms, *c.* 1950
Lawrence Stone (*Elizabeth Stone*)

Isaiah Berlin (*Isaiah Berlin Literary Trust*)

Christopher Hill (*Master and Fellows of Balliol, Oxford*)

Hugh and A.J. Ayer listen to a speech by Arthur Koestler at Congress for Cultural Freedom, Berlin 1950

About to set out with Alan Clark, Boxing Day 1947 (*Jane Clark*)

Bernard Berenson examines a picture (*I Tatti*)

As Robert Blake's best man, 1953

With Mary Roxburghe and Mollie Buccleuch at Drumlanrig, Dumfriesshire (*Xenia Howard-Johnston*)

A.L. Rowse, 1950 (*Getty*)

Lady Alexandra ('Xandra') Howard-Johnston, May 1948 (*Xenia Howard-Johnston*)

Xandra at Armistice Day, Edinburgh 1937 (*Xenia Howard-Johnston*)

'Johnny' Howard-Johnston (*Xenia Howard-Johnston*)

Xenia Howard-Johnston (*Xenia Howard-Johnston*)

James Howard-Johnston (*Xenia Howard-Johnston*)

Earl Haig ('Dawyck') (*Xenia Howard-Johnston*)

The Regius Professor and his wife on the leads at 8 St Aldates, August 1957 (*Mark Gerson*)

THIRD SECTION

With scholar's hat and gown during the Chancellorship election, March 1960 (*Getty*)

A televised debate with A.J.P. Taylor, chaired by Robert Kee (*BBC Photograph Library*)

A delegation to China organised by the SACU, September 1965

LSE Oration Day, 5 December 1968 (*Getty*)

The Trevor-Ropers in Pakistan, spring 1972 (*Xenia Howard-Johnston*)

With Edward Heath, Harold Macmillan and Harold Wilson, 25 September 1973 (*Press Association*)

With Pope John Paul II, 14 January 1992

Maurice Cowling conducting a supervision (*Master and Fellows of Peterhouse, Cambridge*)

The Dacres aboard a Cambridge punt (*Country Homes and Interiors*)

At the offices of *The Times* (*Lebrecht*)

Rupert Murdoch (*Getty)*

'Piece in Our Times', May 1983 (*Private Eye*)

Returning to England after the disastrous *Stern* press conference, 25 April 1983 (*Press Association*)

The historian in old age (*Ellen Warner*)

Acknowledgements

My greatest debt is to Hugh Trevor-Roper's friend and literary executor Blair Worden, who has helped me at every stage in the writing of this book. His knowledge of my subject has been a most valuable resource. He read each chapter as soon as it was written and offered useful feedback, but never attempted to impose his perceptions on mine, or dictate what I should or should not write. We have held many long and enjoyable conversations about my subject, in a variety of settings: striding along a river bank, watching a cricket match, in cars and car parks, in various restaurants (mainly Greek), cafés, and most of all in pubs. I am enormously grateful to him for his guidance throughout. I am especially grateful too to another of Trevor-Roper's executors, his stepson James Howard-Johnston, who gave me several long and revealing interviews, entertained me to lunch and dinner at his college, and made many useful comments on my typescript, steering me away from social gaffes with skill and tact.

Another person who read my book as it was being written is my old friend Richard Davenport-Hines, who covered my typescript pages with perspicacious comments in green or red ink. I thank him warmly for his generous help. I am grateful to him too for providing transcriptions of letters from the archive at I Tatti. I must express special thanks also to Judith Curthoys, Colin Kidd and Valerie Pearl, each of whom read the complete text in typescript and offered helpful comments: and to thank those who read and commented on passages from the book, including Xenia Dennen, Sir John Elliott, Timothy Garton Ash, Ted Harrison, Eric Hobsbawm, Sir Peter Ramsbotham, John Robertson and Graham Stewart. Besides these, several other individuals who preferred not to be mentioned by name read either the complete text or part of it on my behalf. I am grateful to them all, and my book has benefited from their constructive criticism. However, I have not always taken the advice I have been given, and I bear sole responsibility for the account that follows.

Many other busy people have given up their time to write to me or talk to me about my subject. I have been almost overwhelmed by the hospitality and generosity shown to me by complete strangers, many of whom invited me into their homes and some of whom put me up for the night. I have been entertained to lunch, and consumed many cups of tea and glasses of wine. I am grateful to all of them, and I only wish that I had more space to thank them more graciously than in the following list: Donald Adamson, John Adamson, Lord Armstrong, the late Peter Avery, Michael Banton, Hugh Bayley, the late Lord Beaumont, Alan Bell, Michael Bentley, Michael Binyon, the late Lord Blake, Lord Briggs, Peter Brown, Peter Burke, Lord Carlisle, Sir Raymond Carr, Jeremy J. Cater, Jeremy Catto, Edward Chaney, Mrs J.C. ('Nim') Church, Barry Collett, I.J. (John) Croft, Tam Dalyell, Cliff Davies, Edward Devereux, Jessica Douglas-Home, the late Nan Dunbar, Sir John Elliott, Marion Elliot, Richard J. Evans, Robert Evans, Charles and Lady Kitty Farrell, Lady Antonia Fraser, Chris Friedrichs, Janice Furze, Irene Gaddo, Timothy Garton Ash, Sir Martin Gilbert, Frank Giles, the late Lord Gilmour, Trevor Grant, Hugh Griffith, Mark Griffith, the late Earl Haig, Raina Haig, Henry Hardy, Sir Brian Harrison, the late Sir Nicholas Henderson, Roger Highfield, Eric Hobsbawm, David Hopkins, Sir Peter Hordern, Sir Michael Howard, Angela Huth, Richard Ingrams, Eberhard Jäckel, Harold James, John Jolliffe, Hugh Kearney, the late Sir Ludovic Kennedy, Paul Kent, Bob King, Phillip Knightley, Lord Lawson, Mary Lefkovitz (Lady Lloyd-Jones), Magnus Linklater, Brian MacArthur, Father James McConica, Alan Macfarlane, Piers Mackesy, A.F. ('Freddie') Madden, Noel Malcolm, the late John Mason, Derwent May, Henry Mayr-Harting, Karl Miller, Alasdair Milne, Leslie Mitchell, John Morrill, the late Richard Ollard, Peter Oppenheimer, Nicholas O'Shaughnessy, Alasdair Palmer, Sheila Pargeter, Bill Parry, the late David Pears, Roger Pemberton, Andrei Pippidi, Nick Price, Sylvia Pritchard, Lord Quinton, Theodore K. Rabb, Sir Timothy Raison, Sir Peter Ramsbotham, Professor Piyo Rattansi, Lord Rees-Mogg, Richard Rhodes, W.R.B. Robinson, Michael Rogers, Paul Lawrence Rose, Lord Rothschild, Lady Mary Russell, Mark Seaman, Richard Searby, James Shiel, Jonathan Steinberg, James Stourton, John Stoye, Hartmut Pogge von Strandmann, David Sturdy, Virginia Surtees (formerly Ashley Clarke), Nicholas Tate, Gina Thomas, Lord Thomas, Sir Keith Thomas, William Thomas, Christopher Thompson, the late A.F. ('Pat') Thompson, Nicolas Thomson, D.R. (Richard) Thorpe, Sir Crispin Tickell, Lady Juliet Townsend, the late Patrick Trevor-Roper, Graham Turner, Penny Tyack, Colin Webb, Charles Webster, Lord Weidenfeld, Francis Wheen, Brian Young, Simon Young, Theodore Zeldin. If inadvertently I have omitted anyone I apologise.

Several current Fellows of Peterhouse, and those who were Fellows of Peterhouse at the time when Lord Dacre was Master (some of them now Emeritus or Honorary), granted me interviews, but since most of them asked or even pleaded not to be named in my acknowledgements it seems invidious to mention any. I am grateful to them all the same. In breach of this policy I should like thank the late Neil Plevy, who died at a tragically young age after this book was complete. I am very sorry that he did not live to see it in print.

I am also grateful to those, too numerous to name, who responded to my advertisements in *The Times Literary Supplement* and *Christ Church Matters*, or who responded to my circular letters to the old boys of Charterhouse or the old members of Christ Church.

The staff of various libraries and archives have lent me their professional help and guided me when I was lost. Most of all I want to thank Judith Curthoys, archivist at Christ Church, where Trevor-Roper's papers are kept. Judith allowed me to continue working on these despite the fact that the archive was officially closed for much of the time. I am hugely grateful to her for her assistance, her flexibility, and her unfailing good humour. I am grateful too to the staff of the Christ Church library for their hospitality, and for allowing me to join them during tea breaks, and even to share their chocolate biscuits. I must also extend special thanks to Rob Petre, who generously agreed to store the Trevor-Roper Papers at Oriel while the Christ Church archive was closed. As well as these two, I should like to thank the archivist of Trinity, Clare Hopkins, and Joanna Parker, Librarian of Worcester, for allowing me to examine papers in their possession. Julian Reid, archivist of Merton, gave me access to the college archives and patiently answered a number of my queries: as did Robin Darwall-Smith, archivist of both Univ and Magdalen. Dr Norma Aubertin-Potter, who presides over the Codrington Library at All Souls, granted me access to the Sparrow Papers, and Dr Simon Green kindly supplied me with information about Trevor-Roper's failed application for a Fellowship there. I am also grateful to the staff of the University Archives for supplying me with information on Trevor-Roper's university appointments, and for giving me access to records relating to the Ford Lectures; and to the staff of the Bodleian Library, especially Colin Harris and Helen Langley, for allowing me access to several of the collections within the Department of Western Manuscripts, particularly the papers of the late Harold Macmillan. Dr Martin Maw, archivist of the Oxford University Press, allowed me to examine material from the OUP archives, where I was amused to find a folder of letters and memoranda which I had written more than thirty years before.

I should like to thank Dr Patricia McGuire, archivist of King's College, Cambridge, for granting me access to the Annan Papers; Bill Noblett of the Cambridge University library, for access to the papers of the late J.H. (Sir Jack) Plumb and several others in their collections; and the staff of the Churchill Archive Centre at Churchill College, for access to the papers of Randolph Churchill, and for answering my questions about other collections. I am grateful also to the staff of the National Archives and Liddell

Hart Centre for Military Archives at King's College, London, and to the staff of the archives of the London School of Economics and Political Science, the Warburg Institute and the Royal Historical Society. I am especially grateful to Jeff Walden of the BBC Written Archives Centre at Caversham for his expert guidance, and for helping me with follow-up queries.

The Archivist of Macmillan Publishers, Alysoun Sanders, was a helpful and patient host. Dr Arnold Hunt, Curator of Historical Manuscripts at the British Library, showed me the out-letter books of Macmillan Publishers, and drew my attention to relevant letters in other collections. I am grateful to them both; as I am grateful to Helen Fraser of Penguin for permission to examine papers in the Hamish Hamilton collection, and to Rosemary Wynn, the assistant archivist for Special Collections at the Arts and Social Sciences Library of Bristol University, for showing these to me.

I should especially like to thank Dr Donald Adamson for providing me with transcriptions of letters from A.L. Rowse's largely unsorted papers.

I am particularly grateful to the editors of both *The Times* and *The Sunday Times* for giving me special permission to examine the files relating to the Hitler diaries affair ahead of the thirty-year embargo; and to Nicholas Mays, archivist of News International Limited, for facilitating this and for allowing me access to the other files relating to Trevor-Roper's thirty-five years as a contributor.

I must also thank Ann Wheeler, former Archivist at Charterhouse, and Michael Osborne, Headmaster of Belhaven Hill, for allowing me to examine material in the school archives and for showing me around the schools. Elizabeth Cripps kindly showed me around Chiefswood, and John Simms around No. 8 St Aldates; Philip Toothill showed me the rooms Trevor-Roper had occupied as an undergraduate and then as a Student of Christ Church.

I am indebted to all those who kindly supplied me with copies of Trevor-Roper letters in their possession, most of which (with specific exceptions) will be deposited in the Dacre archive at Christ Church. I also wish to thank all those who supplied me with pictures, particularly Trevor-Roper's stepdaughter Xenia Howard-Johnston and Andrew Threipland, who kindly lent me the albums entrusted to him by Hugh's brother Pat.

It is a little unusual for a publisher to feature as a character in a book appearing under his own imprint, but Lord Weidenfeld is an unusual publisher, without whom post-war publishing in Britain would have been less interesting and less fun. His acquaintance with Hugh Trevor-Roper began in the early 1950s, when he asked the young historian to edit *Hitler's Table-Talk*. Around this time Trevor-Roper became involved with a married woman, Lady Alexandra Howard-Johnston, and I discovered that for their clandestine assignations in various country hotels they registered under an assumed name, using Weidenfeld's London address – a revelation which delighted him fifty-five years later, when he generously took me to lunch at the Wolseley. Weidenfeld remains active in the firm that bears his name, and is still avid in pursuit of his quarry. On my mentioning the manuscript of an unpublished work in Trevor-Roper's archive, he instantly demanded whether the rights were available. I replied that, to the best of my knowledge, the rights were already his, since he had made a contract for the book some months before I was born.

I have been lucky enough to have had two sympathetic editors at Weidenfeld: Ben Buchan, who took on the book and looked after it in the early stages, and Ion Trewin, who stepped into Ben's shoes (and had been a champion of the book from the start). I am grateful to them both. It was particularly appropriate that Ion should handle the book, since he has recently completed a biography of Trevor-Roper's pupil Alan Clark. In 1963, after his book *The Donkeys* had gravely offended Lady Alexandra, Clark had written to his former tutor that 'our biographers will have fun with this correspondence'; we did. I am grateful to Ion for his many helpful suggestions. Another enjoyable aspect of being published by Weidenfeld has been the opportunity to work with my old friend Alan Samson, whose leftovers I inherited twenty-five years ago when I joined Macmillan. A further essential member of the editorial team has been Bea Hemming, one of the best young editors I have encountered in over thirty years' experience of book publishing. Linden Lawson made what seemed to me an excellent job of the copy-editing. I am grateful to her for her skill and professionalism.

Two other old friends from my publishing days have contributed to this book. Alan Williams has given me expert legal guidance, for which I am truly grafeful, even if I have sometimes appeared reluctant to accept it. Douglas Matthews has once again produced an excelled index, as he has done for my three previous books. I wish to express my gratitude to them both.

I also want to thank my agent Andrew Wylie, for always being there when I needed him.

Lastly, I want to express my great gratitude to my wife Robyn, for her support and encouragement throughout. Without this the book could not have been written.

Foreword

I have written several biographies, but none until now about an individual whom I had met. But I did meet Hugh Trevor-Roper, and came to know him fairly well. Writing his life has therefore been a departure for me.

I first met him at an Oxford party in 1977. He was then sixty-three, and Regius Professor of Modern History, with a worldwide reputation. I was in my early twenties, and a junior editor with Oxford University Press. I had forgotten the circumstances of this meeting until almost thirty years later, when I found in the OUP archives a letter I wrote to him the next day. I do remember that I approached him cautiously, aware that he could be acerbic, but found him surprisingly affable. Subsequently I invited him to lunch with two of my colleagues, which turned out to be a stiff occasion. Only later did it occur to me that he might be shy, causing him to retreat behind a screen of reserve.

We were in sporadic contact over the next dozen years, as I pursued my early career in publishing. I came to know him better in the early 1990s, while I was writing my first book, a biography of A.J.P. Taylor. He granted me several interviews and gave me copies of his letters from Taylor. He also read and commented on my draft typescript. I was grateful that he made no attempt to dictate my account of those episodes in which he had participated, in particular his contest with Taylor to become Regius Professor in 1957. 'Your version is not my version,' he said afterwards, 'but you have every right to tell it in the way that seems true to you.' He reviewed the book favourably when it was published in 1994. At the Oxford Union he and I re-enacted the debate between Taylor and Trevor-Roper over *The Origins of the Second World War* (I took Taylor's part). By this time we had become friendly, and I visited him now and then at his house, the Old Rectory in Didcot. One cold winter morning I arrived to find Hugh and his wife Xandra in a state of agitated distress, as water from a burst pipe streamed down the wall of their dining room, damaging wallpaper and pictures. The plight of this elderly couple, by then both infirm, made a pathetic impression. Though no plumber, I climbed into the roof-space and succeeded in stopping the leak.

At some stage the possibility arose that I might write his life. Until recently I had persuaded myself that the proposal came from him, but correspondence in his archive indicates that it originated from me. (This has been a salutary reminder of the unreliability of memory.) In any case he welcomed this tentative suggestion. 'I'm not sure if I'm worth a biography,' he said with feigned modesty, 'but if anyone is to write it, I should like it to be you.' We made no formal agreement, but talked regularly about his past, and he offered me glimpses of his dauntingly voluminous archive. He introduced me to his friend and literary executor, Blair Worden, who also encouraged me to write the book.

I last saw Hugh about ten days before his death. He was then in a hospice, and aware that the end was near, but he remained interested in the outside world to the last. 'What news,' he would ask, 'from the Republic of Letters?' I was never convinced that I was qualified to answer this question.

After Hugh's death I was given exclusive access to the biographical materials in his archive, then at Didcot, now housed at Christ Church. These include letters, notebooks, diaries and a draft memoir of his early life: a rich mine for a biographer to quarry. The materials in the archive were supplemented by a succession of further finds, including hundreds of love letters between Hugh and Xandra, then married to another man, during their clandestine affair – a correspondence of the most intimate and revealing nature. The letters emerged after Hugh's death from drawers in both his desk and hers, including a cache discovered in a secret drawer by the sleuth Alan Bell. Another box of letters, this time to his mother, was found by Hugh's stepdaughter Xenia Dennen at the bottom of a wardrobe when the house in Didcot was being cleared. Perhaps the most miraculous discovery of all was made by a college porter, who rescued more than a hundred of Hugh's uninhibited letters to an Oxford classicist (together with other treasures) from a Walton Street skip.

Hugh did not like being treated with too much reverence, and often quoted Gibbon's preference for praise 'seasoned with a reasonable admixture of acid'. He insisted that I should write whatever I liked, and his executors have given me a free rein. It is nevertheless possible that in writing Hugh Trevor-Roper's life I may have been influenced by feelings of loyalty, affection and gratitude. It would be false to deny the existence of such feelings. The reader must decide whether they have been a help or a hindrance to my understanding of his character.

In the book that follows I refer to my subject by his first name.* Though I knew him as 'Hugh', this is not the only reason. He took the title Lord Dacre when he became a peer in 1979; I felt that it would be awkward to

---

* I adopted the same policy in my biography of A.J.P. Taylor, referring to him as 'Alan', and I have been amused to note that one subsequent biographer refers to him as 'Taylor' and another as 'Alan Taylor'.

refer to my subject by one name for four-fifths of the book, and then by another for the remainder. There was a further difficulty, in that he continued to write under the name Hugh Trevor-Roper. It seemed simpler and clearer to refer to him as 'Hugh' throughout.

There is another policy which may require explanation. A number of people who were important to Hugh are not mentioned in this book: for example, several of those younger friends who enlivened his last two decades. A book which listed all those who played a significant part in Hugh's life would be tedious to read. In general, I took the view that individuals were as likely to feel relieved as they might be aggrieved to find their names not listed in the index.

The unreformed law of defamation has provided a further restraint. On legal advice I removed or modified a number of passages from my first draft. Informed readers may not be surprised to learn that a high proportion of these were taken from the chapters covering my subject's stint as Master of Peterhouse.

It has been my experience that historians, trained to be scrupulous about the use of evidence in their study of the past, are as susceptible to gossip as those in any other discipline. In researching this book I have been told certain stories which I have subsequently discovered to be untrue, and others which I suspect of being so. For example, it has been said that as a boy Hugh was not invited to children's parties at Alnwick Castle, resulting in a permanent sense of exclusion, which manifested itself in a longing for social acceptance. This is one of those theories difficult to disprove; but what I do know makes me sceptical. For one thing, Hugh's father Bertie was a respected member of local society. After the Duke of Northumberland he was the next person in the locality to own a car. He acted as family doctor to the ducal family, though discretion inhibited him from advertising the fact. So if there were parties for children of prominent local families, then the Trevor-Roper children were likely to have been invited. It is probable that they were not invited to the Christmas parties held at the Castle for the children of estate workers, but if so, this would not have been a cause for grievance. Far from being excluded, the Trevor-Roper family owned a key allowing them private access to the Castle grounds.

Another such legend, easier to disprove, is the story that the historian Lawrence Stone had been Hugh's 'fag' at Charterhouse. Surely (it is said) this is the clue to explain the 'love/hate' relationship between the two men? Alas, when you insert the key into the lock, it fails to turn. The two schoolboys were not in the same house, so that even if they had overlapped, Stone could not have been Hugh's fag. But in fact they did not overlap at Charterhouse: Hugh left the year before Stone arrived. I am reminded of one definition of tragedy, ascribed to Samuel Butler, which Hugh often cited: a beautiful theory spoilt by an inconvenient fact – or in this case, two facts.

There are more such legends. For example, it is said that Oxford University Press had a contract to publish Hugh's 'big book' on the Puritan Revolution, and turned it down. But searches in the OUP archives and in the archives of his literary agent reveal not a shred of evidence to support this claim, and it seems inherently implausible. For one thing, Hugh had an existing contract to publish the book with Macmillan, which was not cancelled until long after he abandoned the project. For another, he had a low opinion of OUP's history publishing which he expressed frequently, not least in an eight-page memorandum to the Waldock Committee in 1967.

No subject attracts curiosity so much as sex. There has been speculation about Hugh's sexuality since he first rose to notice. A number of those whom I interviewed for this book indicated that they believed him to be homosexual, though when pressed for proof, could produce only second- or third-hand anecdotes at best. Such hearsay is of dubious value. I do not say that Hugh had no homosexual feelings, but I have found no convincing evidence of homosexual activity in his life, even when he was at an all-male boarding school.

Doubtless some of these myths arise from misunderstandings, or confusion. Others may be malicious in origin; there has been no shortage of those willing to denigrate him. Yet others may have originated from Hugh himself: he was certainly capable of embellishing a story to raise its entertainment value. I have endeavoured to avoid booby traps laid in my path, deliberately or otherwise.

It is now more than fifteen years since I first discussed the possibility of this biography with Hugh. It has been a long journey, and sometimes I have paused for rest. But my subject has been an amusing and invigorating companion, from whom I now part with regret.

Adam Sisman
February 2010

1

Boy

In later life, Hugh Trevor-Roper was sometimes referred to as 'Roper'. The tale – perhaps apocryphal – is told of a grandee who persistently addressed him as such. '<u>Trevor</u>-Roper', Hugh eventually protested. 'But my dear fellow, I don't know you that well,' came the reply.[1]

The sting in this story comes from Hugh's assumed mortification at such a snub. It was a common charge against him that he was a snob, preferring the company of his social superiors, and aspiring to be accepted as one of them. The English upper classes have made a practice of adopting hyphenated surnames, so that both can be retained when a member of one notable family marries another. Calling Hugh 'Roper' could therefore be interpreted as a put-down. It perhaps adds piquancy to the story that the forename 'Trevor' has plebeian connotations.

In fact Hugh was proud of his Roper origins, which could be traced back to the beginning of the fifteenth century. There is a great 'Roper Roll' (a form of family tree) at Nostell Priory in Yorkshire. The Roper family had established their descent from the brother of Archbishop Chichele, founder in 1438 of All Souls College, Oxford; as 'Founder's Kin', they were entitled to claim college fellowships. This hereditary right was abolished by Act of Parliament in the nineteenth century.

In the reign of Henry VIII a William Roper* had married the eldest daughter of Sir Thomas More; and after his father-in-law's fall and execution had written his biography. The Roper family became guardians of More's memory, remaining faithful to the Church of Rome for generations, beyond the time when it was prudent to be so. Hugh, who gained a reputation as a scourge of twentieth-century Catholics, was amused by this family tradition. In St Dunstan's Church near Canterbury there is a Roper Chapel, where (according to him) two priests are obliged to sing regular masses on behalf of the family in perpetuity.

In 1608 William Roper's nephew John was granted the manor of Teynham in Kent, and eight years later he was created Baron Teynham, after paying the then extraordinary sum of £10,000 for the title.[2] Hugh was

---

* William Roper was one of the principal characters in Robert Bolt's play *A Man for All Seasons*, first performed in 1960.

descended from the Teynhams, via a younger brother of the 9th and 10th Lords Teynham; conscious of this connection from an early age, he was always aware that, were a dozen or so intervening cousins to perish *à la Kind Hearts and Coronets*, he would inherit a peerage.

The Ropers clung to their faith throughout most of the seventeenth century, but after the Revolution of 1688 they decided that the struggle was no longer worth continuing and conformed to the established Church. About a hundred years later Hugh's great-grandfather, Cadwallader Blayney Roper, inherited the estate of Plas Teg in North Wales from his aunt, one of the Trevors, a Welsh family of similar antiquity, and took the surname Trevor-Roper to acknowledge both sides of his inheritance. His aunt had earlier married one of the grand Dacres who owned vast tracts of the North of England. The Trevor-Ropers maintained the connection by continuing to use the Dacre name through subsequent generations, long after contact between the families had come to an end.

The principal house on the Plas Teg estate was a magnificent stone mansion, perhaps the finest Jacobean country house in Wales.[3] It had been built around 1610 by Sir John Trevor, to a design attributed (without any solid evidence) to Inigo Jones. Charles Dickens stayed at Plas Teg during one of his lecture tours and described his host, Hugh's great-uncle – another Charles – as a jolly country gentleman: one of a long line. Among Charles Trevor-Roper's younger brothers was Hugh's grandfather Richard, who inhabited one of the lesser houses on the Plas Teg estate. Grandfather Richard and his wife had thirteen children, the youngest of whom, Hugh's father Bertie, was born in 1885. One of Bertie's earliest memories was of his father being laid on the kitchen table, which had been placed beside the bath, for his tuberculous leg to be sawn off. Hugh's grandfather did not survive this operation. Eleven years later, his grandmother married again, to her late husband's cousin Hugh; Bertie's eldest son would be named after this stepfather. The Trevor-Ropers had a habit of marrying within the family; Richard's elder brother George, for example, married another cousin, one of his sister-in-law's sisters.

The senior line of the family was almost severed in 1917, when Charles's grandson, a soldier, was killed at Passchendaele – but a son was born during the war, inheriting the estate which would otherwise have passed to a cousin under the terms of the entail. This fatherless son, Richard Dacre Trevor-Roper, was a wild boy, expelled from Wellington College for running an underground inter-school gambling syndicate.[4] Subsequently he raced cars and was rumoured to have climbed the outside of a skyscraper. In the Second World War, after being cashiered from the Army, he joined RAF Bomber Command, becoming famous as one of Guy Gibson's Dambusters, a rear gunner known to his colleagues as 'Trev'. Hugh would often remark that his cousin Richard Trevor-Roper, who was awarded the DFC and the DFM, had been much more distinguished than he would ever be. But 'Trev' too was killed in action, over Nuremberg in 1944;* once again, the male line of the Trevor-Ropers had apparently been cut. After the war the estate was sold at auction – bought by the auctioneer, who cut down the trees and built new houses in the grounds, allowing the mansion to fall into ruin once he had stripped out its saleable contents. In the late 1950s he applied to have it demolished, but this application was refused after a campaign of protest. Hugh inspected Plas Teg, then standing empty and dilapidated, and toyed with the idea of buying it, but his wife vetoed the proposal. His brother bought the house instead and, with grant aid, restored it; and though almost two decades later he was compelled to sell it, the house had been preserved from destruction. Meanwhile the surrounding estate, which once had extended to more than a thousand acres, had shrunk to a mere garden.

There was a postscript to this dual tragedy of father and son. Years later it emerged that, on his final posting, to an air base near Skegness, 'Trev' had married a local woman. Unknown to him, he had fathered a child: a boy named Charles, who would grow up in difficult circumstances, with only one parent, bereft of the privileges which he might have enjoyed had his father survived. Hugh delighted in this story and befriended Charles, by then running a hotel in Torquay, whom he acknowledged as head of the Trevor-Roper family.

Hugh's father Bertie chose medicine as a profession. After taking a degree at Manchester University, and qualifying as both a physician and surgeon, he applied for a position as a medical officer in India, but was rejected as a 'bad life' because of his asthma – though in fact he would live to be ninety-two. His asthma may also help to explain why he did not serve in the Great War, which began while he was still in his twenties. As a doctor he was unlikely to have been conscripted, and in any case married men were among the last to be called up. In 1910 he had married Kathleen Davison, daughter of a Belfast businessman who had retired to Cheshire. That same year he bought a practice in Glanton, in the Cheviot Hills of rural north Northumberland. Why he and his wife should have wanted to make their lives in that part of the country is unclear. There was no obvious family connection with the area, though the Dacres had once owned a large estate near Morpeth. Northumberland is a Border county, a wedge of English territory projecting into Scotland. From Alnwick northwards it is especially isolated: there England narrows to a funnel not more than twenty-five miles wide,

---

* Two other Trevor-Roper cousins were killed on active service during the war, one in Normandy in 1944, and the other flying over Norway in March 1945.

hemmed in by mountains on one side and the sea on the other. Glanton itself was (and remains) a modest village of plain stone houses, most of two storeys, less than ten miles as the crow flies from the Scottish Border, across the looming Cheviot Hills.

In 1912 Kathleen gave birth to her first child, a daughter whom they named Sheila; two years later, on 15 January 1914, Hugh was born, at Glanton; and in 1916 a third child followed, called Patrick and known as Pat ever after. Pat's second name was Dacre; Hugh's was Redwald, originally a seventh-century king of East Anglia and apparently a Davison family name. Hugh came to dislike the name Redwald (perhaps because it was embarrassing to a shy schoolboy), and preferred it not to be mentioned. He felt himself to be the least popular of the three children, and Pat, by nature outgoing and amiable, to be the favourite. By the time Pat was born the Trevor-Ropers had moved a few miles east, to the historic county town of Alnwick, where Bertie had bought another practice. Though he retained the original practice in Glanton, and shuttled between the two, working single-handedly without a partner, Alnwick was henceforth the family home. As a boy Hugh often accompanied his father on the short journey to Glanton, and sat in the waiting room while his father saw the patients. In the early days of his practice, Bertie did his rounds on horseback; afterwards on a motorcycle, and eventually by car. Much later, when he had learned to drive, Hugh sometimes chauffeured his father on his rounds.

Hugh did not need to look far for evidence of Alnwick's dramatic history. It is a medieval town, with cobbled streets, narrow alleys and handsome stone buildings. Fortified gates and fragments of surviving wall provide clues to a violent past. In 1424 the Scots sacked Alnwick and set it alight. A stone memorial outside the walls marks the site where a Scottish king was killed during a siege. Dominating the town is a Norman castle, one of the largest in England, stronghold of the Percy family for the past seven centuries. The Percys became the most powerful barons in the North, at war with the Scots for generations. The most famous of them, known as Hotspur, was brave to the point of recklessness; it was this Hotspur whose qualities Shakespeare contrasted with those of the young Prince Hal. In the eighteenth century the Percys acquired the defunct title of Dukes of Northumberland; they adapted the castle for a more peaceful age, and enclosed their now picturesque estate with a wall, more suited to keep out trespassers than armed raiders.

The Trevor-Ropers lived in that part of the main street of Alnwick known as Bondgate Without, because it was outside one of the old town gates (the part inside is known as Bondgate Within). Their house was a substantial stone building (now a small hotel), large enough to be used as a surgery as well as a home. All four local doctors were clustered along a stretch of

Bondgate Without known locally as 'the Doctors' Mile', and each worked in turn at the local infirmary, a short distance further out of town. Bertie Trevor-Roper also served as a Medical Officer of Health, both within Alnwick itself and the surrounding countryside. It seems that he was successful in his profession, sought out by wealthy and titled patients, including the Percys, though the fact that he was treating them was kept confidential. After the Duke, Bertie Trevor-Roper was the next person in the district to own a car, a black Ford. Poorer patients often turned up at the kitchen door, hoping to be treated free of charge. The Trevor-Ropers kept a house-maid who lived in a small room at the top of the house, and who doubled as a receptionist for the surgery, answering the doorbell. To kitchen-door patients she offered a doorstep diagnosis, sending them away if she judged the problem to be a minor one, with the comment that 'the doctor is too busy to see you'.

In an obituary written by a colleague, Bertie Trevor-Roper would be described as a good surgeon and a kind physician, always affable and generous and never censorious or self-pitying, with an enviable dry wit.[5] To his sons, however, Bertie exuded the air of a man thwarted by life. Elegantly turned out in trilby and country suit, he was to them a distant, reticent figure, who seldom spoke to his children. He took no part in the conversation at meal-times. Even when they rode with him in the car on his rounds he discouraged chat. (One reason may have been that he was having affairs; the children noticed that they had to wait a long time outside when he was attending to certain attractive female patients.) He maintained that he would converse with them once they reached the age of reason, which he put at sixteen, but by then it would be too late: they had nothing to talk about. As was usual at the time, the children addressed him respect-fully as 'Father', just as they addressed Kathleen as 'Mother'. Because of his remoteness Bertie seemed to his three young children intimidating, even frightening, though he was never harsh or cruel. On the contrary, his photographs suggest a gentle, rueful character. Later his grandsons would find him relaxed and fun. Hugh eventually decided that his father had contracted out of parenthood. Bertie can have had little experience of his own father, who had died while he was still an infant. On the other hand, the fact that he named his eldest son after his stepfather suggests that he and the older Hugh were at least on amicable terms.

Neither of his parents seemed to Hugh to have any intellectual or cultural interests, certainly none that they shared with their children. The only books that Hugh could remember his father reading were on horse-racing. Aside from his profession, the Turf was Bertie's chief interest in life. He took the family to race-meetings across the North of England and southern Scotland, including the point-to-points of the various hunts. In due course

Hugh became interested in racing himself, though it never absorbed him as it did his father. Bertie was a gambling man; as well as betting on horses, he and Kathleen spent evenings at the roulette tables in the casino at Monte Carlo, on winter excursions to the South of France, from which the children were excluded. At weekends the family sometimes drove into Newcastle for lunch at Tilley's smart tea-rooms in Blackett Street. Hugh discovered an antiquarian bookstall in the market, which yielded many treasures. Family holidays were taken in the late summer at a cottage near Howick on the Northumbrian coast, a few miles north-east of Alnwick. Bertie stayed behind to work, joining them at weekends.

According to Hugh, there was never any sign of intimacy between his parents. His mother Kathleen was rigidly conformist, lacking in humour, and cramped by what seemed to Hugh in retrospect a stifling class-consciousness and accompanying sense of decorum. She never hugged her children, and refused to allow them to mix with those she considered to be their social inferiors, not even their neighbours. They were forbidden to invite home the daughter of the lawyer who lived opposite, for example, even though she took lessons with Sheila. The Trevor-Roper brothers remembered sitting on the garden wall, gazing down at the local children playing in the street. Their society was confined to the offspring of their parents' friends, almost exclusively in the Glanton area. The 'Alnwick people' were shunned. Though the genteel seaside resort of Alnmouth, only a few miles downstream from Alnwick, was frequented by the families of well-to-do businessmen not unlike Kathleen's own father, they never went there: to mix socially with such types was 'inappropriate'.

Until social barriers began to crumble in the 1960s, class 'distinction' in England to a large extent dictated how individuals would relate to each other – or more often, not relate to each other. These barriers were high walls that were scaled only rarely, with the help of beauty, talent or cash, or in exceptional circumstances such as in wartime. Most people remained confined within the class they were born into – particularly in the country-side, where the status of the upper classes was displayed by their possession of land and grand houses. The Trevor-Roper family occupied a precarious position, straddling one of these barriers. Bertie came from a background of faded gentry, a family dispossessed of most of its lands and therefore on the slide. His role as a country general practitioner gave him access to the great houses of the area, and the confidence of their inhabitants; but his status remained that of a middle-class professional. Bertie seems to have been indifferent to his plight; but to Kathleen it mattered desperately. While despising the lethargic Trevor-Ropers, she was determined to assert their family claims at every opportunity.

Hugh was dragged to children's parties in country houses, which he found boring, indeed loathsome. At one of these parties, in the festive season, a man dressed as Father Christmas was taking presents off a tree lit with candles; utterly bored, Hugh was facing the other way when he became aware of a commotion behind him. He turned to see Father Christmas engulfed in flames, his red flannel costume ablaze. The children were hurried out of the room and taken home by strangers. Nothing was said about the incident, but over the next few days and weeks neighbours and other adults he encountered when out on walks with his nanny would ask after his father, whom the children had not seen since the party. Hugh gradually came to the conclusion that Bertie had been the burning Father Christmas, and, though denied by his mother, this was eventually confirmed. It was a long time before his father returned home from hospital. What was so unnatural about this episode was the silence surrounding it, as if it were an embarrassing incident to be kept quiet.

Adult behaviour seemed bewildering, governed by rules that were never explained. Perhaps in response to such mystification, both Hugh and his brother would develop a thirst for truth, seeking rational answers to problems, believing that these could always be found if one sought them in the right place. Truth was simple, but people complicated it. When Hugh remarked innocently, 'I worry a great deal how it is that babies are born,' his horrified mother ran out of the room. Theirs was, the two brothers would subsequently agree, a grim household, without warmth, affection, encouragement, spontaneity or natural feeling of any kind. Expressions of emotion were unwelcome. Conversation was discouraged. Enquiries were rebuffed with the standard reply, 'Curiosity killed the cat'.

Starved of affection, and even of attention, Hugh became a very abstracted child, lost in thought much of the time and unheeding of those around him. He did notice, however, how much more agreeable other people's parents were to him than his own, and took this to be the general rule, commenting to his sister Sheila that on the whole parents disliked their own children and preferred other people's. After some discussion the two of them reached the conclusion that this could not be true; presumably parents merely pretended not to like their own children, for obscure adult reasons.

Looking back, Hugh saw his early childhood as a dismal period. Perhaps he did not see it as such at the time because he had nothing to measure it against, but when jovial adults asserted that this was 'the happiest time of your life', he contemplated the future with pessimism – though he also wondered if he might not remain a small boy for ever. For a while he suspected that children were a servile class, kept in perpetual subjugation by the promise that one day they would become the masters. He saw no empirical evidence that children grew up into adults, and speculated that the whole thing was a myth, a conspiracy to keep them down. He looked forward gloomily to a life of dreary servitude.

He was a solitary boy, frail, reserved and awkward in company. This was accentuated by his short-sightedness, which compelled him to wear spectacles from an early age, making it hard for him to participate in team games, for which he never showed the slightest aptitude. Anyway he had few friends, and none within easy reach. He found solace alone, in reading and thinking. To protect himself from ridicule he developed a shell of self-mockery: one that hardened, and endured even when he no longer required its protection. Not all the privations of childhood could repress his innate sense of fun, however. Hugh had little in common with his bubbly older sister, whom he would later dismiss as 'a flibbertigibbet', and his brother was too young to share many of his interests; even so, the three of them perforce spent much of their time playing together. They produced their own magazine, entitled *Ogo Pozo*. Hugh also wrote several fully scripted plays in doggerel verse, which the three of them ('The Roper Dramatic Company presents ... ') performed before an adult audience, showing a professional attention to detail, right down to handwritten programmes, with a list of the cast in order of appearance (each child of course taking several parts), a description of each scene, and a mocked-up advertisement for a local café.

Sheila was a keen horse-rider from an early age, and in due course Hugh took lessons from a local spinster who kept stables; he became an enthusiastic though inexpert rider, somewhat accident-prone. He went fishing on the River Till or the River Aln within the Castle park, to which the family had their own key, allowing them private entry. Hugh also took long walks and bicycle rides, exploring the surrounding countryside and decoding its history. For an imaginative child, evidence of the past was everywhere in Northumberland: in prehistoric hill forts; in the defensive barrier of Hadrian's Wall, northern boundary of the Roman Empire, some of it still intact two thousand years after the Romans had left; in the ruined abbeys – most romantic of all, the abbey on the Holy Island of Lindisfarne, abandoned by the monks in the eighth century when the Vikings came; in the imposing castles of Bamburgh and Dunstanburgh, built on outcrops of rock projecting into the sea; in the Pele towers to be found scattered throughout the county, small fortified keeps which provided a secure retreat during raids; in the deserted hamlets and farmsteads; and in battlefields such as Flodden, where in 1513 one of the Dacres had played a prominent part in the devastating defeat of the Scots. Until the Union of the two kingdoms Northumberland had been part of the 'Debatable Land', the Border area claimed by both England and Scotland and fought over for centuries, the very landscape soaked in blood.

Hugh was born too late to remember the Great War, as it was then known, though one of its effects was obvious to him as a child: a shortage of young men, and a corresponding preponderance of widows and unmarried women. As well as the immediate family, the Trevor-Roper household comprised a cook, a maid, a nanny and a governess. The children did not eat with their parents, but took their meals with the nanny and the governess, both Scottish. The latter was a Miss Amos, daughter of a Presbyterian minister, who lived nearby with her two sisters, both also unmarried. It seems that she was an excellent teacher who made lessons enjoyable. Hugh never forgot his excitement at learning to read, and at the realisation that doing so opened up a world infinitely larger than the narrow confines of the nursery. Reading remained one of his principal pleasures throughout his life, until he was too blind to continue. He devoured the few books in the house indiscriminately, absorbing esoteric information from an early Victorian encyclopaedia in three volumes that he found slumbering on an upper shelf. He learned how to identify the constellations of the stars, how to deduce the distance and diameter of the moon, the dynasties of the Pharaohs of Egypt, the Kings of Assyria and Babylon, and much else. His erudition evidently did not go unnoticed in the family. At the end of a letter to his mother (then away on holiday) he signed himself 'Professor H.T-R.'

One of the first books he read was called *Line Upon Line*, the Bible story in simple language; and following this he was made to learn some hymns and two psalms from the Book of Common Prayer, becoming, as he later put it, 'thoroughly grounded in Christian orthodoxy'. He pressed Miss Amos for an explanation of the sentence 'He did not abhor the Virgin's womb', but found her replies disappointingly evasive.

Bertie Trevor-Roper showed no interest whatsoever in religion, but his wife conformed to the Church of England, insisting that her children went regularly to Sunday services. These were conducted by the local vicar, who was also Archdeacon of Lindisfarne, and dressed accordingly in shovel hat and gaiters; he attended obsequiously on the ducal family. Red-nosed and toad-like, he delivered unctuous sermons. To Hugh, the service was a meaningless ritual; his mind was occupied by the prayer book to be found in each pew, containing tables which allowed the reader to compute the date of Easter for any given year, and other important dates in the ecclesiastical calendar. Hugh passed the time in such calculations. There were also bibles which confidently listed the dates of events mentioned in the Old Testament. The Archdeacon's fruity voice went unheard as Hugh memorised these dates and attempted to reconcile them with the Assyrian and Babylonian chronologies he had absorbed from the family encyclopaedia.

The three children became devoted to their governess, despite her habit of rapping them on their fingers when they made a mistake; in their adult years they often visited her at the houses she shared with her sisters, first in Alnwick, and afterwards in Alnmouth, where they were always greeted with the affectionate welcome so lacking from their parents. As a boy Hugh would bring back flowers he had gathered from the hedgerows and shells he had picked up from the beach to present to Miss Amos; she would identify these and encourage him to bring her more. From his governess he learned the names of plants, animals and birds; this was the beginning of a lifelong interest in nature. In particular he learned to love the landscape of Northumberland: its hills, its rivers, its bare moors and secret valleys, and its dramatically beautiful coastline. Here the sun can burst through the cloud on even the most dismal day, revealing huge skies and dramatic views across hedgerows, undulating fields and desolate moorland. Even at the end of his life, when he had become too blind to make out his surroundings, the Northumberland countryside remained vivid in his mind.

In May 1923, soon after his ninth birthday, Hugh was sent to board at a preparatory school in Derbyshire, Stancliffe Hall, near Matlock, a large, ugly house built by a Victorian engineer as his home. Bertie would have been content for him to go to the Duke's School in Alnwick, but as usual Kathleen's ambition for her sons triumphed. In order to maintain one's place in the social hierarchy, correct schooling was necessary. Why she should have chosen this particular school, almost two hundred miles to the south, rather than one of the much nearer schools in North Yorkshire favoured by the local squirearchy, is unknown, the only clue being that one of Bertie's distant relatives had attended Stancliffe Hall some thirty or forty years earlier. Private schools vary in quality: what was a good school in one generation may not be so good in the next, and vice versa. So far as Hugh was concerned, this one was an early-twentieth-century version of Dotheboys Hall.* Its long corridors stank of slop-pails and stale fish. The dormitories were even more unpleasant, Hugh's particularly so as the boy in the next bed was incontinent. Despite the boys' protests, the slovenly dormitory maids wiped out the 'jerries' and the tooth-glasses with the same rag, so that the latter always smelt of stale urine. When there was an outbreak of influenza in the school, the Matron ladled out doses of 'Scott's Emulsion' to all sixty boys, using the same spoon, which was never washed from the first spoonful to the last. The food was unpalatable. At lunchtime the boys would be served cold mutton, consisting almost entirely of solid white fat, or smelly blue meat, full of tubes, which they knew as 'cat's meat'.

---

* Stancliffe Hall closed in 2000. Two years later it was used as a location for the film *Stig of the Dump*.

Tea was presided over by a squat, middle-aged master with a sneering, cynical voice known to the boys as 'Twitch', an elaboration of his initials 'TWH'. The whole school assembled in the hall, organised by forms. On a table in the centre was an enormous tea-urn, serving tea so hot that it had to be diluted with cold water, and a large pile of buttered bread. Twitch would invite the boys to advance and take a slice, beginning with the top form; if any remained after the last boy in the lowest form had gone up, the ritual was repeated; but boys in the lowest form were seldom offered a second helping.

One of Hugh's earliest experiences at Stancliffe Hall was of being hurled into the swimming pool and ordered to swim. This was a skill he had yet to acquire. He floundered desperately to the side, and clung to the rail until rescued.

On arrival, Hugh had been placed automatically in the lowest form, and was shocked to find himself in the company of boys who could not read. He wrote to his parents complaining about this, with the result that he was suddenly moved up several forms, but it made little difference. In three terms at the school he learned nothing, except the names of the Judges and Kings of Israel down to Zedekiah.

Discipline was enforced by the Headmaster, Colonel Bedford-Franklin, with his cane. A more immediate threat was the slipper wielded by the most senior boy in Hugh's dormitory. As punishment for any behaviour that this junior tyrant considered impertinent, he would inflict a beating on the bottom, which might entail as many as seventy-five strokes. One such beating was enough for Hugh; afterwards he lay silent as a mouse in his dormitory bed, listening to the dreary churchbells of Darley Dale, which always seemed to toll their most doleful sequence at bedtime.

There was a bully in the school called Jones, accompanied everywhere by an acolyte who assisted him in persecuting other boys. This pair soon identified Hugh as easy prey. One day he was approached by these two and politely asked if he would participate in an experiment. Naïve and anxious to please, Hugh readily agreed, and metal terminals with wires leading from them were placed in each of his hands. At the press of a button he was convulsed by an electric shock, so powerful that he found it impossible to release the terminals: the greater the pain, the tighter his hands gripped them. The two bullies laughed as Hugh danced in agony.

The spiritual needs of the boys were attended to by a local clergyman, who conducted services in the school chapel. One of his sermons described two boys walking together along a country road, discussing the existence of God, which one maintained and the other denied – until God himself terminated the dialogue with a thunderstorm, causing a tree to fall on the head of the infidel. Hugh did not find himself convinced by this example, especially after he had put it to what he described many years later as 'a simple empirical test'. His faith shaken, he decided to give God a second chance. He longed for a triangular Cape of Good Hope stamp to make good a deficiency in his collection, so he tore an ordinary 2d stamp to shreds and placed it under his pillow before going to bed, and prayed fervently for it to be changed into an intact stamp of the kind he coveted. The next morning, he groped eagerly under his pillow to verify the miracle. 'I was disappointed, of course, at what I found there; but I accepted, without flinching, the intellectual consequences of my experiment, and that morning God was silently dropped from my universe, to which he has never returned for more than brief and temporary visits.'[6]

Stancliffe Hall was too far from Northumberland for Hugh to go back and forth easily, so he remained at school during half-term holidays. The mother of another pupil took pity on him and invited him home on one occasion, but she did not take to him, describing him afterwards as 'smug'. Perhaps this was a mask for unhappiness. His brother later described Hugh as having been 'miserable beyond belief' at Stancliffe Hall. Looking back on his time there when he was nearly thirty, Hugh decided that this had been the most wretched period of his life.[7]

Even so, his spirits were irrepressible. His letters home were illustrated with comic sketches, a habit which remained with him all his life, and enlivened by comic verse of his own composition. At Stancliffe Hall he produced his first book, Trevor-Roper's *Bible of Ghosts* – apparently very popular with his fellow schoolboys – which subdivided ghosts into their *genera* and species, with full descriptions and illustrations. In adult life he could only remember the Skittywakky Ghost, which issued out of mouse-holes and wore elaborate headdresses, like Queen Mary.

Back in Northumberland for the Christmas holidays, Hugh collapsed during a bitterly cold bicycle ride. After staggering home, he was sent to bed. His return to school was repeatedly postponed, pending his recovery, until he had missed the whole spring term. No one ever explained what was wrong with him, though his sister told him that she had overheard the words 'rheumatic fever'. During his convalescence his mother took him to Cornwall for a holiday. By May he had at last recovered enough to be sent back to Stancliffe Hall for the summer term. Afterwards, when he returned home for the holidays, he was informed that he would not be going back there for the next school year; he would be sent instead across the Scottish Border to a new school, Belhaven Hill, in Dunbar. Hugh was very distressed at this news and broke down in tears; his parents, aware of how unhappy he had been at Stancliffe Hall, could not understand why. The reason was quite simple. Not knowing any better, Hugh assumed that all schools were the same: they were prisons, where one had to serve out one's term. He had learned how to endure one prison; moving to another meant having to start afresh. Fortunately his new school proved very different.

Belhaven Hill is now established as one of the most prestigious preparatory schools in Britain, but in September 1924, when Hugh arrived there at the age of ten, it had been in existence only four terms and had fewer than thirty pupils. The school had recently moved into the building it still occupies, a Georgian house with projecting bays at each end, just outside Dunbar, twenty-eight miles east of Edinburgh. The house commanded views of the sea, and at night the boys could often hear the eerie sound of the foghorn on the Bass Rock, out on the approaches to the Firth of Forth, its wailing borne down on the wind as this beat against the dormitory windows. The school was run as a partnership by two young bachelor masters, Brian Simms and Wilfrid Ingham, who between them did all the teaching. According to Hugh, Simms was a kindly man who ran the school well and discouraged bullying, though other pupils remember him as formidable and as a stern disciplinarian. During the war he had been a conscientious objector, a sign perhaps of determination and strength of principle; later he became a clergyman. Ingham, known to the boys as 'Bungey' on account of his springy step, was more unpredictable, and liable to lose his temper. The boys speculated that, having served during the war in South-West Africa, he was used to beating up natives and had found it hard to curb this habit. Exasperated by Hugh's incompetence on the playing field, Ingham once hurled a football boot at him in the changing-room. But in class Hugh was Ingham's favourite, held up to other boys as a model.

Both Ingham and Simms seem to have been diligent and effective teachers. Under them Hugh learned Latin and Greek to a high standard, as well as studying all the other usual subjects, including French, which he had already begun to learn with Miss Amos. Simms taught history by making the boys learn by heart the Kings and Queens of England, their dates, and the principal events of their reigns – perhaps not the most interesting method, but one which provided a framework for future study.

Another important person at the school was the Matron, Miss Rutherford, known to the boys as 'Miss R'; she presided over high tea, and afterwards told stories which were very popular with the boys, almost all of whom were Scottish. The gist of these was always the same: the superiority of the Scots over the English. The Union between Scotland and England in 1707 remained a subject of sentimental regret more than two centuries later. In class, Lord Belhaven's lament for Scottish independence was held up to the boys as a model of classic eloquence.

It is hard to believe that Miss R's homilies did not provoke a reaction from Hugh. In later years he described being surrounded at Belhaven Hill

by xenophobic Scottish boys uttering the ritual incantation of 'Ban-
nockburn'.[8] His letters home contained plenty of cracks against the
'Scotch' – 'shows the ignorance of the Scotch', reads one of them – suggesting
that he expected these to be received well by the Trevor-Roper household.
Pat soon joined Hugh at Belhaven Hill. By school convention first names
were never used, so that even the two brothers addressed each other by
their common surname.

On Sundays the boys were segregated, according to whether they
attended the Scots or English Church, i.e. Presbyterian or Episcopalian.
Hugh, unaware of the difference, plumped for 'English'. One sermon from
that time remained in his memory, given by the Bishop of Edinburgh, who
suggested, in passing, that the British Empire might not last for ever. To
the schoolboy Hugh, accustomed to seeing a map hanging on the wall
showing a large proportion of the world coloured red, the idea seemed
absurd.

Conditions at Belhaven Hill were Spartan by modern standards. The day
began at 7.00 a.m. with the sound of the school bell. The boys, wrenched
from sleep, queued shivering for a bath, usually cold but hot twice a week.
Pupils dressed in knickerbockers except in high summer, when grey flannel
shorts were allowed. Bathtime was followed by fifteen minutes of physical
training; boys who failed to perform to the required standard were dispatched to run around a gravel path. After breakfast came a further period
of outdoor exercise and then morning prayers, followed by lessons, which
commenced just after nine o'clock. All the senior boys shared one lavatory,
outside in the stables. As there was no electricity in the building, the school
was lit by gas. When asked by an anxious prospective mother how the
dormitories were heated, Simms replied that when it was really cold,
Matron would light the gas lamps half an hour before the boys went to bed,
and this sufficed.

At weekends Ingham led the boys on walks into the countryside and
along the seashore, welcoming Hugh's curiosity about plants, animals,
birds and marine life, just as Miss Amos had done. Every afternoon of the
summer term, whatever the weather, he marched the whole school down
to Belhaven Sands, and would swim out to sea before floating on his back,
to keep an eye on the boys inshore. On Saturdays this excursion was
extended to include a picnic of sandwiches and 'pop', sprawled among the
sand dunes.

On Sunday evenings Simms read aloud to the boys, adventure stories
such as Alexandre Dumas's *The Three Musketeers* or Conan Doyle's
'Brigadier Gerard' stories. Hugh supplemented these with his own reading:
the historical romances of Baroness Orczy, for example. In one letter to his
mother Hugh asked whether a copy he had ordered of *The Lost World* had

arrived; in another he mentioned that he was reading *Dr Dolittle's Post Office* (then only recently published).[9] There was a small library at the school, which Hugh, encouraged by Ingham, ransacked for novels, history and natural history in particular. Some of this reading, Hugh subsequently decided, was premature: he acquired a set of Theodor Mommsen's multi-volume *History of Rome*, which even Ingham thought was carrying his zeal for learning too far. He read several of Dickens's novels far too early to understand or appreciate them, with the unfortunate result that he never returned to Dickens later in life. But the historical novels of Sir Walter Scott absorbed Hugh, set as many of them were in the Border country between England and Scotland; and Scott's *Tales of a Grandfather* provided him with a highly coloured introduction to the history of the region up to the time of the '45 Jacobite Rebellion. Robbery, blackmail, raiding, arson, livestock-rustling, kidnapping, murder and extortion had been rife throughout the Debatable Lands. 'Reiver' families such as the Armstrongs and the Scotts roamed the wild moorland of the Borders, often in bands of marauding horsemen; while 'Warden' families such as the Buccleuchs and the Dacres maintained frontier garrisons and tried to enforce the rule of law. This was history dramatic enough to excite any schoolboy, a turbulent past still echoing in the landscape around him.

In the less restrictive atmosphere of Belhaven Hill, Hugh began to relax, and a mischievous, subversive side to his nature emerged, which would lead him into later indiscretions. He wrote his own magazine, *Bathos*, a skit on school life, illustrated with his own comic sketches and enlivened by his comic doggerel, in the style of Belloc's *Cautionary Tales*. One such poem ostensibly described the frolics of prehistoric animals, in a manner which transparently lampooned aspects of the school. *Bathos* proved too subversive for the Headmaster, who banned the magazine after its first issue.

In 1927, aged thirteen, Hugh was taken by his mother to London – his first visit – to sit the scholarship examination for Charterhouse, alongside another Belhaven Hill boy called Goode. Soon after their return to Belhaven it was announced that both* had been elected junior scholars at Charterhouse, and a third boy had won a scholarship to Eton. The whole school enjoyed a half-holiday in celebration.

Years afterwards, Hugh mused on Wordsworth's belief that after the intense delights of childhood,

> Shades of the prison-house begin to close
> Upon the growing Boy . . .

* Goode finished ahead of Hugh.

His own experience was the opposite. Childhood had been a form of prison, a sentence to be endured, a grey period with little pleasure to colour it. When not mocked or despised, he had been ignored. He had survived by withdrawing into himself, seeking safety in isolation, protected by a self-created barrier of reserve. Only later would he discover a capacity for uninhibited pleasure.[10]

Carthusian

Charterhouse was founded in 1611 by the immensely rich Tudor benefactor, Thomas Sutton. Today his statue stands in front of the school, in the area known as Founder's Court. Sutton's foundation established a school and a 'hospital' (almshouses), which for more than two and a half centuries occupied the same site on the edge of the City of London (now known as the Old Charterhouse). In 1872, however, the school moved out of London into open countryside, on the outskirts of Godalming. There, among the Surrey beech woods, on a site running down to the River Wey, a set of buildings in the Gothic style was erected, whose soaring towers, reminiscent of ecclesiastical architecture, dominated the locality. A cloister had been added in the early twentieth century, to commemorate the many Carthusians* who had served in the Boer War, the foundation stone being laid in 1901 by the hero of Mafeking, Old Carthusian Robert Baden-Powell. To one side was the new chapel, designed by Giles Gilbert Scott and dedicated only three months before Hugh's arrival. Indeed the building work was still incomplete. The new chapel was on a monumental scale, its plain stone walls rising sheer to an impressive height. The austere interior created a solemn effect, like that of a tomb. The chapel had been commissioned in memory of the Great War, in which the school had suffered a horrifying number of casualties, including 687 Old Carthusians dead. Robert Graves, who left Charterhouse in 1914, estimated that at least one in three of his generation had been killed; most of the survivors, if not permanently disabled, had been wounded two or three times. To build the chapel had been the personal vision of the Headmaster, Frank Fletcher, determined, like so many of his contemporaries, that this should have been the 'war to end wars'.

Hugh felt that there was something dead about the school itself. Little had altered there since the mid-nineteenth century, though the world outside had changed beyond recognition. While British society struggled to adapt itself to successive shocks, Charterhouse remained inflexible. Tradition there was so strong, wrote Robert Graves, that even the school buildings were impregnated with 'the public school spirit'. Although the prestige of the 'bloods' – members of the cricket and football elevens –

---

* Pupils at Charterhouse are known as 'Carthusians'.

had diminished under Fletcher, nevertheless, according to a history of the school, he 'stood for the old world'.[1] A small, distinguished-looking man who exercised quiet authority, he was notably formal in his approach, his reserved manner contrasting with the flamboyance of some other public school headmasters of the inter-war period.[2]

Three boarding-houses had been included in the original design of the new school, and further houses were added or purchased and adapted over the decades that followed, each named after their first Housemaster. Hugh found himself allotted to Daviesites, named after G.S. Davies, later Master of the London Charterhouse. This was a large, three-storey Victorian house with decorated gable-ends and dormer windows projecting from the roof, one of a group of boarding-houses on a hillside facing the school, but divided from it by a sunken road. This road was spanned by a bridge, to which the Daviesites had established special privileges: only they were allowed to use the pavement on one side, and any boy from another house who presumed to trespass on it would be driven off. Many years later, Hugh was reminded of this behaviour when observing monkeys in India. The Housemaster of Daviesites was a clergyman, Lancelot Allen, a nervous, fidgety man rumoured to employ boys as spies, and to patrol the dormitories at night, wearing carpet slippers in the hope of catching his charges unawares in forbidden activity. Though Allen taught French, he was never heard to express interest in French culture, or in culture of any kind. Many years later Hugh would describe him as having been 'the most reactionary man in the school'.[3] He joked that their Housemaster had turned out more agnostics than any other clergyman in England.

Charterhouse was a bewildering place for a new boy, with its own arcane terminology and quaint customs, some of which survive to this day. At first Hugh was rather lost in this unfamiliar and confusing environment, and it took him a while to find his bearings. Fortunately there was a system by which each new boy was allotted an experienced older boy to initiate him into these mysteries, known as a 'father'. As in other places, the school year was divided into three terms, but here they were confusingly known as 'Quarters': the autumn term being known as the Oration Quarter, the spring term as the Long Quarter and the summer term as the Cricket Quarter. Masters were referred to generically as 'beaks' (a term familiar from elsewhere) or, more particularly, 'Brooke Hall', after the building that served as Masters' Common Room. New boys were 'new bugs', another familiar term, and scholars were 'gownboys'. Swots in general were known as 'hash pros', since 'hash' meant lessons. Prep was 'banco'. Misdemeanours were 'black books', after the colour of the punishment book, in which they were recorded. There was a complicated system of privileges known colloquially as 'postees' (from the Latin *post-te*, meaning 'after you'), denoting status and seniority. In one's first year, for example, all jackets had to be fully buttoned. In the second year one button could be left undone, and in the third year, two. Monitors (prefects) could wear their jackets open. From photographs taken at the time it seems that the most senior boys could turn up their jacket collars. Black socks were compulsory in the first year; 'clocked' socks (black with a stripe down one side) allowed in the second, and coloured socks in the third. There were other 'posties' which could trap the unwary. Only monitors were allowed to walk four in a row, for example; Hugh and three others were beaten for transgressing this rule.

As at other schools, the younger boys 'fagged' for their elders, carrying out chores and running errands. Academic or sporting excellence provided escape routes out of this servitude. In all the other houses a boy ceased having to fag once he had been at the school two years; but at Daviesites, those who were insufficiently academic or athletic might continue to fag until they left the school. With Allen's tacit blessing, Daviesites maintained the brutally termed tradition of 'rooting in cocks', whereby a boy accused of impertinence to one of his seniors could be taken to the washing-room, bent over a washbasin, with one knee raised to his chin, and kicked – perhaps with football boots – up the bottom. Hugh's friend Pat Lancaster, who was later captured by the Japanese in the fall of Singapore, would comment that having been a boarder at Charterhouse had been good practice for a prisoner of war.

Scholars bypassed the lower forms, and Hugh was further promoted after only one Quarter; in consequence he was able to escape fagging after his first year. He was one of nine new pupils who stuck together and defended themselves from attack. According to one of his contemporaries, Hugh remained 'normal' and 'well-liked' despite being obviously 'very brainy', which made him often impatient with those slower than he. This boy sat next to Hugh each evening at banco and, finding Latin difficult, would often push across his work in a plea for help, to which Hugh cockily replied, 'How would you like it, in prose or blank verse?' Hugh persuaded one of the masters to teach him Spanish, which he learned within only a few weeks. He took pride in his ability to put on a virtuoso performance. On one occasion he accepted a bet that he could not list all the Books of the Bible from memory. Despite a momentary blankness when he reached the Book of Isaiah, he managed it easily.

As one of the elite of public schools which placed a high value on academic excellence, Charterhouse encouraged fierce competition between the cleverer boys. A system of ranking provided a constant measure of performance. Hugh blossomed in this hothouse environment. Academic success earned him prestige beyond his capability on the sports field. Striving to excel offered him an opportunity to demonstrate his intellectual superiority – not just over other pupils, but over masters too. One of those who taught him Latin later admitted that he had to sit up all night revising in order to keep one jump ahead of his precocious pupil.

At the end of two terms at Charterhouse, Hugh was placed fourth equal out of twenty-three in his class: a creditable performance, if not exceptional. Top of the class was a boy from Kent named Bowes. By the end of his second year, Hugh had begun to hit his stride; he was placed second in one of the two sets (known at Charterhouse as 'divisions') of the Fifth form which studied classics, and awarded a senior scholarship. Again, Bowes had his nose in front. In 1929 Hugh's brother Pat arrived at Charterhouse, having similarly won a scholarship from Belhaven Hill, and was likewise allotted to Daviesites. In due course Pat too would be awarded a senior scholarship.

Hugh's rapid climb up the school compelled Allen to make him a House Monitor, entitling him to his own study at a much younger age than was usual. Studies provided living as well as working accommodation, allowing the occupier more space and privacy. It was in his study, when he was fifteen, that Hugh glimpsed a new world of poetry, on reading Milton's 'Nativity Ode'. His passion for Milton would never waver, though in later life he would become less tolerant of Milton's Puritanism and his republican politics. That same year he took part in 'The Masque of Charterhouse', an open-air pageant of the school's history with a large cast in appropriate costumes, presented for the first time since 1922. His part, as one of six foundation scholars, was not too demanding. The figure of Thomas Sutton was represented as an Elizabethan sea-dog, surrounded by small boys pulling imaginary nautical ropes: a depiction that Hugh would later describe as 'entirely mythological'.

Around this time Hugh was again very ill: perhaps a recurrence of the rheumatic fever he had suffered at Stancliffe Hall. To assist his recovery the Trevor-Ropers decided to take him and the other two children with them to Menton in the South of France that year. This was the first time that Hugh had been abroad. Being under twenty-one, the children were not allowed to accompany their parents on their evening expeditions to the casino. This luxurious holiday – foreign travel was comparatively much more expensive then – suggests that the Trevor-Ropers had not suffered unduly from the 1929 Slump. Hugh apparently made a complete recovery. Having been a frail child, he was growing into a vigorous and robust young man, slightly taller than average. Back at home, in an attempt to compensate for his otherwise sedentary existence, he tried to cultivate an enthusiasm for golf. Photographs taken in this period show him dressed in a loud check suit with plus-fours, like a character from a P.G. Wodehouse novel, his nose adorned with circular spectacles and his neatly parted hair plastered to his forehead, ending in a quiff. Hugh would go solo around Alnwick's nine-hole course, playing against 'bogey', but he soon became bored with this. Instead he developed a taste for beagling, which combined in one activity exercise, the pleasure of being out in the countryside and a certain hearty companionableness.

Carthusians were required to join the Officers' Training Corps (OTC); the Daviesites platoon 'under the command of Corporal Trevor-Roper' won the Recruits' Cup. Most of Hugh's extra-curricular activities at school were solitary ones, however. At the age of sixteen he boldly announced that he would take no further part in school games. Afterwards, his only school sport was long-distance running, which he did alone. He took up sketching in earnest, and developed a facility for caricature, which found a counterpoint in the extravagant metaphors that adorned his prose. The two were connected, in that Hugh claimed to be unable to understand anything that he could not present to his imagination in pictorial form; correspondingly, when he comprehended anything vividly, it was always in terms of some visual image. Many of the most striking metaphors he would employ derived from his fascination with the natural world: he interpreted the world of men in terms of wobbling jellyfish, confused sheep, performing sealions, scuttling crabs, sinister spiders and lazy trout.

Nature was very important to him. When he had arrived at Charterhouse Hugh had been astonished at the green-ness of the surrounding countryside, so different from the bleaker moors of Northumberland to which he was accustomed. He soon discovered species of butterfly that he had known only from books: ones unable to tolerate the harsher northern climate, orangetips and swallowtails for example. He became a lepidopterist, alone pursuing his quarry with a butterfly net through the woods for miles around, making a prize catch of a White Admiral near the then unspoilt village of Gatwick.

By the end of his third year, in the Under Sixth, Hugh was placed first in his division. This was the moment when boys chose the subject in which they would specialise in the Sixth form. The Headmaster summoned Hugh and asked for his choice. Hugh answered 'mathematics' – curiously, because it was not a subject in which he had previously excelled. But it was one that he enjoyed and believed himself good at: justifiably so, since in the Sixth form he would win the mathematics prize. Fletcher was not impressed. 'Clever boys read classics', he pronounced, and showed Hugh the door.

Whatever he may have felt at the time, Hugh afterwards acknowledged his deep gratitude to Fletcher for guiding him away from 'a juvenile flirtation with mathematics' towards the study of classics. The school had a proud tradition of excellent classical teaching; in the preceding century several of the masters there had been fine classical scholars, one indeed General Editor of the Loeb Classical Library. From the time he entered the

Sixth form, Hugh was taught classics by A.L. Irvine, known as 'Uncle', who
made the boys learn by heart passages of Greek and Latin literature which
he had selected and published for the purpose. Though rather mechanical,
this method left pupils enriched. Even into old age Hugh could quote long
passages that he had learned in this way. He was taught too by Fletcher
himself, who introduced the boys to Tacitus, the man Hugh considered the
greatest of all Roman historians, whose work was to influence the book
many rate as Hugh's masterpiece, *The Last Days of Hitler.* Fletcher also led
the boys through his own favourite Greek tragedy, the Agamemnon of
Aeschylus. But it was his introduction to Homer that ignited Hugh's passion
for classics. At first he struggled with Homer's archaic vocabulary and the
unfamiliar form, but once he had broken the code (as he later put it), he
found he could read Homer's verse easily. Looking back a dozen years later,
Hugh would count this as one of the most memorable moments of his life.
'On I read, far past the appointed terminus, till late at night, fascinated;
and all my leisure hours for long afterwards were spent in reading Homer,
till I knew all the Iliad and Odyssey.'[4]

Irvine was encouraging about Hugh's prospects. 'I see no reason why the
highest scholarship should not be beyond his reach in due course,' he wrote
in an end-of-year report; 'He also has an unusual breadth of reading at his
command. The only thing I at all fear is his facility: I sometimes wish things
caused him a little more difficulty.' In Irvine's reports there are several
references to Hugh's 'fatal facility', and warnings about the dangers of over-
confidence.

Looking back, Hugh qualified his gratitude at being so well taught at
Charterhouse with this reservation: 'one element of education was, as it
now seems to me, entirely missing. That missing element was thought.'
Perhaps, he wrote in an autobiographical fragment, 'one should not expect
schoolboys to think. Perhaps, at that age, when the mind is quick to absorb
rules and facts, but is otherwise still immature, they should be drilled in
the discipline of language and mathematics, [and] build up a repository of
factual and linguistic knowledge, the essential tools for later exploration.'
Yet for Hugh learning, valuable though it was, would never be enough in
itself. His questioning mind would constantly search out problems, and
seek to answer them.

During his final year in the school Hugh edited *The Carthusian,* the
school magazine. His editorials were mildly facetious, but there was
little trace yet of the distinctive Trevor-Roper style. Contributions to *The
Carthusian* were unsigned, so it is difficult to single out those that might
be his.

By the time he had reached the Sixth form, Hugh had confirmed his
position as one of the academic stars of the school. In his first year he was

placed third overall, winning prizes for divinity, modern history and the essay prize, as well as one of the prizes awarded to those who had achieved the highest aggregate scores across a range of subjects. In the following year, his last at Charterhouse, he was placed top of the Classical Sixth, acknowledged as the highest form in the school, thereby winning the form prize, and scooped up a fistful of other prizes: for classical composition, for English literature, for divinity (again), and for the study of classical literature. Hugh had also become a school monitor, and was by now Head Monitor of Daviesites, where, according to one of his contemporaries, he was 'held in respect but not fear'. As such, he was acknowledged as the second boy in the school, after the Head Monitor.

Hugh applied to Christ Church, where three exhibitions, each worth £90 a year,* were reserved for Carthusians. In this he was influenced by Irvine, who himself had been at Christ Church, which he reckoned to be the only good Oxford college. Hugh sat the exam and won a scholarship to read *Literae Humaniores* (classics, philosophy and ancient history), beginning in the Michaelmas (autumn) term† of 1932. He was awarded the Talbot Scholarship, worth £20 per year, with a prize of books to the value of £5; and one of the five school exhibitions of £80 per year, each tenable for four years. Another school exhibition, worth a further £80 per year, was at the disposal of the governors, and in 1932 this was awarded to Goode, Hugh's compatriot from Belhaven Hill, who won a scholarship to Trinity, Cambridge. Hugh's other rival, Bowes, also won a scholarship to Christ Church to read Greats, though disappointingly he would only manage a second-class degree. Hugh did not much care for him. After both had left Oxford, he wrote a satirical ode celebrating Bowes's appointment as a schoolmaster at Brighton College. 'Bowes', he wrote to his brother, 'is about as interesting as cold cabbage, and certainly much less witty.' Bowes would be killed on active service in 1942.

Hugh left Charterhouse at the end of the 1932 Summer Quarter. 'I hope his career at Oxford and in life will fulfil the high promise of his school record,' Fletcher wrote in his final report: 'if so, he will do <u>very</u> well. His memory powers, scholarship, and capacity for rapid and effective expression are exceptionally good.'

In September Hugh set out on a walking holiday in the Scottish Borders with two companions, which formed the basis of a light-hearted article he contributed to the Charterhouse literary magazine *Greyfriar*, his first signed appearance in print. This was an account of a local figure he had

---

* This was a substantial sum, worth approximately fifty times as much in today's money.
† The University calendar consists of three eight-week terms, called Michaelmas (autumn), Hilary (spring) and Trinity (summer).

encountered in the pages of Walter Scott: Thomas of Ercildoune, the thirteenth-century soothsayer known as Thomas the Rhymer – an apt subject for Hugh's satirical pen, enabling him to poke fun at the credulousness of the Scots. He introduced his account with a self-mocking description of the holiday, claiming that his companions had 'nipped in the bud all my stories' and 'allowed none of my Scottish ballads to proceed beyond the second line'. His piece was illustrated with two satirical sketches, depicting himself peering through round spectacles, dressed in cap, tweeds and plus-fours, bearing a knapsack, equipped with walking-stick in one hand and map in the other, and puffing unconvincingly at a pipe.

In the following spring another piece of his would appear in *Greyfriar*, purporting to be 'an ancient romance', sung by a minstrel to the accompaniment of a harp in the year AD 2934, of events that had happened a thousand years earlier. The supposed minstrel told of a hunt for the Loch Ness Monster (then much in the news), led by the mighty Lord Rother of the Mere, sailing in his ship *Dilly Mail*, much to the chagrin of his rival, Lord Beaver of the Brook. This ludicrous squib was illustrated by two more of Hugh's cartoons.

At the end of the first week of October, refreshed by his strenuous holiday, Hugh went up to Oxford.

3

Undergraduate

Christ Church is the grandest of the Oxford colleges. An undergraduate who went up to Christ Church just after the Second World War compared it to the Brigade of Guards: 'just as the British Army was said to consist of the Brigade of Guards and a few attached troops, so we considered that the University consisted of Christ Church and a few attached colleges'.[1] Other colleges barely registered in the minds of Christ Church men. One pre-war undergraduate is said to have requested a taxi from a college porter at the main gate; when asked where he was going, the young man answered vaguely, 'Oh, Pembroke'. The porter was understandably bemused. Pembroke College stands on the opposite side of St Aldates, just across the street.

Christ Church's generous size suggests its superiority. Other colleges seem cramped by comparison. To its side stretches Christ Church Meadow, a field running down to the river, itself almost as big as the rest of the University combined. Christ Church's quadrangles include the magnificent Tom Quad, the largest in Oxford. Wren's Tom Tower, above the Great Gate that forms the main entrance to the college, is one of the city's landmarks. For his first year Hugh was allotted a set of rooms, comprising a bedroom and a separate sitting-room, on the ground floor of Staircase 2,* overlooking St Aldates – ideal for undergraduates who wanted to climb in at night after the gate was locked. One contemporary enviously described Hugh's as 'the most luxurious chambers in Tom'.

The college originated in 1525, and was first known as Cardinal's College after its founder, Cardinal Wolsey. 'The establishment was planned on a magnificent scale,' Hugh would write in a brief guide to the history and architecture of Christ Church, published after the war, 'and picked young men were drawn thither from every source, even from Cambridge.'†[2] After Wolsey's fall in 1529 it was inherited by King Henry VIII together with the rest of the Cardinal's property, including Hampton Court Palace. For

---

* The set no longer exists, most of it now forming part of the Porters' Lodge.
† Hugh wrote this booklet on his own initiative. Christ Church's Governing Body licensed its publication in 1950 as an official guide (though Hugh ensured that he retained the copyright himself), for sale to visitors, and it was presented gratis to every undergraduate on arrival. A second edition was produced in 1971, and a third in 1985. It is still in print today.

almost twenty years afterwards it was a meagre, stopgap affair, but in 1545 the King, flush with the confiscated wealth of the monasteries, dissolved his former foundation and, next year, 'refounded' it as Christ Church.[3] From the year of the refoundation the Cathedral itself has formed part of the college, which explains why Christ Church is known as 'the House', a reference to its Latin name, *Aedes Christi*, the House of God. The Dean of the Cathedral is always head of the college, and until an Act of Parliament in 1867 the Dean and the Chapter alone constituted the Governing Body, so that the professional teachers (known, confusingly, as 'Students') were not independent Fellows but mere subordinate employees, with no say in the running of the college. After 1867 these teachers were elevated to the status of governors like the Fellows of any other college, though they remained known as 'Students'. Two of the canonries were then abolished, and all save one of the remaining six attached to University professorships; yet there remained (and remains) a tension within the college between the clerical and the secular.

Socially, Christ Church had long been a cut above the rest. For generation after generation, it was the obvious choice for young aristocrats. Recalling his time as an undergraduate at Magdalen in the late 1920s, John Betjeman remarked how Christ Church men always seemed to give the impression that they were just dropping in at Oxford on their way to a seat in the House of Lords, shortly to be vacated on the deaths of their fathers; or that they were coming into college for a term or two, but spending most of their time away in country houses.[4] Among the preponderance of under-graduates from the great English public schools could be found the occa-sional foreign princeling, young count or maharajah, or the son of a Greek or American plutocrat. The intake of ninety-one freshmen who came up to Christ Church in 1932 included Lord Hugh Percy, Earl St Aldwyn, Lord Lyell and the Master of Elphinstone. This was a much grander society than the predominantly middle-class environment of Charterhouse.

Christ Church has always prized brains as well as breeding; one third of the undergraduate places were reserved for scholars, who sat at a separate table in Hall and wore a longer gown to distinguish themselves from the commoners. Nevertheless, the college traditionally took a relaxed attitude to the lacunae of young men from the right backgrounds. As late as 1964, for example, Christ Church had the largest proportion of public school boys of any college, and the largest proportion of undergraduates failing their Finals.[5] As Hugh would observe, 'social grandeur is not always or necessarily equivalent to intellectual eminence'. Over the centuries many a young squire had been advised by his chaplain to go to Christ Church 'if only for a term or so', with the assurance that there was not the least occasion to open any books there except 'those excellent works', the Stud

Book and the Racing Calendar.[6] It was argued that the presence of such men added to the gaiety of the college, enlivening what might otherwise become a grey meritocracy, though of course snobbery played a part too. Dean White, head of the college when Hugh went up in 1932, was said to tremble with pleasure at the mention of a duke.[7] A very small man, he wore a top hat, which he raised ceremonially whenever he met an undergraduate who happened to be a member of the peerage.

Soon after his arrival at Christ Church, Hugh received an invitation to tea with the Dean. Entering the deanery, he found one other new undergraduate had been invited: a Parsee from India. Why the two of them had been combined was unclear. The Dean greeted Hugh with the words, 'Mr Trevor-Roper, I think that you come from Northumberland. I always say that so long as we have the Percys and the Cecils, Christ Church can hold up its head among the colleges of Oxford.' The conversation advanced awkwardly, the two undergraduates sitting silent most of time while the Dean's American wife loudly scolded a novice footman for a succession of blunders.

This patrician predominance gave its own character to the college. Free-spending Christ Church men drove sports cars, followed country pursuits, gave extravagant parties and treated the dons much as they might servants.

Life could be difficult for the few proletarians who made it through the gate. One of these was A.L. Rowse, an earnest left-winger when he came up to Christ Church in 1921. As Rowse recalled more than forty years afterwards, he was persecuted by a group of 'toughs' who had no intellectual interests whatsoever. When they got drunk he would close his outer door (an action known as 'sporting your oak', indicating that you did not want to be disturbed); they 'would shout and scream and beat on it, sometimes attempting to pour water through the letter-box, while I sat it out within, heart palpitating with fury and indignation as much as fear'.[8] Rowse described Christ Church as 'a very stuck-up place in those days, insufferably complacent'. Half a lifetime later he remained aggrieved at not having been elected to a History lectureship at his old college, after he had been encouraged to apply.[9]

Harold Acton, high priest of the Aesthetes, had been a contemporary of Rowse's at Christ Church. The fascinated Rowse described him as 'a bird of brilliant plumage', mincing his way through the mob with an odd, affected carriage.[10] Leaning from his window, Acton had recited Eliot's *The Waste Land* to his fellow Oxonians through a megaphone. When Hugh arrived ten years later Acton's acolytes could still be found there, despite the philistine hearties who rampaged through the quadrangles, smashing glass and de-bagging those undergraduates suspected of having 'artistic' tendencies. A handful of celebrated 'Queens' combined a flamboyant

appearance with a studied formality of manner.[11] In his first term at Christ
Church Hugh was shocked to be introduced to 'a real horror' at a tea party,
whose appearance and manner left him at a loss for words; in trying to
describe him, he could only quote a complaint in the Junior Common
Room book that 'hermaphrodites' were being allowed into the JCR.[12]

The more sophisticated environment of Christ Church unsettled Hugh.
Having been a big fish in the small pond of Charterhouse, he now found
himself diminished and exposed in an open sea. He envied the easy manners
and effortless self-assurance of the Etonians or the intellectual repertoire
of the boys from Stowe, who would casually drop the names of Marx or
Freud, Pirandello or Pound, while he could only quote Sophocles or Seneca.
Hugh longed to escape from his own identity, which he despised as provincial and gauche. Sitting with the scholars in Hall, he gazed admiringly
at the young men at the other tables, whose open and carefree ways contrasted with the timid, inhibited and introverted qualities of mouse-like
scholarship boys like himself. Hugh found his work comparatively straight-
forward, so he began to loosen up, drinking fine wines and champagnes,
dining on oysters and salmon, and throwing lavish lunch parties. Often he
would be drunk in the evening. He bet on horses to fund his increased
expenditure. The bottle and the turf played a large part in this new life,
which he described in expansive letters to his brother Pat, then still a
schoolboy at Charterhouse.

Whenever possible Hugh liked to be outside, tramping through the
countryside after a pack of beagles, or riding to hounds, not gathering
mould in some fusty library. These were activities that could occupy most
of the daylight hours, starting soon after dawn and continuing until early
afternoon. Afterwards he would relax over several pints of beer and darts
in a pub – especially The Sportsman at Quainton, where Hugh became
friendly with the local farmers. After closing time he would often go on to
a cottage for a supper of bread and cheese and pickled onions, washed
down with more beer from a barrel, when songs would be sung and the
blacksmith's son would entertain them on a mouth organ. At last there
would be the jolly drive back to Oxford through the dark and the fog,
blowing bugles and hunting-horns, the car weaving across the road, or into
a ditch – or, on one memorable occasion, into the duck pond at Marsh
Gibbon. Once both car lights failed, and they crawled back towards town
with Hugh crouched outside on the running-board to shout directions to
the driver.

In the early mornings Hugh would sometimes run around Christ Church
Meadow, racing a friend. At other times he would stroll around the
Meadow, engaged in earnest discussion with companions, or alone, deep
in thought.

A.J. Ayer, who took his degree from Christ Church in the year Hugh arrived, observed in his memoirs that in those days there seemed to be time for everything.[13] Undergraduates tended to adopt the attitudes of a leisured class, whatever their social backgrounds. Such attitudes were fostered by the material advantages the young men enjoyed, living in sets of rooms attended by college servants, known as scouts, who supplied coal for the fire and hot water for shaving, and waited at luncheon and dinner parties. The day began with a roll-call at eight o'clock. Undergraduates were meant to be fully dressed for the roll-call, but in practice it was sufficient to turn up wearing an overcoat over pyjamas. Afterwards scouts would bring breakfast, which could consist of as many as four courses, to their rooms. Lectures could begin at any time from nine o'clock onwards, but few lecturers chose to start before ten, and attendance was not compulsory in any case. Teaching consisted of a weekly tutorial, often taken individually or at most with one other, at the outset of which the undergraduate would read his essay aloud; the rest of the tutorial would be taken up with a discussion of the essay's subject. When not at lunch parties, undergraduates would generally take a cold lunch in their rooms or in the Junior Common Room. Afternoons were left free for leisure activities. Tea was served in the JCR, and tutorials taken in the early evening, before dinner in Hall or, on warm evenings, outside on the grass lawn, which began at 7.15 p.m. In those days dons invariably dined in evening dress, but undergraduates were merely required to wear gowns over their normal clothes, as they were at lectures and tutorials. Nor were they obliged to dine in Hall, though since they were charged for at least four dinners a week, most chose to do so. Those who wanted to dine out gravitated towards The George, a fashionable restaurant on the corner of George Street and Cornmarket, though the food was no better than in Hall and considerably more expensive. After dinner one could go out on the town, perhaps to visit undergraduates in other colleges. The cinema was a legitimate attraction, as was the Oxford Playhouse, with a programme largely consisting of farces and Agatha Christie murder mysteries, with the occasional new work by Noël Coward or Bernard Shaw, or revivals of plays by Barrie or Galsworthy. Hugh took advantage of a visit to Oxford by the D'Oyly Carte Opera Company to see *Trial by Jury*, *The Pirates of Penzance* and *The Yeomen of the Guard*. But the city's pubs were out of bounds to undergraduates, patrolled by proctors to ensure compliance. Alternatively one could entertain guests in one's rooms until the main gate closed at twenty minutes past twelve – except women guests, who had to be ushered out by ten. The rules strengthened the society of the college. Undergraduates were not allowed to sleep out of college during term. Misdemeanours could result in the culprit being 'gated', i.e. confined to college in the evenings.

One night in his first term Hugh attended 'a somewhat immoral College Debating Society', which, as he explained in a letter to his brother, 'provides ample refreshment and is quite amusing. I gave an eloquent harangue upon one of the Canons of the Cathedral who is the most repulsive man I have ever seen, who is fat and glistening, and who, in the words of a Don at the said meeting "sweats – I say it with a shudder – sweats while he eats, winter and summer".' Hugh's distaste for religiosity was becoming apparent. 'I have already got into disfavour with certain religious beings by con-tinually refusing their invitations to religious tea-parties.'[14] Nonetheless Hugh attended the occasional Sunday Cathedral service. Soon after his arrival in Oxford he heard the Dean preach a sermon entirely devoted to praise of the Japanese, whom he extolled as models for people of other nations. Since the Japanese had recently invaded Manchuria, and there set up a puppet government notorious for its brutality and oppression, the Dean's panegyric struck Hugh as odd.

Continuing the military training he had begun at Charterhouse, Hugh joined the cavalry section of the University Officers' Training Corps (OTC). He does not seem to have taken this very seriously; perhaps he just wanted an opportunity to ride. At weekends Hugh sometimes went back to Charterhouse for the day, or took a long walk in the Oxfordshire countryside. Early in his second term, during a cold spell, when even the Mercury pool in the middle of Tom Quad was frozen hard, Hugh boasted to Pat that he had been for 'a short stroll' of thirty-eight miles in the Cotswolds.[15]

Classical scholars undertook a four-year course, studying first the classical languages themselves (Honour Moderations or Mods), and then ancient history and philosophy (Greats). There were examinations at the end of both parts of the course, marked separately. Hugh soon showed his excep-tional qualities. 'An exceedingly intelligent and capable scholar', wrote one of his tutors, Denys Page, at the end of his first term; 'he should do very well indeed, assisted by exuberant but not unfounded self-confidence. I have nothing but praise for his work.' Page was only a few years older than Hugh, a man of gaiety and charm, but with a tendency to dogmatism that sometimes led to ferocious quarrels. A grammar school boy, he had won a scholarship to Christ Church in 1926, where he had been awarded several of the most coveted University-wide prizes, and obtained first classes in both Mods and Greats. He had received special coaching from J.D. Dennis-ton at Hertford College, a philological specialist who became one of Hugh's closest friends. It was probably at Page's suggestion that Hugh was farmed out to Denniston for a term.

After Hugh's first term his other tutor, J.G. Barrington-Ward,* predicted 'many triumphs'. Barrington-Ward was a very efficient teacher though, like Page, he showed no interest in the classics as literature, which to Hugh was one of the main reasons for reading them. Instead of studying the classics as presenting an exemplary model of life, and as a means of understanding the civilisation and culture of antiquity, Barrington-Ward saw them, so Hugh felt, as an opportunity for a kind of learned crossword puzzle. Hugh would come to feel that there was something sterile about this approach to classical studies, exemplified above all by the scholar A.E. Housman, who had neglected ancient history and philosophy altogether.

After the Trinity term 1933, Page was even more enthusiastic, describing Hugh as 'a brilliant scholar, painstaking and ingenious'. He had already been honourably mentioned for the Gaisford Prize for Greek Verse, and Page saw this as merely 'a prelude to very considerable distinctions'. Such tutors' reports were delivered in Hall in the end-of-term 'Collections', at which the Dean would pass judgement on the performance and behaviour of the undergraduates in question. Dean White was famous for his *faux pas* on such occasions, often delivering a damning appraisal to the wrong man.

It had been impressed on Hugh at Charterhouse that a classical scholar ought to be able to read the writings of the dominant figure in classical studies, Ulrich von Wilamowitz-Moellendorff. He therefore decided to teach himself German, by the method he had used to learn Greek: first mastering the structure, and then reading a book of sufficient length and intrinsic interest to enable him to 'break the code'. He chose for this purpose Gregorovius's *History of the City of Rome in the Middle Ages* (1859–72), a dauntingly monumental work in eight volumes. At the back of his mind was another motive. Hugh had no very clear idea of what to do after he finished at Oxford. His uncle Claude, one of his father's older brothers, offered to have him articled as a solicitor in his office in Manchester, but Hugh did not relish this prospect. Another uncle, his mother's brother Jim, suggested that he might join the family firm in South America, which sounded much more romantic; but his mother stamped on the idea of his working in 'trade'. Hugh was not attracted either by the notion of becoming a schoolmaster, or even a don teaching classics. Many of the cleverest young men of his generation aspired to a career in the Foreign Service, for which one needed French (which he had studied since his lessons with Miss Amos fifteen years earlier) and German. The life of a diplomat sounded pleasant,

---

* One of his older brothers was Robert Barrington-Ward, then chief leader writer for *The Times* and deputy to the Editor, Geoffrey Dawson, who in 1941 would succeed Dawson as Editor. Like Dawson, Barrington-Ward was a strong supporter of the Baldwin and Chamberlain Governments' policy of appeasement towards Nazi Germany.

with the glamour of postings abroad. In so far as he had an ambition, this was it.

To speed his understanding of this new language he arranged to spend part of his first long vacation in Vienna* with an undergraduate friend, another classical scholar called Robert Beaumont. The custom in those days was for visiting students to lodge with a local family. The people to whom they applied could take only one of them, and so passed on the other to neighbours. (In retrospect, it seemed surprising that these two families should have been on cordial terms, since one of them was Jewish, and the other Nazi.) The two young Englishmen read in the mornings, and divided their evenings between the cinemas and the beer gardens.[16] Vienna was then in ferment, with a socialist mayor confronting a conservative Chancellor. Meanwhile Hitler had come to power in Germany, encouraging Nazi agitators in his former homeland. Within a year an Austrian civil war would erupt; the Chancellor would be murdered by the Nazis, while the showpiece Karl-Marx workers' flats in Vienna would be shelled by the Austrian army. None of this tension was apparent to Hugh, however. At the time he was entirely apolitical. In domestic politics he had assumed the unthinking conservatism of his parents and their circle. Indeed the local MP for the Berwick-on-Tweed division of Northumberland, which embraced Glanton and Alnwick, the conservative Captain A.J.K. Todd, was a close family friend. Hugh did not bother to cast a vote in the general election of 1935, the first in which he was eligible to vote, when Todd was defeated by the Liberal candidate, Sir William Seely. The National Government embraced moderate opinion from all three main political parties. Two factions of Opposition Liberals competed for the support of a dwindling number of Liberal MPs. The unpalatable alternatives were either the rump of the Labour Party on the Left, or the fascist party being organised by Sir Oswald Mosley on the Right. The turbulence within almost every country on the European mainland discouraged Britons from extremist politics. Young people displayed ambivalent feelings towards the German revival, many sympathising with German complaints at the harsh terms imposed on them by the victorious Allies in the Versailles Treaty. Some wanted to make friends with Germans: the poet Stephen Spender took this so far as to sleep with young Germans as a gesture of reconciliation.

Hugh was disinclined, both by background and by temperament, from taking an interest in politics. Though he had joined the League of Nations Union (LNU) at Charterhouse, this was the kind of worthy cause he had since discarded, together with much of his schoolboy identity. There is no

---

* Hugh may have been influenced by Page, who had spent the year 1930–1 studying in Vienna after taking his degree.

record of his speaking at or even attending the debates at the Oxford Union during his undergraduate career – in contrast to his contemporary Max Beloff, later a conservative historian, who in those days invariably championed the progressive cause. Hugh was certainly not present for the notorious debate on 9 February 1933, when the motion 'This House will in no circumstances fight for its King and Country' was carried, by a majority of 275 votes to 153. The result was greeted with outrage in the patriotic press* and was widely believed to have encouraged Hitler to think that 'England' would not fight, though the evidence for this is flimsy.[17] Whether the vote was truly representative of undergraduate opinion as a whole may be doubted.[18] The Union attracted the most politically minded under-graduates, which in the 1930s meant those on the Left. In the second debate of the Michaelmas term of 1932, for example, the motion was carried that 'This House believes that the Russian experiment is succeeding, and welcomes its success'. A few weeks later, the House decided that socialism offered 'the only solution to the problems facing this country'.

The Union President at the time of the 'King and Country' debate was a Christ Church man, Frank Hardie. Indeed Christ Church in the 1930s was a very political college. The Senior Common Room contained several parliamentary candidates, three of whom – the physicist Professor Frederick Lindemann (later Lord Cherwell), and two younger dons, Frank Pakenham (later Lord Pakenham, and later still, Lord Longford), who taught politics, and the historian Patrick Gordon Walker – would attain ministerial office, albeit the first two as peers. Gordon Walker stood as Labour candidate for Oxford City in 1935, while the economist Roy Harrod, biographer of Keynes, stood as the Liberal. Several other dons had strong political contacts. Former Christ Church men such as Randolph Churchill and Quintin Hogg maintained close links with their *alma mater* while noisily engaged in politics.

Though Hugh was indifferent to all this political activity, even he could hardly remain oblivious to the stream of Jewish refugees from Nazi Germany, who arrived in Britain in increasing numbers. In particular, a conspicuous figure appeared at Christ Church that summer: Albert Einstein, then the most famous scientist in the world. He had been per-suaded to come to England by Lindemann, who toured Germany in his chauffeur-driven Rolls-Royce, seeking out distinguished Jewish scientists displaced by the Nazis. Einstein boarded with Roy Harrod and his wife Billa in their St Aldates house. With his brown suit and unruly shock of white hair, he stood out among the other dons dining in Hall. That same

---

* The *Daily Express* blamed 'practical jokers, woozy-minded Communists and sexual inde-terminates' for the vote.

June, some very different Germans arrived in Oxford: a group of Nazi students on a 'private visit'. In November, Mosley addressed a meeting of the British Union of Fascists at Oxford Town Hall, a short distance up St Aldates from Christ Church; according to the *Oxford Magazine*, hecklers were 'very roughly handled' by Mosley's 'private army'. In the mid-1930s Mosley was a frequent visitor to Oxford, where a small number of Black-shirts could be found in most colleges. In November 1934, for example, he was guest speaker at the University Fascists' Dinner. In May 1936, Mosley held a packed meeting at the Carfax Assembly Rooms in Oxford, at which protesters were set upon by Blackshirt 'stewards' armed with truncheons.[19] Hugh reported to his mother on the event. 'Great damage to the Blackshirts was done by one of the dons of Christ Church, who, being struck over the head by a Blackshirt with a steel chain, was roused to a berserk fury.'[20] This was Frank Pakenham. An undergraduate strolling around Tom Quad late that evening heard a commotion outside and a battering at the gate, which was opened immediately; in staggered the tall figure of Pakenham, blood pouring down his face from a scalp wound.

For his second year Hugh moved into rooms in the Victorian Meadows Building. There he gave a lunch party for Ann Sitwell, presumably a friend from Northumberland – 'you know, the wench everyone fought to have as a permanent opponent at Mr Rea's tennis tournaments', he explained to his brother. Apparently she was a desirable young woman; Hugh was certainly disappointed when she cut him dead the next time they met. 'I suppose she prefers the pseudo-intellectual shits with whom she seems to associate,' he complained.[21]

At the end of the Michaelmas term 1933, a note of criticism crept into his tutors' reports for the first time. 'A very able man who does exceptional work and a lot of it,' wrote Page: 'he has unfortunately not yet grown out of a certain childish superciliousness which has a strong and bad effect on his attitude to his work, and even on the work itself.' By the end of the Hilary term 1934, Page could report that 'he has far more patience and sympathy with his subject than of old'. During this term Hugh sat Honour Moderations, and emerged with a first. He had already won the Craven Scholarship, a prize won by many of the country's leading classicists over the years. Hugh was in all probability the best classical scholar in his year.

But by this time he had decided to change course. Instead of continuing to read Greats for the second half of his degree, he switched to modern history. One reason was that he did not relish the prospect of being taught Roman history by 'Bobbie' Longden, whom he actively disliked, and indeed despised; or Greek history by R.H. (Robert, known to his friends as 'Robin') Dundas, notorious for his prurient cross-examination of shy and lonely schoolboys. 'I forget,' Dundas would say in his curious, pinched voice, once he was alone in his rooms with a newly arrived undergraduate, 'are you a bugger?' But there was a more fundamental reason for Hugh's decision. He had become disenchanted with classical studies as they were then taught at Oxford. Classical scholarship seemed to him to have reached a dead end, consisting of editing and re-editing the same texts, 'tinkering with texts', as he later described it. By this time, as he later recalled, 'I had read all the classical literature worth reading, and much that was not. Why scrape the bottom of the barrel?'[22]

Hugh was thinking about his future. The study of modern history seemed appropriate to the diplomatic career he envisaged. To join the Foreign Service depended on passing a special examination, which could be undertaken no sooner than two years after graduation. In the meantime he would fund himself by obtaining a Fellowship at All Souls, the postgraduate college reserved for the cleverest scholars, an established first step on the route into the Diplomatic Service. And he would continue to improve his French and German, with the intention of becoming fluent. In the pursuit of this aim, he spent the spring vacation of 1934 in Provence, and the summer in Burgundy, staying as a paying guest in a suite of rooms in a château. 'Do you know', he wrote to Pat, with the air of a man of the world, 'that prostitutes in Paris can be had for 6 francs?'[23] Though he affected an air of authority on the subject, there is no evidence that Hugh took advantage of the bargains to be had in the French capital, or indeed that he had any experience of sex at this age. It seems likely that he was still uncertain of his sexuality, like so many of his contemporaries. Perhaps sensing this, a Moorish soldier propositioned him in the Palace of the Popes in Avignon, a fact of which Hugh later boasted to his prurient friend Logan Pearsall Smith.

In the Trinity term 1934 Hugh began to read modern history, taught for one term only by J.N.L. (Nowell) Myres, who had taken firsts in both classics and modern history, and who specialised in Roman and Anglo-Saxon Britain. 'Has made an excellent start,' reported Myres; 'he reads the sources with avidity and has views of his own: he should do very well.' Modern history was the most popular school in Oxford, regarded as a soft option, suitable for those sons (and a few daughters) of wealthy men whose academic abilities were limited.[24] Of those modern history candidates taking Schools* in 1935, only 8 per cent obtained first-class degrees.[25] The course covered the whole of English history, from medieval to modern, at a superficial level, with a century or so of foreign history, and then a special

---

* The exam taken at the end of the BA course, more commonly known nowadays as 'Finals'. The term 'Schools' is also used for the Examination Schools, the building where undergraduates sit their exams.

subject which one would study from primary sources. In the year in which Hugh took up modern history, the syllabus was in the process of being reformed, with the inclusion of a general paper (which embraced 'development and methods of historical writing'), and the extension of the period that could be studied into more recent times.[26] Hugh took advantage of this extension to study European history from 1815 to 1914.

Far from abandoning classics, Hugh continued reading and studying classical literature for two more terms, in parallel with his historical studies. It was during this period that he won two more of the most prestigious classical prizes, the Hertford ('for the promotion of Latin') and the Ireland ('for the promotion of classical learning and taste'), and was again honourably mentioned for his efforts to win the Gaisford Prize for Greek Verse. The following year he was *proxime accessit* (runner-up) for the Gaisford. 'Brilliant work,' commented Page at the end of the Michaelmas term 1934, 'done in odd moments stolen from his History tutors.'

Those tutors, Keith Feiling and J.C. (John) Masterman, were equally enthusiastic about him. 'The ablest man I have taught for several years,' reported Feiling at the end of his first term: 'I have the highest hopes.' Feiling, a courteous, kindly man who spoke with a stutter, had been a tutor at Christ Church for almost a quarter of a century, and was soon to retire from teaching to concentrate on research, particularly on the history of the Tory Party, which became the subject of two of his major works. He kept up a wide range of political contacts, including Winston Churchill, who sought Feiling's guidance on his life of his ancestor John Churchill, 1st Duke of Marlborough, published in four volumes from 1933 to 1938. A pupil who shared tutorials with Hugh remembered Feiling coming in late, and explaining, by way of apology, that he had just come from a meeting with 'Winston'. Feiling was a serious scholar of an old-fashioned kind, who seemed to Hugh out of touch with modern historical thinking of the type taught by the younger men, almost all of whom were on the Left.

Though very different in temperament, Feiling and Masterman formed a highly effective partnership, ensuring that in the inter-war years the Christ Church history school achieved more first-class degrees than that of any other college.[27] Hugh compared Masterman to the best kind of public school master, who never did any research and whose emphasis was entirely on teaching. Indeed there was some thought that he might become Headmaster of Eton. However, his approach was too limited for the cleverest pupils: Rowse, for example, who had been bored by Masterman's tutorials, which he had found intellectually lacking.[28] A fine athlete, Masterman had played hockey for England and lawn tennis at Wimbledon, and was selected for an MCC tour of Canada as late as 1937, when he was in his mid-forties. According to A.J. ('Freddie') Ayer, who joined the Christ Church Senior

Common Room in 1932 as a lecturer in philosophy, Masterman's outlook on life resembled that of a character in a John Buchan novel.[29] An easygoing bachelor don, he was, like Feiling, well connected with those in power, and assiduous in helping pupils of whom he approved to find jobs. Hugh reckoned that one could judge how high one ranked in Masterman's estimation by the club at which he invited you to lunch. (Hugh was always invited to the best club.) Masterman's reports show that he found Hugh 'a very pleasant pupil to teach' and 'a most agreeable pupil'.

In contrast to Feiling and Masterman, the young Patrick Gordon Walker had embraced Marxism. He was determined to reform and modernise the teaching of history at Oxford. He summoned first-year students to his rooms and there explained that history was not an art, but a science. The Marxist interpretation had predicted the course of events since Marx's own time with such remarkable accuracy that it could now be regarded as scientifically valid. This seemed very exciting to Hugh at the time. 'The vast pageant of history, hitherto so indeterminate, so formless, so mysterious, now had, as it seemed, a beautiful, mechanical regularity, and modern science had supplied a master-key which, with a satisfying click, would turn in every lock, open all its dark chambers, and reveal all its secret workings.'[30]

Hugh found his historical studies undemanding, allowing him time to relax and enjoy himself. 'I am leading a fairly sober life just now, getting frequently bottled but never drunk,' he informed his brother in a typical communication; 'but will be very tight on Friday night when I am going to such a blind as one doesn't find more than once a year.'[31] Hugh was now on friendly terms with several of the younger dons, including Freddie Ayer and Frank Pakenham. Early in 1935 he boasted in a letter to Pat, who had gone up to Cambridge to read medicine, that he had been lunching at The George with the famous Maurice Bowra, rated by Ayer as 'by far the most influential don in the university'.[32]

A classicist, Bowra was an unequivocal admirer of the values he identified in Greek literature. According to Anthony Powell (a Balliol undergraduate in the mid-1920s), Bowra 'openly praised the worship of Pleasure'.[33] Though he revelled in malicious gossip, he would not tolerate criticism, and was savage to those whom he thought guilty of disloyalty. Bowra was admired especially for his bons mots, which caused generations of undergraduates to fall off their chairs laughing. His conversation could be bullying, even brutal, though it was rarely dull. A short, bullet-headed man, Bowra spoke rapidly, in a loud and resonant voice, which gave power to his witticisms. As a raconteur he was a welcome guest at the salons of hostesses like Margot Asquith, Ottoline Morrell and, latterly, Ann Fleming. He cultivated undergraduate followers, known as 'Bowristas': some of the most brilliant students of the inter-war years came into his orbit, including Noel Annan, Freddie Ayer, Isaiah Berlin, John Betjeman, Kenneth Clark, Cyril Connolly, Cecil Day-Lewis, Hugh Gaitskell, Stuart Hampshire, Osbert Lancaster, Anthony Powell, John Sparrow, Stephen Spender, Rex Warner, Evelyn Waugh and Henry Yorke (Henry Green).[34] The ethos of Bowra's 'Immoral Front' was homoerotic, like those of Mallarmé or Stefan George, though this was more a matter of style than practice. For most of his undergraduate acolytes, Oxford was an interim stage between single-sex boarding schools and adult heterosexuality. Bowra did not prey on young men, as Sparrow later did. Indeed, no one could be certain whether Bowra ever had sexual relations of any kind. Noel Annan later described Bowra as the Immoral Front's 'non-playing captain'.

Bowra preached freedom of thought and 'not playing the hypocrite more than necessary'. He told a visiting Nazi that he looked forward to using his skull as an inkpot. Hugh was stimulated by Bowra's often outrageous talk. He enthusiastically adopted Bowra's vision of life as a struggle between the cultivated and the philistine, the gay and the drab.

In the same letter in which he mentioned lunching with Bowra, Hugh enthused to his brother about the essays and notebooks of Samuel Butler (published in two volumes in 1912 and 1934). Many years later he would describe Butler as 'his earliest literary hero', who had 'loosened, refreshed, and redirected' the 'long-misused energies' of his mind. Hugh first encountered Butler during his freshman year, in an anthology of prose and verse he had purchased with the money he had received from a school prize. This contained a passage from Butler's novel *Erewhon* (1872), which inspired Hugh to read the whole book, and he had been so captivated by this witty satire of Victorian values that he had gone on to read everything Butler had written. Hugh particularly liked *The Fair Haven* (1873), 'that splendid spoof which ruined his reputation'. Butler had originally published this book under a pseudonym, as if it were a sincere defence of religious orthodoxy in the form of a memoir. Though the whole work was meant ironically, some reviewers failed to see the point, and praised it for its piety and naturalness. They were therefore made to look foolish when Butler published a second edition under his own name, with an explanatory foreword. Reviewers and readers alike were wary of him thereafter.[35]

Listening to Bowra and reading Butler helped to liberate Hugh. Following Butler's example, 'I turned my back on the prim, traditional paths of classical learning'. Though he retained strong ethical views, for example in defence of elementary justice and intellectual freedom, he rejected orthodox morality – 'social & sexual conventions, religion, and all the apparatus of God & Sin'. These, he decided, were merely 'the systems people make out of their repressions'. They might make an interesting psychological study: 'but when people attach importance to them, I don't argue, I flee'.[36]

Butler wrote about a friend who, though rather a cad, was extrovert, genial, good-looking and carefree. In contrast, Butler felt himself to be crotchety and difficult, self-conscious and awkward. 'Why am I not more like my friend?' Butler had asked. When he read this passage Hugh experienced a shock of recognition. 'That's me,' he said to himself; 'that's exactly how I feel. I'm Samuel Butler!'

In the spring vacation of 1935 Hugh went to Germany, to improve his fluency in the language. He had arranged to stay with a family in Freiburg-im-Breisgau,* a medieval university town on the western edge of the Black Forest. It did not seem strange to him to be visiting Nazi Germany. Half the countries in Europe were ruled by unpleasant dictators of one sort or another; for a young Englishman with little interest in international politics, there seemed no reason to think Hitler particularly sinister. In 1936 John Stoye, another Christ Church undergraduate who became an historian, spent a vacation living with a Nazi family in Munich, without even noticing the political situation. Hitler was trying to woo the British, arguing that there was no need for 'England' and Germany to be enemies. Nazi zealots were encouraged to proselytise to visiting Britons about the new Germany.

Hugh experienced this even before he had arrived at his destination. En route to Freiburg he stopped at Bingen, to spend a day walking along the right bank of the Rhine (the left bank was still demilitarised, and until a few years before had been occupied by French troops). Pausing to examine a hideous monument to the Prussian triumph over the French in 1870, he was waylaid by two Germans, father and son, in ecstasies before this 'splendid' memorial to 'a happy time'. The father proceeded to lecture Hugh about the virtues, the peaceful intentions and the greatness of the *Führer*. When at last Hugh felt able to resume his walk, they accompanied him, continuing in the same vein, rehearsing him in what he should say about Germany when he returned to England. Desperate, Hugh cast around for a means of escape. It took some time before he was able to give them the slip. This was a hazard that he would encounter whenever he ventured out alone. After an apparently innocent, friendly greeting, the ubiquitous Nazi proselytiser would soon warm to his theme. How do you find the new Germany? How eager Germany is to be understood in England! The peace-loving *Führer* was noble and virtuous. What will you say about Germany when you arrive back in England? And so on, in a seemingly unending stream . . .

---

* Eduard Fraenkel, a prize pupil of Wilamowitz's, had been professor there until displaced by the Nazi codes forbidding Jews from holding university chairs. He came to Oxford as a refugee, and in 1935 he was living in rooms at Christ Church. Possibly he influenced Hugh's choice of destination.

In Freiburg Hugh lived with a widow, a cultivated lady who had a son of about the same age as Hugh, studying at the university. He was a keen Nazi and introduced Hugh to his young Nazi friends. His mother was more reserved. Hugh formed the impression that she looked down on the Nazis as crude and vulgar, as he did – though she supported the regime for want of a better alternative. On one occasion Hugh rashly referred to the persecution of the Jews. '*Das ist refugieten quatsch*,' she snapped angrily – that is refugee nonsense.

Hugh was taken up by this group of young Nazi students and drawn into their world. Not having any other contacts, he went along with them. He was made to watch parades of marching Nazis carrying fluttering swastikas, and to hear harangues by Party bosses at rallies. Far from converting him to the merits of National Socialism, however, these experiences had the opposite effect. He was nauseated by what he witnessed, revolted by the inflammatory rhetoric and appalled by what he saw as the abject conformity of the German people. The final straw came when he was taken to a demonstration, part of a violent propaganda campaign throughout Germany against the government of Lithuania, which like many other countries in Central and Eastern Europe had a substantial minority of ethnic Germans. There a group of young Nazis had been convicted of treason, and four of them condemned to death. In Freiburg, Hugh stood among the baying crowd as a Nazi demagogue addressed them from the balcony of the town hall. 'What is Lithuania?' he screamed, and then spat out his answer: 'A miserable little state which has no right to exist.' The crowd roared its approval.

Disgusted by such bullying talk, Hugh decided to cut short his stay in Freiburg. He took his leave of his landlady, and headed for nearby Baden-Baden, an attractive spa town, with the added appeal of a casino. Hugh had never been inside a casino before and was intrigued to see what one was like. His father always seemed to be trying out new 'systems' for winning at the roulette tables or on the racecourses – without much success. Hugh was therefore dubious about such systems, but during a long country walk he had devised a complex one, to occupy his mind as much as anything else. On his arrival at Baden-Baden, he checked into a little hotel not far from the casino. That afternoon he took his place at the roulette table. At first he only watched, to ensure that he understood the rules. Then he started to play, applying his system, which proved unexpectedly successful. By the early evening he had accumulated a useful sum. He left the table and went back to his hotel for dinner. Afterwards he returned to the casino and resumed gambling, again applying the system he had devised. Again he kept on winning. By the time the casino was about to close he had a large pile of counters in front of him. It was worth, by his standards, a very large amount.* When the time came for the last spin of the roulette wheel, Hugh's system showed that it was time for zero to turn up. He decided to risk all. One could double the maximum stake by placing the sum on each side of the table. This Hugh decided to do, betting on zero on both. He watched with feigned indifference as the wheel spun, and was agreeably surprised when the ball ended on zero. Hugh collected his winnings, tipped the croupier, and walked out of the casino with the air of a practised gambler.

This unexpected bonus presented a problem. Hugh was nearing the end of his stay in Germany. He knew that there were strict laws forbidding the export of currency, and harsh penalties for those caught doing so. He left Baden-Baden the next morning and spent a few days in Heidelberg contemplating what to do. The best course, he eventually decided, was to post the money back to England. He changed the money into high-denomination notes to reduce its bulk and crammed it into an envelope, which he addressed to himself at Merton. He would wait until the last moment before posting it in Cologne, intending to be safely across the Belgian border if the package was opened and his ruse discovered.

Hugh spent some of his last day in Bonn, where he was due to change trains for Cologne. He planned to take a few hours to walk around the town. But he had barely left the station when he was once again pounced upon by another Nazi missionary. How do you find the new Germany? Et cetera ... The man would not let Hugh interrupt, and promised to accompany him wherever he wanted to go. When Hugh attempted to escape, the man seized him by the shoulders and pinned him against the wall, while continuing his monologue. Hugh broke free, and made his escape. That was the last he saw of Bonn. He ran back to the station and caught an earlier train to Cologne, where he found a postbox, waited until the last collection had been made, and posted his package. Then he caught a night train across the border. In due course the package arrived unopened in Oxford.

Back in England, Hugh reflected on his experiences. He did not like the new Germany, which seemed full of Nazi 'bores', and warned Pat, who was contemplating a holiday in the Black Forest, against this peril.[37] Hugh decided that he never wanted to visit Germany again. On the positive side, he had achieved a certain fluency in the language, which he had originally taken up, at least in part, in order to read Wilamowitz. But this too had proved a disappointment. Hugh had read Wilamowitz's *Sappho und*

---

* It is difficult to estimate how much. Hugh enjoyed telling this story, and with each telling the amount seemed to grow.

Simonides in Freiburg, and found it ponderous and silly. It seemed to him that Wilamowitz had been overrated. He decided to waste no more time learning German.

At the end of the Trinity term 1935, Feiling's report praised Hugh for some 'distinguished work', though he qualified this with the comment, 'perhaps a little too lofty and independent of advice'. Hugh was now living in digs; Feiling commented that his pupil had been in 'rather mediocre health this term'.

A letter to his father from Geoffrey Latimer, a pupil who shared tutorials with Hugh, gives a snapshot of him at this time. 'Trevor-Roper is reputed by some to be the most brilliant brain in the college,' wrote Latimer. 'He's got a first in Mods, and everyone says he will walk away with a first in history.' Latimer described Hugh as 'frightfully nice, ascetic looking, thin face and spectacles and an inveterate punter – he lost all his "safe bets" last week, he was telling me.' The two of them always sat together for Masterman's lectures in Christ Church Hall. Latimer took copious notes, but Hugh never wrote a word, just sketching horses' heads throughout. Latimer cheerfully described the dispiriting experience of being Hugh's tutorial partner. It was evident to him that Masterman was far more interested in what Hugh had to say, even when his star pupil had a hangover. When Latimer finished reading his essay, Masterman just murmured a vague 'yes', and then turned away to talk to Hugh.

One Saturday early in December, Hugh read what was described as 'a provocative paper' on the Romantic Poets to a college essay club.[38] No record of its content survives, but the subject indicates the breadth of his interests. The following April an article appeared in the *Oxford Magazine* under the heading 'Homer Unmasked!' signed 'H.R.T-R'. This piece skilfully combined two areas of Hugh's expertise to prove his hypothesis that Homer was 'a bookie', analysing equestrian references in *The Iliad*. 'Let there be no cavilling by fractious professors,' he warned. Though this was an entertaining piece, Hugh was rash to publish it only a few weeks before Schools. One wonders whether he undertook it in answer to a drunken bet.

Towards the end of April, Hugh complained to Pat that his brain was 'not very different from an over-ripe Gorgonzola'. He ascribed his state to 'impending Schools, which even now hang before me like some dank, threatening cloud, while behind me lie a series of wasted years, like odious nightmares of the past'.[39] Hugh sat the exams a few weeks later, and in due course, to nobody's surprise, was awarded first-class honours.

Researcher

Immediately after taking Schools Hugh went to live on a Cotswold farm, to prepare for the examination for All Souls, due to take place at the beginning of the Michaelmas term. He stayed there alone, studying those topics he thought most likely to arise. On the appropriate day he presented himself for the exam, which included a general paper, a history paper and an oral. The arrangements for the oral examination struck him as odd. Among the Fellows of All Souls at the time were such grandees as Viscount Halifax, then Lord Privy Seal and Chancellor of Oxford University; Cosmo Lang, Archbishop of Canterbury; and Geoffrey Dawson, Editor of *The Times*. Though few of these had been involved in any kind of academic work for decades, and many of them had not sat an examination themselves for half a lifetime or more, they expected to play a part in the election of new Fellows. Hugh was nonplussed to find his viva conducted by the Home Secretary, Sir John Simon.

He was not elected. In fact he did not even make the shortlist of four. Perhaps his flippancy counted against him. In later life he could remember little about what he had written, though a passing reference in his diary for the following year provides a clue. In one of his papers he had referred to Rousseau's *Confessions* – a book he had not read – as 'a lucid journal of a life so utterly degraded that it has been a bestseller in France ever since'. (When he came to read the book six months later he would describe this judgement as 'a trifle hard').[1] In their collective report on the seventeen candidates, the assistant examiners remarked that 'Trevor-Roper has a good knowledge but is apt to spoil his effects by a display of cleverness and his work lacks grip'.[2] These comments were made on behalf of all five assistant examiners, but they bear the stamp of the historian Llewellyn (E.L.) Woodward, an influential figure within All Souls in the 1930s. The two successful candidates that year were Stuart Hampshire (Balliol) and Dennis Routh (New). Hampshire would have a distinguished career as a philosopher; Routh a rather less glittering one as a civil servant. Routh had been at Winchester, a school which at the time provided more successful candidates to the college than any other, so the fact that he was a Wykehamist may have worked in his favour.*

---

* Another possible factor was that he was descended from Martin Joseph Routh (1755–1854),

The examiners conceded that this had been a 'particularly strong' year, and that in a weaker year, the college would have felt justified in electing one, or two, from the group of men who had failed to make the shortlist. The other unsuccessful candidates included Max Beloff* and the Arabic scholar Albert Hourani, who was later to become University Reader in Middle East history. Indeed, some of the most important living historians had failed to gain All Souls Fellowships: Lewis Namier, for example, who in 1911 had been deemed the most outstanding candidate intellectually, but whose 'race' (he was a Jew) had prevented his election.

In later life Hugh decided that this setback had worked in his favour. All Souls, he would argue, had often proved to be a graveyard of talent. Members of that very exclusive club led a privileged life; he might not have possessed the strength of character to resist its charms. At the time, of course, this rejection must have been a huge disappointment. It slammed the door on the career in the Diplomatic Service that Hugh had envisaged for himself. Moreover, it was the first failure in a life that until this moment had been crowned with success. Hugh's subsequent references to 'Ye Old Soles Club' were noticeably sour (nor was he above the occasional jibe at Wykehamists). In honour of Routh's achievement, he composed a sarcastic ditty, 'Song on the Fatal Error of All Souls College', which he recited as he passed the college one drunken evening to the accompaniment of loud blasts from a hunting-horn:

> ... But I'll not care! With merry din
> I'll thank the Lord that I'm not in,
> Nor can contract from Dennis Routh
> Syphilis or foot-and-mouth ...

A.L. Rowse, who had been elected a Fellow of All Souls on leaving Christ Church eleven years earlier, could seldom resist an opportunity to rub salt into the wound. Hugh's papers, he told anyone who would listen, had been 'very bad'. It was a pity that All Souls had abolished the tradition of 'Founder's Kin', Rowse would continue, because Trevor-Roper would never get in any other way. In fact, Hugh might well have been more successful had he reapplied in either of the following two years, when the competition was less intense. He suffered a further rejection when he was unsuccessful in his application for a teaching Fellowship at Wadham.†

President of Magdalen for sixty-three years and a famous figure in Oxford, responsible for the often quoted advice, 'You will find it a very good practice always to verify your references, sir'.
* Beloff later became a Fellow of All Souls when he was elected Gladstone Professor of Government.
† The successful candidate was F.W. 'Bill' (later Sir William) Deakin, Warden of St Antony's College, 1950–68.

Before taking Schools Hugh had been offered (subject to obtaining an adequate degree) a University Senior Studentship,* an award which would provide him with a salary of £200 for a period of two years in order to undertake research leading to a thesis. This had been a fall-back position, on which he now fell back. Though it was a University rather than a college award, he was given the run of the Christ Church Senior Common Room. His original proposal was to study 'The influence of the Puritan Revolution in determining the character and organisation of the Anglican Church'; in time, the focus of his interest would migrate towards the years before the Revolution. David Ogg, a Fellow of New College who specialised in the seventeenth century, was helpful to Hugh at the start. In January 1937 Hugh visited the Public Record Office in Chancery Lane for the first time. He was not impressed: 'dinge, incredible dinge, must, fust, and influenza germs'. The PRO, he decided, 'is no place for a gentleman'.[3] He had asked Feiling to act as his supervisor, who declined on the ground that he was insufficiently acquainted with the material, and Hugh had then tried Ogg; but instead he had been ensnared by 'fluffy old Jenkins'.[4]

Canon Claude Jenkins, then in his sixtieth year, had been Regius Professor of Ecclesiastical History since 1934. He was an Oxford eccentric, who dressed in a low-crowned hat and antiquated clerical garb, collected cigar butts to smoke later, and surreptitiously pocketed fingers of toast from the breakfast table. Piles of books on both sides of the steps up to his rooms left only a narrow corridor for visitors to ascend, before they squeezed into a study so stuffed with books as to be almost impenetrable. Even the bath was filled with them. Jenkins's mind was as chaotic as his rooms. He lectured all morning on the hour, each lecture commencing directly after the other. An alarm clock hanging from a string round his neck served as a prompt to change subject, though his few listeners (sometimes as few as one) found it hard to distinguish one lecture from another.

Hugh felt that Jenkins had been imposed on him. He resented being consigned to the care of this dotty old man, who became a focus for his developing anti-clericalism. Indeed one could regard Hugh's thesis as an expression of this resentment, its arguments calculated to irritate his supervisor.

One result of Hugh's failure to win an All Souls Fellowship was to accentuate an already noticeable anti-intellectual tendency in him. In the future there would be less work and more play, and more time devoted to the pursuit of pleasure, often in the company of carefree undergraduates, rather than serious men studying for higher degrees.

---

* Under a scheme administered by the General Board of the Faculties; 1936 was the last year in which such an award was made.

Hugh enjoyed many lively evenings with his friends, particularly at the Gridiron Club ('The Grid') above the Midland Bank on Carfax, where exuberant young men smashed glasses, upset tables, and snatched off table-cloths during the meal, with the inevitable results. As he was entering the Gridiron, Robert Blake, then an undergraduate at Magdalen and later to become one of Hugh's closest allies in Oxford, narrowly escaped being hit by an empty magnum of champagne that Hugh had heedlessly tossed from an upstairs window. Often Hugh would drink himself into oblivion, carousing through the streets and quadrangles late into the night, so that he would wake up hung-over, with little recollection of what had happened the previous evening. Sometimes he would find that he had slept in a chair, or gone to bed with the light on, or still wearing his clothes. He ruined a pair of trousers climbing out of a friend's rooms after the gate had been locked. Unlucky drinking companions might find themselves de-bagged, pushed downstairs in a mêlée, or dunked in Mercury. On several occasions Hugh would be fined by the college censors for such late-night mis-demeanours.

He never became a member of the exclusive Bullingdon, the dining club limited to twenty blue-blooded members, though he was their guest on at least one occasion.[5] He was, however, a member of Loder's, another largely aristocratic club restricted to Christ Church men, most of them under-graduates but with the occasional don in attendance. Its President, Peter Wood, who subsequently became President of the Bullingdon, was a close friend of Hugh at the time. Loder's had originally been founded (so it was said) for Bible reading on Sunday nights. This function had been superseded with the passage of time, replaced by wine and song. On Sunday evenings Wood led by example, circulating the room while hanging from the picture rail, singing all the while. These evenings culminated in a solemn ceremony, at which the most junior member present was timed while drinking cheap port from a silver cup known as 'the Lady', and taunted if he was too slow.[6] Hugh conscientiously drank a Lady-full of champagne at a Loder's dinner in November 1937, though he disliked doing so after drinking burgundy. 'I take a low view of Loder's,' he noted afterwards in his diary. Hugh was also a member of the more secretive 'P' (the Pythic) club, for which both students and Students were eligible, by invitation only. In 1937 he organised the biannual 'P' dinner at the Café Royal.

This was almost entirely a male world, not dissimilar to the environment of a public school. The only women he encountered in Oxford were land-ladies, the mothers of friends, or the daughters of the elder dons. Back in Northumberland for the vacations, he met girls at evening parties or hunt balls, but he does not seem to have become involved with any of them. There is no record of any sexual activity. The type of girl he met socially was very unlikely to have gone to bed with a man unless married or at least engaged to him. He does not seem to have visited prostitutes. Several of the dons in his circle were homosexual; if Hugh did sleep with anybody, it was most likely to have been one of these.

He often travelled up to London for a night on the town, usually return-ing to Oxford on the last train back, the so-called 'Flying Fornicator'. On several occasions he fell asleep in the carriage and had to be woken when the train was standing in Oxford station, to prevent his being carried on to Birmingham. On one boozy evening in London he wandered drunkenly around the Oxford and Cambridge Club, surprising the staff in the kitchens and servants' quarters, and announcing to those members relaxing in each of the four sitting-rooms that the club was full of 'bishops and other bores'. When riding on the Underground after a dinner in town he gallantly offered his seat to a female passenger, only to find himself, as he confessed in a letter to his brother, too drunk to stand.[7]

Hugh relished his epicurean existence. He portrayed himself as an eighteenth-century character, with the habits and hearty appetites of a country gentleman from the pre-industrial age. He began writing a diary, which he inscribed 'The Journal of H.R. Trevor-Roper (gent.)'. A night of copious alcohol and much merriment would be described as 'an old-fashioned evening'. Alongside Homer, his other favourite author, he decided, was the fox-hunting squire R.S. Surtees.[8] Occasionally the two sides of Hugh were uncomfortably juxtaposed. Over a jolly lunch he and a friend laughed heartily at the sort of people who took rubbings of old brasses in country churches; the very next day found him on his knees in a parish church, taking a brass rubbing.[9]

One of Hugh's young friends, who would play an important part later in his life, was Earl Haig, known to his friends as Dawyck,* and owner of Bemersyde, a castle near Melrose that Hugh had noticed on his walking tour in 1932. Haig had inherited the title from his father, the Field Marshal, when he was only nine. Four years younger than Hugh, Haig had been educated at Stowe and had come up to Christ Church in the autumn of 1936; the following May he would be one of the pages of honour to King George VI at his coronation.† To be the son of such a famous father was a daunting legacy. At the time of his death in 1928 Field Marshal Haig was a national hero, regarded as The Man Who Had Won the War. The body of the former Commander-in-Chief had lain in state for several days as long queues of mourners filed past, before being taken on a gun carriage to

---

* Pronounced 'Doyg'.
† Among the pages were two other heirs of prominent war leaders, George Jellicoe and Henry Kitchener.

Westminster Abbey in a solemn funeral cortège, escorted by the most senior surviving generals from the First World War, including Marshals Foch and Pétain from France. After them followed the Prince of Wales and three of his brothers, leading a vast concourse of slow-moving men. But at the end of the 1920s attitudes to the war had undergone a revolution; what had so recently seemed a glorious victory became perceived as a tragic waste. Only a year or so after his father's death Dawyck Haig found himself tormented by his fellow schoolboys, as the son of a military leader whose tactics had caused unnecessary slaughter on a horrifying scale.

In mid-January 1937 Hugh settled into new digs at No. 59 St John Street. Two nights later, as he stood at the front door fumbling for his key, he heard his next-door neighbour urging a parting guest, 'Remember, except ye become as a little child – a little child, mind you – ye cannot be saved.' Hugh was appalled. 'Have I fallen among Buchmanites?' he asked in his diary. 'Good Lord deliver us!'

Frank Buchman was an evangelical American preacher who some years before had founded the 'Oxford Group', a virulently anti-Communist Christian crusade. (In the late 1930s it became known, topically, as 'Moral Re-Armament'.) Though the Oxford Group was a misnomer in the sense that it had no particular connection with the city, it attracted devotees in Oxford as elsewhere. The 1930s was a decade of religious revival, which witnessed a strong Roman Catholic resurgence; in England alone there were some 12,000 Catholic converts each year.[10] Catholic proselytisers targeted the young of the ruling classes, whom they saw as the leaders of the future. Their newly built Oxford headquarters, the Jesuit college Campion Hall, was conveniently located alongside Pembroke, just across the road from Christ Church. The Jesuits had already identified one potential Christ Church convert in Frank Pakenham, the unworldly son of an Irish peer, who, so Hugh rather unkindly liked to say, had turned from Canterbury to Rome after being hit on the head by a Blackshirt – just as some years earlier he was said to have become a socialist after falling from his horse onto his head during a New College 'grind' (point-to-point). It was the other way around in Pakenham's memoirs: he had become a socialist after being beaten up by Blackshirts, and became a Catholic only later. Pakenham's conversion to Catholicism was orchestrated by the fascinating Father Martin D'Arcy, Master of Campion Hall. It was said that Pakenham had pledged to Father D'Arcy to enlist a trio of sinners, all Christ Church men: Freddie Ayer, the 2nd Earl Birkenhead* (another Freddie), and Hugh Trevor-Roper. If so, he was unsuccessful with all three.

---

* He had succeeded to the title from his father in 1930, while still an undergraduate.

D'Arcy was receiving into the Church a stream of prominent converts, including the novelist Evelyn Waugh, who had 'gone over' to Rome in 1930, in a period of personal uncertainty and distress. D'Arcy's success, and that of his colleagues, alarmed those who regarded the Catholic Church with suspicion. For centuries, English Catholics had been depicted as potential traitors, owing their allegiance to a foreign Pope, and by extension to menacing Catholic powers like France or Spain. 'Mary's Dowry' had offered to deliver the nation into the arms of the enemy; since her time the English had been vigilant to avoid being ruled by a Catholic monarch. The national story was one of Protestant freedom and prosperity, contrasting with Catholic tyranny and backwardness. The Church of England was identified with the nation, its structure intertwined with the institutions of the state. Its very insipidness provided reassurance. Those who clung to the Old Religion seemed stubborn, or worse, fanatical. Though the threat of a Catholic coup had dwindled in the eighteenth century, and the laws discriminating against Catholics had been repealed in the nineteenth, English Catholics remained outside the Establishment, tolerated but not entirely trusted. Catholics still prayed for the conversion of England.

D'Arcy had studied philosophy and ran seminars on Aquinas for Christ Church undergraduates; Waugh described the mesmerising combination of his 'El Greco looks' and 'fine, slippery mind'.[11] To Patrick O'Donovan, later foreign correspondent for *The Observer* and columnist for the *Catholic Herald*, D'Arcy was 'the epitome of all that was brilliant or dangerous within the Roman Church, of all that was sensitive or guileful among the Jesuits'. Pakenham's wife Elizabeth, herself a Catholic convert, also thought D'Arcy dangerous: 'his elegant figure, dark wavy hair, aristocratic features, intent eyes and air of subtle sophistication immediately made me think of Mephistopheles'.[12]

Early in 1937 Hugh seems to have been susceptible. He attended Church of England services almost every Sunday, and dined several times at Campion Hall, where the guest nights had a reputation for brilliant conversation.[13] Father D'Arcy was charming and amusing; and there was delicious food, fine wine, plenty of port and stimulating company. At a more profound level, Catholicism – like Communism – offered a comprehensive belief system that compelled unconditional surrender to its tenets. Each offered an end to doubt, a comfortable refuge among the Faithful, or among those devoted to the Cause of the Party. Perhaps the absence of Hugh's mentor Maurice Bowra, who was spending the academic year in Harvard, created a vacuum. Bowra described organised religion as 'marvellous rot', to be respected but not taken seriously. He was deeply suspicious of Catholicism; Rome was 'a haven for those who feel a natural aversion to thought'.[14]

One evening Hugh dined in Campion Hall with his friend Peter Wood:

among the others present was Sir Edwin Lutyens, the architect who had
designed the new Campion Hall to D'Arcy's commission. Lutyens was 'very
tight, sometimes funny, sometimes just rude'. Father D'Arcy gave them a
tour of the college's art collection of Murillos, Donatellos and Titians –
known to some as the *objets d'Arcy*. On the way home afterwards Hugh
admitted that he admired the Jesuits, but still distrusted them. Wood
remarked forcefully that he would far rather dine with the Jesuits than
Nonconformists. Hugh agreed that dining with Nonconformists was a
contradiction in terms.

Peter Wood was the second son of Lord Halifax, owner of extensive
estates in the North of England. Like his father, Wood was passionate about
hunting, becoming Master of the Christ Church beagles; and like both his
father and grandfather (who had led a campaign for reunification of the
Christian Churches), he was High Church in his beliefs. At the beginning
of one Hilary term, after Hugh had spent the vacation as usual with his
parents in Alnwick, he and Wood motored down from the North together,
Hugh driving Wood's dilapidated car while Wood himself followed in a
van full of hounds. They had spent the previous night at Garrowby, the
Halifax house on the edge of the Yorkshire Wolds. Hugh had slept in
Golgotha, a guest bedroom equipped with a comfortable four-poster bed
and a fire burning hospitably in the grate. On the wall at the foot of the
bed was a square niche, concealed by miniature curtains; Hugh opened
these to find a human skull, a grisly reminder of mortality.

Wood took Hugh to Pusey House – founded in the nineteenth century
as an Anglo-Catholic centre by a canon of Christ Church who had been a
leading figure in the Oxford Movement – to hear a sermon preached by the
Bishop of Bradford, the man who two months earlier had precipitated the
Abdication Crisis by denouncing (in coded terms) the King's liaison with
Mrs Simpson. Hugh was impressed by the Bishop's sermon, though he
found the High Church ritual hard to stomach. As for the congregation, he
thought them 'a drab lot'. He was not surprised that they sought beauty
external to themselves. 'They might have come, all in a bunch, straight
from the Bodleian.'[15]

Hugh's flirtation with Catholicism (and indeed Christianity) ended suddenly, for no obvious reason – unless there is a clue in a letter from
Freddie Birkenhead, written half a lifetime later, in which he refers to having
'narrowly escaped rape' at D'Arcy's hands.[16] In a notebook entry written
during the war Hugh described a moment of revelation as he walked around
Christ Church Meadow one afternoon. 'I suddenly realised the undoubted
truth that metaphysics are metaphysical, and having no premises to connect
them to this world, need not detain us while we are denizens of it. And at
once, like a balloon that has no moorings, I saw the whole metaphysical

world rise and vanish out of sight in the upper air; where it rightly belongs; and I have neither seen it, nor felt its absence, since.'*[17]

Theology disappeared with metaphysics, and was to trouble Hugh no more. On another walk around the Meadow in mid-April, he listed to a friend those whom he would willingly consign to a great *auto-da-fé* to illuminate the Meadow on Coronation Night, then only weeks away: all the Jesuits in Oxford, Dundas, Longden and the Archbishop of Canterbury. Early in May, during yet another walk around the Meadow, he shocked Peter Wood by telling him that he had scrapped all his previous High Church views, 'together with all the foundations on which such views must necessarily rest – original sin, divinity of Christ, and suchlike mumbo-jumbo'. Though still attending the occasional church service, he now did so in 'a spirit of critical amusement'. Visiting a country church to examine the medieval tombs, he was embarrassed when his companion fell to his knees in prayer. Subsequently he entertained himself by concocting blasphemies. At the inauguration of a new Bishop of Oxford later in the year, Hugh was amazed by the large number of clergymen in attendance, whom he described in his diary as 'parasites on the credulity of the mob', paid to repeat 'a lot of hocus-pocus which no one believes in'. Hugh annotated an earlier diary entry, recounting one of his conversations with a Jesuit priest, to emphasise the reversal in his opinions. 'One ought to change one's furniture at regular intervals,' he reflected; 'the furniture of one's mind too. Or else, of course, to have no furniture, which saves a lot of trouble.'[18]

In a notebook entry written a few years later Hugh linked his rejection of theology with the beginning of his interest in the economic basis of history, which would form the philosophical underpinning for his historical writing over the next two decades.[19] It is tempting to speculate that he exchanged one faith for another, Catholicism for Communism. But this would be too neat. Though Hugh's thinking was certainly *Marxisant* in the 1930s, so was that of almost every other young historian, indeed of most young intellectuals. It is hard to explain Hugh's brief dalliance with Catholicism, except as part of his search for an identity. In this period of his life he tried on many different hats until he found one that suited. For example, he joined the freemasons, an odd affiliation for someone so sceptical of 'flummery'. In due course he became embarrassed about 'this Masonic mumbo-jumbo', concerned that his Masonic paraphernalia might be discovered were he to have an accident and his room be cleared.[20] Late one

* These lines, written in 1942, seem to echo Logan Pearsall Smith's description of an equivalent moment: 'One Sunday afternoon in June, when I was up a cherry-tree picking cherries, the whole supernatural scheme of things seemed to fade away into the blue sky, never to return.'

night he stuffed his apron, square and compasses, and all other vestiges of his Masonic existence into a suitcase, and dropped it over a bridge into the river.

Hugh claimed to Pat that he was trying to 'canalise his frivolity and anti-clericalism' into an article, in order to keep both out of his thesis. This article seems to have been a satirical one entitled 'The Recall to Religion':* a reference to an evangelical campaign initiated by the Archbishop of Canterbury, who in a radio broadcast called the nation to a renewed faith after the coronation of George VI in 1937. Hugh showed his article to several of his friends, one of whom thought it partook 'a little too much of the sledge-hammer, and too little of the rapier'. It was obviously provocative, because he was advised to submit it to publishers anonymously. Apparently it was never published. In any case, Hugh failed in his attempts to keep his opinions out of his thesis. This had now coalesced into a biographical study of William Laud, Archbishop of Canterbury in the reign of Charles I, who had been impeached by Parliament and executed in 1645. It puzzled Hugh that any man could go to the block for his religious beliefs, and he set about trying to understand how this had happened.

Laud's record within Oxford reinforced his reputation as a narrow-minded disciplinarian. He had been first a Fellow and later President of St John's, and then Chancellor of Oxford University. In this capacity he had extended and clarified the powers of the Chancellor, including his right to examine the religious conformity of every University member. Laud had also revived and strengthened the University's traditional requirements on discipline, residence and teaching. The Laudian Code, which remained in force until 1854, imposed strict controls on the conduct of undergraduates, and even afterwards provided the basis for the rules excluding them from pubs. 'I have come to the conclusion that Archbishop Laud was an interfering old bugger,' Hugh wrote to Pat, adding that his supervisor disagreed.[21]

Hugh's remarks on Laud echoed Macaulay's, who expressed his contempt for Laud as a 'ridiculous old bigot'. The great Whig historian had seen Laud as the embodiment of autocratic clerical governance, unthinking support for monarchical absolutism, and High Church narrowness. But in the Victorian period Laud had become a cult figure to the Oxford Movement, his works being reverently republished in the *Library of Anglo-Catholic Theology*. In his biography Hugh would portray Laud as a man of limited understanding, increasingly out of his depth. Those who had written about Laud in the past, he claimed, had generally been one of two types: High Anglican clergymen concerned to puff Laud, or doughty dissenters

---

* A book was subsequently published under this title, the work of several hands; its contributors included the Bishops of Bristol, Lichfield and Exeter, and the Dean of Exeter.

determined to slate him. 'Laud's clerical biographers,' he wrote, 'since they approach him on their knees, are naturally unable to see very far.' Hugh depicted the modern Church satirically, as having withdrawn from the 'rough-and-tumble' of political life: it was 'an unmolested cipher, neither loved nor hated, and approached with the decent, if meaningless, reverence allowed to the dead. Churchmen sometimes looked back wistfully to her great days and, drawing a mistaken inference, said that the world had been religious then, when really it was that religion had been secular; and laymen, judging the religion of the past from that of the present, thought it incomprehensible that men could have been driven to revolution in defence of a set of implausible conjectures.'[22]

'Old Jenkins has just written a letter of protest against my thesis (the high-church old humbug),' Hugh recorded in his diary; apparently Jenkins had accused him of 'trailing your coat provocatively',* and 'deliberately setting out to make the examiners angry'. Jenkins was useless, even to the point of agreeing, without consulting Hugh, to supervise another research student on the same subject. Hugh made unsuccessful attempts to engineer a transfer, and when these failed, decided to do without a supervisor altogether.[23] He augmented his salary by teaching four hours a week at Balliol during the Trinity term 1937, for a fee of £36.[24] On 9 June he entertained the brightest of his Balliol pupils, Rodney Hilton, to lunch at 'The Grid'. Hilton was a grammar school boy, active in the Labour Club and a member of the Communist Party, a Marxist who would subsequently make a successful career as a historian of medieval England. 'I liked him,' wrote Hugh in his diary; 'we had plenty of conversation. He is an economic historian, & – I think – rather Labour: but no philistine in the matter of food or conversation, & we found plenty of subjects on which to agree & in which to find amusement.'

During the same term Hugh learned from Masterman that he had been nominated and accepted to cover for Patrick Gordon Walker, while the latter was away on sabbatical. He was offered a salary of £300 a year, a dining allowance, and use of Gordon Walker's rooms in Killcanon. This was a tempting offer. But Hugh had another iron in the fire: Merton had created a Junior Research Fellowship in history, to begin in the academic year 1937–8 and to run for three years. The appointment would be made at the beginning of the Michaelmas term. Such Research Fellowships offered a route into an academic career. Hugh decided to apply.

Oxford feeling was strongly in support of the Spanish Republican government in its civil war with the Nationalist rebels, led by General Franco and aided by 'volunteer' legions from fascist Italy and Germany. Hugh

---

* A phrase Hugh incorporated into the published *Archbishop Laud* (page 74).

54

shared in the unease about the aggressive policies being pursued by Hitler and Mussolini. In February he had heard an after-dinner talk by Alfred Duff Cooper, the Secretary of State for War (and the official biographer of Field Marshal Haig), on the need for extensive military training. The Government was beginning a programme of rearmament in response to the worsening international situation, though conscription remained anathema. Duff Cooper's talk prompted an uncharacteristically sombre response from Hugh. 'He spoke well and with conviction,' Hugh noted in his diary. 'What is needed is not originality – which amuses and is then forgotten – but sameness repeated with such emphasis as will ensure effect.'

In the early summer of 1937 he attended a week-long OTC camp at Tidworth on Salisbury Plain with an undergraduate friend, Kenneth Swann. It seems to have been a high-spirited occasion, with plenty of hospitality on offer. On the penultimate evening they were guests of the Gunners at Larkhill. 'Kenneth and I found a knot of dingy infantry sergeants talking shop after dinner, exuding ignorance and officiousness, scarcely anthropoid. The temptation was too great, and seizing a soda-water fountain I squirted it into their midst. A riot ensued, and Kenneth and I were set upon by troops of infuriated sub-humans, who very nearly succeeded in de-bagging us: but we escaped with great subtlety under the tent-flaps & let the tent down on our baffled adversaries.'[25]

One evening towards the end of the Trinity term 1937 the physicist Professor Lindemann invited Hugh back to his rooms for further discussion after they had dined together in the Christ Church Senior Common Room. A vegetarian and a teetotaller, Lindemann was a bachelor of private means, rich enough to afford a full-time servant who combined the roles of butler, valet, secretary and chauffeur. He had calculated mathematically how to recover an aircraft from a spin – until then almost inevitably fatal to the pilot – demonstrating the effectiveness of his theory by deliberately inducing a spin in a plane he was flying himself. This dramatic coup captured the imagination of Winston Churchill, of whom 'The Prof' became a close ally and confidant. Though himself of German origin, Lindemann was profoundly suspicious of German militarism. He expressed himself forcefully, without tact, bulldozing aside opponents in discussion, believing himself to be a realist surrounded by fools, while others thought him incorrigibly ultra-conservative. 'You cannot hunt with the tiger,' Lindemann would say, impatient with what he saw as the woolly thinking of Labour and Liberal politicians, who saw no inconsistency in arguing for a firm line against the fascist dictators while simultaneously advocating disarmament. Hugh enjoyed talking with the Prof, though he thought his views outrageous, and was repelled by his 'dogmatic illiberalism'. After spending the evening with Lindemann Hugh realised that his host believed him to be more conservative in his opinions than he really was, 'and so is welcoming me with open arms, as an offset to all these young socialist dons!'[26]

Back in Northumberland for the summer, Hugh set aside his research into Archbishop Laud to concentrate on a new work, which he first called 'Paradise Reformed' and then 'Fr. Loligo'. No trace of this survives, and it is impossible to be certain what it was, but it may have been a novel,* possibly influenced by Samuel Butler's *Erewhon*. Hugh offered it to several publishers, all of whom turned it down. One night he dreamed of seeing a copy of the printed book in the window of Blackwell's bookshop, 'with the most pungent of its epigrams exposed on the yellow jacket as a blurb'. He had written the book under trying conditions: constantly chivvied and badgered by his disapproving mother, who repeatedly went into his room to read disjointed bits of the manuscript which she could not understand. In his diary he recorded her unhelpful criticisms: 'I am wasting my time writing stuff which no one will ever want to read, & why do I do it, & why don't I stop, & why haven't I more sense . . .?'[27]

Relations with his mother were as bad as ever. Back in the spring vacation, Hugh had threatened to cut short his stay at home because 'Mother's attitude had become so intolerable'. Now he raged in his diary about his mother's lack of hospitality towards a friend whom he had invited home for dinner after they had been beagling together. 'Mother has a fixed idea, it seems, that it is the duty of everyone to feed rigidly by families (horrid thought!): only rarely, and then formally, inviting anyone else to join in: and then they must come into a hushed room, with due ceremony, & talk demurely about golf & the weather, say thank you very much, & go home for good. If anyone comes in suddenly, & fails to respond to hints to go away as he is keeping us from our food, he is fed: & then he is disparaged & I am blamed afterwards!'[28]

At the end of September Hugh returned to Oxford, to be scrutinised by the Merton electors to their Junior Research Fellowship. 'I hope I impressed them more than they did me,' he wrote in his diary after dining with the Fellows, 'at least, I do not mind if I didn't, as I am rather hoping to fail, & have only entered at JC's insistence.' A week later, however, Hugh learned that his application had been successful.† In celebration he bought a car, a 1927 Morris Oxford, for £10. His new appointment carried no teaching responsibilities and provided him with a measure of security, allowing him

---

* 'Loligo' is a form of squid attracted to the light, as Hugh, with his interest in natural history, would have been aware.
† E.T. 'Bill' Williams was elected a Junior Research Fellow in history at the same college meeting.

to renounce his candidature for the postgraduate degree, then regarded by historians as unnecessary and indeed rather *infra dig*; though he continued to work on Laud, as a book rather than as a thesis. Relations with his former supervisor had deteriorated to such an extent that Jenkins wrote a formal letter to the Christ Church Librarian, complaining about Hugh's failure to return some books and describing his former pupil's behaviour as 'intolerable'.[29]

The Merton electors allowed Hugh to take Gordon Walker's Christ Church pupils and to inhabit his rooms until the end of the year. As a resident senior member he was given a key, allowing him access to Christ Church at all hours. Perhaps because he was not living in Merton, the Senior Tutor Idris Deane-Jones urged him to dine there as often as possible. Unfortunately Hugh found his new colleagues 'a drab lot of fellows'. He 'decided that only drink could make the dinner tolerable'; he resolved to bring 'one of my livelier undergraduate friends to Merton every Monday night to brighten it up, as they are a painfully dingy lot'. A Christ Church friend, the philosophy tutor Gilbert Ryle, commented that the Merton dons looked 'as if they had never drunk anything except water from a stagnant duckpond'. This was not an accusation that could be levelled at Ryle himself, who impressed locals at The Sportsman by downing a pint in five seconds. Dining at Merton about a month later, Hugh met, 'for the first time, one congenial Fellow' – the poet and literary journalist Edmund Blunden – 'with whom I talked & listened & talked & listened again almost till bedtime, on philosophy & literature & everything else'. After that he and Blunden often enjoyed each other's company. But later that month he dined again at Merton, 'where I ate the worst dinner I have ever eaten among the dullest people I have ever met'.[30]

In striking contrast was Peter Wood's twenty-first birthday party, held in a private upstairs room at the Gridiron. This began with champagne cocktails, and continued over an excellent dinner. There were about thirty guests, including several of Hugh's undergraduate friends: 'the Bullingdon, the peerage, & me!' During the fish course, a trout, thrown from a distance, disintegrated in mid-air, and struck Hugh a glancing blow. After the savoury course, the tables were overturned: 'to this I attribute two large bruises on my knees. The other unaccountable bruises I attribute to the period after leaving The Grid & before reaching my rooms, during which the faculty of memory was suspended.'[31]

Though Hugh relished such wild evenings, he also enjoyed more sophisticated company. Following a disappointing dinner of the Canning Club, for example, he went back to Gilbert Ryle's rooms with Freddie Ayer, 'when the conversation flowed with much more grace, relevance, & wit'.[32] After dining in college Hugh would often call on Ryle or Ayer for a stimulating chat before retiring to bed. The two philosophers were utterly different in style: Ryle a plain bachelor, while Ayer was an elegant womaniser, who would marry four times. But they had much in common too. In particular both stressed the need for clarity of expression, a quality that Hugh also valued very highly. Indeed he believed it to be a duty of any writer. When Ayer was asked to give a speech in Latin on the state of the Bodleian Library, he appealed to Hugh for help, offering to divide the fee. Hugh composed an 'elegant & facetious' address; Ryle pronounced it afterwards 'a wow', and the Dean went even further, saying that it had given the Bodleian Oration a new lease of life. 'My colleagues do not think this an advantage,' Hugh noted sardonically in his diary.[33]

Ryle was then in his mid-thirties, a tall, slim man of military bearing, though he had been too young to serve in the First World War. Hugh enjoyed his incisive and witty mind, and appreciated his direct and unpretentious manner. They exchanged scurrilous epigrams, and Hugh recorded in his notebooks some of his favourite 'Gilbertiana'. During an earnest discussion in the Common Room between some visiting undergraduates, the question was put: 'What is the difference between the soul and the intellect?' Without pausing for reflection, or lifting his eyes from his beer glass, Ryle replied coolly, 'The intellect is that part of you with which you read books other than the Bible.'

Ayer was a gregarious and animated conversationalist, whose rapid speech indicated the speed of his thought. Like Hugh, he had failed to gain an All Souls Fellowship, perhaps for similar reasons. He exhibited the same irreverence and cocksureness which infuriated many of their elders. At the age of only twenty-six Ayer had made his name by publishing *Language, Truth and Logic*, a highly influential book which popularised the Viennese concept of 'logical positivism', repudiated metaphysics, and incidentally ridiculed religion of all kinds. Father D'Arcy reviewed the book in *Criterion*, and in a letter to Evelyn Waugh described Ayer as 'the most dangerous man in Oxford'.[34]

Ayer rejected propositions which could be categorised as non-sense or tautology. Hugh employed Ayer's categories as a purgative for his prose, rejecting rhetoric, slovenly language, ambiguity or emotive obscurity, and aspiring to limpidity and austerity of style. It became one of his cardinal rules that no sentence of his should have to be read twice in order to be understood. No concept was too difficult to be expressed clearly. A useful test of lucidity was to translate a phrase from English into Latin; the necessary effort of understanding revealed any non-sense, tautology or ambiguity.

Unlike Ryle, Ayer enjoyed discussing details of other people's private lives. 'I hate gossip,' he claimed over lunch with Hugh, 'but I do love truth.' After another lunch at the Gridiron, which had been prolonged by a snowstorm outside, they 'demolished' several reputations. 'I think we bring out the worst in each other,' Ayer commented. In his memoirs Ayer would provide a portrait of Hugh at this time. 'Though some might think him lacking in charity, he was a zestful companion and a staunch friend. I admired his intellectual elegance, appreciated his malice, and was delighted to find that he shared my anti-clericalism and my irreverence for authority.'[35]

Isaiah Berlin was another young philosopher whom Hugh came to know around this time. They may have been introduced by Ayer, since both were members of a group of philosophers that used to meet in Berlin's rooms to thrash out their ideas in debate (another was Stuart Hampshire). Berlin had won a Prize Fellowship to All Souls in 1932, the first Jew ever elected there; in 1938 he took up a teaching Fellowship at New College, where he was to remain until after the war. A plump figure, 'a baby elephant' as Stephen Spender described him, invariably dressed in a shabby three-piece suit, Berlin wore round spectacles which magnified the appearance of his dark eyes and accentuated the effect of his short-sighted stare. Though his habitual expression was deadpan, he always seemed to be stifling a smile. His most outstanding characteristic was his talk, delivered at high speed in long, intricately structured and controlled sentences which echoed his prose style. Berlin was a cultivated person, with a liking for high society. He and Hugh enjoyed each other's company, especially when trading malicious gossip about their drearier colleagues.

Around this time Hugh acquired another car, a dark green Sunbeam-Talbot, slightly sporty in appearance and capable of being driven very fast. At the beginning of the Trinity term 1938 he moved into rooms in Merton, though he contrived to retain the key allowing him out-of-hours access to Christ Church. Following a Canterbury Club dinner one February evening, Hugh stayed up late talking to a group of friends, including Ayer, in the rooms of an undergraduate friend, Edward Fitzgerald 'Gerald' Heathcoat-Amory. Much wine was consumed, before Hugh eventually left around 1.30, wearing a top hat 'of doubtful provenance'. He used his key to let himself and another guest out of the college gardens, and collapsed onto his bed at Merton, after what he described as 'an excellent evening – intoxication as a work of art'. Next morning, while he was still dressing, he received a visit from Michael Foster, the Christ Church Senior Censor, responsible for disciplinary matters, who curtly demanded to know what information Hugh could provide about the case of Professor Lindemann's bicycle. Apparently somebody had taken a bicycle from outside Lindemann's rooms through a locked gate, ridden it around a garden, and then discarded it, damaged, in a flower bed. After Hugh had indignantly denied any part in this crime, Foster next accused Ayer, who called on Lindemann early in the morning, angrily protesting his innocence. Later one of the undergraduates present confessed to Hugh that he had been the culprit.[36]

During the course of another lively evening, Heathcoat-Amory shot Hugh in the thigh with an air pistol. Hugh got his doctor out of bed to dress the wound, as he was hunting the next day. He was drinking prodigious amounts. After one day's hunting he downed four pints of ale at The Sportsman and then a fifth at another pub before driving back to Oxford 'at shocking speed', arriving just in time for dinner at Merton. Afterwards, instead of retiring to the Common Room with the other Fellows, he slipped out and drove up to Wolvercote, where he consumed a further two pints at The Trout. On his way back to college after closing time he called on a friend in Leckford Road and drank 'about half-a-pint of neat whisky', a drink which he normally avoided, and which even he admitted was 'a very injudicious move'. He reached Merton safely enough, but then became convinced he had dropped something, and set out again by car. 'I suddenly became aware that I was speeding at about 40 mph over Carfax on the wrong side of the islands'. Failing to notice a policeman trying to stop him, Hugh drove on, parked the Sunbeam-Talbot in Merton yard, and quickly let himself into the college. The pursuing bobby tried to gain admission, but fortunately failed. Next morning Hugh received a visit from the police, and confessed to the charge of 'driving without due care and attention', without admitting to being anything but sober at the time. Over lunch at the Gridiron, his undergraduate friends 'laughed inordinately at this misadventure'. In due course Hugh was convicted, and fined £2.[37]

In the winter months Hugh used to go hunting a couple of days each week. According to Tim Beaumont, whose father Michael was Master of the Bicester, Hugh was a brave but not a good horseman. Indeed he was regarded as a figure of fun because he was always falling off his horse. 'A day's hunting isn't a day's hunting without one or two cracking falls,' Hugh would say. He would often be seen on his knees, scrambling around trying to find his spectacles. Hunting with the Bicester in mid-January 1938, he attempted to ford a brook which turned out deeper than he thought. His horse disappeared entirely below the surface. Hugh, entangled in the reins, was dragged underwater by the floundering mare. After a frightening few moments he struggled free, and both horse and rider swam independently to the river-bank. Unfortunately he had lost his spectacles, without which he was helpless, and had to be driven home, leaving his car behind to be collected later. On another day's hunting Hugh's mount slipped as he was galloping towards a brook, somersaulting him through the air. In the course of this fall he was kicked twice in the hat, but survived unhurt. On yet another occasion his mare, frightened by two ponies, suddenly shot side-ways. Hugh's knee cracked against a gatepost, with which his stirrup became entangled. As the mare moved off Hugh was dragged from the saddle and left hanging upside-down with his head trailing on the ground. Fortunately he was wearing detachable stirrups, or he would certainly have broken a leg.[38]

Hugh's enthusiasm for fox-hunting motivated him to undertake some research into William Somerville, 'the poet of the chase', which formed the basis of an article in *Country Life*. He introduced Somerville as a poet influenced by Milton, 'praised by Peter Beckford and Surtees, and (more faintly) by Dr Johnson'. In life, Somerville had attempted to contradict Addison's opinion that a man could not be both a Whig and a fox-hunter. He had kept his own hounds and beagles and had been enthusiastic for all forms of hunting, 'except coursing, which, like Surtees, he despised'. Somerville's 'close observation and enthusiasm' was evident in his writing. Hugh drew attention to his 'keen perception of nature' and his 'sympathetic description of the incidents of the chase'. He may have been steered towards *Country Life* by Peter Wood (an occasional contributor), and was disappointed to discover that the magazine did not propose to pay him for his learned contribution.[39]

In January another article signed 'H.R.T-R' appeared in the *Oxford Magazine*, this one entitled 'A Modest Proposal'.* Its satirical tone was scarcely likely to enhance the author's popularity with his colleagues. The author deplored the fact that 'fine old traditions are in danger of extinction, now that tutors are actually expecting well-connected undergraduates to work'. He referred to 'the frequent complaints of friends of mine (mostly reading Agriculture)' that 'learning will soon be the ruin of the University – surely the last place one would have expected to be tainted with so formidable an innovation!' The article recommended (in the Laudian tradition) that all heads of college should at once be ordained and, if possible, made bishops, while other dons should be compelled to be in holy orders too. 'As regards the ejected Professors, I cannot but think the Continental methods a little too severe.' He saw no reason why professors who yielded their posts quietly 'should not be permitted to keep licensed digs for undergraduates'. New Fellows should be 'of a sober, unoriginal and insignificant character (there will be little need for change here)'. As a precautionary measure, the 'most harmless among them' should be allowed some outlet of 'inoffensive study', such as 'a study of the Origins of Ludo, or the non-alcoholic drinks of the Ancient Chinese'. These were 'the broad outlines' of a plan 'to restore Oxford to her former glory, and to encourage

* A reference to Swift's savagely ironic *Modest Proposal*.

ancient families' to 'send their sons thither, without any fear that they might be infected with sedition, heresy, learning, or other forms of immorality'.[40]

In the spring of 1938 Hugh took a motoring holiday in France with an undergraduate friend, John Carver. They caught the ferry to Boulogne and drove to Paris, where they stayed at the Hotel Bougainville near the Invalides. After consuming plenty of wine on their first evening they found themselves in a brothel, drinking cognac with 'two fantastic tarts', one of them black. The Englishmen claimed to be Finlanders who had come for the races at Auteuil, and extracted themselves around one o'clock in the morning by explaining that their wives would become suspicious if they were absent much longer. The next day they set out for Burgundy, stopping at regular intervals to see the sights or do a bit of fishing. In the evenings they devoured a succession of huge meals, washed down by plenty of wine; one night the two of them consumed five bottles. A self-conscious note in Hugh's diary describes a sunny spring evening in Vézelay, when the two young men ambled slowly around the ruined city walls, beneath trees laden with apple and cherry blossom, gazing into the infinite distance, while Hugh carried a book under his arm – 'a fine picture of post-war, decadent youth!' Hugh was reading Bertrand Russell and 'the great Sigmund Freud'. In the next few years he would regularly record his dreams, and made several attempts to analyse himself, before becoming disillusioned with Freudian ideas.

In Oisilly Hugh took Carver to call on the family he had lodged with as an undergraduate four years earlier; the two of them stayed at the château for a large tea, followed by early-evening cognac. This was as far as they ventured; afterwards they started back, pausing to spend a few more days in Paris, 'accosted by tarts, pimps and vendors of pictures wherever we went, as the natural result of wearing English cloth caps'. On their last night they ate a splendid meal in the Avenue Gabriel, downing three bottles of wine between them and finishing with brandy more than seventy years old. Afterwards they climbed into the locked gardens of the Tuileries, playing hide-and-seek in the dark, before staggering back to their hotel on Boulevard St Michel. As they lurched up the stairs towards their third-floor room, Hugh's companion lost his balance and grabbed at him. The pair of them tumbled down two flights of stairs together, gathering speed as they fell.[41]

In the Trinity term 1938 Hugh saw Maurice Bowra often. They regularly 'exchanged malicious conversation', just as he did with Freddie Ayer. One afternoon they discussed the Chancellor of the Exchequer's new Budget while walking around the Meadow together. Both deplored the possibility of a tax on luxuries. Necessities might well be taxed, as they could dispense with these – but luxuries, never. A week or so later Hugh dined in Bowra's rooms at Wadham. They drank German wines, followed by 'buckets of brandy'. *Inter alia* they discussed 'the beastliness of the Germans', and their apparent readiness to suffer martyrdom in the attempt to force it on others. Bowra thought that the Germans would 'beat us in war, as we have no wish to fight while they are all so anxious to die'. 'I must say,' added Bowra, 'that I don't blame them. If I were a German I should wish to die too!'[42]

Hugh showed Bowra a paper he had written questioning the authorship of the Greek tragedy *Prometheus Bound*, conventionally attributed to Aeschylus.[43] He acknowledged the difficulty in saying anything definite when the evidence was so fragmentary, but he made his case with verve, confidence and wit, especially in assessing what the scholiasts of antiquity had written. 'We know that they were frequently wrong,' he wrote, 'quite devoid of critical faculties, completely ignorant of critical methods, and credulous to a degree remarkable even in scholars'. Bowra responded enthusiastically to this 'very entertaining and exciting' paper. 'So far as I know, most of it is new'. At Bowra's suggestion Hugh read his paper to an audience of Oxford's senior classicists.[44] This was a remarkable performance for a young man who had abandoned formal classical studies after only a few terms as an undergraduate; his interpretation anticipated some of the arguments of modern scholars.[45]

'I am often astonished by the depth and extent of my learning,' Hugh noted a few years later. '"Hugh Trevor-Roper", I say to myself, when this bewildering revelation breaks upon me, "you must be careful, or you will be buried, obliterated, beneath the burden of this stupendous erudition. Go slow! Be canny! In the interest of learning, you should devote more time to beagling, foxhunting, drinking, fishing, shooting, talking; or, if you must read, read Homer, Milton, Gibbon, who cannot harm the brain."'[46]

Hugh's wit was dangerous; his tongue could run away with him. On paper, the risk was greater still. Bowra was humiliated to receive a postcard from Hugh drawing attention to an error in his *Oxford Book of Greek Verse in Translation* (1938): he had mistaken a dirge for an epithalamium, confusing a funeral lament with a wedding-song. It was mortifying to have such a howler pointed out by one of his protégés, a man who wasn't even a classicist – all the more so to have it exposed to casual scrutiny on a postcard. Bowra couldn't bear to lose face in such a way, and nursed his resentment for years, though he maintained friendly relations on the surface.[47] Hugh seemed oblivious to the pain he had caused. Perhaps, though, this was an act of rebellion, conscious or otherwise. Bowra set the terms for his friendships. He demanded submission; and Hugh was unwilling to submit.

Hugh's mistrust of 'that old serpent D'Arcy' had deepened into active dislike. He and several others boycotted a dinner of the Canterbury Club when they learned that Father D'Arcy had been invited. Nevertheless he joined the company, which included Frank Pakenham, for brandy afterwards and found it 'quite a convivial evening'. A few weeks later he dropped by Dawyck Haig's rooms in Tom Quad after dinner to meet a friend of Haig's, the French painter Paul Maze. There he found 'a lot of mellow & stupid aristocracy admiring the sophistry of Fr. D'Arcy', among them Peter Wood and even Gavin Astor, one of those who had boycotted the Canterbury Club dinner. D'Arcy was holding forth about art, a subject in which his host had a particular interest, and had begun to argue that a religious painting was a higher form of art than a secular painting, when Maze boldly dissented. In the Louvre, continued Maze earnestly, there was a picture of the Crucifixion by Salvator Rosa, and beside it a picture by Rembrandt, of a joint of raw meat. 'A far less hackneyed topic,' interposed Hugh, joining forces with Maze against D'Arcy, by dwelling for a while on 'the relatively unexploited artistic properties of butcher's meat, particularly sausages, offal, and the like'. Confronted by this attack, D'Arcy responded by 'shrugging his shoulders & smiling & looking round at the mute aristocracy'. Infuriated, Hugh was 'more plain-spoken than I need have been', and shocked Peter Wood by remarking that 'Rembrandt knew what he was doing, & that a hunk of beef is a damned sight better subject for a picture than Jesus Christ'. At this point D'Arcy suavely took his leave, shaking hands with everyone present before being escorted to the gate. Talking with Paul Maze afterwards, Hugh agreed that 'D'Arcy is evil & is trying to catch Dawyck in his papal net'.[48]

It was understood that Junior Research Fellows could supplement their meagre income with teaching work. Schools often contacted dons to ask if they knew anyone suitable when a vacancy occurred. In May 1938 Hugh received a telegram from the Headmaster of Uppingham,* inviting him to teach the Sixth form history for three weeks, starting at once. He was wanted to replace a master who had been taken ill with mumps. After consulting Masterman and the Warden of Merton, Hugh agreed, on the grounds that it might be quite interesting (and at any rate was not long enough to be boring), and that the extra money would be useful. 'I may be able to scrape together enough boodle to pay my income-tax,' he wrote to Pat. 'I understand that the austere intellectual pursuits which I follow are severely frowned upon in Uppingham, & teaching confined to Christianity,

---

* John Wolfenden (later Sir John, and later still Baron Wolfenden), who until 1934 had been a philosophy Fellow at Magdalen. He later became a distinguished public servant, best known for chairing the committee on homosexual law reform and prostitution in the mid-1950s.

morals, & games. The food will be execrable & I shall probably have to go
to Chapel.'[49] Another motive for taking up the invitation was that it might
please Magdalen, the Headmaster's old college, where Hugh had put in for
a vacant teaching Fellowship at Masterman's suggestion. Soon after his
return from Uppingham, Hugh dined at Magdalen with the President and
Fellows. He was irritated not to be offered anything to drink throughout a
long dinner, not even a glass of water. After the meal the President, the
literary scholar George Gordon, offered him whisky and a cigar, both of
which he refused. A little later he introduced Hugh to one of the Fellows.
'Mr Trevor-Roper is a man of remarkable abstemiousness,' the President
explained, 'who neither smokes nor drinks.' Hugh did not get the job,
which went instead to a lecturer from Manchester some eight years his
senior, A.J.P. Taylor, who came with an impressive set of references, from
two distinguished Manchester professors, Ernest Jacob and Lewis Namier,
and from Llewellyn Woodward, who had acted as an external examiner at
Manchester.

Hugh was still working steadily on his Laud book; by mid-July 1938 he
had finished six chapters, and a week later he had written another. This
much he considered sufficient for the time being, so he was delighted when
Gilbert Ryle suggested driving up to Newcastle together. They left that
same afternoon, and Hugh was back at his parents' house in Alnwick the
following evening. He stayed there all of August and most of September,
walking, beagling, fishing and bathing in the river with his father and
brother. They had a favourite place at the river-mouth known as 'The
Sinister Pool', where the tidal race made swimming dangerous but exciting.
Hugh took a sensuous pleasure in being out in the countryside. Walking in
the Castle Park on a day when the weather was warm and the air fresh, he
jumped all the gates from sheer *joie de vivre*. Nature exhilarated him. On
one magnificent spring day he had taken a long walk in Buckinghamshire
with an undergraduate friend. The trees were all in flower and the birds in
song; 'the air was quite vinous', so as to make him feel 'gloriously pagan:
everything was so fresh & smiling that it was impossible to contain my
happiness within myself, but broad smiles shaped themselves on the faces
of sheep & lambs & rabbits, & all the inhabitants of Quainton & their
dogs & cats. Never have I felt so drunk with Spring & Buckinghamshire!'[50]

Hugh was now twenty-four years old. Five years later, looking back over
this period in his life after re-reading his diary for 1938, he was astonished
that he had been able to do any serious work:

> From that diary I get the impression that I did nothing but hunt foxes and hares,
> and dine out, and drink, and talk, and exercise my horse on Sundays, and go to

occasional race-meetings, and enjoy low-life, and exercise hounds in the sweet air early on Sunday mornings. And the amount one drank in those forgotten days of cheap and plenteous wine! Never less than three bottles of claret or burgundy, or two of port, between two people, to keep the conversation going after a convivial dinner. There was no introspection then, no hesitancy or doubt ... [51]

Cadet

'If ever there was a time for impersonal despair,' Hugh wrote in his diary on 20 September 1938, 'it was tonight, at the melancholy face of politics in Europe.' For Hugh to write seriously about public affairs in his diary was almost unprecedented; but this was a time for seriousness. War seemed imminent, despite British readiness to accept almost any German demand. The policy of Neville Chamberlain's Government was to appease German grievances, signalling that neighbouring territories with significant German populations might be returned to the Reich – but only by negotiation, not by force. Lord Halifax had said as much to Hitler on a private visit to Germany in 1937, and soon afterwards Halifax had been appointed Foreign Secretary. To Hitler, it seemed that he might have whatever he wanted, without needing to fight. His invariable response to concessions was to ask for more. Since 1937, he had been threatening Czechoslovakia, one of the few remaining democracies in Europe. Hitler demanded autonomy for the German-speaking minority congregated in the Sudetenland, near the frontier. In May 1938, reports of German troop movements had prompted Halifax to warn Germany that the French were bound by treaty to defend Czechoslovakia, and that Britain would almost certainly support France. This firm stand had caused Hitler to back down. But in mid-September events reached a new crisis: Hitler announced that he would annex the Sudetenland. German troops began mobilising. Chamberlain flew out to see Hitler at Berchtesgaden – a decisive action, far more impressive then than it would be now – but failed to persuade him to moderate his demands. Unable to influence Germany, the British and French governments put pressure on the Czechs to accept, backing away from their earlier commitments. Hitler had called Britain's bluff.

Hugh was ashamed of his country's spinelessness in the face of German blackmail. 'What possible advantage can we draw from this surrender?' he asked in his diary, before providing his own answer – 'a brief respite'. Even leaving aside the moral issues and taking the most 'realistic' view, the British Government had involved itself still further in Europe, while undermining the position of its democratic allies. 'Chamberlain's peace indeed!' snorted Hugh. Hitler must now know, he wrote, 'that the democratic front is a collapsed house of cards, & that the spoils of all Europe are his for the taking'.

Hitler's intransigence forced the reluctant democracies to choose between confrontation and humiliation. On 22 September Chamberlain again flew to meet Hitler, this time at Godesberg, again without success. Hugh was at home in Alnwick, drinking port with Gilbert Ryle, when he heard on the radio of the breakdown in negotiations. It was too late for peace: the tiger was out of the cage. 'Now (I fear) we can only come into a war, & perhaps help to win it, not prevent its outbreak. Now I must lay aside my Horace & take up Clausewitz, Machiavelli, & Mein Kampf, suspend enquiry, abandon the individual pleasure of the bottle & the chase – unless – can it be that Hitler will yield now?'

A period of suspense followed, as the British people prepared for war. At a meeting attended by Hugh's father, local doctors were informed of a War Office communication indicating that war might begin within only a few hours. On the night of 27 September Chamberlain made another radio broadcast. 'How horrible, fantastic, incredible it is that we should be digging trenches and trying on gas masks here,' the Prime Minister exclaimed, 'because of a quarrel in a far-away country between people of whom we know nothing!' Hugh understood from this speech that 'there was by now pretty well no hope of peace left'. Early the following morning he caught a train to Oxford, with the intention of putting his affairs in order; he calmed his nerves on the journey by reading *The Iliad*. 'Everything here is in a frightful mess, what with wars and rumours of wars,' he wrote to his brother on his arrival. 'Merton College has been active all day preparing a gas-proof, sandbag-lined refuge in the Stores; and I have been to the Town Hall to sign on for the volunteer clerical canteen & odd work if necessary.'[1]

That same afternoon the Prime Minister announced to the House of Commons a last-minute reprieve: a conference would be held in Munich the next day between Britain, France, Germany and Italy (the Czechs were not invited). Hugh felt that the enthusiasm which greeted this announcement was premature. Like so many of his compatriots, he did not know whether to be relieved or apprehensive. He was sceptical of Hitler's assurance to Chamberlain that this was his 'last territorial demand in Europe', given his record of broken promises and worthless guarantees. 'Can we trust such a man?' Hugh asked himself. 'Is he not like Cromwell, a knave self-deluded by his own idealism?' Hugh was well aware that war might mean defeat and disaster. 'For war I have myself nothing but loathing & fear; but the meaning of peace which is still in danger of being accepted under dictation, is equally dubious & perhaps more sinister.' In the Merton Common Room he listened with disgust while a humanitarian colleague solemnly explained that the British Government should not allow moral considerations, 'which alone are valid, to be in the least affected, even to be supported, by strategic considerations, which are inherently immoral'. It was such remarks, Hugh felt, which 'had made the word academic into a synonym for ridiculous'.[2] He was contemptuous of his colleagues who waited until the arrival of the latest issue of the *New Statesman* in order to know what to think. 'Oh how these petulant socialists exasperate me!'

The Munich conference agreed a settlement of the Czechoslovakian issue over the heads of the Czech government and people: the Sudetenland was awarded to Germany. Chamberlain flew back to England bearing a statement of good intentions signed by the *Führer*, which he proffered to a cheering public at Heston Airport. 'I believe it is peace for our time,' he declared. Hugh noted sardonically how Chamberlain had been welcomed 'by hysterical & enthusiastic crowds evidently incapable of distinguishing between his laudable efforts for peace & his disastrous policy which has brought the necessity of such last-minute efforts upon us'. In the House of Commons the Munich Agreement was denounced by, among others, Churchill and Duff Cooper, who resigned from the Government in protest.* Hugh was equally dismayed. Ayer recommended that he should send a telegram to the Prime Minister, addressing it from Christ Church since he believed that a protest from the college carried more weight.

Hugh was impressed by an article published in *The Spectator* a week after Chamberlain's return from Germany. The author was R.C.K. Ensor, who had become a Senior Research Fellow at Corpus, Oxford, after retiring from a successful career in journalism. Hugh had heard Ensor read 'an excellent paper' to the Stubbs Society the previous year on the influence of the press lords. Ensor was the author of *England, 1870–1914* (1936), the most recent volume in the *Oxford History of England*, in which he had argued that Germany had been responsible for the First World War, against the prevailing consensus that everyone and therefore no one was guilty.† Now his *Spectator* article would have a profound influence on Hugh's thinking. Ensor claimed to have predicted the Munich crisis some years earlier, having read *Mein Kampf* in German even before Hitler had come to power. 'To do so is the beginning of wisdom in contemporary foreign affairs,' wrote Ensor, 'for never did statesman show his hand more frankly than Hitler did in that book.' Few Britons had read the German edition of *Mein Kampf* (1925 and 1926), which outlined Hitler's plans for a series of aggressive wars of conquest; an English translation had been published in 1933, but this was an anodyne abridgement, carefully censored by the German authorities. As

---

* He had become First Lord of the Admiralty in 1937.
† Anticipating by a quarter of a century the revisionist arguments of the German historian Fritz Fischer.

a result Britons tended to discount Hitler's wild rhetoric. The British media played up the absurdities, the theatricalities and the bombast of Nazism. Hitler himself was depicted as a 'tin-pot demagogue'.[3] Ensor, on the other hand, believed that Hitler 'was not a man of words only, but would try to perform what he preached'.[4] Hugh was persuaded to read the book himself, not in the sanitised English version, but in the original German; though this was a penance because, as he confessed, he had turned his back on all things German after returning from Nazi Germany in 1935, and had neglected them since. Like Ensor, he reached the reluctant conclusion that Hitler had to be taken seriously.

The Munich Agreement stimulated passionate debate within Oxford, as it did throughout the nation. The arguments cut across conventional party lines, dividing families, severing longstanding friendships and uniting former foes. In particular, the issue revealed a cleft between the generations: on the whole, young people believed in standing up to Hitler, while their elders favoured appeasement of German grievances. It was the young who had most at stake, because if war came it was they who would have to fight. On Hugh, as on many others of his generation, Munich had a radicalising effect, alienating him from the complacent consensus of support for the Government. He despised senior dons like Feiling who clung to their faith in Chamberlain.

An upcoming by-election in Oxford provided an opportunity to test these new alignments. Christ Church was at the centre of the action: the Conservative candidate, Quintin Hogg, was a Christ Church man, as was the Labour candidate, Patrick Gordon Walker. Roy Harrod took the initiative by calling for the Opposition parties to unite in a popular front against the Government, in public letters to the *Manchester Guardian* and the *Oxford Times*, and private communications with Churchill and the Liberal leader, Sir Archibald Sinclair. After some hesitation the Liberal and Labour parties agreed to withdraw their candidates* in favour of the Master of Balliol, A.D. Lindsay, who stood as an 'Independent Progressive'. Maurice Bowra (now Warden of Wadham) and Gilbert Ryle were among those prominent Oxford figures who endorsed Lindsay's manifesto. The Conservatives adopted the slogan that 'A vote for Hogg is a vote for Chamberlain'; it was wryly suggested that a vote for Hogg was a vote for Hitler.[†] Among those campaigning for Lindsay against the official Conservative candidate were two future Tory leaders, Harold Macmillan and Edward Heath. Other active supporters of Lindsay included the future Labour

* Gordon Walker stood down against his will, and was replaced as the Labour candidate at the next election by Frank Pakenham.
† This slogan has been attributed to the classicist (and politician) Richard Crossman and the philosopher J.L. Austin, among others.

Deputy Leader Denis Healey, and the young Balliol historian Christopher Hill, both then members of the Communist Party. In the poll Hogg defeated Lindsay, though his majority was halved.

Hugh voted for Lindsay, and became a committed opponent of the Government. He was exultant when an anti-Government candidate was successful at another by-election in mid-November. A few days later he and Ryle queued to see Picasso's 'Guernica', then on display in Oxford.[5] The destruction of the small Spanish town of Guernica by German bombers in April 1937 seemed a terrifying portent of what was likely to happen on a huge scale if it came to a European war. British Government estimates suggested that 600,000 people would be killed in the first few months of aerial bombardment, and many more injured. As it turned out, these figures were absurdly exaggerated: civilian deaths (including those of civil defence personnel) attributable to enemy action throughout the entire war amounted to just over one-tenth of this figure.[6]

In March 1939, Hitler seized control of the rump of Czechoslovakia; Poland was his next obvious target. In response, Britain and France guaranteed to come to Poland's aid if she were attacked. By this time it had become clear to Hugh that war was unavoidable. He was determined to play his part, and schemed to avoid a medical examination which would certainly have disqualified him from active service because of his very short sight. He already had a Territorial commission as a result of his service with the OTC. In the summer of 1939 he served a month's attachment to the Life Guards, then encamped at Pirbright in Surrey.

Hugh dated the beginning of his disillusionment with Marxism to this period. The great problem of the 1930s was the sudden and apparently irresistible rise of aggressive dictatorships. This was the challenge to Hugh's generation. Neither Marx nor any of his followers had prophesied the rise of fascism, for all their claims to be able to predict the future. As the expected European war drew near, their *ex post facto* rationalisations were beginning to look very thin. Ever since fascism's appearance, Communist ideologues had been arguing that it should be ignored, as irrelevant to the class struggle and doomed to fail, according to the inexorable laws of historical progress. Now that the menace of fascism was becoming impossible to ignore, such a policy seemed as misguided as that of the conservative appeasers, perhaps even more so. Though he remained receptive to Marxist ideas, Hugh came to believe that Marxist historical science had failed to meet the crucial test of the age.[7]

If Hugh felt fatalistic about the future, one reason might have been the deaths of many of his young friends, several of them as a result of accidents. Rowse had noticed the same phenomenon among his contemporaries, and speculated that 'they lived more exposed, more highly strung lives, took more chances'.[8] In August 1938, Hugh heard the melancholy news that his friend Robert Beaumont, with whom he had gone to Vienna, had been killed while climbing. Hugh felt a degree of self-reproach in that he and Beaumont, who had recently begun teaching ancient history at Corpus, had drifted apart. He reflected gloomily that of the friends he had made in his first year at Christ Church, four were already dead – and a month later there was a fifth, killed in an aeroplane crash in Wales. Earlier in the year one of Hugh's closest friends from Charterhouse had been killed when his aeroplane crashed in Scotland. And a few weeks after the Munich crisis, Hugh's favourite Merton colleague, Lascelles Abercrombie,* died after apparently recovering from an illness, 'a terrible and irreparable blow'. It was for Abercrombie's name (even more than Blunden's) that Hugh always looked when he signed on to dine in Hall: 'now that he is dead I shall feel alone in a swamp, without light or guidance or company'.[9]

Hugh attended the memorial service for Abercrombie, which he thought 'a drab and melancholy affair'. There was not a single sentiment in hymn, psalm, prayer or lesson with which Abercrombie would not have violently disagreed, he felt; and thought much the same about Beaumont's memorial service, lamenting that 'this ridiculous mummery and mumbo-jumbo' should be the only way we know of paying tribute to the dead. 'To think also that such a farce may be performed over myself,' he railed: 'that one day some old gaffer may intone to a sceptical congregation that I am now seeing my Creator face to face, & similar undiluted rubbish.' Hugh consoled himself by reflecting on the advantage of set prayers, 'which is that no one need pay any attention to their meaning, or associate himself with the meaning of his own utterances'. Unfortunately, wrote Hugh, 'I myself am incapable of such detachment or such hypocrisy.'[10]

Hugh's disdain for religious dogma and his implicit acceptance of determinist ideas of class struggle were evident in his contribution to a vigorous debate on the letters pages of *The Spectator* in the summer of 1938. This had been unwittingly inaugurated by A.L. Rowse in a review of *A People's History of England* by A.L. Morton – published by the Left Book Club – evidently a crudely reductive work which Rowse summarised as 'bad history, and possibly bad politics too'. However, he had cited approvingly Morton's view that 'the Reformation was in essence a political movement in a religious guise, part of a long struggle by the European moneyed classes for Power'. This comment, remarked Rowse, 'is essentially sound and in

---

* Lascelles Abercrombie (1881–1938), Fellow of Merton and Goldsmiths' Reader in English, formerly Professor of English Literature in Leeds and London, and the author of volumes of his own verse as well as of literary criticism.

keeping with the best modern research'. Dissenting letters in subsequent numbers of the magazine, by those doubting whether the inconspicuous martyrs of the sixteenth century had been motivated by class interest, elicited contemptuous responses from Rowse: 'One thing that history teaches us is that there is hardly any limit to the nonsense human beings will believe.' After a further letter from the assertive medieval historian G.G. Coulton, Hugh entered the correspondence on Rowse's side. His contribution was scornful of those who believed that 'theological niceties' and 'academic doubts about immaterial things' could bring about 'a redistribution of political power and the overthrow of ancient institutions'. Hugh dismissed the 'pious pretence that what is really important in this world is the conjectural constitution of the next'. In the following number Rowse referred to Hugh's 'brilliant' letter, with which he agreed 'almost entirely'. This is what the younger people think, wrote Rowse, with characteristic firmness.

Although Rowse was then, broadly speaking, on the Left and Hugh on the Right, they concurred in their analysis. Both then believed economics to be the motor of human history. Hugh agreed that the German Marxists had 'laid the foundations of a new historical system, and so changed the whole basis of historical study that no subsequent student can altogether ignore them'. This was an exciting period to be an historian. A new paradigm had rendered obsolete all earlier historical writing: the entire past needed reinterpretation. In particular, the period from the Reformation to the Revolution in England assumed a new significance. 'It was no longer a merely constitutional struggle, which could have been avoided if the Stuarts had had a little more political sense; it was the crisis in the change from medieval to "capitalist" society; and as such it needed a complete overhauling.'[11]

Hugh's understanding of the Protestant Reformation was shaped by the ideas of one of the leading social theorists of the twentieth century, Max Weber. In his *The Protestant Ethic and the Spirit of Capitalism* Weber had developed a new sociology of religion. In particular, he argued that the system of capitalism which had brought into being the modern world had been made possible by the Protestant mindset, by Calvinism in particular.[12] This was a theory that would preoccupy Hugh for the next quarter of a century or more. Weber's ideas had come to him via R.H. Tawney, Professor of Economic History at the London School of Economics and Political Science and President of the Workers' Education Association. Tawney wrote the foreword to the first English edition of Weber's book, published in 1930, a copy of which was in Hugh's library. A Christian socialist who abhorred the destructiveness of unbridled capitalism, Tawney was widely admired, even revered, both for his scholarship and his principles. In person he was modest and unassuming; as one of Hugh's colleagues would remark, he exuded 'an aura of sanctity'. He refused public honours; when offered a knighthood, he was said to have protested, 'What harm have I ever done the Labour Party?' Tawney was a leading member of the Fabian Society, and Hugh would subsequently use the term 'Fabian historians' as a form of shorthand to describe his followers. Tawney's *The Agrarian Problem in the Sixteenth Century* (1912) had characterised the period as one of economic strain, agrarian dislocation and social upheaval; and his *Religion and the Rise of Capitalism* (1926) had added a moral dimension to Weber's thesis. Tawney located the 'transition from feudalism to capitalism' in England, in the decades leading up to the English Civil War. In this period, argued Tawney, bourgeois society had been born. A Church weakened by the Reformation was no longer able to protect the poor by moderating the undesirable effects of economic competition. In the 1630s Laud had tried to reassert the power of the Church as a force for good, and failed. Protestantism had replaced social solidarity with individualism; economic and ethical interests became separated. In the opening pages of his *Archbishop Laud*, Hugh would quote Tawney approvingly: 'Calvin did for the bourgeoisie of the sixteenth century what Marx did for the proletariat of the nineteenth.' Another important influence on Hugh's thinking was the American historian John U. Nef's monumental *History of the British Coal Industry* (1932). Nef identified the origins of what he called a 'proto-Industrial Revolution' beginning as early as the sixteenth century. This fitted with Tawney's ideas about the emergence of a capitalist economy in the same period.

Tawney's work influenced the whole generation of young British historians and political thinkers who came of age from the late 1920s onwards. 'Perhaps no man has stimulated the study of English history in the sixteenth century more effectively than Prof. Tawney,' Hugh would write in 1953; 'the century from 1540 to 1640, the century which separates the Dissolution of the Monasteries from the Great Rebellion, may almost be defined, thanks to his reinterpretation of it, as "Tawney's century".'[13] Indeed, it was thanks largely to Tawney that the early modern period – broadly speaking, the three centuries (1500–1800) between the Middle Ages and the Industrial Revolution – became a focus of intense interest for English-speaking historians in the mid-twentieth century. This was the era in which capitalist society began to emerge, when conditions were established that would enable England to become the first country to experience an industrial revolution.

Hugh's letter to *The Spectator* anticipated the argument of his biography of Archbishop Laud. The polemical style is similar. The underlying assumption is that differences of doctrine are merely masks for political differences.

In his introduction to the book, Hugh would insist that Laud be viewed 'in that secular spirit from which alone an impartial view can come'. He stated his belief in the axiom 'that human nature does not change from generation to generation except in the forms of its expression and the instruments at its disposal'. Though the actions of men such as Laud appeared to have followed rules entirely different from those familiar to the modern world, they were comprehensible if one understood religion to be 'the ideal expression of a particular social and political organisation'. Viewed in this light, the willingness of men to fight and die for what might appear in retrospect to have been unimportant differences in religious practice seemed no more absurd than their willingness to do the same in modern times for what might appear to be equally unimportant differences, such as the colour of a shirt, or the form of a salute.[14]

Early in February 1939, Lovat Dickson, an editor from the publishing house of Macmillan (and himself a published poet and biographer), called on Hugh at Merton and took away with him two chapters of the biography of Archbishop Laud. Hugh was soon in correspondence with Harold Macmillan who, though a backbench MP, was active in the family firm. From the outset Hugh made it obvious that he meant business. 'It had always been my intention to submit my manuscript to Jonathan Cape,' Hugh wrote to Harold Macmillan on 25 February, 'but since you have shown an interest in it, I shall be prepared to consider its being published by Messrs Macmillan, to the extent of giving you the first sight of the completed manuscript.' By the middle of May Hugh had delivered a complete typescript.

'It is written from a detached, rather critical – even Gibbonesque – point of view,' Harold reported to his brother Daniel, the senior partner in the business: 'I feel sure that this young man is a good writer and a clever man. We certainly ought not to miss the book.'[15] An opinion was sought from H. Maurice Relton, Professor of Dogmatic Theology at King's College, London. 'Where I find myself feeling very uncomfortable in the perusal of some of Mr Trevor-Roper's pages,' wrote Relton, 'he leaves me with the uneasy feeling that possibly he may be right in what he says, and my ideas of the life and significance of Archbishop Laud's work may have in consequence to be revised.' Relton recommended the book for publication, while warning that 'it may quite well meet with a cool reception in clerical quarters'.[16] Daniel Macmillan informed the young author that he and his colleagues were 'very interested in your book'. He hoped that Hugh would not mind waiting a little longer, 'as we want to have the book read by our regular historical advisor, who, we may tell you in confidence, is Dr Keith Feiling, and who will be returning to London in about ten days'. Hugh protested, insisting that if it had to go to Feiling, it should also be sent to someone better qualified to comment: Ogg or Rowse, for example.[17] In the meantime Harold Macmillan called on Hugh during a visit to Oxford.* Afterwards he wrote making a formal offer of publication for the book, 'which we recognize to be a most original and important piece of work'.[18]

Feiling had confirmed Relton's favourable view of the book. 'Of his ability there is no question, as his all-round academic record, both as classic and historian, shows,' he wrote. 'Very few men of his age from Oxford are more likely to write books of real mark.' However, though some parts of the book were 'beautifully written', the introduction was 'written in a spirit highly offensive to churchmen'. If the clergy still read such books, Feiling warned, they would find this provocative. In conclusion he observed that the early seventeenth century was a period 'ripe for re-examination and addition'.[19]

Hugh accepted the terms offered, including an advance of £50, payable on signature of the contract. He used the money to buy a mare with the 'palpably ridiculous' name of Faleria, which he considered changing to 'Royalty' or 'Macmillan' in consequence of the deal. In the end he called her 'Rubberneck', because of her habit of turning her head round to look at him in the saddle.[20] Wild and irresponsible, the horse was 'a creature after my own heart', one which Hugh believed shared his own weaknesses. 'It is a snob,' he wrote in a wartime notebook. 'It revels in its speed and virtuosity. It loves showing off, and hurls itself, out of sheer *joie de vivre*, at the most impossible obstacles; and it doesn't give a twopenny damn when it takes a tremendous fall in consequence. It despises all dull and easy ways. It exhibits a malicious delight in the discomfiture of its rivals. And it never gives up.'[21]

Towards the end of May 1939, Hugh was interviewed for a Fellowship at University College, Oxford. 'Univ' was then a small college, very much the antithesis of Christ Church, with only fourteen Fellows, of whom two were historians. Perhaps a little jaundiced, Hugh afterwards remarked of Univ that it was 'a sort of Oxford Tibet, with primitive inhabitants, strange superstitions, and few attractions for colonising powers'.[22] The Master was Sir William Beveridge, who had come there from the LSE two years earlier. Beveridge took Hugh for a long walk at the time of the appointing process, leading Hugh to believe himself to be the Master's candidate. This, he subsequently realised, was fatal to his chances. His application was unsuccessful; the Fellowship was awarded to a medievalist, A.D.M. (David) Cox,

---

* They met in Hugh's Merton rooms at four o'clock on a Friday afternoon. At 6.30 that same evening Macmillan saw C.S. Lewis at his hotel; and later he played bowls and dined at Magdalen with A.J.P. Taylor, when the two men closed an agreement to publish Taylor's *The Hapsburg Monarchy* (1941).

who had been a Prize Fellow of All Souls in 1937, but whose early promise was not fulfilled.

Meanwhile Hugh had been appointed a Second Lieutenant in the Territorial Army. He spent a month that summer in camp with the Life Guards near Woking, 'inundated' by galley proofs of *Archbishop Laud*. Other sets of proofs had gone to Gilbert Ryle and David Ogg; and to C.V. (Veronica) Wedgwood, a former pupil of Rowse's, who had written a biography of Laud's ally, the Earl of Strafford. Ryle's comments proved invaluable: 'like Eve in paradise, [he] ranged through the whole wilderness, weeding out solecisms, trimming the luxuriant phrases, and unmixing the metaphors'.[23] Ogg congratulated Hugh on 'such a vigorous piece of work', and commented that he had been right to tone down some of the references 'which might alienate readers of an orthodox or deeply religious type'. He offered some stylistic advice: 'it is a good plan, in the final revision, to delete a good number of adjectives'.[24]

The Life Guards was a cavalry regiment, then still unmechanised, and Hugh spent much of his month on manoeuvres galloping up and down the sandy knolls of Surrey on a steaming black charger. Afterwards he went to visit his parents in Northumberland. Gilbert Ryle was staying with his twin sister nearby in Newcastle, and he and Hugh took long walks together. When Hitler invaded Poland at the beginning of September, the two young dons decided to return at once to Oxford. They drove in Ryle's car, taking turns at the wheel. After it became dark they were stopped by a policeman, who ordered them to switch off the headlights. With war expected imminently, a blackout was already in force. They continued without lights, inching forward cautiously to avoid an accident, and arrived very early the next morning.

Next day Hugh reported for duty and was told to wait. Britain was not yet at war; Chamberlain was still vainly hoping that Hitler might retreat. Oxford seemed very empty, though Merton was busy preparing to accept refugees. In the evening Hugh wandered round to Christ Church to see Frank Pakenham, and found him already in bed – not his usual bed, but an uncomfortable camp bed – to prepare himself, Hugh noted wryly, for the rigours to come.

Soldier

The first few months of war were a frustrating time for Hugh, as for so many others. He continued to live at Merton while awaiting his call-up papers. Meanwhile he was given a clerical task, receiving University volunteers into the Army and recording their details. He was also lecturing to the Oxford University OTC four days a week, on the Bren gun and the anti-tank rifle, having been trained in their use; though as he cheerfully confessed, his poor sight disqualified him from using them himself, and he had scored zero in his firing test. Every Friday he hunted with the South Oxfordshire Hounds. An attempt to persuade the War Office to pay for the upkeep of his horse was unsuccessful.[1]

This period of limbo did not last long. On 3 December 1939 he confided to his brother that a friend had been taken on to do 'a hush-hush job', and had offered Hugh the post of his deputy, which he had accepted, after obtaining leave to do so from his commanding officer. 'I am told the job may be extremely dull, but might turn out very exciting.' At least it promised to be more stimulating than the likely alternatives once the Army discovered his short sight. The new job would be based in London, so he was looking for a flat.[2]

The un-named friend was the Bursar of Merton, Walter Gill, a lecturer in electricity known to his colleagues as 'Gilly'. A genial character, utterly indifferent to status, and with little respect for bureaucracy, hierarchy or convention, Gill was a practical man who believed in getting things done rather than waiting for them to happen. He had jolted Merton into modernity by introducing electric lighting into the quadrangles. According to Hugh, most of Gill's colleagues regarded him as a handy chap who could mend a wireless set when it went wrong or fix the lights when these fused, but otherwise as one who only by a charitable definition could be included among the educated. During the First World War Gill had served with the wireless (radio) intelligence section of the Royal Engineers in the eastern Mediterranean; in Egypt he had used the Great Pyramid as a mast for wireless interception. He had published a book about his experiences entitled *War, Wireless and Wangles* (1935). Though in his mid-fifties at the outbreak of war in 1939, Gill was determined to become once more involved, and 'wangled' his way into a new organisation called the Radio Security

Service (RSS), part of MI8, the department of the War Office responsible for communications. Gill became head of the RSS's discrimination section, the 'brains' of the set-up.

RSS was a child of the fear of bombing. Its function was to search for radio signals emanating from German spies operating within Britain. It was believed that these signals would be used as beacons, directing German bombers to their targets. Once such signals had been detected, the transmitters would be located with the help of the Post Office, which possessed a fleet of direction-finding vans, used in peacetime to detect unlicensed radio operators. The spies would then be rounded up by MI5, the internal Security Service. Such, at any rate, was the theory. In fact the RSS was founded on a false premise. The only two German spies active in Britain at the outbreak of war had already been detected and were now controlled by MI5. German bombers were guided not by head-beacons placed alongside their targets, but by tail-beacons in Germany. RSS was created to hunt a quarry that did not exist.

MI5 had relocated out of central London to Wormwood Scrubs, displacing the prisoners, who apparently very much resented their evacuation to safer, rural locations. The infant RSS nestled in the bosom of MI5. Lieutenant Trevor-Roper found himself working alongside Major Gill in a cramped and poorly ventilated prison cell on the first floor; like the other cells, this clung to an exterior wall of the huge prison building, and was reached by a metal walkway which overlooked its vast, empty interior. The elderly but still upright Director-General, Sir Vernon Kell, who had run MI5 since its foundation thirty years earlier, could be seen during the coffee-break after lunch in the area formerly used for prisoners' exercise, casting an appreciative eye over the secretaries, who tended to come from 'good' families. They were said to be chosen, like racehorses, for their legs and their breeding.

Hugh told his brother that he was working in 'the most God-forsaken part of London', with nothing but 'a vast extent of council-houses' in the vicinity.[3] He took up Gill's invitation to share a flat in nearby Ealing, at No. 29 Mount Park Road, a house belonging to the historian John Wheeler-Bennett and occupied by Wheeler-Bennett's secretary. Soon after Hugh moved in, the flat next door was hit by a German bomb.

In the months that followed Hugh made several friendships that would afterwards prove valuable to him, particularly with those working in the counter-espionage ('B') section of MI5, then run by Brigadier Oswald ('Jasper') Harker. In June 1940 Kell would be dismissed and Harker appointed acting Director-General of MI5; he would be succeeded as head of 'B' section by his deputy, Guy Liddell, a cultivated, sensitive man who had won the Military Cross in the First World War. The two MI5 officers

Hugh came to know best were both in their early thirties: 'Dick' White, like Hugh a former pupil of Masterman's at Christ Church, who after the war would become successively head of MI5 and then MI6, the only person ever to hold both posts; and T.A. Robertson, known by his initials as 'Tar', architect of the outstandingly successful 'Double Cross' system. From the beginning of the war Robertson and his colleagues took the far-sighted decision to 'turn' enemy agents and leave them in place whenever possible. This enabled them to be used for deception purposes, which would prove invaluable in the latter stages of the war. Robertson and his colleagues could justifiably claim to have controlled the German espionage system operating in wartime Britain.[4]

Hugh's generally good relations with MI5 enabled him to argue successfully against the arrest and imprisonment of Arthur Bryant, the historian then best known for his three-volume biography of Pepys (1933–8). Bryant's notoriously pro-Nazi book, *Unfinished Victory*, was published by Macmillan* in the spring of 1940. This was enough to raise a clamour for his arrest under Rule 18B of the Emergency Powers Act (1939), which allowed for the internment of those suspected of being Nazi sympathisers. Even Lovat Dickson asked Hugh if he thought that Bryant should be interned. To his MI5 colleagues, Hugh maintained that Bryant's personality was dominated by the desire to ingratiate himself with authority; accordingly he could be 'turned', to become a lucid propagandist for the Allied cause. Hugh's prediction proved correct: once convinced of his mistake, Bryant bought up the unsold copies of his offending book and swiftly embarked on a new career as a writer of patriotic histories, beginning with *English Saga*, published in the same year as *Unfinished Victory*. Towards the end of the war, as Hugh was walking on the South Downs, a small Labrador bounded up to him and began licking him vigorously. The dog's anxiety to please put him in mind of Arthur Bryant. To his amazement the great man himself then appeared, and invited Hugh to his nearby cottage for tea.[5]

RSS received intercepted signals from a variety of sources. The first of these was the Post Office, which, in order to catch unlicensed radio transmissions, had established three permanent receiving stations at the furthermost corners of the United Kingdom, at St Erth in Cornwall, Thurso in Scotland and Lympne in Kent. Next, it received unidentified material from the monitoring services of the Armed Forces, the BBC and the cable companies. Complementing these professional sources was a countrywide network of enthusiastic radio hams, the so-called 'Voluntary Interceptors'.

---

* Harold Macmillan was said to have defended his decision to publish Bryant on the grounds that 'We are publishers, not policemen'.

These 'VIs', forbidden during the hostilities from chatting to each other over the airwaves, were only too happy to harness their hobby to the war effort. By the autumn of 1940 RSS would consist of three MI8 staff officers, supported by a twenty-strong headquarters, about a thousand Post Office and technical staff, and a further thousand Voluntary Interceptors.[6]

Hugh's job was to comb through the mass of miscellaneous material that arrived at Wormwood Scrubs daily for suspicious signals. This proved an unrewarding task, though it did offer occasional light relief: for example, when he discovered, in the summer of 1941, the passionately worded dialogue between P.G. Wodehouse, then living in Berlin and determined to benefit by broadcasting to America on German radio, and his shocked literary agent in New York, who implored him to stop.

At first, the failure to find any signals emanating from German spies in Britain was attributed to the technical difficulty of detecting high frequency radio messages except at very short or very long range. This led Gill to look at the problem the other way around, and to search for transmissions to agents based in Britain from their controllers in Germany. 'If the agent can hear his replies,' he reasoned, 'so can we.' By intercepting such communications RSS was straying beyond its remit, but in doing so was fulfilling a function for which no other provision had been made. 'Tar' Robertson guided Gill towards the source of signals received by captured German agents and the type of messages agents might expect to send and to receive. In particular, MI5 had identified a wireless station in the Hamburg area in communication with a German ship off the Norwegian coast, which was reporting on the movements of neutral shipping. This ship was suspected of relaying radio traffic between agents operating in Britain and their controllers in Germany.[7] The signals were enciphered, but the accompanying operators' chat was in German. RSS had standing instructions to pass any such signal traffic to the Government Code & Cipher School (G.C. & C.S.), responsible for the decryption of encrypted German radio communications, producing what became known as 'Ultra' intelligence. G.C. & C.S. had recently relocated from central London to Bletchley Park, a late-Victorian mansion set in its own grounds, about midway between Oxford and Cambridge. Accordingly Gill and his young subordinate gathered together as much as they could of this traffic and sent it to Commander Alistair Denniston, head of Bletchley. His response was discouraging: the material was of no interest and no more need be sent. Why Denniston should have reacted in this way remains unclear. There may have been a simple failure of communication between the infant Radio Security Service and the rapidly expanding Government Code & Cipher School. Or perhaps the message was intended to divert the two RSS officers from further investigation of matters outside their remit. G.C. & C.S. was controlled by 'C' (or, more properly, 'CSS', meaning 'Chief of the Secret Service'), head of the Secret Intelligence Service (SIS, also known as MI6), which jealously protected its jurisdiction over foreign intelligence against feared encroachment by MI5. Distribution of Bletchley's intelligence 'product' was closely controlled by SIS's counter-espionage section (known as Section V), headed by Major Felix Cowgill.

Neither Hugh nor his commanding officer was satisfied with this rebuff, however. They believed the signals might be significant, and continued to study this material out of hours. Between them they possessed the necessary skills: Gill had some experience of cryptography, while Hugh was familiar with German and equipped with the mathematical aptitude he had demonstrated at Charterhouse. There was not much else to fill their drab Ealing evenings anyway: all of London was blacked out after dark. The German cipher provided a welcome alternative to *The Times* crossword. A code given to a German agent who had been 'turned' by MI5 provided a possible crib.[8] After much trial and error, Hugh broke the cipher one evening while lying in the bath, to the drone of German bombers overhead. It was a simple transcription cipher: once you had the key, German words and sentences appeared as if by magic out of what had previously been gibberish. The two RSS officers deciphered more and more of their store of signals, and as they did so, it became obvious that they were reading the radio transmissions of the *Abwehr*, the German secret service.

This was not, of course, an Enigma cipher, which the *Abwehr* used when transmitting radio signals between two secure locations where the Enigma machines could be safely housed. It would require the extraordinary intellectual, technical and material resources of Bletchley to decipher Enigma messages: and it would be two years before Bletchley started reading *Abwehr* Enigma. Hugh had broken one of the hand-ciphers used by the *Abwehr* when communicating with out-stations where an Enigma machine could not be risked, for example from a ship, or from an insecure location in a neutral country. Thus the *Abwehr* office in Madrid used the Enigma machine located in their embassy when communicating with Berlin, but a hand-cipher when communicating with out-stations in other parts of Spain or North Africa. Soon RSS was reading much of this traffic, having cracked further ciphers used in intercepted signals sent to and from ships in the Baltic and a number of land-based stations. One direct result was the arrest of several enemy agents as soon as they landed on British soil.[9] More generally, these intercepts acted as a gradually widening peephole, through which RSS could begin to observe and analyse the activities of the *Abwehr*, and provided a continuing source of technical intelligence about *Abwehr* use of wireless. Such intelligence would prove essential to the eventual breaking of the *Abwehr* Enigma cipher.

Gill and his deputy were understandably excited at what they had discovered, as was their commanding officer, Colonel J.P.G. Worlledge. An
upright, old-fashioned individual, Worlledge lacked the political agility
required to manoeuvre his way through the hazards of the secret world.
After he had circulated news of RSS's findings, Worlledge received a 'rocket'
from his MI8 superior, who instructed him that in future RSS was not to
interest itself in cryptography, 'since that is the province of G.C. & C.S.'
Gill greatly enjoyed this order. Denniston reacted with alarm, hurrying
down to Wormwood Scrubs, accompanied by his senior cryptographer,
Oliver Strachey (brother to Lytton). Hugh would always remember the
smart click of Denniston's shoes on the metal stairs of the prison, as he
negotiated his way up them with naval expertise. During the course of the
ensuing discussion it was agreed that Bletchley should set up a separate
section under Strachey to handle the *Abwehr* traffic RSS had discovered.
Soon afterwards the two RSS officers paid a return visit to Bletchley, the
first of many for Hugh, who was now promoted to captain. Despite these
new arrangements, the next four *Abwehr* codes to be broken were cracked
within RSS, not at Bletchley.[10]

The work of RSS, initially confined to the detection of enemy agents
operating within Britain, now expanded to encompass enemy wireless
communications anywhere in the world. Early in 1941 the first foreign units
of RSS would be set up in Gibraltar and Cairo. Gill's unit directed the work
of the interceptors, pointing them towards the likely sources of the most
valuable intelligence. The number of enemy signals intercepted grew from
a trickle into a flood; by the end of the war RSS had passed more than a
million such messages to G.C. & C.S.[11]

Towards the end of 1940 Worlledge would commit another blunder. RSS
had intercepted signals from an *Abwehr* substation in North Africa which
provided a comprehensive picture of its organisation in Morocco.
Worlledge ordered Hugh to write a report on the subject, which he then
naïvely forwarded to his usual customers, with a covering note: 'The
attached memorandum, the work of Captain Trevor-Roper, seems worthy
of circulation.' SIS's Major Cowgill was incandescent at this breach of
security: 'Trevor-Roper ought to be court-martialled', he fumed. He was
irritated that Hugh's report had been circulated to MI5, of which SIS was
always jealous; and furious that the report had gone to the Post Office, a
civilian organisation which had no business with such secret matters. For
ten days or so RSS was summarily excluded from the distribution of
intelligence emanating from Strachey's section at Bletchley, until the situation was rectified at the insistence of MI8. For Cowgill, the matter emphasised the anomalous position of RSS, and the resulting lack of what he
considered proper control over its activities.[12]

*

Early in 1940 Hugh had received finished copies of *Archbishop Laud*, his first book, a proud moment in the career of any author. Subsequently he liked to dip into it. 'I am for ever discovering yet more exquisite beauties,' he wrote in a notebook, 'lurking unsuspected among yet profounder truths.'[13] He had hoped that it might have been published towards the end of the previous year, but Macmillan had deferred publication because of the outbreak of hostilities. Even so, the spring of 1940 was not the ideal moment to publish a biography of a seventeenth-century archbishop – 'especially one that is calculated to provoke the hostility of all sects of every religion on earth', as one of Hugh's colleagues predicted.[14]

Hugh had tried to ensure that the book had a good start by squaring the reviewers. 'By titillating strings or listening to importunities, I have already made the following arrangements,' he wrote to Lovat Dickson early in 1940, listing four reviewers he had lined up, including A.L. Rowse in the *New Statesman* and C.V. Wedgwood in *The Listener*. 'With this my small supply of influence runs out,' he continued, 'but if you can exert any, I should be very grateful. The general rule, I think, should be that the book is sent to historians rather than clergymen.'[15] The response from the reviewers was mixed. A.L. Rowse praised the book (praise he later retracted), but, as Hugh had anticipated, clerical reviewers were generally hostile. One condemned it as an amalgam of Lytton Strachey and Karl Marx: irreverence mixed with subversion. While attending Sunday service at St Margaret's, Westminster, Pat heard his brother being denounced from the pulpit.* An exception to these clerical critics was Herbert Henley Henson, the former Bishop of Durham and a Fellow of All Souls, who reviewed the book in *The Spectator*, describing it as detached, discerning and 'brilliantly written'. Frank Pakenham, whom Hugh met by chance on a visit to Oxford, told him that *Archbishop Laud* 'reminded me of Gibbon'. Hugh was initially delighted by this apparent praise. Pakenham frowned. 'I mean', he continued, 'that it made my gorge rise.'

The publishers were pleased with the controversy, however, and wanted more from Hugh. Over a celebratory lunch he and Lovat Dickson discussed a new book provisionally entitled *A Don at Arms*, 'a display of the exuberant spirit of youth'. Presumably this would have explored the gulf between the generations exposed by the arguments over Munich. Afterwards Dickson wrote to say that he had discussed the idea with 'Mr Harold', and that they wanted to pursue the matter further. Hugh's response was discouraging;

---

* Early in 1949 Patrick Trevor-Roper heard his brother denounced again from the same pulpit, this time for writing a light-hearted article in *The Spectator* entitled 'The Myth of Charles I'. The denouncer was the irascible Rector, Canon Charles Smyth.

evidently he had reconsidered. Possibly he felt his new role to be incompatible with personal publicity. 'As to your other suggestion, that I should write gossipy indiscretions,' he wrote in reply, 'mention it not again. I have decided that I have survived the stage of exhibitionism & not yet reached that of anecdotage, so I'm writing nothing about myself.' After the war, he promised, 'I'll write you a learned treatise on Archdeacons in the tenth century, or something like that'.[16]

Hugh was especially gratified to hear from his Oxford friend Nevill Coghill* that the celebrated bookman Logan Pearsall Smith admired *Archbishop Laud*, and had been asking about him. Apparently Smith had written Hugh an appreciative letter, though this had never arrived. As an undergraduate Hugh had been delighted to discover Smith's *Trivia*, a series of slight volumes of maxims and observations, spiced with malice. While encamped with the Life Guards the previous summer, Hugh had carried these with him; 'and well I recall the pleasure they gave me,' he wrote afterwards, when 'after grooming my horse, I would linger in the shadow of my tent, with some profane pot-companion, exchanging the shining aphorisms of *Trivia*'.

Hugh wrote to Smith to explain why his letter had not been acknowledged, and Smith responded by urging Hugh to call at his home in St Leonard's Terrace, Chelsea, overlooking the gardens of the Royal Hospital. In due course Hugh arrived, dressed in khaki, and impressed himself on his host as 'a charming, erudite young man' by reciting from memory many of Smith's bons mots.[17]

Smith, then almost seventy-five, proved to be a fidgety bachelor, a large man with a slight stoop that concealed his height. A pair of spectacles perched on a long, pointed nose helped to give him the appearance of a well-to-do clergyman.[18] Born into a prosperous Quaker family in Pennsylvania, Smith had studied at Harvard, Berlin (where he met Matthew Arnold) and at Balliol, where he had been a favoured pupil of the Master, Benjamin Jowett. Instead of going into the family glass-making business as expected, he had decided instead to dedicate himself to literature. After living in Paris for five years, he returned to England and lived alone in the country, while he sought to develop a pure prose style he could call his own. The remainder of Smith's family joined him in England, taking a house not far from his in Sussex; this new home attracted progressive intellectuals, among them Bertrand Russell, who married Smith's sister Alys. Another sister, Mary, married the art historian and connoisseur Bernard Berenson. After the death of his mother in 1911 Smith moved to London, which would remain his home for the rest of his life. He was an omnivorous and tireless reader.

---

* Fellow and tutor in English literature at Exeter College, Oxford.

'People say that life is the thing,' he wrote, 'but I prefer reading.' During the dark winter months Smith withdrew from society and read historical works; like Hugh, he was particularly interested in the seventeenth century. He edited the poetry of John Donne and the prose of Jeremy Taylor, and had written a biography of the poet and diplomat Sir Henry Wotton. In 1938 he published his autobiography, *Unforgotten Years*, an elegantly written work which Hugh had read with delight. By this time many of 'the old familiar faces' Smith had known were no more; but 'the Sage of Chelsea' attracted a younger generation of disciples, including Cyril Connolly, Robert Gathorne-Hardy and Raymond Mortimer. Now Hugh would join their number. He became a frequent visitor to the house in St Leonard's Terrace, and a correspondence began between the two men. Very soon he and 'Logan' were on first-name terms.

In the weeks leading up to the Battle of France in 1940, RSS intercepted radio traffic between *Abwehr* controllers in Germany and agents in Holland, Belgium, Luxemburg, and France, who were asked to provide information about defences, roadblocks, troop dispositions and so on. Studied together, these messages should have indicated where the German onslaught would come. But despite the new arrangements for co-ordination between Wormwood Scrubs and Bletchley, no one was analysing the radio traffic in its entirety; as a result, the devastating German attack through the Low Countries took the British and French by surprise.[19] Evaluation of radio intelligence was failing to keep pace with interception and decryption. There was a need to scrutinise, contextualise and explain this material. In a report on the interception work of RSS, Gill put in an urgent request for more resources, including two extra intelligence officers to work alongside himself and Hugh.[20]

Meanwhile Hugh's health collapsed and he was sent on leave. Perhaps the strain of working so hard, in an ill-ventilated and poorly lit prison cell, contributed to his collapse. He was suffering from acute sinusitis, resulting in repeated headaches and pressure behind the eyes. Hugh's condition was debilitating enough to necessitate half a dozen courses of palliative treatment as a hospital in-patient during 1940; he was off-duty for such a long time that he was relegated to half-pay. No doubt it was humiliating for him to be *hors de combat* as a result of such a condition, at a time when many of his peers were being treated for wounds received in action.

That summer Hugh underwent an operation at the Westminster Hospital to remove the septum or dividing cartilage of the nose; unhappily, this was botched, forcing him to submit to a second operation after only a couple of months; even this was not wholly successful, and a third operation would be required a dozen years later.[21] It was dispiriting to undergo repeated operations to no good effect. Hugh sought advice from a Harley Street specialist to whom he had been recommended. The medicine he prescribed provided some relief, though Hugh abandoned this when the chemist refused to identify it. Years later he discovered that it had been cocaine.

'I'm absolutely sick of sinuses,' Hugh complained to his mother; 'it's very dreary living life like a permanent invalid.'[22] Two years afterwards Hugh would record in a notebook that the year 1940 had been 'the most miserable period of my life'. The months spent in and out of hospital had been 'an aimless, hopeless period of disappointed and despondent waiting'; more than once he had abandoned hope of a cure and plunged into the deepest depression, to the point of despair. Yet even during this bleakest of times, there were 'a few momentary bubbles of delight that broke through that gloomy marsh'. In June, after the catastrophic defeat of the Allied armies and the evacuation from Dunkirk, Hugh was in the far south-west of Cornwall, walking through the flower-filled fields above Lamorna. He had been sent there nominally to inspect the receiving station at St Erth, in reality to recover from his ailment. 'It was warm and sunny, and the air was laden with the smells of hay and hedgerows,' so that it was 'a delight almost beyond the imagination to be alive'. On a stone bridge above a brook he sat for hours in the sunshine, reading Dante, refreshed by the sound of running water. Returning at last to Penzance, he learned that Paris had fallen that very morning. A few days later France surrendered; Britain stood on the brink of a precipice. Yet instead of feeling downcast, 'I merely reflected that we had no more speculative allies, & knew where we stood.' In retrospect, Hugh would be astonished at 'the serene, effortless confidence with which we accepted, and reacted to, the most colossal of disasters'.[23]

At this moment of crisis, with the whole nation on alert for an expected German invasion, Hugh became involved in a pair of absurd incidents. Strolling through the Cornish countryside, his uniform unbuttoned and so scruffy that 'he looked as though he had fallen from the moon', he was brought up short at an improvised roadblock and arrested on suspicion of being a spy. Apparently the Local Defence Volunteers* of two separate villages had been mobilised to round up this dangerous stranger. Despite his War Office pass, he was marched at the point of a double-barrelled shotgun to the police station at Marazion to account for himself. After his release, Hugh was foolhardy enough to take a rowing boat out into the Fal estuary, to fish for mackerel; he had strayed some considerable distance out to sea when a squadron of German aircraft suddenly appeared overhead, and began to strafe him as the anti-aircraft defences on the shore opened fire. The sea erupted under the impact of machine-gun fire and falling

---

* Better known as the Home Guard.

shells, while the air filled with the deafening noise of diving aircraft and ack-ack. Half an hour's frantic rowing brought him to land, somehow unscathed. Soon afterwards he was admitted for further treatment to a Falmouth hospital, where a nurse greeted him with the words, 'Oh, you're the German spy; how lovely!'[24]

Later that summer Hugh underwent a second operation on his septum. While still in hospital recuperating he heard that the flat he shared with Gill had been destroyed by a German bomb, which had landed in the front garden. Hugh lost most of his remaining personal belongings – but at least he was spared the ignominy suffered by Pat, who had been forced to flee through the streets in his pyjamas after his flat had been bombed.[25] RSS, along with its host, MI5, had been dispersed to other locations after Worm-wood Scrubs was hit by high-explosive bombs; buried in the ruins were Hugh's typewriter, his German dictionary and his copy of *Mein Kampf.*

After his discharge from hospital Hugh returned to the site of the charred flat in Ealing, where he 'found the stairs hanging like a cobweb in the burnt, roofless building, while in what had been our drawing-room the tops of chairs projected like islands from a sea of roof, rubble and miscellaneous wreckage'. He was struck by the high morale of the Londoners he encoun-tered, 'so bright and cheerful among the blitzes that to be among them seemed like a holiday'.[26]

After so much illness and misery Hugh engineered his own recovery by 'a great act of faith'. Analysing his condition, he observed that he was equally incapable of intellectual work and physical activity, and reasoned that it was only by doing both that he could do either. So against medical advice he decided to resume hunting. After two months of training to get fit enough to stay on a horse, he went out with the Bicester, wrapped up in warm clothes and fortified with a hip flask; 'and behold, it worked'.[27]

While Hugh was recuperating, high-level discussions were taking place about the future of the Radio Security Service. Three Whitehall depart-ments were involved: the War Office, which controlled MI8, and which had decided to abandon its troublesome offspring; the Home Office, which controlled MI5; and the Foreign Office, which controlled SIS. Viscount Swinton, the newly appointed Chairman of the Security Executive, adju-dicated. There was an obvious need to tighten RSS security and to integrate its work with that of the other services involved in secret intelligence. It seemed sensible to place RSS under the control of either MI5 or SIS. But which? There was no obvious answer. MI5 was responsible for internal security, SIS for intelligence-gathering and counter-intelligence outside the British Empire. Radio waves were oblivious to such demarcation. According to its original remit, RSS should have become part of MI5, where it was already embedded. RSS was providing valuable intelligence to support the work of MI5 in rounding up German agents, indicating when and where these would arrive. As the war progressed, RSS's monitoring of *Abwehr* communications would prove crucial to MI5's deception operations. But SIS controlled distribution of the product of G.C. & C.S., the goose which, as Churchill said, laid the golden eggs. It was desperate to cling on to this goose because its larder was otherwise empty. SIS had suffered a catastrophic defeat soon after the war began, when two of its most senior officers had been lured to a meeting at Venlo, near the Dutch border with Germany, supposedly to meet representatives of the German High Command who were planning to overthrow Hitler. This was a Gestapo ruse; the two Britons had been kidnapped and smuggled across the frontier. During interrogation, they had revealed all they knew. As a result SIS's intelligence network had been compromised. Subsequent German conquests robbed SIS of most of its stations on the Continent. In the absence of human intelligence Bletchley's product seemed even more significant, and since RSS had by accident become one of Bletchley's most important suppliers, SIS wanted to control RSS too. By doing so it could ensure that there would be no further lapses in security of the kind allowed by Worlledge.

In May 1941 RSS was disgorged by MI8 and swallowed up by SIS. Colonel Worlledge, who had resisted the change, was dropped, and Gill transferred to other duties (and demoted to captain). A new receiving station using the latest American equipment was built and manned at Hanslope Park in Buckinghamshire, dedicated to the requirements of SIS and thus dispensing with the need for Post Office involvement. RSS would henceforth come under the control of SIS's radio communications section, known as Section VIII and led by Colonel Richard Gambier-Parry, a flamboyant Old Etonian who in peacetime had been sales manager for an American manufacturer of radios. Gambier-Parry appointed his old friend Ted Maltby as 'Controller, RSS'.

Hugh despised Maltby, 'that farting exhibitionist', whom he likened to 'those baboons on Monkey Hill, exhibiting to all in turn their great iridescent blue bottoms'. Maltby failed to understand the need for intelligence direction, though without it RSS resembled a lumbering dinosaur, a powerful body without much brain.[28] But Hugh could not help liking Gambier-Parry, whom he had known before the war, when both had regularly gone out hunting with the Whaddon Hounds. 'In the world of neurotic policemen and timid placemen who rule the secret service, he moves like Falstaff, or some figure from Balzac, if not Rabelais.' Gambier-Parry the huntsman had cut a 'loud, Levantine figure in a risqué chocolate uniform, beltless and betabbed, his brass hat slightly awry, thrusting merrily forward on a heavyweight hunter, & closely followed by two modish blondes, his secretaries'. In the evenings afterwards he would bang the bottle on the table and boast of his success: 'led the field all the way'. When appointed as head of Section VIII, Gambier-Parry had seized an opportunity to establish his headquarters at Whaddon Hall, which was not far from Bletchley. There he lived like a colonial governor, with a fleet of camouflaged Packards at his disposal. Having taken over the house, he lost little time in taking over the Whaddon Hounds, and commandeered the huntsmen to his personal staff if they were in danger of being called up. Under Gambier-Parry's patronage, meets of the Whaddon would assemble on the lawn outside the house in true aristocratic style.

After the bombing of Wormwood Scrubs, RSS had been transplanted to the village of Arkley, near Barnet, on the northern edge of London, where the built-up suburbs gave way to open countryside. Various large houses in the area were requisitioned as billets. MI5 set up a liaison section at Arkley, as well as its own intelligence section to work on RSS material. As RSS's sole remaining intelligence officer, Hugh now became head of its intelligence section, known henceforth as the Radio Analysis Bureau (RAB), which was subordinated to Cowgill's Section V. This was a fudge. Logic suggested that if RSS was to be integrated into SIS, to become a mere supplier, its intelligence function should be shut down. But RSS's intelligence work was too valuable to discard. Hence the unsatisfactory compromise of creating RAB as a separate RSS intelligence subsection within Section V. The contradictions in this arrangement were immediately apparent. Hugh refused to move to St Albans, where SIS had relocated from central London to avoid the bombing, and insisted on remaining with RSS in Arkley, so that he could provide it with intelligence guidance. Interception could be improved by studying the call signs, frequencies and other technical features of enemy wireless.[29]

In his new role, Hugh was now serving two masters: as an officer of Section V he was responsible to Cowgill, but as part of RSS he was responsible to Maltby and, through him, to Gambier-Parry. He was able to exploit this dual chain of command to achieve considerable autonomy in his work, often appealing to Gambier-Parry to overrule instructions given him by Cowgill. Relations between Cowgill and his awkward subordinate were never cordial. Hugh regarded Cowgill with contempt, as 'a purblind, disastrous, megalomaniac', and stubbornly refused to be cowed; while Cowgill condemned Hugh as 'an independent character'. He suspected Hugh of 'irreverent thoughts and dangerous contacts'.[30]

Cowgill had been recruited from the Indian police, and retained the attitudes of a policeman. He was suspicious of academics and intellectuals, and constitutionally averse to sharing intelligence; for him, security was paramount, and intelligence was to be disseminated strictly on a 'need to know' basis. Later in the war Cowgill denied MI5 access to intelligence material merely on the grounds that he 'did not like the look of the people to whom it was going'. Hugh's instincts went the other way. For him, intelligence-gathering was pointless if it was only to be hoarded. Releasing it piecemeal was to misunderstand its usefulness. The essence of intelligence was not the discovery of specific information to be used for a specific purpose, but the assembly of fragments which, taken together, provided a larger picture. The individual pieces of intelligence revealed by reading *Abwehr* signals were not necessarily significant in themselves, and indeed could be misleading if taken in isolation; but evaluated together, they provided a working model of the organisation, from which *Abwehr* operations could be not only detected but predicted. To understand the *modus operandi* of the *Abwehr*, and to mount successful operations against the enemy – particularly the deception operations which were to prove so crucial later in the war – required continuous and detailed study and evaluation. This was best done by circulating intelligence as widely as possible, to enable appraisal from multiple sources. Hugh's emphasis on intelligence evaluation ran counter to the orthodoxy within SIS, which was to supply raw intelligence free of comment or analysis.* This philosophical difference between Hugh and his SIS superiors would be the cause of much conflict over the coming years.

'So I found myself in the Secret Service,' wrote Hugh many years later, in an autobiographical fragment:

> that mysterious and powerful organisation of which, in my boyhood, I had read – admittedly in the form of novels – in the works of John Buchan, Baroness Orczy, E. Phillips Oppenheim, and so many others – such romantic and tantalising accounts. It had a myth about it in those days, a myth of ubiquity, infallibility, colourful exploits, dark doings, brilliant results; a myth, moreover, accepted abroad, where its very name inspired awe and emulation ... Foreign intelligence services envied the British secret service: it was their idealised model; but how could they imitate it if they could not discover it? Its members were unidentified, its chief – CSS, or C to the initiated – never named. So it enjoyed the reputation of an invisible, implacable force, like the Platonic world-spirit, operating everywhere. The Soviet government, seeing conspiracies all around it, imagined the British secret service as their universal organiser. To the Nazi government, it was at the same time a bogey and an ideal. Four years later, in conquered Berlin, picking through the rubble of the bombed Gestapo head-

---

* There was a parallel with medieval historians, who tended to cherish 'pure' historical records and be suspicious of any form of analysis.

quarters in Prinz Albrechtstrasse, I found official handbooks, stamped 'secret', describing the structure and operation of the British secret service. I have them still and turn to them occasionally for light relief. The British secret service, I there read, penetrates all the institutions of British life; the Anglican Church, the Boy Scout movement, you name it. It was the most powerful instrument of British *Machtpolitik* ... The reality, I soon discovered, was rather different.

Major

Hugh's boyhood illusions about SIS did not survive his first visit to St Albans. He was 'appalled' by the 'cosy, puerile' atmosphere he discovered within Section V, which reminded him of an isolated public school, amazed by the lack of interest in and understanding of intelligence, and struck by the contrast with the orderly efficiency of MI5. Hugh came to see SIS as an example of a closed, inward-looking society, recruiting by patronage, feeding on fantasy and self-perpetuating illusions, and increasingly isolated from reality. Its members, he felt, tended to come from one of two unimpressive groups: rich men of limited intellect whose egos were boosted by membership of a secret organisation with a romantic past; or retired officers of the Indian police, whose experience had been limited to harassing innocent Indians suspected of Communist leanings. On the one hand, empty-headed members of the upper class, clubland habitués; on the other, unimaginative policemen whose brains had been scorched by the Indian sun. Such men could not begin to comprehend the new techniques of scientific intelligence made possible by the systematic study of radio intercepts. Since the perceived threat in the inter-war years had come from international Communism – from the Left and not from the Right – these men were unprepared, ideologically as well as practically, to change direction. Little was known about Nazism; none of Hugh's new colleagues appeared to have read *Mein Kampf.*

Few graduates entered SIS – indeed, its Assistant Chief was emphatic that he wanted none. At its head was the newly appointed 'C', Colonel (later Major-General Sir) Stewart Menzies, who had been in the service since 1919, and whose world (as Hugh saw it) was circumscribed by the Life Guards, the Beaufort Hunt and White's Club. The Duke of Buccleuch, who had been Menzies's fag at Eton, later told Hugh that none of his contemporaries could understand how so unbelievably stupid a man could have ended up in such a position. To Hugh he resembled a thoughtless feudal lord, living comfortably at court on income produced from the labour of peasants whom he had never seen, working estates which he had never visited.

Menzies believed himself to be the natural son of Edward VII, whose portrait dominated his office. He was indulgent towards Hugh, tolerating the clever young man's disregard of orders and indifference to rank. At the end of the war Menzies would tell Guy Liddell that he 'had always backed Trevor-Roper'.[1] Unfortunately Menzies allowed himself to be dominated by quarrelsome subordinates: Claude Dansey, Assistant Chief of the Secret Service, and Valentine Vivian, Deputy Chief. These two were not on speaking terms. They represented the two types of SIS men: Dansey, described by Hugh as 'a snob, a bully and a shit', recruited young men into the service from the bar at Boodle's; while Vivian, a serpentine character 'reminiscent of Uriah Heep', had been an Indian policeman and surrounded himself with others from the same background, such as Cowgill.

Hugh was exasperated to be working with such 'boneheads'. One exception was 'Kim' Philby, who arrived at St Albans to run the Iberian subsection of Cowgill's Section V. As the *Abwehr* had stations in Madrid and Lisbon, and substations elsewhere in Spain and Portugal, Hugh's work required liaison with Philby, whom he found 'an agreeable and effective person', good company and good at his job: 'intelligent, sophisticated, even real'.[2] At the time Philby seemed to Hugh someone who could bring some much-needed mental stimulus into the 'philistine world' of SIS; though in retrospect he would question Philby's intellectual credentials. 'Except for one reference to Marx, he never mentioned a book in my presence, nor could I get him to talk on serious topics: he would always keep conversation on a superficial plane, in ironic, Aesopian language, as if he knew of the differences which would divide us should we break the surface on which, till then, we could happily and elegantly skate.'[3] At the time, though, Philby's shrewd mind and sophisticated talk made him a welcome contrast to most of his colleagues.

Philby's name had been familiar to Hugh since the early 1930s. A Christ Church contemporary of Hugh's, Ian 'Tim' Milne, had been at Westminster with Philby before coming up to Oxford, and had often mentioned his former schoolmate in conversation, referring in particular to motorcycling holidays in central Europe with 'my communist friend Philby'. Far from deterring Hugh, Philby's left-wing background came as a relief from the unthinking conservatism of most SIS members. In any case, all that now seemed to be in the past. Several of Hugh's young friends had considered themselves Communists in the early 1930s; most had since become disillusioned, particularly after the signing of the Nazi–Soviet Pact in August 1939.[4]

Hugh was more in sympathy with the codebreakers at Bletchley than with most of his SIS colleagues at St Albans. Commander Denniston had actively recruited 'men of the Professor type' to fill the ranks of his fast-expanding team. As well as mathematicians, he sought out archaeologists and scholars in ancient history or orthography, those who in peacetime specialised in reconstructing the past from surviving fragments of evidence. Soon there were dozens of dons complementing the professional crypt-ographers at Bletchley, supported by hundreds of translators, technicians and administrative staff. From a nucleus of about 150 at the outbreak of war, the number working at Bletchley rose to 3,500 by late 1942, and would eventually reach 10,000 or so by 1945. They worked in shifts to provide twenty-four-hour coverage: essential since the Enigma settings changed daily and speed was of the essence. All were billeted out to surrounding towns and villages. The mansion soon proved too small to contain the river of people flooding into Bletchley, which overflowed into the various outhouses and into a succession of crude, single-storey huts erected in the grounds.

The raw product emerging from Bletchley in ever-increasing quantity was often arcane; even specialists found it difficult to understand. Hugh, following Gill, saw the role of his subsection as one of analysing and interpreting such material. From August 1941 the Radio Analysis Bureau began to issue 'Vw' (Section V, wireless) reports on the *Abwehr* and its activities in theatres around the world, including the occasional 'Who's Who' of local enemy agents, known as 'Purple Primers'. Over the next few years the RAB (and its successor, the RIS) would circulate more than eighty such reports, describing *Abwehr* activities in impressive detail. One modest example provides an illustration of the benefits brought by such close scrutiny. In a report on Axis intelligence in Southern and Eastern Africa, Hugh was able to show that the Italians drew much of their infor-mation from their German allies. He identified an error in the translation of an intercepted German telegram, indicating that an enemy agent in South Africa was not supplying information on Allied shipping direct to German submarines, as had previously been thought. This was a conclusion of immediate practical interest to the Admiralty.[5]

His reports were highly valued by MI5 and by the secret intelligence departments of the three services, and indeed by the Bletchley codebreakers themselves, who found them useful in deciding which lines of research should be investigated first.[6] Hugh was anxious to ensure that Vw reports were given the widest possible circulation. But Cowgill was determined to deny Hugh's subsection direct contact with bodies outside SIS. As the official history of British Intelligence records, the result would be 'a running battle' between the two men, 'sustained by personal animosities'. At one point Cowgill ceased to circulate Vw reports altogether, leading to a row with MI5.[7] The fact that many of Hugh's natural 'customers' were men that he knew socially heightened Cowgill's mistrust. The Army intelligence section was headed by Brian Melland, a distant cousin of Hugh's; Melland's RAF equivalent was the art historian John Pope-Hennessy, whom Hugh had met through Logan Pearsall Smith. Hugh also formed an excellent working relationship with Ewen Montagu of the Admiralty's Naval Intelligence Division, a barrister in civil life. At Bletchley, Hugh's old tutor, Denys Page, arrived as a replacement for Oliver Strachey. As for MI5, its officers had worked with Hugh on rounding up enemy agents since early 1940. The effect of Cowgill's intransigence was to create an unofficial network through which information was surreptitiously exchanged. His authority was consequently diminished.

There was strong pressure from MI5 for radio intelligence to be circulated more freely than Cowgill would allow. In May 1941 a joint SIS and MI5 Wireless Committee was formed, in an attempt to reconcile the demands of the two services. This committee met fortnightly, 'to the accompaniment of continuous disputes'.[8] Among those regularly attending were Guy Liddell and Dick White from MI5, Maltby and Cowgill from SIS, and Page from G.C. & C.S. Another MI5 officer who sometimes attended was Captain Anthony Blunt, Liddell's personal assistant. Hugh acted as committee secretary. His 'scholarly approach' impressed Liddell, who noted in his diary that Hugh had 'perhaps a better understanding of the system than anybody else'. Liddell qualified his praise by adding that the young don was 'something of an intellectual snob'. But he felt that the intelligence emanating from RSS was 'pure gold and everything should be done to develop it'. He pressed SIS to recruit more staff for RSS, including more intelligence officers to work alongside Hugh.[9] In the summer of July 1941 Hugh acquired an assistant, in the shape of the twenty-one-year-old Charles Stuart, who had left Christ Church with a first-class degree in history only weeks before. Vigilant and meticulous, Stuart came recommended by Masterman, who extolled the 'ice-blue clarity of his intellect'. Like Hugh, Stuart was a keen huntsman. A tall, wiry, stooping figure, he walked with a rapid stride, suggestive of his impatient mind.

A couple of months after Stuart, Gilbert Ryle arrived at Arkley. He had been serving with the Welsh Guards, which he found stuffy and boring, and had written to Hugh in the hope of escape. Ryle's keen and original mind, his insistence on clarity of expression, his droll and subversive wit and his utter lack of pretension made him an ideal colleague. His companionship did much to relieve the tedium and frustration that Hugh often experienced in his work. 'How one longed, in those drab, mechanical days, to escape from routine work and routine postures and to discuss ideas!'[10] Ryle's relaxed common sense did much to calm the spirits of his frequently volatile commanding officer. Hugh's irritability was exacerbated by illness; during the summer and autumn of 1941 he was again 'haunting Harley Street', seeking treatment for his sinusitis; in September he told Guy Liddell that his doctor had advised him to winter abroad, but he was concerned about the possibility that his team might be broken up in his absence, and did not want to go unless he could be sure that the work he was doing would be allowed to continue. Hugh put the case for a separate bureau to study radio intelligence. In his diary, Liddell recorded that there was 'much to be said for this suggestion, and were it not for the difficult personality of T-R and his quarrels with Felix [Cowgill] the whole matter could have been settled months ago'. Indeed, the 'personal quarrel' between the two men had 'driven a wedge' between MI5 and its sister service.[11]

In November, while he was ill in bed, Hugh read Ryle two pseudonymous 'self-appreciations' lent to him by Logan Pearsall Smith.* At Ryle's insistence, Hugh composed his own 'self-appreciation', of five handwritten pages. 'Pride is my chief fault, and will be my undoing,' he predicted. He listed some of his other weaknesses – 'imprudence, ostentation, volubility, and the need for company' – about which he was 'quite unrepentant'. Two years later Hugh would compose a more revealing self-portrait, which he headed 'Autopsy', and which he would return to and revise in 1950. He confessed that he sometimes suffered from deep depression, to the extent that he would break down completely, and afterwards feel humiliated and ashamed. In the depth of his depression he felt intellectually helpless, doomed to ineffectiveness and oppressed by a sense of utter solitude. 'I crave affection and consolation, but am afraid to solicit it and so emphasize my isolation.'[12]

At the beginning of 1942, the three Christ Church men were joined by Stuart Hampshire, who had been languishing with the infantry in Sierra Leone. His recruitment suggests that Hugh had overcome any resentment he may have felt towards Hampshire as one of the two candidates preferred to him for All Souls Fellowships in 1936. A subtle thinker, Hampshire was a gentle and unworldly man, with an acute moral sense. His sensitive, imaginative approach to his work contrasted with Stuart's rigorous precision, just as his egalitarian, socialist politics contrasted with Stuart's elitist conservatism.

These four RAB officers, two historians and two philosophers, made a 'formidable Oxonian combination', as Philby would acknowledge in his memoirs. Patrick Reilly, a Foreign Office mandarin who became personal assistant to Menzies in 1942, believed that they constituted 'a team of a brilliance unparalleled anywhere in the Intelligence machine'.[13]

On Christmas Day 1941 Lord Swinton visited Arkley, in his role as Chairman of the Security Executive. He had already made some changes within MI5, and he was now turning his attention to SIS. At the end of his official

---

* Smith had published them in 1897 in *The Golden Urn*, a short-lived review he edited with his future brother-in-law, Bernard Berenson. The two 'self-appreciations' were by Bertrand Russell and Sir Hubert Miller, an evidently sophisticated Hampshire squire.

inspection, which lasted most of the morning, he casually asked Hugh if he was free for lunch. Later Hugh would discover that Lindemann had recommended Swinton to speak to him. Swinton proposed the Carlton Club, so the two of them climbed into the Minister's official car and drove into London. They found the club burnt out, after an air-raid the previous evening; but the Junior Carlton Club on the other side of Pall Mall was still operating, and indeed offered a full Christmas menu, albeit in its basement, where the ceiling was supported by scaffolding. Being the only two lunching there, they were able to talk freely, and as the meal progressed Hugh found himself answering a series of questions from the Minister about his work, which he answered 'with decreasing discretion as the port followed the burgundy'. In truth, Hugh was only too keen to tell Swinton about his frustrations, his impatience with Cowgill in particular. Eventually the lunch came to an end. Hugh rode in the Minister's car back to Arkley, to be greeted with momentous news: Bletchley had succeeded in breaking the *Abwehr* Enigma. This triumph would produce a flood of *Abwehr* intercepts, many of them communications at the highest level. Because the Germans believed the Enigma ciphers to be unbreakable, they were very open in what they said in such messages.

For the next few days Hugh boasted of a political coup, in securing the ear of such a highly placed auditor as Lord Swinton. In reality, as later became obvious, Hugh's conversation with Swinton deepened the mistrust in him already felt by his superiors. Ryle punctured Hugh's pride with a characteristically downbeat comment: 'Many a bull, emerging from a blood-stained china-shop, has congratulated itself on its Machiavellian diplomacy.'[14]

'I enjoy your company more than that of anyone now living,' Logan Pearsall Smith wrote to Hugh in September 1942. His letters were often sweetened with such expressions of affection, though almost always accompanied by a seasoning of vinegar. 'I will allow myself to say that I find your company the most delightful in the world,' he wrote in the summer of 1941; adding, 'I am not sure that you are altogether a nice person.'[15]

Smith recognised in Hugh a fellow-spirit, one who shared his taste for mischief and malice. A capricious old man of some means, Smith was not above teasing his younger attendants with the expectation of future inheritance. He cultivated rivalry between 'the social queens, the elegant, foul-mouthed spinsters & the clerical and other boy-friends who form my usual society'.[16] It was a habit of Smith's to entice visitors with the promise of books from his library after his death. 'Greedy ghouls' were encouraged to paste their own book-plates inside the covers, in anticipation of the time when such 'blackmailers and hyenas' might take possession of the volumes themselves. Some of the most desirable were already spoken for, of course; but a new plate could be pasted over that of a transgressor. This was a game which Smith relished, a minor variant of his 'will-shaking'.

Cyril Connolly, who had been his secretary-companion, tired of Smith's waywardness and moved on. Robert Gathorne-Hardy took his place, and submitted to humiliating treatment in exchange for the uncertain status of Smith's 'heir'. The old man's erratic behaviour had been accentuated by the late onset of manic depression, on a cycle regulated by the seasons: in spring and summer he was euphoric, but in the winter months he sank into a deep gloom, when he would be almost incapable of speech, and took not the slightest pleasure in company. Hugh was careful not to visit him during these moods.

Towards Hugh, Smith posed as an ageing coquette – 'your virginal octogenarian boyfriend' – one moment flirtatious, the next coy.[17] Homo-sexual innuendo permeated his facetious letters. He showed a prurient interest in Hugh's private life, repeatedly complaining about Hugh's 'implacable' reserve, and always wanting 'the low-down on you'. He solicited a copy of Hugh's 'self-appreciation'. He admitted to being irritated 'at the way when my soul (if I have a soul) is like an open window to you, and all my failings apparent enough to your observation (and ironic comment), you keep on your mask in my company, & envelop yourself in enormous fig-leaves.'[18]

Hugh resisted Smith's relentless probing. He left Smith's eightieth birth-day party early when he became irritated by Smith's teasing questions. His letters offered no hint of emotional or sexual entanglements – or even of sexual inclination. In his private notebook, he observed that 'formless, sentimental women' reminded him of 'over-ripe pears'. He confessed that 'in general, women repel me'. Hugh opened his mind on this subject to Stuart Hampshire, who remarked on the 'ugly gait and soft complaisant grimaces' of so many women – to which Hugh added other details, 'their foolish birdlike minds' and 'their twittering voices'. In his 'self-revelation', Hampshire admitted to wishing that he was more than 'slightly homo-sexual', because he very much preferred the society of men to that of women. Hugh qualified his distaste for women by reminding himself of those whom he liked, 'who belie their sex by possessing features and under-standing the art of growing old; aged dowagers with aquiline faces, who sit erect and stately in their high chairs, giving orders to their servants, and disapproving the low standards of the age in life, taste & manners'.[19]

Soon after their friendship commenced, 'Logan' began to hint that Hugh would benefit from his will. He wanted, he said, to leave his money to someone who would thereby be enabled to follow his own example and devote himself to the undeviating pursuit of literature.[20] Smith warned

Hugh not to be unduly elated, 'as I don't mean to die next week or the week after either, & I so enjoyed disinheriting my supplanted heirs that I may want to taste again this tipsy pleasure'. In January 1943 Smith sent Hugh a copy of a will which named him as principal beneficiary.[21] But unlike Gathorne-Hardy, who had become a dependant, Hugh refused to play Smith's game. He responded to Smith's jibes with jibes of his own. Such 'effrontery' only increased his attractiveness for the older man; verbal sparring characterised their encounters. 'One of the things that makes me like you is the masochistic pleasure I derive from the scornful way you treat me,' Smith told Hugh.[22] 'You must have observed that though no flattery is unwelcome,' he wrote on another occasion, 'the breath and faint garlic of derision in the salads you prepare, the drops – I won't say of poison, but of not unfriendly irony you infuse in your sauces, is especially to my taste'.[23]

For Hugh, Smith's home in Chelsea provided an escape from the drudgery of his work and the limitations imposed by its secrecy. He had one day free each week, and during the summer months he often used this day to visit Smith. At St Leonard's Terrace he found a house filled with fine books, many of which would come to bear his book-plate. There he would meet civilised guests such as Rose Macaulay, Cyril Connolly, Desmond Mac-Carthy and Osbert Sitwell. Above all there was his host, whose talk poured forth in a seemingly never-ending stream. Smith's conversation was sophisticated and uninhibited, and very much to Hugh's taste. Though he affected not to like gossip, Smith adored news from what he called the *beau monde* (a phrase that Hugh adopted for himself). And when reminiscing, Smith could recall encounters with many famous figures of the past sixty years, including his close friend, the poet Robert Bridges; Walt Whitman, a family friend; his Harvard contemporary, the philosopher George Santayana; Henry James and his philosopher brother William; the painter James Whistler and the critic Roger Fry; the novelist George Moore; men of letters such as Walter Raleigh and Edmund Gosse; Virginia Woolf; and many others.

Smith had coined his own phrase for pressing books on friends, 'cram-throating'. He sent Hugh regular parcels of books through the post. As Hugh later recalled, these 'provided me with elevating relief from the routine and squalor and philistinism of much of my work'.[24] Reading filled the long hours of inactivity, particularly when he was ill in bed, or in hospital. For a while Hugh kept a record of the books he had read each year. In 1940, for example, he read sixty-five books; in 1941, seventy-two; in 1942, eighty-four; and in 1943, one hundred and nineteen. His reading ranged very widely, from poetry to politics, from Sallust to Saki: including Boswell and Gibbon, Chaucer and Dante, and modern authors like Rose Macaulay, Robert Graves and Arthur Koestler. He re-read the classics in

Latin and Greek, plenty of books in French, and a few in German and Italian. Instead of confining himself to historical works about the early modern period, he concentrated on those of philosophical or literary value, by such authors as G.M. Trevelyan, Benedetto Croce and Henri Pirenne. He also read books by his contemporaries A.J.P. Taylor, A.L. Rowse and E.H. Carr. It was not all solemn stuff: among the titles he listed were Surtees's *Mr Sponge's Sporting Tour* and Erskine Childers's thriller *The Riddle of the Sands.*

At this period of his life it was by no means obvious that Hugh was destined to become an academic historian. There remained a tension within him, between the careful, scholarly side of his character and the more easy-going, showy side. It seemed certain that he would write more history, but he appears to have considered himself as a writer first, and historian second. Among the projects he discussed with Smith was a book of seventeenth-century portraits, in the manner of Aubrey's *Brief Lives.*[25] Hugh also contemplated writing biographies of Louis XIV and Marlborough. The latter idea came from A.L. Rowse, who was much courted by publishers after the best-selling success of *A Cornish Childhood* (1942), chronicling his struggle to escape rural poverty and to get to Oxford. Privately, Hugh condemned the 'shrill, vulgar, boastful, hysterical, over-dramatised, and often irrelevant outbursts which frequently intrude in that otherwise prim narrative'.[26] Rowse now proposed that Hugh write for a new series he was editing, which would 'capture historiography from trashy female novelists' and 'compare with the best volumes in the Home University Library'. Hugh liked the idea of writing a short study of Marlborough, and envisaged a book along the lines of Lytton Strachey's *Elizabeth and Essex* (though 'rather better') – until he received a contract from the publishers, with a flyer explaining the scope of the 'Teach Yourself History' series: 'a set of manuals in yellow boards,' he wrote disdainfully in his notebook, 'to be sold on railway-stations to mugging but conscientious artisans'. He wrote to Rowse withdrawing from the agreement, politely explaining that he had evidently misunderstood the scope and nature of the series. In response he received a four-page letter of 'boastful, hectoring, rude, condescending abuse': the first of several such over the years to come. In the 1930s Rowse had been one of those Hugh had most wanted to know, attracted by his more appealing qualities: his insistence on readability, his hot Celtic character, his unusual career, his baroque mind and his complicated prejudices. Increasingly, however, he would come to think of 'poor old Rowse' as absurd. Rowse's self-importance, his touchiness, his vanity and his greed were subjects of derision within the Oxonian world of the Radio Analysis Bureau. Hugh now found it 'incredible' that he had once admired Rowse. He reluctantly acceded to Rowse's request for an introduction to Pearsall Smith, though he 'boggled at the responsibility of introducing a shrill exhibitionist to a venerable and fastidious sage'. Smith was not impressed. 'I found that he hasn't read any history,' he told Hugh afterwards. 'He has never heard of Gregorovius. Milman's *History of Latin Christianity* wasn't even a name to him. Why, I don't believe he has even read Gibbon.'[27]

Hugh wrote a portrait of 'Logan Pearsall Smith in old age', which he sent to his subject for approval. In it he summarised the philosophy of 'the Sage of Chelsea' thus: 'that humanity is ridiculous, but that there is a pleasure in observing its antics even amid our own gesticulations, and that it is redeemed from utter meaninglessness by its ideals, though many even of these are very odd; and that style is an ideal too, style of living, style of writing, born of disinterested thought and sweat to ennoble and preserve the thoughts and memory of an else insignificant existence'.[28] He repeated one of Smith's aphorisms: 'The indefatigable pursuit of an unattainable Perfection, even though it consists in nothing more than the pounding of an old piano, is what alone gives a meaning to our life on this unavailing star.'

Smith was as much concerned with style as with scholarship. He endlessly polished his *Trivia*, seeking Hugh's suggestions for improvements forty years after the first edition had been published. No care was too great in the quest for perfect prose, no effort too much. 'Words & phrases are the only things that matter,' he wrote to Hugh early in their friendship. Two weeks before his death in 1946, Smith was asked if he had discovered any purpose to life. 'Yes,' he replied: 'there is one thing that matters – to set a chime of words tinkling in the minds of a few fastidious people.'[29]

Smith's influence revived Hugh's interest in prose style. In his revolt against the fussiness of classical composition, and in his rejection of any ideas that could not be verified by reason, Hugh had neglected literary considerations. Following Ayer and Ryle, he had formed the view that clarity of expression was the sole criterion of good writing. In his book on Laud, he had 'consciously ignored the temptation of style'.[30] Now Hugh shifted his stance. Clarity alone was not enough; bare prose was like an undecorated house. Under Smith's tutelage, Hugh aspired to a sophisticated style, adorned with metaphor and irony. 'Though your style is good,' wrote Smith, 'I think it might be enriched & made more amusing by choice phrasing & freshness & surprise of epithet.'[31]

Smith encouraged Hugh's literary ambitions. He regularly praised Hugh's 'enchanting' and 'delicious' letters, which, he said, he often re-read; 'the mingling of mockery & friendliness & the perfect phrasing is a potation of which I never tire'. He kept them carefully, as he kept the letters of Virginia Woolf, Henry James, George Santayana and Walter Raleigh: 'yours perhaps the best'.[32]

In 1944 Hugh sent Smith a manuscript entitled 'A Vision of Judgement', an apocalyptic satire featuring archetypal characters such as the Jew, the Nazi, the Widow and the Airman. One of his principals was God himself, who is troubled by doubts about his own existence. The manuscript has not survived and the correspondence does not establish whether it was in verse form, like the *Visions of Judgement* of Southey and Byron to which its title obviously refers. Smith found the work unsatisfactory, though 'witty & very pleasant to read, & the Voltairean irony is just the sort of thing I like'. Hugh followed his advice to put the work aside, to ripen in his mind.[33]

That Smith was sincere in his high opinion of Hugh's talent was evident in a letter he wrote after the end of the war to Edward A. Weeks, Editor of the *Atlantic Monthly*. Smith provided Weeks with a list of new writers the magazine might like to publish, rating Hugh as 'the ablest', and adding that Cyril Connolly shared his opinion. Among the other young writers Smith mentioned were Kenneth Clark and John Russell, who would become chief art critic of *The New York Times*.[34]

It was one of Smith's rules that an aspirant writer should keep a notebook; another that he should mark any striking passages he read in books and keep an index of these inside the back cover, a habit Hugh adopted and continued all his life. In 1942 Hugh began keeping his own notebooks, which he continued for several years. They contain observation, reflection, character study, self-revelation, travelogue, aphorisms, descriptions of dreams, comments on books he was reading and striking passages from these, scraps of memorable conversation, and satirical ballads, in both English and Latin, and occasionally Greek. They record both high spirits and deep gloom. Their form owes something to Smith's *Trivia*, as well as to the notebooks of Samuel Butler, though they are distinct from both. It is unclear whether Hugh meant them for eventual publication. They are not spontaneous expressions of thought and feeling, but careful literary constructions; at least some of the content has evidently been transcribed from earlier drafts. Hugh entitled them τττερόεντα, an abbreviation of the Homeric formula for introducing speech ἔττεα τττερόεντα, meaning 'winged words', perhaps implying that what they contained was intended to be communicated.

On the other hand, it seems clear that some of what he wrote, whether in the notebooks or elsewhere, was for himself alone. There was the sheer pleasure of exercising his skill, like a runner sprinting along an empty beach. There was also the need to express thoughts and feelings that might be too personal to share. Some of his private prose is self-consciously experimental: he poses, like a woman trying on different outfits before going out in the evening. Moreover, writing helped him to order his thoughts. Articulating his ideas was part of the intellectual process. There was a therapeutic purpose, too. It seems that in later years, whenever he was particularly troubled about something, he would write about it, in the form of a memorandum to himself. In this way, perhaps, he was able to externalise his anxiety.

One function of the notebooks was to relieve his irritation at the ignorant complacency of his slow-witted colleagues. 'How can I describe it?' he wrote of SIS in March 1942:

> A colony of coots in an unventilated backwater of bureaucracy? A bunch of dependent bumsuckers held together by neglect, like a cluster of bats in an unswept barn? O for a broom, I cry, to drive them twittering hence! But expostulating voices say, No! for it is a consecrated barn protected by ancient taboos. And so another image rises in my mind, of the high-priests of effete religion mumbling their meaningless ritual to avert a famine or stay a cataclysm. And then I remember the hieratic indolence of those self-inflated mandarins, their Chinese ideograms, their green ink, their oriental insincerities, their ceremonious evasions of responsibility, their insulation from the contemporary world, and the right image has come, of Palace eunuchs in the Great Within.'[35]

During the winter months, when Logan Pearsall Smith withdrew into his library and ceased to receive visitors, Hugh sought every opportunity to go fox-hunting. Hunting in England continued throughout the war, albeit on a diminished scale, and with less flummery, the meets attended for the most part by rich, middle-aged men, local farmers and officers stationed nearby. Hugh managed a day out with the Whaddon or the Bicester Hounds most weeks during the season, though this required careful planning. Having laid up his car for the duration of the war because of petrol rationing, he had no transport of his own. He still kept his mare, Rubberneck, at Quainton, and on hunting days would arrange for her to be taken early in the morning to a convenient pick-up point on a main road near the meet, which he would reach by hitch-hiking forty miles or more from Arkley. Often he would set out before dawn, wearing his captain's uniform, relying on lifts from passing lorries or service vehicles to make his rendezvous. Hugh would try to time his regular visits to Bletchley to coincide with meets of the Whaddon, which meant that he could enjoy the luxury of travelling by staff car.

Hunting was not without risk: in 1943 Hugh would spend eight days in hospital after falling from his horse. But vigorous outdoor activity provided a relief from the vexations of Hugh's work as an intelligence officer. On one occasion, while Hugh was out hunting with the Whaddon, these two parts of his life were brought suddenly and unexpectedly together, when the chase led the hounds to Bletchley itself. The fox darted into the Park, followed by the pack in full cry. The sentry at the gate was powerless to stop them, but he detained the huntsmen and the whips at the gate, while the baying hounds fanned out through the Park in pursuit of their quarry. Hugh had a nightmare vision of their bursting into the huts where the Ultra signals were deciphered, and emerging with precious decrypts gripped between their teeth, to be scattered across the north Buckinghamshire countryside. Flashing his pass at the sentry, he spurred his horse into the Park to round up the hounds before they could do any serious damage. Meanwhile the sly fox had made his escape.

Logan Pearsall Smith often teased Hugh about his love of fox-hunting. From time to time Hugh seems to have asked himself whether it was a becoming activity for one who aspired to live the life of the mind. Soon after he had resumed hunting following his long illness in 1940, he had been reproached by Tom Armstrong, Organist and Choragus (choir-master) at Christ Church. Armstrong told him that he was being 'false to your own intellectual nature' in going fox-hunting, and 'being such a snob', and 'loving worldly rather than intellectual things'. He begged Hugh to consider that he had an intellect, and therefore should be an intellectual and strive to realise his intellectual vocation. Armstrong said that he was speaking on behalf of a group of friends, disturbed at Hugh's evident wish to waste his talents in the pursuit of false values. To combine the tastes of a scholar and a country gentleman had been possible in the eighteenth century, but now the two were incompatible; one must choose between them, and choose aright.

Hugh was 'bitterly hurt' by these charges. He conceded that he might once have been snobbish, but not now, and he was aggrieved that someone he liked as much as he did Armstrong should not have noticed his growing 'intellectual idealism' and 'distaste for high society without aristocratic ideals', and the 'burning contempt' he now entertained for those motivated solely by the lure of 'shabby success', such as Feiling, Elton* or Bryant. Hugh poured out his pique in his notebook. 'My love of foxhunting is real,' he insisted, 'and unconnected with its social implications, which I despise.'[36]

Years later, Hugh would write that fox-hunting had saved him from 'going mad' during his time with SIS. Early in 1942 his exasperation with his colleagues erupted in a long letter to Lindemann – to whom he had evidently grumbled before about 'the mess' SIS was making of 'this new world of intelligence'. This time Hugh's beef was not with Cowgill, but with

---

* Godfrey Elton, former Fellow and tutor in modern history at Queen's College, Oxford. A strong supporter of Ramsay MacDonald, he wrote the first volume of MacDonald's biography. MacDonald's son Malcolm had been his pupil. In 1934, while MacDonald was still Prime Minister in the National Government and his son an Under-Secretary of State, Elton was raised to the peerage, prompting Namier's quip: 'In the eighteenth century peers made their tutors under-secretaries; in the twentieth under-secretaries make their tutors peers'.

Maltby and Gambier-Parry in their direction of the 'technical department', i.e. RSS. Hugh described how his 'consistent efforts to get technical policy related to intelligence aims' had been thwarted; the memoranda he had submitted through the ordinary channels 'have always been silently suppressed'; his pleas that intelligence chiefs 'take cognisance of the defects in the policy of the technical department' had been fobbed off with a muddled and unsatisfactory response. 'I'm very much afraid that I may have no alternative but to resign,' he told Lindemann, and asked for suggestions of any other job he might do. 'If there is any position in which I could use my understanding of interception technique and research to better purpose than that of merely recognising mismanagement, I would be glad to take it.'[37]

As the Prime Minister's scientific adviser and long-term confidant, Lindemann (who had been elevated to the peerage as Lord Cherwell the previous June) was a man of influence, as Hugh knew well – though appealing to such an influential outsider to resolve an internal dispute was unlikely to endear Hugh to his superiors. Gambier-Parry was certainly very annoyed when he learned what Hugh had done. It is unclear whether he saw the letter to Cherwell; if he did, he cannot have relished Hugh's description of himself and Maltby as 'gramophone salesmen and others from the commercial world', who were 'quite unable to judge the possibilities themselves'. Furious, Gambier-Parry demanded that Hugh be removed from any connection with RSS. Hugh was summoned by Menzies, and, in the presence of Vivian, rebuked for 'telling tales out of school'. The session lasted three hours. Hugh remained unrepentant, though he consented to write a letter of apology to Gambier-Parry, 'on the understanding that this did not involve a withdrawal of my statements'; while Menzies agreed to receive a proposal from Hugh for the future operation of RSS which he had been previously forbidden from submitting. Gambier-Parry reluctantly accepted Hugh's apology, though he considered it somewhat grudging. 'The storm has broken around my head,' Hugh wrote afterwards to Lord Cherwell, 'but on looking round after it, I find that the damage is slight, and in some places the air is clearer & the countryside more refreshed.'

A few weeks later Hugh submitted a document entitled *Interception and Intercepted Intelligence*, which argued that a special office should co-ordinate intelligence on the *Abwehr* and study it intensively. Hugh sent a copy of his report to Cherwell, asking him, 'if you think it advisable', to show it to Desmond Morton, Churchill's personal assistant; 'and then if he'll see me, I would welcome the opportunity'.[38] Morton, as the filter through which Churchill received Ultra intelligence from Bletchley, was in a good position to judge the validity of Hugh's claims. Whether or not anything came of this initiative, the problem persisted. At the end of the year Guy Liddell minuted his boss Sir David Petrie, who in April 1941 had succeeded Harker as head of MI5, arguing much the same line as Hugh had done. 'RSS always described themselves as "the technical tool", with Gambier-Parry and Maltby as "the chief plumbers", wrote Liddell. 'It seemed to me that there was a tendency by the plumbers to try and direct intelligence, whereas intelligence should try to direct the plumbers.'[39]

In sharing his concerns with the likes of Cherwell and Morton, Hugh risked losing his job. But he was not a career intelligence officer, and the special circumstances of the war legitimised extraordinary measures. Servicemen were dying because of the failure to exploit intercepted intelligence. Hugh frequently complained that the 'professionals' who had joined SIS before the outbreak of hostilities acted as if the war were a dangerous interruption to more important concerns. Nor was he alone in by-passing his superiors when the need was urgent. In October 1941 several of the leading codebreakers at Bletchley appealed directly to the Prime Minister, after the failure of their repeated applications for more support staff.[40] Churchill responded by issuing one of his 'Action this Day' memoranda, ensuring that their demands were met 'on extreme priority'. Afterwards the codebreakers were rebuked by Menzies for wasting the Prime Minister's time.

Hugh was impatient of bureaucratic restrictions and procedural niceties; his high-handed behaviour often generated friction. Around the time of his interview with Menzies, he clashed with Commander Edward Travis, the new operational head of G.C. & C.S. who had succeeded Denniston two months earlier. Hugh believed that the significance of his work entitled him to liaise directly with the specialist sections at Bletchley Park, particularly when he felt that the big picture was being obscured by a mass of detail. Travis explained to Menzies why he had denied Hugh access to the huts where these sections worked. 'Captain Trevor-Roper either suffers from delusions or he has deliberately tried to mislead you,' he wrote. 'It was on account of complaints, which on investigation showed that there was no justification for his intrusion into Huts 3 & 4, that I refused permission for him to enter these sections again.' Travis indicated that Vivian agreed with him.

In a mild memorandum to Hugh, Menzies suggested that Ryle might be attached to Bletchley (where his cousin was working as a codebreaker) as a liaison officer, but Hugh imperiously rejected this compromise as 'impracticable'. Travis's objections were 'interfering with work of proven importance', and seemed to be personal rather than logical. 'If Commander Travis has made allegations which you consider sufficient to justify such action, I hope I may be allowed the usual privilege of being made acquainted with them and answering them.'

Menzies forwarded Hugh's response to Travis, who showed it to his deputy, Nigel de Grey. 'Trevor-Roper seems unable to speak the truth even by accident', commented de Grey:

> Is it necessary to argue with a junior officer or is this part of the service background? Personally if he were in my employ I should tell him to shut up – if he persisted I should sack him.
>
> The real danger to my mind is that his own master does not seem able to control him. How then can we confide our secrets to him?[41]

Within Bletchley, there was a tension between those responsible for intelligence and those responsible for security. The latter tended to resent SIS's control over the distribution of their hard-won secrets, and to suspect that they were not being guarded carefully enough. Hence there was pressure on Cowgill from Bletchley itself to restrict the distribution of Ultra intelligence. There was a sense of 'them and us': within G.C. & C.S., SIS was known as 'the other side'. The professional codebreakers had a poor opinion of much of the intelligence emanating from SIS, mostly tittle-tattle picked up from foreign businessmen and other dubious sources. Ironically, Hugh was identified with his SIS colleagues, though he shared the Bletchley codebreakers' contempt for their amateurishness.

A fortnight later Travis reported back to Menzies after consulting on the matter. His tone betrayed his irritation. 'Were I to allow everyone who asks to enter B.[letchley] P.[ark] we should have very few secrets, and were I to spend as much time arguing as I have in this case I should do no other work.' Both Vivian and Cowgill agreed that there was 'no reason' why Hugh should have access to the secrets of Bletchley, and even if there were, continued Travis, 'he is not a suitable person to be allowed to do so'.[42] For Hugh, it was doubly frustrating to find his superiors within SIS siding against him. As so often before, he turned to his notebook to unload his feelings about his colleagues:

> I am sick of them, sick to death of them, that nest of timid & corrupt incompetents, without ideals or standards, concerned only with the security of their own discreditable existence, bum-sucking under the backstairs of bureaucracy. Weak men on the defensive, who will do and say anything through fear, they dread improvement, for improvement means change, and change may mean the shaking of a few old somnolent moths out of long undisturbed curtains and the brushing of cobwebs from dark, un-noticed corners.[43]

'The strain of continually fighting with highly-placed fools, combined with the rigours of the English climate, having proved too much for my health, I've come here to recover in the milder and less controversial atmosphere of Dublin,' Hugh wrote to his brother on 25 February 1942, three days after his letter to Cherwell complaining about Maltby and Gambier-Parry, 'and am going on, on Sunday, to Co. Limerick for some fox-hunting, the prospect of which is already beginning to revive me.'[44]

This was Hugh's first visit to Ireland, which remained neutral throughout the war. He had gone there at the suggestion of a friend from his undergraduate days, Dickie Dawson, whom he had met by chance in London. Dawson's father trained racehorses near Dublin, and Dawson frequently crossed the Irish Sea to escape the restrictions of wartime Britain. Although civilians needed special permission to visit Ireland during the hostilities, this rule did not apply to those in the Armed Services. Hugh checked the position with Cowgill, who gave his verbal approval to go.

Hugh planned to spend a few days in Dublin before joining Dawson in the country. While still in England he had telephoned his Irish friend, Frank Pakenham, hoping for introductions. 'Frank, I'm going to Dublin next week,' explained Hugh: 'hadn't you better come and have lunch with me tomorrow and give me the low-down?' There was an embarrassed silence. 'As a matter of fact I won't,' replied Pakenham at last; 'Dublin's one of the few places where my credit is still fairly high, and I'm not going to spoil it by sponsoring an obvious spy.' When Hugh laughed, Pakenham became serious. 'British intelligence officers have been murdered there,' he warned: 'I advise you not to go.' Hugh protested that he was only going fox-hunting. 'Of course you will have your cover,' Pakenham replied stonily. Though a British civil servant (after being invalided out of the Army), Pakenham had convinced himself that the struggle against the Axis was a ploy to conceal British designs on Ireland.

Like most of his Oxford colleagues, Hugh considered Pakenham a little 'touched in the brain'. He wrote a 'Ballad of Sir Pakenham', gently mocking his old friend, whom he compared to Don Quixote:

> Don Pakenham de la Mancha
> Has gone on a crusade:
> The bees sing in his bonnet,
> He waves his two-edged blade;
> And his emblem of the Double Cross
> Is gallantly displayed.

And so on, for several stanzas.

Hugh approached another Irish don, Nevill Coghill, who happily provided him with an introduction to the American Ambassador to Ireland. As a result he was invited to lunch at the American Embassy in Dublin, where he found himself seated next to Dawyck Haig's sister, Lady Alexandra Howard-Johnston, wife of an officer in the Royal Navy and pregnant with her first child. He seems to have made little impact on her, as subsequently she had no memory of meeting him.

When he joined Dawson in a small country town, Hugh found waiting for him a letter from his former boss, Colonel Worlledge, who had learned via the local bush telegraph that he was going to be in the area. Worlledge lived nearby, having returned to Ireland after being informed by the War Office that his services were no longer required. He invited Hugh to stay a night at his home, Glenwilliam Castle, and over a convivial dinner each outlined to the other what he knew of the takeover of RSS by SIS. Life in Ireland had not changed much over the centuries; next morning Hugh returned to the local town by pony and trap.

Hugh greatly enjoyed his visit to Ireland, though he found himself assumed to be a British spy wherever he went. Before parting, he and Dawson agreed to return a few months later in the year, for a week's walking in Connemara. The early summer found them back in Dublin, lunching together at the Unicorn restaurant, when Frank Pakenham walked in with another man. Hugh gave his old friend a genial wave; Pakenham glanced at him in fright and shepherded his guest to the farthest corner of the dining-room. Determined not to be ignored, Hugh waited until he had finished his lunch; then he sauntered over to Pakenham's table and began chatting about his plans for the holiday, despite Pakenham's obvious embarrassment. Though clearly loath to do so, Pakenham was obliged to introduce Hugh to his guest, Frank Gallagher. Hugh left after securing a promise from Pakenham to join him and Dawson at their hotel for an evening drink, on their return from the west.

A week later he and Dawson were back in Dublin, refreshed after an energetic holiday. When Pakenham failed to appear at the appointed time, the two of them went out to dine and then returned to their hotel for the night. Hugh was due to leave by ferry early the next day, so he packed his suitcase, asked for an early morning call and went to bed. Some time after midnight he was woken by a knock on the door. It was the hotel 'Boots', who announced that there was a 'gentleman' to see him. Hugh sent him away, grumbling that he could see no one at that time of night. A few minutes later the Boots returned. 'The gentleman says it's very urgent.' Hugh reluctantly agreed to allow the visitor to come up. A minute later he heard the sound of heavy feet climbing the stairs; the door was flung open, a voice shouted 'Police!', and four hard-faced men entered, each clutching a pistol. Hugh sat up in bed, watching astonished as the intruders spread out to the corners of his bedroom. Then one of them told him that they wanted to search his luggage. Hugh demanded to see a warrant and, on being shown an official-looking document, motioned his assent. His carefully packed suitcase was upended and its contents poured out onto the floor, where they were carefully sifted. The search revealed nothing more sinister than a pair of silk stockings, unavailable in wartime England except on the black market. The man holding them looked up and grinned. 'We shall have to tell our friends in the Customs about these,' he said. 'Are ye sure there are no firearms?' asked another of the quartet.

A pyjama-clad Hugh was cross-examined about his movements in Ireland while the plain-clothes policemen scanned his letters and papers, noting down the names of anyone mentioned in them. Eventually, after confiscating his undeveloped camera film, the four withdrew in some disappointment, leaving their host to ponder the significance of what had happened. Clearly they had expected to find something. Someone had alerted them to his presence in Dublin, and someone had suggested that he was there on some covert mission. Trevor-Roper suspected that he had been 'fingered' by Frank Pakenham.

By the time the policemen had left, dawn was approaching: too late to go back to sleep. Hugh was in a quandary about what to do next. The story of what had happened here this night was bound to get back to England, where it was sure to cause him embarrassment, or worse. Though innocent of any blame, Hugh was concerned about the possibility that his superiors might not see it that way; they might take the view that there was no smoke without fire. Cowgill and Vivian would be only too pleased to be rid of him. Hugh resolved to postpone his departure so that he could report the incident to the British High Commission in Dublin, where his friend John Betjeman was working as a press attaché.* He arranged to have lunch with Betjeman at the Unicorn. It was a jolly, indeed hilarious, occasion; both were familiar with Pakenham and knew his eccentricities. Pakenham's lunch guest Frank Gallagher, Hugh learned, was Director of the Irish Government Information Bureau, a former IRA man and a close associate of de Valera's. Long afterwards, Hugh discovered that it had indeed been Gallagher who had tipped off the Irish police about the presence of a suspected British spy in Dublin, after his suspicions had been aroused by Pakenham.

Returning to England a day late, Hugh made his way straight to MI5, where Guy Liddell's brother Cecil was in charge of the Irish desk. 'Oh, if it's only Frank, we can stop that,' Liddell said reassuringly after Hugh had explained himself; 'nobody takes him seriously.' Liddell told several amusing stories about Pakenham's contacts in Ireland, all tolerantly observed by MI5. But he had spoken too soon: a check revealed that a report of the incident had already come in, and had been passed to SIS in the routine manner. In due course Hugh was interviewed about what

---

* While in Dublin Betjeman sometimes described himself as a spy, but there seems to be no firm evidence that he was involved with intelligence matters.

had happened in Dublin by a member of SIS's security department, who reported that he seemed to feel 'got at'. In response to a mild admonitory note from Cowgill, who instructed him that any future such incident should be reported to SIS, not MI5, Hugh replied defiantly that the incident had been a personal one, unconnected with his work; accordingly it seemed appropriate to report it to MI5 rather than SIS.

Vivian was infuriated by Hugh's unrepentant attitude. 'This passion for being different from ordinary mortals amounts to insubordination,' he fumed. For this junior officer to 'bandy words' with his superiors 'verges on impertinent'. If Trevor-Roper was unable to accept a direct order, continued Vivian, 'he is a not an officer I wish to retain'. Vivian was further provoked by Hugh's presumption in writing his response in green ink. Within SIS, green ink was the traditional prerogative of the Chief (and red reserved for his Deputy). For a junior officer to write in green was a serious breach of protocol.

Hugh wrote to Pakenham, regretting that they had missed each other in Dublin, 'especially as you might have been able to explain a curious episode that occurred on my last night there'. Pakenham replied by telegram, signing himself 'Unicorn'. They met for dinner in the Savile Club. At first Pakenham pretended not to know what Hugh was talking about, but towards the end of the meal he opened up. 'Of course you must see that you put me in a very awkward position,' Pakenham insisted, when Hugh teased him about his behaviour. 'But Frank, I don't see ...' Hugh began. 'Well, in that case you can't see very far,' Pakenham interrupted irritably.

Cowgill's reluctance to share intelligence was a persistent irritant to MI5. Guy Liddell complained to Vivian several times about the difficulty of working with him. At a top-level meeting between SIS and MI5, attended by Petrie, Vivian and Liddell, among others, 'all present agreed that the real difficulty was Felix's personality. He had grossly overworked himself and had in consequence taken up a very narrow bigoted attitude.'[45] Early in 1942 officers of MI5 were incensed to discover that German intelligence intercepts relating to identified or suspected British spies (the 'ISBA' series) were being secretly withheld from them, thus putting their agents at unnecessary risk. The first MI5 officer to become aware of this was Herbert Hart, who worked for Dick White in MI5's 'B' section. Hart was a brilliant young barrister, who after the war would be elected a Fellow in philosophy at New College and who eventually became the University's Professor of Jurisprudence. He claimed that a typist's error had brought the existence of these intercepts to his attention. This explanation was a cover, however; more than half a century later Hugh admitted to having 'leaked' to Hart the information that these messages were being silently subtracted from the circulated services. Hugh, aware that the Germans numbered their messages consecutively, and perhaps prompted by Page, had noticed that some numbers were missing.*[46]

'We are constantly finding matters which are important to us and to our links abroad have for some unknown reason been withheld,' Liddell briefed Petrie in May 1942.[47] SIS's reluctance to distribute intelligence, particularly the evaluations produced by the Radio Analysis Bureau, was the source of much friction between the two services, leading Petrie to propose that SIS's Section V be amalgamated with MI5's 'B' Division. Menzies fended off this suggestion, and towards the end of 1942 took steps to strengthen SIS's control of Hugh's unit, which became fully integrated into Section V. But though he now reported solely to Cowgill, Hugh was no more subservient than before. At the thirty-eighth meeting of the Joint Wireless Committee on 3 December, Hugh sided against his boss, who had put forward Vivian's proposal to disband the committee. The result was a humiliating defeat for Cowgill, whose only supporter was Maltby. Liddell noted in his diary that there was 'an obvious desire' to see Hugh 'eliminated'. He warned Vivian that if his idea was 'to get rid of Trevor-Roper', he was making a great mistake. To kick him off their committee would be 'highly detrimental to their discussions, to which he contributed almost more than anyone'. While recognising that Hugh was in some ways 'a troublesome person', Liddell liked him and had a high opinion of his ability. Hugh had been badly mishandled, he thought. 'Had his views, many of which were obviously right, been given more sympathetic consideration, many difficulties might have been avoided.'[48] Hugh seemed to despair of any change, because less than a week after Liddell's conversation with Vivian, he wrote again to Lord Cherwell in search of alternative employment. 'I think as much as can be done in my present position has been done, and a much greater amount that ought to be done will never be done, since no radical change can be expected in a department protected by so much secrecy and mumbo-jumbo.'[49]

As in the past, the sublime beauty of the English countryside provided a respite from his struggles within SIS. In the middle of his dispute with Cowgill, Hugh experienced a day 'of undiluted felicity' hunting with the Bicester, beginning when he caught a passing lorry at Apex Corner as dawn was breaking:

> I arrived at Ham Green far too early for the meet, but it was a mild morning, and I walked abroad, and the fields were still dewy and the bare woods black, dead black, against the white morning sky; and I sat on a gate, my senses dwelling

---

* Afterwards Hugh would regularly use the term 'ISBA' as a verb, meaning to deprive someone of information to which he was entitled.

on the scene, and read in my pocket Horace of the pastoral world of Calabria, and Liris, now Garigliano, the silent stream, and Galaesus, and the creaking oakwoods of Garganus. But later, in the early afternoon, when the colours were up, we checked during a merry hunt, and I paused on the top of Finemere Hill with all the world beneath me; and there, before and below me, like a vast, undulating smoky-brown sea, stretched the Big Woods; and the pleasure of that sight remained and remains with me ... [50]

In November 1942 RAB produced its most important report to date, headed 'Canaris and Himmler' and written by Stuart Hampshire. This paper, which was based on a new source discovered by RSS and decoded by G.C. & C.S., argued that Himmler's SS intelligence organisation, the *Sicherheitsdienst* (SD) was encroaching on the work of the *Abwehr*. Admiral Canaris, head of the *Abwehr*, was suspected by the Nazi Party of not only inefficiency but disloyalty, and Himmler was attempting to oust the Admiral and take over his organisation. The report concluded that this struggle for secret intelligence was a symptom of a wider struggle for power between the Nazi Party and the German General Staff. It implied that there was an opportunity for the Allies to exploit this widening rift.

Such reports could not be distributed without approval from Cowgill, as head of Section V; but since he was out of the country when this particular report was submitted, it went instead to his deputy, Kim Philby, who refused to allow its circulation. When asked why, he gave no reason. Puzzled, Hugh sent Hampshire to St Albans to discuss the matter with him, with Stuart in support as the RAB's *Abwehr* expert. These two sat on the other side of Philby's desk while he went through the document, dismissing its conclusions as 'mere speculation'.

The RAB officers were baffled by Philby's obduracy, particularly since they thought of him as more rational and enlightened than Cowgill. 'There's something *wrong* with Philby,' insisted Stuart after their meeting – though it would be two decades before they learned what this was. In suppressing their report Philby was almost certainly acting under instructions from his Soviet controllers. 'It would have been dangerous for the Russians to think that we were dickering with the Germans,' he commented in his memoirs.[51] It was not in the Russian interest that the Western Allies should establish contact with the conservative opposition within Germany, while the Red Army was still too far away to intervene.[52] In 1944, Philby would suppress another important report from Hugh's unit, this one arguing that a conspiracy was being hatched against Hitler. In his paranoia Stalin feared that if Hitler was overturned, the Western Allies might join forces with the defeated Germans in a fresh crusade against the East. While this fear failed to take account of political realities in Britain and the United

States, it stemmed from Stalin's own actions. Had not the Soviet Union itself made a pact with Nazi Germany in the summer of 1939?

Though Philby gave no reason for his decision, it was defensible on policy grounds. In venturing beyond the normal limits of intelligence, the 'Canaris and Himmler' report had strayed into a forbidden zone. SIS was supposed to gather intelligence about the enemy, not suggest how such intelligence might be exploited. While Hugh and his colleagues might argue that such a distinction was an artificial one, it remained the Whitehall orthodoxy. The Venlo disaster had made SIS wary of contact with the enemy. This RAB report posed questions that no one would like to have answered. Churchill had stipulated that he wanted no dealings with Germans claiming to be opposed to Hitler, and had laid down a policy of 'absolute silence' in response to any such approaches.[53] The slightest whiff of negotiations could prove poisonous to the delicate relations between the Allies.

Frustrated by Philby, Hugh resorted to Cherwell, with whom he often lunched at the Carlton Grill – apparently the only place in London where the chef knew how to prepare a meal of egg white and lettuce as the Prof liked it. Over one of these lunches Hugh mentioned casually that his unit had detected signs of a power struggle in Germany. Cherwell took the bait: he asked to see a copy of the suppressed paper, which Hugh subsequently forwarded to him. He was disappointed when nothing seemed to come of this ruse. On 12 April 1943 Guy Liddell gave him lunch. Hugh seemed 'very depressed' and told Liddell that 'he had really nothing to do, since whenever he produced a document based on his product or made any suggestions, he was told that this was already being dealt with by Section V'. Hugh talked gloomily about taking another job abroad, but feared that this might lead to the break-up of his section, which Liddell thought would be 'a disaster'.[54]

One day in early May Hugh received a telephone call from Miss Pettigrew, Menzies's formidable secretary, to say the Chief wished to see him. Far from being alarmed, Hugh felt gratified by this attention from on high. He did not connect it with the paper he had shown Cherwell. By this stage of the war the danger of bombing had diminished and SIS was in the process of moving back into its permanent headquarters at Broadway Buildings, near St James's Park Underground station. On the appointed day Hugh travelled into town for his afternoon meeting with Menzies, taking the opportunity to have a proper lunch at the Savile Club beforehand, washed down with half a bottle of Puligny-Montrachet. His good cheer diminished as he sat outside Menzies's office, waiting for the green light to indicate that he could enter. He noticed that Miss Pettigrew seemed less welcoming than he expected.

The atmosphere in Menzies's office was formal. The Chief was seated behind a table, with Colonel Vivian beside him. Menzies explained that questions had been raised about Hugh and that he proposed to leave Colonel Vivian to pursue the matter. The latter began interrogating him: did he know Lord Swinton? And if so, how? How did he know Lord Cherwell? It rapidly became clear to Hugh that this was a form of trial, though the charges remained unstated. Vivian, who appeared to be fishing for evidence to be used against him, was the prosecutor; Menzies the judge. Fortified by the Montrachet, Hugh defended himself boldly. Vivian seemed to fumble, and appealed to Menzies. 'Of course, sir,' he said on two separate occasions, 'whatever the outcome, it will be impossible for Trevor-Roper to remain in the organisation after this.' Menzies remained non-committal. Then Miss Pettigrew entered, carrying a tray bearing a China teaset, and placed it before her boss. 'Do you take milk and sugar?' Menzies asked politely, and Hugh relaxed, feeling that the crisis had passed.

Once they had finished their tea, Hugh was asked to wait outside, leaving Menzies and Vivian alone together. After a short while Vivian emerged and stalked past Hugh without meeting his eye. Then the green light came on again, and Hugh went back in. 'I sent for you in order to sack you,' Menzies told him genially. 'I thought I had no alternative. But I have changed my mind.' He ordered Hugh to write him a formal letter of apology for communicating with Lord Cherwell. Then he announced that Hugh would no longer be subservient to Cowgill, and through Cowgill, to Vivian; indeed, he would never set eyes on either of them again. The Radio Analysis Bureau was removed from Section V, and renamed the Radio Intelligence Service (RIS). It would be responsible directly to Menzies, through his personal office. From now on Hugh would have direct access to the Chief.

Hugh returned to Arkley dazed by this development. His three colleagues were quicker to grasp what had happened. 'You don't seem to realise', they told him, 'that you have won a great victory.' Gradually it dawned on Hugh that they were right. He was promoted to Major, in accordance with his new status as head of his own section. One of the first acts of the new RIS was to distribute the suppressed report 'Canaris and Hitler', albeit in a bowdlerised form. Half a century later, Hugh would discover that Cherwell had indeed shown the report to Churchill, and that Churchill had raised the matter with Menzies, who was embarrassed to admit that he knew nothing of it.

About two months after Hugh's 'trial', he was telephoned by R.L. Hughes, MI5's liaison officer at Arkley, who said that he had something to show Hugh, which he had been ordered not to allow out of his possession. When Hugh arrived at his office, Hughes handed him a document. It was unsigned, but the style was recognisably Vivian's. It took as its starting-point the incident in Dublin the previous summer, when Hugh's hotel room had been ransacked by the Irish police. The author speculated on the reasons for Hugh's trips to Ireland, and remarked on the fact that he had visited Colonel Worlledge. He went on to suggest that Hugh was motivated by resentment against SIS for its treatment of Worlledge, and of Gill in particular. The document concluded with a hair-raising allegation: that Hugh had gone to Dublin to betray the Ultra secret to the Germans.

The charge was treason, which if proven in court-martial carried a punishment of execution by firing-squad. Even if it remained unproven, Hugh could have been incarcerated under Rule 18b of the Emergency Powers Act. Hugh raised the matter with Dick White, who told him not to worry: MI5 had long ago taken the measure of Vivian and found him both petty and vindictive. Though reassured, Hugh remained puzzled as to how this document could have found its way to MI5. It was only in 1994, when a book drawing on interviews with Cowgill was published, that the full story became clear to him. It seems that the allegation had originated with Cowgill, who, deranged with hatred for Hugh, had drawn up a charge-sheet in the hope of having him court-martialled. Vivian had then rewritten Cowgill's draft into his own style. When Menzies had dismissed the charges as fantastic, one or other of them had passed the document to MI5, in the vain hope that someone there would take it more seriously.

Now liberated from Cowgill's restraining influence, Hugh's RIS was free to work more closely with MI5 and others outside SIS. His help was particularly valuable in deception planning. Hugh had long since recognised the necessity to study the *Abwehr* in order to manipulate it successfully, and to predict how it would react. To feed this beast the delicate morsels of misinformation one wanted it to swallow, one needed to know its habits and its appetites. The rivalry between the German bodies responsible for collecting intelligence enhanced the possibilities for deception. Once a deception operation had been launched, Ultra decrypts of messages between the *Abwehr* and the German High Command provided a means of monitoring its effectiveness, a technique known as a 'closed-loop' deception system. In the summer of 1943, for example, RIS provided essential intelligence feedback on the success of 'Operation Mincemeat', the deception plan to mislead the Germans about the invasion of Sicily. The enemy was led to believe that the Allies planned to invade Greece and Sardinia, and withdrew two Panzer divisions from the Eastern Front in anticipation of this. Analysis of Ultra decrypts prompted a cable to be sent to the Prime Minister, then in the United States: 'Mincemeat Swallowed Whole'. The enemy was indeed completely taken in by this deception operation: two weeks after the invasion of Sicily, the Germans remained convinced that it was a feint to disguise an attack on Greece and Sardinia. In fact they were still debating the subject when Mussolini was overthrown in a coup.

Similarly, RIS and RSS technical staff would be crucial to MI5's superbly successful 'Double Cross' ('XX') system, which used enemy agents in order to feed misinformation back to the Germans. The enemy agents were run by MI5 case officers, their work co-ordinated by a committee chaired by Hugh's former tutor, J.C. Masterman. Such manipulation of enemy agents would form a principal part of 'Operation Fortitude', the deception plan designed to induce the Germans to believe that the main invasion of France would occur in the Pas de Calais rather than in Normandy. The planners needed to be sure that there were no unidentified enemy agents in Britain who might betray the Allies' true intentions. In searching for these, RSS intercepted no unexplained transmissions, and quickly identified transmissions from double agents even when these came without warning and from previously unused locations.[55] Ultra decrypts enabled Allied intelligence to monitor how successfully the enemy had been hoodwinked. Hitler continued to believe for some weeks after the landings that the main invasion would come in the Pas de Calais, withholding Panzer divisions from Normandy which could have been used to repel the attackers.

From the summer of 1943 onwards Hugh and Gilbert Ryle were invited to attend a monthly committee in the War Cabinet offices of the London Controlling Centre for strategic deception. This high-level committee existed to define the probable German appreciation of Allied intentions for the benefit of deception planning.[56] It was a case of 'what do they think our intentions are?' Meanwhile RIS continued to analyse enemy intelligence operations around the world and to issue reports on its findings. By this time Hugh and his three colleagues had come to know the *Abwehr* intimately. In his continuing study of the enemy secret service, he was amused to detect many similarities with his own. The *Abwehr* turned out to be the mirror image of SIS, with many of the same weaknesses and absurdities; they too had their Vivians, their Cowgills and their Danseys. Indeed Admiral Canaris was in many respects similar to Major-General Menzies: a deeply conservative, weak, but fundamentally honourable man. There was even a personal connection: Canaris had a mistress in Vienna, whose sister was married to Menzies's brother. In August 1943 RIS circulated a report entitled 'Abwehr Incompetence'. Hugh observed that in the paranoid atmosphere of Nazi Germany, the *Abwehr* did not dare to winnow the operational intelligence it gathered, for fear of being caught out, but supplied it unprocessed to commanders in the field.[57]

In retrospect, Hugh decided that issuing this report had been a tactical error; his SIS colleagues believed that they were wrestling with giants, and disliked being told otherwise. A report written by Gilbert Ryle dealt with the *Abwehr* department responsible for sabotage. They had mounted only one operation, Ryle concluded, parachuting an agent disguised as a missionary into Africa: the unfortunate agent had dropped into Lake Chad. Among his subsequent messages back to his controller had been requests for a medicament used in the treatment of venereal disease. Ryle described him as 'an unpromising evangelist'.

As time passed, the predictions made in the 'Canaris and Himmler' paper, which Philby had dismissed as 'mere speculation', proved prescient. In March 1944 RIS issued a 'Top Secret' report headed 'Decline of the Abwehr': Admiral Canaris had been placed on indefinite leave, and the SD had assumed operational control over the *Abwehr*. 'There is a definite revolutionary atmosphere among the Generals,' the report concluded. In an RIS report on 'German Strategic Deception', issued just before D-Day, Hugh observed that it was 'a very piecemeal affair'. The *Abwehr* lacked any initiating or co-ordinating machinery for strategic deception. The Germans seemed to have little awareness of its possibilities, and had shown themselves innocent of deception techniques.[58]

Back in March 1943 Dick White had suggested that Hugh should be sent to the Middle East for three months. 'I can think of no single officer, either in MI5 or MI6,' he wrote to Liddell, 'who possesses a more comprehensive knowledge of the Abwehr organisation, particularly on its communication side, than Capt. Trevor-Roper'. White believed that Hugh would be 'the most appropriate person' to introduce a wider perspective into the parochial outlook of counter-espionage officers working in the Middle East. He cited a paper which Hugh had recently written that had been of the greatest interest to Colonel Dudley Clarke, controller of deception policy out there.[59]

The proposal for Hugh to go to the Middle East came to nothing at the time, perhaps because of fears that the Radio Analysis Bureau (as it then was) might be broken up in his absence. But early in 1944 Hugh spent six weeks abroad, on a tour that took in Gibraltar, Algiers, Cairo, Beirut, Basra, Karachi, Delhi and Calcutta. Afterwards he calculated that he had spent 130 hours in the air. Though he had seen the imperial architecture of New Delhi, the Pyramids of Egypt, Roman ruins in Syria and North Africa, Vesuvius in full eruption and Etna capped with snow, his heart remained untouched; his overwhelming feeling was nostalgia for the green earth of England, 'with its woods and streams and hills, its hedgerows flowering in the springtime, its haystacks and cornshocks in the autumn, and, in winter, a pack of hounds streaming over the grassland and the plough'.[60]

Soon after D-Day, Hugh heard that Gerald Heathcoat-Amory* had been killed in Normandy, only a few days after Kenneth Swann. These two were among those undergraduate friends, many of them Etonians, with whom Hugh had consorted as a frivolous young Research Fellow. The war claimed their lives in a relentless tide. One had died in 1940, during the retreat towards Dunkirk; another was killed at El Alamein; another drowned, when his ship was sunk off Tobruk; another had been killed in Tunisia, after winning a Victoria Cross for destroying an enemy machine-gun nest single-handedly, with a bayonet; yet another had gone missing in Italy. Now the last of them was dead. On a visit to Oxford, Hugh encountered an elderly don who could barely contain his tears, as he recounted the deaths of the young men who had made up his reading-parties. Hugh was surprised not to feel more affected himself. To him, it seemed merely that his former life, which had been slowly fading since the war began, was now extinguished. Viewed 'from a colder, darker epoch', that life seemed to him romantic:

> How effortlessly we lived, in that golden period, in Oxford, in Northumberland, abroad; hunting foxes and hares, drinking and talking, reading new books and old books, walking hounds in the early summer mornings through Garsington and Cuddesdon and Coombe Wood, watching for the emergence of each new wildflower in those comfortable fields and hedgerows and water-meadows, making new intellectual discoveries in those hours of infinite, astronomical leisure. How delightful to sit in a beautiful Oxford room, south-facing through great bow-windows over the Christ Church Meadow, rook-racked, river-rounded, writing a book, after an early walk, amid pleasant interruptions ... [61]

While on leave in Northumberland, Hugh received a letter from Logan Pearsall Smith. 'I am rather under the impression that you are taking a pause or holiday to consider your future and your fate, to decide what you want to make of your life; what are your real wishes, and how you can best attain them,' wrote Smith. 'Now how did he know?' Hugh asked himself indignantly, for Smith's letter seemed to encapsulate all that he had been thinking and feeling. 'I take it you are about 30,' Smith continued: 'a turning-point in life, when one has more or less to decide on the future path one wants to pursue. Here we are in life; something has got to be done about it; one has ventured on various paths which have seemed to lead to nothing; snatched at fruit which has turned sour; knocked at doors which have either remained shut, or, if they have opened, have led into what seemed likely to be prisons, or penitentiaries, or bordels, from which one

---

* His elder brother Pat (a contemporary of Hugh's at Christ Church), had been killed in 1943, and his middle brother, Michael, had been killed in a flying accident before the war.

must flee to save one's life'. It's quite true, reflected Hugh: 'I'm 29; and those are my sensations. The world, which I have so enjoyed, seems now dull, insipid, tasteless.'

> Dramatising, as always, my predicament, I thought of those among the great whose crisis came also at this time; of St Paul and St Augustine, grim figures, tortured by sterile learning, & seeking, amid those flinty rocks for a simpler path; of Dante, who, at thirty, contemplated Heaven & Hell, and never looked on earth with the same eyes afterwards; of Sir Thomas Browne, who seemed at thirty to have outlived himself and to begin to be weary of the sun ... I thought of Samuel Butler, who, at thirty, heard these pugnant words, '*Et maintenant, monsieur, vous allez créer?*'

In his letter to Hugh, Smith wrote of his own experience at this stage in life. At thirty-one, after five years in Paris, when he had fallen under the influence of Flaubert and de Maupassant, he had published a volume of short stories. The volume had failed, and Smith felt that he had taken a wrong turn. But he had tasted 'of what I consider the richest cake which is baked in the oven of the gods: the ecstasy and the exasperation of the art of writing'. To indulge in 'this secret vice' in peace, he had gone to live alone in the country, and there produced *Trivia*, 'the centre & the secret of my life: what else I have done isn't of much importance, but to write this little book was I think worthwhile'. He urged Hugh to emulate his example, advice he repeatedly reiterated; even to have failed in such an effort 'seems to me better than success in any other kind of ambition'. He quoted Sancho Panza's eulogy of his master: 'Though he did not achieve great things, yet did he die in their pursuit.'[62]

In his notebook Hugh laid out the options for his future. 'Shall I, like Horace, retire to the country, to this Northumberland perhaps, which I so love, there to polish style, to hunt and fish, and aim ambitiously at an unattainable literary perfection?' But then he thought of Wordsworth, 'who also retired to the country to worship an ideal, and there, for lack of society and intellectual stimulus, became a dowdy, platitudinous, egotistical, moralising bore'.

Or should he instead 'plunge into a life of action, madly seeking the stimulus of force'? Hugh considered volunteering to be sent to Yugoslavia, to live among the rebels there. He was inspired by the example of the RAF pilot Richard Hillary, 'the Byron of our age', who had overcome appalling injuries to return to active service, only to be killed at the controls of his own plane. 'Should I court death, for at least that is better than taking one's own life dingily, in a garret or gunroom, in despair of life and its purposeless, vertiginous calm? How happy was Gibbon, who could live untroubled by such thoughts, executing a life's work in perfect peace! How happy is Gilbert, whose temperament has never experienced the anguish of intellectual self-division, who makes his cracks morning & evening, and goes on uninhibited, now drunk, now sober, from day to day!'

Hugh did not solve this 'great enigma', partly because he received a telephone message from Barnet ordering him to return early to duty. 'Meanwhile,' he lamented, 'I am becalmed.'[63]

Sleuth

'I am no longer becalmed,' Hugh announced in his notebook, almost a year afterwards: 'I know what to do. To write a book that someone, one day, will mention in the same breath as Gibbon, – this is my fond ambition.' He quoted the same sentence from *Don Quixote* that Smith had quoted to him a year before.

Hugh had found 'The Solution', as he described it. 'Having discovered this truth, how easy it all becomes! The vast chaos of the universe arrays itself at last in an orderly pattern; the great enigmata of the world resolve themselves like melting snow.' Now this was resolved, 'the pleasures of society, and the taste of divine solitude' were sufficient to keep melancholy at bay.[1]

It remained only to find the theme. In the spring of 1943 he elaborated a plan for his magnum opus: 'A History of the English Ruling Classes'. He would begin, he decided,

> with the silent, patient, nibbling rat-faced country landlords and lawyers of early Tudor days, slowly surveying, undermining, & circumventing their predestined parcels of abbey-lands; and then I picture this same class, raised by revolutions in agriculture, industry & commerce from parochial squireens into the splendid renaissance gentry of Elizabethan & Jacobean times, those cultivated stylists who held elevated conversation among the terraces & fountains & colonnades of their elegant Palladian houses ...

continuing the story right through to 'the champagne age, the loud, bounding, commercial aristocracy of Edward VII and P.G. Wodehouse, cosmopolitan & exotic, Oriental Sassoons, American Astors, the Indian Aga Khan, the last mutation of this long fantastic history of a class now dead as the mammoth and the mastodon'. For an epilogue, he considered various possibilities: perhaps ending the book with a description of the teetotal socialist Countess of Carlisle, 'emptying the cellars of Naworth Castle into the River Eden', or with Lord Lonsdale, 'his coal-mines nationalised, his castle bare, his race-horses sold, his yellow-liveried flunkeys dismissed, his packs of hounds disbanded, wearing out his faded splendour in a villa in Surrey'. The more he thought about this idea, the more he liked it; though two years later he was still wondering how to impose a form on so vast a subject. Meanwhile he was pondering another work:

> I want to examine fully and seriously the social and political significance of religious revivals, on which I think I have something to say which will be worth saying. I shall divide religious revivals into two categories: ideologies (like early Christianity, and Lutheranism, and Calvinism, and other phenomena of the Reformation), which are not really revivals but innovations, though the formal conservatism of men has represented them as revivals, nor exclusively religious, as that word is commonly understood, since they embrace also our modern ideologies of Marxism and Fascism; and real revivals, such as the Oxford Movement in England, and the parallel movements on the Continent ... I think that such a study will show that ideologies, though in part an intellectual retrocession, are an essential means of changing the basis of society, and can therefore be weapons of progress, but that revivals are always a phenomenon of social as well as intellectual reaction. And in defining the concepts and terminology necessary to my study, I shall incidentally show, firstly, that social progress consists exclusively in the raising of the standard of living of a society, and that those who attempt to attach to it a spiritual or any other kind of significance, are invariably fostering social reaction (as St Paul, and the Gnostics, and the Mystics, and Gandhi); and, secondly, that there is no direct relation between artistic and social values, – indeed that artists have often been reactionary in their politics, and that high civilisation, in an artistic sense, is generally a social anachronism, occurring in societies in which the ruling class has become, through security, negligent of its proper function (which is of ruling), and only retains an economic supremacy ... On this subject it seems to me important to be clear; to let it be known that there is no such conception as 'progressive art'; that the form of society influences only the details of an artist's work and his relations with the public; and that the last word on the matter was said by Whistler: 'Art happens.'

But it would not be prudent to publish such a book yet, he decided: 'what would the monks and mandarins of Oxford say?'[2] He did not want to jeopardise his chances of returning there. When Hugh had last dined at Christ Church, the Dean had invited him to apply for a Studentship (the Christ Church term for a Fellowship) after the war, and Trevor-Roper had said that he would. After a pause the Dean edged gingerly towards a further point. Was he anti-clerical? Or did he merely dislike certain clergymen? For of course, continued the Dean, that was bound to weigh with some of the electors. Hugh was bewildered by these questions, and floundered in his replies. Back in Barnet, he examined his position, so that he might answer clearly next time he was asked about the subject. Religion had no validity for him: the 'fundamental pillars of Christian doctrine are, intellectually, trash; and so is the doctrine of all other religions too'. The real basis of religion, he decided, was psychological: for the individual, it filled an important void. It was also valuable in providing the invisible cement of the social order. For these reasons it was 'impractical as well as unnecessary to denounce it as untrue, and proper to find out, and recommend (or avoid opposing) that form of it which is most commendable, or least objectionable. Those forms are least objectionable which are socially most appropriate, and which incidentally preserve, or support, important secular values.' Like his Merton colleague Garrod,* Hugh claimed to be an Anglican, not a Christian; and like Hume, he commended the Church of England for its very indifferency.³

Hugh had identified his vocation: he would go back to Oxford and write a Great Work. And yet each time he returned there, he was disappointed:

> I find a few thwarted old men conspiring furtively in alcoves, devising schemes to perpetuate their momentary, accidental and disastrous ascendancy. 'We must have less irreverence in future,' I overhear them saying, 'less study; more religion perhaps, certainly more games. We have sinned in the past, and have paid for it dearly; we must elect more carefully in the future; thought is an unhealthy thing. The advance of culture is a mistake; it must be stopped; it is leaving us behind. It's intellect that does all the damage; what we want is a good third and a hockey-blue. Pass the port, Muggins!'⁴

In September 1944 Hugh travelled up to Newcastle for yet another operation, this time to remove his appendix. He remained in hospital for ten days afterwards, and then spent a fortnight convalescing at his parents' house in Alnwick, a period made tolerable by a parcel of books sent by Logan Pearsall Smith. One of these, a collection of essays by H.A.L. Fisher, prompted a joshing exchange between sender and recipient. 'More and more, as I read history,' wrote Hugh, 'I believe in the Whig historians. There is no getting away from the fact: they are right.' Of those who dissented from their interpretations, he thought the Fabians best, though dull; 'and then there are the Marxists, who are tiresome, though often valuable, and sometimes amusing'. Of the neo-Tories, 'Feiling is perhaps the least disreputable'. Of the Roman Catholic historians, 'it is most charitable to say nothing'. In response, Smith teased Hugh about 'your persistent deep-dyed disgusting Whiggery, ... your philosophic radicalism, your greasy Jacobinism & your dry dialectical Marxism – it makes me sick to think of it. I believe in the Church as by law established, private property, the family & the Throne.'⁵

Hugh returned to London in time for Smith's eightieth birthday party,

---

* H.W. Garrod (1878–1960), literary and classical scholar, was a Fellow of Merton for more than half a century.

attended too by London literati and members of the *beau monde*, including the society hostess Sibyl Colefax and several Sitwells. While Hugh had been in hospital, Cowgill had made one last, unsuccessful attempt against RIS. He suggested promotion and dispersal for Hampshire, Stuart, and Hugh himself, while Ryle was to be allowed to return to Oxford, where he had been appointed *in absentia* Waynflete Professor of Metaphysical Philosophy. Ryle torpedoed this suggestion in a brisk minute. Cowgill was on the slide, deserted by Vivian and double-crossed by his protégé Philby, who was appointed head of the newly re-formed Section IX, dedicated to counter-espionage against the Soviet Union. Cowgill resigned in a huff. Back in 1943, Hugh had accurately predicted to Reilly that 'as each area becomes really important, it will have to be given to Philby, and thus, in the end, he will control all, and Cowgill and Vivian and the rest will drop uselessly from the tree, like over-ripe plums'.[6]

Hugh had not been unduly concerned at Cowgill's attempt to dismember RIS because he felt that the time had almost come for it to be disbanded anyway.[7] By the winter of 1944 the Allied armies had broken out of their bridgehead in Normandy and had driven the Germans back to the Rhine. It was obvious that the war would soon be over; intelligence was of less use now that the enemy was in retreat; attention turned to new problems, such as rounding up suspected war criminals and suppressing the anticipated guerrilla resistance to occupation. The Allies decided to establish a 'War Room' under the auspices of the Supreme Headquarters, Allied Expeditionary Force (SHAEF) to collect, collate and analyse counter-intelligence material, and to advise staffs in the field on all aspects of enemy clandestine activity. Under the direction of 'Tar' Robertson (now Lieutenant-Colonel), its staff consisted of experts from SIS, MI5 and the American Office of Strategic Services (OSS), the forerunner to the CIA. Hugh was appointed to run the research side of this new body, which became active on 1 March 1945. A few days later he moved into the MI5 offices in St James's Street, taking with him Hampshire and Stuart. Ryle remained behind at Arkley, genially presiding over the demise of RIS while writing his book *The Concept of Mind* (published in 1949).

The work of the former RIS officers was in some respects much the same as it had been. They continued to study enemy radio traffic and issue regular reports, but now they were able to draw on much more information, including captured enemy documents and transcripts of prisoner-of-war interrogations. For the past couple of years RIS had assisted MI5 with interrogations, providing briefings to check that prisoners had told everything they might be expected to know.[8] Hugh had taken part in at least one of these, and in his new capacity as head of the research section of the War Room, he often interrogated German prisoners himself, frequently flying back and forth to liberated France and occupied Germany for this purpose.[9]

In April 1945 the research department of the War Room produced a manual for counter-intelligence officers in the field after victory, entitled *The German Intelligence Service*. Later that summer Hugh produced a more detached and considered account of the same subject, 'The German Intelligence Service and the War', which was not printed and had a more limited circulation. Addressed to his superiors and successors, this document was effectively Hugh's testament as an intelligence officer. In it he analysed the few successes and frequent failures of German intelligence, drawing on captured documents and interrogations of German prisoners – particularly Walther Schellenberg, boss of the SD and, following the fall of Canaris, head of all German intelligence. During his interrogation by Stuart Hampshire, Schellenberg had been amazed to discover how much the British already knew; and he had been humiliated by the contrast with his own ignorance of British intelligence.

Hugh acknowledged the enormous benefit the Allies had derived from 'certain most secret sources', i.e. Ultra. But his report also showed how structural weaknesses had contributed to German intelligence failures. Hugh stressed the lack of centralised evaluation of raw intelligence, of the type RIS had provided. Similarly he highlighted the lack of co-ordination in German deception operations. This absence of centralised control was but 'one aspect of a phenomenon which was of much wider relevance in Nazi Germany': the administrative structure, in theory 'pyramidal', was in reality nothing of the kind – not a unitary structure at all, but 'a vortex of personal ambitions'. German intelligence was a microcosm of Nazi society as a whole, with rival ministers 'running independent personal intelligence bureaus in competition with each other'.

Hugh's interpretation ran contrary to the consensus. Contemporary observers found it difficult to resist the impact of Nazi propaganda, which celebrated a German people united under the rule of their *Führer*. Hitler's Germany appeared unified and ruthlessly efficient, as evidenced by the revival of the German economy in the 1930s, followed by the succession of rapid military victories which established German dominion over the European mainland. Since the war, however, historians had come to realise that the reality of Nazi Germany was very different from the image it projected. Far from being a smooth-running machine directed from above, the Nazi state was a tangle of competing institutions with overlapping responsibilities, each trying to anticipate, rather than respond to, the wishes of the *Führer*. Hugh's wartime analysis of Nazi Germany now appears prescient.

His report was sceptical of the value of spying. Individual agents operating in enemy-controlled territory were of limited worth, he concluded, and indeed could prove 'a positive and serious danger to their employers' if used by the enemy as a channel for disinformation. Intelligence received from such agents should always be centrally evaluated, in conjunction with the results of cryptography. In his concluding paragraph Hugh argued that the centralisation necessary to sophisticated deception operations had been achieved by the British largely because of the existence of 'special sources' (i.e. Ultra intelligence), whose effective exploitation so evidently involved central study.[10]

Some of his criticisms of German intelligence might equally have applied to SIS. Dick White was impressed by what he read. It was this report, he said many years afterwards, that persuaded him to ask Hugh to undertake an investigation of the utmost importance.[11]

In the last few weeks of the war in Europe and the first few weeks of the peace Hugh was able to take some leave and begin picking up the threads of his academic work. He had resumed his historical studies with a visit to the Public Record Office (PRO) as early as October 1944. In April 1945 he travelled up to Ushaw College, a Roman Catholic seminary in County Durham, to examine records in the library. Its President, Monsignor Corbishley, greeted him hospitably: 'a delightful man, of antique simplicity and quiet courtliness, who led me round those vast corridors, and showed me great chambers, chambers of horrors, some full of grotesque statuary, some of relics, some of stuffed birds and uteruses, equally grotesque, so that it was only by his devout genuflexions, or the omission of them, that I could distinguish the sacred from the profane'. Despite his suspicion of proselytising Catholics, Hugh felt a weakness for the 'old' Catholics like his Roper ancestors. 'I like to think of the quiet rural existence of those families in the North, and in old Lancashire, and in folds of the Cotswold and Chiltern Hills, whom the Reformation passed by, and whose old faith has survived because their lives were simple and elemental, outside the developments of time.'

One May morning, when he had no work to do, Hugh reflected that he had never been to East Kent, where some branches of the Roper family still lingered: 'unadventurous dynasties, who had cultivated their cornfields and cherry-orchards unobtrusively for six centuries or so'. So he took a train to Chatham, and hitched a lorry-ride along Watling Street to Teynham, to begin his investigations. He strolled through the orchards heavy with blossom. Enquiries led him to the Roper-Dixons, distant relatives who pressed him hospitably to stay to lunch, and told him their history. He asked about the nearby Elizabethan house of Lynstead, home to another branch of the Roper family, which had parted from the main trunk quite recently, in the reign of Queen Anne. But the Roper-Lumley-Hollands had fled to Brazil at the outbreak of war, 'pursued by the just execrations of all classes among their neighbours', and meanwhile the Army had taken over Lynstead. So instead of going there, as he had intended, he walked on through fields and lanes until he found a lorry driver to take him back to London and the present, out of the antiquated, feudal, genealogical Kentish past.[12]

A few days before the end of the war in Europe Hugh went to stay, not for the first time, with his SIS colleague Malcolm Muggeridge and his wife Kitty in East Sussex. They took walks and spent many convivial hours in country pubs, often in the company of the biographer Hesketh Pearson, who lived nearby. Muggeridge had spent most of the war in Portuguese East Africa; Hugh had met him in Algiers in 1944, and again in Paris early in 1945. He was now back in England, idling in other people's offices and about to take up a job with *The Daily Telegraph*. 'I like poor old Malcolm Muggeridge,' Hugh wrote in his notebook; 'of course, having no interest in the truth, he is obstinately wrong in most of his opinions.' Muggeridge had written a study of Samuel Butler, which Hugh thought utterly wrong-headed. 'But, like Boswell, "I have ever delighted in that intellectual chymistry which can separate good qualities from evil in the same person"; and so I shall continue, I hope, to enjoy his company, while leaving his books, of course, unread, and his arguments, of course, unheeded.' Muggeridge noted in his diary that he found Hugh 'nice but argumentative'; while Hugh observed in his notebook that dining with Muggeridge was like picnicking on a volcano: 'one can never be quite sure that there won't be an eruption'. Hugh saw plenty of Muggeridge around this time, and through him came to know several of his literary friends, including Anthony Powell, Hugh Kingsmill and George Orwell – though Muggeridge was always sneering at Orwell, which infuriated Hugh, who admired him greatly. One afternoon in July Hugh and Kingsmill joined Muggeridge, Orwell and Powell, who had been lunching together at a London club. Hugh observed that Orwell wrote like Johnson, but Kingsmill disagreed, shouting 'Cobbett, Cobbett!'[13]

'I found Malcolm's company and conversation, at the time, agreeable,' Hugh reminisced many years later:

> ... indeed, he could be very attractive for a short period. The trouble was, he never mounted a hobby-horse but he rode it to death; and he was entirely destructive. He touched nothing that he did not disintegrate; he belonged to no society that he did not undermine. He could be witty and his cynicism could be amusing – if only he had known when to stop. I got on well with him *à deux* or in small parties, when he was under control; but when he had a docile audience, he could be insufferable.[14]

*

Early in May 1945, Hugh was due to fly out to Germany to interrogate another important captive, SS General Gottlob Berger. Before doing so, he was keen to talk to John Elphinstone, senior officer of the *Prominente*, the 'celebrity' prisoners of war who had been incarcerated at Colditz Castle. Elphinstone was the Queen's nephew; other *Prominente* included the King's nephew, Viscount Lascelles (who became Lord Harewood in 1947); Dawyck Haig; and Churchill's nephew, Giles Romilly. These men had been earmarked as potential hostages and separated from the other prisoners. In the last few days of the war Hitler had given orders for their execution, but General Berger, who was responsible for the prisoners, ensured that they escaped to safety. Elphinstone had negotiated their release with Berger.

Elphinstone was staying with the Royal Family at Buckingham Palace, following his return from Germany a few days before. Hugh already knew him slightly, as they had been contemporaries at Christ Church. Through Elphinstone's brother Andrew, who was working for SIS, Hugh arranged to meet him at the Palace on 8 May. This date carried a significance that neither could have known at the time the arrangement was made. On 7 May the Germans surrendered; accordingly 8 May was designated for the victory celebration. On VE-Day more than a million excited people converged on central London in a mood of euphoric release, and impromptu dancing erupted in the streets. Several times during the afternoon and evening the King and Queen appeared on a balcony of the Palace to greet the jubilant crowds massing below. Around five o'clock in the evening, Hugh collected Andrew Elphinstone from the SIS headquarters at Broadway Buildings, and the two men walked across St James's Park together. The thronging crowd in front of the Palace was impenetrable, but Andrew Elphinstone had been given a key to a garden gate around the back and they were able to enter this way, with only a nod from the policeman on guard duty. Inside the Palace they shared a lift with the two young princesses,* the elder dressed in ATS uniform, who were going to join their parents and the Prime Minister on the balcony, and who later that evening would mingle incognito with the crowds outside. Elphinstone entertained his guests with whisky. His rooms were on the second floor overlooking the garden; from time to time Hugh would interrupt the interview so that the three of them might cross to the bathroom opposite, to gaze out at the sea of people stretching back along The Mall. By craning his neck Hugh could look down on the heads of the Royal Family, waving to the crowd from the balcony below.

*

---

* i.e. the future Queen Elizabeth II and her sister Princess Margaret.

On 20 June 1945 Hugh was appointed to a research lectureship at Christ Church, a post often given as a form of probation for a Studentship. An historian was needed to replace Patrick Gordon Walker, who would not be returning to the college; later in the year he would take his seat in the Commons, having won the first by-election of the new Parliament. Another historian, Steven Watson, was appointed at the same time as Hugh. Watson's election was unopposed, but Hugh's election was split, five members of the electoral committee voting for and two against. The Governing Body had approved the committee's recommendation after 'long but motionless discussion'. The contrast between the two votes seems significant, given that Watson, unlike Hugh, had no previous connection with the college. Christ Church was still a very conservative place. After war service with SOE, Freddie Ayer had sought to come back there; but when he asked the Dean what his chances were, he received the discouraging reply that there would be less opposition to him than there had been previously. Ayer's impatience with college tradition had been obvious in 1939, when Dean Williams had left to become a bishop. Ayer had joined with Ryle in putting forward a plan to laicise the college, to allow for the possibility of its being governed by a layman, but the proposal proved too radical for the Governing Body and it was easily defeated. This left the college headless, until Ryle suddenly remembered a young Canadian who had rowed with him in Trial Eights and who had gone on to take a first. After further reflection he remembered the name: John Lowe. The Canadian had taken holy orders, and was now teaching in a Canadian seminary. In due course Dr Lowe became Dean of the college.[15]

'I'm *very glad* about Ch. Ch.', Garrod wrote ambiguously from Merton, 'tho', perhaps, I will miss you here. But Ch. Ch. will give you better than some other colleges that variety without which you wilt. And your faults – always obvious – will be lost in the crowd of mixed temperaments.'[16]

Hugh was due to take up his post at Christ Church at the beginning of the Michaelmas term. He applied for early demobilisation from the Army and meanwhile continued his War Room work. Listening to secretly tape-recorded conversations between captured staff officers who had waited on the Nazi leaders, he was struck by the bizarreness of Hitler's inner circle – 'scenes of nihilistic bombast uttered among high Wagnerian mountains, against a more immediate background of spinsterish tea-parties, Bavarian rococo woodwork, cuckoo-clocks and cream-buns'. Hitler and Himmler, these once-terrifying figures who had commanded the fate of millions, relied, like Roman emperors, on random influences, on masseurs, quack doctors and astrologers. As the Third Reich imploded, Göring lounged in his Karinhall, his fleshy body encased in a toga, painting his fingernails blue. 'What poor, inflated vulgarians, what weak pretenders they all turn out to have been, how absurd and byzantine that fantastic court at Berlin and Berchtesgaden and in the peripatetic *Führerhauptquartier!*' Hugh contemplated a book on the subject:

I should like to see a complete study made of the last months of that exotic circus, from 20th July 1944 to the end, when the Thousand Year Reich was breaking up, when the *Führerprinzip* had no more validity, and that vast, vaunted pyramid of obedient discipline had become a contracting cage in which all were fighting against all; when grandiose plans were being declared, plans of Alpine Redoubts and Scorched Earth and Werewolves and Wagnerian Twilights, and no one had any time to consider them, for every man was busy with his own plans for negotiation or deception or denunciation, and escape, in the face of that inevitable defeat which, to the very last, none might even mention to the demented tyrant.

Berger's interrogation provided an intimate portrait of the last months of the Third Reich. The SS general had gone with Himmler to see Hitler in the besieged capital of Berlin on 22 April 1945, the day the *Führer* had dismissed most of his staff and withdrawn into the bunker. Berger last glimpsed his leader unable to stand without propping himself up, his head shaking, his leg twitching, shouting 'Shoot them all!' Himmler had ended his life a naked prisoner, biting on a cyanide capsule. 'At least,' reflected Hugh, 'compared to this sordid ending, there is, in Hitler's demented finale, in the mystery which envelops its circumstances, something of a *Götterdämmerung.*'[17]

Both before and after the end of the war Hugh made frequent visits to the headquarters of the 21st Army Group (which became the British Army of the Rhine in August 1945), based first at Aachen and later at Bad Oeynhausen, a pleasant nineteenth-century spa town in Hanover. Until a new state could be constituted Germany was under military occupation, divided into four zones administered by each of the victorious Allies (Britain, America, Russia and France) and governed by a 'quadripartite' Control Commission. While visiting Bad Oeynhausen Hugh stayed with Dick White, now a Brigadier and head of counter-intelligence in the British Zone. White had requisitioned an elegant eighteenth-century *Schloss* about thirty miles south of Bad Oeynhausen, formerly occupied by a snobbish crony of Ribbentrop's. In the previous tenant's place White had introduced an hotelier and his family, who were anxious to ensure that their British guests wanted for nothing. 'It's a colonial life,' remarked White, 'an easy, splendid life' – though he also observed that it was artificial and mind-closing, like life in Kenya. 'Better to live in a two-roomed flat in foodless, servantless, overcrowded, undersupplied

England,' White continued, 'where there is at least some pressure on the mind.'

Hugh made several visits to White's *Schloss* in September 1945, days that he remembered as 'among the happiest in my recollection'. There he lived like a guest at an aristocratic house party, eating splendid meals and taking siestas after drinking plenty of excellent German wine at lunch. He particularly enjoyed the company of Major Peter Ramsbotham, a clever and sophisticated graduate of Magdalen who had gone into the Intelligence Corps after leaving Oxford, and who would subsequently make a distinguished career as a diplomat. One morning White, Ramsbotham and Hugh meandered over the gently rolling Teutoburg Hills, 'talking of abstract propositions, such as Truth and Validity, and concrete propositions, such as the Canons of Christ Church, for ten unnoticed miles'.[18]

A casual conversation during one of these visits was to change the course of Hugh's life. He was drinking hock with Dick White and Herbert Hart one evening when the three of them began to discuss the issue of the moment: what had happened to Hitler? More than four months after the German surrender this question remained open. The circumstances of Hitler's last days were mysterious; it was still uncertain whether he was alive or dead. Far from becoming clearer, the problem had become more obscure as the months passed. On 22 April 1945, as the Red Army completed its encirclement of Berlin and Russian artillery began shelling the city centre, Goebbels had told the German people in a radio broadcast that the *Führer* had resolved to remain in the capital until the end; but nobody could trust a word Goebbels uttered. Nine days later Hitler's successor, Admiral Dönitz, announced that Hitler had died, 'fighting to the last breath against Bolshevism'. But at the time Dönitz was far away in Flensburg, near the Danish border, and in the chaos of collapsing Germany his information was not to be relied upon. On 5 June, when the Allied commanders-in-chief met in Berlin to set up the machinery of quadripartite government, Russian staff officers told their American counterparts that they were 'almost certain' Hitler was dead. A body had been recovered and identified 'with fair certainty'. But four days later a statement issued by the Soviet commander of the Russian Zone of Occupation, Marshal Zhukov, denied that Hitler's body had been identified.[19]

With so much in doubt, the fate of the *Führer* had become the subject of intense and often wild speculation. Some said he had been murdered by his own officers in the Tiergarten; others that he had escaped from Berlin by air, or from Germany by submarine. He was living on a mist-enshrouded island in the Baltic; in a Rhineland rock-fortress; in a Spanish monastery; on a South American ranch; he had been spotted living rough among the bandits of Albania. A Swiss journalist made a deposition to testify that, to her certain knowledge, Hitler was living with Eva Braun on an estate in Bavaria. The Soviet news agency Tass reported that Hitler had been spotted in Dublin, disguised in women's clothing. No doubt his moustache had betrayed his identity.[20]

Dick White had recognised from the start the importance of solving this mystery. Hitler had captured the imagination of the German people; so long as the possibility remained that he might be still alive, the stability and security of the occupied zones could not be guaranteed. This man had been responsible for the most destructive war in the history of the world, causing the deaths of tens of millions; the slightest chance that Hitler might return, as Napoleon had done, was too terrible to contemplate. The ghost haunting Europe had to be laid to rest. White had convinced Field Marshal Montgomery, Commander-in-Chief of the British Zone, of the need for an inquiry into Hitler's fate. After the German surrender he had gone, with Montgomery's blessing, to Berlin, where the Russians assured him that both Hitler and Goebbels had committed suicide, and that their bodies had been burnt. White had been shown a set of false teeth identified as Hitler's. But the Russians had since changed their story. On 26 May Stalin had told President Truman's envoy, Harry Hopkins, of his belief that Hitler had escaped and was in hiding, together with Goebbels and Bormann; and on 6 June he had told Hopkins that he was 'sure' Hitler was still alive. Since then the uncertainty about what had happened to Hitler had become a serious problem, straining the fragile relations between the victorious Allies. The Russians were now accusing the British of secretly harbouring him. White described the situation as 'intolerable'.

This was the position when Hugh discussed the subject with Hart and White at the *Schloss* near Bad Oeynhausen. Over the third bottle of hock Hugh outlined what he had discovered about Hitler's last days from captured German officers, giving an account of a shoot-out in the Berlin Tiergarten which he later realised was complete fantasy. 'But this is most important!' exclaimed White, his eyes popping as they sometimes did when he was excited. White asked Hugh if he would undertake a systematic study of the evidence surrounding the fate of Hitler. He would be given all necessary facilities to carry out his inquiry, and have the authority of a major-general to interrogate prisoners, to call on the services of the occupying forces, and to pursue the evidence wherever it led. The Russians would have to be informed, though he could expect little co-operation from them. But the Americans would help, and so, in theory, would the French. Hugh accepted the offer without hesitation. Here was a unique opportunity for a young historian: to investigate one of the most dramatic stories in the history of the world, while the trail was still fresh. How could he refuse?

First he had to obtain clearance from his superiors. On 10 September

White requested Hugh's release from 'Tar' Robertson. After outlining the problem, he proposed a solution. 'The man who has kept the closest tabs on the matter appears to be Trevor-Roper,' he wrote. 'I believe that a job like this, unless it is done now, will never get done and unless it is done by a first-rate chap, won't be worth having.' As well as being useful in calming relations with the Russians, White believed that the inquiry should be 'a work of considerable historical interest'. Hugh flew back to England for a talk with Robertson. 'I agree with you entirely that the idea of clearing up this business about Hitler is essential and that it should be done now,' Robertson replied to White afterwards. He had given his permission for Hugh to 'get on with your job immediately'.[21]

Hugh withdrew his application for early demobilisation and returned to Germany in mid-September to begin his inquiry, using the cover name 'Major Oughton'.* He was already familiar with much of the background, of course. As a member of the War Room he had been on the circulation list for transcripts of interrogations or buggings of German prisoners, and he had access to a mass of captured documents, including the papers of the Dönitz government in Flensburg. Hugh's penetrating scrutiny dissolved the clouds of fantasy obscuring his subject. 'How easy all problems are,' he would remark after his inquiry was complete: 'how infallibly the darkest mystery yields to the deadly force of pure reason!' He was quickly able to dispose of some of the wilder stories concerning Hitler's fate. The truth was more difficult to establish. The only conclusive evidence that Hitler was dead would be the discovery and identification of his body. In the absence of such evidence, the next best proof consisted of accounts from eyewitnesses who were either familiar with Hitler's intentions or actual witnesses of his fate. Hugh viewed such evidence sceptically, aware that all witnesses are fallible, especially when recalling events that had taken place five months earlier. They were particularly unreliable on dates; 'they could not possibly be otherwise, living as they did, perpetually underground, not distinguishing night from day, in circumstances of siege and bombardment'. He therefore relied on external evidence to establish when events had taken place.[22] He was a skilful and experienced interrogator, alert to inconsistencies and quick to detect when he was not being told the truth. By identifying and tracing a sufficient number of key witnesses, and confining his questioning to the essential facts, Hugh planned to be able to accumulate enough evidence to establish beyond doubt what had happened. Not that

---

* In private, the late Professor Norman Gash, who served in military intelligence during the war and rose to the rank of Major, and afterwards made a distinguished career as an historian, claimed to have been involved with Trevor-Roper in the investigation into the death of Hitler. I have been unable to corroborate this claim, which is not supported by the extensive documentation on the investigation in Trevor-Roper's own archive or in the relevant files in the National Archives.

it would be easy to locate individuals in the chaos of defeated Germany. Many of those being sought had gone to ground, fearing a charge of war crimes.

He concentrated his search on the 'dark period' between 22 April, when Hitler had ordered much of his staff to leave Berlin, and 2 May, when the Russians had taken the city. The *Führer* had retreated to an underground bunker below the Chancellery to escape the Russian shells; the remainder of his life would be spent in its eighteen small and windowless rooms. Hugh focused on finding survivors who could provide eyewitness testimony for those ten days. Goebbels was believed to have committed suicide, Bormann to have perished in a last-minute attempt to escape from the bunker. Most of the surviving senior figures were in custody in one or other of the Allied Zones, though some of the prisoners had not been identified, and the significance of others had yet to be recognised. Those of Hitler's entourage who had left on 22 April had flown to Obersalzburg, where they were now in the custody of the Americans. By questioning these individuals Hugh was soon able to discover the names of colleagues who had been left behind after the exodus. For example, Dr Morell, Hitler's physician, had left on 22 April, but his surgeon, Dr Stumpfegger, had remained. Two of the *Führer's* secretaries had left, but another two had stayed. Those guards who had gone could name those who had remained, and so on. In this way Hugh was able to draw up a fairly complete list of those who had stayed in Berlin. He circulated thirty-three names of potential witnesses to prisoner-of-war camps in all the Allied zones, asking to be notified if any of these individuals were being held. Neither the Russians nor the French ever replied; the Americans, on the other hand, proved co-operative. Peter Ramsbotham co-ordinated the search in the British Zone, and was soon able to report that several of the witnesses on the list were in captivity and available for interrogation. As for those who had evaded capture, Hugh reasoned that they were most likely to have sought refuge in or near their old homes, or with close relatives, so he made enquiries with the British Field Security Police or the American Counter-Intelligence Corps in the relevant districts. In this way further individuals on his list were located.

At an early stage in his investigation Hugh flew to Berlin to examine Hitler's bunker. The former capital of the Reich was under four-power occupation and still open to free circulation, though the Soviet Zone surrounding the city was closed. His first impression of the bunker was one of negligence. Its entrance beneath the wreckage of Speer's once-grand Chancellery building was guarded by two slovenly Russian soldiers, who were happy to grant him admittance in exchange for a cigarette each. Inside, all was dark and flooded ankle-deep. Hugh had expected the bunker to have been sealed, its contents carefully removed for expert study; he was amazed to find that they had been left undisturbed, a prey for the casual visitor. Light-fingered officers had removed souvenirs such as Hitler's hairbrush. A British officer had picked up and subsequently handed to Hugh a copy of Hitler's engagement diary, which recorded his appointments, hour by hour, in the last six months of his life. Groping down the dark corridors, Hugh sketched out a plan of the interior. Gradually he deduced the function of each room, a layout that would be a crucial aid to his interrogations.

He would return to Berlin several times and spend many hours exploring the bunker and its immediate surroundings. On one of his flights into the city he was accompanied by Noel Annan, a Fellow of King's College, Cambridge, who would become a lifelong friend. During the war Annan had served with distinction in the Intelligence Corps, latterly as a member of the Joint Intelligence Staff Committee; he was now a political adviser to the British Military Government, though in conformance with security practice he did not reveal this, and it would be almost half a century before Hugh would discover what his friend had been doing.[23]

As well as those who had remained behind in the bunker after the exodus on 22 April, Hugh also sought out those known to have visited the bunker during the last days, such as Albert Speer, the architect whom Hitler had made Minister of Armaments and War Production. Speer had gone there on 23 April to confess to the *Führer* that he had disobeyed his order to destroy much of the industrial infrastructure of the Reich. He feared execution, but Hitler had forgiven him, and he had been able to leave, to join Dönitz in Flensburg. Hugh was impressed by Speer's dignified demeanour, contrasting strongly with the abject behaviour of most of the others whom he interrogated. Nevertheless he would describe Speer as the 'real criminal' of Nazi Germany, because he epitomised the *trahison des clercs* which had allowed the educated elite to comply so willingly and so readily with the murderous Nazi regime.

Hugh spent much of the next few weeks driving by jeep along empty roads to interrogate potential witnesses. Sometimes he was driven by a young soldier, though often he was completely alone; even so, he never felt threatened. The German people were completely quiescent; the expected resistance from fanatical Nazis was conspicuous by its absence. Indeed, at the end of his investigation Hugh looked back on his travels around Germany on those days of late summer and early autumn as almost idyllic. 'It was a fascinating piece of historical research – a fig for Archbishop Laud; he never led me, or could have led me, on those delightful journeys, motoring through the deciduous golden groves of Schleswig-Holstein, and coming, on an evening when the sun had just set but the light had not yet gone, and the wild duck were out for their last flight over the darkening waters, to the great Danish castle of Ploen, gazing like a sentinel over those white autumnal lakes.'

In general his witnesses, once cornered, spoke freely. They exhibited little loyalty to their former master, or to their colleagues; most were concerned merely for themselves. Nazi officials who had so recently strutted now grovelled. Hugh was disgusted by their shameless cringing. He was non-plussed by Hitler's butler, Artur Kannenberg, who immediately offered his services, presenting a handwritten list of his qualifications. All that was lacking was a testimonial from his most recent employer.

On 1 November 1945 a handout based on Hugh's findings, 'The Last Days of Hitler and Eva Braun', was distributed to the press at the Hotel am Zoo in Berlin. Hugh himself presented a summary to the assembled journalists. Nine days later he submitted his report, 'The Death of Hitler', to the Quadripartite Intelligence Committee. It concluded that Hitler had committed suicide by shooting himself and Eva Braun on 30 April, and that their bodies had subsequently been burnt. Goebbels had committed suicide the next day. Hugh was satisfied that the seven witnesses to the 'dark period' whom he had located and interrogated could not have combined to concoct a story robust enough to have withstood his questioning. 'The evidence from the sources at present available is entirely consistent in all material points, and this consistency is noteworthy since the groups of witnesses are quite independent of each other.' Hugh was confident that further findings were unlikely to add anything significant, and indeed facts which have emerged sub-sequently have confirmed the accuracy of his report in almost every detail. He disposed crisply of alternative accounts of Hitler's fate. 'Other versions have been circulating suggesting that Hitler is not dead at all. These have been examined and found to rest on no valid evidence whatsoever.' Hugh finished his report with a list of suggested questions to be raised at the next meeting of the Committee, most of them directed at the Russians. The Russians noted these requests but never answered them. 'Very interesting' was the only response they would make.

Hugh returned to England. After a few days in London he retrieved his car, obtained some petrol and drove to Oxford, 'looking forward, after a suburban life in Barnet, and an urban life in London, and a colonial life in Germany, to books and drink and intellectual society once more'. He had been allocated a set of ground-floor rooms facing into Tom Quad. It seemed to him delightful to walk down Broad Street again on a clear, cold November day, allowing his eye to rest complacently on a decaying nose of one of the Roman emperors who guarded the Sheldonian Theatre. 'How exhilarating is the intellectual life, how buoyant the air of a learned place, how beautiful its architecture and associations!'

On his first night at Christ Church he sat next to Keith Feiling. 'The outlook is very black,' Feiling muttered gloomily, filling a large glass brimful with port; 'there is no faith, no hope, no morals; and the political situation is worse, infinitely worse, than in 1938.' Hugh enquired politely about Feiling's progress with his life of Neville Chamberlain, and Feiling brightened a little. His studies, he said, had convinced him that Chamberlain was an even greater man than he had supposed. Turning tactfully to speak to his other neighbour, the philosopher Michael Foster, Hugh learned that he had been addressing the Governing Body on the need for a new era of austerity. In future, Foster emphasised with melancholy relish, there would be no drink and no dances and no gaudies and no pleasure of any kind at all; and as a supererogatory mortification he had suggested to the Governing Body that the dons should in future have the same food as the undergraduates. Avoiding this contentious subject, Hugh spoke of a book he had just obtained, Karl Popper's *The Open Society and Its Enemies*, which seemed to him important; what did Oxford think? Foster said he had not heard of Popper; he considered that C.S. Lewis was undoubtedly the most important philosopher in England today. Hugh was struck dumb. By the next morning's breakfast he was sufficiently prepared not to be astonished by Feiling's remark that Arthur Bryant was 'growing every year in stature'.

> 'What a set of old crashers!' I said to myself; Shall I ever stick it out? And my heart, that volatile organ, sank heavily down towards my stomach, which itself was feeling weak and hollow after a Christ Church breakfast; and I wondered why I had ever returned to this world of disconsolate reactionary gloom.[24]

Hugh had been in Oxford only about ten days when he received a telephone call from Bad Oeynhausen. A document had been found, which appeared to be Hitler's will.[25] Was it genuine? Hugh had already seen a telegram referring to a 'personal testament' among Dönitz's papers, so he was predisposed to believe it so. He was soon able to examine it himself, after a 'photostatic copy' was couriered to him.

Accompanying this personal testament was a political testament, appointing Dönitz as Hitler's successor and expelling both Göring and Himmler from the Nazi Party for their treachery in opening negotiations with the enemy. These documents had apparently been signed by Hitler at four o'clock in the morning on 29 April 1945, the day before his suicide. Also attached was an appendix signed by Goebbels, in which he explained his decision to disobey the *Führer's* order to flee Berlin and instead to die by his side. They had been discovered sewn into the lining of a coat belonging to a man who claimed to be a journalist from Luxemburg.* In fact, as his interrogation revealed, he was Heinz Lorenz, a press secretary on Hitler's staff, whose principal responsibility had been to monitor enemy radio broadcasts. It was he who had brought the *Führer* news of Himmler's attempt to negotiate with the Allies. After Hitler's death Lorenz had been ordered to deliver the documents to the Party archives in Munich, a duty which he had abandoned as impossible. According to Lorenz, there had been two other sets of documents, one given to Major Willi Johannmeyer, who was ordered to take them to Field Marshal Schörner, commander of Army Group Centre, then engaged in a desperate attempt to withstand the assault of the Red Army along the Czech frontier; and the other to SS Colonel Wilhelm Zander, who was to convey them to Admiral Dönitz at Flensburg. If these two sets of documents could be traced, this should establish the authenticity of the will beyond doubt. Hugh flew to Germany to resume his hunt for Hitler.

Hugh had never heard of Zander, but he was familiar with the name of Johannmeyer, whom he knew to have been on the staff of General Burgdorf, Hitler's chief adjutant in the bunker. Indeed Burgdorf had witnessed and signed Hitler's will, together with Bormann and Goebbels. After the death of his *Führer*, Burgdorf had committed suicide.

Johannmeyer was soon traced, living quietly with his parents in Iserlohn. Hugh had him detained and interrogated; but he denied everything, and his interrogator, the twenty-two-year-old Captain Robert Maxwell,† was inclined to release him. Dissatisfied, Hugh decided to go to Iserlohn to interrogate Johannmeyer himself. Eventually, after long questioning, Johannmeyer admitted that he had been in the bunker, but he continued to deny any knowledge of Hitler's will. His story was that he had been ordered to escort Lorenz and Zander through Russian lines. He understood them to be carrying documents, but claimed to be ignorant of what these were. Even when shown them he insisted that he had never seen them before. He was a simple soldier, no more.

Frustrated, Hugh gave orders that Johannmeyer should be kept in detention over the Christmas period, and returned to Bad Oeynhausen. There he heard from Peter Ramsbotham that the military high-ups were panicking: no one wanted the responsibility of deciding what to do about Hitler's will. The decision had been passed up the line to the Joint Intelligence Committee (JIC) in London. 'This is an historical document,'

---

* According to one account, they were discovered when a British sergeant shoved the recalcitrant prisoner and, as he did so, felt something inside Lorenz's coat.
† Maxwell was from a Czech-Jewish background. In his childhood he was called Jan Koch; after he fled to England in 1940 he was known respectively as Leslie du Maurier, Leslie Jones and Ian Robert Maxwell.

protested Ramsbotham; 'who are these brass-hats that they should feebly demand the suppression of an historical document?' Equally exasperated, Hugh made a bold proposal. Zander's home was in Munich, in the American Zone. 'Give me a car, for ten days, and I will look for Zander, and if I should find him and his documents I should of course have to hand the documents over to the American authorities; and if they should choose not to suppress but to publish them, that would be too bad, but it would be no business of ours: for the choice is theirs.'[26]

There had been no trace of Zander since he had left the bunker. His wife, who was living in Hanover, claimed to have heard nothing from him; she had convinced her relatives that he was dead. Hugh comforted himself with the conviction that all problems are soluble, and set out for the American Zone. He went first to the American internment camp in Frankfurt to search their records and, finding nothing, drove on to Munich, where he located Zander's flat and ransacked his belongings, but again found nothing. It was now Christmas Eve. In the Munich headquarters of the American Commander-in-Chief, the soldiers detailed to help Hugh were disappearing for a week's holiday. Frustrated, Hugh began to gather up his papers from his temporary desk. He would have to return to the British Zone and confess to Ramsbotham that he had failed.

Two Americans walked past. One of them, glancing at his papers, murmured to the other, 'Zander again!', and walked on. Hugh pounced on him: 'What did you mean?' The American assured him that it was nothing. Hugh protested that it must be something. He had come, he explained, all the way from the uttermost north only to look for Zander. Was he alive or dead? And if alive, where? The American replied merely that the German girlfriend of a friend of his had once been the closest friend of Frau Zander. But there had been a bitter quarrel, and now the girl would tell anything she knew to sweeten her revenge.

Within a short time Hugh had established that Zander was living under a false name in the village of Aidenbach, near the Austrian frontier. Two days later, after driving all day and all night in an American jeep through mud and sleet and snow, Hugh stood outside the house at three o'clock in the morning. He posted an American soldier with a revolver at each corner, and knocked on the door. There was no answer. Hugh ordered a German policeman to climb through the window and open the door. Inside, they found a man in bed who claimed to be a merchant named Wilhelm Paustin. Hugh made him dress, and then drove him all the way back to Munich for interrogation. Perhaps because he was by then so weary, the man made no resistance, and admitted to being Zander. He revealed that he had deposited the documents for safe-keeping at the home of a friend, where they were duly located and found to match the documents discovered in Lorenz's coat. Hugh drove straight to the headquarters of the American Third Army at Bad Tölz, and reported his findings to the commanding officer, General Lucian K. Truscott. As soon as Hugh had left, Truscott called a press conference at which he announced the discovery of Hitler's will, just as Hugh had predicted. Back at Bad Oeynhausen, Ramsbotham informed Hugh that the JIC had referred the decision on what to say about Hitler's will up to the Cabinet; but by then it was too late, as its discovery was being announced in banner headlines in newspapers around the world.

Hugh sent for Johannmeyer, who arrived by truck early on New Year's Day. All morning they wrestled; but Johannmeyer was too tough to be bullied and too proud to be cajoled. Hugh had warmed to this youngish German officer, who seemed decent and honest, though stubborn. He resolved to try reason instead, and led Johannmeyer through all the evidence which made his story incredible. 'And now,' Hugh asked, 'if you were in my place, could you possibly believe that story?' The German replied that he could not; 'but it is nevertheless true'. In despair, Hugh left the room. They were alone in the headquarters; everyone else had left for the holiday. Hugh had nowhere to put Johannmeyer. He decided that he must admit failure and summon a truck to take him away. But while Hugh was out of the room, trying to make a long-distance call, Johannmeyer had leisure to think. When Hugh returned, and resumed his mechanical questioning – rather to fill in the time than out of any hope of success – he became aware of a change in his prisoner's attitude. Instead of blocking every assault, Johannmeyer was seeking guarantees in case of surrender; and when Hugh responded appropriately, he said quietly, '*Ich habe die Papiere*' ('I have the papers').

'Where?' demanded Hugh.

'At my house in Iserlohn,' he replied, 'buried in a glass bottle in the back-garden.'

On the long drive back to Iserlohn they stopped for a meal. While they were eating Hugh asked Johannmeyer why he had changed his mind. 'In your absence from the room,' replied Johannmeyer, 'I went over the matter in my mind, and it seemed to me that if those other two, who were both Party members, and had done well out of the Party, had so easily betrayed the trust reposed in them, then it was quixotic in me, who was not a member of the Party but only a soldier, to defend the position they had abandoned.' At Iserlohn they left the car some distance away, at Johannmeyer's request; he didn't want the neighbours to see a British staff car outside his parents' home. The two men walked together through the cold night to the house. It was now night-time, and the ground had frozen hard. Johannmeyer took an axe from the hall and together they walked out into the back garden. It was only at this point that Hugh belatedly recognised the precariousness of his situation. He was alone and unarmed, with a tough young German army officer bearing a large axe. Johannmeyer had been detained for a week at Hugh's insistence and had resisted his interrogation for almost all that time. Perhaps he had given way only to lure Hugh to this spot? It was dark, and nobody knew where he was. The story of the buried papers might be a ruse. But his anxiety was short-lived: Johannmeyer found the place, broke the ground with the axe, and dug up the glass bottle. Then he smashed the bottle with the head of the axe and drew out the documents: the third copy of Hitler's private testament, plus a vivid covering letter from Burgdorf to Schörner describing the circumstances of its dictation, 'under the shattering news of the treachery of the *Reichsführer* SS'.

Fifteen years later, Captain Maxwell, by now a millionaire publisher, asked Hugh about Johannmeyer. There was a problem that had been vexing him ever since: 'How did you manage to get that German to talk?' Having been unsuccessful himself, Maxwell assumed that Hugh must have either bribed or bullied his prisoner into revealing where the will was hidden, and was nonplussed to hear that he had done neither.

Hugh returned to England early in 1946 with a reputation as a Hitler expert. His triumphant successes, first in establishing what had happened to Hitler, and then in tracing the missing copies of the will, meant that his name would ever more be associated with Hitler's. These discoveries were announced at press conferences and reported in headlines across the world. Over the years that followed Hugh would be the first choice to examine and authenticate Nazi documents, to appear as an expert on radio and television programmes, to write articles on Nazi subjects for newspapers and magazines, and forewords to volumes of Nazi memorabilia. The appetite for such material was strong, and would remain so. By writing an article entitled 'Hitler: New Light on a Dark Career', published in March 1946, Hugh opened his account with *The New York Times*, 'from which an infinite, endless, golden shower of American dollars flows ceaselessly into my pockets'.[27]

———

Student

Hugh saw Logan Pearsall Smith for the last time early in January 1946, after he returned from Germany and before going up to Oxford. Smith was in bed, weak but euphoric, talking incessantly, without restraint. Hugh tried unavailingly to calm him. Finally he took his leave. On the stairs he met Smith's sister Alys, clearly in a nervous state. It was obvious to him that his friend was being very troublesome.

A few weeks later Hugh heard that Smith had died. Though he had been ill for months, his death came as a shock. 'A great section of my life seems to me to have ended,' lamented Hugh. 'No-one else has had such an effect on my personal history.' In his notebook, he traced the course of their relations, and reflected on how much he owed to his elderly friend. 'My whole philosophy seems, now that I consider it retrospectively, to have come from him, and what I would have been without him I cannot envisage, cannot imagine.'

> For it was Logan who afterwards re-interested me, in a time when the war had separated me from desperate academic study, in style & the world of sensation, & enabled me thus to fill in the hard structural pattern of thought which I had thus evolved; and how can I express adequate gratitude for such an experience? – who showed me that life is short, & three parts routine, and most of it comedy, and can only be saved from triviality and given significance by some ideal to which all else, or at least much else, and that much including many humane pleasures and meritorious aims, and especially power and success, must be sacrificed, as by the merchant who sold out to re-invest all in one pearl of great price; and that style is an ideal worthy of this sacrifice. This I learnt from him and believed, & I still believe it, and shall, I hope, continue, like Gibbon, to value reading above the wealth of India. For in his life and conversation, among the tinkle of coronets and the wild extravagant gossip, and the exquisite relish of high life and *la comédie humaine*, of which it was also witness, he illustrated this philosophy to me so vividly that if it has not become mine, at least mine can never be altogether emancipated from its influence.'

It emerged soon afterwards that Smith had made a new will less than a month before he died, superseding the will of 1943 by which he had left the bulk of his estate to Hugh. Except for a few personal bequests and a life-interest to his sister (then aged seventy-nine), he bequeathed all his property, valued at almost £13,000,* to John Russell, a young man whom he had known for only a short time. Hugh received nothing, except the books that already bore his book-plate. There was no bequest either to Smith's former secretary-companion Robert Gathorne-Hardy, who felt bitter that he had endured so much for no reward, and complained strenuously that he had been unjustly treated. He tried to have the will set aside, on the grounds that Smith had been insane at the end, unaware that he would have benefited no more from the earlier will. Eventually Russell agreed a settlement with him. Alys Russell had been indignant on Gathorne-Hardy's behalf about her brother's behaviour. 'You know, he made an iniquitous will,' she said feelingly when Hugh called on her.

Hugh was wise enough to rise above the acrimony that followed Smith's death. Unlike Gathorne-Hardy, he had never trusted the capricious old man's promises, and showed no disappointment when these proved empty. In due course, when the jockeying for Smith's inheritance became clearer to him, Hugh would write a long private memorandum on the subject. In 1949 Gathorne-Hardy published a memoir entitled *Recollections of Logan Pearsall Smith*, which Hugh reviewed in a Third Programme radio broadcast. The BBC legal department raised a number of objections to Hugh's script, which they thought potentially libellous of Gathorne-Hardy. There were sharp exchanges between Hugh and the producer, P.H. Newby,† before a final version was agreed. Hugh explained that though he was a friend of the author, he had also been a friend of the subject, whose character the book traduced. Though Gathorne-Hardy's book had 'many of the qualities of a work of art', it was marred by a 'shrill personal note' of resentment, and the result was 'a distorted picture'. The broadcast elicited a pained protest from Gathorne-Hardy, and a brisk rebuke from Alys Russell.[2]

'You can't believe how frightful Oxford is,' Hugh wrote to Charles Stuart after he had been back there a week or so.[3] The pay was poor, the college food almost inedible, there was little to drink and any hint of fun was frowned upon. 'Oxford is very full, and the life of dignified ease which one used to associate with my profession seems to have evaporated,' Hugh complained to a correspondent who had known Christ Church in the 1930s; 'everyone is extremely busy, everything is difficult to get or get done, and no one seems to have any time for scholarship'.[4] The University was filling up with young men demobilised from the Forces whose higher education

---

* Worth over £400,000 in today's money.
† A novelist, who had published his first book in 1945. In 1969 he would be the first winner of the Booker Prize with his novel *Something to Answer For.*

had been interrupted or postponed, in some cases for five years or more. Such mature undergraduates tended to be more serious about their studies and less inclined to puerile junketing than beardless youths arriving straight from school. On the other hand some of these ex-servicemen might not have qualified for admission in normal times.

One of the most energetic of the Christ Church 'returnees' was Lawrence Stone, who had first come up to the college from Charterhouse on a history scholarship in 1938.[5] Masterman was then on sabbatical, enjoying the hospitality of maharajahs in India, so Stone had been 'sent out' for his special subject to John Prestwich of Queen's. In 1940, after two years' study, he had joined the Royal Naval Volunteer Reserve (RNVR), and served as an officer in destroyers for the next five years, in both the Atlantic and Pacific theatres. He had already introduced himself to R.H. Tawney, and cultivated Tawney's company whenever he was in London on shore leave.[6] By the time he became Hugh's pupil, Stone was twenty-six (Hugh was then thirty-one) and married. He had already published an article in the scholarly journal *History*, written at sea from secondary sources supplied by the London Library. Even more remarkable was the fact that in 1946, while still an undergraduate, Stone was commissioned by Nikolaus Pevsner to write a volume on medieval sculpture in the *Pelican History of Art* series.

'His work for me is quite excellent,' Hugh commented in his tutor's report for Collections. 'He works very fast, almost impatiently. He should certainly get a first-class. Please commend.' The audacious Stone cut a very different figure from the usual deferential undergraduate. He is said to have stormed out of a revision class Hugh was conducting, because he considered such humdrum work beneath him. Nevertheless the two men became friendly, perhaps because they were similar in temperament and shared many interests (including driving fast in powerful cars). Tall and rangy, Stone was dandyish, dressing in sharp suits, his fingers festooned with rings, so that he was often described as Byronic in appearance. As Hugh had predicted, Stone took a first in history Schools in 1946; he was immediately elected to a Bryce Research Fellowship, becoming a lecturer at Univ, a year later. In the same year he had been proposed for a lectureship at Christ Church. Though two members of the History Lectureship Committee (one of whom may or may not have been Hugh) voted for him, another candidate, the medievalist D.M. Bueno de Mesquita, was appointed instead.

In March 1946 Robert Blake was elected to fill the vacancy at Christ Church for a tutor in politics left by Frank Pakenham, who had gone to the House of Lords as a Minister in the new Labour Government.[7] Hugh, who had become friendly with Blake while both were serving with SIS, claimed credit for his election.[8] Good-humoured and courteous, Blake disguised a sharp intellect beneath the persona of a rubicund country squire. Three years younger than Hugh, he had read Modern Greats (Philosophy, Politics and Economics) at Magdalen, taking a first in 1938. When war came he joined the Royal Artillery. Captured near Tobruk in 1942, he had been a prisoner of war in Italy for eighteen months before making a daring escape that earned him a Mention in Dispatches. He had spent the last months of the war and the first months of the peace in SIS, working for Kim Philby, whom he found an agreeable colleague, as Hugh had done. The war had deepened Blake's interest in political history, and he abandoned plans for a legal career in favour of academe. A shrewd operator, he became one of Hugh's closest allies in Oxford intrigues. Soon afterwards they were joined by Charles Stuart, returning to Christ Church as a replacement for Master-man, who had been elected Provost of Worcester. Keith Feiling was also leaving Christ Church, to occupy the Chichele Chair in Modern History at All Souls. Hugh thus became the senior history tutor, his Studentship ratified at a Governing Body meeting on 19 June.

Stuart was a quiet man, content to ride in Hugh's slipstream. Their collaboration at Christ Church was an extension of their working rela-tionship within SIS, when Stuart had been one of Hugh's subordinates. Letters between them were peppered with intelligence jargon.* As Blake later recalled, these three 'formed a small pressure group which might be described as radical Tory'. Yet Hugh and his colleagues were not confined to the Right. They saw themselves as Cavaliers fighting Oxford's pleasure-loathing Puritans: a Party of Light to scatter the 'forces of darkness', and a Party of Gaiety to relieve the belt-tightening measures adopted during the war. Maurice Bowra, whose politics (in so far as he had any) were Left-leaning, saw himself in much the same way, and used similar terms. Noel Annan observed that in Bowra's world the Legions of Darkness were in perpetual warfare with the Children of Light. The flame of Bowra's Wadham was rekindled at the House.

The 'Christ Church Mafia' of Blake, Stuart and Trevor-Roper intrigued to insert their allies onto every college committee, and to banish their enemies. 'Whom can I ruin next?' Hugh asked, as he paced Tom Quad, after ensuring that a philosopher he considered unsympathetic was not elected to a Studentship. The constant refrain of the Party of Light was 'confusion to the canons': their policy, resistance to 'the clerical party and any increase in the chapter fund'. This was not a call to revolution. On the contrary, Hugh believed in outward conformity to the established orthodoxies, however archaic or absurd these might appear to the rational mind. He saw nothing contradictory about attending and participating in

---

* For example, they used the term 'V-Man' to refer to a confidential source: a corruption of V-Mann (*Vertrauensmann*), a term used by German intelligence, meaning 'trusted man'.

church services, while scoffing at religious belief. In later years he would declare that he belonged to the Party of Rimmon,* meaning that he conformed without believing. At the beginning of 1948 he would accept the role of Junior Censor, which included among its duties reading the lesson in the Cathedral at evensong. 'The young should always be brought up in the Established Faith,' Blake commented to Hugh on one occasion. 'They can then have all the more fun in deviating from it later.'[9]

Hugh and his allies wanted Christ Church to reassert itself as one of the richest Oxford foundations, 'to *behave* like a rich college', to pay the dons properly and to exert a corresponding influence within the University as a whole. They believed that the college should entertain lavishly. This meant opposition to Dean Lowe, whose idea of hospitality was to serve 'well-watered white wine cup'. One undergraduate described the Dean as a 'walking frost-pocket'. He gave a party for the undergraduates at which sherry was served in minuscule glasses. The young men were advised to fill the glass to the brim, 'as this is the only one you'll get'.

The year 1946 was the 400th anniversary of the college's refoundation. Shakespeare's *Henry VIII* was performed in Hall, with Michael Howard, a newly demobilised infantry captain whose undergraduate career had been interrupted by war service and who would later become a distinguished military historian, taking the part of Cardinal Wolsey. The performance drew plaudits from the young Kenneth Tynan, then an undergraduate at Magdalen and just launching his career as a critic, who attended dressed in his usual purple suit and golden shirt.[10] The climax of the celebrations came in October, with a dinner to honour King George VI, the college Visitor, at which the Queen was also present. Champagne flowed, and the loyal Christ Church men sang 'Here's a Health unto His Majesty' with verve and vigour. Hugh described the festivities in a letter to his friend and former Christ Church colleague Solly Zuckerman, who had recently accepted a chair in anatomy at Birmingham University. 'I signalised Their Majesties' visit by extreme intoxication,' he confessed. 'My hand still trembles, my mind is cloudy, and I am crippled by mysterious bruises.'[11]

Half a century later, Michael (by then Sir Michael) Howard speculated that it must have been hard for his tutors, Trevor-Roper and Masterman, to return to the routine of teaching after six years in secret intelligence. 'Christ Church was anyhow far too gentlemanly a college to make its undergraduates work any harder than they felt inclined.'[12] The attitude of most of the dons towards undergraduates was lax to the point of negligence. Hugh made little attempt to disguise the fact that teaching bored him. 'Pupils are a terrible distraction,' he moaned.[13] He was at his best with the

---

* 'He bowed in the house of Rimmon', 2 Kings 5:18.

most able and high-performing students, and impatient with the dim. Immediately after the war, because of the pressure of numbers, he would hold seminars for three or four students at a time; afterwards he reverted to the more usual Oxford system of one-to-one tutorials. During these he listened in silence as the undergraduate read his essay aloud, interrupting only to correct misuse of English. He pounced on mixed metaphors; 'The floodgates of disaster stalked through the land' was a favourite. When one undergraduate suggested that a certain historical event was 'inevitable', he snapped back: 'Nothing is inevitable until it has happened.' Once the reading was finished, he would launch into a disquisition on the subject of the essay while he prowled about the room, often emphasising his argument by brandishing a paper knife. In more extreme cases he might resort to a hunting-crop. His exposition was always lucid and often witty. In selecting historical examples he delighted in the dramatic and the absurd. He was determined to push an interpretation as far as it would go, arranging it in a large and satisfying synthesis. The more perceptive of his undergraduate listeners recognised that their tutor was 'doing a turn', using the opportunity to work his words into a state of high polish. Nevertheless they were dazzled by these brilliant performances.[14]

Schoolboys going up to the House to read modern history received a reading list from Hugh in the preceding spring. Among the books he recommended were Gibbon's *Autobiography* ('the best in the language') and his *Decline and Fall of the Roman Empire*, Macaulay's *History of England*, Churchill's life of his ancestor Marlborough, Clarendon's *History of the Rebellion* and Mandell Creighton's *History of the Papacy from the Great Schism to the Fall of Rome*. 'You will have less leisure to read these books when you are up,' Hugh's letter explained, 'as you will have to write a weekly essay.' For Graham Turner, a grammar school boy from a working-class family who came up to Christ Church on a scholarship, Hugh was the most terrifying of tutors. Turner was not taught by Hugh in his first two terms; their initial encounter had come at Collections, when hapless undergraduates were obliged to walk the full length of Christ Church Hall and then stand before a panel of dons to receive verdicts on their performances during the term just finishing. Hugh, who was substituting for the Dean as chairman, glanced at the tutors' reports on the table in front of him. 'Well, Turner,' he said witheringly, 'if I were you, I should just go home to Macclesfield.' This was not an encouraging start, and things became worse once Hugh began tutoring him. By this time Hugh had moved from Tom Quad to an elegant set of panelled rooms facing south on the first floor of Peckwater Quad, so it was to these that Turner came for his first Trevor-Roper tutorial. After he had read aloud an essay on some aspect of Tudor history, Hugh remarked damningly that it was 'full of small-town metaphors'. During another tutorial Turner incautiously mentioned the Elizabethan Monopolies Act. 'Most interesting,' commented Hugh; 'Just run me through the history of monopolies in the Elizabethan period.' Turner entered his tutorials dreading the ordeal ahead, and emerged afterwards shaken, needing to steady himself with a large whisky. On sober reflection, he decided that he faced a choice: either he succumbed to the onslaught, or he raised his game. He chose the latter course. In the seventh week of that term, he read an essay on the 1630s. 'That is a very good essay,' his tutor opined. Turner glowed with satisfaction. He conceded afterwards that Hugh's hectoring, which had seemed unkind, had helped him to improve.

Turner's awe was deepened by the fact that his tutor seemed to move in lofty social circles. Once, in mid-tutorial, the telephone rang. Hugh picked it up and answered, 'Ah, Prince Obolensky!' The young man was perhaps more impressed than he should have been, unaware that the Russian prince was a member of the Christ Church Senior Common Room, an historian of Byzantium and Eastern Europe. But he formed the view that there was no social gathering in England in which Hugh would not be at his ease.[15]

Hugh's intimidating reputation preceded him. David Hopkins, another grammar school boy, the son of a wholesale grocer from Worthing who had come up to the House on an exhibition, approached his first Trevor-Roper tutorial with trepidation, having heard stories of Hugh's savagery. He read his set essay, on Henry VII, expecting a mauling. To his astonishment he was told at the end, in a voice so low that he could hardly hear it, that he had produced a 'damn fine essay'. But, said his tutor, he had used the expression 'more or less'. Which did he mean? Hopkins was quick to learn the lesson, and more exact in his choice of phrase afterwards.

Another pupil, Michael Banton, later a sociologist, was one of those whose education had been interrupted by war service, in his case with the Royal Navy. He was therefore some years older than the typical undergraduate, and less easily cowed. Reading an essay aloud, Banton became irritable as Hugh walked about the room, sorting out letters, filing, and carrying out other routine tasks. Surely, he thought, he deserved at least some show of attention from his tutor, who was paid to listen to his undergraduate pupils, however boring this might be. His irritation was compounded when he had to pause in mid-flow, after the Dean knocked on the door, entered, and then began to discuss some college business. Eventually the Dean left. As the door closed, Hugh – to Banton's amazement – repeated back to him, word for word, his entire last sentence. The young man's protests died in his mouth.[16]

Hugh's first words to Theodore Zeldin (later the historian of modern France) were an order: 'Take your hands out of your pockets!' Despite this daunting start, Zeldin found tutorials with Hugh 'wonderful'. He likened them to an operatic duet: first he would read his essay, and then Hugh would take up the theme, in a soaring aria that might last as long as half an hour. To the receptive listener, this was an exhilarating intellectual experience. Other English historians tended to be parochial in their interests, their knowledge limited to a finite period; Hugh's learning was Europe-wide, and ranged across the centuries.

He lectured in the cavernous Christ Church Hall or the Examination Schools, the grand neo-Jacobean building on the High Street erected in the late nineteenth century. His lectures were beautifully constructed, and usually well attended. Most thought him a witty and brilliant speaker who held his audience with ease, though a minority of undergraduates found his presentation too 'scripted'. In lecturing on the Puritan Revolution, for example, he discussed the standard history in many volumes by S.R. Gardiner (1829–1902), completed after his death by C.H. Firth. 'As you make your way through the volumes of Gardiner and come to the penultimate volume, you find that Gardiner has come to life. In fact what has happened is that Gardiner has died.' The metaphors that Hugh employed remained memorable more than half a century later, as in his description of the peers' response to the Revolution: 'Some cowered in caves as the avalanche thundered overhead; others clung to the revolutionary toboggan as it hurtled downwards.' Hugh often spoke in long sentences, consisting of multiple subordinate clauses – so many of these that on at least one occasion the audience began to applaud. He wore a rose in his buttonhole. Occasionally he would interrupt his flow to read a quotation, take a sip from a glass of orange juice, or correct his text with his fountain pen.

An undergraduate crossing Peckwater Quad one evening encountered Robin Dundas, who asked where he was going. 'I'm going to a party of Mr Trevor-Roper's,' the young man replied. 'Good heavens,' exclaimed Dundas in mock astonishment, 'have you come into some money?' Hugh confessed that it was always the 'socially presentable' undergraduates whom he seemed to invite to his parties. He did so with a guilty conscience, because he felt that he ought to invite those who did not go to many. But just because of this, they were not so easy to entertain: they arrived on the dot of six o'clock, knew none of the other guests, and made awkward conversation. 'So I slide into the easy path of pleasure instead of the stern, rugged, cobbled path of duty, and my parties are crowded not by severe poor scholars but by elegant upper-class flibbertigibbets'.[17] One such was Francis Dashwood, a pupil of Robert Blake's, an Old Etonian and heir to a baronetcy. He was a flamboyant character, who strove to recapture some of the style and zest for living of the eighteenth century. Hugh was a guest at several of the spectacular parties thrown by Dashwood at the family estate, West Wycombe Park in Buckinghamshire.

Nevertheless, he could be surprisingly considerate to socially inexperienced young men whom he wanted to encourage. David Hopkins, who came from a teetotal Baptist family, was unsure whether to accept Hugh's invitation to a cocktail party. His host assured him that it was perfectly all right to attend without drinking alcohol, and so that Hopkins would not feel conspicuous, confined himself to orange squash that evening, to the amazement of some of the others present.

As a young bachelor don, living in college, Hugh was welcome at parties given by undergraduates. He would appear in formal evening dress, offset by bright red socks. Occasionally his presence at such parties would be at odds with his duties as Censor. After attending a party given by one young Scotsman, an Old Etonian and the heir to a baronetcy, Hugh combined gratitude and censure in one succinct missive. 'Your splendid party which I so much enjoyed seems to have deteriorated somewhat after I left,' he began. There followed a description of various resulting misdeeds, together with a summary of the penalties imposed.[18] In his role as Censor Hugh found himself being interviewed by officials from the Thames Conservancy on the morning after the 1949 Commemoration Ball, when a rather cross-looking swan was discovered afloat on Mercury, wearing a black evening tie. The officials who bagged and removed the bird were not much amused by the Porter's suggestion that it had flown in like a helicopter; or that the swan had donned the tie so as not to be found improperly dressed.

On social occasions Hugh could be disarmingly silent. One conversational gambit after another would fail, until his interlocutor, by now desperate, hit on the right subject. Then he would respond, perhaps with a soliloquy lasting several minutes: how Elizabeth I kept her favourites and her advisers separate, where the Goths came from, a scandal in the *beau monde*, or the best way to cook a lobster. One of his undergraduate pupils, later a colleague, likened the process to feeding a fruit machine: you kept pushing coins into the slot, one after another, until at last the machine would light up and produce a shower of gold.[19]

Hugh often took undergraduates on expeditions to examine churches or country houses, amassing material for his writings on the early modern period. One such companion was Nicholas Tate, another Old Etonian, from the family of sugar magnates. They visited various houses not open to the public; Tate was impressed to find how many doors were open to his tutor. The highlight was a visit to Althorp to see the Sunderland Papers. Lord Spencer greeted Hugh with the words, 'How nice to see you again', before giving them a personal tour. Hugh gossiped freely from behind the wheel as they drove back and forth to these destinations, from time to time swivelling his head to emphasise a point to his passenger. On one such occasion, he avoided an innocent milk float only by a violent swerve, hurling his passenger from his seat.

Richard Law, an undergraduate reading Greats, knew Hugh socially. Tired after taking Schools, he encountered Hugh crossing Tom Quad and fell into conversation. When asked what his plans were after leaving, Law explained that he was going to stay with friends in Tuscany before coming home to look for a job. 'Well,' said Hugh lightly, 'I'll give you a lift, if you like, as far as Turin.' The young man seized on this offer. The journey was a liberal education, punctuated by frequent halts which led into disquisitions on French medieval church sculpture, the economics of domestic architecture in Troyes or Soissons, or misreadings of inscriptions on Hellenic tombs. 'Come on! You know some Greek', urged Hugh. 'Jot this down while I hold the torch.'

Another pupil whose company Hugh enjoyed was the playboy Alan Clark, who would become better known as a military historian, a right-wing Conservative MP, and a startlingly frank diarist. His father, the art historian Sir Kenneth Clark, had been appointed Director of the National Gallery at the age of only thirty-one; he had also been Surveyor of the King's Pictures, and held both posts until 1946, when he arrived in Oxford to take up an appointment as Slade Professor of Fine Art. 'K' Clark (as he was known) was a man of learning and taste, who had inherited a fortune. He used his money to collect pictures, acting as a patron to young artists such as Henry Moore, Graham Sutherland and John Piper. His eldest son Alan was a disappointment to him, being neither intellectually distinguished nor particularly cultivated: remarkable then chiefly for rushing about in fast cars, as a result of which he became known as 'Klaxon Clark'. Hugh was more tolerant of the young Clark, a strikingly handsome Old Etonian whose zest for life he found exhilarating, and whose antics resembled those of the young bloods he had admired in the 1930s. The two of them often went on long country walks together. Clark kept in contact with Hugh after taking a third-class degree in 1949, and indeed insisted on his admiration and affection for the older man, though the latter deplored him as 'an unemployed *roué* in the smart-crooked sub-world of the metropolis'. Following a visit from Clark in 1953 Hugh likened him to 'a weak-minded rake who every now and then goes to confess, with exemplary piety, to a grave, respectable old priest' – by which, of course, he meant himself.[20]

Johnny Dalkeith, heir to the Duke of Buccleuch, was a more dignified character, despite being a member of the raucous Bullingdon Club. He had come up to the House after war service, having enlisted in the RNVR in 1942 as an ordinary seaman. Like Lawrence Stone, he had served in destroyers; in due course he had been commissioned, and had ended the war a Lieutenant-Commander. He would succeed to the dukedom on his father's death in 1973, inheriting the vast family estates; on his own death in 2007 he was said to be the largest private landowner in Europe. In the spring of 1948, Hugh accepted an invitation to spend a weekend with the Duke and Duchess at Boughton,* their Northamptonshire house, vulgarly known as 'the English Versailles', where the 11,000-acre estate encompassed five villages. This was a period when owners were struggling to hang on to large estates; but Hugh found that the Buccleuchs 'still contrive to knock along quite comfortably in spite of capital levies, etc. – no nonsense about shutting up any of the 400 odd rooms, or cutting down any of the trees in the seventy miles of avenue'.[21]

Hugh was unabashed about assisting well-born young men to gain places at Christ Church. He described the admissions policy of the college as 'justice tempered by prejudice'. It was obvious that he was more at ease with public school boys from 'good' families. Some found this embarrassing: Jacob Rothschild, for example. But it was obvious too that he favoured intellect most of all, and this was a quality common to young men of all classes. After he came to know Bernard Berenson in 1947, Hugh would often suggest that pupils visiting Italy should call on him; in doing so he would not discriminate between those from grand and modest backgrounds. In 1949 he asked Berenson whether David Hopkins might call. 'He is quite the best pupil I have at present,' wrote Hugh. 'He is very young & very enthusiastic and has a very clear mind and is an engaging character. He hasn't had many opportunities of moving in the world,' Hugh continued, 'but his intellectual purity, which I find very attractive, makes him at ease anywhere.'[22]

'Socially, I am a snob,' Hugh confessed:

I like the world of grace and leisure and the opulence necessary to maintain it. But in fact, though I always look for it there first, I seldom find it in its traditional haunts, and recognise that the upper classes more often betray than cultivate their natural opportunities. I am continually disgusted by the triviality and vulgarity of the great world, and bored by its lack of education. And yet, since it remains the likeliest haunt of the virtues it has refused to cultivate, I suppose I shall always be more at home there than in the virtuous dwellings of the poor.

Hugh relished the *beau monde*. He spent weekends at country houses, carried there at high speed in Lancias and Lagondas, and darted down to London for parties. In the summer of 1946 he attended 'a very grand dance' at Claridge's, as he boasted to his brother, 'Winston was there, and the King

---

* One of three family seats, the others being Bowhill House in the Borders and Drumlanrig Castle in Dumfries. The family also owns Dalkeith Palace in Midlothian.

of Yugoslavia, and of course the Prof (who never misses a social function); and there was plenty to drink; so I quite enjoyed it.'[23] Some years later Pamela Berry* would remark that Hugh had been taken up by all the great London hostesses, and that she was always meeting him at every grand party.[24] In 1951 he would be one of about a hundred people 'of diverse talents, artistic and social' invited by Lord Rothermere, proprietor of the *Daily Mail*, and his wife (soon to become Mrs Ann Fleming) to a party, after the first night of Noël Coward's play *Relative Values*. To his dismay Hugh found himself next to Princess Margaret, notorious for being difficult and offhand, even rude, when bored; but according to Lady Rothermere he acquitted himself well, making the Princess laugh before being supplanted by the Master himself. He had met Coward before, at the bedside of the ailing Sybil Colefax: obviously a lively occasion, because she wrote to him afterwards that their 'wonderful meeting' had 'gone the round of London'.[25]

His private life was a mystery to colleagues and pupils alike. Some assumed him asexual, others homosexual. A fragment of overheard conversation provides a possible clue. An undergraduate, in his rooms for a tutorial when the telephone rang, heard a female voice at the other end say, 'You can come over now. He's gone out.' He assumed that his tutor was having an affair with a married woman.

At Christ Church Hugh was determined to revive some of his pre-war indulgences. His enjoyment of eating and drinking was so conspicuous that among the undergraduates he acquired the nickname 'Pleasure-Loper'. He resumed hunting with the Whaddon and the Bicester. In the early mornings he could often be seen exercising a pack of hounds in Christ Church Meadow. One of his pupils never forgot the sight of him clanking into the Cathedral to read the lesson at Evensong fresh from the chase, wearing a surplice over hunting gear. Hunting-horns littered his rooms. In 1946, at a meeting of the XX Club, which combined young unmarried dons with the older undergraduates returned from war service, Hugh spoke against the motion, proposed by Gilbert Ryle, that 'Hunting is the pursuit of the uneatable by the unspeakable'. Ryle accused his opponent of suffering from a severe dose of 'Tallyhosis'. Hugh wrote a dialogue on fox-hunting, continuing the debate which he had begun with Tom Armstrong by arguing with himself: which he tried, unsuccessfully, to get Cyril Connolly to publish in *Horizon*, a serious, high-minded magazine of literature and the arts. His protagonist in the dialogue attempted to prove that fox-hunting, far from being a 'reactionary, unscholarly pursuit' as his colloquist claimed,

---

* Pamela Berry, only daughter of Viscount Kemsley, owner of *The Sunday Times* and the *Daily Sketch*. In 1941 she had married the Marquess of Huntly.

was in fact 'the most intellectual pastime in the world, the sole relaxation worthy of a philosopher's leisure'; before admitting that 'I go hunting, and have gone hunting, and shall, I hope, continue to go hunting, for pleasure, pure pleasure'.[26]

Like Hugh, Dick White was a history graduate, a former pupil of Masterman's. He had appreciated the historical importance of Hugh's inquiry into the death of Hitler from the outset, and urged him to use the material that he had gathered to write a book. Journalists were already conducting their own investigations, willing to speculate when facts were unavailable. As Hugh recognised, the subject provided an opportunity to write a classic. Most works of contemporary history are quickly superseded as new evidence becomes available. But in this case the circumstances were exceptional, even unique. 'The theatre in which the action took place was closed; the actors were few and known; there were no seats for the public or the press; no reviews; no bulletins. The primary documents were few, and these were in my hands. Theoretically therefore the story could be told without fear of later correction.' Time has shown this theory to be correct. Hugh's book *The Last Days of Hitler* remains in print, more than sixty years after its first publication; and though others have written on this subject subsequently, no one has significantly altered the picture first drawn by him.

The dramatic possibilities of a study of the last months of the Third Reich had occurred to Hugh the previous summer, when his interrogation of General Berger had provided barely credible details of that disintegrating regime in all its exotic strangeness. Back in 1943 Hugh had read transcripts of conversations between two captured German generals recorded without their knowledge, in which the pair fulminated about the bizarre behaviour of the Nazi leaders, Göring in particular. Hugh boggled at the extraordinary details revealed in these eavesdrops.

His subsequent inquiry into Hitler's fate had further fired his imagination. Stumbling down the dark stairs and wading through the flooded passages and noisome, cell-like rooms of Hitler's bunker, Hugh had been overwhelmed by a sense of terrible irony. An all-powerful tyrant, whose bullying oratory had electrified vast crowds at mass rallies, had passed his last weeks hiding underground in this squalid burrow, ranting to a dwindling entourage. As he fingered the sodden, disintegrating papers that the Russians had unaccountably left undisturbed, Hugh identified the megalomaniac architectural plans that Hitler and Goebbels had studied together, while overhead the Russian shells rained down constantly on their ruined capital, and the ground shook under the impact of their detonation. 'And yet, however circumscribed, however insulated from reality, from the great

events around it, the action in the bunker was somehow not trivial or parochial or irrelevant, for it symbolised and shadowed the greater drama
outside: the drama of a not few days but of a whole generation.' The last days
in this small shelter encapsulated 'the last convulsions of a European agony'.

> How could I fail to reflect on this nemesis of a pernicious ideology and the stu-
> pefying insolence of absolute power? What historian could fail to respond to such
> a challenge, such an opportunity? As for presentation, the situation itself was so
> dramatic, so bizarre, that it needed no rhetoric: it merely had to be set out.[27]

Hugh took as his starting-point the 'July Plot' of 20 July 1944, when a
group of middle-ranking army officers failed in their attempt to assassinate
Hitler and overthrow the Nazi Party. This was followed soon after by the
Allied breakout from Normandy, opening 'the last act in the tragedy of
Germany'. The remainder of the drama was determined by the inexorable
advance of the Allied armies. Hitler's Germany contracted, pressed from
each side by overwhelmingly superior forces, shrinking to a cramped,
underground bunker. This was a story with its own dynamic, moving
inexorably towards an apocalyptic end.

First there was a hurdle to clear: since Hugh had gathered much of his
source material in an official inquiry, any book arising out of this would
need official approval. In practice, this meant that it would require authorisation by the Joint Intelligence Committee, of which White was then
secretary. He advised Hugh not to submit the idea for approval beforehand.
'No government committee will ever sanction a proposal of which they
cannot foresee the effect,' he warned; 'but if you were to write it first, and
take the risk of their decision, and then submit the text to them, they would
at least be able to see the limits of what they were allowing'.[28]

Hugh began to write, working in the evenings during term time. He had
already formed a mature view of his subject. His wartime observations had
convinced him that 'the Nazi state was not (in any significant use of the
word) totalitarian; and that its leading politicians were not a government
but a court – a court as negligible in its power of ruling, as incalculable in
its capacity for intrigue, as any oriental sultanate.' In his opening chapter –
'Hitler and his Court' – Hugh used the same terminology that he had
employed in 'The German Intelligence Service and the War', the booklet
he had written in his final few months in the War Room. 'The structure of
German politics and administration, instead of being (as the Nazis
claimed), "pyramidical" and "monolithic", was in fact a confusion of private
empires, private armies, and private intelligence services.' Hugh depicted
the leading Nazis as unscrupulous courtiers, greedily feasting off the spoils
of conquest, jostling for favour, ever ready to belittle a rival and even,
in the end, to abandon their leader. The story demanded a satirist: the

characters were so absurd, their behaviour so grotesque, their ideology so horrible; only ridicule could touch them. Like the historian Tacitus, Hugh chronicled the death of a tyranny; and, like the satirist Juvenal, he skewered his victims by making them ludicrous.

It would become a maxim of Hugh's that a good book should be written 'for someone'. His book on the last days of Hitler was written for Logan Pearsall Smith, 'in the sense that I had him as a critical reader before my eyes when I wrote it'[29] – though now that he was dead his criticisms could never be other than conjectural. It had been Smith who had inspired in Hugh the ambition to write a work of lasting value: a book 'that someone, one day, will mention in the same breath as Gibbon'. The comparison was bold, but irresistible: had not Gibbon too chronicled the fall of a once-mighty empire? Gibbon's example was constantly in Hugh's mind as he worked on the book, even if he disclaimed the comparison. In a letter congratulating Freddie Ayer on obtaining a Chair in philosophy at University College, London, Hugh said that whereas he had little chance of becoming a second Gibbon, Ayer should not lightly sacrifice his own prospects of emulating Hume.[30]

He wrote in longhand, in the pages of an exercise book, working very fast. A pencilled calculation on the manuscript indicates that he kept a running total of the number of words written. Dates stamped at intervals in the pages of the manuscript suggest that more than two-thirds of the book was written in a mere four weeks, between 18 February and 15 March 1946. Hugh was producing around 2,000 words each day: a creditable pace for a journalist rushing out a topical work, but one almost unheard-of for a serious scholar. It helped that he had already assimilated all the material and had formed his conclusions in the course of carrying out his inquiry. Even so, his fluency remains impressive.

In the spring vacation Hugh flew to Nuremberg, where those accused of war crimes were being tried, to collect further evidence. He had cadged a lift on an RAF plane, thanks to his friend Solly Zuckerman, formerly Chief Scientific Advisor to the British Bombing Survey Unit. 'It was all arranged (like so many such arrangements) over a glass of port in Oxford. All Oxford dons, I find, have been, for the past six years, controlling enormous and highly secret <u>rackets</u>; so that in an Oxford common room almost <u>anything</u> can be arranged with the greatest ease.' Though now demobilised, Hugh was allowed to interrogate several of the prisoners awaiting trial in the guise of a British officer. One of these was the SS doctor Karl Gebhardt, soon to be notorious for his surgical experiments on concentration camp inmates, particularly women; he would be convicted of crimes against humanity and sentenced to death by execution. In his role as a press representative, Hugh claimed a front seat at the trials of several leading Nazis. 'I got great pleasure from Ribbentrop's defence which completely sabotaged Göring, and incidentally hasn't defended Ribbentrop either.'[31] While in Germany he was able to interview a few more of those who had been present during the last days in the bunker and who had surfaced since his inquiry had been completed, including two of Hitler's secretaries.

By mid-May the manuscript was substantially complete. Hugh sent it to White, who had expressed himself eager to read it. The book was considered by a JIC sub-committee on 14 June. Hugh rightly anticipated that Menzies would be opposed to publication, out of instinctive timidity rather than for any logical reason. 'Tim' Milne, now promoted to Colonel, attended the meeting as Menzies's representative, but prevaricated ineffectively under pressure from the committee chairman, Harold Caccia. JIC gave its approval, subject to the condition that no 'M' material (obtained from clandestine tape recordings of high-ranking German prisoners of war) was to be used. Another stipulation was that the book should not be published until the trials of the principals at Nuremberg were complete. The committee recognised that, far from being harmful, publication of the book offered propaganda benefits in helping to prevent the creation of a Hitler myth. It recommended that 'some responsible commander in authority at the time of the incidents described' be asked to contribute a foreword, as a means of adding weight to the book. Two individuals were mentioned by name: Field Marshal Lord Montgomery and Marshal of the RAF Lord Tedder, who had been Deputy Supreme Commander of the Allied Expeditionary Force under Eisenhower.[32] Of the two, Hugh greatly preferred the latter. Tedder accepted his invitation, supplying a short foreword in October after reading the proofs. Hugh had approached Tedder via Solly Zuckerman, who had worked closely with Tedder in the British Bombing Survey Unit. Zuckerman also agreed to write to Alfred Hitchcock about the possibility of a film based on the book, which led to a meeting with Hitchcock's associate, the impresario Sidney Bernstein.

From an early stage Hugh was alive to the book's commercial possibilities. He sought advice from Dick White, whose brother worked in publishing. 'I was thinking of Hamish Hamilton,' he explained. 'Macmillan published my first book on Laud,' he continued, 'but are rather mugwumpish, I think.' He mentioned other publishers, including Faber. Collins 'have some advantages, but seem to me pretty low, as do Hutchinson (only lower)'. White recommended Hugh to check that the prospective publisher would have sufficient paper available, given the shortages arising from wartime exigencies. Before the book had been given the go-ahead by the Joint Intelligence Committee Hugh wrote to Hamish Hamilton, an enterprising publisher who had approached him speculatively the previous November. Hamilton had already lured Hugh's lively colleague A.J.P. Taylor away from Macmillan. Hugh's letter explained that he was unable to submit the manuscript of the book for consideration until it had been approved by the relevant authorities. He was writing in similar terms to Macmillan, and asked for answers to various questions: how much paper would be made available for the first printing; the speed at which the book might be published; and the prospects for sales in America. He cited advice he had received from White, that a first impression of 25,000 or possibly 50,000 might be justified. Hamilton responded enthusiastically, but when Hugh asked him to propose terms, he declined, pointing out that it was difficult to give any undertaking about the number he would print or the royalties he would offer without having read a line of the script. Hamilton was sceptical of the need for such a large first printing. Since (as he now understood) Hugh was under an obligation to show it first to Macmillan, 'it would be irregular for me to suggest terms before they have reached a decision'.[33] Hugh was offended by this half-hearted response.

Macmillan had the advantage of an opinion from one of their authors, John Wheeler-Bennett, the historian specialising in modern Germany whose Ealing house Hugh had occupied with Walter Gill at the beginning of the war. Wheeler-Bennett read the book in typescript, and was clearly bullish about its commercial value, because Macmillan moved rapidly to secure the rights. While still in discussion with Hamish Hamilton, Hugh wrote to Lovat Dickson at Macmillan, confirming his understanding of a verbal offer of terms: a royalty of 15 per cent on the first 5,000 copies sold, and 20 per cent thereafter, 'dependent on your being able to produce the book fairly quickly'.[34] A month later, once the book had been approved by JIC, Hugh sent Dickson the manuscript by registered post, and two days afterwards returned to him a signed contract for the book.[35] Hugh was still at work on an epilogue, in which he attempted to answer a question posed by Harold Caccia (who described the book as 'enthralling'): how had this 'collection of monkeys' been able to control Germany and come close to conquering Europe? Hugh incorporated Caccia's monkey image into his text.[36] By 14 July he was able to tell Charles Stuart that his book was finished.[37] He planned to call it *Hitler's End*.

There then followed a lull, while the book was set up in proof. Hugh resisted pressure from Macmillan's American company to publish quickly, pointing out, *inter alia*, that he was under an obligation to delay publication until after the judgments at Nuremberg. Having worked so hard, he wanted a holiday. 'I am leaving to be abroad on 14 August,' he informed Dickson, 'and will be out of reach of correspondence for perhaps a month.' He had reserved a passage by ship to Iceland – 'faute de mieux', he told his brother, referring to the fact that travel in Europe was very difficult immediately after the war. Meanwhile, he arranged for 'some critical friends who have been associated with me in the war' – Ryle, Hart and 'the Prof' – to read the proofs in his absence.

Hugh spent three weeks in Iceland, alone for much of the time, strolling along the seashore, walking in the mountains, watching the birds, fishing for trout and char and camping in the wilderness. In his notebooks he gave a rather mannered account of his holiday. He wrote that his only companions on these expeditions were his books; he carried with him editions of Horace and Herodotus, and the letters of Charles Lamb. At last, one afternoon, he 'felt a thirst for a pint of English beer', and made his way to Reykjavik, but when he enquired for a boat home, he was told that there would be none sailing that way until at least the following spring. A chance meeting in the street with an old Faroese sea captain whom he had befriended on the voyage out led him to an Icelandic trawler-owner, on the brink of sending his ship to England to sell his catch of fish. 'So I leapt aboard, and after four days of sousing tempest, night and day, gladly I saw the rock of St Kilda, and dropped at last into the lee of the Hebrides, and glid in calm water down to Fleetwood, and took train to Northumberland, and was at home again.'[38]

On 18 September he wrote from his parents' house in Alnwick to inform Dickson that he was once more 'in operation'. Dickson had reported that Macmillan's American company was anxious to call the book *The Last Days of Hitler* rather than *Hitler's End*. Hugh sensibly assented.[39] Also waiting for him on his return were messages from his proof-readers. 'I have been merciless about commas of which I think you use too many,' commented Ryle; adding blandly, 'It is a good story & well told.' Lord Cherwell was more enthusiastic. 'I think the book is most excellent, quite fascinating reading and in my view sure to be a best-seller,' he wrote. Cherwell provided a number of editorial suggestions, most of which Hugh incorporated, though he baulked at Cherwell's assertion that Hitler had been a coward, on the basis of a clipping from the *Sunday Express* of an article on the subject by a psychiatrist.[40] 'I like having my opinion of professional psychiatrists confirmed,' commented Hugh, '& also my opinion of the worthlessness of unchecked human testimony, which I have derived from this enquiry. The psychiatrist, you will remember, quotes Göring's graphic account of how he & Hitler together saw the pictures of Mussolini's body hung upside-down in Milan ... In fact Göring saw Hitler for the last time on 20 April. Mussolini was executed on 28 April. Hitler shot himself on 30 April. Göring may have seen pictures of Musso's body in his American captivity, but not before. Hitler can never have seen any.'[41]

One task remained. On 25 October, back at Christ Church, Hugh drafted a succinct preface. He acknowledged those 'many friends, both British and

American, who have helped me in the composition of this book', but named only one: Dick White. It was White who had conceived the idea of the inquiry into Hitler's death, and who had invited Hugh to undertake it; and it was White who had then encouraged Hugh to write the book. 'He is thus both the first parent and the ultimate midwife of this book; and I dedicate it to him.'

Good news followed over the next few weeks: *The Daily Telegraph* agreed to serialise the book before publication, and it was taken by the Book Society, a book club. Hugh was pleased by these developments, but irritated that the Americans intended to print only 5,000 copies, which seemed to him 'excessively unambitious'. Macmillan's London office planned a first printing of 30,000, of which 15,000 were for the Book Society.* This was 'very satisfactory', he commented in a letter to Dickson; 'do you think that it can be used as a lever on the New York Company?'[42]

One startling development was an anonymous letter from a Zionist organisation in Lisbon sentencing Hugh to death 'by new and sudden means'. Presumably those who made this threat misunderstood the nature of the book. Dickson was 'aghast' at the news, though he deduced from Hugh's cool tone that 'I take the announcement more seriously than you seem to do'. Hugh sent this 'elegant fan-letter', together with the envelope it came in, to Guy Liddell at MI5.[43]

The Last Days of Hitler was published on 18 March 1947. Hugh gave a dinner in Oxford to celebrate. Dick White thanked him afterwards for 'a really magnificent' evening. Hugh wrote to Peter Ramsbotham in Germany, lamenting that he could not have been there. 'It was a splendid party. From the ends of the earth they came, Solly Zuckerman from remote septentrional north of Birmingham; Dick White from the Mohammedan East of London; & Herbert Hart was there, & Denys Page, & Charles Stuart; & the oysters that were eaten, & the infinite succession of wines that were drunk, went on till 2.00 a.m., a Sardanapalian beano'.[44]

By this time it was clear that Cherwell's prediction had been correct: the book would be a bestseller. On 22 March, only a few days after publication, Hugh asked Lovat Dickson, on the advice of his accountants, if Macmillan could pay him £1,000 on account of royalties before the end of the tax year on 5 April. The total sum due to him in the first accounting period from sales of the British edition alone would be £3,849.† In America, *The Last Days of Hitler* was selected as a Book of the Month Club 'dual selection' for August; Hugh learned that his share

* On 13 December 1946 Dickson informed Hugh that in 1940 Macmillan had printed 1,500 copies of *Archbishop Laud*, of which 562 remained unsold.
† Hugh's annual stipend as a Student of Christ Church was £150, plus rooms and dining rights. He earned a further £300 p.a. as a History Faculty lecturer.

of the take would be a cool $30,000, 'a frightful sum of money', as he described it.* Success bred success. Offers arrived from newspapers willing to fund trips abroad; everybody wanted to hear from the 'young don who at the moment has the attention of the whole English-speaking world'.[45] An old friend wrote from Northumberland to tell him that 'I can't pick up a paper or switch on the wireless without hearing the name Hitler or Trevor-Roper'.[46] A week or so after publication, Hugh informed Stuart that he had 'been having a tremendous economic battle with the BBC, which I have thoroughly enjoyed'. The battle was over the fee payable for a radio adaptation, broadcast on the Third Programme. Hugh had successfully resisted the Corporation's attempt 'to fob me off with contemptible sums', though this hard bargaining prompted a disturbing thought: 'Am I becoming a Rowse?' The book would be translated into French, Flemish, Danish, Finnish, Swedish, Norwegian, Icelandic, Polish, Czech, Serbo-Croat, Hungarian, Greek, Italian, Spanish, Portuguese, Hebrew and even Thai. Pirated editions appeared in Bulgaria and Romania. To Hugh's amusement, the Bulgarian edition was suppressed by the Communist authorities on the grounds that it was 'too objective'; he delighted in this detail. 'Printing presses are at work throughout Europe, translating Hitler,' he boasted to Stuart. 'At this very moment a polysyllabic printing press is operating on it in Finland. Can Rowse beat this?'[47]

The one country where the book was not published was Germany. Though there was strong evidence of demand for a German edition, the Allied Control Commission, the only body at the time able to undertake such a venture, firmly declined to do so. The Control Commission's press office was quoted as saying that their policy was 'not to devote too much time to the past, but to concentrate on the positive tasks of reconstruction'. (Hugh looked into the possibility of obtaining compensation from the Foreign Office for lost sales in Germany.[48]) German language rights were sold instead to a Swiss publisher, Amstutz and Herdeg of Zurich, causing many later problems. The Prime Minister himself, Clement Attlee, made enquiries about a German translation after reading the book, because he felt that such 'a damning exposure of the character and intrigues of the Nazi leaders' ought to be distributed in Germany as widely as possible.[49] Discussions about a film based on the book petered out, and the possibility of a stage play, dramatised by R.C. Sherriff, came to nothing. Hugh was advised that, on top of the advance of $2,500 that he had already received, approximately $37,500 would be due to him from Macmillan's American company at the end of the first accounting period.

---

* The conversion rate in 1947 was $4.03 to the £.

His accountants advised him to buy an expensive car, rather than lose the money in tax. He contemplated buying a Rolls-Royce, but settled in the end for a grey Bentley, which he parked ostentatiously in Tom Quad.

Traveller

The Last Days of Hitler received prominent and enthusiastic reviews. *The Times* hailed the book as a masterpiece. 'Here is a bestseller, if ever there was one,' declared *The Spectator*'s reviewer, Alan Bullock, a Fellow of New College, Oxford, who was himself to write a bestselling biography of Hitler.* His review was headed 'A Theme for Gibbon'. Noel Annan lauded the book in the *New Statesman*, describing it as 'a triumph of scientific investigation'.[1] Alongside such public praise Hugh received many private letters of congratulation, from friends and strangers alike. One of these came from Lewis Namier, the eminent historian of eighteenth-century England, who had a special interest in Nazi Germany. 'I read your book, if I may say so, with the greatest interest and admiration,' wrote Namier. 'You have made a truly excellent job of it and combined very thorough scholarship with lightness of touch and a style which I am glad to see is not yet extinct in Oxford.' Praise from such a quarter was welcome. 'I am very glad,' replied Hugh; 'there is no one whose judgement on the subject I value more highly.'[2]

Robert Gathorne-Hardy told Hugh that he had been 'dazzled' by the book; 'the name Gibbon kept coming into my mind'. He recognised that it had been written – 'as we all try to write still' – for Logan Pearsall Smith, who 'would certainly have approved of it'. Lawrence Stone (by this time a college lecturer) was another admirer. 'The first chapter I found particularly illuminating and the whole, a most suggestive picture of court politics from which perhaps wider applications might be drawn on the general problems of personal government.' Stone addressed Hugh by his first name, an indication of their closeness at this time.[3]

Dawyck Haig was another who wrote to Hugh congratulating him on *The Last Days of Hitler*. This appears to have been the first time Haig had made contact since the 1930s, as he took the opportunity to thank Hugh for a letter he had received as a prisoner of war in Italy. 'It must be very pleasant to be just an ordinary don after all that,' mused Haig, 'but I suppose things have sadly changed since our days with regards to eating, drinking and hunting. Apparently there are few dons now who like to see "the young

---

* *Hitler: A Study in Tyranny* (1952).

gentlemen in top hats and tail coats". Towards the end of the year Haig came to Christ Church as Hugh's guest for an evening, and afterwards wrote to express his pleasure at seeing him again after so long 'just the same (you might say uncoarsened by success)'.[4]

Malcolm Muggeridge, on the other hand, thought Hugh 'rather full of himself' when he came to dinner, 'as a result of the great success of his book'. Muggeridge noted in his diary afterwards that 'when we asked him a few simple questions about Hitler: as what sort of pictures he liked, had he slept with Eva Braun, he seemed quite unable to give a cogent reply'. Muggeridge concluded that this was 'very typically donnish'. In fact Hugh had felt unable to discuss Hitler's sex life in front of Muggeridge's wife, Kitty, as he explained in a subsequent letter to Muggeridge. 'I was too discreet to announce last night the interesting fact that, according to medical files, Hitler derived sexual satisfaction from delivering speeches before great crowds of people, having confessed to experiencing orgasms at such times. I should add that this conclusion had been independently deduced by others, from the style and tempo of his oratory!'[5]

A substantial number of letters praising *The Last Days of Hitler* came from America, and among them was one from the economist John Kenneth Galbraith, who in his capacity as a director of the US Strategic Bombing Survey had been in Germany immediately after the surrender. Galbraith revealed that he had contemplated preparing his own record of the last days in the bunker based on eyewitness accounts, and to this end had questioned several of the Nazi leaders while they were still being held at Flensburg. 'On reading your account I felt rather happy that I had abandoned the notion,' he wrote to Hugh; 'you have done it with so much skill, precision and historical sense that any lesser effort would have seemed sorry indeed by comparison.' Galbraith offered his own impressions of Speer, whom he had interrogated at length. He had decided that Speer was 'a really superb actor', presenting himself in the manner most likely to create a favourable opinion in his captors. Hugh was very interested in Galbraith's account, and conceded that he might be right about Speer.[6]

In the midst of all the praise one aspect of the book stood out for criticism. Hugh had not been able to resist the opportunity to take a few sideswipes at organised religion. 'The author has not yet entirely outgrown the adolescent anti-clericalism which disfigured the opening and the concluding pages of his life of Laud,' declared the *Church Times* reviewer, who particularly objected to Hugh's remark that Hitler 'had no trouble from the Churches'.[7] The same jibe upset the suffragan Bishop of Munich. 'In my opinion,' wrote the Bishop, 'you could only have reached this judgement in ignorance of the facts.' Hugh agreed that individual Christians had fought actively against Nazism, but he could find no evidence that the

Churches had done so, other than in trying to defend their jurisdictions.[8]

Catholics found his barbs especially wounding. He had described Goebbels as 'the prize-pupil of a Jesuit seminary' who 'retained to the end the distinctive character of his education'. This analogy between the methods of the Nazis and the Jesuits was offensive to many Catholic readers. 'As the Jesuits created a system aimed at preventing knowledge,' Hugh had written, 'so Goebbels created a system of propaganda, ironically styled "public enlightenment", which successfully persuaded people that black was white.' He gave further offence by likening Himmler to the recently beatified Cardinal Robert Bellarmine,* on the grounds that both men were kind to animals. Hugh soon found that by straying into casual criticism of the Catholic Church he had trodden on an ant-heap. A review in *The Tablet* by a Jesuit priest, Father James Brodrick, questioned his authority for his sneers. The Jesuits, Brodrick maintained, had been among the victims of Nazism: 'We, the living members of the Society of Jesus, are sufficiently capable of looking after ourselves, but we cherish the memory of our martyred dead and very much resent any furtive and despicable attempt, worthy of Goebbels at his worst, to plant swastikas on their graves.'[9]

Alongside such public criticism *The Last Days of Hitler* elicited a number of private letters of protest. One of the most good-tempered came from Father Bernard Basset, SJ, who as a student at Campion Hall had known Hugh in the 1930s. After congratulating him on 'your latest triumph', Basset gently remonstrated with him for making 'what appears to me to be a very unfair attack on the Jesuits'. He received a friendly though unapologetic reply; but when Basset continued to debate some of the points he had raised, Hugh sent him a stinging response, accusing him of malice. Basset, clearly shaken, apologised, bringing an abrupt end to the exchange.[10]

Among this correspondence was a sneering letter correcting 'inaccuracies in your popular study' from a stranger, on writing-paper headed with the elaborate monogram 'EW': the novelist Evelyn Waugh, a writer whose prose Hugh greatly admired. Waugh proceeded to challenge a number of references in the book to the Catholic Church. The tone of his letter was 'exquisitely offensive', Hugh recalled later. 'Don't answer,' ended Waugh. 'But if you find you are wrong, why not put it right in subsequent editions?'[11]

This apparent lack of concern was deceptive: Waugh decided to attack Hugh in public. Before doing so he wrote to Maurice Bowra to find out more about his intended target. 'Trevor-Roper is a fearful man,' Bowra replied; 'short-sighted, with dripping eyes, shows off all the time, sucks up to me, boasts, is far from poor owing to his awful book, on every page of

---

* Bellarmine had been one of the judges who sentenced the philosopher Giordano Bruno to be burnt at the stake for heresy. He had also cross-examined Galileo.

which there is a howler.'* Bowra's spite is surprising, indeed shocking; though according to Noel Annan, who had known Bowra well, outbursts against even his dearest friends were common in his letters. Perhaps he was still smarting from Hugh's humiliating exposure of his blunder in *The Oxford Book of Greek Verse in Translation*. 'Please persecute him as much as you can,' Bowra continued. 'Something in The Tablet would wound him a lot. He is very thin-skinned.'[12]

Waugh duly wrote to *The Tablet* appending a note to Father Brodrick's review. 'There was not the smallest reason why Mr Trevor-Roper should introduce Catholic theologians into his nasty story,' his letter concluded. 'They are dragged in ignorantly, maliciously and irrelevantly. Mr Trevor-Roper had a sensational subject. Apparently he thought it too good an opportunity to be missed for giving wide currency to his prejudices.'[13] Though Hugh replied to Brodrick's review, he ignored the comments appended by Waugh. Shortly afterwards he learned that an abusive, possibly obscene, letter had been sent under his name to a titled lady;[†] her secretary, shocked by its contents, had referred the matter to the police, who identified Waugh as the writer.[14] This was the beginning of a feud, which continued for years, occasionally surfacing in public. Society hostesses schemed to bring them together, to spice up their parties, but Hugh contrived to avoid such a confrontation, aware that while he might match Waugh in print, he could not hope to equal Waugh's rudeness in person. These two antagonists were more similar than either might like to admit.[‡] Both had cultivated in Oxford a romantic vision of aristocratic grace and ease, contrasting with their middle-class backgrounds. Both had been attracted to Catholicism by Father D'Arcy, at a similar stage in life. The difference was that Hugh had not succumbed to the lure of the Mother Church.

Organised protests by American Catholics severely embarrassed the Macmillan Company of New York. At least one of these hinted that if the book were not withdrawn, Catholic schools might boycott textbooks published by Macmillan. The President, George P. Brett Jr, proposed to tell complainants that the book would be corrected in its next printing. Hugh refused to allow this. Lovat Dickson attempted to act as mediator. Over lunch he told Hugh frankly that he thought the references to Jesuits which had so upset Catholics in America were 'gratuitous', and that 'the pain they

---

* On 10 August 1991 (twenty years after Bowra's death) Hugh replied to Waugh's biographer, Martin Stannard, who had sent him a copy of this letter, with the assurance that he did not object to its publication, 'though I did raise my eyebrows on reading it. I had always thought of Maurice as a friend: clearly an error.'
† Almost certainly Lady Pamela Berry, the attractive wife of the proprietor of the *Daily Telegraph*.
‡ In his *Times* obituary of his Peterhouse foe, Maurice Cowling would write that 'in all but religion, Trevor-Roper was almost an exact replica' of Waugh.

gave to a great many people must have very much outweighed any moderate satisfaction you could have got through uttering them'. But Hugh would not be cajoled, or bullied. He was willing to consider modifying or removing objectionable passages in the course of any general revision of the text for a second edition, but he was determined not to surrender to 'blackmailers'. Brett threatened to allow the book to go out of print rather than reprint it unchanged; Hugh responded that he would take legal advice about the voiding of the contract, seek to reissue the book with another American publisher, and announce the reasons for this change to the press. At this point Harold Macmillan intervened and successfully calmed each side in the escalating dispute.[15]

Hugh removed some of the passages that had incensed Catholic readers from the second edition of *The Last Days of Hitler*, which appeared in 1950. He found that he was mistaken in believing Goebbels to have been educated by Jesuits, and deleted the flippant inferences he had drawn from this. He also toned down his portrayal of Hitler's pilot, Hanna Reitsch, who had threatened legal action. These were very minor changes. More significant was the addition of a long introduction, explaining how the evidence on which his narrative rested had been accumulated. 'This is an incomparable book, by far the best book written on any aspect of the second German war,' purred A.J.P. Taylor, reviewing the second edition in the *New Statesman*: 'a book sound in its scholarship, brilliant in its presentation, a delight for historian and layman alike. No words of praise are too strong for it.'[16]

On the day that the first edition of *The Last Days of Hitler* was published, Ronald Lewin, later a military historian but then a BBC radio producer, wrote to Hugh proposing that he should give a talk about the book. Discussions stalled over the fee, since the amount Hugh demanded was much larger than usual. As a result the project eventually had to be abandoned. This tussle ran concurrently with the battle over the fee for the radio adaptation of the book. Hugh gained a reputation within the BBC for driving a hard bargain, and thereafter producers would be wary in their dealings with him.

In January 1947 he had made his first broadcast on the BBC, reviewing the Hitler–Mussolini correspondence which had just been published. A few weeks later A.J.P. Taylor suggested that he should contribute a talk on Disraeli to a series on nineteenth-century British prime ministers. Hugh cribbed most of his material from Blake, who was at work on a biography of Disraeli. Afterwards the producer assessed his script as 'excellent', his enunciation as 'good' and his voice 'slightly academic and plummy'. The producer of a later broadcast would describe his voice as 'clear, slightly nasal'; and another as 'a little like a tipsy bishop'.

Hugh's high profile led to further invitations to broadcast, despite his demands for high fees. Another BBC producer reported that Hugh's 'clear baritone' voice was 'easy to listen to', with only the 'slightest suggestion of superiority', and commented that Hugh was 'alive to his own importance'.[17] Later the veteran producer Anna Kallin would summarise in-house opinion of Hugh: 'He is an excellent broadcaster, with a great gift of the gab, well-constructed scripts and always flashes of wit. But one must be <u>very</u> careful scrutinizing scripts for libel, or simply gratuitously offensive remarks about contemporaries. His great bee in his bonnet is Catholicism, and he can bring that in to almost anything ... Having said all this, I would still recommend him as a most lively, entertaining and witty speaker.'[18]

Less than a fortnight after the publication of *The Last Days of Hitler*, Hugh returned to Germany, funded by *The New York Times*, to gather material on the German opposition to Hitler. This was the culmination of months of activity. While in Iceland the previous summer, he had been commissioned by a local magazine to write an article on the 'July Plot', the failed attempt to assassinate Hitler and to overthrow the Nazi regime. He had returned from Iceland 'so exhilarated in morale that I am contemplating writing another book', as he told Stuart Hampshire soon afterwards. He envisaged a 'prequel' to *The Last Days of Hitler*, in the same style and using the same type of evidence. Hugh had become interested in the German opposition while in SIS. He was fascinated by the details of the Plot: such as the fact that Count von Stauffenberg, who had been so maimed while fighting in North Africa that he had only one hand with three fingers remaining, and as a result had been compelled to use his teeth to remove the fuse from the bomb before bringing it into the conference room. The Plot had been 'the only determined act of opposition to Nazism in twelve years of dictatorship'. Hugh was keen to find out more about the plans of the conspirators, both for the coup itself and for what would happen afterwards. It was a tragic story, of considerable historical importance in itself. Moreover, there was wider significance in studying both how dictatorships could be overthrown, and the terrible risks involved. In Tacitus's account of the conspiracy against Nero in AD 65, Hugh saw an exact prefiguration of the motives and weaknesses and betrayals of the plot against Hitler.

Unfortunately it was very difficult to establish the facts about the Plot. Most of the conspirators had been executed or murdered by the Gestapo soon afterwards. Many of the records had been destroyed, or had fallen into the hands of the Russians, 'which for practical purposes is the same thing'. The evidence of individual witnesses was unreliable. 'Just as all

Frenchmen, in 1945, turned out to have belonged to the Resistance Movement, so all Germans are now turning out to have belonged to the Opposition, and most of them to have had a hand in the Plot.' Hugh believed that the study should be made quickly, before memories faded and the surviving evidence was lost or destroyed.[19]

He began busily collecting information on the subject, from both official and unofficial sources. An ever-increasing number of works on the German opposition were being published, in English and German, and Hugh devoured these as soon as he could lay hands on them. Through his MI5 contacts he gained access to captured documents and prisoner inter-rogations; and from a former War Room colleague, Major Burrows Smith of the American Counter Intelligence Corps, he obtained more of the same; Peter Ramsbotham sent over 'a great haystack' of papers from Germany; Hugh exchanged material with other writers working on associated sub-jects, including John Wheeler-Bennett, Basil Liddell Hart and Chester Wilmot;* and he contacted journalists who had reported on the Plot, such as Donald McLachlan of *The Times*. He also endeavoured to get in touch with surviving members of the German opposition and their families; this had been the primary purpose of his visit to Germany in March 1947. He wrote an account of the Plot for the BBC Home Service, to be broadcast on the third anniversary of the attempted coup; portions of the narrative were dramatised, with actors speaking the parts of the participants, intercut with extracts from Hitler's broadcast to the German people immediately after the failed assassination.[20]

Just as he was getting going, however, he had received from Macmillan's American company proofs of *Day of the Whirlwind: the Story of Germany's Underground*, a new book by Allen W. Dulles, head of the Office of Strategic Services in Switzerland during the war, which proved to cover much of the same ground. Hugh thought highly of Dulles's book and recommended Macmillan to publish a British edition. 'An American has got in ahead of me,' he wrote disconsolately to Ramsbotham. Nonetheless he went ahead with his visit to Germany, where he met Stauffenberg's brother, among others.

In his disappointment, Hugh was tempted by an approach from the educational publishers Evans Brothers to write a different book (no record of the proposed subject survives). He floated the possibility that he might accept this commission past Harold Macmillan, who responded firmly: 'I can assure you that an author makes a great error in not concentrating all his books under a single publisher.' He referred to the book on the July

---

* Wilmot put him in touch with Peter Bielenberg, a figure on the fringes of the July Plot, who was staying in England before settling in Ireland.

Plot. 'I have been looking forward to that volume, which I feel sure will be of considerable importance.' He urged Hugh to turn down the approach from Evans. 'If we thought that you would like to vary your work by having some other book on hand, such as a Life of Disraeli,' he continued, 'we should of course be very glad to publish it for you.'[21] Later that year Hugh received another approach, this time not from a publisher but from J.R.M. Butler, the Regius Professor of Modern History at Cambridge. Butler had been appointed chief military historian and Editor of the official military history of the war and was looking for contributors to this massive, multi-volume project.[22] But Hugh had too much on his plate already to contemplate helping himself to more.

Over the next few years he maintained his interest in the July Plot, though he pursued it with less energy than before. In March 1948, for example, he told Dietrich Bonhoeffer's brother-in-law it was 'not quite true' that he was writing a book on the German Resistance Movement, 'though I have collected a good deal of material and hope to have the opportunity of using it in some form or another'. In 1950 he admitted to a German professor that he had contemplated writing a book on the July Plot. 'But on examining the matter closely, I decided that a complete account could not be made at so early a date, and I have not, in fact, gone farther with the plan, although I am interested in the subject and continue to collect information.'[23] Some years later he reviewed Constantine Fitzgibbon's 'scholarly and sensible' book on the subject.[24]

Hugh had been wryly amused to find that Dulles had made use of the 'M' material that he himself had been forbidden from quoting in *The Last Days of Hitler*. He began corresponding with Dulles, and called on him at Claridge's when Dulles visited England in May 1947. It was a useful contact; in 1953 Dulles would be appointed the first civilian head of the CIA.

In the package that Hugh sent to Dulles after their meeting was an article he had written on the German opposition. This had been published in *Polemic*, a new publication which described itself, somewhat inaccurately, as a 'magazine of philosophy, psychology, and aesthetics'. In fact *Polemic* was willing to publish intelligent articles on almost any topic. Like Stuart Hampshire, Hugh had been introduced to *Polemic* by Freddie Ayer, a member of its editorial board. Its Editor, Humphrey Slater, was an ex-Communist who had fought on the Republican side during the Spanish Civil War. Slater tried to rise above the crude pro- *v.* anti-Communist mud-slinging which characterised so much intellectual discourse in the immediate post-war period, though he was not always successful in this.

These post-war years were a time of much hand-wringing about the need for a new philosophy to revive Western civilisation. The nightmare of Nazism, and the disastrous failure of the democracies to contain it, had created a void, with no lack of candidates willing to fill it. On one side were the Communists and 'fellow-travellers', who exerted a degree of influence on British intellectual life almost impossible to contemplate today. On the other were anti-Communist zealots, many of them former Communists themselves. Hugh was opposed to both. Intellectually he was anti-Communist, but he was mistrustful of those who advocated an anti-Communist crusade. He was repelled by prophets such as Arnold Toynbee who claimed to offer a spiritual solution to the moral problems of the post-war world. And in view of the supine attitude of the Vatican throughout the period of fascist rule in Europe, he found the hunger of certain English-speaking Catholics to secure the moral fruits of victory 'somewhat indecent'.

In an earlier number of *Polemic* Hugh had reviewed Karl Popper's *The Open Society and Its Enemies*, a defence of intellectual and social freedom against what Popper called 'historicism', the belief that human society is predestined and therefore predictable. He praised the book as 'a magnificent and timely achievement', closely reasoned and written in forceful and lucid prose. Popper's was 'by far the most important work of contemporary sociology', which had 'utterly demolished the philosophical basis of historicism'. Hugh liked the dichotomy advanced by Popper, between the 'Closed Society, in which men are governed by man-made, normative laws to which, nevertheless, divine origins and sanctions are naively attributed', and the 'Open Society, in which a distinction is made between objective facts and normative conventions which can be made and altered by free decision'. The Open Society was, in fact, rational society – the society to which Hugh wanted to belong.

Popper had attacked 'the three great tyrants of philosophy, Plato, Hegel and Marx'. Hugh's comments on the latter reveal the continuing impact of Marx on his thinking:

> As for Marx, the errors of his scientific system – his Hegelian dialectic, his false theory of value, his doctrine of class-war, the relativity of ideas and institutions (that most absurd and disastrous of his dogmas), the inevitable triumph (and cohesion) of the proletariat, the withering-away of the state – all these fallacies have now been exposed so often that Mr Popper can find little further to subtract from them. Nevertheless, in spite of these enormous errors, Marx remains in a class by himself. Not an aesthete like Plato, nor a toady of power like Hegel, he was at least inspired by a genuine humanitarianism; and even after his errors have been counted, the residue of his work has altered our whole intellectual world. We can no more think him away than we can live without electricity ... [25]

Polemic was never a commercial success; it appeared at irregular inter-vals, and ceased publication altogether after only a few years. Another member of its editorial board, whom Hugh got to know better around this time, was George Orwell. Though Orwell came from the activist Left and Hugh from the apolitical Right, they had plenty in common, sharing a mistrust of both Communism and Catholicism. Indeed Orwell frequently linked the two, as enemies of intellectual freedom.[26] Hugh developed a deep respect for Orwell's independence, integrity and clear thinking. He was particularly impressed by Orwell's essay 'Politics and the English Language', published in *Horizon* in April 1946. In this and in other essays (and in his novels), Orwell stressed that just as oppression begins with the misuse of language, so freedom of thought requires clarity and simplicity of expres-sion. Hugh's exceptional sensitivity to language made him especially recep-tive to Orwell's message. His experience as an intelligence officer had nurtured in him a loathing for the euphemisms used by bureaucrats. For the rest of his career as a college tutor he would press Orwell's essays on undergraduate pupils as models of English prose.

In July 1947 Hugh left Oxford for the Continent in his new Bentley, with Robert Blake as his passenger. *The Observer* had offered him £60 a week* ('an immoral amount') to act as a special correspondent, reporting on political conditions in Western Europe – particularly France and Italy, both of which seemed vulnerable to Communist takeover in the late 1940s, as they struggled to recover from the economic devastation caused by the war. Hugh reached the conclusion that Communist strategy was contradictory. In trying to appeal to the 'obstinately conservative' peasantry, the Party in both countries adopted policies – for example, on food prices – contrary to the interests of industrial workers in the cities, the class which (according to classical Marxist theory) provided revolutionary impetus. In the first of his *Observer* articles, Hugh stated his firm belief that 'fascism can never revive in Italy'. Subsequently he reported on the policy of General de Gaulle's new political movement: anti-Communism and a presidential state. De Gaulle's appeal, he said, was the same as Louis Napoleon's a century before: 'My name is my programme.'[27]

The two Englishmen spent six weeks away, heading first for Italy, calling on Hugh's pre-war hosts at Oisilly en route and making a brief pilgrimage to Voltaire's château at Ferney, before taking the car over the Alps at the Simplon Pass. They remained in Italy until the end of July, then stayed three weeks in France on their way back, a week in Toulouse and a fortnight in Paris. In spite of living, so he claimed, in 'eremetical squalor and roman-

* Worth almost £2,000 in today's money.

tic austerity' in Paris, Hugh found afterwards that he had spent £200 there: two-thirds of his annual income as a university lecturer. In Italy, by contrast, he had lived 'in great opulence and comfort and plenty'.[28] Moreover he met Bernard Berenson, who was to become an important figure in his life, filling some, though not all, of the vacancy left by the death of Logan Pearsall Smith.

It was Logan's sister Alys Russell who had urged him to visit her brother-in-law. 'BB will love to see you to talk about Logan & books & politics,' she assured him.[29] Hugh telephoned Berenson as she had suggested, and found him not at I Tatti, his exquisite villa near Florence, but at Casa al Dono in Vallombrosa, his equally exquisite mountain retreat about twenty miles south-east of the city, where he retired to escape the summer heat. The two young dons were invited to lunch. Berenson proved to be a very small man with a white beard, immaculately dressed, with an imperious manner. Their hostess was Berenson's com-panion* Nicky Mariano, a large, serene woman with benevolent eyes and a sweet smile, described by Kenneth Clark as 'one of the most universally beloved people in the world'.[30]

Then in his early eighties, Berenson had for many years been celebrated, not only as the world's leading expert on Italian Renaissance art, but as a man of great gifts, almost a sage. In the public mind he was 'BB', more a phenomenon than an individual, identified with the Tuscan villa where he had lived since the beginning of the century and where he still held court, receiving distinguished visitors from around the world. Not the least of his achievements had been to overcome deprivation and disadvantage to enjoy a life of comfort and sophistication. He had been born in Lithuania, in what was then the Pale of Settlement, in 1865 (the same year as his future brother-in-law, Logan Pearsall Smith). His family, fleeing anti-Semitic pogroms, brought him at the age of ten to America, where his father worked as a pedlar. The young Berenson's outstanding intellectual qualities were soon evident, and these, combined with a capacity for hard work, took him first to Boston University, and then to Harvard, where he studied Oriental languages and fell under the influence of the philosopher William James. Afterwards he travelled in Italy and Greece, wandering on foot from place to place and living almost on air, enraptured by nature and by art. He began to study Renaissance painting; struck by the prevalent confusion about who had painted what, he resolved to introduce scientific principles into the process of attribution.

---

* She had been part of Berenson's household since 1919, when she joined as librarian. Berenson's wife Mary died in 1945, but long before that Miss Mariano had become, as Kenneth Clark put it, 'in effect, the second Mrs Berenson'.

In nursery clothes, c. 1917.

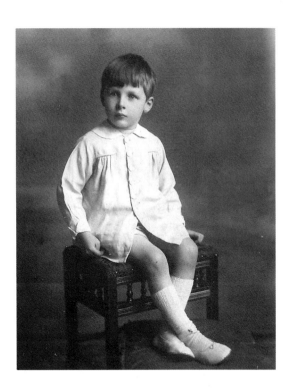

Hugh, wearing a tie a few years later, with his sister Sheila and younger brother Patrick.

'A man thwarted by life'.
Hugh's father, Dr Bertie Trevor-Roper, with Susie, in the garden of the family house in Alnwick.

'She never hugged her children.'
Hugh's mother, Kathleen Trevor-Roper.

'A solitary boy, frail, reserved and awkward in company.' Hugh on the Northumberland shoreline.

Belhaven Hill preparatory school, c. 1927. Hugh is seated in the second row on the left of the picture; his short-sightedness is already apparent as he peers at the camera. Next to him is his rival Goode, who (like Hugh) would win a scholarship to Charterhouse; further along are the two masters, Brian Simms and Wilfred 'Bungey' Ingham. Next to Simms is the formidable Scottish Matron, Miss Rutherford. Hugh's brother Pat is in the back row, third from the left.

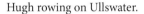

Hugh rowing on Ullswater.

As Head Monitor of Daviesites, Charterhouse, *c.* 1932, seated next to the housemaster, Lancelot Allen, who nurses a pet dog. Note Hugh's upturned collar, a mark of seniority.

'Like a character from P.G. Wodehouse'. Aged seventeen, with his siblings in the garden at Alnwick, 1931.

With 'Hazel' (otherwise unidentified), at St Abb's Head on the Berwickshire coast, mid 1930s.

Hugh was a keen walker. On a bitterly cold Sunday in his second term at Christ Church, for example, he went for a 'short stroll' in the Cotswolds of 38 miles.

An expedition up Mont St Victoire, southern France, spring 1934. Hugh was then a second-year undergraduate at Christ Church.

Until he broke his back in a riding
accident in the winter of 1948–9, Hugh
regularly rode to hounds, though he
endured criticism from some of his
colleagues, who deplored fox-hunting as
an unsuitable pastime for an intellectual.

'People say that life is the thing, but I prefer reading.' Hugh's mentor Logan Pearsall Smith.

Below left 'The best kind of public schoolmaster, who never did any research and whose emphasis was entirely on teaching.' Hugh's tutor and patron, J.C. Masterman.

Below The Jesuit priest Father D'Arcy, with his 'El Greco looks' and 'fine, slippery mind', both fascinated and repelled Hugh.

'I am told the job may be extremely dull, but might turn out very exciting.' Lieutenant Trevor-Roper, around the time he joined MI8, in December 1939.

'His first impression of the bunker was one of negligence. Its entrance . . . was guarded by two slovenly Russian soldiers, who were happy to grant him admittance in exchange for a cigarette each. Inside, all was dark and flooded ankle-deep.'

A series of books followed, establishing his credentials as the pre-eminent critic in his subject. Printed in these were lists of paintings he considered authentic. Never a modest man, he became increasingly dogmatic as his reputation spread. His procedure before a picture seemed almost magical. 'He would come very close to it and tap its surface and then listen attentively, as if expecting some almost inaudible voice to reply. Then, after a long pause, he would murmur a name.'

Berenson's expertise had commercial as well as academic value. This was a period when wealthy Americans, awash with dollars but lacking in knowledge, were buying European paintings by the yard, relying on certificates of authenticity – though of course these were always ques-·tionable and sometimes bogus. Kenneth Clark, who worked for Berenson in the mid-1920s, compared the issuing of these certificates to the authentication of relics in the late Middle Ages. Nevertheless, American buyers insisted on them. Like most other art historians and critics of his era, Berenson was willing to supply this demand, and as the most respected of them all, his opinion was more valuable than any other. He was soon making a great deal of money, enough to allow him to lease, and then to buy and restore, the sumptuous villa of I Tatti, with its surrounding estate of fifty acres. Berenson entered into confidential commercial arrangements with art dealers. The sums involved were huge. In 1928, for example, he signed a contract which gave him a commission of 10 per cent on sales of pictures he had authenticated, plus a retainer of £10,000 per annum.* After Berenson's death, Kenneth Clark described his former employer as 'perched on the pinnacle of a mountain of corruption. The air was purer up there. He would not have kept up his position if he had done anything flagrantly dishonest; on the other hand, he could not get down.'

As the years passed, Berenson's dogmatism began to rebound on him. It was galling for him to be continually criticised for mistakes he had indeed made but which he had been the first to detect. Though he might wish to revise some of the unqualified judgements he had given in the past, he found himself compromised. Those who had bought paintings on the strength of certificates signed by him did not want their authenticity challenged. 'Consistency requires you to be as ignorant today as you were a year ago,' he unhappily complained. He became irritable, demanding, sensitive to criticism, intolerant of rivals, even to the point of vindictiveness and vituperation, impatient and increasingly autocratic. Yet he retained many attractive qualities: a well-furnished mind, intellectual curiosity, a passion for reading (and being read to), a lack of cant, pleasure in sophisticated conversation, hospitableness and interest in (if not sympathy for) other

* Worth almost half a million pounds in today's money.

people, especially the young. When he spoke his diction was pure, his rapid mind darted from one subject to another, and he could draw on a rich reservoir of experience to freshen his thinking. These were qualities Hugh valued. He relished the talk around Berenson's table, ranging from abstract ideas to high-class gossip. There he was never awkward or tongue-tied, as he often was at home. It was nothing to him if Berenson was sometimes unfair or unkind. So was he.

The two men took to each other straight away, though Berenson was almost half a century Hugh's senior. They had many qualities in common, besides a shared delight in the give and take of conversation: scepticism; a keen interest in history, and in politics; a love of literature, and of elegant prose; sensitivity to nature; and enthusiasm for walking. To Hugh, Berenson was a true cosmopolitan, a man interested in everything, with a depth and breadth of outlook rarely found in England and never encountered in grand country houses there. Moreover Berenson himself was bound up with the place where he had chosen to live. Like many Englishmen before and since, Hugh was astonished by Italy; by the art, by the beauty, by the light, by the ancient yet still vital culture. In his mind Berenson was inextricably linked to all of this. To Berenson, Hugh represented an ideal. The day after the two young Englishmen's visit, Berenson made a note in his diary. 'Why do I feel more attracted to the Englishman than to the American of the same abilities, equal achievement and success? It can only be that the Englishman is more of a work of art to be enjoyed as such particularly, whereas the American with rarest exceptions can be admired only. In other words, it is a question of breeding.' As a young man Berenson had dreamed of going to study in Oxford and spending his life there; he idealised Oxford men as 'very clever, brilliant, serious even although without too much gravity, and well-taught, just the men whom I admire and even adore'.

After his return to England Hugh wrote to Berenson, beginning a lively correspondence that would continue until Berenson's death twelve years later. Often he would write to Nicky Mariano, in the knowledge that she would read his letters aloud to Berenson. Hugh's letters were deliciously witty and laced with high-grade gossip. Their tone was respectful, though not deferential, indeed occasionally irreverent: in his first letter, for example, Hugh referred to Casa al Dono as 'your oracular mountain cave'. He hinted that he would return, if invited. The following March he came to stay a few days at I Tatti, and afterwards he would often be a guest there. It became one of his favourite places to visit, where he contrived to go, on average, once a year, despite the currency restrictions introduced by the Labour Government in 1947 which made foreign travel difficult. 'The whole atmosphere of the house appealed to me,' he recalled thirty years afterwards. 'I felt it was a sophisticated, civilized world where the conversation was on an intellectual level.' Hugh enjoyed too the comforts of the house, the peace of its splendid library of 50,000 volumes where he could withdraw to work and write letters without giving offence to his hosts, and the beauty of its setting, with its grand avenue of cypress trees and its 'numinous' ilex grove, where he could wander at will. 'There is no place where I so enjoy the leisure I find there and feel myself so happily at home,' he wrote gratefully to Nicky Mariano after one of his visits.[31]

It was possible to see Berenson as an old fraud, a man who had squandered his talents in the pursuit of money, and whose personality had shrivelled in the process of trying to defend the indefensible. But Hugh would never allow criticism of his friend. To him, 'BB' was a great man.

'Life without travel is inconceivable to me,' Hugh told Berenson.[32] Boxing Day 1947 found him buttoned into a thick overcoat, ready to set out for Czechoslovakia in an open-topped Lagonda. Hugh was then thirty-two; for a chauffeur-companion he had chosen the nineteen-year-old Alan Clark, dandyish in full-length coat with fur collar, who had borrowed the car from his parents. The pair of them might have been bound for Monte Carlo or some other rakish resort; instead, Hugh's mission was to report for *The Observer* on Czechoslovakia's precarious politics. This was the front line in the developing Cold War between East and West. Elections in 1946 had led to the formation of a coalition government under the pre-war President, Edvard Beneš, with Communists taking control of many of the most important Ministries. But now there was deadlock within the coalition between the Communists and their allies over whether to participate in the American-led Marshall Plan for economic recovery. Ominously, Stalin had summoned the Communist Prime Minister to Moscow for discussions.

Travel abroad in the immediate post-war years required regular skirmishes with officialdom. At Harwich they were told it was impossible for them to proceed without a *carnet* certifying that the car was not for export. Hugh persuaded the relevant official to write out an authorisation for 'temporary export', and they boarded the ferry to Antwerp, only to encounter customs officers who demanded the equivalent of £600 in Belgian currency as a pledge of the car's return. Fortunately they found a rich shipping magnate willing to deposit this sum on their behalf. They then made for the German border, flying a Union flag from the bonnet to suggest the presence of a British general within. 'Rightly deducing that no British official would be on duty at such an hour, we craftily drove up the frontier at 7.00 o'clock on Sunday morning,' Hugh wrote gleefully to Stuart. 'A few sharp words in German to the German on duty had an electrifying effect on his conditioned reflexes, and we floated effortlessly into Germany.' In the snow-bound Bavarian mountains, however, their car suffered a head-on collision with a chauffeur-driven limousine. Luckily they were travelling slowly at the time, so the impact was less disastrous than it might have been. After running repairs they were able to continue across the Bohemian border into Czechoslovakia. The Czech officials spoke no English, which prevented them from detecting that the documents presented by the visitors were invalid.[33]

Hugh was not disappointed by Czechoslovakia. Prague fascinated him: 'it reminded me more of Dublin than Rome, the great palaces and buildings of a foreign aristocracy gradually crowded out by the shoddy hutches of a peasantry come to town.' Politically he found it 'most interesting'. He called on Jan Masaryk, the foreign minister and son of Czechoslovakia's founder, Tomáš Masaryk, who seemed 'in excellent form', lying in bed in a vast and luxurious apartment in the Czernin Palace while he wrote private letters in violet ink and read Gogol's *Dead Souls*. In a letter to Berenson, Hugh predicted that the curtain* would not fall soon, a prediction he made also in an *Observer* article.[34] He was utterly wrong: only weeks afterwards the coalition collapsed, leading to a Communist takeover. Masaryk's body was found below a window in the courtyard of his own Ministry. Beneš resigned in June and died three months later.

Hugh was due to go on another tour with Alan Clark in the summer, this time to Lapland, but the young man let him down at the last moment. Instead he went to Italy for the second time that year, spending four days in Venice, two days walking in the Dolomites, and visiting Padua and Ravenna, before staying twenty-four hours with Berenson in Vallombrosa. Earlier in the summer he had gone to Ireland, to stay at Glenveagh Castle in County Donegal as the guest of Henry P. McIlhenny (known to his friends as 'Henry P'), a wealthy Philadelphia art collector he had met in Italy. Witty, clever and welcoming, McIlhenny was an amusing man who combined gusto with delicacy. Hugh reported to Berenson that after meeting 'your engaging *bon-viveur* friend' in Italy, he had invited him for a weekend at Christ Church, and McIlhenny had reciprocated by having him to stay in Ireland, at the house which he and his mother had bought in 1937. Glenveagh Castle was a romantic nineteenth-century concoction of towers and battlements in a barren landscape, located close to the place where McIlhenny's grandfather had lived before emigrating to America in 1843. 'Bogs to bogs in three generations,' McIlhenny commented cheerfully.

---

* In a speech given at Fulton, Missouri, in March 1946, Winston Churchill had announced that an 'iron curtain' had descended across Europe; all the nations behind it were subject to a very high and increasing measure of control from Moscow. He had singled out Czechoslovakia as the only country in the 'Soviet sphere' where there was still true democracy.

The garden was adorned with Roman busts and the neighbouring hill crowned with an obelisk.[35]

Hugh was prevented from returning to Ireland towards the end of the year, for some hunting with Michael Beaumont, formerly Master of the Bicester,* by a serious accident, when his horse rolled on him. One of his pupils witnessed an apparently insensible Hugh being carried back to his rooms in Tom Quad on a stretcher, one red-clad arm hanging limp over the side.[36] He had broken his back, and would spend the next three months encased in plaster. Dick White was horrified. 'I feel bound to protest at the daily more numerous hazards you accept as background to the intellectual life,' he wrote.[37] This was the second such accident within a year: during the previous January Hugh had spent five days recuperating in bed after his horse rolled on him from head to foot in a Buckinghamshire quagmire.[38] Perhaps deciding not to push his luck any further, he reluctantly abandoned the sport. A little later he sold his hunter to one of his wealthiest pupils, Tommy Baring. It amused him that this transaction had taken place during a tutorial.

He had not recovered in time to go to the USA at Christmas, as he had originally intended. But by the end of the Hilary term 1949 he was fit enough to travel, and in mid-March he flew to America, the first time he had crossed the Atlantic. 'My life is spent in a succession of cocktail parties,' he wrote to Stuart, 'I can scarcely open my mouth to speak without a Bronx or Manhattan being shot into it.' In New York he attended a grand dinner given by Mrs Cornelius Vanderbilt, 'where 26 bores sat down to dine off gold plate and 26 Irish footmen stood behind their chairs'. After dinner, 'to escape the tedium of talking or listening to each other, we were all shepherded into a state-room & made to look at an indescribably dull colour travel film taken in Europe by Cornelius Vanderbilt jnr. This I find is a regular feature of American dinner parties – one better, because less effort, than bridge.'[39]

Hugh remained in America four weeks. After mixing in the high society of New York, Boston and Harvard, he passed his last week driving south into Virginia, accompanied by his former pupil Francis Dashwood, sharing motel rooms. Afterwards, he told Berenson that he had enjoyed his time there, contrary to expectations, 'because it was so new and strange. And, *very strange*! I still feel inarticulate about it, as one who has returned from the Moon; and in some ways depressed. Their standard of education is really very saddening! Harvard depressed me a great deal, & New York

---

* Beaumont was a wealthy man, and a former Conservative MP. His son Timothy was reading agriculture at Christ Church. In 1947 Beaumont senior sold Wotton, his superb Soane house near Aylesbury, to escape the punitive rates of tax imposed on those with high earnings by the post-war Labour Government. One of its pavilions is now owned by Tony Blair.

I found rather too hard; but I greatly enjoyed Washington, and met some really delightful people there'.[40] One of those he encountered during his stay in America was Alexander Kerensky, Russian Prime Minister immediately before the Bolshevik Revolution in October 1917. During their brief conversation Kerensky dwelt on the days of his glory, when he had been hailed by Lloyd George as the saviour and reformer of his country, and implied that it was by a mere fluke that he had been displaced by Lenin – someone, it seemed, had most unfortunately been absent from a vital committee meeting.[41]

In the summer Hugh went back to Iceland to fish for salmon. Each morning he made a two-hour journey on the back of a pony to reach the river from the farm where he was staying. The weather was 'beastly', the north wind incessant, and while playing a fish he plunged into the icy water, which flooded into his waders, leaving him soaked. After the long ride back to the farm he sank into a torpor, prostrate with painfully inflamed sinuses. (This familiar condition had afflicted him in Italy the previous year, when he had been forced to curtail his holiday and take to his bed. The hotel, thinking that he was dying, exported him to a hospital run by nuns.) However, he was rescued by an elderly fisherman camping nearby, and taken back to Reykjavik, where gradually he began to recover. His accidental host turned out to be the Icelandic Prime Minister, who reminisced about an earlier guest: Admiral Canaris, who had come to dinner in 1934 when his German battleship had put into the port. Hugh recorded these reminiscences in a letter to Charles Stuart. 'At dinner Canaris had expanded in a most un-Menzies-like way, & told a great number of stories about his early life', which Hugh detailed. 'So you see,' he concluded, 'that important additions to Truth can be made even here.'[42]

He spent the next Christmas vacation in Italy, going first to Capri, where he got to know 'that old *roué*' Norman Douglas:* 'the last real pagan before Christianity and barbarism closed in, for the second time, on our civilization'. Hugh attended Douglas's eighty-second birthday party, during which his inebriated host fell down a steep flight of stone steps. But otherwise he was rather bored; as he told Berenson afterwards, 'that world of decayed *rentiers* and social casualties doesn't attract me'. He was much happier when he moved on to Rome, to spend Christmas with Sylvia Sprigge, correspondent for the *Manchester Guardian*, one of Berenson's most regular guests. Through Sprigge he met Frank Giles, Rome correspondent for *The Times*. Afterwards he moved on to I Tatti. He was evidently on fine form, drawing this comment from Berenson after he had

---

* Norman Douglas (1868–1952), novelist and travel writer, exiled from England after a sexual scandal involving a teenage boy.

left: 'Hugh is a wonder of historical and political culture and insight, and a great gossip.'[43]

In March 1947, the same month that *The Last Days of Hitler* was published, Solly Zuckerman, acting on behalf of Tedder, had suggested that Hugh should write a new book, 'a popular edition' of the overall report being produced by the British Bombing Survey Unit (BBSU). In tandem with a similar American body, the BBSU had been set up at the end of the war to study the effects of strategic bombing in Europe. More than a thousand experts had studied the economic, operational and scientific aspects of strategic bombing, and a series of research panels had produced their findings, to be combined into a report which of its nature was bound to be technical. Tedder now wanted a 'potted version' written for the general public. The subject was of course a controversial one. Not only had the bombing campaign consumed substantial resources; it had entailed the attrition of bomber crews. Some doubted whether the sacrifice had been worthwhile. Few then questioned, as they have done since, whether the bombing was morally justifiable; but even so the deaths of civilians could not be altogether ignored, especially the deaths of civilians in occupied countries.

Hugh was attracted to the idea, but demanded a free hand; he did not want to produce a work of propaganda for the RAF, and asked for guarantees that the information he required would be made available and that no alterations would be made to his conclusions without his agreement. Zuckerman was concerned that Hugh had misunderstood the character of the task required. He seemed to be under the impression that fresh research was called for, which was hard to justify in view of the enormous amount already undertaken. 'But even if further research into sources were called for,' Zuckerman wrote privately to Tedder, 'Trevor-Roper is certainly not the person to do this work.' He confessed to feeling diffident about expressing such doubts, given his friendship with Hugh and the fact that he had suggested Hugh's name in the first place. 'The trouble is, he is not an economist, and not a scientist, but a professional historian with a literary flair. It was the latter of his talents on which we wished to call.'

Zuckerman was anyway sceptical that Hugh would take it on, and promised Tedder to look around for 'a second string'. More than a year later, however, Zuckerman was impressed to find Hugh 'at work' on the report. He told Hugh that 'the big explosive never to be mentioned' (i.e. the overall report) was now about to be published. 'The final proofs are with the Stationery Office, and in about three weeks' time I shall see a dummy copy, complete with figures and index, in the form in which it is not going to appear on railway bookstalls.' Hugh promptly asked to be relieved of his burden. He had written three chapters of the proposed work,* but the pressure of his college duties had meant that he had been unable to devote as much time to it as he had hoped.[44]

This was the second book which Hugh had begun and then laid aside, an ominous portent. The problem was disguised by the huge success of *The Last Days of Hitler*. But even this success was ambiguous. His worldwide reputation as a Hitler expert meant that he was constantly in demand, distracting him from historical research. He began to refuse work on the grounds that his German was inadequate. 'I only read the German language with difficulty and distaste,' he told Lovat Dickson in 1950, returning a book unread on which his opinion had been sought; 'and I am really too busy at present to struggle thro' a novel in it.'[45] Other evidence suggests that Hugh was a fluent German reader, though not a fluent speaker. He was such a good linguist that he found it easy to master any language. While working on *The Last Days of Hitler* and when researching the book on the July Plot he had rapidly read and digested not only printed works but also documents, often of a specialised or technical nature. In this case, and probably in others too, Hugh exaggerated his difficulty in reading German as a get-out. 'It is a laborious process to me to read German,' he informed a correspondent in 1948 who had asked him to read a manuscript, 'and I am really rather anxious to detach myself from my accidental connection with Nazi history, and to revert to my proper work!'[46]

---

* On 4 September 1998, Noble Frankland, co-author with Sir Charles Webster of the official history of the Strategic Air Offensive, wrote a letter to *The Times* about the BBSU reports, in which he mentioned Hugh's involvement. 'He wrote a first chapter of startling and characteristic brilliance. His second chapter declined into confusion, and before he had completed the third he abandoned the project on the ground that it was not a feasible operation.' Frankland explained that following Hugh's withdrawal the project had been referred to him; in due course he had advised that any attempt to make sense of the BBSU was bound to fail, because the reports were 'fatally flawed'.

Historian

'Proper work' meant his studies into the sixteenth and seventeenth centuries. This was his chosen period, about which he was teaching and lecturing to undergraduates. In fact he had resumed 'proper work' in the Public Record Office within a fortnight of returning from Germany after finding Hitler's will. Alerted by a chance find, he had discovered an important new source; but writing *The Last Days of Hitler* meant that he would be unable to exploit this for some years.

Browsing on his favourite antiquarian bookstall in Newcastle before the war, Hugh had picked up a seventeenth-century tract, *England's Grievance Discovered*, a diatribe about the malpractices of the Newcastle coal merchants. He had been surprised to find references to Thomas Sutton, who, so it was claimed, had controlled a substantial portion of the local trade in coal, and had thus been able to raise its price considerably. This was the first indication to Hugh that Charterhouse's founder, whose name had been so familiar to him as a schoolboy, had been anything other than a worthy benefactor. No Carthusian could have been unaware of the imposing statue in Founder's Court; nor was it possible for a boy to attend the school without being exposed to the devotional literature portraying Sutton as an Elizabethan hero – responsible, among other feats, for the defeat of the Spanish Armada. In Nef's two-volume *History of the British Coal Industry* (1932), Hugh came across Sutton's name once more. He discovered that Sutton's early wealth had indeed derived from his lease on the coalfields around Newcastle, the richest in Europe, and that at this stage of his career he had lived in Alnwick. A footnote described a casual conversation between Nef and a Shakespearean scholar ransacking the more arcane Elizabethan and Jacobean archives in the PRO, who had noticed Sutton's name occurring repeatedly in an obscure sequence of documents known as the Recognizances for Debt. These references had pricked Hugh's interest; but before he could investigate the subject further, Hitler had invaded Poland.

These were the documents that Hugh had gone to the PRO to study in January 1946.* He found them a fascinating source, and made a thorough

---

* He had begun examining them while on leave towards the end of 1944, but his duties as an intelligence officer prevented him from studying them in detail until he was demobilised.

study of them. They exposed the workings of a system for raising money, originally devised for the use of London merchants but adapted for the use of anyone who could provide adequate security. In the late sixteenth and early seventeenth centuries a number of prominent English families had been forced to part with their lands in order to pay their debts. In doing so, they suffered social disaster. The Recognizances for Debt showed this process in operation. They revealed that Thomas Sutton had been the greatest moneylender of his age, an activity glossed over by Carthusian historians. In an article for the school magazine published in 1948, Hugh would show how the character of Sutton had been sanitised over the 350 years since the school's foundation. For example, in his book *Charterhouse in London* (1921), presented to all school monitors on leaving, the former Master of the London Charterhouse, G.S. Davies, had denied that Sutton was a moneylender; he assured readers that Sutton only occasionally obliged friends with a loan – though in his day he had been known as the greatest 'usurer' in England, and was believed by many to have been the original of Ben Jonson's Volpone, the miser who became a recluse after his wife's death, 'fed several with hopes of being his heir' and in the end deceived them all.[1]

Hugh also studied Sutton's own papers in the London Charterhouse, apparently the first time that anyone had done so since the eighteenth century. As a result of his research he developed a view of Sutton as a pioneering entrepreneur. He had been impressed by an essay by the Belgian historian Henri Pirenne,* who had observed that when a new form of economic organisation arises, it necessarily calls into being a new class to direct and control it. Thomas Sutton was one of the first of such a new class. In 1948 Hugh told Berenson that he had for some time contemplated 'a little work consisting of accounts of the lives of four such figures, who in different ways can illustrate the social & economic changes of the 16th–17th century in England'.[2] One of these figures was Sutton.†

The Recognizances for Debt provided a previously unexplored means of studying the economic pressures forcing social change in the period leading up to the English Revolution. Tawney had made this subject topical. In a series of articles, the most famous of which, 'The Rise of the Gentry', was published in 1941, he had presented a picture of an aristocracy sinking into ruin through personal extravagance, poor husbandry and political ineptitude; while a lesser class, 'the gentry', was acquiring wealth, land, confidence and power at their expense. This shift

---

* *'Les périodes de l'histoire sociale du capitalisme'* (Brussels, 1914).
† The other figures were John Dudley, Duke of Northumberland; Sir Thomas Bodley; and Richard Boyle, 1st Earl of Cork.

in the centre of social gravity had led to a political upheaval: the Civil War, in which the House of Commons, the mouthpiece of the gentry, had asserted its authority over both the Crown and the House of Lords. Tawney's ideas fitted neatly into the model constructed by Engels, making it appear that the first 'bourgeois revolution' had taken place in England. His work had an electrifying effect on historians of the period. As a result, everything that had previously seemed settled was open to reinterpretation.

At the end of the war Hugh was very much under Tawney's influence. This was obvious in an article he published in the journal *History* in 1945, to mark the 300th anniversary of Laud's execution. The article reviewed how historians had portrayed Laud through the intervening three centuries. Surveying the current state of understanding of the subject, Hugh assumed the intellectual predominance of the 'Fabian school of English historians', i.e. Tawney's followers. By contrast, he believed that there was 'no end to the nonsense that has been produced by neo-catholics and neo-tories' – a sentence that might have been written by A.L. Rowse; or at least the pre-war Rowse, since by this time Rowse was on his way to becoming a neo-Tory himself. Laud's attempt to assert the authority of the Anglican Church was explained in Tawney-esque terms. Laud had 'set out to halt, and in many ways to reverse, a process which had been going on for a century ... the process by which the essentially static, feudal society of the Middle Ages had been replaced, or was being replaced, by a modern, competitive, capitalist society'.[3]

A few weeks after his return to Oxford from war service Hugh read a paper to the Stubbs Society, in which he outlined some of his tentative findings from these new records. He described how Sutton had acquired the lease on the Durham coalfields, which he afterwards sold at vast profit, coming south with two packhorses laden with money, the foundation of his fortune. In this paper, afterwards published in the *Durham University Journal*, Hugh announced his intention to draw on the same original material 'in a completer study of the general problem'.[4] This intention would be reiterated in his successful* application for a University lectureship, a five-year appointment worth £300 annually. 'I propose to undertake a study of the economic and social changes in the period 1540–1660 in general.'[5]

Before he could do this, however, Hugh had become absorbed in writing *The Last Days of Hitler*. When, in October 1946, he had been approached by Oxford University Press to prepare an edition of Clarendon's *History of the Rebellion* for the World's Classics series, he had felt

---

* Hugh was appointed a University lecturer with effect from 1 October 1949.

obliged to decline 'a task which I should otherwise really enjoy', regretting that the pressure of work was such as to make it 'temporarily impossible for me to go on with the research in which I am interested; and I should have to regard the anthologising of Clarendon as a secondary matter'.[6] The huge success of *The Last Days of Hitler*, the tempting offers it brought in its wake and the demands of his work as a tutor and lecturer postponed his return to this research for several years. Hugh's letters from this period are full of complaints about the many demands on him. The problem would become worse when he took on the college office of Junior Censor at the beginning of 1948, and worse still when he became Senior Censor in 1950. As the Dean was then Vice-Chancellor,* Hugh had to fulfil most of the duties normally undertaken by a head of college.

Following his paper to the Stubbs Society, Hugh had been visited by Lawrence Stone, who was keen to discuss the subject further. Sutton was of course as familiar a figure to Stone as he was to Hugh, and the two clever Carthusians may have enjoyed chuckling over the less than heroic picture of their school's founder that was emerging from the records. Stone was especially interested in the Recognizances for Debt. Hugh showed his enthusiastic young colleague transcripts he had made from the originals in the PRO. Stone asked if he might borrow these, and Hugh readily agreed to lend them to him. About three weeks later Stone returned them, saying that he had found them very interesting. Some marginal notes suggested that he had been to the PRO to examine the sources himself. After that they did not meet for a long time.

Stone was a charismatic person who inspired intense admiration, even hero-worship in his colleagues. When he went to Princeton in the 1960s his graduate students dubbed him Lorenzo Il Magnifico. War service had obliged him to delay becoming an historian for five years; as a result, he was the quintessential young man in a hurry. Some years later, once Hugh had become disillusioned with Stone, he described how his former friend and pupil had 'rushed around England & France, attending conferences; pushed himself before the notice of professors; advertised himself, through his father-in-law, a French medieval historian called Prof. Fawtier, in France; and then wrote articles which, by the triple technique of a challenging thesis (generally a mere exaggeration of a borrowed thesis), a dogmatic *ex cathedra* style, and a portentous array of documentation –

---

* The principal administrative officer of the University (the post of Chancellor being purely honorific in recent times). The convention (now lapsed) was that heads of College became Vice-Chancellor on two-year terms by rotation. Dean Lowe was appointed Vice-Chancellor at short notice in 1948, after his predecessor (the Principal of Brasenose) had fallen to his death in stepping from a moving train. Lowe remained Vice-Chancellor until 1951.

appendices, footnotes, statistics – were taken everywhere, even by the elect, as being important contributions to scholarship'.[7]

In later life Stone admitted that he saw nothing wicked about going into a different field of study 'with a pickaxe and digging out the gold and getting out fast'. Disconcerting reports reached Hugh that Stone was working in the PRO on the Recognizances for Debt, though he heard nothing more from Stone himself. Then, in 1948, Stone published the product of his labour, in the form of a long article, 'The Anatomy of the Elizabethan Aristocracy', that opened and almost completely filled the number of the journal in which it appeared, the *Economic History Review*. From his opening sentence, Stone took his cue from Tawney; his points were forcefully expressed, and there was a moral undertone to his case just as there had been to Tawney's; but he pushed Tawney's argument a stage further. Stone portrayed a bankrupt Tudor aristocracy living beyond its means in an attempt to keep pace with social conventions. 'Snobbery and foppery, gluttony and gambling were all more important than changes in price structure or land tenure.' Stone went on to assert that 'the group of aristocratic rebellions of the late sixteenth century have been generally misunderstood. Their political or religious motivation was slight. Fundamentally they are important only as indications of the growing financial malaise of the noble class.' This line was of course satisfying to those who believed that there had to be an economic cause for every significant political change. Stone's argument was analogous to one Hugh had made in his article on Sutton, in which he had suggested that indebtedness, rather than religious resentment, had been the real cause of the Gunpowder Plot. Stone's portrayal of an aristocracy in crisis was resonant in the late 1940s, a time when estates which had remained in the same family for generations were being sold or broken up, and great houses demolished or falling into dereliction. His thesis was supported by impressive statistical evidence, including twelve pages of appendices. Almost all of these figures were drawn from the Recognizances for Debt.

Stone had consulted Tawney about the article before publishing it, and asked for comments and advice on the prospects of publication. 'I suppose it is much too long for the Economic History Review,' he had written speculatively. As President and founder of the Economic History Society, Tawney was in a position to answer this question. Apologising for the trouble he was giving, Stone explained that 'there is no-one in Oxford to whom I can turn for advice on 16th century economic history, and I value your advice above that of anyone else in any case'.[8]

This article established Stone as an historian. It was the kind of work that attracts the admiration of historians: an imposing edifice of argument, founded on archival research and buttressed by statistics that gave it an appearance of invincible solidity. 'All the professors at once . . . bowed down in servile adoration,' wrote Hugh. Even the great French historian Fernand Braudel admitted to Hugh that he found Stone's argument '*une thèse séduisante*'. It became the new orthodoxy, regularly regurgitated by undergraduates. Stone was made a member of the Council of the Economic History Society, and was 'pressed for professorships'. W.K. Hancock, Professor of Economic History at Oxford until 1950, gushed that 'in ten years' time no economic historian in England will be able to hold a candle to Stone'; his successor Hrothgar (John) Habakkuk, one of the Editors of the *Economic History Review*, suggested that 'to economic historians now there can only be one question of interest, and that is, what is Stone working on now?'[9]

Years later, Hugh would describe having been 'shocked' when he read Stone's article to find it 'grossly erroneous'. That is not what he said at the time. On the contrary, he complimented Stone. 'I think it is really excellent and am very glad that you have done it,' he wrote, adding that he had admired not only the content but also the style in which it was written. 'I think Lawrence's article is very good and drop all potential criticisms,' he told Charles Stuart. 'I shouldn't have done it nearly as well, and the work is nearly all his own.' A few weeks later he was evidently feeling less enthusiastic about his protégé, when he disclosed to Stuart that Stone, whom he satirically dubbed 'the professor-designate of modern history at the University of Brisbane', had replied 'coldly' to his letter of praise.[10] In the meantime Hugh had received a letter protesting in vehement terms about Stone's 'brazen theft' of his work. It came from Menna Prestwich, an historian of the early modern period at St Hilda's, who was married to John Prestwich, the medievalist who had taught Stone as an undergraduate; the pair formed a powerful partnership in the confined world of the Oxford History Faculty. Her letter made it obvious that she was writing on behalf of the two of them. She referred to Stone's 'purloining' of Hugh's research. 'It is the most monstrous piece of historical and literary theft that can have occurred,' she fulminated. 'We are astounded by it.' The purpose of her letter was to tell him how much she resented Stone's 'thievery', and to say how sorry she was about it. 'It would be very nice if you could manage some kind of counter-attack.'[11]

Hugh continued to push the career of his former pupil. In the winter of 1949/1950 he was Stone's principal sponsor for a history Fellowship at Wadham, replacing Bill Deakin: the post that Hugh had unsuccessfully tried for in 1937, after failing to gain a Fellowship at All Souls. Even so, he was piqued by what seemed to him a neglect of academic propriety. Stone had recognised that Hugh had discovered a significant source of new evidence, in an area of intense interest to historians; he had exploited their personal relationship to learn more; and he had then worked speedily and secretly to forestall Hugh, ensuring that he would be first to make use of it in print. His behaviour had been, at the very least, underhand. This, at any rate, is how Hugh came to see it, and he was not alone in this view. 'One had known before that Stone did not possess the virtue of honesty, but one had not realized how debased a criminal he was,' raged Menna Prestwich.

Stone had written 'the completer study of the general problem' that Hugh had intended to write himself. Though he had acknowledged in a footnote his debt to Hugh for calling his attention to this valuable material, the benefit from the discovery was his alone. Moreover, Stone had ventured to correct a suggestion his former tutor had made in the published version of the paper given to the Stubbs Society, the means by which he had been alerted to the Recognizances for Debt in the first place.[12] Hugh therefore had cause to be doubly offended. Still more serious for him was the fact that he had stumbled on such an important new source and then failed to make use of it.

This was a damaging failure. Hugh's reputation as an historian was far from secure. His book on Laud was thought by many to have been excessively polemical. *The Last Days of Hitler* had won admiration around the world, but less esteem within Oxford. Though hailed as a masterpiece of historical writing, it was not a work of 'history'. By its very nature it was not a work of archival research. Its colourful style left donnish readers uncomfortable. There was an element of jealousy in this reaction, of course. *The Last Days of Hitler* had made Hugh famous. He had begun to write for the newspapers, a dangerous activity for a don. It had also made him rich, a fact made obvious by the Bentley parked prominently in Tom Quad. Blake teased Hugh that he was thought by his colleagues to be 'rolling in money'.[13] Academics unqualified to judge the historical worth of the book (and some who had not even read it) nevertheless felt able to make derogatory comments about it, in common rooms and tutorials. 'There was a general feeling that Hugh allowed himself to be deceived in that book,' one -remarked opaquely.

Hugh was conscious of how he was seen in Oxford, and often made sardonic references to this. One reason why he resisted pressure from publishers to write a book about Hitler's mind, he told Berenson, was that 'such a book might (*horresco referens*)* succeed!' He implied that he was working hard in the PRO as a form of penance, 'writing silently away at that infinitely dull book which, I fondly hope, *may* rehabilitate me in the learned world after my unforgivable lapse into the shocking crime of *success!*'[14] His arrogance did not enhance his popularity with his colleagues.

---

* 'I shudder at the thought.'

He was particularly disdainful of the kind of work prized by many medi-evalists, the minute examination of rolls and suchlike, which he referred to contemptuously as 'nuns knitting'.*

Stone's success was galling to him. 'The Anatomy of the Elizabethan Aristocracy' had attracted far more acclaim from historians than anything he had written. The pupil had eclipsed his master. The contrast between them was painfully apparent. In the same year that Stone's article in one of the most serious scholarly journals had been recognised internationally as a major contribution to the understanding of the period, Hugh's output consisted of a centenary piece on 1848 for *The Cornhill* and his lightweight article on Sutton, lacking any scholarly apparatus, for *The Carthusian*. He was contemplating a book called *The Army in Politics, 1640–1660*, and became engaged in complicated discussions with Macmillan's American office about the possibility of publishing this on a commission basis in the USA. These plans were rooted in a tax avoidance scheme; Hugh was determined to leave as much money as possible in America and was pre-pared to fund the production costs of the proposed book in return for a proportion of the profits. The discussions stretched out for months, testing the patience of his publishers. Of the book itself, there was no sign.[15]

By the end of the 1940s Hugh's plan to write 'a little work' about four figures whose lives illustrated the social and economic changes of the period had been concentrated into a biographical study of Sutton. He found it slow going. Part of the problem may have been his subject. Hugh had recognised from the start that Sutton was not an inspiring personality. 'Although, in his last years, he was a figure of almost mythological wealth, an English Midas, envied and flattered by the spendthrift court of King James, he remains an impersonal, enigmatical figure. The truth is, he was a very dull dog; a man without tastes or ambitions except in money, a man who amassed money not to share it, not to spend it, but to increase it; not to found a family (he left his illegitimate son penniless), not to gratify an ostentatious spirit, nor to relish exorbitant pleasures, but merely as a means to more money.' Sutton was, Hugh had already concluded, 'a perfect example of Max Weber's sociological type, the Spirit of Capitalism'.[16] Another reason, perhaps, for his slow progress was that the appearance of Stone's article in 1948 had deprived his work of its currency. Had Hugh's

* He produced a spoof and scatological lecture series, 'The Meaning of Medieval Civilization', as follows: '(1) Some curious postures in late Roman chamber pottery (with lantern-slides); (2) A perforated fragment from an early Merovingian toilet-roll; (3) The exploitation of surplus value in monastic laundry-charges, 1066–7; (4) Two emendations in a newly discovered cartulary of Keble College; (5) Purl or Plain: the dilemma of a thirteenth-century Irish nunnery; (6) Gryphon couchant or wyvern futuent? An unsolved mystery in the arms of Clare; (7) Some bastards, concubines and catamites of a fourteenth-century curate in Lincolnshire.'

study of Sutton appeared in 1947, it would no doubt have been received as a valuable contribution to the discussion launched by Tawney. It would have been particularly welcomed as the first work to draw on an entirely fresh source. But following Stone's article it would have seemed much less remarkable. In the race to publish scholarly research, the winner takes all.

Even while working on his Sutton book, Hugh was gathering his forces for an attack on Stone. Criticism of his own failings sharpened his desire to cut Stone down to size. Maybe he disliked Stone's portrayal of a spendthrift, feckless aristocracy, and his puritanical message, so much in tune with the times and so antipathetical to Hugh's cavalier instincts. On examining 'The Anatomy of the Elizabethan Aristocracy' more carefully, he realised that it was riddled with errors. In working so fast, Stone had paid the price of his haste. He had not taken the trouble to understand the system of loans by recognisance; his figures were therefore misleading; he had seriously misinterpreted the documents; and, worst of all, he had often mis-transcribed them, perhaps deliberately. Stone, Hugh concluded, was 'a charlatan'. But no one else, apart from himself, had examined the documents upon which Stone's erroneous article was based. In the circumstances Hugh decided that it was his duty to reply to the article and expose its falsity. One of his undergraduate pupils, Alastair Parker, was startled to find his tutor, ill with sinusitis, sitting up in bed and clutching a file labelled 'Death of Stone'.*

In January 1951 Hugh outlined his intentions to Wallace Notestein, a septuagenarian specialist on seventeenth-century English history and for many years Professor of English History at Yale, who had spent the academic year 1949–50 in Oxford as a visiting professor. The two men were linked also by their acquaintance with Berenson: Notestein's wife was a close friend of Berenson's sister, and the couple had made the first of several visits to I Tatti in 1950. 'I have decided to liquidate Stone,' Hugh announced:

> While I was working on Sutton in the summer I kept finding such gigantic statistical errors in Stone's 'Anatomy of the Elizabethan Aristocracy' that I decided I must clear him out of the way before publishing conclusions which will be in many ways radically different from his. Of course once I began checking all his ms and even printed references, I found the situation far worse: it is a case not merely of haste and inexperience but deliberate falsification on a shocking scale, and I have decided to blow this pirate ship out of the water in order to make the seas of 16th century historical scholarship safe for legitimate commerce.[17]

---

* Another undergraduate, George Engle, spotted the same file on Hugh's desk as he stood waiting to see the Senior Censor, then engaged on the telephone.

Energised, Hugh began 'working furiously, scribbling away, night and day, deleting in the evening all that I have written in the morning, in the usual manner of authors, emptying inkpots and filling wastepaper baskets without much other effect, and thoroughly enjoying myself, to my own surprise, in the process'. He lamented to Dawyck Haig that he never had enough time. 'If only there were no undergraduates! If only term began in November instead of October! But scratch, scratch, a page a day, and I move slowly over the paper, envying no one.'[18] He took great care to verify his figures, employing a researcher to check his references carefully.

In September 1950 he submitted the first draft of his 'reply to Stone' to the Editors of the *Economic History Review*. His covering letter explained what he was about. 'In this article I contest, fundamentally, all the figures and calculations which are basic to Stone's article *The Anatomy of the Elizabethan Aristocracy*.' He was particularly anxious that it should be published as early as possible, he continued, 'since I am finishing a book on a related topic, and wish it to be clear in advance why the figures I shall there use are so radically different from those already published by Stone. I imagine the topic is of some general interest also,' he added. Simultaneously Hugh sent his draft to J.E. Neale, Astor Professor of Modern History at University College, London, an authority on the Elizabethan House of Commons. 'I want to be armour-plated at every joint,' he told Neale, 'and your scrutiny of the joints will be most valuable!' Neale responded the next day, explaining that he had found the article so fascinating that he had been unable to stop reading it. 'Of course you are right,' he replied: 'crushingly, overwhelmingly so.' Hugh also asked Rowse to scrutinise his article, and the Prestwiches. 'We enjoyed the article enormously,' responded John Prestwich: 'There can be no doubt of its annihilating effect. What is shattering is not so much the proof of Stone's hastiness but the decisive proof of his dishonesty in quoting evidence which he must have known not to support his points.' Encouraged by this, Hugh submitted the final text of his article. 'I feel that it has really become necessary to expose Stone's thesis,' he explained. 'The parade of footnotes and appendices is so impressive that people are easily persuaded of their solidity, and I am continually bothered by their effect on good undergraduates. It is only by checking all his sources that I have realised the astonishing extent to which he has consistently emended his sources in order to sustain his thesis.'[19]

In a private letter to his co-Editor, Professor Michael Postan, Habakkuk conceded that Stone had been 'extraordinarily cavalier in his use of evidence'. He thought it 'as well' that Stone's article should have been corrected, though he wished that it had been done by somebody more 'charitable'.[20]

The two Editors of the *Economic History Review* were understandably embarrassed. Both asked Hugh to tone down his wording. After discussion with Habakkuk, Hugh indicated that he had 'softened the adjectives here and there', and made other changes in response to their suggestions. 'I should like to send a copy of the article, when in proof, to Stone,' he stated, 'as a matter of civility to a victim.' He went so far as to draft an explanatory letter to Stone, but then decided not to send it. In fact Postan had already warned Stone that he had received 'a very damaging refutation of your article on the Elizabethan aristocracy from Trevor-Roper'. Stone was grateful for the early warning. He asked for the right of reply in due course, and made a comment that did not accord with Hugh's recollection of events. 'In view of the fact that we have had long discussions on this subject, in which I now assume he was collecting ammunition, he is, perhaps, acting with some discourtesy.'[21] Later in that same month Stone sent Hugh a note indicating his awareness of the impending attack.[22] 'Postan isn't at all pleased, having invested so heavily in Stone,' Hugh confided to Notestein; 'but he must cut his losses; and doubtless there will be grumbles in other quarters – but you know I really rather <u>enjoy</u> a fight!'[23]

Hugh reacted badly when his article did not appear in the March 1951 issue of the *Economic History Review* as expected. He telephoned Habakkuk to complain that he had been 'double-crossed'. An indignant Habakkuk informed Postan that Hugh had accused him of 'suppressing' his article. In an apologetic but defiant letter to Postan, Hugh denied that he had made such an accusation, and claimed that his use of the phrase 'double-crossed' had been mere '*badinage*'.[24] Hugh's 'The Elizabethan Aristocracy: An Anatomy Anatomised' duly appeared in the next issue. This article has been described as a 'magnificent if terrifying work of destruction', and as 'one of the most vitriolic attacks ever made by one historian on another'.[25] Ruefully reflecting on Hugh's assault more than thirty years afterwards, Stone described it as 'an article of vituperative denunciation which connoisseurs of intellectual terrorism still cherish to this day'.[26] In fact, Hugh's language was not vituperative, though it was pitiless. He began quietly, before enumerating error after error. The cumulative effect was devastating. The result of Stone's multiple mistakes, Hugh believed, 'is not an analysis, it is a caricature of Elizabethan England'. The Elizabethan aristocracy were not, as a class, on the verge of bankruptcy; on the contrary, they had, in general, retained their lands; 'it was the gentry who were the sellers'. Far from being on the rise, the gentry were on the decline.[27]

Such a remorseless attack would have destroyed the confidence of a lesser man. Stone responded a year later with 'The Elizabethan Aristocracy – A Restatement'. He admitted to having misunderstood the system of Recognizances for Debt, and that he had made many regrettable mistakes of detail. But he maintained that many of Hugh's charges were incorrect, 'and many more are misapplied or only partly true'. His theory that the Elizabethan aristocracy was in economic decline might need modification, but it remained essentially intact. There was a personal sting in his final comment that the truth was most likely to emerge from 'lengthy research, rather than by the cultivation of a fierce polemical style'.[28]

Hugh wrote a rejoinder to Stone's 'Restatement', but Postan declined to publish it, explaining that 'we cannot continue a controversy indefinitely'. He suggested that 'the most acceptable way of continuing this discussion would be for you to produce an independent and non-polemical study of the same, or even a broader subject, in which the facts of Elizabethan society as you see them are expounded in full'.[29] Tawney wrote to congratulate Stone on his response to Hugh. In reply, Stone conceded that 'my earlier article was undoubtedly careless on detail and Trevor-Roper was right to point it out. But he need not have been so rude and I am convinced that on the main issue he is quite wrong.'[30]

The differences between the two men were elaborated in their lectures to Oxford undergraduates throughout the 1950s. Both were effective and even scintillating speakers. One day Stone argued persuasively that the Stuart aristocracy was in such severe financial difficulty that its members were at risk of being forced to sell their estates; the next, Hugh would equally convincingly argue the opposite, that their assets were sufficiently large to enable most of them to withstand temporary periods of indebtedness. For some students this was bemusing; others enjoyed the whiff of intellectual controversy.

Stone felt that Hugh 'had it in' for him, and that he would never obtain preferment in Oxford while his antagonist wielded influence there. There is some evidence to show that his suspicions were correct. A letter from Blake to Hugh reveals that they intrigued to prevent Stone from obtaining a readership in economic history early in 1951.[31] There may have been other such instances in the years that followed. Stone certainly believed that the promotion ladder was blocked to him.[32] Eventually he left for America. Some said that Hugh had driven him out of Oxford.

'What this whole business goes to show,' remarked the Regius Professor of Modern History, the medievalist V.H. Galbraith, 'is that Stone is no scholar and Trevor-Roper is no gentleman.' Galbraith cordially disliked Hugh, while conceding that he was 'as clever as a monkey'. Hugh reciprocated the dislike.

His brutal attack on Stone won him many admirers but few friends. In the midst of it all he had applied for the recently created Chair of Modern History.* This had become vacant upon the resignation of its first

* Worth £1,900 p.a.

incumbent, Llewellyn Woodward, who was leaving to take up a research professorship in the Institute of Advanced Study at Princeton. (Hugh's application may have been one reason why he was so impatient for his article to be published in the *Economic History Review*.) The Trevor-Roper campaign was conducted with military precision by his two lieutenants, Blake and Stuart. They advised him not to show his hand early, so as not to alert those hostile to him until the last minute. Having ascertained that both Masterman and Feiling were electors, he was counselled to look elsewhere for referees. Stuart vetoed Hugh's suggestion of Isaiah Berlin: 'he is not an accepted member of the History Faculty, and he would be pooh-poohed only too easily'. Besides, Stuart continued, 'he is clever & known to be clever: it is bad enough to have a clever candidate, but to have him recommended by a clever man would be too much'. As for Namier – often described, not entirely fairly, as a bore* – he would be 'entirely fatal'.[33] Hugh settled on three referees: Neale, his supporter against Stone; John Wheeler-Bennett, who, though not an academic, commanded immense respect for his scholarship; and E.T. 'Bill' Williams, now a Fellow of Balliol, who had been a Junior Research Fellow alongside Hugh at Merton in the late 1930s. Williams replied to Hugh's request by postcard. 'I have just been reading the Economic History Review and realise for the first time the meaning of the cliché about leaving no Stone unturned!' he wrote. 'It would be splendid if you were elected. The fact that you took part in the war will no longer count against you,' he continued: 'age and experience might.'[34]

Galbraith was determined not to have Hugh, and threatened to resign if he were elected. Masterman, another elector, was equally determined not to elect Hugh's most obvious rival, A.J.P. Taylor. The Chair was offered instead to a Fellow of Worcester, R.B. (Bruce) Wernham: a compromise candidate, one who had not even applied and who expressed understandable surprise at his appointment. Wernham had not published a single book. 'I have never heard of him,' confessed Namier.[35] Taylor dismissed Wernham as a 'nonentity'. Some years later Hugh described Wernham as 'a mouse, who had never been heard of before, and who has never been heard of since'.[36]

He was very disappointed. 'After a long and violent and acrimonious struggle, which I have found exhausting to the nerves, I have been defeated,' he told Dawyck Haig, 'and I feel enveloped in gloom and contrition at having thus failed to justify the efforts and confidence of my friends.' His morale needed raising after this setback. 'Do not, I beg you, have the

* Hugh himself described Namier to Berenson in May 1951 as 'the greatest living historian writing in English ... also, without doubt, the greatest living bore.' Berenson expressed a different view when Namier and his wife visited I Tatti in November 1953: both, he wrote to Hugh, were 'good company'.

slightest qualms of conscience about the outlay of energy on the part of your Friends,' urged Blake. 'There is nothing that they enjoy more than a fight in the eternal struggle against mumping* and grubbery.' He entreated Hugh not to be downcast, pointing out that in a few years' time Galbraith was due to retire as Regius Professor. He recommended that Hugh should have a word on the subject with Masterman, 'and listen very carefully to what he may have to say, especially to the oblique half hints and sagacious nods with which no doubt the conversation will be accompanied'.[37]

Trevor-Roper and Taylor, the two rival candidates for the Chair spurned in favour of Wernham, had much in common. Though their political allegiances were different, their temperaments were similar. Both were sharp-witted and sharp-tongued. Both despised the medievalists who dominated the Oxford History Faculty. Both were combative characters, unafraid to express controversial opinions in public and willing to give offence if necessary. Both contributed articles and book reviews to the national press, and both broadcast on the BBC, in a period when their stuffier colleagues felt such activities to be demeaning to a don. Both were thought to be interested in money, and both liked to drive a hard bargain. Both took a keen interest in the recent history of Germany, and in central Europe generally. Like Hugh, Taylor had visited Prague after the war, where he had a memorable audience with President Beneš.

Taylor was a small, bespectacled, pugnacious man with a severe stare that collapsed into a gleeful grin when he was amused. He was the only son of a wealthy Manchester cotton merchant; his flat Northern vowels betrayed his Lancashire origins. Taylor was a man of the Left, but more significant to Hugh was that he was an independent thinker, as Orwell had been. Though never intimate friends, he and Hugh were on good terms. Taylor's marriage had broken down, so that he was leading a bachelor existence. Hugh's post-war diaries show that in this period he and Taylor would often meet for a drink or a meal. Sometimes Taylor would call by Hugh's rooms and the two of them would take a walk together. Both were strenuous, indefatigable walkers: hardy men as historians go.

In June 1950 Hugh was one of 118 prominent writers, scientists, artists and philosophers from about twenty countries invited to participate in the 'Congress for Cultural Freedom', which took place in Berlin. The Congress was funded with American money (revealed years later to have originated from the CIA) and organised by Melvin J. Lasky, a young New Yorker attached to the American High Commission in Germany. It was intended

---

* A word often used in the correspondence between these two; its meaning was apparently somewhere between mumbling and grumbling.

as a counterblast to the Communist-backed 'Congress of the Intellectuals', held two years before in Wroclaw, Poland. The Wroclaw Congress had been disrupted by Hugh's colleague A.J.P. Taylor, who had broken with the Party line by rejecting 'wild slogans about American fascism', and who had concluded his impromptu speech with a plea for intellectual honesty, tolerance, love and the pursuit of truth. He had given Hugh an account of the Congress on his return to Oxford.

These congresses were set-piece occasions in the cultural Cold War between the United States, the 'Leader of the Free World', and the Soviet Union, the sponsor of international Communism. The decision to hold the Congress for Cultural Freedom in Berlin was an act of defiance in itself, as a report in *The Economist* recognised. Here the Cold War was at its chilliest. The city was an anomaly, a forlorn island surrounded by a Russian sea. It was accessible from the West only along restricted road and rail links, and by narrow air corridors. In 1948 the Russians had sealed the land links and tried to starve West Berlin into submission, but a continuous airlift had kept the city supplied for more than a year, until the Russians had relented and lifted the blockade. Afterwards Germany itself had become divided into two separate states, the Western-backed Federal Republic and the Communist German Democratic Republic.

It was therefore questionable whether it was possible to stage such a congress at such a time and in such a place, where pure intellectual discussion was bound to become contaminated by politics. Even while the Congress was taking place, Communist speakers in the Russian-occupied sector of the city denounced it. Cold War rivalry influenced every debate, penetrating every subject. Scholars found it difficult to avoid taking sides, even those in the physical sciences. The struggle between the two rival ideologies had spread across the globe, subsuming all other conflicts. The day before the Congress opened, troops from Communist North Korea invaded South Korea. In the temporary absence of the Soviet Union,* the United Nations Security Council passed a unanimous resolution condemning the North Korean aggression. Two days later President Truman pledged to use American military might to support the South Korean regime.

The week-long Congress opened with a series of set speeches, preceded and followed by Beethoven overtures, before an invited audience 2,000-strong; it would culminate with a further set of speeches delivered in the open air before an estimated 15,000. The core of the Congress was to be four public panel discussions, one on each day. Hugh had been asked to

---

* The Soviet Union was boycotting UN Security Council meetings, in protest against the fact that nationalist China (Taiwan) and not Communist China held a permanent seat on the Council.

participate in the first of these, on 'Science and Totalitarianism' ('Science' was taken to include the social sciences). He prepared a paper under the heading 'Truth, Liberalism, and Authority', in which he argued that, in the past as in the present, 'the war on science' had been 'a corollary – almost an automatic corollary – of ideological power struggling to establish or maintain itself'. A parallel for the current 'totalitarian war on science' could be found in the Counter-Reformation. Those committed to a doctrine of absolute truth, such as Marxists or Roman Catholics, would always resist free scientific enquiry. The duty of intellectuals was to 'clear their minds of cant': to resist the prohibition on free scientific enquiry demanded by those advocating such intolerant doctrines.[38]

The panel was opened by another of the British delegates, Freddie Ayer, whose paper soberly examined the philosophical justification for tolerance. This was heard in disapproving silence by the listeners, as much too 'low-key'. Afterwards the chairman dismissed Ayer's argument as irrelevant, since 'our enemies are too intolerant to be tolerated'. Hugh was persuaded to jettison his paper and to confine himself to a brief and reasoned plea for the impartial examination of the methods and aims of free enquiry. This too was received coldly. As the day went on, it became obvious that many of those present were not interested in debate.

There was much talk at the time about the responsibility of the intellectual to make public statements of belief. Earlier in the year *The God That Failed* had proved a bestseller in America. In this book six well-known writers from Europe and the United States – Louis Fischer, André Gide, Arthur Koestler, Ignazio Silone, Stephen Spender and Richard Wright – explained why they had renounced Communism. Several of the contributors to the book had been invited to the Congress.

Hugh had agreed to attend the Congress anticipating free intellectual discussion, and was disappointed when it turned out to be a political demonstration. The proceedings were hijacked by ex-Communists, led by Arthur Koestler and James Burnham,* who declared that the only choice open to the world was either to embrace Communism or to attack it. According to them, there was no middle way. Koestler attacked the British, and the Labour Party in particular, as parochial and isolationist for refusing to see the problem in such clear terms. Hugh disagreed. He believed that there were valid alternatives, of which socialism was only one. If forced to take sides, he feared that many French and Italian workers would choose Communism.

* American political theorist and author of the now largely forgotten *The Managerial Revolution* (1941). A Communist in the 1930s, Burnham moved rapidly to the Right, becoming an aggressive Cold War warrior. He attacked liberalism, which he saw as 'a syndrome', in his *Suicide of the West* (1964).

The crisis in Korea heightened emotions in the hall where the speeches were being delivered. Several of the speakers extolled the American decision to intervene in Korea. Both Ayer and Trevor-Roper were repelled by the frenziedly partisan atmosphere, and thumped the table to express their dissent. Indeed Burnham appeared to be advocating nuclear war. Hugh deplored such belligerent, irresponsible talk. On his transcript of Burnham's address he scribbled: 'a speech totally inappropriate to this congress'.

As the Congress continued, the more moderate delegates became increasingly uneasy. One especially demagogic speech, delivered by the Austrian writer Franz Borkenau, was received with thunderous applause by the excited Berlin audience. Hugh was appalled, both by the rabble-rousing rhetoric and by the 'hysterical German applause which greeted it', all too reminiscent of scenes he had witnessed in Germany before the war. He felt that the Congress had exposed an unholy alliance between ex-Communists, displaying all the zeal of the recently converted, and German nationalists, united in their detestation of Russia. He was not alone in deploring the tone of the speeches. After Borkenau had finished, one horrified Scandinavian delegate remarked that it was obviously time for Dr Adenauer to make way for Herr Otto Strasser.*

The Congress was due to close with the publication of a manifesto representing the unanimous view of the participants. The British delegates, backed by the Scandinavians and the Italian novelist Ignazio Silone, refused to accept the wording. They threatened to stage a walk-out unless the amendments drafted by Hugh were accepted. In particular, they objected to the sentence: 'Totalitarian ideologies which deny intellectual freedom have no right of citizenship in the republic of the spirit.' This was bad English and bad politics, appearing to justify the anti-Communist witch-hunts then being conducted in America. In the face of such strong opposition the offending sentence was withdrawn, and almost all the other amendments accepted, though the hardline ex-Communists continued protesting until the end. Afterwards they felt bitterly towards their two English guests. 'We were very unpopular, especially as we won in the end,' Hugh informed Berenson. 'No more aeroplanes, I'm afraid, will be sent to fetch us, in luxury, to international congresses: at least of that kind. But I enjoyed the fight!'[39]

In a piece for the *Manchester Guardian*,† Hugh regretted that the

---

* A dissident but unrepentant Nazi, then living in Nova Scotia and barred from Germany, who hoped to return and found a new political party.
† Lasky wrote two letters for publication in the *Manchester Guardian* disputing the version of events at the Congress presented by Hugh, and the two subsequently exchanged polite letters elaborating their differences in private. American officials expressed their dismay at Hugh's stance to the Foreign Office.

Congress had not been more constructive; 'it was simply Wroclaw in reverse'. He referred to a suggestion once made by Silone: that the coming struggle would be between Communists and ex-Communists. 'After the sterile congresses of Wroclaw and Berlin I am confirmed in my view that a more satisfactory solution will be offered by those who have never swallowed, and therefore never needed to re-vomit, that obscurantist doctrinal rubbish whose residue can never be fully discharged from the system.'[40]

Around this time Hugh found himself courted by the publisher Hamish Hamilton, known to his friends as 'Jamie'. Having missed the chance to publish *The Last Days of Hitler*, Hamilton was keen to right his mistake. Meanwhile he had come to know Hugh socially, partly as a result of a mutual friendship with Bernard Berenson. Hamilton and his Italian wife Yvonne had first visited Berenson in June 1947, only a month before Hugh, and subsequently they were frequent guests at I Tatti or Casa al Dono. In the early 1950s Hamilton began corresponding with Berenson regularly, around the same time that he came to know Hugh. In January 1950 he sent letters of introduction for Hugh to acquaintances in Capri, and later that year Hugh reciprocated by inviting Hamilton to a gaudy at Christ Church. He dined with Hamilton and his wife at their North London home (in Hamilton Terrace), and they often met at parties.

Hamilton's letters to Berenson provided glimpses of Hugh. At a Boughton weekend party, for example, 'Hugh Trevor-Roper was there, and we found ourselves wondering if one so young and gifted ought to spend quite so much time hating people. He has hardly a charitable word for anyone, and seems to relish the discomfiture even of those he is supposed to like. A strange mixture, and rather a frightening one.' Some months afterwards Hamilton dined alone with Hugh, who was 'entertaining as always, but the arrogance and vindictiveness make me uneasy'. On several occasions Hamilton forwarded letters from Hugh that he thought Berenson might like to see. Returning one of these, Berenson commented that it contained 'nothing that he has not told me, but with a verve, a brilliance, a panache, an illumination that is all but unique. Trevor-Roper is a good talker, a fine historian, but above all a superb letter-writer. *Floreat!*'[41]

Hamilton wanted to lure Hugh onto his list. Thus began a flirtation: Hamilton made frequent advances which Hugh rebuffed, but in a manner suggesting that future advances might not be unwelcome. In 1950, for example, Hamilton asked Hugh to write a life of Mussolini: an offer Hugh declined, while making it clear that he was not bound to Macmillan.[42] However, there was an awkwardness that had to be overcome if Hugh was to enter the Hamish Hamilton stable. Just as Hamilton was justifiably proud of the eponymous publishing company that he had founded in 1931, so he was anxious to edit from the record any story that suggested incompetence or lack of enterprise. After a lunch in Hampstead with the Kenneth Clarks, the Hamiltons offered Hugh a lift to Paddington station in their car. He was surprised when Hamilton pulled over well short of their destination. Hamilton turned to him with a grave expression, while his wife gave him an imploring look; it was obvious that they had rehearsed this moment. Hamilton then instructed Hugh <u>never</u> to mention the fact that he had missed the opportunity to publish *The Last Days of Hitler.*

Destroyer

'Someone someday will do to Tawney – whom I honour – what you are doing to Lawrence Stone,' Notestein had predicted, after receiving Hugh's letter announcing that he planned to 'liquidate' Stone. In his reply, Hugh had demurred. 'I am critical of Tawney, whom I also greatly admire, and I have contested him on one point in my article. You will see whether you agree with him or with me on that. But I don't believe that anyone will be able to do to him what I am doing to Stone, i.e. proving (as I submit) that he is neither honest nor a scholar.'[1]

Nevertheless, the research he had undertaken for his attack on the disciple had led him to question the teaching of the master. Stone's article on the Elizabethan aristocracy had been founded on the Tawney thesis of the rise of the gentry at the expense of the aristocracy. The data that Stone had used in support of his argument had been shown to be worthless. But might the thesis itself be mistaken? Hugh's experience was leading him to scrutinise his early *Marxisant* assumptions. Like almost every other historian of his generation, he had accepted certain fundamental tenets of Marxist dogma, believing in the omnipotence of economics and the inevitability of class struggle. Tawney's thesis fitted neatly into this orthodoxy. By 1950 it was becoming more difficult to subscribe to the Marxist creed. The intellectual dishonesty of Communist ideologues had become lamentably evident. An approach that had once seemed progressive and modern now seemed tired and clichéd. 'Marxism has been a great stimulus to historical study,' Hugh wrote in 1950, 'but by now it has long succumbed to intellectual sclerosis.'[2]

Tawney was no Communist, of course. But he had explained the upheavals of the seventeenth century in Marxist terms. He had identified the gentry as the 'middle class', enabling him to depict the upheaval in the mid-seventeenth century as a 'bourgeois revolution'. Hugh was now ready to break with the faith. 'I used to think that historical events always had deep economic causes,' he told Berenson; 'I now believe that pure farce covers a far greater field of history, and that Gibbon is a more reliable guide to that subject than Marx.'[3]

Early in 1951, before his attack on Stone had appeared in print, Hugh requested an offprint of his 'Rise of the Gentry' article from Tawney.[4] In retrospect this seems a disingenuous request, because two years later he would publish a critique of Tawney's thesis, arguing for a radical reinterpretation of the period. One does not usually ask a favour of a man one is about to attack. But perhaps, when he asked for the offprint, Hugh had not then reached the conclusion that Tawney needed to be challenged.

Hugh was still working on Sutton. In April 1951 he was hoping to complete the book during the summer. In fact he would write five chapters before putting them aside. He had not warmed to his subject. 'Millionaires – those of them who have made their own millions – are seldom interesting personalities,' he began. It was an unpromising opening for a biographical study. By mid-summer, after the disappointment of not being elected to the Chair of Modern History, he was sick of Sutton. He complained to Dawyck Haig that he had reached 'the 185th foolscap page* of an infinitely dull book which I am writing, and it is duller than even I had ever conceived, and now I realise that I don't really want to go on with it, and all is wasted labour'.[5] He did not altogether abandon the book. There remained the possibility that he might return to it later. He continued to collect material on Sutton, as he did on the July Plot. In 1955 he was still insisting that he would 'publish something fairly short about him before long'.[6]

In the early summer of 1952 Hugh delivered to the Editors of the *Economic History Review* the first draft of a long critique of Tawney's 'Rise of the Gentry' thesis. He began respectfully enough, by acknowledging the stimulus Tawney had provided to the study of the period; historians could 'no more think of it now in pre-Tawney terms than sociologists can think of society in pre-Marxist terms'. But the evidence for Tawney's thesis was weak. The gentry had not risen at the expense of the aristocracy. 'The rise of aristocracy under the Stuarts is far more significant than any decline they may have experienced under Elizabeth … the decline of the declining gentry in the early seventeenth century is at least as significant as the rise of the rising gentry.' Indeed, the economic distinction between aristocracy and gentry was an arbitrary one: both relied on land for their income. Hugh pointed out that most of the great new fortunes acquired in this period derived not from the profits of agriculture, but from either trade or the benefits of holding office under the Crown. The crucial distinction was not between aristocracy and gentry, but between Court and Country, between those who held offices and those who did not.

Hugh painted a vivid picture of impoverished and discontented country squires, the declining 'mere gentry', jealous of the fortunes made by merchants and office-holders and resentful of taxes. It was this class, the 'Independents', overlooked or dismissed by Tawney, who had given a

* The surviving manuscript has 184 consecutive numbered pages, plus several pages of inserts.

revolutionary quality to the century. Far from being a progressive 'bour-geois revolution', this had been a revolt of the decaying and backward-looking classes, those who longed to return to a decentralised, stable and stagnant society. He contrasted the 'Country gentry' with the 'Court gentry', citing *inter alia* the example of his own ancestor Sir John Roper, who with his great legal fortune had been able to purchase the barony of Teynham, and thus ascend into the aristocracy.

The style of Hugh's article was lofty, with much use of the personal pronoun – 'I will allow … ', 'I suspect … ', 'I doubt … ', 'I have already shown … ', and so on. 'If my thesis is correct,' he concluded, 'Prof. Tawney's thesis must be revised.'[7]

Though recognising it to be 'a very learned & able piece of work', Postan was embarrassed by this attack; Tawney was, after all, President of the Society which published the *Review*. His name appeared on their letterhead. 'He must modify – I mean mollify – the tone of his references to RHT', Postan wrote to his co-Editor, Habakkuk. 'The tone would have been excessively polemical even if the object of his strictures had been mere Stone. We certainly cannot allow this tone in reference to a man of RHT's academic eminence and personal character. I suspect T-R does not realise himself how offensive his asperities are.'

Habakkuk agreed. 'I find it difficult to decide whether T-R is a fun-damentally nice person in the grip of a prose style in which it is impossible to be polite, or a fundamentally unpleasant person … using rudeness as a disguise for nastiness.'[8] In fact, Hugh was well aware of the unease his article would cause. 'I am preparing a little aluminised bombshell on the English 17th century,' he confided to Berenson, 'and then, when it has been placed under the hieratic throne of the most respected of our professors, I shall retire in haste, to avoid the explosion, to the timeless, cultivated security (if the right of asylum is still granted to me) of I Tatti.'[9]

Habakkuk advised Hugh that the tone of his references to Tawney was, on a number of occasions, 'excessively polemical'.[10] There was a further problem in that the article was much too long: more than 20,000 words, far more than the journal's usual limit of 8,000 words. In this case Habakkuk was willing to publish an article of up to double this size, but no longer. Rather than edit his article down to 16,000 words, Hugh offered it instead to Macmillan, proposing to elongate it to 30,000 words, to make a slim book. Meanwhile he tried to discover what Tawney himself thought about the situation from the writer and artist Richard Rees, whom he had met while both were guests of Dawyck Haig in Scotland. Rees was a close friend of Tawney's and would become his literary executor. (He had also been close to George Orwell, and was Orwell's literary executor.) 'The fact is that I would like to publish the article in such a way as would irritate him least,'

Hugh confided to Rees, 'but various incidents cause me to be uncertain of the method to employ. I would be inclined to invite him to read it first, but I fear that he might regard this as impertinent. I do not know him personally, and I am told by people here that he has expressed strong antipathy to me and my work.' He explained to Rees that Professors Postan and Habakkuk – 'as shifty a couple as ever were hatched by your old University'* – had stated that his article was too long for them to publish. 'I am making arrangements to publish my article as a pamphlet (making it clear, of course, that the Econ. Hist. Rev. has refused it). But I would like to know how to handle Tawney, to whom I suspect I have been slanged by Postan. If you can give me any information about his attitude of mind – and how much he knows, or has been told (or misinformed) about my article – I should really be most grateful.'[11]

Rees assured him that he was quite wrong: there could be no question of dislike or disapproval. On the contrary, 'the Sage' never referred to him without praise and cut his articles out of the *New Statesman* to keep. Encouraged, Hugh wrote to Tawney, offering him a preview of the article. Tawney thanked him for his offer, but replied that he was too busy to take advantage of it. 'Besides, I should, in any case, feel some embarrassment in criticising criticisms on myself, even if I felt tempted to do so.'[12]

Hugh had gone so far as to sign a contract with Macmillan, from which he asked to be released when the Economic History Society relented, offering to publish his article as a separate supplement.[13] This was an innovation for the Society, the first of a small series of such supplements. Hugh delivered the final text on 1 December 1952 and the supplement was published, under the title *The Gentry 1540–1640*, early the following year. At Postan's urging, Hugh agreed to change the wording of his first footnote, referring to Stone's rejoinder to his 'Anatomy Anatomised'. He had originally written: 'his citations of my words there are of a piece with his previous handling of other sources'; he modified this to read 'he anyway seldom quotes me correctly'.[14]

The Gentry 1540–1640 was widely noticed, even earning a mention in the *Malay Mail* and a short summary review in the *North Borneo News* – an indication of how topical the subject seemed. Hugh received compliments from Namier and Neale. 'History would indeed have been much the poorer if this essay had not been published,' wrote Neale; he was sure that Tawney would not resent 'so brilliant and persuasive a re-interpretation of the problem'. Professor J.H. (Jack) Hexter, an American specialising in British history of the early modern period, praised *The Gentry* as a 'wonderful' essay. 'I think you have achieved a masterpiece of total devastation', he

---

* Cambridge.

wrote; 'The Tawney century just ain't there any more – *Spürlos versunkt!*'*[15]

Tawney published a short article responding to Hugh's criticisms. Its tone, though restrained, nevertheless revealed Tawney's distaste for such personal censure. 'An erring colleague is not an Amalekite to be smitten hip and thigh,' he protested.[†] 'My correction of some of Mr Hugh's misconceptions has, I trust, been free from the needless and unpleasing asperity into which criticism, to the injury of its cause, is liable on occasion to lapse.' He went out of his way to praise Stone's 'admirable' article 'The Elizabethan Aristocracy – A Restatement'.[16]

Hugh was irritated by what he perceived to be 'the smug, Olympian spirit' of Tawney's article, and particularly irritated by his praise of Stone. He wanted to continue the argument, but Postan refused to allow him space for this purpose. Hugh asked his Christ Church colleague Roy Harrod if the *Economic Journal* (of which Harrod was joint Editor) would publish his reply to Tawney. 'I think it is time that "economic historians" like Tawney & his school learnt a little honesty in <u>method</u>,' he declared; 'otherwise economic history will get nowhere.' He wanted to write a short article entitled 'Fabian Tactics' analysing Tawney's arguments. 'Having just reviewed[‡] the last four volumes of Arnold Toynbee's pretentious *Study of History* which is similar in its dishonest method I feel that the whole science of history is being vitiated by these methods whereby theories are first stated as facts on the basis of illustrations arbitrarily selected and then, when challenged, defended by dishonest tricks and a deferential editorial guillotine.'

Nothing came of this proposal. In subsequent correspondence Hugh continued to fulminate about 'Postan's somewhat disingenuous methods of editing', which, he claimed, had prevented the *Economic History Review* from becoming a free forum for discussion. As one of Harrod's colleagues remarked, 'T-R is rather notoriously at loggerheads with Postan'.[17] Hugh tried to resurrect the debate on the letters pages of the *Times Literary Supplement*, arguing that Tawney's thesis had 'supplied the orthodoxy – I would say the error – of a generation, which has been accepted with cries of ideological delight by Marxists and Roman Catholics alike'.[18] His letter was not published.

---

* 'Sunk without a trace'.

† This is a misquotation: it was the Philistines who were 'smitten hip and thigh' (Judges 15:8), not the Amalekites, who were indeed smitten (1 Samuel 14:48 etc.), but not hip and thigh. Possibly Tawney was remembering the account left by Darwin's friend Sir Joseph Hooker of the famous debate in 1860 between Thomas Henry Huxley and the Bishop of Oxford, Samuel Wilberforce, in which he made the same error.

‡ In *The Sunday Times*, 17 October 1954. Hugh had met Toynbee at Alys Russell's in September 1947.

In his attacks on Tawney and Stone, Hugh acknowledged the help of another Oxford historian, J.P. (John) Cooper, a Fellow of Trinity. Cooper was of the same generation as Stone. He had been a grammar school boy, a pupil of the Magdalen medievalist K.B. McFarlane; his undergraduate career had been interrupted by war service in the Army. After taking a first-class degree in modern history in 1947, he became, successively, a lecturer at Manchester University and a Fellow of All Souls. In 1951–2 he worked alongside McFarlane as a junior lecturer at Magdalen. A letter from him to Hugh acknowledged the latter's help in his election to a Fellowship at Trinity in 1952.[19] Cooper was known to have imbibed McFarlane's scrupulously high standards, and he showed little tolerance for those who failed to meet these. His criticisms carried corresponding authority. An irascible, moody character, with an intimidating exterior, he inspired fear in those of whom he disapproved. His career, like that of his mentor McFarlane, showed a reluctance to publish his own findings, combined with a readiness to criticise the work of those less inhibited. 'As you may know,' Notestein wrote to Hugh before the 'Anatomy Anatomised' article was published, 'John Cooper has been exceedingly critical of Stone's conclusions, and Cooper is a careful scholar.'[20]

Cooper provided a statistical appendix to Hugh's *The Gentry*. The acknowledgements to Cooper in both this and the 'Anatomy Anatomised' article indicate that he and Hugh discussed both pieces in detail as they were being written. According to one who knew them both, Hugh was 'slightly frightened' by Cooper. Though Postan refused to allow Hugh to continue the argument in the pages of the *Economic History Review*, he did accept a contribution from Cooper, which mercilessly exposed the inadequacies of the statistics quoted by both Tawney and Stone. Tawney's numerical evidence, which had persuaded a generation of historians, was shown to have been erected on an error in classification – a statistical mirage reared on a taxonomic illusion. His method of estimating landed fortunes by counting manors, Cooper concluded, seemed to have effects dangerously akin to the counting of sheep: 'it introduces us to a dream world, in which, as in our own dreams, reality may not be entirely absent, but appearances are often deceptive'.[21]

Controversies between academics are not uncommon, but this one was unusual in its ferocity, and in the attention it attracted; indeed, it became a *cause célèbre*. In 1958 *Encounter* published Jack Hexter's overview of the debate, 'Storm over the Gentry: The Tawney–Trevor-Roper Controversy'. This was a substantial article of more than 12,000 words, and it prompted a correspondence stretching over several subsequent issues, including contributions from Hugh himself and from Christopher Hill, as well as younger historians like Patrick Collinson and J.G.A. Pocock. Half a century later, it seems surprising that a magazine aimed at the general reader in Britain and America (albeit the highbrow general reader) should have allowed so much space to such an academic argument. It shows how topical the events of the 1640s and 1650s seemed in the 1950s, when the interpretation of the causes of the English Revolution seemed central to the ideological struggle between East and West. Hexter stressed the emancipating effect of the debate.[22] By then the storm had blown itself out: despite the havoc left behind, the air was clear. Hugh had challenged a theory that had become orthodoxy; in doing so he made it possible for a new generation of historians to examine the subject afresh.

'There is nothing so exhilarating as a good battle, I find,' he wrote jauntily to Dawyck Haig, after successfully defending himself against a prosecution for dangerous driving; 'especially if one wins it!' Combat stimulated him, rousing him from lethargy and curing depression. To Haig, he affected to be ashamed of his 'sudden deviations into aggression and bellicosity' – war against the clergy at home, war against 'impertinent' adversaries abroad, controversies in the learned journals, battles in the University – while insisting that, for him, these were 'absolutely necessary to the morale'.[23]

Early in 1950 he had criticised Oxford University Press in the pages of *The Times Literary Supplement* for its strict enforcement of its perpetual copyright in Clarendon's *History of the Rebellion*. The issue had arisen from the publication of an anthology of documents illustrating the social significance of the Great Rebellion of 1640–1660, *The Good Old Cause*, edited by Christopher Hill and Edmund Dell.* The editors had wished to include passages from Clarendon, but had been forbidden from doing so by the OUP. The extracts had already been set up in page proof, and had to be expensively removed. The fact that the Press had effectively allowed Clarendon's great work to go out of print added insult to injury. Since the late nineteenth century, Hugh suggested, 'the copyright has been used not to publish but to prevent the publication of Clarendon's works'. This was, perhaps, a strange policy for a university press, and he speculated on its cause. 'It cannot be economic,' he continued, 'and it can hardly be supposed,' he remarked cuttingly, that 'the Delegates of the University Press are actuated by a bigoted zeal for the suppression of learning' – especially as the Delegates, the governing body of the Press, were themselves dons. He suggested that their motive had been to protect their copyright, and argued that their interpretation of copyright law was faulty. 'Clearly,' he

---

* Edmund Dell (1921–99), then a lecturer in modern history at Queen's, later a successful Labour politician and company director. In the 1950s Hugh reported to MI5 on suspicions that Dell was a covert Communist. Ironically, Dell would later have difficulties with left-wingers in his constituency and ended as a Liberal Democrat supporter.

wrote, 'the present policy of the Oxford Press in this matter is either deep and obscure or very silly.'[24]

Though the Press relented, and announced that in future the Delegates would allow extracts from Clarendon to be quoted in books printed by other publishers, the officers of OUP were upset by Hugh's 'rude frontal attack'. The Secretary to the Delegates, Arthur Norrington, admitted to his opposite number at the Cambridge University Press, B.J.L. Kingsford, that he had been 'considerably startled by it'. Replying, Kingsford deplored Hugh's 'offensive' letter. 'What a nuisance these loud-speakers are!' he exclaimed.

'The affair is heat-provoking, not so much for its matter as its manner,' Norrington grumbled to G.N. Clark, Editor of the *Oxford History of England*. To another colleague Norrington commented that this action had been 'infernally uncivil of T-R'; it was generally known that he was 'fond of a fight'.[25] A few months later the OUP editor Dan Davin reported to the Publisher, Geoffrey Cumberlege, that he had dined with Hugh at Christ Church. 'We got along very well and he seemed to be much more reasonable than I had expected,' Davin reported. Cumberlege replied that he was glad to hear it. 'I have met him and I think I found him pleasant. I am not certain, however, that he is not one of a large class whom one gets on very well with in conversations but who behave very differently when the excitement of an academic or legalistic problem offers itself.'[26]

Hugh's innate combativeness may have been exacerbated by a chronic recurrence of his sinus difficulties, with the accompanying headaches which drove him to seek refuge in bed, the curtains drawn against the light. A notice was often pinned to his outer door indicating that 'The Senior Censor is in bed', and redirecting undergraduates elsewhere. On the train journey back from a stay at I Tatti over Christmas 1951, he was again 'struck down by that repeated and therefore boring complaint to which I periodically surrender'. By the time he reached London he felt able to go no further, and begged a bed from friends, where he remained a week. This renewed affliction decided him to have a further operation to remove part of his septum, a decision he had been avoiding for some years. This was a similar operation to the two he had undergone in 1940. Though not serious, it was extremely unpleasant in its immediate consequences. Such repeated problems with his sinuses cannot have sweetened his temper.[27]

One day in the vacation, Hugh was impatient to leave the college to drive to the airport, where he was booked on a flight to Iceland. To his annoyance he found his Bentley's exit blocked by another parked car. There was no sign of the owner. The car was locked, but 'by elaborate mechanical ingenuity' he managed to open it and release the handbrake, and then petulantly pushed it out of his way. Unfortunately it ran backwards and smashed against the stonework. It was not until he had reached his destination that Hugh learned the identity of the owner: Lord Cherwell. He wrote a letter of explanation, half-apologetic, half-defiant. 'My dear Prof,' he began; 'Had I known it was yours, I should have called on you & asked you to move it, which would have been much easier; but I'm afraid that (since I associate Overlords with more splendid limousines) I assumed that this car (like others near it) was an improperly-introduced tourist car.' 'I am sorry that you should have treated even a tourist's car the way you treated mine,' replied Lord Cherwell, 'but I take it that the Censor is above the restraint applying to ordinary people. I am sending the car to be repaired by Hart-wells and will tell them to send the bill to you. I was surprised to get an envelope marked Reykjavik but I assume that the stamp with the volcano on it was chosen to symbolise your temperament.'[28]

In 1952 Hugh placed his literary affairs in the hands of an agent, A.D. Peters. (Peters also acted for Evelyn Waugh; the combination of these two antagonists with one agent was the source of amusement on occasion.) At the outset of this new arrangement Hugh summarised the state of his literary earnings. He explained that his ordinary book publishers in England were Macmillan; he was under no contractual obligation to them for any future books 'but my relations with them are good'. On the other hand, he was determined not to publish another book with the Macmillan Company of New York after the pusillanimous way in which the firm had buckled to pressure from American Catholics objecting to passages in *The Last Days of Hitler*. He wished to write a number of longer articles on historical subjects which could in time be recycled in a book of historical essays, together with the most substantial book reviews. In the late 1940s he had written the occasional review for *The Observer*, as well as acting as a special correspondent overseas; but in 1951 he had been lured to *The Sunday Times*, which paid him 180 guineas a year for up to nine book reviews. Two years later this agreement was upgraded to a retainer worth £1,000 a year,* giving *The Sunday Times* first call on his services to write book reviews and 'special articles ... as may be agreed upon with the Editor'. This valuable contract was the beginning of a relationship with the newspaper that would last half a lifetime. An important element in the deal was that he would travel abroad and report on his findings.[29]

As he explained to Peters, he also wrote for the *New Statesman*, which paid him between £5 and £10 for a review, depending on the length, and £21 for a more substantial 'Books in General' piece. Before the arrival of the formidable Janet Adam Smith as Assistant Literary Editor in 1949, he

* Worth over £20,000 in today's money.

had written only a handful of reviews for the magazine, but from that year onwards he became a regular contributor. In the 1950s the *New Statesman* was an important influence on the Left of British politics, with a circulation approaching 100,000 and a claimed readership of 'nearly half-a-million thinking people'. Janet Adam Smith became Literary Editor in 1952, and assembled a glittering team of star reviewers, including Richard Crossman, Malcolm Muggeridge, J.B. Priestley, V.S. Pritchett and Hugh's colleague A.J.P. Taylor. As a result, the magazine gained an unrivalled reputation for intellectual weight. It was often remarked that in her time the second half of the magazine, where the reviews were printed, became essential reading for all sorts of people who had little sympathy with the first half. On the whole Hugh would review books on sixteenth- and seventeenth-century history in the *New Statesman*, and books on Nazi Germany and more general history in *The Sunday Times*. In those days the *New Statesman* was willing to print reviews of academic books (such as *Studies in the Agrarian History of England in the Thirteenth Century*), of such a specialist nature as to test the resolve of even *The Times Literary Supplement.*

Hugh's regular reviewing for the *New Statesman* and *The Sunday Times*, and his reporting as a special correspondent for *The Observer* and *The Sunday Times*, kept his name constantly in front of the reading public. He earned a reputation as a brilliant mind and a scintillating writer. By the early 1950s he was recognised too as an international commentator on Germany, on the Soviet bloc, on European politics, and even what he called 'The Barbary Coast', viz. North Africa. As a prominent intellectual, in a period when intellectuals commanded attention and respect in the media and public life, his opinions were sought on a wide variety of subjects. In 1951 he was invited to join the panel for *Question Time*, a half-hour radio programme of spontaneous discussion of listeners' questions. Though this programme was part of the 'London Calling Asia' service, heard only in the Far East, Hugh's appearance was followed by others on the Home Service and the Third Programme.* In February 1952, for example, he was part of a panel discussing the question, 'Can we hope for another Elizabethan Age?'

In the spring vacation of 1951 Hugh took a walking holiday in Greece. The country was still recovering from a bitter civil war; few tourists dared go, or at least to stir outside Athens. The result was that he never met another foreigner. 'It was heaven,' he wrote. In one three-day trek he covered eighty miles: 'the most terrible, but also the most wonderful walk,' as he described it in retrospect. 'I rather like discomfort, and sleeping out-of-doors, or in peasants' huts.' At dawn he had waded waist-deep across the River Alpheus,

---

* Now known as Radio 4 and Radio 3 respectively.

then in flood and ice-cold; the stony river-bed felt like knives to his bare feet.[30] But it was worth braving the dust and the heat, the squalid inns and the physical exhaustion, he wrote to Dawyck Haig (whom he had tried to persuade to accompany him there), in order to glimpse the Temple of Bassae, still almost perfect and hidden in the Arcadian mountains eight miles from the nearest road.[31] He had an alarming experience in the Peleponnese town of Megalópolis, reminiscent of events in wartime Dublin, when his hotel bedroom was invaded at 3.00 a.m. by enraged soldiers who stabbed his mattress with their bayonets. They accused him of being a Communist spy – 'not for the first or the last time', he reflected wryly many years later.[32] On his return home from Greece he stayed a relaxing week at I Tatti. Afterwards he wrote to Berenson enthusing about Gibbon, 'the greatest of all historians', whom he had begun re-reading 'for the nth time' in Crete and on Mount Hymettus. 'What a splendid writer he is! If only historians could write like him now! How has the art of writing footnotes altogether perished and the gift of irony disappeared!'[33]

In the summer of that year Hugh visited Spain for the first time, with a diversion to Portugal. He didn't much like the latter, but the former was a revelation, particularly the 'high, endless, golden emptiness of the Castilian plateau'.[34] He had gone there with an undergraduate, Michael McCreary, and they had often slept out under the stars to save money. 'I was fascinated altogether by that extraordinary, incongruous, accidental, isolated appendage to Europe,' he told Berenson.[35] He confessed to Dawyck Haig that he had conceived 'a romantic passion' for 'that strange peninsula'.[36] He became convinced that familiarity with Spanish history was essential for understanding developments in early modern Europe as a whole.[37] He realised, too, that the Spanish archives were relatively unexplored. 'What wonderful subjects of history there are in Spain, if only there were historians to explore them,' he remarked, while contemplating a visit to Spain to work in the Simancas national archive.[38] Over the next few years he would return to Spain several times on behalf of *The Sunday Times*. A.J.P. Taylor congratulated him on an article he wrote about General Franco. 'What a good writer you are,' exclaimed Taylor; 'the only contemporary historian with a Gibbonian turn of phrase and wit.'[39] Hugh began to review books on Spanish subjects. His interest in the country had been kindled by reading Gerald Brenan's *The Spanish Labyrinth: an Account of the Social and Political Background of the Civil War* (1943) – 'an astonishing work', as he described it to Berenson. 'The richness of the historical knowledge, the heroic intellectual integrity, the rejection of all ready-made formulae, the monumental learning behind it, the burning lucidity of the style – it made everything else written on Spain seem pitifully shoddy.' *The Spanish Labyrinth* took its place alongside C.M. Doughty's *Arabia Deserta* as one of Hugh's favourites.

Though the book ostensibly dealt only with the run-up to the Spanish Civil War, Hugh made his best pupils studying sixteenth- and seventeenth-century Spain read it, because of the profound analysis of Spanish history 'between the lines' of its pages.[40]

Brenan was then in his late fifties, a figure from the fringes of the Bloomsbury Group (he had been Dora Carrington's lover). He had not been to university and was entirely self-taught; after almost twenty years living and studying in Spain he had been forced to return to England at the outbreak of the Spanish Civil War. Years afterwards Hugh would tell Brenan that he was 'my ideal historian – you see the past in the present, and the present in the past, imaginatively, and yet with corrective scholarship, and you express it in perfect prose'. He had begun corresponding with Brenan by a fan letter. 'Since my admiration for your works grows rather than diminishes with time,' he wrote in 1952, '(as does my curiosity about certain problems in Spanish history which, I become more and more convinced, only you can relieve), may I consult you, either in writing, or, if that is not even more inconvenient to you, by personally calling on you if you should be at leisure?' Hugh outlined to Brenan his notion of an antithesis between Court and Country, which he believed was far more fundamental than religious differences to an understanding of seventeenth-century England. He wondered whether a comparable dichotomy was detectable in seventeenth-century Spain.[41]

Soon afterwards he was invited to visit Brenan, then living near Marlborough, and found that he liked both Brenan and his wife 'enormously'. Hugh wrote of Brenan that he had 'an almost heroic integrity, a hatred and impatience of humbug which reminds me of George Orwell; than whom however he is much more genial and sociable'. In 1953 Brenan and his wife were allowed to return to Spain and settle in Andalusia, where he would remain, almost continuously, until his death in 1987, at the age of ninety-three. In subsequent years Hugh was often a guest of the Brenans in their simple Spanish home. 'There is nowhere where I feel that conversation is as uninhibited, as intelligent, and as general.' Though he could not pretend that the house was comfortable, he found it 'the most interesting, most intellectually stimulating place that I know'.[42]

Hugh's new interest in Spain was a mark of his unceasing intellectual curiosity, even while in the thick of the most ferocious controversy in English history for a generation. His admiration, indeed veneration, for Brenan showed his readiness to learn from the most unconventional scholar, one quite outside the main current of academic life.

While travelling in Spain in 1951 Hugh read a volume of *Hitler's Table-Talk*, which had just been published in Germany. As he explained to

Berenson, he thought this a book 'of great historical importance', an interesting corrective to the fashionable view that Hitler had been 'a pure charlatan, only accidentally placed in a position of absolute power' – a view which seemed to him 'not only wrong but, by its almost inevitable political consequences, disastrous'. Hugh was convinced that, contrary to all received opinion, Hitler had possessed a powerful mind, a conviction he had formed from his reading of *Mein Kampf* before the war. 'I contemplate (if I can find the time) writing something on *The Mind of Hitler.*' He told Berenson that he had mentioned this project 'with casual boastfulness, under the influence of your splendid hospitality' to Jamie Hamilton; 'forgetting (under the same influence) that I was surrounded by pouncing publishers'. But, as he explained to Hamilton, he envisaged it as only an article; if it developed into a book, he would feel obliged to offer it to Macmillan.[43]

A year later Hugh learned that what appeared to be a more authoritative text of *Hitler's Table-Talk* was to be published in France. The copyright was claimed by one François Genoud, a businessman from Lausanne who had come to a financial arrangement with Hitler's sister Paula, his only surviving relative. But the issue of who owned Hitler's copyrights was untested in the courts, and the position was further complicated by the claim of the stenographer who had taken down the table-talk and who had licensed the German edition. Genoud was the son of a Swiss wallpaper manufacturer and a half-English mother. As a teenager he had been sent for his education to Germany, and in 1932, at the age of seventeen, he had shaken hands with the *Führer*, who became his lifelong idol. Since the war he had cultivated prominent surviving Nazis and the families of the former Nazi leaders. In time he would come to control the literary estates of both Goebbels and Bormann.

Hugh approached Genoud about publishing an English translation of *Hitler's Table-Talk*. They arranged to meet at the Hotel Kléber in Paris. Hugh had suggested this project to Macmillan, without success. Instead he was accompanied by George Weidenfeld, 'a smart, smooth, enterprising émigré from Vienna' whom he had met through Isaiah Berlin.[44] Weidenfeld had recently set up his own publishing house in partnership with Nigel Nicolson, and was beginning to display the deal-making skill that was to make him one of the most successful international publishers of his time. He had already published an English-language edition of the memoirs of Hjalmar Schacht, Hitler's Minister of Economics. But Schacht had never been a member of the Nazi Party; it was another matter to publish the anti-Semitic rants of the *Führer* himself. Hitler rested awkwardly on the list of a Jewish publisher. Weidenfeld decided that he was willing to publish Nazi source material, provided that it was prefaced and annotated by respectable historians. He had recently married Jane Sieff, heiress to the Marks & Spencer fortune. At the time of the meeting with Genoud, the couple were staying at the Paris home of her aunt, Lady Marks. Though Weidenfeld was rather secretive about the appointment, the two women wormed out of him that he was meeting a distinguished Oxford historian and a Nazi sympathiser with access to important source material.

Genoud proved to be an intense, nervous man with dark hair and Mediterranean, almost Semitic features. He and Weidenfeld rapidly agreed terms for an English edition. During the conversation, while the three men were huddled together in the hotel lobby, Weidenfeld's wife walked past with her aunt. The two women glowered at the Nordic-looking Hugh, whom they understandably mistook for the Nazi.[45]

The English-language edition of *Hitler's Table-Talk* appeared in 1953. In his introductory essay, 'The Mind of Adolf Hitler', Hugh argued that Hitler could not be dismissed as either a mere visionary or a mere adventurer; 'he was a systematic thinker'. Historians had said little of Hitler's mind, or dismissed it as non-existent – 'partly, no doubt, because of its repellent character'. His table-talk did indeed exhibit his 'coarseness and crudity, the dogmatism, the hysteria, the triviality', and was 'cluttered ... by much tedious and much disgusting matter'; but it also contained 'the kernel of his thinking'; it was 'the mirror of his hideous genius'. Hugh argued that Hitler's programme was fixed from the moment he left prison in 1924; every subsequent glimpse 'shows its consistency'. The last words he was recorded as having written were an exhortation 'to win territory for the German people in the East'.

The book received mixed reviews. In the *New Statesman* Leonard Woolf dissented from Hugh's view of Hitler and gave his opinion that 'this book does not add much to our knowledge'. Alan Bullock, writing in *The Observer*, remained unconvinced that Hitler 'had read either so widely or so deeply as Mr Trevor-Roper appears to think'.* Gordon Craig gave it an indifferent review in *The New York Herald Tribune*. Writing in the *Manchester Guardian*, A.J.P. Taylor praised the introduction as 'beyond doubt, the most penetrating study of Hitler yet made'. Its inevitable fault, argued Taylor, was to be too rational: 'it tries to pin Hitler down within the confines of systematic thought'. Hugh had stressed Hitler's geopolitical ambitions; Hitler had certainly predicted that the 'decisive struggle' would be that between Germany and Russia, but 'he had talked earlier of the decisive struggle with France, and he might just as well have talked later of the

---

* This was a response to Hugh's review in *The New York Times Magazine*, earlier in the year (22 May 1953), of Bullock's *Hitler: A Study in Tyranny*. While praising Bullock's biography as 'comprehensive, clear and well-written', Hugh deplored his 'lack of interest in Hitler's mind'.

decisive struggle with the United States'. Taylor thought that *Hitler's Table-Talk* revealed no more than what was uppermost in his mind at that moment.[46]

The book proved a profitable publication, and was revived in fresh editions over subsequent decades as new material emerged. It is still in print today. Hugh received a handsome fee of 300 guineas for writing his introduction to the first edition and 'doing such editorial work as you feel necessary', which turned out to be very little.[47] He and Weidenfeld had another meeting with the 'seedy Swiss' in September 1953, when they lunched with Genoud to discuss the 'literary remains' of Martin Bormann.[48] The following year Weidenfeld published *The Bormann Letters*, with another introduction by Hugh, who received a fee of 100 guineas, plus another 100 if the book was serialised (it was), and a further 100 if it was sold to an American publisher (it was).[49] The letters provided revealing insights into the personal relationships of the Nazi leaders. 'Bormann, ever the perfect bureaucrat, not only sent his wife's letters home so that she could file them, but also included the love letters written to him by an actress, whose seduction he triumphantly reported to Gerda.'[50]

Perhaps the strangest of the controversies with which Hugh became embroiled as a result of his investigation into the death of Hitler was that surrounding the role of Himmler's Estonian masseur, Felix Kersten. This reached its climax in 1953. The royal family of Sweden became involved; diplomatic messages were exchanged between Stockholm and London. But the facts remained confused, and the issues potent enough to be still the subject of partisan dispute in the twenty-first century.

After the publication of *The Last Days of Hitler* Hugh had received a long, civil letter from Count Folke Bernadotte, whose grandfather had been King of Sweden and whose uncle was then on the throne. Bernadotte complained that Hugh had downplayed the importance of the humanitarian mission he had undertaken in the last months of the war, when he had gone to Germany as a representative of the Swedish Red Cross to negotiate with Himmler. Tens of thousands of Scandinavian prisoners, including several thousand Jews, had been rescued from German concentration camps as a result.[51] 'I thought that Bernadotte was pitching his claims rather high,' Hugh noted, 'but I replied saying that I had not touched on these subjects because they were not relevant to my subject.' Following a request from the Swedish publishers he allowed them to include this exchange of letters as an appendix to the Swedish edition of the book.[52] In 1948 Bernadotte was assassinated by Zionist terrorists, while acting as a mediator in Palestine on behalf of the United Nations.

Two years later a biography of Bernadotte appeared, written by the former *Daily Mail* journalist Ralph Hewins. To Hugh, it bore the signs of being a sponsored work, financed by Bernadotte's widow, an American millionairess who had inherited a fortune founded on asbestos manufacture. Some years before the book was published, Hewins had written to Hugh in the guise of an old Christ Church man interested in *The Last Days of Hitler*, without providing so much as a hint that he was contemplating a book himself. Hewins had then quoted in his book from Hugh's reply remarks that were never intended for publication. To make matters worse, Hewins had included a three-page appendix denouncing Hugh in what the victim described as 'very abusive language'. In his foreword Hewins had acknowledged *The Last Days of Hitler* as a principal source, alongside Bernadotte's memoirs; but he had not acknowledged that he had both sought and been granted permission to quote from it, and he criticised 'Professor [*sic*] Trevor-Roper's' treatment of Bernadotte as 'unfair and unhistorical'. Thus, as Hugh complained to Lovat Dickson, 'he had deliberately concealed the discreditable fact that he has been fed by the hand he is biting'. According to Hewins, Hugh had seldom lost an opportunity 'of rating Bernadotte down'. His 'prejudices' against neutrals accounted for the 'error and misconceptions' in *The Last Days of Hitler*. 'I draw attention to these points,' Hewins concluded, 'partly because I am anxious to expose and condemn the prejudices which they connote, partly for the sake of the record.' Hugh told Dickson that Hewins was 'perfectly entitled to be as ungrateful, as ignorant, and (short of defamation) as offensive about me as he likes'; but he was annoyed that Hewins had, as he saw it, 'behaved badly', and asked Dickson to seek redress from Hewins's publishers, Hutchinson.[53] Hugh believed that this and other such attacks were motivated by those trying to justify Swedish neutrality in the war, for whom Bernadotte was their 'mascot'. To Hugh this stank of hypocrisy. In his view, Swedish neutrality had been motivated at best by a desire for self-protection, with a large measure of self-interest. Swedish industry was dependent on access to German markets.

Hewins's book contained no mention of Himmler's masseur, Felix Kersten: the man who, so Hugh's researches convinced him, deserved much of the credit which had accrued to Bernadotte for rescuing prisoners from concentration camps. Through a technique of 'manual therapy' which he had devised himself, Kersten had been able to relieve the agonising stomach cramps from which Himmler suffered, and as a result had gained a unique position of influence over the terrible *Reichsführer*-SS, one of the most powerful men in Europe. 'All tyrants, isolated in dangerous eminence – especially if they are fundamentally weak men,' wrote Hugh, 'require confidants whom (perhaps wrongly) they suppose to be outside the vortex of political rivalry around them.' Court fools, astrologers, priests and mistresses had filled this role in the past; modern despots relied on doctors. Himmler had allowed Kersten great liberties; and, so it seemed, Kersten had repeatedly interceded with his patient to save lives. In 1941 Hitler had ordered that three million Dutchmen be transported to Polish Galicia, and charged Himmler with this task; Kersten claimed that to have used his influence to postpone this appalling scheme until the war was over. In recognition of his intercession the Dutch government proposed Kersten, unsuccessfully, for the Nobel Peace Prize. Hugh endorsed the proposal.[54]

In Sweden, however, where Kersten made his home after the war, his contribution was minimised and his name tainted by association with Himmler, though of course it was this very association which, so he claimed, had enabled him to help so many prisoners under the control of the SS. In 1944 Kersten had secured the release of Swedish businessmen arrested in Warsaw on charges of espionage, and had escorted several of them back to Sweden. As a result of this comparatively minor incident he had established contact with the Swedish Foreign Ministry. In the last winter of the war, when it became clear that German defeat was imminent, Hitler had given orders that prisoners in the concentration camps should be slaughtered to prevent their being liberated by the Allied armies. It was Kersten who had put the Swedish Foreign Minister in touch with Himmler, resulting in the release of the Scandinavian prisoners. Bernadotte's role, so Hugh came to believe, was no more than that of a transport officer. Indeed Bernadotte had at first refused to take any Jews and, when Kersten protested, had warned him to keep quiet unless he wanted to create difficulties for himself and his family in Sweden.

Kersten flew to Stockholm and protested to the Swedish Foreign Minister in person. This led to what Hugh described as 'one of the most ironical incidents in the whole war'. On 21 April 1945, Norbert Masur, a representative of the World Jewish Congress, entered Nazi Germany, protected only by a Swedish passport, for a secret meeting with Himmler, convened at Kersten's country house. Himmler greeted the visitor: 'Welcome, Herr Masur. It is time you Jews and we Nazis buried the hatchet!' Two days after this bizarre interview, Himmler gave Bernadotte permission to take as many prisoners as he wanted from the camps.

When Hugh met Kersten in Holland in the early 1950s, he found him an insensitive character. But that was not the point. Hugh was outraged that Bernadotte had been credited for saving these prisoners while Kersten had been ignored. Moreover, he was provoked by Hewin's criticism. He decided that the issue should be aired publicly, and that he would support Kersten's cause by writing an article for the English-language press. This was accepted by the American magazine *The Atlantic Monthly,** for publication in their issue of February 1953. Hugh anticipated that his article would upset those who venerated Bernadotte as a humanitarian hero. To criticise Bernadotte was tantamount to sacrilege. Hugh had long wanted to visit Sweden, and decided to go there before 'all social doors in Stockholm will be shut against me'.[55] In January he journeyed to Sweden with an American friend, Harvey Poe, bearing a letter of introduction from Berenson. The envelope was addressed simply, 'The King'.

'I greatly enjoyed my visit,' Hugh reported afterwards to Nicky Mariano; 'I did everything I intended to do; visited the places that I went to see, studied in the libraries where I meant to study, and returned enlightened to Oxford.' The King, a regular guest of Berenson's, 'was extremely kind to me for the sake of his friends at I Tatti'. He had taken Hugh to the royal residence at Drottningholm, shown him everything that he wanted to see there, told him all about Queen Christina's pictures, arranged his visits to the museum, and seen to it that all his needs were 'admirably supplied'. Embarrassed, Hugh had felt obliged to tell the King, 'as seemed only fair', that he had written an article 'which might not be welcome in Sweden'; though His Royal Highness had seemed 'not too well pleased', he received the information calmly. While in Stockholm, Hugh had called on Kersten, who had shown him 'some fascinating documents', including records of his conversations with Himmler.[56] The authenticity of these documents would later be questioned.

Hugh's article elicited the anticipated protests. The Swedish Ambassador in Washington complained to *The Atlantic Monthly*. The Swedish Foreign Office released a communiqué to the press on the subject, categorically denying that Bernadotte had refused to transfer Jews to Sweden. Hugh issued his own statement to the press in reply. Sir Roger Stevens, British Ambassador in Stockholm, sent a dispatch to London deploring the *Atlantic Monthly* article. 'Count Bernadotte is generally regarded in Sweden as having been a man of high principle and exemplary character,' he wrote. 'Thanks to his work in Germany at the end of the war he became a symbol of Swedish humanitarianism – a necessary balm to many Swedish consciences for escaping the war; and his murder in Palestine transformed his memory into a legend. Mr Trevor-Roper's unexpected attack on his reputation naturally caused a considerable sensation.' Stevens thought it unfortunate that Hugh had used his powers of historical detection to blacken the memory of Count Bernadotte. 'By doing so he has caused needless pain to many Swedes and in particular to members of the Swedish Royal Family, who have mentioned the subject to me with evident distress.'

---

* Now known as *The Atlantic*. Isaiah Berlin had suggested publishing the article there.

A Foreign Office official commented that 'Mr Trevor-Roper's bent as a historian is as a "de-bunker". I do not think he would ever allow his work to be much affected by other people's feelings.' The official was sure that it would be 'quite useless for us to try to get him in any way to recant'. The incident was 'best forgotten'.[57]

Hugh, meanwhile, was beginning to have doubts. One of the documents which Kersten had shown him purported to be a copy of a letter from Bernadotte to Himmler, dated 10 March 1945. If authentic, it was very damaging to the sender. Not only had Bernadotte offered to supply information to enable German V-weapons to find their targets in England; he had stated bluntly that he did not wish to take any Jewish prisoners back to Sweden. This appeared to confirm what Hugh already believed from other sources, and had alleged in his *Atlantic Monthly* article. But the language of the letter was maladroit, and seemed incompatible with the status of an experienced negotiator like Bernadotte. What was the source of this document, and where was the original? After Hugh voiced these doubts, Kersten produced an affidavit attesting the document's authenticity from Gottlob Berger, former head of the SS Office, the same General Berger whom Hugh had interrogated in 1945. A sworn statement from such a source did not impress Hugh. On the balance of probabilities it seemed to him likely that the document was a forgery, and that Kersten had forged it. If this were so, might not the other documents in Kersten's archive have been forged too? His confidence in Kersten was shaken.

There was a sub-plot to this rivalry between Kersten and Bernadotte. Norbert Masur had not been the emissary originally chosen to meet Himmler; that honour was intended for Hillel Storch, chairman of the Stockholm World Jewish Congress. It was Storch who had undertaken the preliminaries, in the expectation that he would be the one to enter the ogre's den. Like Masur, Storch had shown heroic courage in his willingness to confront the arch-enemy of his people to save his fellow-Jews. He was not a Swedish citizen, however, but a Latvian, a citizen of a nation swallowed up by the Soviet Union and therefore a stateless person; and for this reason it was decided at a late stage that Masur should go instead. After the latter returned in triumph from his meeting with Himmler, Storch was not altogether pleased. He felt that his contribution had been unfairly overlooked. When Masur subsequently published an account of his extraordinary mission, an unseemly squabble erupted between the two of them. Both petitioned Hugh, first by telephone, then in person, each denouncing the other. Hugh was reluctant to take sides in this internecine dispute.

In 1956 Kersten's memoirs were published in English, with an introduction by Hugh, who was careful to include a footnote disassociating himself from the Bernadotte letter.* Once again there was uproar in the Swedish press. The Swedish Foreign Office issued a 'White Paper' on the Swedish Relief Expedition, censuring Hugh's account as 'consistently anti-Bernadotte' and insisting that Bernadotte had played the leading part in the negotiations for the release of the prisoners, while conceding that Kersten had made 'energetic and successful representations' to Himmler on their behalf.[58] Another acknowledgement of Kersten's contribution came when he was finally awarded Swedish citizenship, after a wait lasting years. It was nevertheless awkward for Hugh to be so publicly associated with a man whom he suspected of having forged evidence to support his own case. In May 1956 an article appeared in *The New Republic* opposing Hugh's line on Bernadotte, to which he replied in a subsequent issue.[59] Further attacks on Hugh appeared from time to time in the Swedish press, including one by an elderly Norwegian psychiatrist, Dr Johan Scharffenburg, who demanded that Hugh should be prosecuted or at least disciplined by Oxford University, or otherwise brought to heel.

Kersten died in 1960, but the controversy surrounding his rivalry with Bernadotte continued to dog Hugh. 'Scarcely a year passes without some reminiscent echo of his name,' Hugh wrote towards the end of his life, 'and behind the name I see once again that gross peasant figure with his huge hands kneading the stomach of the most sinister destroyer in modern history'. In 1994, a book about Bernadotte's assassination added yet another twist to the story.[†] The real target of the book was the former Israeli Prime Minister Yitzhak Shamir, who had been implicated in Bernadotte's killing. To denigrate Shamir the author had restored Bernadotte to his pedestal, dismissing Kersten's claims to share his glory. A lengthy epilogue criticised Hugh for rebuffing the author's requests for an interview to discuss the matter. Hugh insisted that he had no record of having received such a request.[60]

He had long since reached the conclusion that Kersten was a dubious character whose documentation could not be trusted.[61] But he continued to uphold Kersten's central claim to have saved thousands of lives by interceding with Himmler. If Kersten was shown to have subsequently forged documents to support his story, that did not prove the story untrue. Hugh came to believe that Kersten had resorted to forgery in a desperate attempt to secure the recognition of which he had been defrauded, and to wreak his revenge on Bernadotte, who had defrauded him. Whether this judgement was realistic or naïve remains hard to assess. In 2002 the Swedish historian Sune Persson published an article supporting Bernadotte's claims

---

* *The Kersten Memoirs, 1940–1945* (London, 1956).
† Kati Marton, *A Death in Jerusalem* (New York, 1994).

against those of Kersten, using Swedish documents not seen by Hugh. But though his arguments were convincing, they were not conclusive, and were undermined by his assertion that the accusations against Bernadotte levelled by Trevor-Roper and others were 'obvious lies'.[62]

The controversy surrounding Felix Kersten was unusual, but not unique; a host of bizarre stories and claims emerged from the collapse of Nazi Germany, and Hugh was called upon to evaluate many of them. In these investigations he was able to consult former colleagues in military intelligence on an informal basis. His cousin Brian Melland, who had become responsible for the Cabinet Office Historical Section after the war, regularly provided off-the-record advice, of a type generally unavailable to other writers on these subjects. Such a combination of access and expertise made Hugh an invaluable source to newspapers, magazines and book publishers in Britain, America and other European countries. This work was a very profitable sideline for him. It did, however, come at a cost, consuming time which he might otherwise have spent on his 'proper work', and distracting him from study which required sustained concentration. Repeatedly, Hugh would interrupt scholarly research to undertake an urgent commission, again and again sifting the debris of the Third Reich for gold among the rubble.

Lover

'How complicated the problem of living is!' Hugh exclaimed in a letter to Dawyck Haig in the spring of 1950; 'but it must be soluble without using one's friends as emotional laundry-baskets.' He confided that he suffered from 'abject depression'.[1] Characteristically he made light of his periodic affliction, though at such times his work seemed to him futile and the demands on his time overwhelming. Recurrent sinus problems further sapped his morale. He felt that he might never write another book to equal *The Last Days of Hitler*. At times it felt as if he might never write another book of any kind. Bowra summed up the prevalent view within Oxford when he described Hugh to an American friend as 'a robot, without human experience, with no girls, no real friends, no capacity for intimacy and no desire to like or be liked'.[2] Berlin echoed Bowra. 'He doesn't have any human perceptions: he's all glass and rubber.'[3]

Hugh felt able to confide in Haig because he too had been a victim of depression. In 1945 Haig had emerged from captivity with amoebic dysentery, weighing under eight stone, his body covered in boils. Afterwards he had suffered a breakdown. Some years later Hugh discovered that Haig had been seeing a psychoanalyst. 'I do hope you will not worry about yourself too much,' he wrote. 'I think that happiness is to be found neither by ignoring inhibitions nor by worrying about them, but by <u>first</u> discovering what they are and <u>then</u>, when one has discovered them, <u>disregarding them</u> – as it is easy to do once they are known.'[4]

Haig's recovery had been helped by studying fine art at Camberwell, where he had come under the influence of 'Euston Road School' of painters such as Victor Pasmore, Lawrence Gowing and William Coldstream. Afterwards Haig began to build a career as an artist himself. This provided him with an identity of his own, enabling him to become something more than 'my father's son', the phrase with which he would entitle his memoirs.[5] Nonetheless his father's legacy remained important to him. In 1949 Haig asked Hugh to undertake the delicate task of editing the Field Marshal's diaries; instead Hugh proposed Robert Blake, who skilfully negotiated the family sensitivities to produce an edition that was published in 1952.*

---

* A new edition of Haig's war diaries and letters, edited by Gary Sheffield and John Bourne, was published in 2005.

In the winter of 1947 Haig returned to Bemersyde, the estate in the Scottish Borders presented to his father by a grateful nation after the First World War. Hugh was invited there in the summer of 1949, and in the following few years he would be a regular guest. It was a romantic situation: a fortified house developed from a pele tower and almost five hundred years old, surrounded by natural gardens brimming with wild flowers, set on high ground above the Tweed; a track snaked down through woods to the river, where salmon lurked in dark holding-pools. To Hugh, Bemersyde was a haven, and Haig an ideal host. 'There is no place that I visit with such pleasure, or leave with such regret,' he wrote after a visit in the spring of 1950: 'My dear Dawyck, infinite thanks: your house is the humanest place I know, – you make it so.'[6]

On moving back to Bemersyde, Haig had resumed the duties of a laird and his role as head of the family. He took his part in local society, officiating at ceremonies of the British Legion and becoming Deputy Lieutenant of the county. In 1948 he celebrated his thirtieth birthday. Tall and slim, he cut a dashing figure, whether on the hunting-field or in the ballroom. As a good-looking young bachelor, he was sought after by aristocratic hostesses. 'He is rather an attractive character,' Hugh wrote to Berenson, introducing Haig in 1948; 'has intellectual interests without intellectual stamina,* & has both the limitations and the qualities of sensitivity, made conscious by experiences in the war.'[7] Others remarked on Haig's gentleness and unassuming modesty.

Hugh often said that he was 'devoted to Dawyck'. Their friendship, renewed after the war, became closer in the early 1950s. He revealed his feelings to Haig in a way that he seldom, if ever, did to anyone else at the time. 'I have no more valued friend than you,' he would write in 1954, at a time when their relations had come under strain through no fault of either.[8] Haig was an exemplar of that golden generation of blue-blooded young men whom Hugh had admired in the 1930s, so many of whom had been killed in the war; indeed, Haig was one of very few survivors. Though Haig took no part in court, Hugh liked to envisage him in this capacity, performing with grace, charm, and elegance – though perhaps not with ease or altogether undivided attention, as he knew that Haig never liked to be away from Bemersyde for long. He tried unsuccessfully to persuade Haig to accompany him on walking holidays abroad, and jokingly awarded him the title 'The Hermit of the Tweed' as a mark of his reluctance to venture far from home. 'Even Greece, even the mysterious beauty of Delphi, failed to lure you out of your hermitage,' he wrote, in another vain attempt, this time to attract

* Haig left Oxford with a fourth-class degree.

Haig to a dinner in Oxford. 'How then (I sadly ask) can I possibly lure you to the familiar quadrangles of Christ Church?'[9]

Haig had three sisters, the eldest of whom, Lady Alexandra Henrietta Louisa Howard-Johnston, was eleven years his senior.* Known to her friends as 'Xandra', she was a tall, handsome woman with aquiline features and an erect carriage, married to a naval officer, Clarence Dinsmore Howard-Johnston (known as 'Johnny'), by whom she had three children, the youngest still an infant. The two elder children were at boarding-school, and the youngest often stayed with his nanny. As wife to the naval attaché in Paris in the late 1940s, Xandra required an extensive wardrobe for the many formal dinners and state functions that she had to attend. She dressed exclusively at the house of the couturier Jacques Fath. He lent her evening and day dresses each season, aware of the publicity that this would give his house. Since her figure was identical to that of his mannequins, his model dresses fitted her perfectly. If there was a dress that she wanted to keep, he allowed her to buy it at sale price at the end of each season. In 1948, during a special gala in honour of Princess Elizabeth and her husband the Duke of Edinburgh at the Théâtre National de L'Opera, Xandra and her husband had been mistaken for the royal couple by the Garde Nationale, which sprang to attention when the Howard-Johnstons started to climb the marble staircase.

Xandra was interested in music and had studied singing in Paris under Pierre Bernac; in the years after the Edinburgh Festival was founded in 1947 she brought Bernac and her friends Yehudi and Diana Menuhin to Bemersyde. But she had been inadequately educated, and inhabited a milieu in which learning was little valued, even in boys; one of her sisters expressed dismay at the prospect that Xandra's elder son might win a scholarship to Eton, thereby becoming a despised 'tug'. Confined to aristocratic society, within which interlopers were regarded with suspicion, Xandra had little experience of ordinary life; Hugh later discovered, to his amazement, that she had never eaten fish and chips. After the death of her father in 1928, her increasingly erratic mother had developed a violent dislike of Xandra, and she had been taken in by the Buccleuchs, who continued to show a quasi-parental interest in her welfare. Nervous and unconfident, she was regarded within the family as 'difficult' and 'highly strung', and was mocked by her less sensitive younger sisters for her interest in clothes and music, for repeatedly 'getting into hot water', and for enjoying the company of creative people. At such times she looked to her brother for protection.

---

* The other two were Lady Victoria ('Doria'), who was divorced from her husband Claud ('Andrew') Montagu Douglas Scott in 1951, and Lady Irene ('Rene'), married to Gavin Astor.

Hugh met Xandra while staying at Bemersyde in April 1953. He was then thirty-nine; she was forty-six. She was recovering from a skiing accident, her leg encased in plaster from hip to ankle. Having spent months in plaster himself after breaking his back, Hugh was especially sympathetic. He offered to drive her to the hospital in his Bentley on the day she was due to have the plaster removed. Afterwards they had a celebratory lunch *à deux*, during which he reminded her that they had met eleven years earlier, at a lunch party in Dublin.* One evening he took her with him to dine with his friends the Reays, who lived nearby in the Borders.

Xandra's husband (now a Rear-Admiral) was away, serving in a NATO post at Fontainebleau, while she was living alone at Birchfield, not far from Bemersyde in Melrose. In theory she was due to join him in France in the autumn, once a house was ready for them to occupy; in reality their marriage was in difficulty and neither of them was looking forward to cohabiting again. Xandra mentioned to Hugh that Sir Thomas Beecham was going to conduct a Delius opera in Oxford in a fortnight's time, when she would be on her way south to France; he took the hint, suggesting that she should make a detour to Oxford, and promised to make all the necessary arrangements.

She arrived a fortnight later, in time to accompany him to the concert. He had arranged a small supper party with some of his friends afterwards, at which vintage champagne was served, before he escorted her back to her hotel. Next morning he presented her with a leather-bound copy of *The Last Days of Hitler*, before seeing her off on the train back to London. 'My dear, dear Hugh,' she addressed him from her husband's flat in Dolphin Square, 'I am quite overwhelmed by your generosity & sweetness & hospitality ... I feel like the Princess in the opera who kept saying "Am I dreaming?"' She was leaving early the next morning for Fontainebleau, 'and I do not look forward to it'. But she was due to return after a week, and wondered if they might meet again. 'Did you <u>really</u> mean that it would not bore you to show me around Oxford?' A few days later she wrote to him from Paris. 'I have been reading your book,' she told him. 'What beautiful prose you write!' She was 'proud beyond words' to have been given 'this beautiful book' by its author. 'You <u>must</u> write another,' she insisted. 'It seems to me a crime that you should waste your talents in eye-catching newspaper articles, but I suppose they bring in lots of money.' She confessed to having been 'utterly miserable' in Fontainebleau, and now she

* In 1971 she was quoted by *The Sunday Times* as saying that Hugh had 'made no impression on me at all' when they had met in Dublin during the war. 'The day I really remember was years later ... He was staying at the home of my brother, who was with him at Christ Church. The daffodils were out and the Queen Mother of the Belgians had dropped in. It was simply lovely.'

was uncertain whether his invitation had been sincerely meant. 'I am full of misgivings – you cannot want me to turn up at Oxford so soon again – you probably don't like females – my "thank you" letter was, perhaps, too fulsome – other doubts crowd round.'[10]

In response, Hugh sent her a masterful telegram: 'DISCARD ALL DOUBTS RETURN AS PLANNED AND FOLLOW DETAILED INSTRUCTIONS AWAITING YOU IN DOLPHIN SQUARE'. These required her to meet him on Saturday evening at Wheeler's Oyster Bar in Old Compton Street, from where they would go on to the St James's Theatre to see a highly recommended performance of Racine's *Britannicus*. Afterwards he drove her to Oxford, and they spent the next day together, sightseeing, walking in the gardens, listening to a Handel anthem that nearly made her cry, meeting Isaiah Berlin with Hugh's Christ Church colleague Roy Harrod and his lively wife Billa and finally dining together in a country pub, before he put her on the train back to London. As they talked he was delighted to discover that she had been to Bassae, 'that infinitely romantic spot in the wilds of Arcadia', one of the places to which he had attempted to lure her brother.[11]

'How I wish I was a pupil coming at 10.00 a.m. to your rooms,' she sighed the next morning. 'What fun it would be if Dawyck could be persuaded to come for a trip abroad with you, and if I could come too!' She hoped that he might travel up to Scotland for the Edinburgh Festival in the summer; she would be alone for three weeks in July when the children were away, as 'Johnny does not wish to spend his leave with me'. Hugh ignored this hint in his measured reply, though for the first time he signed his letter 'with love', in response to her 'love from Xandra'. She had enclosed a newspaper cutting about Hugh headed 'The lively young don', though she observed that the accompanying photograph 'does not give that impression!!' We are not all that amused, commented Hugh in a droll reply, especially as he had received the same cutting from several other sources describing themselves as 'well-wishers', 'pro bono publico', etc.; 'but could generally be identified, behind their smug anonymity, as ironical mockers and irreverent malicious friends'. At a party 'one of my pupils admitted to a conspiracy to send me a red carnation from my alleged feminine admirers, etc, etc'.[12]

Xandra was 'enchanted' with his long and witty letter, and responded with a twenty-page bulletin of her own. 'I love getting letters & I love writing letters, as you already know to your cost!' This was the beginning of an intense correspondence. Whenever they were apart they wrote to each other, and while a few of these letters were comparatively short, only a couple of pages or so, most were much longer. Though her letters were often repetitive and sometimes emotional to the point of incoherence, most of his were carefully composed, and must have taken hours to craft. She wrote in a sometimes indecipherable scrawl, while his hand was as clear as his prose. In the twelve months from 1 June 1953 he wrote her more than 165 letters, and she wrote him more than 189. This is an average over the whole year of a letter every couple of days – though in fact the rate was uneven, a period of several days of (often enforced) silence followed by two or even three letters written in a single day. Since letters between Melrose and Oxford arrived within twenty-four hours of sending, it was possible to receive a reply two days after posting a letter if this was written immediately on receipt. The figures are even more striking if one considers that the two of them were frequently together during this period, and that some letters referred to in the correspondence have not survived. A few indeed were deliberately destroyed.

'I have so often longed for a companion who could appreciate the same things as I,' she confided in the twenty-page letter (having first written 'me' and crossed it out); her husband shared none of her interests and indeed derided them. Her lack of self-confidence was manifest. 'I am touched that you should want me to visit Oxford again,' she continued; 'I am always surprised that anyone would like to see me, especially someone so brilliant as yourself.' Hugh met her in London when she returned for the Coronation in early June. 'I find my life very wearing & sometimes get very depressed,' she admitted afterwards; 'it makes me feel less alone, to have you to write to.' They had arranged for her to come back to Oxford for a long weekend a fortnight later. 'I do so look forward to June 12th – don't arrange any parties for me – I infinitely prefer being just with you.' She expressed the hope that she would eventually get him to 'thaw' a little; 'I have never known anyone so reserved as you.'[13]

'I am sorry about the "reserve",' he replied. 'I hope you will just ignore it, or treat it as an unfortunate but unavoidable defect, like short-sightedness or deafness, which one can get round in one's friends by shouting a little louder or gesticulating a little more obviously at them.' He asked her about her experience of the Coronation, which he had watched 'in dignified ease on Lord Cherwell's television-set', in his Lordship's comfortable but 'hideously furnished' rooms.[14]

'Please refuse all invitations', she entreated a few days later; 'if you have any writing to do, I will be very happy to sit on your sofa with a book. I don't need to be entertained in any way'. She addressed him for the first time as 'My dearest Hugh', adding that she had been having 'a terribly difficult time with my husband. He has written me some horrible letters'. She chided Hugh for being self-effacing. 'How can you say you have so little to offer when you possess all the qualities that really count – in your mind – You open a new & wondrous world to me – I have never ceased to be surprised that you, with your brilliant intellect, should sometimes seem to quite like being with me. I have never dared to admit that sometimes you use words of which I do not know the meaning!!' She again urged him to write more books, and playfully threatened to 'use pressure' to persuade him to do so. Her letter ended in a wounding postscript: presumably an afterthought, as its tone contrasted with what had gone before. 'You ask if you are forbidding – the answer is "no" – just cold, aloof, impersonal – Any slightly warm feelings I might have towards you are nipped in the bud by your frostiness – If we approach a slightly personal topic you shy away from it like a frightened horse … You appear loathe [*sic*] to be alone with me.'[15]

Why did she lash out in this way? She was lonely and hungry for human contact; more than that, she was miserable in her marriage. She had married 'Johnny' Howard-Johnston in 1941, in a blaze of passion; he was a handsome man and a brave and skilful naval officer, and at that time of national emergency these had seemed qualifications enough for a husband, despite the worrying fact that he had been married before. Once the fire had dimmed, however, she had discovered that they had nothing else in common. He was bullying and boorish, preoccupied with his career; for some time they had not shared a bedroom; she suspected, rightly, that he was a serial womaniser.* He sneered at her 'artistic' interests, told her that she was 'mad' and overruled her decisions. On at least one occasion he hit her.[16] The two older children had come to dread his visits, because of the angry scenes which always seemed to start within five minutes of his arrival. Her brother had rebuffed her attempts to discuss these problems. In Hugh Xandra hoped to have found a friend in whom she could confide.

'How awful!' Hugh wrote in response to the postscript; 'Is that really so? I am filled with remorse, humility (if you think me capable of such emotion – few, alas, do!), and all manner of excuses. … 'I really didn't know – as I do now – how unhappy you have been recently, and therefore I didn't know that what you wanted was not society but (if I may so express it) a kind of refuge; and not knowing this I felt that it would be presumptuous to confine you (or indeed anyone) to my company, which I feel is dull for anyone.' He had already posted this letter when a telegram arrived from Xandra: 'DISREGARD PPS HAVE EXAGGERATED'. He sat down to write her another letter, explaining that 'it is genuinely because I do not think that my personal life is interesting to anyone that I seem to shy away from personal discussion'. He asked her, not for the first or for the last time, to forgive his 'irrepressible levity: it is really, as the psychologists would say, a superficial defence mechanism, elaborated against others, not you: for you I have only, in spite of the icy formalism which surrounds

---

* Not long after she met Hugh she found a stock of 'French letters' in her husband's pocket book, and punctured each one with a pin.

them and which I shall try to discard – but then I should feel as naked &
exposed as a snail without its shell – the warmest feelings'. There was an
element of self-parody in his letters which sometimes eluded Xandra. He
told her that he was 'very determined' to write another book; 'the fear that
I shall not do it, or shall be prevented from doing it, is one of the strongest
motives that shapes my otherwise erratic activities'.[17]

Three more letters from Xandra arrived in the next few days. 'I am filled
with remorse,' she lamented; 'how could I have written such a cruel PPS
to my letter when you have always been so angelic to me? ... I know only
too well, from bitter experiences, at a cost I shall go on paying for till my
death, that show of feeling means <u>nothing</u> ... My pen ran away with me
but, alas, not in the right direction ... If you will ask I will tell you some of
the bitter experiences I have been through ... I am <u>terribly</u>, <u>terribly</u> sorry
if my thoughtless PS has hurt you in any way.'

'I shall feel I have done some good if I can help you to get down to
writing your book,' she declared the next day. 'Dearest Hugh, I long to help
you in this way.' In his letters to Xandra, Hugh often complained about the
distractions preventing him from writing, particularly during term time.
'How is one ever supposed to do any scholarship at all in this absurd
university city?' he grumbled. 'I think I must retire into a hermitage or a
monastery if I am ever to write another book.'[18]

Xandra had different plans, however. 'In theory I should like to fling my
arms and thank you for all your kindness to me,' she hinted, the day before
her arrival in Oxford for the planned weekend visit, 'which would horrify
you in your monastic surroundings.' During the weekend that followed her
theory was put into practice; they made love at least once in his rooms. On
the Saturday night he had taken her to see *Antony and Cleopatra* at Stratford,
and on the Sunday he arranged a dinner party for her with the Harrods,
the Pakenhams and Robert Blake. On her final evening they had dined at
The Rose Revived, a romantically situated pub where the River Windrush
flows into the Thames. Afterwards she poured out her feelings in a torrent
of emotion. 'I am like someone who has been in a concentration camp,
who has become numb into misery & sunk in apathy – I thought I couldn't
feel anything anymore or love anyone – I cannot <u>believe</u> that, after all these
years, someone is going to bring me to life.' Perversely, however, she urged
him not get too involved with her; 'I am too old for you,' she argued: a
problem that would always trouble her.[19]

But Hugh was already committed. 'The question is: what are we to do?'
he asked after their weekend together, and in a sequence of numbered
paragraphs he laid out in detail a series of questions which he hoped that
a good lawyer would be able to answer. His choice of words suggests that
he already regarded her problems as his own. From the start he had adopted

a stance of calm authority, in contrast to her wavering self-doubt. He apologised for the cold and practical content of his own letter. 'I am most touched by the affection which you have shown me, and which (having been bitten once or twice & having bitten back!) I had hardly expected from anyone.' Xandra appealed to his chivalrous instincts. He had been shocked by the letters from the Admiral which she had shown him; 'he has plainly treated you abominably'.[20] Her feminine vulnerability was appealing; he was the knight in shining armour who would ride to her rescue. Insensibly, perhaps, he found himself arguing that she should divorce her husband and marry him. It was surprising that he should thus commit himself to a woman whom he had met less than two months before, and with whom he had spent only a few days; still more so, given that she was middle-aged, indeed significantly older than he, and married, with three young children whom he had yet to meet. No doubt the fact that she came with a title added to her allure. Maybe his fondness for her brother made her seem familiar. And perhaps he relished the prospect of a struggle with the Admiral.

'I have never found anyone with whom I felt so happy,' she wrote a few days later. She had taken his advice to consult a lawyer about her marriage. 'My husband means nothing to me,' she insisted to Hugh; 'I have only persevered because of the children.' In another letter she complained at how rudely the Admiral spoke to her, 'just as he would address a rating who had done something wrong'.[21]

Hugh's tone was light-hearted and flirtatious, avoiding declarations of emotion. He thanked her for a gift of new towels which, he said, had 'most impressed' his scout. Though he encouraged her to write, he teasingly pretended to believe that she would be distracted from doing so by social engagements. 'Only let me know occasionally, by means of a 30-page-or-so letter, how you are faring and feeling. Throw in just a little social gossip from stony-hearted duchesses to season it (for I must admit that, unlike many virtuous people, I don't hate gossip!).' Hugh liked to portray her as 'a gay social butterfly', fluttering prettily between the great houses of the Borders; Xandra protested that she was a mere housewife – albeit assisted by a nanny, a daily woman and a cook, plus a gardener two days a week.[22]

A fortnight after her weekend in Oxford Xandra confided to her brother that she wanted to separate from her husband. To her surprise, he was sympathetic. 'He did not know how I had stood it so long,' she told Hugh; 'he said that there is an appalling atmosphere in the house when we are together.' Haig was 'absolutely delighted' to hear of her feelings for his friend, 'it is the best thing that could have happened for Hugh,' he said, and wrote to Hugh confirming that he was 'so glad to hear the news from Xandra that you are helping her, and giving her support, and comfort'. He felt that 'only good can come from a relationship between you both'. He hoped that 'Johnny' could be persuaded to agree to a quiet divorce, and was anxious to avoid an action for cruelty, which he believed would be 'disastrous for all concerned'. Haig was apprehensive of the embarrassing publicity that a contested divorce case might attract, and perhaps he also felt concerned at how his sister would handle herself in court.[23]

Despite her brother's support, Xandra was now very unsettled. She was nervous of her husband's reaction, and feared that he might hit her again; 'I am now absolutely petrified of meeting him,' she admitted to Hugh. Once again she urged him not to get involved with her. 'I feel I am taking advantage of your kind and chivalrous nature (which the sharp exterior so effectively disguises!),' she wrote. 'I do feel it is now too late for anything – I am too old.' She telephoned him in Oxford, and complained at his 'cold and professorial manner' on the telephone. He asked her to consider that he might have someone in the room when she called.[24]

Xandra was volatile, one moment aggressive, the next apologetic; elated, then despondent. Hugh repeatedly tried to steady her in a series of sensible, almost businesslike letters, in which he set out the circumstances and calmly considered their options. This was not what she wanted. She complained that 'there was not enough love' in his letters. But when he was in more lively form, she was easily hurt by his wisecracks. He reflected on 'the awful truth' contained in 'that severe warning' from Logan Pearsall Smith's *Trivia*: 'Quality folk are seldom at their ease with intellectuals, among whom they make a great deal of mischief.'[25]

In mid-July they met in Paris, where Hugh had gone ostensibly to undertake some research. They had been there only a day or two before she received a warning from a friend: the Admiral had discovered that she had come to France and was looking for her. Hugh sent Berenson a telegram asking for refuge and received an encouraging reply. The lovers took a night train to Florence, arriving at I Tatti tired and bedraggled after sitting up for the whole journey. Berenson noted his impressions of Xandra in his diary: 'Youngish woman with wooden angular profile, Celtic blond colouring, fairly good figure, no interests or talk to entitle her to frequent us or to be travelling with Hugh. She is Dawyck Haig's sister and daughter of the general of the First World War, and perhaps that is enough. Hugh, awkward gestures, shrill yet pleasant laugh as of musical glasses. No flow of continuous talk.' The next day he observed that 'Lady Alexandra improves on acquaintance. Would not know she had ever read a book, but of good judgment and sound sense about people, and she seems to know many of the governing class societishly as well as politically.'[26]

They stayed three days at I Tatti. Afterwards Xandra would complain that Hugh had been 'cold and distant' to her while they were there. She longed for him to come to her room in the evening to talk over the events of the day, but she had no time alone with him until after they had left I Tatti, when they spent two blissful days in Siena and Urbino. They made the return journey incognito, as Hugh subsequently reported to Nicky Mariano: 'Xandra's husband, having discovered that she had gone abroad by Newhaven & Dieppe, and knowing that she would have to be back on 28th July, with great craft had all the boat trains from Newhaven met; but we, with superior craft, had the tickets changed in Paris and returned *via* Calais and Dover, thus giving him the slip.'[27]

Hugh returned to England in high spirits. In a thank-you letter to Berenson he described his activities. 'Since I came back, I have been sitting entirely alone in my rooms in Oxford, writing a wicked little book on the Roman Catholic Revival in 19th Century England which will no doubt, on its publication, cause many a social door to shut against me.' He hoped – 'perhaps it is too much to hope' – that it might cause a paralytic stroke to his old enemy Evelyn Waugh. It was certainly meant to be provocative. 'I keep alive on the malicious prose which I am distilling about those poor papists,' he boasted to Xandra. 'When I feel low, I just think of the rage which I hope to cause in them!'[28]

This was a neglected subject, perhaps deliberately so. In his wartime notebooks Hugh had fulminated about the 'dishonesty' of Catholic historians. Now he said the same in so many words. 'Thanks to the careful reticence of the RC historians, the facts are almost forgotten, buried, where the cowed Catholic will not find them, and the boldest Protestant will not seek them.' Within English Catholicism there was a constant tension between the laity and the clergy, between the moderate 'Cisalpines' and the uncompromising 'Ultramontanes'. Hugh distinguished between the 'old' Catholics, who were essentially aristocratic, and the newer converts. The old Catholics had survived by showing a willingness to adapt to the demands of the state, while the 'papists' remained intransigent. The change that occurred in the nineteenth century was 'essentially, the victory of the clergy over the laity'.

By the end of the eighteenth century the Catholic threat had receded; Catholics were tolerated in England, informally if not legally. The Act of Union with Ireland in 1800 had widened these divisions: 200,000 English Catholics were subsumed by 6,000,000 Irish Catholics. From then on Ireland and Italy were the two poles between which English Catholics 'were necessarily suspended'. Hugh depicted the laxly enforced penal laws as 'a positive protection' to the Catholicism of the laity. 'By cutting them off from Protestant society, they had protected them from the doctrinal contagion of that society.' Emancipation was therefore a danger. For this reason it was resisted by Bishop Milner, the dominant Catholic polemicist in early-nine-teenth-century Britain. 'As the high-priest of a native community, trying to preserve its culture though surrounded by a superior and more powerful civilization, he saw the chieftains of his tribe continually seduced by the white man, joining their clubs, seeking admission to their schools, and acquiring "advanced" ideas quite unsuitable to the kraals of Basutoland.'

'I have just written a particularly malicious account of conversions in the peerage,' Hugh gleefully disclosed to Xandra.[29] After Catholic Eman-cipation in 1829 the conversion of the Romantically inspired upper classes 'continued apace, and became one of the major occupations of the Roman clergy in England'. Hugh pointed out that this had been a two-way process: though the Earls of Longford had converted to Catholicism in the nine-teenth century, the Ropers, Lords Teynham, had abandoned their Catholic faith. And of the aristocratic families that converted to Catholicism in this period, only a minority remained so one hundred years later. With the re-establishment of the Catholic hierarchy in England, and the appointment of the ultramontane Cardinal Wiseman as the first Archbishop of West-minster, 'English Papist leaders found themselves committed to a policy of unqualified intellectual reaction'. This process continued under Wiseman's successor, Cardinal Manning, who insisted on the doctrine of papal infal-libility despite the misgivings of Newman and other Catholic thinkers. Newman was made to 'grovel as abjectly as an Apulian peasant before a bottle of tinselled pig-bones in a tawdry southern church'. Hugh drew an explicit parallel between Catholics and Communists in their readiness to submit to dogma. 'What are liberal principles?' he asked rhetorically. 'Intellectually they are the reliance on human reason and empirical tests, not on authority, for the discovery of truth.'[30]

'My booklet is getting more and more malicious,' he boasted to Xandra, after he had been working on it for little more than a fortnight. 'I am enjoying it hugely,' he continued; 'with any luck they will be furious.' Though he referred to it as a booklet or a pamphlet, it was, perhaps inevitably, growing into a short book. After less than four weeks, however, he stopped writing. 'My pamphlet is embogged,' he lamented, complaining that he was very tired.[31]

On her return to Scotland Xandra discovered that she was pregnant – an unlikely outcome, given her age. She was understandably excited, but nervous of Hugh's reaction. 'The proof of my love for you is that I want to have your child,' she declared; though she offered to 'get rid of' the baby if he did not want it. 'If I have your child that will be a bond between us for ever,' she repeated, in the course of a twenty-eight-page letter, 'but I don't want to tie you to me.' One reason for having the child would be that

'I would, at least, have something of yours when I had to give you up'. She had been upset by a conversation with her brother, who thought it unlikely that 'Johnny' would ever agree to a divorce. The Admiral claimed to want reconciliation. Moreover Haig had planted doubts in her mind about her new lover. 'I know Hugh <u>extremely</u> well,' he had told her; 'he is not a marrying man.' His friend was completely self-contained: 'I don't think he could ever fall in love with anyone'. Xandra was sure this was untrue. Hugh had told her that he loved her, and had confided too that he had been 'genuinely in love' with a girl before, whom he had wanted to marry.* This young woman's parents had eyed him with chilling disapproval, perhaps aware that he was still involved in another affair at the time – as he freely confessed to Xandra. To his lasting regret, this love had foundered, not because of the other affair, but as a result of his extreme difficulty in showing emotion. He asked Xandra whether she might like to meet this girl, but she declined the offer.

Xandra was showing signs of cold feet. She wondered whether her brother might not have been right when he remarked that 'Hugh is different from you and me; we need someone else but he does not'. Perhaps the affair had become more serious than she had intended. Many years later she admitted that she had not contemplated marrying Hugh at first, expecting that she would remain married while having him as a 'boyfriend': an arrangement reached by several of her friends. Perhaps influenced by his younger sisters, Haig appeared to be backtracking in his support for the lovers. Though he still hoped 'your friendship will go on', he now advocated that Xandra should continue with her husband if possible. He doubted whether Johnny would give her a divorce. 'The best she could hope for would be a separation,' he believed, and warned that if this were to happen, the Admiral was unlikely to allow her more than the minimum allowance. He suggested that Hugh might find it hard to meet her demands. 'Wonderful though Xandra is in most ways, she is a luxury girl in some, and needs a fairish whack to keep her going. If things are not to her liking she does not hide it. This makes her sometimes an uncomfortable companion.'[32]

Hugh's pride was stung by this letter. He told Xandra that he did not wish to be kept in the background 'as a sort of convenient safety-valve'. The secrecy of their position was 'uncongenial', he found. 'The conspiratorial side of our journey abroad had, of course, an enjoyably adventurous quality – for that brief time. But I don't like <u>living</u> conspiratorially, or under

---

* Many years later, on a balmy evening in the Loire Valley, Hugh's pupil Blair Worden felt emboldened to enquire whether he had ever contemplated marrying before he met Xandra. 'Yes, twice,' he replied, and continued after a pause: '<u>since you ask</u>.' Then the shutters came down, and the talk moved on to a less personal topic.

false pretences.' He insisted that he was 'not as self-contained as Dawyck evidently thinks'; and 'since you are so kind as to say that you would want, in an ideal world, to live with me, I should want, if it were possible, to live with you.'[33]

In a second letter written on the same day, which she burnt after reading, he seems to have reproached her for acting irresponsibly in not taking precautions to avoid becoming pregnant. 'But, surely,' she remonstrated with him, 'you did not expect me to have a contraceptive in my hand-bag that first evening when I stayed in your rooms?' She protested that she was not that sort of woman. 'I agreed at once to stay with you that evening because I love you.' She complained that he never made his feelings clear. 'I must now confess that, for some time, I had serious doubts whether you could ever love anyone,' she wrote; 'I even thought, at one moment, that you liked men! (Don't be furious with me – but you always went on trips abroad with young men & undergraduates & always seemed to be with men.) I <u>know</u> Dawyck thinks you are quite neuter.'[34]

Hugh was understandably irritated. 'You think I am ironical when I am serious and serious when I am ironical – or at least you pretend to do so; is it just calculated feminine perversity, or is my language really so "ambiguous"?' He assured her that 'I do indeed love you deeply, more deeply (I am sure) than anyone before,' and admitted that when she had pressed him for short, simple answers, he had dodged the pressure, 'feeling that complex situations don't provide such simple answers'. As for under-graduates, he liked them, or at least some of them, 'not for the reason that you supposed', but because they did not defer to him. 'Of course there are other reasons too – they are energetic, willing to rough it and do chores, and interested in experiences: they like seeing and learning and discovering new things and don't look on everything with that *blasé* affectation of boredom which older people so often do. All this makes them good travel-ling companions.' He hated being deferred to as 'a famous writer': there was no more certain way of driving him back into 'an opaque, impenetrable reserve' than being treated as such. 'It maddens me when people introduce me in such terms: I'm afraid I always retreat into a sulky silence.'[35]

He was beginning to realise that in becoming closer to the sister, he had become distanced from her brother. 'He has been a very good friend to me for a long time,' he told her, 'and yet I now feel that perhaps we have been on false terms, and that I, insensitively, have not been aware of it.' Xandra's occasional revelations of what his friend Dawyck had said about him hurt him deeply; *inter alia*, she suggested that Haig found his company boring. Always unwilling to believe that anybody liked him, Hugh had begun to question the assumptions on which their friendship was based, and to ask if he had not exploited Haig's kindness and hospitality. A 'great cloud of incomprehension' had revealed itself between their two minds. Though he had felt accepted at Bemersyde, he now wondered if he had been mistaken. He felt vulnerable socially: Xandra had already chided him for failing to address her envelopes to 'The Lady Alexandra Howard-Johnston', the correct form for the daughter of an earl. He looked down and saw the social abyss yawning at his feet. An immediate effect of these misgivings was to make him reluctant to impose himself on Haig for the period of the Edinburgh Festival, as she had urged him to do.[36]

Xandra too was feeling raw, not least because there were signs that she was having a miscarriage. 'The words you have used in letters to me lately have hurt me very much,' she protested. 'You wrote that you were "gratified" and "flattered" that I wanted to have your child. Now "gratified" to me is a cold, harsh, pompous word that exerts a chill on me. "Fond" equally is a lukewarm, rather meaningless word.' She proposed to tell her brother that 'there is no other answer to the problem but "goodbye".[37]

Hugh protested that he had not deserved such a 'monstrous' letter. 'I have terrible, almost physical difficulty in expressing emotion,' he admitted in his reply, begun at 2.30 in the morning. The problem originated in the coldness of his upbringing. 'When I was a child I never saw, in my own home, any evidence of any emotion whatever; and it was somehow conveyed to me that any show of it was not only improper but ridiculous. I felt that if I ever showed any, I would be publicly mocked; and mockery made me very miserable.' It was painful for him to reveal that he 'never heard a word of affection' pass between his parents, or from either of them to any of their children. 'This has been a great personal difficulty for me and has interfered with every emotional affair I have had.'

> Then you come along. We find common interests; I find I am delighted with your conversation and company and gaiety; I also find that you are terribly unhappy and have long concealed that unhappiness under that gaiety, and I am terribly sorry for you; I find that you are in love with me; I am delighted to have such affection; and insensibly (this is the order of events: I have no secrets from you and pretend nothing to you) I find that I am in love with you ...
>
> I give my heart to you – rather a complicated object, you may say, like a sea-urchin, prickly outside and untempting within; but you asked for it and must connive at some of its limitations. If you would take it without too many questions ... then, by not raising too many difficulties, or knocking our heads against the brick walls, or rushing against the thorns, and by not insisting on detailed declarations which you must see that I have difficulty in expressing, we might have some happiness together without fruitlessly and endlessly discussing the terms of it ... But no; you insist on prodding the sensitive angularities of my heart; you try to tear off skin to see what is underneath; you report on it to

> Dawyck and compare notes; you invite me to exhibit it to Dawyck so that he can make further observations – and you invite me to do so just at the time when the bridge upon which I have so often and so pleasantly met Dawyck – a delightful, half-serious, sham-gothic, rural-estate bridge – seems, by the internal gnawing of invisible death-watch-beetles, to have dissolved; so that if I go to meet Dawyck I now feel that I shall find only an unbridged gulf between us, and then (since I suffer from social vertigo) I shall draw back from the edge and be able to say nothing. And then, when I, being in pain from this pressure, utter what is perhaps an undignified squeak ... you direct against me that terrible document ...

'You cannot believe what it costs me to utter this egotistical autobiography,' he concluded: 'I hate it.'[38]

But Xandra was 'delighted' to have coaxed such a confession from him, so much so that she immediately sent him a telegram. 'I am touched that you should have "bared your soul" to me,' she affirmed in a subsequent letter. 'You need never fear that I shall mock you – I really do believe that it is good for you to overcome your inhibitions, gently, by degrees.' She was now on holiday with her husband and children, staying at her aunt's house in Anglesey. 'I live on tenter-hooks here,' she wrote; 'I seem to do everything wrong.' The Admiral was suspicious, quizzing her about where she had been and with whom. She told him that she had been staying with an old man of nearly ninety (i.e. Berenson). Hugh urged her to take good care of his letters, and to keep them out of her husband's reach.[39]

Robert Blake was married in August, with Hugh as his best man. This followed Charles Stuart's wedding two years before. The bachelor triumvirate who had formed the Party of Light was being dispersed, as each married and moved out of college. Xandra was invited to Blake's wedding in Norwich; she decided that the time had come to take him into her confidence. 'I was enormously interested in what you say about you and Hugh,' Blake replied. 'It was a secret which, I must admit, I never guessed, or even began to guess.' Blake warned Hugh that he was unlikely to be able to 'keep things secret, even from Johnny, for very long'. He urged the lovers to 'be careful in the extreme' if they wanted to prevent Xandra's husband from gaining sole custody of the children.[40] In the 1950s divorce was unusual in Britain, and carried a social cost; divorced women in particular were stigmatised. Those found 'guilty' of adultery were considered unsuitable mothers, and could be deprived of their children as a result. Moreover, exposure could jeopardise Hugh's academic career. To be named in a divorce case could be disastrous. Even a hint of scandal could be damaging. Stuart Hampshire, for example, was prevented from obtaining a teaching post at

Oxford for several years after the war because of his involvement with Renée Ayer, though her husband had cheerfully encouraged their relationship. Divorce was disapproved of by many who turned a blind eye to sexual relations outside marriage. In 1952 A.J.P. Taylor was the first college Fellow ever to retain his post after a divorce.[41] His re-election was opposed by two of his Magdalen colleagues, though he was the injured party and his wife had been unfaithful to him over a long period.

Hugh spent early September in the Borders. 'My morale is almost indecently high,' he told Berenson.[42] He had been appointed a Special Lecturer in modern history, a position valid for five years and worth £650 annually. He visited his parents at Alnwick, and spent a day with Xandra, when he met her children for the first time – James, then in his last year at preparatory school, Xenia, two years younger, and Philip* (always known as 'Peter'), still an infant.

A few days at Bemersyde reassured Hugh that the 'gothic bridge across the imaginary gulf' was still standing. Then he and Xandra stayed at Drumlanrig, as guests of the Duke and Duchess of Buccleuch, where the 'worldliness' of their hostess was a 'great assistance to us' – presumably in allotting them adjoining rooms. Afterwards Hugh returned to Oxford, from where he thanked Xandra for 'your friendly guidance through the otherwise (to me) frightening *Beau Monde*'. He had seen his brother in London and 'told him all'. Pat, now an eye surgeon, offered the lovers the use of his Wimpole Street flat for three weeks in October while he was in hospital for a minor operation. Xandra could enter through his consulting rooms to throw any watchers off the scent. Hugh had gone to London to lunch with George Weidenfeld and François Genoud. 'How is your charming friend Lady Alexandra?' asked Weidenfeld, who knew that they had been guests of the Buccleuchs. 'It is mortifying to think that *nothing* is ever secret,' Hugh complained to Xandra.[43] In this period he was a frequent visitor to Weidenfeld's house in Chester Square. The publisher remembered him pacing up and down and gesticulating belligerently as he outlined plans for sinking the Admiral.

Xandra came down to London to stay a few days with Hugh at the Wimpole Street flat towards the end of the summer vacation, before he went on a short trip to Holland. The Admiral suddenly surfaced. Arriving at their Dolphin Square flat, he telephoned Xandra's friend Virginia Ashley Clarke to check on his wife's whereabouts; she bluffed it out, and afterwards tried to warn Xandra that he might appear at the station while she was seeing her lover off onto the boat train. Fortunately no such confrontation occurred. Xandra returned to Birchfield to spend the holidays with the

---

* Named after his godfather, the Duke of Edinburgh.

children. Hugh stayed with his friend Lord Reay at Ophemert, his moated castle. Aeneas Reay's family was half-Scottish and half-Dutch. He had been an SIS colleague, a warm, good-humoured giant of a man with a zest for life; they had enjoyed many jolly evenings during the war, on one occasion tumbling down an escalator on the London Underground together while drunk. Reay and his wife Charlotte joined Hugh for what he described as a *bon repas bourgeois* with Felix Kersten and his wife. Hugh also took the opportunity to have lunch with the Dutch historian Pieter Geyl, whom he described to Berenson as 'one of the best of living historians, indeed in a class by himself, or perhaps a class which he shares with Namier, Braudel, and one or two others'. He recommended Geyl's pioneering lectures on historians, which had recently been published in book form in America.[44] Like Hugh, Geyl was critical of Arnold Toynbee, then at the peak of his fame.

While Hugh was away, disaster struck. In mid-October Admiral Howard-Johnston arrived at the marital home in Scotland for the half-term weekend. One morning he came into Xandra's bedroom and started cross-examining her. 'I really felt as if I was up before the Gestapo,' she explained to her lover afterwards; 'he never stopped questioning me.' He asked why she had gone to Oxford in May. She pretended not to remember. 'You went to France with Hugh Trevor-Roper,' declared her husband. 'All Paris is talking about it.' He claimed to have evidence too that she had been to Italy with an Oxford don. Under pressure, she crumbled. 'Have you made love to him?' the Admiral demanded. 'A woman doesn't do that,' she replied demurely. 'Has he made love to you?' he continued. She confessed that he had.[45]

A series of angry scenes followed. 'If I ever see Trevor-Roper I'll shoot him in the backside so that he can't sit down for a month,' thundered the Admiral. He threatened that Hugh could lose his job if cited in a divorce case. Xandra was distraught, particularly as she found that she was pregnant again. 'How can I ever escape from Johnny?' she asked in desperation. 'I feel like a prisoner who has been thrown into the deepest, darkest, most airless dungeon, or like a bird fluttering against a window, helplessly battering its head against the glass.' Once her husband had gone she tried to telephone Hugh (who had returned from Holland to Oxford), reversing the charges so that the call would not show on her telephone bill. There were other people in his rooms and he could not talk freely, which meant that his responses were disappointingly muted. Afterwards Xandra was desolate. 'O misery, misery me,' she wailed.[46]

'My God,' she exclaimed a couple of days later, when she realised that her husband had taken a letter from her doctor referring to her pregnancy. Also missing was a letter from Hugh, discussing the reasons for and against having a child. Her diaries for the past eleven years had gone too. 'I am stunned,' she blubbered; 'All, all is lost!' Hugh was understandably irritated. 'I was horrified to hear you had made such admissions to Johnny,' he wrote testily; 'you gave him exactly what he wanted.' Xandra was penitent. 'Please, please forgive me for being such an utter witless fool.' Signs had appeared suggesting that she was having another miscarriage. 'I did so long to have your child & now even that is being taken away from me.'[47]

Hugh was moved to tears by her letter, which proved embarrassing when someone came into the room while he was reading it. 'I am sorry, very sorry indeed, about the miscarriage,' he wrote, telling her not to blame herself any more about the unfortunate loss of his letters. He assured her that although 'I don't show much enthusiasm, I do love you very much, and feel for you, and am anxious to be of help to you, even if I often express myself badly.' He urged her not to deduce too much from telephone conversations. 'For five years, during the war, I was conditioned never to say anything on the telephone which, if overheard, could give anything away to anyone. Consequently, I always use the telephone as if it were a public amplifier, not a private channel, and am always non-committal on it!'[48]

At the end of October Xandra came south, on her way to Paris, where she was being fitted for another Fath dress. They contrived to spend a weekend in Oxford and several nights together in country hotels, registering as 'Mr & Mrs Roper, of No. 11, Chester Square, London SW1' (the address of George Weidenfeld, whose own marital affairs were complicated enough). When she had to leave he drove her to Heathrow Airport. 'Thank you, my darling, for a lovely weekend,' she wrote gratefully from Paris. 'The more I am with you, the more I love you – & I am so happy with all your friends & I love listening to you talking!' Ten days later he picked her up from Heathrow and they stayed two further nights in Oxfordshire hotels, before she left to visit her elder son at his preparatory school in Kent. On returning to Scotland she reported that gossip about them was spreading, both in Paris and in the Borders. But she had been cheered by a conversation with her lawyer in London, who assured her that nowadays custody cases were decided solely on what was best for the children involved.[49]

Hugh was feeling the strain of his competing commitments, and begged her to be understanding. In letter after letter he complained of feeling tired. 'I am terribly exhausted, & find that I simply cannot get any respite,' he groaned; 'I wish that our own affairs were not also so exhausting by their conspiratorial nature and the elaborate arrangements which they necessitate!'[50] He had applied for (and been awarded) a year's leave of absence from his college duties from 1 January 1954. 'In this sabbatical year I had intended to become a hermit and write a book.' Now he feared that he might be distracted by the uncertainty in his personal life. The year might be frittered away. The opportunity, once lost, would not recur.[51]

On 3 December Xandra listened to Hugh's radio talk 'The Empiricist Answer', part of a series of Third Programme broadcasts suggested by Stuart Hampshire around the theme 'Human Nature in Politics'. Hugh's line was to attack utopian political philosophers, 'such dreary and disastrous prophets as Jean-Jacques Rousseau and Karl Marx'. He followed Alexis de Tocqueville in preferring the empirical, unsystematic methods of English government to idealist, doctrinaire French methods. 'I heard perfectly and was most <u>deeply</u> impressed,' gushed Xandra.[52]

Early in December they travelled by train to Italy, heading for I Tatti. Xandra asked if he would be able to visit her at night during their stay. 'Do we still have to keep up appearances now that they know the situation?' she asked. Hugh had booked a second-class sleeping compartment for the two of them. 'What is the name of the other gentleman?' enquired the travel agent; 'Lady Alexandra Howard-Johnston,' came the firm reply. 'I <u>thought</u> that he boggled a little,' Hugh told Xandra in a letter, 'but if so he corrected himself and suddenly & rather artificially asked if I was at the Varsity Match yesterday.' Despite his firmness Hugh found that they had been placed in separate sleeping compartments, and was forced to telephone the agent again to insist that they were together.[53]

He suffered a further attack of sinusitis before they left. Xandra was solicitous, wanting him to take vitamins to ward off illness. She imagined herself in the future looking after him, cooking him meals and making a home for him, providing him with the leisure to write great books. Before they left for Italy he told her that he hoped to do some work in the library while at I Tatti, preparing some old essays for re-publication as a book, and asked if Xandra would like to help. 'I am delighted & proud & amazed,' she replied; 'I would <u>adore</u> to do that: I will be your willing slave.' A week before their departure Hugh was still undecided whether they should go to I Tatti, dreading the presence there of the society painter Derek Hill, an inveterate gossip. 'The thought of his trivial *couturier*'s mind makes me shiver,' he confessed to Xandra. 'The consciousness of that torpid, complacent, epicurean social vulture perched on an overhanging bough, observing every detail of the morsels which he would afterwards select for his repast, would freeze me into entirely mechanical postures. You know how difficult it is for me to make myself natural even for a photographer.' Xandra, by contrast, rather enjoyed Hill's company. He was a friend of her brother's and had given her one of his paintings. 'Dawyck is very attractive to pansies,' Xandra observed; 'I have noticed this.'[54]

Despite his aversion to Derek Hill, Hugh was comfortable in homosexual company, as was Xandra. In later years both would often spend weekends in the largely homosexual household of Long Crichel House, Dorset, which Hugh's brother Pat shared with two like-minded friends, the music critic Desmond Shawe-Taylor and the writer Raymond Mortimer. During the period while Hugh and Xandra were conducting their affair there was a press campaign against homosexuality, which Hugh regarded as absurd, 'a highly farcical witch hunt'.[55] He felt that the legal persecution of individuals for their private morals was 'monstrous'.[56] In 1955 Hugh's brother was one of only a handful of men courageous enough to give evidence to the Wolfenden inquiry into the law relating to homosexual offences, insisting that homosexuals presented no 'threat' to heterosexual young men. Later Hugh would advise his sister that neither of her boys, then in their teens, were 'in danger' from their uncle.[57]

After staying a few days at I Tatti, Hugh and Xandra travelled to Rome, where they were entertained by Virginia Ashley Clarke and her husband, who had recently taken up the post of Ambassador. Then Hugh flew on to Israel on behalf of *The Sunday Times*, while Xandra returned to Scotland to spend Christmas with the children and her husband, who was in uncompromising mood. What she needed, he told her, was 'a bloody good thrashing'. He had a good mind to give it to her, 'only then you would have a bruise to show, which is just what you want'. He had already announced that he wanted her to see a doctor chosen by his lawyer, and to have electric shock treatment. Now he delivered an ultimatum. Either she stopped seeing Hugh, or he would stop her allowance, shut up the house and remove the children to Fontainebleau. 'I am having a ghastly time,' she moaned. 'I wonder so, so much how you have got on in Israel.'[58]

Snow fell on Hugh's first night in the Holy Land. A full programme had been organised for him by the Israeli authorities, anxious to demonstrate the progress achieved by their new nation (then only five years old) to the outside world. 'My head whirls vertiginously and information is shoved into it promiscuously, from every side, as it whirls,' he complained to Xandra; 'I have been passed from professor to professor, politician to politician, institute to institute, library to library.' His first day was spent touring Jerusalem, his feet soaking in the wet slush; the next inspecting farms and factories in the Negev, stumbling through the mud and tearing his clothes on thorns and prickly pears. He stayed that night in a kibbutz, where he was lent the simple room of an old woman, an immigrant from Germany: evidently well educated, for there was a little case of German books, among them the complete works of Goethe and Heine. 'It makes the Nazi persecution seem particularly vivid to find such refugees, with these few relics of their culture, working as labourers in collective farm settlements on the edge of the Arabian desert.'

'Certainly one should never come to Israel in search of *douceur de vivre*,' he continued; 'but since I never expected to find such a thing, I am not disappointed: indeed I am feeling well, my morale is high, and I am learning a great deal. If only I could get a glass of wine, how completely happy I should be!' He particularly enjoyed his visits to kibbutzim. 'I find these lay-monasteries, these idealist pioneering agricultural communities, quite fascinating.'[59]

The next day found him in Sodom. He longed to send a postcard to Billa Harrod with that resonant postmark, but none was to be found; indeed, there was nothing in that forlorn spot but a potash factory. His tour continued with visits to river diversion projects on the upper Jordan and swamp reclamation projects above Lake Hula, Roman ruins and Crusader castles, and another night in a kibbutz, this time in the north, near Haifa. In the special series of articles on Israel Hugh wrote for *The Sunday Times*, he examined the 'extraordinary phenomenon' of Zionism, 'one of the great human movements of the age'; the precarious state of the Israeli economy; the prospects for another Israeli–Arab war; and the utopian, collectivist ideals intrinsic to the young nation. 'I have an immense amount to report to BB on this squalid, bouncing, pioneering, combustible, fascinating country,' he wrote to Nicky Mariano from Tel Aviv. Berenson could not understand why he had gone to Israel at all, and speculated that perhaps it was a 'secret mission'.[60]

Back in Jerusalem on Christmas Eve, Hugh was taken to a dismal carol service which put him in irreverent mood. At a restaurant dinner with his hosts afterwards he was at last able to drink some wine and, fearing that he might be 'treated' to a midnight Mass, launched into a sacrilegious story. His Jewish audience was convulsed with irreligious mirth as he became increasingly outrageous. One said afterwards, 'I have <u>never</u> heard an Englishman speak like that before.'[61]

While Hugh was still in Israel, an Italian newspaper announced that it possessed evidence that Bormann had died in Italy in 1952. 'As George Weidenfeld is even now bombarding me with the proofs of my introduction to the Bormann letters,' he wrote to Xandra, 'I feel that I ought to clear up this last-minute mystery before passing them for the press.' He duly flew to Rome to investigate the matter and found that, much as he had expected, there was nothing in it. This was one of a succession of blind alleys up which he was led in pursuit of the missing Nazi. Bormann's disappearance after leaving the bunker would prove a favourite subject for the gullible over the ensuing decades, and Hugh was regularly called upon to evaluate sightings in Argentina, Paraguay and elsewhere. His attitude remained sceptical throughout – except for a moment in 1960, when he received what purported to be a personal message from Bormann, in circumstances which convinced him, for a short while, that it was genuine.[62] In 1972 the German Federal government identified human remains uncovered not far from the bunker as those of Bormann; and in 1998 DNA tests confirmed that Bormann had indeed been killed in May 1945, while trying to escape from Berlin.

From Rome, Hugh took the train to Florence, to stay a few more days at I Tatti before returning to England. Though he had been away only a fortnight, he struck Berenson as 'looking handsomer, more distinguished, as well as more mature than when he left'.[63] At I Tatti he found two frantic letters from Xandra, supplemented by a panicky telegram which arrived not long after he did. She was in a highly emotional state, distraught at the choice that seemed to face her: between her lover and her children. Without her brother, who had left for an indefinite stay in Rome, she lacked support. Hugh tried to allay Xandra's fears and to stiffen her resistance to her bullying husband, who now seemed to be insisting that she should come and live with him in France.[64]

On returning to England Hugh succumbed to a fever, as his temperature shot up to 103 degrees. 'Do you think E. Waugh, in conformity with his obsolete superstitions, is sticking pins into me?' he asked Xandra. The two men were fighting another round of their long-running feud. In a *New Statesman* book review Hugh had taken a swing at Waugh, who retaliated in a letter to the Editor. 'Since Mr Trevor-Roper has introduced my name, rudely and irrelevantly, into his article,' wrote Waugh; 'may I offer some reflections? Why does this contributor write so very often about the Catholic Church, a subject on which he is conspicuously ill-informed ...?' He deplored the spectacle of a tutor in modern history who 'so clumsily and offensively attacks the Catholic religion'. In a reply appended to Waugh's letter, Hugh stated that in the ten years he had been writing articles for the *New Statesman* he had written three times on the English Catholics, 'i.e. as often as on the English Quakers and a good deal less often than upon the English Protestants. This seems to me to show a sense of proportion.' The scrap continued over several subsequent issues, with Hugh giving as good as he got. Waugh referred to Hugh's 'hobby of introducing opprobrious references to the Church'; Hugh accused Waugh of 'falsifying documents, concealing relevant evidence, and relying on abuse'. When Hugh argued that he understood these matters better because he came from a recusant family, Waugh was ready with a sneer: 'I cannot accept that because Mr Roper's family apostatised more recently than mine, he has inherited a superior insight into the use of language.'

Hugh's sign-off was dismissive: 'May I recommend to Mr Waugh a period of silent reading?'[65]

*

Xandra's confidence had been shaken by her husband, who doubted whether Hugh really wanted to marry her. 'Ours is a most calm and reasonable love based on mutual interests rather than on sex,' she mused to Hugh. 'His love for me was a violent sexual affair so I suppose he cannot think any other kind of love exists – sometimes I get a bit worried that you show your feelings so little on paper.' She assured Hugh that she had not slept with her husband while they were living in the same house over Christmas. 'But I do appreciate a little touch of jealousy,' she admitted; 'I ferret about in your letters for signs of affection.'[66]

'You should not care so much for the mere husks, the limited and, if often repeated, tedious language of affection!' protested Hugh. 'Do you not think that silent evidence is sometimes as good evidence, if accompanied by acts, as the banal words crooned publicly out from screens and posters in the Odeon cinema? Darling, you must be tolerant of my inarticulacy and consider that there is other evidence besides the evidence of words – which, as the philosophers assure us, were given to us not to express but better to conceal our meaning!'[67]

Xandra asked if Berenson had said anything to him about the discrepancy in their ages. 'Darling, that still worries me <u>desperately</u>,' she wailed. 'I woke up this morning feeling everything was hopeless & that, for <u>your</u> sake, I should not persist but patch things up with J. I felt old & helpless'. This was a continual refrain, which Hugh repeatedly tried to counter. 'I don't feel this, and it does rather embarrass me when you say it, because I don't feel any difference in our age and don't wish to have it rubbed in to me and wish to overlook it, as it is so easily overlooked.'[68]

On 21 January 1954 the Admiral petitioned for divorce in the High Court, on the grounds of adultery. Hugh agreed with Xandra that this action be undefended, provided she retained custody of the children. Such a line would obviate the need for a court appearance, with all its concomitant publicity, an outcome that Xandra's brother was especially keen to avoid. Hugh believed that she might still have a case for cruelty, and urged her to collect evidence from possible witnesses, including the Admiral's first wife, to whom he had apparently been violent. But their position was not as strong as it might have been, had she not confessed to their affair and had she taken greater care to hide Hugh's letters. 'You cannot be too careful at this juncture,' he warned, 'when carelessness has already lost us several valuable points!'[69] At his insistence she deposited his letters in a strongbox at the bank. Moreover, it was essential for them to act discreetly until the divorce was made absolute, in six months' time.

It was not too late to withdraw, Xandra told him. She feared overburdening him with her problems and preventing him from writing. 'I would make it my aim in life to get you to write your book,' she pledged.

'I feel you get waylaid by all the other small commitments of your life & pass by the <u>main</u> commitment of your life – I realise <u>you must write</u> – I could take a pride in encouraging you to do this & in creating an atmosphere that would nourish your writing.' She had been put on her mettle by a statement of Berenson's, that marriage would be the end of him as a scholar. 'After all, you must admit that you have not very much output to show, so far – Archbishop Laud (which you won't let me read), The Last Days of Hitler, some essays for the New Statesman & History Today, an unfinished pamphlet & an introduction to some very unedifying letters'. This was 'not enough', she pronounced. 'As soon as your sabbatical year starts, <u>you</u> are to start writing – I am going to force you.'[70]

Hugh read these 'disdainful references to my tenuous literary output' with mixed feelings. 'I suppose it is rather meagre compared with the majestic stream of scholarly works put out by such thinkers as Dennis Wheatley.* However you have left out certain items; and I would remark that output, in the high-class literary circles in which I move, is judged by its quality, not its quantity.' Xandra was suitably contrite after this rebuke; but her attempt to make amends misfired. 'I <u>adore</u> your letters & think they are witty & scintillating,' she assured him; 'whilst, I must confess, I find your articles are <u>sometimes</u> a little laboured with only flashes of your bright wit here and there'.[71]

'<u>All</u> the London world is saying that I have run away with you,' Xandra informed him. At a dinner party given by Yvonne Hamilton, Hugh took his hostess aside and told her their secret. 'We both feel that marriage will make Hugh more human and perhaps a *soupçon* less malicious,' Jamie Hamilton confided to Berenson afterwards. 'Yvonne is prepared to wager large sums,' he continued, 'that Hugh has never slept with anyone.' Berenson replied that her guess 'may hit the mark'. Women, he believed, and Italian women in particular, 'smell a virgin male from afar'.[72]

Gossip intensified after they were again house guests of the Buccleuchs at Boughton. Hugh communicated to Xandra a report which had reached Isaiah Berlin. 'You and I were never seen but returned late for meals with wisps of hay in our hair, on our clothes, etc. By dint of gentle pressure I discovered that the immediate source of this story was Pam Berry, who ascribed the further source of it to Alan.'† When Xandra went to collect her elder son James from school she broke the news to him that she and 'Daddy' were separating. There was much bluster from the Admiral. If Xandra defended the divorce case and brought a petition for cruelty, he threatened

---

* Dennis Wheatley (1897–1977) was a prolific writer of bestselling thrillers and occult novels.
† Alan Pryce-Jones, writer, critic, journalist and Editor of *The Times Literary Supplement*, 1948–59. A distant cousin of the Duchess of Buccleuch, he was her lover at the time.

to have her lover 'hounded from the country & turned out of Oxford'. Far from intimidating Hugh, however, such threats had the opposite effect. 'The battle must be fought and fought seriously,' he insisted. At a dinner with the Hamiltons, Hugh was 'in sparkling form, mischievous, confiding about his matrimonial projects and complications, and evidently revelling in the whole situation'. His relish for conflict was so evident that he felt it necessary to deny to Haig that he was 'fighting for fighting's sake'.[73]

In early March he was again afflicted by sinus trouble, and took to his bed. He had begun to feel that they were 'getting nowhere' and drifting along, at the mercy of the Admiral's broadsides. He confessed to Xandra that he felt 'very low', and was somewhat ashamed of this. 'Perhaps it is as well that you should know that I have these black moods,' he reflected. 'I do suffer, off and on, from the deepest depression – generally when I feel that I am doing nothing and that time is sliding ineffectually by.' He succeeded in deferring the start of his sabbatical from 1 January until 1 April, and by the middle of March had resumed work on his 'pamphlet'; but he was already 'in despair' about his sabbatical year, 'which looks like being a total waste'. It was maddening that they could not plan for the future. 'I long to have you with me and to be able to work with you in the same house: I feel I should work so much better. At present I cannot work if I see you and working without you I feel lonely and depressed.'[74]

Xandra too was despondent, and castigated herself for her carelessness in leaving her letters where her husband could find them. 'I have thrown away my chance of happiness,' she moaned; 'I shall have to go back to Johnny.' She was weeping as she wrote to him. 'Please write your book. That will be my only consolation in my misery.' She described the mortifying experience of sitting through a sermon in her local church, in which the vicar pointedly attacked those who had lacked a sense of responsibility in marriage.[75]

Hugh remained firm under this histrionic barrage. Though reluctant to impose his will on her, he argued that, having come so far, she could not now retreat. Her marriage had broken down irretrievably. He was still gloomy. 'Nothing I write now satisfies me,' he grumbled. A fortnight later he complained to Xandra that he was 'suffering very much from general depression through the burden of writing when I am not in the mood to write. To write in such a way as satisfies me, I must feel buoyant and resilient.' A few days later he confessed that he had again set it aside. 'I could return to my pamphlet on the RCs – if I weren't mentally so exhausted that I can no longer think.' In a letter to his former pupil Alan Clark, Hugh explained that his private affairs were 'very complex'. He felt that 'if only I could get away for a time at this most delightful season of the year, and not feel too completely alone, I would recover from this depression and be re-inspired with zest for the battles that are looming ahead'.[76]

Help arrived from an unexpected quarter. Xandra reported that her husband was 'furious and seriously disturbed because Lord Mountbatten has written a severe letter to him'. Xandra found it 'amazing' that Mount-batten should intervene on her behalf, because she had met him only once, two years earlier, when he had come to lunch while on a naval visit. But the explanation was not hard to divine. The Mountbattens had recently been staying with the Ashley Clarkes, from whom they had undoubtedly heard lurid accounts of the Admiral's brutish treatment of Xandra. Moreover they were friendly with the Admiral's first wife Esmée Fitzgibbon, whom he had 'almost killed' in a fit of rage. Mountbatten was Commander-in-Chief of the Mediterranean Fleet, which Johnny was due to visit shortly. More important still, Mountbatten was thought likely to become the next First Sea Lord.* Nothing was more important to the Admiral than his career. 'Promotion to Vice-Admiral', his first wife confirmed, 'means more to him than anything else in life.' Though 'livid' that Xandra had contacted naval colleagues to solicit evidence of his cruelty, he became much more accommodating. Xandra's solicitor indicated that 'things are going to turn out the way we want'.[77]

Hugh escaped from Oxford at Easter time, going first to London. There he dined with Cecil Woodham-Smith, author of several works of popular history, and her lawyer husband at their home in Cadogan Place. 'I had an excellent dinner, and of course talked too much,' he told Xandra. 'They all told me that I was very different from what they had expected, and reverted to this topic with almost embarrassing frequency. They seem to have expected a terrifying personality. Do my writings really give such an impression? I had always thought that they breathed out a kind of universal vague woolly sentimentality.' He stayed over the Easter weekend in Sussex with his former pupil Edward Boyle, now an MP and a rising star in the Conservative Party. The experience revived him. 'How glad I am that I came! My health and morale are both much better; the air is wonderfully clear and fresh; I sit in the garden writing this letter among sunshine and flowers'.[78]

Haig had discouraged him from coming to Bemersyde over Easter, while the divorce remained unresolved. Xandra was disappointed that they would not be seeing each other. She was anyway feeling bereft, as the children were going to their father in Fontainebleau for the holidays. She was again working herself up into a state, sending Hugh a succession of increasingly emotional letters. 'I feel very worried that you have shown so little

* Mountbatten was appointed First Sea Lord in 1955, and Chief of the Defence Staff in 1959.

understanding and I now wonder whether our marriage would be a success.' Yet again she suggested that 'it would be better if I withdraw from your life – I am quite sick about the whole thing – & don't think I shall ever recover – J. has succeeded beyond his wildest hopes – he has sown discord between us'.[79] Hugh protested at this 'verbal *Blitzkrieg*'. He found her 'sudden attack' bewildering; 'I think you are being very unreasonable'. Yielding to pressure, he motored up to the Borders and they spent a day together. 'The moment I was with you I forgot all my doubts,' she assured him afterwards. 'I am so glad peace is restored,' he replied.[80]

Another eruption followed a few days later. The possibility had arisen for him to go to South America in his sabbatical year, something he very much wanted to do. He hoped that she might accompany him, for at least some of the time. Xandra's response was coloured by the suspicion that she was 'starting a baby'. She wrote him three emotional letters on the same day. She would not stand in his way, she told him, 'but you must realise that our private plans would be shelved, probably for ever'. If she were not having a baby, 'I would adore to come too'; but if she were, 'it would be a crazy thing to do'. On the other hand, 'I do not think it would be a good start-off for a marriage for you to rush away to South America & I stay by myself & have a baby. Therefore the answer is for me to have it reversed.' She did not want to have to set up house in Oxford by herself.[81] Xandra was relieved when Hugh informed her that he had succeeded in deferring his sabbatical year for a second time, thus postponing any South American trip into the indefinite future. She told him so in a telegram, followed by two further letters written on the same day. 'I am so, so relieved to get your letter this morning,' she told him; 'already, since receiving your letter, I feel quite different!'[82]

Telephone calls between the lovers provided a source of repeated misunderstandings. After she had again protested that he had been 'curt' when she telephoned, leaving her feeling 'rebuffed', he explained that there had been a radio engineer in the room with him, preparing to record a broadcast on developments in Morocco. 'Oh dear, don't you see how frightening it is always to be afraid of being misinterpreted, whatever one does? You are so sensitive that I am afraid of upsetting you if I refuse a call when I am engaged, but then if I take it and hint that I am not free to talk, I am misinterpreted, and you are upset.' This is what he meant when he remarked that she was sometimes 'exacting' – a description which she resented and which often resurfaced in her letters.[83]

'I thought your broadcast was very good,' Xandra commented, 'but I was relieved when you got off the Royal family! I don't think it is a good thing to discuss them! & I do think they work very hard and do a great deal of good.' She received an invitation to a Buckingham Palace garden party, and had decided to go, even though her husband had been invited, 'as it is the last royal party I shall be able to attend'. In the 1950s, divorced women were excluded from events such as royal garden-parties or Ascot. Hugh had been invited too. Xandra was fearful of a confrontation, but he persuaded her to come with him as a gesture of defiance, and her solicitor encouraged this as 'it will be some protection for you from the Admiral, who might other-wise seek you out'. At a party they attended together at Syon House, the Duke of Northumberland 'behaved strangely' towards them. Apparently he disapproved of their plans to marry because of the age difference, believing that Hugh would become restive after a few years and that Xandra would be made very unhappy. More encouraging was the attitude of Maurice Bowra, now taking his turn as Vice-Chancellor, in succession to Dean Lowe of Christ Church. Bowra went out of his way to have 'a great heart-to-heart with Hugh about his girl', as he reported to Billa Harrod. 'He is cracky about her,' continued Bowra. 'I promised 100% support and full alliance of the Immoral Front.'[84]

Billa Harrod was another source of support to the lovers. She and Xandra soon became confidantes. Xandra was able to stay with the Harrods when she came to Oxford in mid-May, and again in June. Billa helped to introduce Xandra into Oxford society. 'I am _so_ grateful to you for saying that you and some of Hugh's friends do not entirely disapprove of me,' she wrote after her first visit, 'unlike what I had been led to suppose. It was _very_, _very_ angelic of you to tell me this, because I felt very worried and thought you might all think that I would ruin his career.' Xandra and her husband-to-be began looking for a place of their own. They knew what they wanted: a Georgian house within easy reach of Oxford. It needed to be large enough to accommodate the three children during the school holidays, plus the nanny and a cook, with a study to which Hugh could retreat from family life. In June she thought that they had found a suitable place with eleven acres in Stanford-in-the-Vale, but this came to nothing.[85]

Any distraction proved an irritant to Hugh, and his simmering frustration boiled over in a letter written at the end of June. 'It is ridiculous that my little book on the RCs should never seem to progress and I must reserve the month of July for it. A lot of the interruptions – legal, financial, administrative interruptions, and of course occasional crises and occasional illnesses – are unavoidable; but social and avoidable interruptions I _must_, for this month, avoid. This means that I really _cannot_ get involved in the vortex of your flying visit to Paris and London, the migrations of your children, the weddings of your neighbours. I must stay quietly in Oxford.' Xandra thought this letter 'unfair & petulant'. She understood that she had to 'keep out of your way' in July, so that he could finish his pamphlet. 'I _must_ admit I dread the effect of its publication on all my RC friends.'

One of these was Sarah, Countess of Haddington, with whom Xandra and her children often stayed in the holidays, either at Mellerstain, their elegant Adam house near Kelso, or Tyninghame, their East Lothian house, whose woods led down to the sea. A Roman Catholic, Sarah Haddington only reluctantly accepted that Xandra's marriage was beyond repair.[86]

Xandra discovered that her husband had been having an affair with a woman in Lausanne for the past two years. Rather late in the day, Walter Buccleuch's sister, the Duchess of Gloucester, now revealed that she had often seen him in London restaurants, during the war, with 'blondes – always the same types, she said – rather common & showy, obvious tarts'. While in Paris, Xandra lunched with an old flame, who happened to be a friend of Bowra's. When she told him about the Admiral's threat to go and see 'the head of Oxford', he roared with laughter and said that it was one of the funniest things he had ever heard. But not everybody would be as relaxed as Bowra, or other members of 'the Immoral party' such as Roy Harrod. Two of Hugh's more conservatively minded colleagues indicated in a friendly manner that being named in the divorce and marrying a divorced woman would damage him personally and damage the college. 'Darling, I am so terrified that you will feel the battle was not worth the spoils, that I am not worth the price you have had to pay,' agonised Xandra.[87]

On 23 July the decree nisi was pronounced, with a formal order for costs against Hugh as co-respondent. The court confirmed an arrangement reached between the solicitors for each side about the children. Neither parent was awarded custody, and both were granted access, with Xandra having care and control. In return for a victory of form, Hugh boasted to Berenson, the Admiral had surrendered all points of substance. They were to be married early in October, as soon as his brother Pat returned from a trip to America: too close to the beginning of term to allow time for a proper honeymoon. Hugh wrote letters of explanation to friends and allies within the University. Masterman rallied to his support; but another whom Hugh had thought of as a friend, Arthur Goodhart, Master of University College, failed to reply, and voiced his disapproval to Robert Blake. Hugh's former Christ Church colleague Nowell Myres, now Bodley's Librarian, responded 'coldly' to Hugh's letter and turned aside suddenly to avoid acknowledging him when the two men encountered one another in the street. The Duke of Buccleuch (an old Christ Church man) wrote a helpful letter to Robin Dundas, in the knowledge that he would feel it his duty to show this to the Dean. The Duke explained that he and his wife were great friends of Xandra's family; that her former husband had 'certain characteristics about which he would prefer to say nothing', and that he had treated her outrageously; that while they would have preferred the divorce to have been 'the other way round', there were good practical reasons for doing it this way; and that he hoped the college would be 'sensible'.[88]

Hugh took Xandra to meet his parents, an episode he described in a letter to his sister. All three parties were prepared for an ordeal: the parents apprehending the arrival of a Mayfair Jezebel, a *soignée*, sophisticated divorcée who had contrived to ensnare their innocent son, Xandra expecting to be eyed suspiciously as such, and afraid of having hysterics if her fiancé's comic account of home life among the Trevor-Ropers proved accurate. As predicted, Bertie opened the conversation by saying: 'Melrose? Oh yes, I know it well. We used to stay there on the way to the Kelso races.' After this effort, he showed almost complete indifference to the remaining conversation, relaxing, like the dormouse at the Mad Hatter's tea party, into the teapot, only occasionally mumbling inconsequentially about Lanark races or Monte Carlo. Kathleen, on the other hand, got on very well with Xandra from the first – although their talk seemed to Hugh to dwell too much on his unsatisfactory character as a child.[89]

When Hugh proposed that they went away together 'somewhere unfashionable' in the summer, Xandra asked her brother if he might come too. 'He said he thought he could be *de trop* with us, but I said we would adore to have him with us for part of the time & I said how devoted you were to him. He was obviously delighted by this – I said I thought the main reason you liked me so much was because you think I am like him ... He said "I like old Hugh too – he is a damn nice chap".' Hugh replied that he would be '<u>delighted</u>' if Haig were to join them, though he could not assent to her rationale. 'You mustn't say that "the <u>main</u> reason" why I like you is that you are like him! That is really rather tendentious! What I would say is that the mental qualities which you and he obviously share are the qualities which I like best in you both – a combination of aesthetic sensitivity, delicacy without primness, fanciful humour, and genuine kindliness.'[90]

In August Hugh drove Xandra to Austria, taking her Hillman car because it was cheaper to run. He had refused her request to study the manual beforehand. From Innsbruck, they took a winding road that climbed high into the Austrian Alps. Above the snowline the engine overheated, and the car came to a stop at a point where the road overlooked a sheer drop into a precipice. Hugh clambered out of the car and lifted the bonnet. He began to consult the manual, his fingers fumbling in the cold. Xandra watched with alarm, terrified that he would step back and blunder over the edge. Eventually he managed to restart the engine.

From the Austrian Alps they continued into Bavaria, passing through the little border town of Branau where Hitler had been born. They spent several days in Munich, and visited Ludwig II's fantastic cliff-top castle, Neuschwanstein. As a contrast to the rich diet of churches and palaces,

Hugh took Xandra for 'a dash of reality' to a couple of German concentration camps. The holiday was not a complete success. One reason was that they could not find anywhere to stay that suited them both; as he had always suspected, she liked more luxurious accommodation, whereas his preference was always for simpler hotels. 'I really think we should not go through with it,' Xandra informed him afterwards. Though he did not take this comment seriously, it was nevertheless disheartening to hear at this late stage. One consolation was that while away he had been able to write most of a 14,000-word article on 'Oliver Cromwell and his Parliaments', his contribution to a volume of essays in honour of the recently knighted Lewis Namier.* On his return, Hugh spent the first half of September working. 'I am now alone, leading a hermit's life in Oxford, writing my book on the English Roman Catholics,' he reported to Berenson. 'I am being very malicious about the RCs, which is raising my morale,' he told Xandra.[91] In mid-September he drove up to Bemersyde, and a few days later they travelled together to Paris, so that she could be fitted for her wedding dress.

Haig's phrase about Xandra's being 'a luxury girl' haunted Hugh. The thing that worried him most, he told her, was 'the feeling that when we are married you may feel that I must become enslaved to the Press, at the expense of my own work, in order to earn enough money. Please help me in this ... I am determined not to be, as it were, sucked into the machine and thereby prevented from writing my books or keeping up my studies.' She assured him that 'of course' she would not force him to work as a journalist. The important thing, she insisted, 'is for you to be a serious writer & not to waste your energies in writing for the press'.[92]

There was still time for a further round of misunderstandings between the betrothed couple. The wedding arrangements remained uncertain until the last moment. They had thought it impossible to marry in church, and had resigned themselves to a London register office, but only a fortnight or so before the set date a minister of the Church of Scotland expressed willingness to marry them in church after all. Then there was a difficulty about the reception: they had planned to hold it at Xandra's brother-in-law's house in Lyall Street, but this proved too small. These late changes delayed the invitations. Hugh became irritated by Xandra's 'apparent indifference' to such problems. 'I get the impression that you really don't care at all,' he wrote. Xandra was 'very hurt' by this comment. 'How cruel your letters are!' she lamented. 'You say I think of nothing but Society & Paris & Fath dresses.' She was 'rather upset' when he spoke sharply to her on the telephone. 'Please don't say things to me like this – it reminds me terribly of Johnny & fills me with doubts.' Hugh admitted to feeling 'very

---

*   Richard Pares and A.J.P. Taylor (eds), *Essays Presented to Sir Lewis Namier* (1956).

depressed' by 'general failure: failure of health, failure of morale, failure to please'. This was not an ideal mood in which to begin married life. They still had not found a suitable home near Oxford.[93]

On 4 October 1954, at four o'clock in the afternoon, Hugh and Xandra were married, at St Marylebone Presbyterian Church in George Street, on the south side of Bryanston Square. He was determined that the wedding should be a high-profile occasion, as a gesture of 'general defiance against such elements in English society as showed a tendency to disapprove of our affairs'.[94] Guests were a mixture of high society and academic luminaries, distinguished by Hugh as the 'sheep' and the 'goats': among them the Duke and Duchess of Buccleuch, Lord Cherwell, Maurice Bowra, Isaiah Berlin, the Harrods and Solly Zuckerman. 'I have never known adultery do so much for a man,' quipped Bowra. The Dean's wife and two of the canons lent respectability to the event. The Pakenhams came too, overcoming their objections to divorce on the grounds that Xandra had never been truly married to the Admiral, since he had been married before. Hugh even invited the fashionable Catholic priest Father Dominic de Grunne. 'I couldn't resist inviting him,' he told Berenson, 'because I knew that, if invited, he wouldn't be able to resist the invitation.' A.J.P. Taylor politely declined the invitation, with the excuse that he would stand out among 'The Quality'. Noel Annan apologised afterwards for having failed to turn up, having confused the date. Both the Hamiltons and the Weidenfelds were invited, and, as a piece of mischief-making, were allotted nearby seats in the church, though sadly the Hamiltons failed to arrive in time for the ceremony. *The Times* reported that 'the bride, who was given away by her brother, Earl Haig, wore a ballet-length dress of beige and gold, and a small beige velvet head-dress. Mr Patrick Trevor-Roper (brother of the bridegroom), was best man.' Hugh's sister and her husband were present, though his parents did not attend the wedding. The two ushers were Gavin Astor and Michael Howard (now a lecturer in war studies at King's College, London). The reception, paid for by Xandra's brother, was held at the Cavalry Club. By the time the Hamiltons at last appeared the bride and groom were on the brink of leaving for Scotland. 'Hugh had changed and wore the usual undergraduate costume of sports coat and grey trousers and looked the part,' Hamilton reported spitefully to Berenson. 'The bride looked like his mother.'[95]

The newlyweds spent a few days together at Bemersyde. Then they motored down to Oxford, Hugh to resume his duties as a college tutor and Xandra to continue the search for the ideal house. Once again she lodged with the Harrods, with her new husband joining her there, as paying guests. She attended some of his lectures, sitting conspicuously in the front row. Within days of returning to Oxford Hugh found time to slate Toynbee's

Study of History in *The Sunday Times*. 'Never have I enjoyed a review more than your pasting of Toynbee,' wrote Noel Annan.[96] Hugh suggested to the BBC that he should broadcast on this 'monstrous piece of humbug imposed on a credulous public', but his proposal was declined. 'I really don't think that T.R. is the man to do it,' commented the experienced Third Programme producer Anna Kallin. She thought his letter 'childish'. The right way to tackle the subject was a discussion between Toynbee and a 'mature' historian – not an 'irresponsible youth' like Trevor-Roper.[97]

Towards the end of October Xandra returned to her house in Melrose, while Hugh moved back into his college rooms, as if nothing had changed.

As he gleefully related afterwards to Hugh, Robert Blake had found himself sitting next to Evelyn Waugh on a trip to Rheims in honour of a new cathedral window. On his other side was Douglas Woodruff, Editor of *The Tablet*. All were drinking champagne. On learning that Blake was from Christ Church, Waugh stated his opinion that it was 'essential' to get Hugh 'removed from Oxford', because of his pernicious influence on undergraduates. Blake was non-committal. Waugh then asked, 'Roper's marriage is a great surprise?'

'Oh no,' Blake replied, 'why should you think so?'

'Surely,' Waugh continued, 'it is surprising that anyone should want to marry that man?'

Husband

Before leaving for Scotland, Xandra had identified a possible home: Cumnor Place, an eighteenth-century house a few miles south-west of Oxford. While she was away Hugh showed it to two other Christ Church wives, both of whom approved. He planned to negotiate the purchase through an agent, aiming to penetrate the 'ring' which he believed to operate in the Oxford area. His agent considered Cumnor Place to be a 'white elephant' and advised that it could be obtained cheaply. As a result Hugh's first offer was £6,000, well below the figure others thought necessary to secure it. He was daunted by the upkeep as well as the outlay, and wondered whether they might not be better-off in a college house, for which rent and rates would be deducted from untaxed income. Xandra was now talking about employing 'two dailies' in the holidays, besides the cook and the nanny, as well as 'someone to come in and wait' when they gave a dinner party. She considered herself expert in interior decoration, and was excited about the challenge of 'doing up' Cumnor Place. 'What <u>fun</u> it will be arranging it all!' she exclaimed.

Though now forty-seven, she still hoped to give her new husband a child. One doctor advised that she was too old; another felt that a small operation would improve her chances. Soon after the wedding she believed that she might indeed be pregnant, and was disappointed when a doctor who examined her pronounced that she was not. 'Darling, I would do <u>anything</u> to have your child,' she affirmed. Hugh tried to console her with the thought that 'many people have no children, and you have three; and if I can provide you with some of the happiness you have missed hitherto, I shall be more than happy myself'.

Eventually he persuaded himself, with the help of some figures from his accountant, to offer up to £8,750 for Cumnor Place. But by then it was too late. Another buyer had offered £9,000, which was accepted. Xandra was furious. She had been longing to find a house where they could live together. His attempts to mitigate her disappointment only enraged her further. Billa Harrod stoked the fire, blaming him for trying to be too clever. 'Poor old Hugh,' she commiserated with Xandra; 'he is such an unrealistic <u>child</u>, full of brilliant and totally irrelevant theories.'[1]

Hugh wondered if the loss of Cumnor Place might not have been a blessing in disguise. He outlined his thoughts in a letter to Xandra. Buying such a house would have implied staying in Oxford permanently, and he questioned whether this was what he really wanted. Supposing he were offered a Chair at Cambridge or some other university: would he want to be prevented from accepting it by the fact of having made a recent invest-ment which anchored him to Oxford? He would not. Far from wanting to stay where he was, he was actively looking for an exit, at least from his work as a college tutor, which was 'merely slowing me up'. Half the year was taken up in day-to-day college business and teaching undergraduates, 'who are largely a drag rather than a stimulus as far as my historical study is con-cerned'. If he were to remain as he was for another twenty-five years, 'I shall find myself being retired at the end of it with a feeling of having buried my talent (such as it is) in a napkin'. If, on the other hand, he was going to write the books that he felt ready to write, 'I must escape'. The courageous thing to do would be to 'cut free from Oxford', or at least leave himself able to cut free, not to tie himself down.

The question was: could they afford it? She had investment income of around £2,350 a year. He would continue to draw his full annual salary of £2,750 during his sabbatical, now postponed until the calendar year 1956. Afterwards, if he ceased teaching, he would still have his University lec-tureship, worth £750 a year, plus the £1,000 he earned from *The Sunday Times*. His literary agent, A.D. Peters, urged him to release himself from the shackle of teaching, guaranteeing that he would earn enough money from writing to compensate for the loss of £1,000 in salary; indeed he predicted that Hugh could earn twice as much. Hugh therefore proposed to Xandra that they should find a place to live near Oxford for the short term, allowing him to take his sabbatical, and then 'break away' from Christ Church, 'or at least convert my present position into a much looser association'.[2]

'Sometimes I worry if I am really married to you,' Xandra lamented in a letter written on 26 December. The end of the 1954 Michaelmas term had not brought the newlyweds together. 'At this moment Xandra is in Melrose, celebrating Christmas with the children,' Hugh informed Berenson in mid-December, 'and I (rather unwillingly in the circumstances) have yielded to the pressure of that literary pasha, the editor of *The Sunday Times*, applied myself to the galley-oar; and am making my way to the Barbary Coast.' He was in Spain, on his way to Morocco to investigate resistance to French occupation, and would not return to England until the second week of January. Xandra was understandably irked by his absence. In response to her reproaches he wrote to her from Madrid, requesting a letter 'containing

<u>no</u> complaints, <u>no</u> protests, <u>no</u> backhanded observations!' In fact he was so upset by one of her letters that he tore it up.[3]

Xandra's agitation was compounded by the Admiral's threat to arrive at their house in Scotland at any moment. The divorce had left unresolved the issue of who owned Birchfield and its contents, resulting in legal complications which would continue for years. Xandra was still frightened of her former husband. She bombarded her solicitor with epistolary missiles. 'Please don't write him <u>too</u> many, <u>too</u> long, <u>too</u> excited, <u>too</u> self-contradictory letters,' begged Hugh. 'The poor man is rather overwhelmed by so many instructions!'[4]

Xandra reported on a conversation with Ian Gilmour, whose wife Lady Caroline was the youngest daughter of the Duke of Buccleuch. Gilmour owned *The Spectator*, and had just given up his career at the English Bar to act as Editor. He expressed strong enthusiasm for Hugh's writing. Over the coming years Gilmour would make persistent attempts to lure him from the *New Statesman*.[5] He offered the prospect of a seat on the board if Hugh would write for *The Spectator* regularly.[6] When Hugh reviewed a book* for *The Spectator*, this elicited a strong protest from Janet Adam Smith, who accused him of treating the *New Statesman* 'rather shabbily'. In response, Hugh pointed out that he had no contract with the *New Statesman*, and after a frank exchange of views they agreed a compromise: that Hugh would give the *New Statesman* first option on his services as a reviewer of historical works after *The Sunday Times*. Immediately afterwards his damning review of Sir Percy Sillitoe's memoirs appeared in *The Spectator*. Sir Percy had taken over from Sir David Petrie as head of MI5 in 1946; on his retirement in 1953, he had been succeeded by Hugh's old friend, Dick White.[7]

Xandra and the children spent Christmas at Bemersyde with her brother. In a letter to Hugh, Haig hinted that this had been an imposition. 'Xandra has a convenient distaste for the kitchen,' he complained, 'and a very convenient and soul-stirring martyr act when it comes to the moment of putting on her apron.' Life was not always 'a glamorous round of sensations and intellectual conversation'. Referring to his eldest sister's 'unnecessarily hysterical frame of mind', he thought that 'a little homely potato peeling with time for meditation might be just what the doctor ordered'. In reply, Hugh tried to clarify his position. 'I am devoted to Xandra, who I think is sometimes unreasonable, and am devoted to you, to whom I think she is sometimes unreasonable, and it is difficult for me to say much to her – on this subject – without running the risk of saying more than you would want me to say.' But he assured Haig that he strongly sympathised with him in such difficulties, and would do what he could to prevent them.

---

* Conyers Read's *Mr Secretary Cecil and Queen Elizabeth*.

'Poor Xandra – in some ways she is not equipped for this world; but I hope I may be of some help to her, and if I may have your support when I need to be firm, I shall always hope to deserve it. I think there are times when she needs firmness, and those are times when I need reassurance.'

Haig assured Hugh that 'you will always have my moral support'. Unfortunately this was called into question almost immediately, when he was exposed to the crossfire between the Trevor-Ropers and the Admiral. Haig's former factor, Ted Ruffman, was now acting as Howard-Johnston's unofficial agent, and had upset Xandra by entering Birchfield on a pretext while she was away. She suspected Ruffman of having stolen the letters which 'Johnny' had used against her in the divorce case, and (which was almost worse) having broadcast their contents to the servants. Because of this, both Trevor-Ropers were determined never to speak to Ruffman again. The situation was further complicated by the fact that Ruffman was 'a former admirer' of hers; at some point in the past he had apparently made a pass at Xandra, which she had rebuffed. Hugh wrote indignantly to Haig, demanding that he too should sever relations with Ruffman, but Haig demurred. Hugh also pressed Haig to use his influence on his aunts to obtain financial help with his stepchildren's schooling, but Haig was reluctant to do so when he was himself short of money. He suggested that the children's education was 'your responsibility'. Furious, Hugh wrote a sharp letter to Haig, which led to a cooling of relations between them for a while.[8]

Meanwhile the Trevor-Ropers had found a temporary home. The Conservative MP Michael Astor* lent them Red Brick Cottage, a Queen Anne dower house in the grounds of Bruern Abbey, near Chipping Norton, twenty-four miles north-west of Oxford. This was too far from town for Hugh to come and go each day, so during the week he stayed in his college rooms. Xandra felt isolated at Bruern, with just Peter (still below school age) and the servants for company; but she was accustomed to being alone. On most weekends there were house parties at the Abbey and the Trevor-Ropers were usually invited to lunch.

Hugh was full of projects, as he told Berenson. He had finished the essay on 'Oliver Cromwell and his Parliaments' and was now at work on another, 'which I hope will be as effective as my essay on *the Gentry* in removing some of the obstructions to historical study in England!'[9] What he meant by this is difficult to ascertain. Back in 1953 Hugh had told Berenson that he planned to use his sabbatical year to write 'a major work' on the rule of Robert Cecil, the 1st Earl of Salisbury, 'which (I believe) may explain a

* A younger son of the 1st Viscount Astor; brother of David Astor, Editor of *The Observer*; and cousin to Hugh's brother-in-law, Gavin Astor, whose father, John Jacob Astor (soon to be ennobled in his own right, as Baron Astor of Hever) owned *The Times*.

hitherto unexplained set of problems in English history'. Cecil, the principal adviser to Elizabeth I and to her successor James I, from 1590 until 1612, had striven to put the royal revenues on a sound footing. The underlying problem, which would become ever more serious as the century progressed and would reach a crisis in the reign of Charles I, was the tension between the swelling demands of the state and the resentment of the taxpayers obliged to meet them. 'My essay on the gentry is, in part, a sample or prefiguration of this work,' continued Hugh, 'but of course only in very small part: it is intended to clear away the cobwebs of controversy so as to make the path plain for a narrative history.'[10] Possibly the essay he was working on early in 1955 was a boiled-down version of this 'major work'; possibly it was something else altogether. There is no record of his returning to work on the Roman Catholic Revival in nineteenth-century England, which he had been writing in the month before his wedding. Three chapters survive, amounting to about 50,000 words, enough for a short book; it remains unclear whether he meant to write more. In any case the book never appeared.*

The spring of 1955 saw the publication by Oxford University Press of a long-delayed work, edited jointly by Hugh and J.A.W. ('Jack') Bennett of Magdalen: *The Poems of Richard Corbett.* The latter was an early-seventeenth-century cleric, a protégé of Laud's and a scourge of the Puritans, who had been Dean of Christ Church (his portrait hangs in Christ Church Hall), Bishop of Oxford and eventually Bishop of Norwich. Corbett was a notorious place-hunter; his poems blatantly flattered his patrons. Hugh admitted that Corbett's verse was 'second-rate', of historical as much as of literary interest.[†] He had proposed this project to OUP as long ago as 1939, immediately after delivering his manuscript of *Archbishop Laud* to Macmillans, and he had evidently done plenty of work on it before military service compelled him to stop. Bennett had been away from Oxford for a few years after the war, and Hugh preoccupied with other work, which helped to explain why the edition had been so long in preparation.[11]

More significant in terms of Hugh's long-term interests was an essay on the sixteenth-century scholar Erasmus, who became one of his intellectual heroes: a scholar whose horizons stretched across Europe, a man who stood for reason and tolerance and moderation against prejudice, bigotry and fanaticism. A portrait of Erasmus hung on the wall of his study. As he explained many years later, Hugh always admired Erasmus for 'his exact scholarship, his humanist philosophy, which rose above that scholarship,

---

* Though it was advertised as forthcoming by Weidenfeld & Nicolson.
† There was a tenuous family connection. The first edition of Corbett's poems, published in 1647, had been dedicated to the wife of Hugh's ancestor, Christopher Roper, 4th Baron Teynham.

his easy Latin style, his wit and scepticism'. In 1951 Hugh had read Marcel Bataillon's *Érasme et L'Espagne*, and had visited Bataillon in Paris. Bataillon led Hugh to see Erasmus both as an intellectual radical and as a spiritual thinker, not merely as a humanist writer. In the course of subsequent reading he realised that though Erasmus had died apparently a failure, his ideas had persisted, not merely in the Protestant world but also in Catholic societies. He traced an intellectual pedigree of Erasmianism through the struggles of subsequent centuries. Hugh came to view Erasmus's time as a brief age of enlightenment, a period of general peace and the relaxation of orthodoxy before the renewed 'ideological' wars of the seventeenth century. 'Political programmes may be defeated entirely, but not ideas: at least, not great ideas. Political circumstances may alter around them, ideological frontiers may be formed against or across them, but such convulsions merely alter the terrain: they may divert or divide, but they do not per-manently dam the stream.' Hugh's use of the term 'ideological' to describe ostensibly religious conflicts was indicative of his relentlessly secular approach. He readily made the analogy between the ideological struggle of the Cold War and the 'ideological' struggle of the Reformation and Counter-Reformation. To him, there were revealing similarities between the two.

The essay on Erasmus was Hugh's first contribution to the new magazine *Encounter*, which quickly established itself as the leading review of its day. It attracted contributions from some of the most admired writers and intellectuals, including Isaiah Berlin, Vladimir Nabokov, Jorge Luis Borges, Richard Ellmann, R.K. Narayan, W.H. Auden, Irving Howe and Bertrand Russell. Unknown to both readers and contributors, however, it was sup-ported by a covert CIA subsidy, and originated in the 'high-minded low cunning' of British and American intelligence agents responsible for running the cultural Cold War. Meeting in Whitehall in 1951, a committee of CIA and MI6 representatives had discussed the idea of an 'Anglo-American left-of-centre publication' aimed at penetrating the fog of neu-tralism which in their opinion dimmed the judgement of so many British intellectuals. *Encounter* was devised as a voice to oppose the 'soft-headedness' and 'terrible simplifications' of the *New Statesman*, and its 'spirit of conciliation and moral lassitude *vis-à-vis* Communism'.[12] The joint Editors of the new magazine, one British (Stephen Spender) and one American (Irving Kristol, succeeded in 1958 by Melvin J. Lasky), were free to publish whatever they wanted, so long as it was not damaging to American interests; but in the extreme sensitivity of the Cold War, when loyalties were tested to the limit, its bias was soon apparent.

Hugh would write several articles for *Encounter* over the next decade, most of them polemical, but he took care to avoid a partisan line. In his article on Erasmus, for example, he referred scathingly to 'the spectacle, five years ago, in Berlin, when the so-called "Congress for Cultural Freedom" mobilized the intellectuals of the West and invited them to howl in unison against the rival intellectuals similarly mobilized in an opposite "Intellectual Congress" in Breslau'. He returned to the attack on those 'doctrinaires and bigots' who conceived of the world in terms of 'ideological blocs systematically opposed to one another in intellectual matters'. The historian of ideas is not interested in 'these stunted McCarthyites', he declared. 'Intellectuals may be citizens; they may even, as such, have to become soldiers; but it is not their business to be recruiting-sergeants. If their rational message is not heard in their time, let them still utter it rather than turn it into a battle-cry; it may still be heard tomorrow.'[13]

That spring Hugh was sent a selection of the letters of the nineteenth-century Swiss-German historian Jacob Burckhardt to review, and this led him to read (or in some cases re-read) other works of Burckhardt's. 'I am still excited by the experience,' he enthused to Berenson, at whose suggestion he had first read Burckhardt back in 1948: 'What a wonderful historical mind!' This enthusiasm never wavered, and would lead him to introduce Burckhardt's writings onto the Oxford undergraduate reading list. In his review he praised Burckhardt as 'one of the profoundest of historians', one who rejected 'the cramping systems which have imprisoned other "universal" historians'. Marx, for example, 'for all his brilliant intuition, never deduced the rise or even the possibility of Fascism; and what he did prophesy shows no sign of coming to pass'. These remarks provoked a rise from the Marxist historian Eric Hobsbawm, a lecturer at Birkbeck College, London, who reproved him for 'making silly statements' about Marx. Hugh hit back, and the debate continued on the letters pages for issue after issue. Hobsbawm was supported by other admirers of Marx, headed by Christopher Hill. 'I am sick of these Marxists,' Hugh railed to Berlin, who joined the correspondence to support him. 'Every time I write in the NS & N* one of the London academic Marxists – Rothstein, Hobsbawm, etc – pops up and lays down the law to me. But I suppose I should relish being selected as their academic enemy no. 1!'[14]

In a contribution to an American publication called *Problems of Communism* (later reproduced, somewhat misleadingly, as the introduction to a multi-author volume called *Why I Oppose Communism*), Hugh likened Marxist historians to Byzantine theologians, or the inhabitants of Lilliput disputing which end of a boiled egg should be broken. 'This is not to deny that there are Marxists who have made contributions to history, but it is never *as* Marxists that they have done so.' Marxist historians, he continued,

* *New Statesman and Nation*, as the *New Statesman* was known from 1931 until 1964.

'incessantly re-write the history of the past and the future, changing the evidence in accordance with the fashion, or the unescapable facts, of the moment, but always maintaining that the new evidence leads to the old conclusions'.[15]

'I meant to ask you this morning, and forgot,' Hugh wrote to Isaiah Berlin in February 1955, 'whether you know anything or can find out reliable information about Moses I. Finley, a Greek historian, Jewish by origin, American by nationality, and now resident at New College, whom we are seriously considering to succeed Dundas.' Finley, who had held a post at Rutgers University, had been persecuted by the notorious anti-Communist committee run by Senator Joseph McCarthy, and was now seeking a refuge in England. Hugh was reading his *The World of Odysseus*, which he would describe in a *New Statesman* review as 'a most exciting, most readable book'. He had also been impressed by Finley personally. But he was concerned about Finley's politics. 'On this subject my view is fixed,' he told Berlin; 'fellow-travellers, apolitical sillies, – yes, if they are good enough; party members, – no, however good. This is a view which I am prepared to defend, and which I am not prepared to change.'[16]

Hugh's objection to Communist Party members was fundamental to his beliefs. Those who chose to follow the Party line rather than think for themselves had committed a sin against his personal creed: they had abandoned their intellectual independence. In this sense Communists resembled those Catholics who unquestioningly accepted the teachings of the Church, abjuring books from the Prohibited Index. Indeed, Hugh suggested that there was tacit collusion between Catholic and Marxist historians, whereby they appeared to substantiate one another's interpretation of the Reformation. In a *New Statesman* review, he described Catholic converts in terms that might equally well have been applied to loyal Party members, as 'casualties of change: intellectuals tired of thinking, aristocrats unable to compete in society, worldlings weary of the world. How well one knows the face of certain converts to Catholicism – that smooth, exhausted look, burnt out and yet at rest, as of a motorist who, after many mishaps and mounting insurance-premiums, has at last decided to drive himself no more, and having found a chauffeur with excellent references, resigns himself to safer travel in a cushioned backseat.'[17] Xandra was apprehensive about the effect of this review on her Roman Catholic friends in the Borders aristocracy. 'Will the children ever be asked to stay at Tyninghame again?' she sadly sighed. Hugh reassured her that none of her friends read the *New Statesman*.[18]

Once he had satisfied himself that Finley was not a Party member, Hugh determined to bring him to Christ Church; after 'a tremendous struggle', and despite opposition from Robert Blake, he succeeded in persuading the

Governing Body to make him an offer. But by then Denys Page had lured
Finley to Cambridge, where he eventually became Professor of Ancient
History, Master of Darwin College and a British subject, ending his days as
Sir Moses Finley.[19]

Although most British intellectuals deplored McCarthyite persecution
of suspected Communists in the United States, there was nevertheless
considerable unease at the time about Communists in academic life, particularly those with access to sensitive scientific and technical information.
The revelation that a number of British scientists had betrayed secrets to the
Russians which had assisted them in the development of nuclear weapons
deepened this unease. The defection of Guy Burgess and Donald Maclean
in 1951 had come as a profound shock, suggesting that Soviet agents had
penetrated deep into British institutions. One result was to cast suspicion
on those who had associated with Burgess and Maclean: for example Kim
Philby, who after the war had been considered as a possible head of MI6.
Philby was interrogated and obliged to resign from the service.

Hugh disliked witch-hunts of any kind. He felt that individuals had
a right to privacy, 'even if they were suspected, perhaps rightly, to be
Communists'. He deprecated the tabloid newspapers' hounding of
Maclean's wife Melinda, and was disgusted by the cant in the press about
an 'Establishment' cover-up.[20] Reviewing a book about the Oppenheimer
case by two American brothers, the journalists Joseph and Stewart Alsop,
Hugh deplored the anti-Communist witch-hunt in the United States. 'In
times of danger men in responsible positions have an absolute duty to resist
general hysteria,' he wrote. 'If some men had not done so, McCarthyism
would not now be, as it mercifully is, at last discredited.' Hugh's interest in
the case arose out of his friendship with Joe Alsop, whom he had met on
his visit to America in the late 1940s. He was embarrassed to have to explain
to Alsop that *The Sunday Times*, which had commissioned the review, had
suppressed it at proof stage on political grounds. After a row with the
Sunday Times's Literary Editor, Leonard Russell, Hugh was able to give
Alsop better news: he had placed the review with *The Spectator*.[21]

A few years later Hugh was approached by Eric Hobsbawm, who had
been invited to lecture at Stanford and was seeking support for his visa
application. Communists found it hard to obtain visas to enter the United
States, and Hobsbawm made no secret of his longstanding Party membership; Christopher Hill had suggested that Hugh might be willing to provide
the support he needed. Hobsbawm approached Hugh diffidently, having
found that several colleagues professing left-wing politics shied away when
asked for such support. 'Please do not hesitate to say that you could not
help me,' wrote Hobsbawm. 'There are, after all, plenty of reasons, all valid,
why you should wish to do nothing about what is, in any case, a slightly

impertinent request, for which I apologize.' But Hugh had no hesitation in endorsing Hobsbawm's visa application. 'I shall certainly give you any help I can,' he replied. 'Would the enclosed letter be suitable?' The application proved successful.[22]

On the other hand Hugh was willing, at least for a while, to supply information to the Security Service about colleagues suspected of Communist sympathies. In the early 1950s he was sometimes asked by MI5 about individuals who it was felt might be 'of interest' to them. He would make discreet enquiries and report back on his findings. One of those whom he regularly consulted was Thomas Wilson, a Fellow of University College, who had been a member of Churchill's Statistical Board of the War Cabinet. Wilson did not relish informing on his colleagues. 'How I hate all this!' he exclaimed to Hugh in a 1952 letter. 'But what can we do if we're to defend ourselves at all against these types?'[23]

Hugh was no Cold War warrior. He was not one of those advocating an aggressive policy towards the Communist bloc. Reviewing a book about Christendom and the Turks in 1955, he stressed the element of co-existence between the two, and drew the moral that 'a frontal struggle between opposing systems' was not inevitable. The theory that the world could not live 'half slave and half free' was simply untrue. Lest any readers should fail to draw the parallel with the present, he twice, in this short review, described the frontier between Christian Europe and the Islamic Turkish empire as an 'iron curtain'.[24]

The Trevor-Ropers surrendered Red Brick Cottage after the end of the Hilary term 1955. Their relationship with the Astors had soured after a dinner party at which a guest had speculated on what Guy Burgess might do if he came back to live in England, and Hugh had quipped that 'he would go to work at *The Observer*'. Furious, their host laid down his cutlery, and declared, 'My father owned *The Observer*, my brother edits *The Observer*, and I will have no one speak of *The Observer* in that offensive way in my house.' The Trevor-Ropers left the party early.[25]

At the beginning of the spring vacation they visited Paris, where they stayed as guests of the Ambassador and his wife, Gladwyn and Cynthia Jebb. They attended a cocktail party given by Nancy Mitford, and spent a night as guests of Lady Diana Cooper, Duff Cooper's widow, at her home in Chantilly. Frank Giles was now Paris correspondent for *The Times* and, like Hugh, had married into the aristocracy. Both husbands liked their wives' titles to be used, even if this caused some confusion. 'She's not "Mrs Giles"; insisted her husband on one occasion. 'Oh, I'm sorry, I thought you were married,' came the response.

Hugh had been invited to Paris to give a lecture at the École Pratique des

Hautes Études, home of the *Annales* school of historians. Its Director, Fernand Braudel, was the last survivor of the triumvirate with whose names the school was associated: the other two being Marc Bloch (a pupil of Henri Pirenne) and Lucien Febvre. Hugh developed a deep respect for Braudel and his colleagues, who aspired to write 'total history', drawing on other disciplines, including sociology, anthropology, economics and even geography. He was one of the first historians in England to appreciate the significance of the *Annales* school, and to take up its cause. 'I am coming to the view that only the French can write history,' Hugh had written in 1951; 'Marc Bloch and his disciples have made all other historians seem trivial.' He had been hugely impressed by Braudel's great work *La Méditerranée et le Monde Méditerranéen à l'Époque de Philippe II*, which he described in 1951 as 'the greatest work produced on the 16th century in my memory'. A quarter of a century later he could still recall the delight with which he first read it. While in Paris with Xandra in the summer of 1953, Hugh had spent an evening with Braudel, who afterwards commissioned him to provide a summary of the 'gentry' controversy for publication in *Annales*. For his 1955 lecture, he chose as the subject 'Social Interpretations of the English Revolution of 1640–1660'. Afterwards he told Berenson that he had enjoyed the experience. 'I was flattered to be invited by them and glad to work for a few days at the École des Hautes Études and get to know the group of historians who, in my opinion, are asking entirely new questions and creating a new type of history.' At Hugh's invitation, Braudel lectured in Oxford the following term. It was a mark of their closeness that when Braudel holidayed in England in 1958, Hugh was the only historian he contacted.

Hugh set his brighter undergraduates reading Braudel. He embraced this new form of history with wholehearted zeal. Most Oxford historians were insular; Hugh was cosmopolitan, and a fluent reader of French, German, Spanish and Italian, with enough Romanian, Portuguese and Serbo-Croat to read the occasional historical work in these languages, and of course Latin and ancient Greek. He took an active interest in the work of scholars in other countries, even isolated places like Romania and Bulgaria. From his perch in Oxford Hugh looked out over the entire European continent.

Encouraged by Braudel, Hugh tried to establish a new historical institute in England, along the lines of the École Pratique des Hautes Études. As a preliminary measure he set up a postgraduate seminar (an innovation in 1950s Oxford) to discuss problems in research on sixteenth- and seventeenth-century history. He solicited support for his project from Bowra.

'I regard you as a man who can get things done – provided of course that

they are in the important interests of learning, rationality and/or pleasure,'
he wrote to Bowra:

> As you know, the capital of historical studies is now in Paris, where a revolution
> has been caused by the work of Marc Bloch and his successors . . . Unfortunately
> these studies, which have had a fertilizing influence in Europe and America,
> have had no effect in England and are totally excluded from Oxford, which
> remains, in historical matters, a retrograde provincial backwater under the
> unhappy custody – to name no others – of that village-idiot-turned-water-
> bailiff, Galbraith.* I don't suppose any of our present history professors have
> any idea of the work being done abroad.

Dismayed by the attitude of the Oxford professors and 'the timid publishers they advise', Hugh concocted plans with a London publisher to
publish a new series of historical monographs under the title *Cahiers*
(following the French lead), for which he would act as editor. 'I have
collected a group of young zealots and am mobilizing arguments and
programmes in order to persuade the Rockefeller Foundation to support
it,' he told Berenson. It would give him some pleasure 'to steal back from
the Marxists some of the clothes they have stolen'. Unfortunately nothing
came of these plans. Perhaps it was unrealistic to contemplate founding
such an institute without the backing of senior figures within the Oxford
History Faculty. Hugh's abrasive manner was ill-suited to persuasion; nor
was his restless nature comfortable with the necessary administration over
a long period. All that materialised of his ambitions was the seminar in the
early modern period.[26]

After her return from Paris, Xandra spent the rest of the spring vacation at
Birchfield with her children, while Hugh preferred to remain in Oxford.
He found the antics of Xandra's youngest child (then still not quite five
years old) especially trying. Gradually a pattern was established: Xandra
would spend part of each vacation with her children, at Birchfield, or
staying with her brother at Bemersyde or her aunt in Anglesey, or with her
friends the Haddingtons at Tyninghame or Mellerstain. Meanwhile Hugh
might go abroad alone, just as he had done before they were married. That
summer, for example, after the two of them had holidayed together in
France, he continued on to Spain and Portugal for *The Sunday Times*.
While they were apart they corresponded in long letters. His were generally
businesslike, though witty and full of descriptive detail; hers were characterised by teasing reprimands, prompting him on one occasion to
respond that 'I seem to hear the reproving voice of one of those severe

---

* i.e. V.H. Galbraith, the Regius Professor of Modern History.

Scottish matrons'. She sometimes complained that he was away so often, or that he had not taken her with him; but she never seemed to appreciate that he was expected to work for his money, and that this involved interviews with industrialists, politicians, academics and bureaucrats, as well as local journalists and British diplomats. Hugh knew that Xandra would not enjoy being abandoned in a foreign country while he was conducting such research, nor tolerate the Spartan conditions he often endured on his tours.

He remained liable to fits of depression. On a walk in the sierra near Madrid,

> I felt very melancholy, being bored and alone and reduced to killing time, which seems to me a crime against nature; and then I felt that you are bored with me too, are no longer fond of me, think that I merely get in the way of the children, etc. etc., and that you would have done better to stay with Johnny. All this made me feel very miserable and I wondered what on earth, in that case, I could do with the now useless fag-end of my life; and then I thought that perhaps it was not quite as bad as that; perhaps my spirits were lowered not merely by real evidence but partly also by lack of food. So, since it was about 3.00, I went into a restaurant which conveniently turned up and had a meal. Afterwards I felt rather better ... [27]

Xandra had returned to Oxford for the Trinity term 1955, taking advantage of a renewed offer to stay as a paying guest at the Harrods' house across the road from the college, while she continued the search for a place of their own. The problem resolved itself unexpectedly. Tom Armstrong revealed that he was leaving Oxford to become Principal of the Royal Academy of Music, and suggested that the Trevor-Ropers might like to take over from him the tenancy of No. 8 St Aldates, an early nineteenth-century building in Bath stone, only yards north of Tom Gate. After only momentary hesitation they agreed. This would become their home for the next quarter of a century. The house belonged to Christ Church and indeed formed part of the college boundary, with a garden projecting into the college grounds. Its interior was fitted with oak panelling, elegant fireplaces, wide floorboards and folding window shutters. Most of the rooms were on the first or second floors, including a substantial first-floor room with a bay window which commanded a splendid view of Tom Tower, which they used as a drawing-room. The house required some alteration and complete redecoration, meaning that they were unable to move in until the New Year 1956. Xandra applied herself happily to the task of choosing colours and furnishing their new home with antiques. She took pride in what she imagined was frugality. A few months after they had moved in she revealed that she had spent £1,100 on furnishings.

Once she was settled in Oxford, Xandra was able to entertain. The Trevor-Ropers hosted regular parties for like-minded colleagues and visitors, including a succession of guests who came to stay at the house. They usually invited undergraduates to lunch on Sundays, serving champagne beforehand. Xandra favoured the 'more amusing' undergraduates such as Jacob Rothschild, Jonathan Aitken, Nicky Gage, younger son of a viscount, and Alexander Weymouth, heir to the Marquis of Bath, to whom she was related on her mother's side.

After the death of Stalin in 1953 the Russians started to release German prisoners of war in a steady trickle. This suddenly became a flood towards the end of the year 1955. Some of these newly released prisoners had been close to Hitler: his valet Heinz Linge, for example, who was allowed to return to Germany in October. One effect was to create 'a temporary boom in Trevor-Roper', as Hugh informed his mother, the day after he had appeared on television for the first time.[28] Funded by *The Sunday Times* and by a lucrative American commission, Hugh made several trips to Germany that winter, to interview witnesses of Hitler's last days previously held by the Russians. These included men who had carried the corpses of Hitler and Eva Braun out of the bunker, supervised the burning of the bodies and buried the remains afterwards. In almost every detail, the testimony of these new witnesses supported the account that Hugh had pieced together in the autumn of 1945. Where he had been obliged to speculate, this new information confirmed the accuracy of his guesses.[29] He boasted to Berenson that his presence in Germany had been required 'to prevent the dangerous possibility of heresy or error on that subject upon which I am now the infallible Pope'.[30]

A third edition of *The Last Days of Hitler* appeared in 1956. The main text was unchanged, apart from trivial corrections and the odd new footnote, but Hugh did add a substantial new introduction, giving a full account of the original inquiry which had led to the writing of the book, and summarising the evidence that had come to hand since the first edition was published – evidence that did not alter the story, but shed interesting light on other matters and, in particular, on Russian attitudes to Hitler.

In December 1955 the Trevor-Ropers visited I Tatti. 'Xandra adores him, and listens open-mouthed, still in love,' Berenson reported to Jamie Hamilton.[31] In the spring vacation they spent a few days in Paris, 'so that Xandra could replenish her stock of exotic hats', as Hugh satirically remarked, before she returned to Scotland for the children's holidays, while he went on to Spain, partly to pursue archival research in the Biblioteca del

Palacio, partly to report for *The Sunday Times*.[32] This trip would provide the basis for two articles, one on opposition to Franco's régime, and another on Spanish relations with Morocco. Spain had a long connection with Morocco, which had just achieved independence from the French; the Sultan of Morocco, newly returned from exile, arrived in Madrid for a state visit while Hugh was there. He spent a couple of days with Gerald Brenan at his home near Málaga; and the Easter weekend at Viladrau, in the mountains of Catalonia, with John Elliott, a Junior Research Fellow of Trinity College, Cambridge, then working on the Catalan revolt of 1640. It had been raining heavily for several days; water cascaded from every mountain crevice, and every stream was swollen. One afternoon, during a break in the rain, they decided to take a walk into the hills. When the rain resumed the two men started back to their hotel, until they found their path blocked by a torrent. Scrambling up and down the bank in the gathering gloom, they searched for a place where they could safely wade across. Elliott forded the swelling stream, and beckoned Hugh to follow. 'I do not trust you,' the older man pronounced sternly, before reluctantly entering the fast-moving current. In the dark they became completely lost, and began to fear the worst, until they glimpsed a light in the distance and stumbled towards it, shouting for assistance. It proved to be a one-room peasant farmstead. The peasant, who spoke only Catalan, lent them an old lantern lit by a candle and guided them onto a path, along which they eventually found their way back to the hotel. They took another walk the next day, this time taking care to return well before dark. Hugh talked all the time. He outlined his plan to write a *cahier* on the European gentry, and asked Elliott to consider writing one on the Catalans.

With the onset of the Trinity term 1956, Hugh's long-postponed sabbatical year had at last arrived. His intention had always been to write a book. But which book? As ever, there were plenty of projects to tempt him. Some years earlier an energetic and Anglophile American publisher, Cass Canfield of Harper's, had proposed to him over lunch in Oxford that he should write a life of Queen Elizabeth I. Hugh told Canfield that he was not interested in 'doing a pot boiler' and recommended him to try Rowse. Canfield's colleague Michael Bessie wrote from New York suggesting a history of Nazism, and when Hugh failed to take this bait, proposed a book on the German character instead.[33] In January 1956 Hugh informed Wallace Notestein that he was 'doing some work on the succession problem at the end of the reign of Queen Elizabeth', possibly related to the proposed book on Cecil's rule. 'I had hoped to write something about it in the course of my sabbatical year,' he told Notestein; but since he understood from John Cooper that Notestein might be working on the same subject, he wanted to clarify the position before starting. Notestein replied that he did not think their plans conflicted. He told Hugh how much he admired his prose. 'There is a new star in the historical world,' he announced: 'No-one, not even Namier, can write like you.' Notestein thought that Hugh's essay on Oliver Cromwell and his parliaments was 'nothing less than a masterpiece', and urged Hugh to write a character study of Cromwell.[34]

But by this time Hugh had settled on another subject. 'I have now begun something on Max Weber and am working slowly at it,' he told Notestein in June. 'I hope to be able to show you the result before too long.'[35] He was not writing a book about Weber himself, but about the Weber thesis, that capitalism had been made possible by the growth of Protestantism. His critique of Tawney's 'rise of the gentry' theory led him to want to tackle the theoretical basis for Tawney's assumptions, and to do so he had to confront Weber. This required him to examine the relationship between religious belief, social change and economic development, not just in England, but across Europe. Early on, he decided that, contrary to what Weber and others had believed, the Reformation and the social changes that occurred around the same time were two distinct processes.[36] The subject was a complex one. He found that there was a significant difference in economic vitality between resident native minorities and diasporas; the Calvinist diaspora, for example, seemed to him much more enterprising than the native minorities already resident in the country. The same applied to displaced Jews. It was the fact that they were immigrants, rather than their religion, that seemed to him significant.[37]

Three years earlier Hugh had discussed with a visiting American editor, Jason Epstein of Anchor Books, part of Doubleday, the possibility of writing a book on the growth of capitalism after the Reformation. The talks were sufficiently encouraging for Doubleday to send Hugh a contract. Nothing more was heard of this for several years. In the early spring of 1956, however, Hugh indicated that he was ready to start. 'I now have plans for a book & you must keep me up to them!' he wrote to his agent, A.D. Peters, in April. Doubleday sent him a new contract with improved terms. Hugh indicated that he would finish the book by the end of the calendar year. Doubleday's London office queried whether they were talking about the same book, because he was now referring to it as 'the book on Weber and Tawney'. Hugh assured Peters that they were indeed one and the same. But he was uncommitted to Anchor Books 'unless they make it worth my while'; all things being equal, he would prefer Macmillan to publish his next book in Britain and Harper's in America.[38]

He found the book difficult to get to grips with. 'I am trying to write something on that controversial subject, the Reformation and the economic growth of Europe,' he reported to Berenson in mid-August:

What a morass I find myself in! What infinite books I have had to read, and in German too! What numerous changes of mind I have gone through! How many pages have I written, only to tear up again! However, it keeps me quiet. For a time progress was very slow; but then I took a firm line. No more social life, no more London balls, no more weekends in the country, no movement from Oxford till I had completed 100 pages; which I have now done, and tomorrow I go to Scotland, whither Xandra – unable to endure this rigorous anti-social régime, and burdened by children – went off last week.[39]

Five weeks later he sent Berenson another report on his progress. 'I scratch away about the 16th century and find that as I solve, or think that I solve, each minor problem, the unsolved problems get larger and more numerous as I approach,' he lamented. 'Then, in despair, I suspend work.'[40]

Hugh was at his most malicious in 'Twice Martyred', a review in the *New Statesman* of a biography by a Jesuit historian of Robert Southwell, a Jesuit missionary to Elizabethan England. 'These Elizabethan martyrs,' he began, 'have become bores. Poor things, they have been martyred again: martyred not by Protestants but, once again, by those more comfortable co-religionists who push them forth, *perinde ac cadavera*,* to maintain an unreal position in a real world.' This time those pushing were not Spanish politicians, 'but convert novelists who puff them from behind'.

> The argument is the same: these innocent men, politically so loyal, were destroyed for religion only. The method is the same: the connection between their dove-like innocence and the serpentine subtlety of their managers is obscured. Unfortunately, the result is the same too. The modern reader, like the Elizabethan Council, remains unimpressed. He feels that his tolerance is being abused. The special pleading is too special. The arguments, references, texts, so plausibly exhibited, have an unfortunately irreducible smell of fish. Consequently, like our ancestors, we cannot take it ... They sent the priests to the scaffold, to cold storage, or back to Flanders; we send their biographies to oblivion, the shelf, or back to Boots.[†41]

This piece prompted the predictable rise from Evelyn Waugh. 'On the rather frequent occasions when he tries to make fun of our religion, he sets us the amusing weekend competition of trying to spot the first howler.' Hugh responded in the next number, with a swipe at converts: 'a tribe

* 'As if he were a lifeless body'; from the *Exercises* of Ignatius of Loyala, founder of the Society of Jesus.
† A reference to the Boots lending libraries, catering largely for female readers.

who have often distinguished themselves by doctrinal ferocity, not always accompanied by knowledge'. Printed in the same issue was a letter from Geoffrey Elton, refuting the argument of another critic of 'Twice Martyred'. Hugh thanked Elton for his support. 'What bores these papists are!' he exclaimed. 'I mean, the Jesuit & convert papists: the sensible ones must be maddened by them!' The ding-dong with Waugh continued over six successive issues, until the Editor declared the correspondence closed.[42] 'I thought Twice Martyred quite the funniest piece, even by you, that I have read for a long time,' wrote Christopher Hill; 'It is delightful to listen to the plaintive squeaks of our mutual enemies the papists as your well-placed blows come home.'

Like Hugh, Hill was an early modern historian specialising in seventeenth-century English history. He had been a member of the Communist Party since his undergraduate days; and though he would leave the Party soon after the Soviet invasion of Hungary in 1956, his understanding of history remained a Marxist one. Despite the political divide between Hill and Hugh, they respected one another as historians. This was apparent in Hugh's commendation of Hill's *Economic Problems of the Church: From Archbishop Whitgift to the Long Parliament.* Hugh had been asked to give an opinion on the manuscript by Oxford University Press, and had not hesitated to recommend – indeed urge – them to publish it, advice which they accepted. Around the time of publication Hugh informed Hill that he had 'read and greatly enjoyed and reviewed – with a prudent mixture of factual agreement & ideological dissent – your excellent book'. His 'very generous' review elicited a grateful letter from Hill. 'With what urbane courtesy you expose my nakedness,' admitted Hill. 'There is little for me do but surrender on most of your points.'[43]

It was natural for Marxist historians to be attracted to the period of the Puritan Revolution. This was one of the most dramatic events in English history, when the world seemed 'turned upside down'. It was in such upheavals that the underlying tensions burst through the surface of society. For Marxists like Hill, it was important to show that the Revolution fitted the Marxist model; those like Hugh who rejected Marxism strove to show that it did not. The evidence was carefully examined by both sides, to see whether it might support their argument. The young Valerie Pearl, a graduate student at St Anne's, undertook pioneering research into the City of London during the outbreak of the Puritan Revolution. When her thesis was complete her examiner, Trevor-Roper, happened to encounter her supervisor, Hill, in the stacks of the Bodleian Library. They began discussing her work, each strongly maintaining that her findings supported his line against the other.

Hugh enjoyed the discomfiture of Marxist intellectuals at the changes taking place in the Soviet Union following Stalin's death.* 'How is X. Hill surviving the destalinisation of history?' he gleefully asked Berlin.[44] He had been offered 'enormous sums of dollars' to write an article for *Collier's* magazine on 'The Last Days of Stalin'.[†] He proposed a deal to Xandra: to use this bonanza to pay for them both to take a trip to Italy. 'May I, in return,' he begged her, 'ask that I am allowed to concentrate on my work, of which this will be yet another interruption, for ever afterwards?'[45] On 11 October 1956 the Trevor-Ropers left England, staying a few nights in Paris, and then going on to Verona, Bolzano, Vicenza, Venice, Ravenna and eventually to Florence, reaching I Tatti on the 21st. While Berenson's guests, they lunched with Prince Paul of Yugoslavia and visited Harold Acton at the magnificent Villa La Pietra, surrounded by one of the loveliest gardens in Italy. Afterwards they returned to England for one night, before flying on to Dublin, where Hugh was due to give four lectures on four consecutive days. On one of these he lunched at the Hibernian Hotel with Colonel Dan Bryan, former head of Irish army intelligence and an amateur historian. Bryan was apologetic about the incident in 1942, when armed police had burst into Hugh's hotel bedroom, and confessed that some years before he had withdrawn from a conference when he heard that Hugh was also going to be present, not wanting to face him. Hugh assured Bryan that he bore no ill-will for the affair.

'The Trevor-Ropers left after a week's stay,' Berenson noted in his diary afterwards:

> She looked haggard and years older than Hugh, but very well dressed, and is not by any means as stupid and dazed as she looks. He is in the first flower of his years and career. Handsome in a Nordic way, though not particularly distinguished-looking. Angular Pinocchio-like gestures, sawing up and down, and finishing arguments with clenched fist. Cock-sure, arrogant, but without insolence, and no effort to assert himself, seems to think it is not worthwhile. Seldom starts, but when cranked up goes on endlessly with infinite detail, and detective awareness and marvellous capacity for taking trouble to convince himself, and to convince his hearers. Seems to have known everybody, or at least everybody who has counted, in the last 30 years. Can recite entire sagas about them. A fascinating letter-writer, indeed an epistolary artist, brilliant reviewer of all sorts of books, very serious historian and formidable polemicist.[46]

'I have been trying, after so much travel, so much pleasure, and so much distraction by political events, to reacclimatize myself to work on the 16th

---

* At the 20th Party Congress in Moscow in February 1956, the new leader, Nikita Khrushchev, had made a speech condemning Stalin.
† This was never published. *Collier's* ceased publication the week before it was due to appear.

century,' Hugh wrote to Berenson after his return to Oxford, 'which I am doing, I fear, very slowly.'

Hugh had been distracted by the Suez crisis. He was at a Dublin dinner party when news came through of the British attack on Egypt. 'I have seldom felt more embarrassed,' he wrote afterwards. He was especially critical of the Prime Minister, Sir Anthony Eden. 'All my worst suspicions of Eden are confirmed,' he confessed to Berenson. This 'vain, ineffectual Man of Blood' had thrown his weight about 'with the uncontrolled, panic-stricken, bewildered irresponsibility of a last-minute convert' to the anti-Arab cause. 'So we are condemned by all, haven't secured the canal, have put it out of action, haven't got rid of Nasser, and look like making a present of the Middle East to Russia. Was ever a good case so wantonly bungled?' The whole affair was 'mortifying'.[47] He wrote to congratulate his former pupil Sir Edward Boyle, who had resigned from the Government in protest against Eden's policy. 'Do get rid of Eden,' he urged. 'It seems to me our only hope of ever being considered honest again lies in repudiating that disastrous liability!'[48]

Hugh was struck by the parallels with the Munich crisis:

> How shall I ever forget Munich? My friends were divided, families were divided, social life was forced into new patterns. The cleavage cut society into novel forms: it did not correspond with any of the old cleavages of political party, economic activity, social class. And while the virtuous Left uttered pacifist nonsense, the Chamberlainites declared, in ever more strident tones, that Chamberlain was the greatest leader we had ever had, a genius, an immortal, a Messiah . . .
>
> It is incredible how similar the atmosphere is today. With the true-blue Tories who, with absolute unanimity, declare forth the genius of Eden, it is quite impossible to argue. However great the losses, those – they say – were a small sacrifice in view of the great gains won by our brilliant Prime Minister (gains which they seldom very clearly specify). And now again, as in 1938, society is divided and it is hardly possible to speak across the divisions.

Ian Gilmour reported on the 'semi-fascist atmosphere' prevalent in London, where it was 'considered treacherous to whisper a word of criticism'. *The Spectator* continued to publish articles critical of the Suez intervention, though 'our readers leave us in shoals'. Hugh reflected on the social basis of 'this irrational support for a policy which seems to me rationally indefensible'; he concluded that there was in England, as in other countries, a fascist world:

> the world of lower-middle-class conservatives who have no intelligence but a deep belief in violence as a sign of self-importance; who hate foreigners, especially if they come from 'inferior' races; and who, gratified with the spectacle of

violence against such people, even if it fails in its object, are prepared to shout in unison, '*il Duce ha sempre ragione*'.* In ordinary times, and given good politics by their leaders, these people remain below the level of public notice, quietly reading the *Daily Telegraph* and cultivating their gardens. But these are not ordinary times and the politics of our leaders is not good; and so out of frustration this extraordinary and disquieting spirit breaks forth.

Hugh was advancing this view to Gilmour in his club when they were joined by an acquaintance from the Borders, a Scottish marquess. Five minutes' conversation with the marquess at White's was enough to show that it was 'by no means only the lower-middle-classes who utter these incredible sentiments'. Gilmour admitted that whenever he came to his club, he was made to feel as if he had been cheating at cards or something similarly vile.

'I am losing all my friends owing to my nonconformity in the present political furore,' Hugh told Berenson. 'I dare not call at the *Sunday Times* office lest I be dismissed for deviation. I think I am the only person in Oxford who refused to sign either of the two petitions, one denouncing the Government for its lack of virtue, the other praising it for its genius. So I must walk warily, uttering (for a time) only sedate platitudes . . .'[49]

---

* 'The Leader is always right', an ironic reference to Mussolini. Hugh was writing to Berenson, who had opposed Mussolini's rule.

Professor

In July 1956 Hugh had applied to be Ford's Lecturer in English History for 1957. The position required the holder to give six lectures, and carried a stipend of £250. No applicant had been appointed since 1944, but then there had been very few applicants during those years; Lecturers were usually appointed by invitation. The appointment was an honour reserved for the very best historians. Ford's Lecturers since the war included Sir Charles Webster, Sir George (G.N.) Clark, Richard Pares and K.B. McFarlane; future Lecturers would include Christopher Hill, J.H. Plumb, Robert Blake, Michael Howard, Geoffrey Elton and Rodney Hilton (the young Balliol Marxist whom Hugh had taught in 1937). The Lecturer for 1955–6 had been A.J.P. Taylor, whose lectures had been condemned by some of his colleagues as frivolous. Hugh offered to lecture on 'England and Spain, 1604–1660', confident that his offer would be accepted.[1] Galbraith's hostility proved insuperable, however, and Hugh's application was spurned. A letter of invitation was sent instead to Sir Llewellyn Woodward (who had been knighted in 1952). Woodward accepted the invitation, on condition that he could give the lectures in the Michaelmas term 1956. The electors were minded to agree; but Charles Stuart circulated a motion opposing such a dangerous precedent and it was defeated in Congregation (the University's legislative body). Woodward withdrew; and a further meeting of the electors on 12 March 1957 came up with a shortlist of five names, among them Hugh's. Changes to the electoral board had improved his chances of success, but even these proved insufficient to overcome the opposition to him, as Hugh reported to his brother. 'After a tremendous struggle, in the course of which Galbraith twice left the room in clownish dudgeon, the board compromised on Norman Sykes, a boring Cambridge clergyman, behind whose name Galbraith had contrived to line up the jellies.'[2]

In 1957 Galbraith was due to retire as Regius Professor of Modern History, generally regarded as the most senior post in the History Faculty. Regius appointments were in the hands of the Prime Minister, acting on behalf of the Monarch. The Prime Minister would consult the Chancellor of the University, who in turn consulted the Vice-Chancellor. At the same time the Appointments Secretary (commonly known as the patronage secretary) canvassed the opinion of those whom it was thought fit to consult. In the case of the Regius Professor of Modern History at Oxford, these included members of the History Faculty and representatives from the college where the Chair was based, Oriel.

In July 1956, Hugh had opened his campaign to succeed Galbraith. He conferred with Blake and sounded several possible rivals, including Steven Runciman and Professor Charles Boxer of King's College, London. The latter was not interested in any circumstances. 'You are the obvious choice for the Chair,' he replied. Runciman, on the other hand, said that if offered the Chair, he would not refuse.[3] Hugh did not confer with his most obvious rival, A.J.P. Taylor. 'It is awkward for us both to be in this mutual admiration society,' Taylor had written to Hugh in 1955, thanking him for a laudatory review of his Bismarck biography:* 'but damn it! Apart from old Namier (who often writes atrociously nowadays) there are only you and me who are any good; and there is no way of hiding it.' Later that year Taylor sent Hugh a postcard, praising one of his articles ('No Popery and Wooden Shoes', in the *New Statesman*) as 'the most brilliant piece you have ever written'.[4]

Taylor was then at the height of his powers. Still in his forties, he had already published half a dozen books of original scholarship, plus three volumes of essays (mostly recycled book reviews). Taylor's *The Struggle for Mastery in Europe, 1848–1918* had appeared in 1954, a major work of old-fashioned diplomatic history. This was the first volume in the *Oxford History of Modern Europe*, an OUP series edited by Alan Bullock and Bill Deakin. Early in 1957 Taylor would be asked to undertake the final volume in the *Oxford History of England*, after the task had been abandoned by R.C.K. (now Sir Robert) Ensor. He also wrote book reviews for *The Observer* and the *New Statesman*, and columns for tabloid newspapers like the *Sunday Pictorial*; broadcast talks on BBC radio; and was a regular member of the panel on the pioneering discussion programme on British television, *In the News*. He was recognised to be a penetrating historian, a scintillating writer and an industrious worker. So when discussions began about the next Regius Professor, he was an obvious candidate. At the end of 1956 Taylor believed he had the appointment in the bag. As an old Oriel man, he was said to be the college's preferred candidate. The Prime Minister, Sir Anthony Eden, had taken the advice of the Vice-Chancellor, Alic Smith, that Taylor should be the next Regius Professor. Smith had himself been advised by Alan Bullock that the History Faculty thought the Chair should go to Taylor. But though Taylor had much in his favour, he also possessed qualities that worked against him. He was prickly and a loner. His success excited

---

* 'Rich, learned, profound and yet highly readable ... Mr Taylor has already written many good books. I have read them all. Of one thing I am sure: this is the best.'

envy, and his brash immodesty offended some Oxford colleagues. His epigrammatic style lent itself to uncompromising judgements. Like Hugh, he allowed his tongue to run away with him. In politics, Taylor was a left-wing populist who enjoyed provoking people. His irreverence struck many as flippancy. His journalism seemed to some at odds with the values of scholarship. None of these qualities recommended him for a Chair.

Hugh had a line to Eden through his press secretary, William Clark, who had read modern history at Oxford in the late 1930s. Early in September he wrote to Clark at great length on the situation. Later in the month Hugh called on his old tutor, J.C. Masterman, who greeted him with the words 'I'm not such an old fool as you think,' pointing to a file marked 'Regius Chair of History' which he had ready. They talked it over for a while. The medievalist R.W. Southern, Galbraith's candidate as his successor, had alienated opinion by acting too openly as crown prince. Affecting no interest for himself, Hugh mentioned Runciman's name; Masterman stroked his nose sagaciously at this suggestion. He announced that he would write to his former pupil, David Stephens, now the patronage secretary. 'And I shall drop a word in the Chancellor's ear,' he continued; 'that can do no harm.' The Chancellor was Lord Halifax, the former Viceroy of India and Foreign Secretary under Chamberlain, who had held the largely ceremonial office since 1933. Masterman added that the appointment had come 'a year too soon', meaning that it was a pity it had not come a year later, when by the system of rotation he was due to succeed Alic Smith as Vice-Chancellor. 'My suspicion is that J.C. may want to run me,' Hugh confided to Xandra.[5] 'I am making a tremendous effort to be <u>discreet</u>,' he told one of his pupils, 'and not to make any of those fatal observations which in a place like Oxford (if there is any other such place) are so disastrously repeated in enemy common rooms.'[6]

In mid-December Masterman summoned Hugh for another talk. He was due to go up to London to see 'them' on the subject of the Regius Chair, and asked Hugh for a letter giving his views on the subject. He then announced that he was going to make one of his 'carefully calculated indiscretions' and produced a letter from his former Worcester colleague, Asa Briggs, whom he had consulted on the matter. Briggs, who had recently taken a Chair of History at Leeds, wrote that there was only one obvious name: Trevor-Roper. Both Southern and McFarlane were too narrow, and Taylor too irresponsible. Hugh nodded gravely. Briggs's support was especially encouraging, in that he was neither a personal friend nor a natural ally. Though nothing more was said on the subject, this interview convinced Hugh that Masterman planned to put his name forward.

Another hint came from Maurice Bowra, who telephoned to inform Hugh that he would be writing to the patronage secretary on the subject of the Regius Chair. He planned to say that the younger and better historians were deeply dissatisfied with the present regime; that Southern, or any nominee of the 'old regime', would be 'fatal'; and that in his opinion the only possible candidates were Runciman, Taylor and Trevor-Roper. In view of both of these developments Hugh wrote to Charles Stuart, in his capacity as 'the undisputed master of electoral mathematics in our generation', announcing that he was now willing to be considered himself for the post. There was one practical objection: 8 St Aldates. Taking the Chair would mean leaving Christ Church for Oriel. Having spent 'a great deal of money, and labour, in arranging the new house', it would be intolerable to move; 'it would kill Xandra'. If forced to choose between house and Chair, he would, reluctantly, choose the house. But if Christ Church would allow him to continue to live there, he would take the Chair, were it offered to him.[7]

The letter Hugh wrote at Masterman's request was therefore a disguised manifesto. He expressed the view that history in Oxford was 'in a bad way'. The seven professors, 'having all, in a sense, elected each other, turn out to be very like each other'. All were narrow specialists, solely concerned with English history, and generally a very short period of English history at that, and all showed a marked reluctance to publish anything. Only one of them had published even one book on an historical subject. They seemed to think it 'positively indecent' to risk error by expressing an opinion. 'How much safer, then, to edit, with learned footnotes, some hitherto deservedly unnoticed monastic laundry-book!' The impression given to outsiders was of undistinguished and timid scholiasts. Research was not directed towards chosen problems; indeed, it was hardly directed at all. Compared with Chicago, Paris, Florence or Stockholm, Oxford now seemed, in this subject, 'a pitiful backwater'. A Regius Professor, unlike the others, was imposed from outside. This provided an opportunity for a change of direction. Hugh outlined the qualities desirable in a new 'Regius': intellectual distinction; some historical ideas; interests wider than merely English history, or merely one century of history; interest in the work being done outside England.[8]

Early in the New Year, the coincidental resignation of both Eden and Smith on the grounds of ill-health in the same week made 'the whole Regius Chair Stakes a different thing'. The new Prime Minister was Harold Macmillan, and the new Vice-Chancellor J.C. Masterman, who lost no time in contacting Macmillan to emphasise that his predecessor's judgement was not to be relied upon. 'The wise bookies have scrubbed the slate clear and now offer one horse only,' wrote Stuart, 'H.R.T-R – odds 6–4 on.' But he warned that 'all this demands extreme moderation and caution from our stable as I know you will agree'. As for No. 8 St Aldates, Stuart assured

Hugh that he had an overwhelming case for fair treatment. Though it was impossible to ensure him permanent tenure, nobody else wanted the house now and nobody eligible was likely to want it for some years.[9]

Blake was even more emphatic. Hugh's publisher was now Prime Minister and his old tutor Vice-Chancellor. 'No combination of circumstances could be more favourable to your interests.' It was 'of paramount importance', he wrote,

> that you should under no circumstances commit yourself in public on the politics of Suez. I know that you feel very strongly about it, and the temptation to make an adverse crack must be almost irresistible. Resist it! The fact that Eden is out makes the inadvisability of such a crack even greater. Remember that they are <u>all in it</u> and are publicly committed, and whatever their private views, doubts, regrets, etc, they will very much resent any rubbing in of the fact that they were bounced by a semi-lunatic into action which should have been pressed to the bitter end or never have been initiated . . . So on no account either in the N.S. & N or the Sunday Times make any attacks on the Government just now. Of course you need not perjure yourself by supporting them. Silence, my dear Hugh, silence, silence is all your old friend, Blake, asks.[10]

The press began to speculate on who would become the next Regius Professor. *The Observer* put Trevor-Roper alongside Taylor as front-runners, claiming that undergraduates referred to the pair as 'the Rich Man's Lucky Jim' and 'the Welfare State's Dr Johnson' respectively. The *Oxford Mail* added Rowse to the list, but quoted an anonymous don: 'You could make a very good book on this, with just as much certainty as on a horse race. Those who seem to have decided on the starters have forgotten the handicappers.'[11] The fact that these three were all well known added to the public interest in a contest not normally controversial. Isaiah Berlin, himself a candidate for the Chichele Chair of Social and Political Theory (for which he was ultimately successful), told one of his sponsors that 'the Chair which is really exciting people is the Regius one of history. Taylor, McFarlane, Southern, Trevor-Roper, Rowse, are all in a great frenzy. The patronage secretary has been down, & saw x & y & z, but not a or b or c – all this leads to speculation and comment & is like a succession of scenes in Trollope.'

Berlin's feeling was that Taylor, 'despite his real ability, has somehow gone too far astray'; he would have preferred his All Souls colleague Richard Pares, Powicke's son-in-law. But Pares was dying of a wasting disease, and had ruled himself out – and 'there is always the tough & heartless but genuinely scholarly & professorbile* Trevor-Roper'.[12] McFarlane wrote to a

---

* A corruption of 'Papabile', meaning 'likely to be made Pope'. See page 287.

former pupil that 'both Trevor-Roper and Alan Taylor are in an awful state of nervous expectancy and acute rivalry'.[13]

In this anxious period of waiting Hugh was sensitive about how he was seen by his colleagues, conscious that his rival was criticised for his columns in the *Sunday Express* and his regular appearances on television as a pundit. This sensitivity helps to explain a letter of complaint that Hugh sent in the middle of March to the BBC Television producer Donald Baverstock, later Controller of Programmes for BBC One. As an undergraduate at Christ Church immediately after the war, newly decommissioned from RAF Bomber Command, Baverstock had been taught by Hugh, and his admiration for his former tutor remained strong. Consequently Hugh was able to speak more frankly to him than he might have done otherwise.

Television was still a relatively untried medium in 1950s Britain. 'In some parts of the educated world T/V is regarded as essentially vulgar,' Hugh wrote to Baverstock, though he went on to make it clear that he did not share this opinion – as well he might, because over the previous eighteen months he had made several television appearances himself, mostly, though not exclusively, on the topical magazine programme edited by Baverstock, *Highlight* and its successor *Tonight*, both of which went out live. Hugh's impression was that these programmes had in the past consisted of 'a series of comments on current affairs, of the same general level of seriousness'. On this occasion Hugh had been asked to say something about Julius Caesar and the Ides of March. Afterwards he wrote to Baverstock explaining why his performance had been poor: he had been 'rather shaken' by the previous item.

> ... when that dreadful couple sang their lower-class music-hall turn and ended in each others' arms before the camera, I felt like walking out rather than taking part; but I couldn't, without making a scene. Nothing I could seriously say on the subject of Julius Caesar, or indeed on any subject, could be worth saying to the same audience as theirs; and when in fact I found myself immediately following them, I felt that the whole programme was simply a succession of knock-about turns in which I would rather not take part. So I am very sorry that I must say that I cannot appear again ... [14]

No decision about the Regius Chair had been announced when Hugh flew out to the Middle East for *The Sunday Times* towards the end of March 1957. His first stop was Baghdad, where he found two former SIS colleagues: Michael Ionides, working for the Iraq Development Board; and Kim Philby, working as a stringer for both *The Observer* and *The Economist*. From Baghdad he joined a small group of journalists following the Iraqi King's tour of northern Iraq as part of 'Development Week'. Philby, who was one of the party, was in an odd position, since he had been accused in public of being a Soviet spy. Sixteen months earlier he had been named in Parliament by an MP as the 'Third Man' (following Burgess and Maclean). Harold Macmillan, then Foreign Secretary, had felt obliged to make a statement denying that there was any evidence against him. Philby had brazened it out, calling a press conference to deny the allegation, which was withdrawn. He was even re-hired by SIS (by now better known as MI6), his journalism providing him with 'cover'. When Dick White took over as head of MI6 in 1956, he was dismayed to find Philby still 'on the strength'. White had suspected Philby of being a Soviet agent since 1951, and had confided his suspicions to Hugh the following year. He knew Hugh to be a skilled and subtle interrogator. Perhaps White hoped that Hugh might succeed where others had failed, in obtaining a confession from Philby. (He would send another officer to Beirut on a similar mission early in 1963.) If so, Hugh's later description of the expedition gave no hint of this. 'I found myself constantly in company with my old friend,' he wrote:

> I was by now satisfied that he had been a Russian spy for over twenty years; but he did not know that I knew this, and I thought it wrong to give any indication of my knowledge. So we mixed again on the old terms; and although I inwardly shrank from him as a traitor, I must admit that I found his company as attractive as ever, his conversation as disengaged, and yet as enjoyable. He had just returned from a visit to his father in puritan Saudi Arabia, and was delighted to be back in an alcoholic country. In our conversation I naturally made no reference to recent history, but I listened carefully for any allusion that he might make. In due course he made it. He wished to date some minor episode, and he chose to date it in an oddly irrelevant way. 'It was about the time,' he said, 'of all that absurd fuss about the "Third Man" . . .' I made no comment; but I thought that he did protest a little too much.[15]

Also on the expedition was the formidable Elizabeth Monroe, a journalist and a scholar of Middle Eastern subjects whom Hugh liked and respected. His admiration for her was a little too obvious in his letters home, provoking a jealous response from Xandra, especially after he referred to being in her company in 'the romantic wilds of Kurdistan'. Hugh remonstrated with Xandra for making 'altogether false and unreasonable accusations'. He insisted that he concealed nothing from her. To reinforce his claim to innocence he pointed out that Elizabeth Monroe was 'about 50' (she was fifty-two); which cannot altogether have appeased Xandra, who had just celebrated her own fiftieth birthday.

On his return from this expedition, Hugh was taken by the British Council representative on a tour of the museums and archaeological sites, including Nineveh and Nimrud, then being excavated by the British

Archaeological School; Hugh had tea with the head of the school, Professor Max Mallowan, and his wife, better known to the world as Agatha Christie.

Afterwards Hugh chose to make the two-day journey by bus over the mountains from Baghdad to Tehran, a decision that his English acquaintances in Baghdad thought eccentric. Apart from two young Germans, he was the only foreigner in the bus, the bulk of the passengers being returning Shi'ite pilgrims. 'I like the sort of people one meets on buses,' Hugh wrote to Xandra, 'and I like observing their habits and customs en route, and the habits and customs of the people one sees on the way.' He was certain that she would not have enjoyed the trip. One of the passengers picked a quarrel with the driver, which became ever more heated. Finally the driver took both hands off the steering-wheel, swivelled around in his seat, and shook both fists at his tormentor. Hugh grabbed the wheel and navigated the bus around two or three bends, before the driver took control again and brought it to a halt.[16]

In Iran, he happened to visit the holy city of Qum, home of the then unknown mullah, the Ayatollah Khomeini. A new oil well had recently been opened nearby, and there Hugh was entertained by a genial, Western-educated engineer rejoicing in this triumph of technological progress, who gloried in the vision of the new society that oil wealth would bring. In twenty years' time, he said proudly, 'we shall have created here a new Iran, a new Iranian man, and those old mullahs there' – he gestured contemptuously towards the old city – 'will have withered away'. Twenty-three years later, soon after the revolution that transformed Iran into an Islamic republic, Hugh remembered this encounter, and wondered whether 'that genial technologist' was still alive. 'If so, he must be very surprised.'[17]

Hugh was piqued by a letter he had received in Tehran from Xandra. 'Oh,' he exclaimed, 'how I wish you would be more understanding!' Her complaints were unreasonable, and he felt 'very bitterly' about them. 'I really do not see why you should nag and peck at me as you do,' he wrote. 'Consider the facts. You expect me to earn more money than I am paid at Oxford. To do this I must write for the *Sunday Times*. The *Sunday Times* wants me to write on foreign politics, and to do this I must go abroad.' But she persecuted him for going on 'holidays' without her. 'Sometimes you make me think that you want to prevent me from doing any of my work, whether as a historian or as a writer. You will not let me stay in Oxford in the vacation and yet you will not let me pursue my work abroad.' He accused her of wanting him to spend his time with her in 'that horrid little house in Melrose', or taking her round the world. 'What then would become of my work, and how would we have the money for such a life? Really, if this is your idea, I feel that you should have married someone else.'

'I have been so dispirited by your letters that I have been in doubt

whether to write to you again,' he wrote to Xandra from Abadan. 'Why
should I write when my letters are either "not proper letters", "not interesting in the least", or, if they are "proper" letters, only excite you to envy
and complaint? I thought I would write to other people, who seem to like
getting letters from me.'[18]

In deciding who should be the next Regius Professor of Modern History at
Oxford, the new Prime Minister sought the advice of his old friend (and
fellow Balliol man), Sir Lewis Namier. Indeed Namier might have had the
Chair himself, had he not been too old at sixty-eight. As the most admired
historian in England, he had been the obvious man the last time around,
following the resignation of the medievalist F.M. (Sir Maurice) Powicke in
1947, but Galbraith had been appointed instead. This time A.J.P. Taylor had
reason to expect Namier's favour. In the 1930s he had worked alongside
Namier in Manchester, and they had become friends. In 1956 he had been
co-editor (with Richard Pares) of a *Festschrift* for Namier, a volume of
essays in his honour. Namier was fond of Taylor; he told Isaiah Berlin that
some of his happiest hours had been spent at Taylor's house. But he had
become stuffy in old age. He often spoke of the dignity of learning, and the
need to keep scholarship pure. Namier could not understand how Taylor
could lower himself to write for the popular press. In a man of learning,
journalism was mere irresponsibility; and 'irresponsible' was one of the
most opprobrious terms in his vocabulary. Furthermore, Taylor had demonstrated his independence by writing an insufficiently respectful review
of a collection of Namier's essays, and in another review had criticised the
work of one of Namier's most devoted disciples, John Brooke. Namier was
clumsy in personal matters, and easily deceived; he took flattery for the
true coin. Often he could not distinguish friends from ill-wishers. Berlin
understood Namier as well as anyone. 'He was an Othello,' wrote Berlin,
'who retained confidence in more than one academic Iago.'[19]

   Hugh had long cultivated Namier.* He contributed an essay to the
Festschrift, and reviewed several of his books favourably. A few days after
Macmillan became Prime Minister, Hugh wrote to inform Namier that his
application to give the Ford Lectures had been spurned. He referred to his
failure to get the 'Third Chair' in 1951, and explained that Galbraith had
prevented his election 'by a three-month campaign of absolute resistance'.
Namier consoled him: 'I am sorry that Oxford continues to run true to
form. Snap your fingers at it; produce a magnum opus, as soon as you can;

* Bowra's poem about the Regius Professorship, 'Sabbatum Regium', suggests that Hugh had
been 'sucking up' to Namier ('Eyes of cod in spawning shoal/Bleared with blinking round the
Pole').

'Pleasure–Loper': photograph taken for the Senior Common Room album, on Hugh's admission as a Student of Christ Church, 1946.

'I have decided to liquidate Stone.' The ambitious young historian in his Peckwater Quad rooms, *c.* 1950.

Lawrence Stone with a worktable, some time in the late 1950s.

Isaiah Berlin, a friend of Hugh's for more than half a century, the two of them particularily enjoyed trading gossip about their drearier colleagues.

'I foresee a terrible time coming when I shall find no point of disagreement betweeen us at all.' Like Hugh, the Marxist historian Christopher Hill specialised in seventeenth-century history.

Congress for Cultural Freedom, Berlin 1950. Hugh and A.J. Ayer listen to a speech by Arthur Koestler, while Franz Borkenau stands behind them. The two Englishmen protested against the anti-Communist rhetoric of the Congress.

Boxing Day 1947, ready to set out for Czechoslovakia in an open-topped Lagonda. Hugh was then thirty-two; for a chauffeur-companion he had chosen his nineteen-year-old pupil, Alan Clark.

Bernard Berenson examines a picture.

Above Sandwiched between two duchesses, Mary Roxburghe (left) and Mollie Buccleuch (right). They are seated on the walls of Drumlanrig, the baroque house in Dumfriesshire owned by the Duke of Buccleuch.

Robert Blake's best man, 1953.

'Why <u>are</u> you so <u>nasty</u> to people?' A.L. Rowse, 1950.

Lady Alexandra ('Xandra')
Howard-Johnston, the eldest
daughter of Field Marshal
Earl Haig, wore this Jacques
Fath dress for the official visit
of Princess Elizabeth and
Prince Philip to Paris in May
1948. Unhappily married, she
began an affair with Hugh in
1953.

The Field Marshal's daughter leads the 1937 Armistice Day parade through the streets of
Edinburgh, flanked by (left to right) Lord Airlie, Sir Ian Hamilton and Lord Haddington.

'Johnny' Howard-Johnston, Xandra's first husband, soon after their wartime marriage.

Xenia Howard-Johnston, Xandra's daughter.

Right Earl Haig ('Dawyck'), Xandra's brother.

Below James Howard-Johnston, Xandra's elder son.

Hugh and Xandra on the leads at No. 8 St Aldates in August 1957, after his appointment as Regius Professor of Modern History had been announced. He was then forty-three; she was fifty.

and the world outside will set right the wrongs of a very small circle.'[20]

There are conflicting reports of what happened next. Namier is said to have given Macmillan an alphabetical list of four names, and provided separate comments on each one, indicating no preference. Another version has it that the patronage secretary handed Namier a list of four names, asking him for comments. According to the first account, Taylor's name was on the list; according to the second, it was not, and Namier was therefore not called upon to express an opinion about him. One name that *was* on the list was that of Lucy Sutherland, Principal of Lady Margaret Hall. She was one of Namier's brightest protégées, a specialist in eighteenth-century history. Macmillan decided to appoint her, and she was inclined to accept, provided that she could remain Principal of LMH. When Hugh heard of this he professed to be indignant, and succeeded in raising an outcry against this alleged 'degradation' of the Chair. The new Vice-Chancellor made his opinion known to the new Prime Minister: the office concerned was so important that it ought not to be held 'in plurality with' the headship of a college. Another historian wrote to Macmillan expressing the same view. Miss Sutherland declined to step down from Lady Margaret Hall; and so another candidate had to be found.[21] Namier then telephoned Taylor and offered to recommend him if only he would renounce journalism. Taylor refused, and the conversation ended angrily.

Two days before the appointment was announced, Taylor wrote to Hugh: 'Sir Lewis Namier asked me to tell you that he had not – as alleged in the press – supported the claims of any one candidate for the Regius Chair to the exclusion of others; & that in particular he had always mentioned you & me in the same breath as Lucy Sutherland. I am sorry to say that I do not give an unquestioned adherence to his statement – but I don't count it against him.'[22] The Chair was offered to Hugh, who accepted. Namier wrote to Hugh offering his congratulations. Hugh replied with his thanks. 'I must admit, I felt a bit of a fraud. I remain stubborn in my belief that Alan Taylor ought to have had the Chair, and that politics ought not to have excluded him; but I suppose he was *vix papabilis*,* so I must try to wear with dignity the mantle which has been stolen from him.'[23]

Hugh received dozens of letters of congratulation, among them messages from Ayer, Bowra, Hampshire, Hobsbawm, Neale, Plumb and Wheeler-Bennett. 'How splendid,' wrote Christopher Hill; 'Now you really will be worth attacking!'[24] There was also a handwritten note of congratulation on his appointment from Lawrence Stone (who no longer addressed Hugh by his first name). 'Inevitably I view it with somewhat mixed feelings,' he

* 'Hardly the sort of person to be made Pope'.

wrote, 'but I am glad that, for a change, it has been given to someone of obvious intellectual distinction.'[25]

'The appointment of Hugh has caused a good deal of pain, but not to me,' Bowra reported to an American friend. 'No one could expect Macmillan to appoint Taylor,' he continued:

> T-R is a very clever man, a good writer, on the right side on all academic matters, and a sturdy fighter. On the other hand he is quite inhuman. He does not like anyone or wish to be liked; what he wants is to impress and be admired. It is not a good way to win friends or supporters. His comic cuckoo wife is much more human than he is but not likely to help him. Also I doubt if he is really a researcher or in the last resort a true historian. But he is a good pamphleteer, an excellent critic, full of energy and very anxious to shine. We could have done a good deal worse.[26]

Hugh also received a telegram of congratulation signed 'Alan', and wrote to Taylor thanking him. In due course it emerged that this telegram had come from Hugh's former pupil, Alan Clark. In fact, Taylor was hugely disappointed. Namier, he felt, had 'betrayed' him. He believed that Namier had not only failed to promote his cause, but had spoken against it. He wrote a 'hideous' letter to Namier, who returned it, not wanting Taylor's angry outburst to stay on the record. But Taylor broke off their friendship; they never spoke again. 'The Regius Chair is a matter of unreserved pleasure to all concerned,' Taylor wrote to his Oxford patron, Sir George Clark, a few days after the appointment was announced. 'It will give just as much pain in many quarters as my appointment would have done; and yet I'm spared all the trouble. Everyone, including Trevor-Roper, knows my qualifications are better than his; and being vain but not ambitious, this suits me down to the ground.'[27]

Taylor persuaded himself to behave graciously towards his rival. 'We mustn't go on exchanging compliments (though they are deserved on both sides),' he wrote a few days after the announcement. 'I am unreservedly glad at the way things have worked out. You were the only person qualified other than me; your appointment will cause quite as much pain to the Powickes and Galbraiths as mine would have done; yet I'm spared all the trouble.' Although, as he told Hugh, his support in the Faculty was the kiss of death, 'it's there for you if you ever want it'.[28]

In contrast, Evelyn Waugh asserted that Hugh's appointment 'showed malice to the Church'. He informed readers of *The Spectator* that he had never voted in a parliamentary election and intended never to do so in the future, because if he were to vote for the Conservative Party, and it got in, he would feel 'morally inculpated in their follies – such as their choice of Regius Professors'.[29]

The author of a profile in the *Sunday Times* congratulated the Prime Minister on 'an excellent appointment'. He outlined Hugh's career to date:

> Appointed at the age of only 43, he has a long career ahead of him. It certainly will not be a dull one ... His life of Archbishop Laud, finished when he was 25, at once stamped him as an historian of high ability, though a certain Voltairean skepticism displeased some people. He first became famous with *The Last Days of Hitler*. Being a bestseller it was of course incontinently dismissed in academic circles as mere journalism. In fact it is a work of acute scholarship, superb narrative, and Gibbonian penetration.
>
> In congenial company, clad in the bright red socks which he wears with his dinner jacket – his one sartorial eccentricity, but devoid of political significance – he is an admirable conversationalist. But as his pupils, and some of his colleagues, at Christ Church can testify, he suffers neither fools nor bores gladly. A formidable glint through his spectacles and an alarming sniff show at an early stage that his patience, like that of the subject of his celebrated book, is exhausted.[30]

'If anyone is inclined to associate regius professorships with ripe wisdom, rotundity, and the mellow after-effects of port, let him turn up an article in the current number of *Encounter*, by H.R. Trevor-Roper, designated Regius Professor of Modern History in the University of Oxford,' urged *The Times Education Supplement*, a week after the appointment was announced; 'it will make him blink.' Described as a 'blistering philippic' by the *TES*, 'Arnold Toynbee's Millennium' accused Toynbee of predicting (and desiring) the political collapse of the West, and of aspiring to found a new religion, of which he himself would be acclaimed as the prophet. In time, this article would be rated as 'one of the most savage and cruel yet justified and effective attacks on one historian by another ever written'.[31] Conscious that it would be controversial, Hugh had delayed its publication until he was sure of the Regius Chair.

Arnold Toynbee was then in his late sixties, with a worldwide reputation. His face had appeared on the front cover of *Time* magazine. His 6,000-page, ten-volume *A Study of History* was an historical Zeppelin. Though experts often tried to shoot it down, their criticisms had no more effect than the pricks of mosquitoes. Indeed, so enormous was it in size and scope that no other historian was qualified to take its measure. The public regarded this floating giant with awe. It was hailed as 'an immortal masterpiece', 'the greatest work of our time' and as 'probably the greatest historical work ever written'. The abridged version of the book became a bestseller, particularly in America. 'As a dollar earner, we are told,' commented Hugh, 'it ranks second only to whisky.'[32] The author, the captain of this floating leviathan, had acquired the status of a sage.

Toynbee's mind offended Hugh because it was fundamentally 'anti-rational and illiberal'. Everything that Hugh valued – freedom, reason, the human spirit – Toynbee found odious. Toynbee hated Western civilisation because it embodied these values. Or so it seemed to Hugh. His taste also rebelled against the obscurity of Toynbee's prose, and his intellect was repelled by Toynbee's pervading religiosity. Moreover, Toynbee's theories were bogus. The volumes he had written pre-war had predicted the end of Western civilisation under the twin assault from fascism and Communism. In fact, the opposite had happened: Western civilisation had defeated fascism and was now holding its own in an ideological struggle with Communism.

In the final volume of his *Study of History*, Toynbee claimed to have been singled out for his task; to have received periodic signs of his election; to have been granted special visions; to have been transported through 'the deep trough of time' to witness the past in action; to feel, in one brief moment, in communion, not just with this or that episode in history, but with 'all that had been, and was, and was to come'; and to have sensed 'the passage of History gently flowing through him in a mighty current, and of his own life welling like a wave in the flow of the vast tide'.

Hugh recognised that it was futile to try to tackle Toynbee on his own terms; satire was the best way to expose the egotism concealed beneath Toynbee's saintly demeanour. The Zeppelin was kept aloft by hot air; once punctured, it would collapse to the ground. Hugh began by separating the volumes of the *Study of History* into two 'Testaments': the pre-war volumes comprising the Old Testament, and the post-war volumes the New. He showed Toynbee to be 'the prophet' of a 'New Universal Church' – not only that, but close analysis of the text revealed him to be the Messiah too. Scholarly scrutiny uncovered 'the authentic record of everything that matters in his Life: the minor prophets who dimly heralded his coming; the Holy Family; the precocious Infancy; the youthful Temptations; the missionary Journeys; the Miracles; the Revelations; the Agony'.

This analysis was preposterous, of course. Yet Toynbee's absurd pre-occupation with himself left him open to this kind of ridicule. As Hugh pointed out, the index entry for 'Toynbee, Arnold Joseph' in *A Study of History* occupied more than twice as much space as the entry for 'History' itself. Even Hugh's use of capital letters echoed Toynbee's grandiloquent capitalising of abstract terms.

Hugh's attack on Toynbee was the subject of newspaper stories across the world, and by no means confined to the highbrow press. 'Two Big Brains Quarrel – I See a Classic Fight', trumpeted 'William Hickey' in the *Daily Express*. 'The generals of the last war have nothing on the dons,' declared V.S. Pritchett in *The New York Times*, reporting on Hugh's 'sustained, violent and personal attack'.[33] 'It is hard to remember when one scholar assaulted another in such a way,' commented 'Pendennis' in *The Observer*. 'There are some who say that Mr Trevor-Roper's vindictiveness, particularly his old-fashioned anti-clericalism, is really a form of adolescent humour,' Pendennis continued. Others are wondering about the influence on undergraduates of a man capable of writing a considered article with such elaborate violence and personal hatred.'[34]

Hugh received a number of letters congratulating him on his deflation of Toynbee. A.J.P. Taylor's response was characteristic. 'Your piece on Toynbee's millennium was the most brilliant thing I have read for many years,' he enthused.[35] A month afterwards he referred to it approvingly in the *New Statesman*. 'The best thing in Trevor-Roper's article was the description of Toynbee's creed as "the religion of mish-mash"; the phrase was mine.'[36]

'We may anticipate a spate of books on Oliver Cromwell,' Taylor predicted in a review written towards the end of 1957. 'Enterprising publishers have no doubt remarked that next year will be the 300th anniversary of his death. We might even get a masterpiece from Professor Trevor-Roper, who is uniquely qualified to write it.'[37]

This was not a new idea. Berenson had urged Hugh to write a full-length biography of Cromwell as long ago as 1948. Mark Bonham Carter of Collins suggested he should write a volume on Cromwell for their *Brief Lives* series in the summer of 1952. At first Hugh had said that he was willing to write the book, but negotiations stalled over the terms.[38] Towards the end of 1956, Hamish Hamilton asked Hugh to write a life of Cromwell, prompted by Taylor, who had advised that Hugh was 'the ideal man' for the task. 'I'm afraid the short answer to your question is that I really don't think there is any need for a new biography,' replied Hugh, then still 'scratching away' on Weber. Taylor kept up the pressure, and in January 1957 reported to Hamilton that Hugh was 'nibbling at the idea' and might do it 'if given a strenuous push'. A week afterwards Hugh told Hamilton that he had been reconsidering the matter and now thought that he should write the book, provided that satisfactory terms could be agreed. 'My *volte-face* is partly due to Alan Taylor,' he confessed, 'who has convinced me that I ought to do it!' Terms were agreed with Hamilton and with the American publishers Harper's, including advances against royalties of £1,000 and $5,000 respectively, and contracts signed. Some time before this Hugh had set up a trust as part of a tax avoidance scheme. In July A.D. Peters wrote to the solicitors administering the trust to explain that Hugh was still working on the research and had not yet started writing. The book was due for delivery in May the following year.[39]

Hugh had already drafted eight chapters of the book on the Weber thesis. He continued to talk of returning to it once the life of Cromwell was out of the way; but the impetus was lost, and he never did.[40]

In July the Trevor-Ropers travelled to Russia, at the invitation of the recently installed British Ambassador, Patrick Reilly. The two men had known each other since the 1930s, when Reilly had held a Fellowship at All Souls, and they had been allies for a period during the war, when Reilly had worked as Menzies's personal assistant. Afterwards he had returned to the Foreign Office. Latterly, Hugh had several times been his guest when he was Minister at the Embassy in Paris.

A visit to Russia during the 1950s was exotic, a peep behind the iron curtain that divided East from West. The Cold War was so all-pervasive that any contact with the Soviet bloc carried with it a *frisson* of menace. While staying at the Embassy the Trevor-Ropers were warned that they would be followed on every expedition, and that every conversation would be bugged. Hugh was sceptical, but after his return he was assured by George Kennan,* the former American Ambassador to the Soviet Union who was spending a year in Oxford as a visiting professor, that there were microphones everywhere; Kennan had found one himself, concealed in the wall behind his desk.

The Trevor-Ropers sailed to Sweden and flew from Stockholm to Helsinki, from where they caught a night train to Leningrad, and a few days later flew on to Moscow. At the British Embassy they were comfortable, but elsewhere conditions were bleak. At a new 'Intourist' hotel they were devoured by bed-bugs. None of the hotels provided soap or toilet paper. There was no plug for the bath or the hand-basin. Hugh found staff happy to accept his nylon socks in lieu of tips. Even the biggest department store provided nothing they wanted to buy. Restaurant food was unpalatable and took inordinately long (an hour or even an hour and a half) to arrive; they were told that the delay was caused by the bureaucratic procedure necessary to prevent pilferage. They adopted the expedient of ordering their lunch at breakfast-time and their dinner at lunchtime. Xandra had been advised by her hostess to bring only old and plain clothes to Russia, but everywhere they went women stared at her as if she were a creature from the moon and sometimes fingered her clothes as they passed.[41] After they had returned to England, Hugh wrote to his brother describing that 'grim, prison-like country which I find it so interesting to have seen, and from which I am so glad to have escaped'.[42]

---

* After meeting him at a dinner party in August, Hugh told Xandra that he had found Kennan 'most intelligent and interesting'.

*

Hugh's *Historical Essays* was published by Macmillan in the autumn of 1957.* Of the forty-two 'essays' in the book, all had been previously published, most of them as book reviews in the *New Statesman*. In his foreword, Hugh posed the question whether it was legitimate to reprint historical essays which had already been published; and answered that it was, 'if they receive an underlying unity from the philosophy of the writer'. Reviewing the book in *The Sunday Times*, Cyril Connolly observed that 'Professor Trevor-Roper ... leaves us to guess what that philosophy is', and cynically suggested that it was a philosophy common to all writers of reviews: 'if they can make a book of them, they will'. Harold Nicolson, in *The Observer*, questioned the use of the term 'essays' to refer to a volume composed largely of short book reviews. Like Connolly, he found much to enjoy in the book, but he deplored the 'absence of even average human compassion'. He hoped that Hugh would acquire more tolerance as he matured. 'Among the strings of his lute there is a wire of hate which is apt to twang suddenly with the rasp of a banjo.'[43]

In fact, Hugh's foreword did advance a philosophy, a bold assertion of the principles he had outlined to Masterman in his letter setting out the qualities desirable in a Regius Professor.

> Today most professional historians 'specialise'. They choose a period, sometimes a very brief period, and within that period they strive, in desperate competition with ever-expanding evidence, to know all the facts. Thus armed, they can comfortably shoot down any amateurs who blunder or rivals who stray into their heavily fortified field; and, of course, knowing the strength of modern defensive weapons, they themselves keep prudently within their frontiers. Theirs is a static world. They have a self-contained economy, a Maginot Line and large reserves which they seldom use; but they have no philosophy. For historical philosophy is incompatible with such narrow frontiers. It must apply to humanity in any period. To test it, a historian must dare to travel abroad, even in hostile country; to express it he must be ready to write essays on subjects on which he may be ill-equipped to write books.

In the concluding paragraph of his foreword, Hugh provided a first draft of what would become one of his most celebrated maxims: 'study problems, not periods'.

There were favourable reviews in the *Manchester Guardian* (Geoffrey Barraclough), *The Economist* (John Prestwich), *Punch* (John Bowle), *Encounter* (Arthur Schlesinger, Jr) and *The Spectator* (Christopher Hill).

---

* An American edition was published by Harper & Brothers early in 1958, under the title *Men and Events*.

The American edition would be positively reviewed in *The New York Times* (Orville Prescott) and *The New York Herald Tribune* (Crane Brinton). Xandra's reaction on reading Hugh's *Historical Essays* was dismay. 'How can you wonder that RCs like Sarah Haddington don't invite you to stay? Almost every essay has a crack against them'.[44] A.J.P. Taylor reviewed the volume in the *New Statesman*. 'Professor Trevor-Roper writes like an angel,' he wrote: 'Each piece has a zest and perfection of a Mozart symphony.' There was a sting in the tail, of course. He observed that the book would enable Hugh 'to conceal for some time the fact that he has not yet produced a sustained book of mature historical scholarship'. Hugh thanked Taylor; and Taylor replied that 'the praise was not flattery but truth – though not grudgingly given'. He lamented that he would miss Hugh's Inaugural, owing to an engagement in Dublin.[45] The reviewer for *The Times Literary Supplement* took issue with Hugh's foreword. 'Any historian worth the name deals with problems in relation to a chosen period or periods,' he insisted. 'Professor Trevor-Roper has, of course, a period – England from the Tudors to the Glorious Revolution: and the few essays in this book that stray outside it are those of the journalist rather than the philosopher.' The unnamed reviewer – *TLS* reviews were then anonymous, and would remain so until 1974 – suggested that Hugh did not know much about Homer or Marx. Stung, Hugh wrote a letter of complaint to the *TLS*, questioning the reviewer's credentials: 'I naturally ask,' wrote Hugh, 'before accepting his judgment, who he is and what authority he has to justify such smug postures.' Hugh thus became embroiled in the campaign against anonymous reviews in the *TLS* led by the literary critic F.W. Bateson. His complaint prompted a lively correspondence, including a further letter from Hugh, and an editorial, before the Editor closed the subject. *The Bookseller* reported on the controversy. Hugh's position was that he did not necessarily reject the principle of anonymous reviewing. The problem, as he saw it, was a lack of editorial control. 'The authors of reviews escape responsibility by being anonymous and the Editor does not assume it.' He was suspicious of the Editor, Alan Pryce-Jones, a Catholic convert, one of those drawn into the Church by Father D'Arcy. Hugh wrote a private letter about the problems with the *TLS* to his brother-in-law Gavin Astor, a director of *The Times*. This was followed by a seven-page memorandum on the subject. He believed that Pryce-Jones was giving out books for review to unqualified dilettanti, many of them Roman Catholics.[46]

A year later Lawrence Stone invited Hugh to join him in a 'broadside' protesting at the *TLS*'s 'malicious and condescending' review of Christopher Hill's collection of essays, *Puritanism and Revolution*. 'Think of the pleasure it would give our friends – and enemies – if you would.' Hugh seems to have politely declined the invitation, but offered moral support.

Pryce-Jones refused to publish the letter until Stone modified his description of the review to 'unfair and silly'; it then appeared, together with a riposte from the anonymous reviewer. Stone speculated that he was 'some obscure undergraduate'. In fact the reviewer was Maurice Ashley, who combined a career as a journalist with that of a seventeenth-century historian. The episode marked a partial rapprochement between Stone and Trevor-Roper, now back on first-name terms. Hugh told 'Lawrence' that he had 'greatly enjoyed' his recent essay 'The Inflation of Honours', published in *Past and Present*: 'how clearly you write!'[47]

On 20 October 1957 Hugh joined the television 'Brains Trust'. This was an adaptation of the hugely successful 1940s radio programme, which at its wartime peak regularly attracted an audience of more than ten million. The radio version had been discontinued in 1949, and revived six years later on television with a panel that varied from week to week; though there were several stalwarts, especially the scientific populariser Jacob Bronowski and the evolutionary biologist Julian Huxley, the only member of the core panel to make the transition from radio to television. Other regulars included A.J. Ayer, Noel Annan and Alan Bullock. Hugh appeared less often but still fairly frequently, taking part twice more in the following couple of months and from time to time thereafter. His contributions were uninhibited; in 1959, for example, he said on air that it would be a good thing if history were not taught at all in schools.[48] Later that year his sister Sheila asked whether he had been 'tight' during a television broadcast.[49]

The 'Brains Trust' went out live from the studios in Lime Grove every Sunday afternoon, with the four panellists seated on easy chairs around a coffee table. The usual procedure was for the members of the panel, the question master and the producer to meet for lunch at Scott's restaurant near Piccadilly Circus. Ayer later described the formula:

> After a good lunch with a fair amount to drink we were driven to the television studios, made up, which consisted in being given a slight coating of powder and a combing of one's hair, assigned our places on the dais confronting the cameras and rehearsed with one or two dummy questions. Nothing like these questions figured in the actual programme and, contrary to popular suspicion, we had no forewarning of what the actual questions were going to be ... About half a dozen questions were dealt with as a rule; never, I think, less than five or more than seven. A fee of £50 was paid to each panellist, which was generous for those days, especially as the work involved no preparation, and the fee was supplemented by a good lunch, drinks after the programme and free transport home. The questions were seldom purely factual, not often literary, and almost never scientific. Politics might be brought in on an international scale, but party politics were

eschewed. Religion was discussable in general terms. Some but not many questions were meant to be facetious. The overwhelming majority of them, at least
in the programmes in which I figured, raised concrete or abstract issues of
morality.[50]

Towards the end of October Hugh took part in another television discussion entitled 'Is Religion Necessary?', part of the *Lifeline* series. Among
the contributors were the Buddhist lawyer Christmas Humphreys and the
Biblical scholar Eric Heaton, a Canon of Salisbury Cathedral. Hugh poked
fun at 'doctrines devised to befuddle the senses of illiterate peasants in the
pre-scientific Middle East', and obliged Heaton to admit that he did not
believe in the Athanasian Creed – the doctrine of the Trinity originating in
the sixth century AD, rarely mentioned by modern clerics. His facetious
tone provoked an angry letter, forwarded by the Archbishop of Canterbury,
Geoffrey Fisher, to the BBC's Director of Television, Gerald Beadle. Typically Hugh exaggerated this story, telling Berenson that the Archbishop
himself had complained to the BBC's Director-General, Sir Ian Jacob,
demanding that 'a young man called Trevor-Roper' should never be allowed
on the air again.[51]

Hugh's inaugural lecture as Regius Professor, 'History: Professional and
Lay', was delivered in the Examination Schools on 12 November 1957, to an
audience of dignitaries including Masterman. 'Mr Vice-Chancellor,' Hugh
began, 'it is no new experience for me to read to you, my former tutor, an
imprudent historical essay, though it is a new experience to do so before
this formidable public audience.' Hugh referred briefly to his predecessor,
who had crossed the Atlantic to avoid having to attend this occasion, before
surveying the history of the post of Regius Professor since its founding in
1724. With satirical zest he traced the long record of strife between professors
and college tutors. Professors had sought 'a superintendence of some kind'
over the history school, which the tutors had stoutly resisted. Hugh sympathised with his predecessors' desire to inculcate a more professional
approach to the subject, but at the same time he insisted that 'history is a
humane study', and that 'the study of the humanities requires a different
method from the study of the sciences'. He stressed the necessity for historians to keep in touch with 'the laity', those outside the profession. He
cited the example of classical studies as a warning: 'professional classical
scholars have assumed they are teaching only other classical scholars; consequently they have killed the subject'. Similarly, there was a danger that
philosophers would kill philosophy, philologists literature, or historians
history. 'The clergy, in any subject, by a kind of natural law, tend to bury
themselves deeper and deeper into the *minutiae* of their own dogma; thus

buried, they tend to forget the outer world which may be radically changing around them; and often it takes the less concentrated mind of the layman, who is more aware of these changes, sometimes his impatient boot, to bring them up to date.'

Historians, he said, had much to learn from economists, sociologists, philosophers, art historians and even anthropologists and psychologists. He cited Max Weber's thesis on the Protestant ethic: 'a thesis of startling simplicity and – in my opinion – demonstrable error. But how much poorer our understanding of the Reformation, how much feebler our interest in it would be today, if that challenge had not been thrown down, and taken up!' In humane studies, 'there are times when a new error is more life-giving than an old truth, a fertile error than a sterile accuracy'.

'I have seldom enjoyed an event more than Trevor-Roper's inaugural lecture,' Isaiah Berlin wrote to a friend in America:

> It was amusing in itself – I must send you a copy – but what was funny were the preliminaries: he had hoped for a large incursion of smart persons from London and deputed Lord Furneaux* and Chips Channon's son† – he wrote them that he gathered that they were socially-minded and would know the faces of Cabinet Ministers and Ambassadors – to act as ushers. He caused four rows of the School to be kept empty for him for the 'quality', it was terrible to see aged dons and white-haired ladies rudely pushed away from these empty places which were waiting to be filled by elegant persons from London. In the end, apart from the Duke of Wellington and about eight members of the Astor family and his own wife and her sister Doria, nobody came and the seats were filled by plebeians … The best moment was when Nancy Lancaster‡ – Ronnie Tree's first wife – who had previously already had it remarked to her that Xandra Trevor-Roper looked like a very young and very sprightly eighty – marvellously fresh and vigorous for her advancing years – when we were all bidden to dinner rushed up to Lady Alexandra, clasped her hands and said, 'Oh, oh, the bride's mother!' There was a deathly silence, but poor Xandra smiled wanly and we sat down to dinner.[52]

---

* Son of Hugh's friend Lord Birkenhead.
† Paul Channon, then a Christ Church undergraduate and later a Conservative MP.
‡ The influential interior decorator, partner with John Fowler in the decorating business Colefax and Fowler. At the time of this dinner she was sixty.

Scholar

'In order to disperse my critics, I am now writing a huge book, in three volumes,' Hugh told Berenson in December 1957.[1] He planned a major work on the Puritan Revolution of the seventeenth century, and confidently proclaimed that this would be his magnum opus, a work to justify his appointment as Regius Professor.

He had been contemplating a book on this subject for almost a decade. As long ago as 1949 he had discussed with Macmillan publishing a history of the period from 1640 to 1660.[2] In 1955 he had told Berenson of his plans to begin a book on the seventeenth century 'as soon as we have a house'. Those plans had been set aside twice, first in favour of the unfinished book on the Weber–Tawney thesis, then for the biography of Cromwell. Once he started work on the latter he found himself writing on the Cromwellian Revolution rather than on Cromwell himself. He soon decided that this was what he should be writing, 'a sustained book of mature historical scholarship', of the kind that he had so far failed to produce: a work that demanded a serious publisher.

Hugh seized on a pretext to tear up his contract with Hamish Hamilton only six months or so after it was signed. Apprehensive that he might be scooped, and to deter other biographers, Hamilton had announced Hugh's life of Cromwell in a booksellers' catalogue. Hugh claimed to be 'horrified' to see this advertisement. 'My hand trembles with rage,' he wrote to Hamilton – but his shaky hand was obviously simulated. 'I am furious with Jamie Hamilton,' he informed A.D. Peters. 'Nothing more certainly prevents me from writing than such public statements, and I now do not want write this book for him. I have written and told him so.' Though Peters explained that Hamilton had obtained his agreement to the announcement, Hugh nevertheless insisted that the contract be cancelled. He would not allow his hand to be forced by such 'cheap tricks', in order to have the book ready for 'this piddling anniversary'.[3]

He was already working hard on the revised plan. 'I am trying to write a work on some aspects of the Puritan Revolution,' he wrote to Veronica Wedgwood. The first volume of her narrative history of the same subject had appeared two years before, and its successor was then in press.* 'I do

---

* *The King's Peace* (1955); *The King's War* (1958).

not think it will in any way be a competitor of yours,' Hugh reassured her, 'as I am mainly concerned with the social side of it.'

The Hamiltons visited the Trevor-Ropers in Oxford in the hope of retrieving something from this muddle, only to be received 'v. frigidly' by their host. '*What* a strange mortal Hugh is,' exclaimed Hamilton afterwards, in a letter to Berenson. A few days after his visit to Oxford Hamilton received a letter from A.D. Peters informing him that Hugh was adamant in his wish to cancel his contract, 'because he finds that what was intended to be a life of Cromwell will turn out to be a 300,000-word History of the Civil War. This, in his view, ought to be published by his regular publishers, Macmillan, who specialize in scholastic works.'[4]

'I am now free from Jamie Hamilton in respect of my magnum opus,' Hugh wrote to Rex Allen, his editor at Macmillan, at the end of 1957. The three volumes would appear under the overall title *The Great Rebellion*. He had already written almost 100,000 words, and expected the first volume, covering the period up to 1644 and entitled *The Breakdown of the Monarchy* (later revised to *The Crumbling of the Monarchy*), to be ready by Easter. A new contract was drawn up for this work with Macmillan, providing a relatively modest advance against royalties of £750. In this instance Hugh was less interested in money than gravitas. By March the anticipated length of the first volume had grown to 150,000 words. The second volume, *The Independent Revolution 1644–1653*, would be about the same length, with a third volume, *The Protectorate of Oliver Cromwell, 1653–1658*, of 70,000 words or so.[5]

Hugh's elevation to the Regius Chair required him to relocate to Oriel: 'the dingiest, dullest college in Oxford,' as he described it to Berenson.[6] In fact Oriel has many fine features; but its charm cannot compare with the magnificence of Christ Church. Hugh's relationship with his new college resembled an arranged marriage: Christ Church had been his first love, and retained his heart. Oriel could never compete with its glamour, its aristocratic cachet, its wealth and its powerful connections. The sophisticated political and social gossip exchanged in Christ Church's Senior Common Room found no echo in Oriel, where the talk was more likely to be about rowing. In the nineteenth century Oriel had been the centre of the Oxford Movement, the home of Newman, Pusey and Wilberforce – not a tradition appealing to Hugh. In more recent times it had attracted many Charterhouse boys, giving it a character which Hugh had spent the past quarter of a century trying to escape.

In the late 1960s, surveying his first decade as a Fellow of Oriel, Hugh provided a disparaging picture: 'The intellectual level was low, very low: whatever method of calculation was used, Oriel always came out at the bottom of the list of colleges, measured by results in Schools. The teaching was ineffective; all mental stimulus had long been extinct; the college societies had all died through lack of it; and the Senior Common Room was characterized by a tepid cosiness which was never disturbed by anything so divisive as an idea.' It seemed to him 'like a country club in Carlisle: an old, half-moribund institution where the local squire, the local solicitor, and the local clergyman gathered occasionally for a glass of port, a rubber of auction bridge, and slow conversation about the weather'. The Fellows were 'as stagnant a body of men as could well be imagined'. The Provost was Kenneth Turpin, a former civil servant with a bureaucratic turn of mind. This trait did not endear him to the new Regius Professor. 'My natural loyalty was my old college, Christ Church, from which I had been wrenched, not to this quiet backwater into which I had been forcibly transported,' wrote Hugh; 'and socially I found no inducement to dine there or take guests thither.'[7]

The Trevor-Ropers continued to live at 8 St Aldates, despite the fact that it belonged to Christ Church, with which they were no longer connected. Though their tenancy was anomalous, the Governing Body of the college was persuaded to grant them a seven-year lease. Xandra had devoted much time and energy to decorating and furnishing the house. In 1957 it had been featured in *House and Garden*, with an accompanying article by Loelia, Duchess of Westminster, who praised the couple for their bold choice of colours: the brilliant magenta satin upholstery in the drawing-room contrasting strongly with the heavy, olive green curtains. An equally brilliant tangerine provided the theme for one of the bedrooms.[8] Once the house was decorated to her satisfaction Xandra felt able to invite her musical friends; among guests who stayed at the house in 1958 were Peter Pears and Benjamin Britten, and the Menuhins. In June that year it was the venue for a remarkable evening, when fifty people crammed into the drawing-room to hear a concert of music by two famous composers who had come to Oxford to receive honorary degrees from the University, the Frenchman Francis Poulenc and the Russian Dmitri Shostakovich. Xandra had become friendly with Poulenc during her first marriage, while she was living in Paris; in 1956 he and the baritone Pierre Bernac had been guests of the Trevor-Ropers at 8 St Aldates when they had come to Oxford to give a concert in the Sheldonian Theatre. Aware that his friend André Gide had received an honorary degree from the University, Poulenc longed for one himself; Xandra had asked her husband if anything could be done, and Hugh had contrived it.

The concert was to take place after dinner, on the evening before the ceremony. Shostakovich, who spoke no English, was staying with the Berlins; he had arrived in Oxford in an official Embassy car, flanked by

KGB minders whom he described in their presence as 'my friends, my great friends', while a nerve twitched in his cheek. Decades of intimidation by his Soviet masters had broken his spirit. At the slightest reference to contemporary events his face assumed an anxious expression, and he lapsed into silence. At the ceremony itself, and on other public occasions, he looked paralysed with fear, starting when anyone spoke to him. On the night of the concert the minders were absent, having been despatched to a dinner elsewhere and then to a play. Nonetheless Shostakovich remained on his guard when guests attempted to make conversation, Berlin and Dimitri Obolensky acting as interpreters. He placed himself in a corner of the drawing-room, occasionally smiling wanly at a witty aside from Berlin.

After the two musicians Xandra had selected had performed Shostakovich's cello sonata, he complained that the pianist was very bad, and that the cellist had played two passages incorrectly. The cellist flushed, and appealed to the score. In a rage, Shostakovich jumped to his feet, ran over to the score and began making violent amendments in pencil, while uttering a stream of protest in Russian. Berlin translated: it seemed that the musicians had been playing from an altered Western score. Shostakovich returned to his corner and listened while songs from Poulenc were sung by a young woman in the Victorian fashion favoured by Xandra, which many people thought ludicrous. Shostakovich writhed, while Poulenc grimaced, though he congratulated the singer politely afterwards. Following a performance of Poulenc's cello sonata, Berlin suggested that Shostakovich might like to play something himself. The great Soviet composer sat down at the piano and performed his own arrangement of a prelude and a fugue in Bach style, playing very loudly with stiff fingers, with such passion and intensity that everything else heard that evening seemed trivial and even decadent by comparison. The haunted expression left Shostakovich's face only while he was seated at the piano.[9]

It was soon obvious that *The Crumbling of the Monarchy* would not be ready by Easter, as Hugh had forecast. 'I wish I could be reading literature instead of my own book, which is so dull,' he confessed to his wife that summer; 'I have now rewritten 170 pages, but I am not much more pleased with it. I simply can't see how to make it, at the same time, intellectually clear and artistically constructed. The Great Rebellion was itself a great muddle; how can one make it both true and clear?'[10] Meanwhile there was plenty to distract him. In the spring of 1958 he spent three weeks in Mexico for *The Sunday Times*; in the autumn, he travelled to Paris as a member of the British delegation to a Unesco conference, held to mark the opening of its new headquarters. 'The whole thing is, I am now sure, a complete racket,' he wrote afterwards to Nicky Mariano; 'When I arrived, I soon found that there was absolutely nothing to do ... I was supposed to make a speech, and indeed took a lot of trouble to prepare it; but when I arrived, the time-table had been changed, the opportunity had already passed, and I never made it ... But Xandra was able to visit her couturier and order a new dress and a new hat; I was able to lay my hands on some new *Hitleriana* and arrange for its publication in *Figaro*.'[11]

This new Hitler material consisted of more table-talk recorded by Martin Bormann, dating from the final months of the war, when Germany's defeat had become obvious even to the *Führer*. It had been procured by François Genoud, whom Hugh met while in Paris. Genoud had already made pro-visional arrangements for its publication in France and America, and was negotiating to publish it elsewhere, including Britain, under titles such as *Hitler's Last Testament, Hitler's Final Conversations* and *Hitler Speaks from the Grave*. Hugh's role was to authenticate the documents; without his imprimatur they were much less valuable. There was a voracious appetite for such material in many different countries, even though the content was often flimsy or banal. And even when the authenticity of the documents was not in question, Hugh benefited from a widespread sense that it was unseemly to publish such material without a scholarly commentary to set it in context. He was the first man to whom newspaper, magazine and book publishers would turn for such a purpose, and was thus able to command substantial sums for his commentaries and introductions; his letters to his agent show that he was alive to his worth, and determined to exploit it to the full.

In the summer of 1958 a husband-and-wife duo appeared at Hugh's early modern history seminar. Both were working for a B.Litt. degree: he on the archdeaconry of St Albans in the sixteenth century, she on the eighteenth-century press. They attended for a fortnight, and then appeared no more. But later in the year Hugh received a letter from their landlady, the daughter of the late Nuffield Professor of Medicine, informing him that her tenants were being 'persecuted', and begging him to help 'these dear people'. Hugh agreed to see the husband, who introduced himself as the Reverend Robert Peters, explaining that he had been ordained a priest in the Episcopalian Church of America by the Bishop of Seattle. Once in Oxford, Peters had been invited by his friend, the Anglo-Catholic vicar of St Barnabas's Church in Jericho, to officiate there, and accordingly Peters had sought permission from the Bishop of Oxford to do so. The Bishop, at first willing, had made an apparently inexplicable *volte-face*: he told the vicar that on no account should Peters be allowed to officiate anywhere in the diocese. Outraged, humiliated and insulted, Peters now feared that the Bishop might intervene to prevent the History Board granting him a degree.

Hugh reassured Peters that the Bishop had nothing to do with the Board. The only way in which it could be persuaded not to admit him to a degree would be if his college, Magdalen, refused to sponsor his application. But Peters strongly suspected that the Bishop had slandered him. Apparently the President of Magdalen had sent for him and asked a series of disquieting questions. 'Do you think,' the President had asked, 'that anyone has been impersonating you?' Hugh offered to mediate. To him, Peters was plausible. A meek little man who seemed older than he claimed to be, he readily answered questions and provided sensible answers. He told Hugh that he had a first-class degree from London University, and had been recommended for postgraduate work by the two professors there. His references sounded excellent. A few weeks later Hugh called on the President of Magdalen, the art historian T.S.R. 'Tom' Boase. The President listened intently as Hugh outlined Peters's case. Afterwards he explained that he had never spoken to the Bishop. He sent for a large file, from which he extracted evidence that told quite a different story.

Peters had been a last-minute applicant to Magdalen, so late that some of the formalities had been overlooked. Soon after his arrival he had courted and won the hand of a pretty young New Zealand girl, a graduate of Lady Margaret Hall and, by special permission of the President, a wedding service had been held in the chapel of Magdalen College. A champagne reception followed, attended by heads of colleges and other distinguished guests. A little later, complaints had begun to arrive from the Principal of St Clare's Hall, a finishing-school for young ladies in north Oxford where Peters had been teaching. Attached to one of these complaints was a letter of application from Peters, in which he claimed to have a first-class degree in modern history – from Magdalen, taken in 1945. The President confirmed that Peters had never been seen at Magdalen until recently. He fished out another letter, from an educational establishment in America where Peters had apparently been employed. Doubts had arisen there about his *bona fides*. Had he in fact been at Magdalen, the letter enquired, and taken a first-class degree? Boase had repeatedly requested from Peters his birth certificate and other evidence of his identity and qualifications, but had been unsuccessful in obtaining a satisfactory response. Mrs Peters claimed that her husband was seriously ill, and unable to see people or write letters. The President demanded a medical certificate. After a delay, a certificate arrived, with an illegible signature.

Boase revealed circumstantial evidence for believing that Robert Peters was not thirty-five years old as he claimed, but forty-five; and that he was identical with one Robert Parkins, who had applied for admission to London University but who had failed in all subjects. Indeed it seemed possible that he was a clergyman who had been defrocked for bigamy some years earlier. In the file too was a brief letter of recommendation from Professor Joel Hurstfield of London University, saying merely that he knew Peters and thought him capable of historical research. Since Hurstfield was a colleague, Hugh decided to write to him, asking what he knew about Robert Peters. In reply, Hurstfield explained that Peters had turned up in London claiming to have a first-class degree from Oxford, and had asked permission to attend the postgraduate seminar in early modern history – just as he had later done in Oxford. After a few weeks he had departed, apparently to take up 'a tutorial post at Magdalen College, Oxford'. It was then that he had solicited the bald testimonial from Hurstfield. Some time later Peters had come back to see Hurstfield, and informed him that he was being persecuted by a disappointed former admirer of his wife.

Meanwhile Hugh had been consulted by a colleague at Lincoln College, a New Zealander, about a senior lectureship in his native Christchurch. An Oxford man had been chosen, and his appointment was about to be confirmed. Though not very impressive in person, he had excellent qualifications on paper. Another point in his favour was that he was married to a New Zealand girl. Originally he had wanted to postpone taking up his appointment, but now he begged that there should be no delay – on account of his wife's illness. The 'Oxford man' was of course the Reverend Robert Peters. In his application he had claimed to have a first-class degree in theology from Oxford as well as a first-class degree in history from London, a Ph.D. from Washington, and to have undertaken research work for Professor John Neale. Hugh advised his colleague to speak at once to the President of Magdalen, and to cable his compatriots in New Zealand, urging them to stay their hand if possible.

Around this time Peters sought an interview with the chairman of the Board of Modern History, Steven Watson. He complained that he was the victim of a campaign of slander, as a result of an alleged offence said to have taken place some years before, the issuing of a false cheque. One of the slanders was that he beat his wife: which, as the chairman could see (Peters had brought his wife to the interview), was manifestly untrue. He had been advised, he said, by the Professor of Colonial History to keep out of the President of Magdalen's way, which he was doing; and complained further that the Bishop of Oxford had taken against him on doctrinal grounds.

After Peters failed to respond to an ultimatum from the President of Magdalen, he was struck off the books of the college. But even then he refused to accept defeat. He maintained that Boase was culpable for losing important documents which provided evidence of his identity and qualifications, and he would appeal against the decision, if necessary to the Chancellor.

With some relish Hugh regaled Xandra with this story, and she happened to mention it to the Regius Professor of Hebrew, Cuthbert Simpson, who later that year would succeed John Lowe as Dean of Christ Church. 'But I know this man!' Simpson exclaimed. He had come across Peters in Canada, and could supply another piece in the jigsaw. After being defrocked for bigamy in England, Peters had gone to Australia, from where he had applied, unsuccessfully, for admission to the General Theological Seminary in New York; and had then contrived to be ordained again, in Canada. One day in Toronto, as he officiated in church, he had been recognised by a young woman who knew his past; and, after an inquiry, he had been defrocked again. 'I will have that man put in prison,' Simpson warned, over dinner with the Trevor-Ropers. The very next day, a Sunday, Simpson attended morning service at the Church of St Mary Magdalen, at the bottom of St Giles's, opposite the Randolph Hotel. On his arrival the incumbent, the Reverend Colin Stevenson, introduced him to his new assistant: Robert Peters. 'I want a word with you,' a tight-lipped Simpson told the surprised vicar, and led him through to the vestry, where he insisted that Stevenson telephone the Bishop forthwith. After an episcopal eruption, a shaken Reverend Stevenson had no option but to inform Peters that he was no longer welcome at St Mary Magdalen.

Realising that he had been rumbled, Peters left Oxford with his wife 'for a holiday in Derbyshire'. They were not seen in the city again for some time. Hugh decided the time had come to inform the police. Later that same month a story appeared on the front page of the *Daily Express*: 'Peters the parson hoaxes Oxford'. The report revealed that he had been married four times and jailed twice, once on bigamy charges, and once for theft and obtaining money on false pretences. As time passed, more facts emerged about Peters's career. While a chaplain at Gresham's School just after the war, he had been dismissed for making improper advances. On trial for bigamy in 1947, he had jumped bail and fled the country. He had been arrested in Lausanne for non-payment of bills. He had abandoned his second wife on a train in India. He had attended a theological college in Ceylon. He had become a Roman Catholic. He had obtained teaching posts at colleges in the United States, before being arrested by the FBI and deported. And so on. Everywhere he went, so it seemed, he had left a trail of forged documents, deserted wives and unpaid bills.

Appalled but fascinated, Hugh began to keep a dossier on Peters, compiled from correspondents across the world; every now and then he received fresh news of 'our old friend', as he applied for posts in Wisconsin, Ottawa, Washington, Illinois, Dublin, Kuala Lumpur and elsewhere. Peters surfaced in a bewildering number of guises, some near, some far: as a research student at Manchester University; an assistant master at The Leys School,

Cambridge; as a part-time lecturer at North-West London Polytechnic; a professor at Hope College, Holland, Michigan; as a copy-editor at the Clarendon Press (dismissed for misuse of unpublished theses); and at an international historical congress in Vienna, where Hugh, dozing through a series of grave statements about heresy in the seventeenth century, was startled into wakefulness when the French president of the session called upon 'Monsieur le Professeur Peters de l'Université de Manchester' to make a learned intervention. At the reception given afterwards by the British Ambassador, Peters began to proposition Hugh's stepdaughter Xenia, then twenty-one (he was forty-seven), until he discovered who she was.

Peters applied as 'a distinguished Oxford historian' to United College, Winnipeg, but the Principal found out the facts in time and cancelled his appointment. In the early 1970s he emerged as Principal of 'St Aidan's' in Shropshire, described as 'an ecumenical theological college' – until exposed in a *Sunday People* article. But Peters was irrepressible, as Hugh discovered. By 1981 he was apparently a member of the Department of Religious Studies at King's College, in the University of Aberdeen, now sporting a doctorate from a college in Geneva; and in 1983 he was director of theological studies at 'University College', Buckland, Oxfordshire.[12] One March evening Hugh turned on the television, intending to watch the news, and was startled to see a familiar figure on the screen, appearing as a contestant on BBC's *Mastermind* programme, dressed in a dog collar, and described as 'Dr Robert Peters, Minister of Religion'.[13]

Hugh became a connoisseur of fraud. Peters's antics provided a source of repeated entertainment, exposing the gullibility of academic and religious institutions across the world.

'I live in nervous fear of your complaints,' Hugh told Xandra; 'it is <u>terribly</u> wearing to be under this continual barrage.' He felt that she was unrealistic about what they could afford. 'I don't know where all <u>your</u> money goes,' she remarked pointedly during a telephone conversation, the kind of comment he found exasperating. 'Why must we always have these arguments?' he asked, after detailing how his money had been spent. One of their squabbles concerned the dedication to his book. 'It is sad that you do not believe in putting your feelings on paper,' she lamented, 'or even dedicating your book to your wife!!' His response was laconic. 'I don't think that I shall ever finish my book, so the problem of dedication won't arise.'[14]

Perhaps as a result of their quarrelling, Xandra lost weight; always very slim, she now became alarmingly so. In the winter of 1958–9, when she was hospitalised with viral pneumonia, her weight dropped below seven stone. As part of her convalescence Hugh proposed a last visit to Berenson, now very frail; but Nicky Mariano replied that he was no longer up to the effort of seeing guests, other than on exceptional days. The Trevor-Ropers went instead to a hotel in Beaulieu-sur-Mer, on the French Riviera, where Hugh soon became bored and restless, and they cut short their stay. On their penultimate day in the hotel they drove over to Menton, to lunch with his parents, who were holidaying there, as had been their habit since the 1920s. On quitting Beaulieu the Trevor-Ropers spent a weekend in the Gard with the art collector Douglas Cooper and his friend John Richardson* before flying home.

Though Hugh often complained about the distractions of family life, he was furious when Xandra took the children to stay at Tyninghame, an invitation from which he was deliberately excluded. He was indignant that Xandra should have accepted on such terms. As for Sarah Haddington, he considered that she had put herself beyond the pale, 'and you must choose between her and me'. Though this was an empty threat, and in fact Hugh would be a guest at Tyninghame the following year, the quarrel was symptomatic of a wider problem: they still had no home of their own. Their hold on 8 St Aldates was tenuous now that Hugh was no longer connected with the college, and in any case it was not an ideal place for the children in the school holidays. Birchfield was no solution: it was too small to provide him with a study, and half of it still belonged to her ex-husband. Hugh felt like a 'supernumerary' whenever he was there. Xandra was keen for them to buy a bigger house in the Borders; Hugh wanted to remain in the south of England, dismissed as 'suburban' by Xandra. 'You often seem to forget that I have my work to do, that all my books are at Oxford, that to earn money I have to keep in touch with London, even in vacation, and that all this makes me want to live, for preference, reasonably near London.' He feared that, in the end, he would be reduced to living in college rooms, so that she could live in her 'dream house' in Scotland.[15]

Eventually Xandra prevailed. Towards the end of May 1959, after looking at dozens of places, they received a telegram from Xandra's brother telling them that a house called Chiefswood was for sale, in a valley just outside Melrose, only a few miles from Bemersyde. Within twenty-four hours they were on their way to Scotland, and the next morning they drove over to Chiefswood. It was a beautiful spring day; the azaleas and rhododendrons were in bloom. A long, flower-filled drive alongside a burn led past a kitchen garden to a Regency house, built of pink stone quarried from a nearby hill. It was on only two levels, its upstairs rooms huddled under

---

* Later Slade Professor of Art History at Oxford, then embarking on his major biography of Picasso. Hugh discouraged him from offering it to Weidenfeld, and recommended him to A.D. Peters. The book was eventually published by Jonathan Cape.

projecting eaves; but it provided four good-sized bedrooms, three bath-rooms and plenty of smaller rooms, and was surrounded by ten acres of its own land.

Chiefswood had been built by Sir Walter Scott for his daughter Sophia when she married his biographer, John Lockhart. The young Disraeli had stayed there twice, in 1825, and in his novel *Vivian Grey* had portrayed it as 'a cottage *orné* in the most romantic part of the principality'. The main frontage was around the far side, overlooking a lawn which disappeared beneath hanging trees, some of them planted by Scott himself. A walk through the woods linked it to Scott's magnificent 'baronial' pile, Abbots-ford. Scott had written his novel *The Pirate* at Chiefswood, riding over from Abbotsford before breakfast to escape the noise of building or the demands on a host of 'the brilliant and constantly varying society' of visitors. He had worked in a small dressing-room above the pillared porch, standing at a desk so that he could gaze up the glen through a small 'Gothick' window when he needed inspiration. The romance of this story appealed to Hugh. 'I could write here,' he told Xandra.

The house was being sold by a system of sealed bids; they put in their offer, and four days later learned that Chiefswood was theirs. Xandra drew up a schedule of improvements and devised an elaborate decorative scheme, turning the kitchen into a dramatic dining-room, with red and white striped awning material slung under the ceiling and crimson parachute silk on the walls, to give the illusion of being in a tent. She furnished the house with fine English and French pieces from the late eighteenth and early nineteenth centuries. It would be Christmas before Chiefswood was ready for them to move into. 'My only fear,' Hugh confided to Nicky Mariano, 'is that the example of Sir Walter Scott may prove too ominous, and that I shall spend the rest of my life writing against time to pay the debts thus incurred!'[16]

'When I am free from writing or delivering lectures,' grumbled Hugh in December 1958, 'or sitting on committees (oh how I hate committees), or being dragged this way or that on social occasions, I go quietly on with that great, unending, formless, and at times dispiriting book which I am trying to write – of which I have already written and torn up and re-written 600 pages.'[17] Several of Hugh's 1959 letters refer to 'furiously writing' and 'writing, writing, writing – or rather, re-writing, re-writing, re-writing'. He told a graduate student that he wrote everything four or five times over before he would let it go to print. The impression of effortlessness required painstaking endeavour.

Many of his letters mentioned the difficulties he was encountering with the form of the book. The essential problem seems to have been one of incorporating analysis of the social structure within a narrative framework. The events of the early 1640s were especially complex; it was no easy task for the narrative historian to pilot the reader through these labyrinthine passages, even without the additional dimension of analysis. In July he informed his publishers that he was hoping to deliver the book 'by the end of this year'. Once again he referred to 'the great difficulty I am experiencing about form'.[18]

Such a complex task required all his energies, and he complained to Berenson of 'the interruptions of life, the necessities of lecturing on quite different subjects, the pressures of this and that occasion, the dislocation of illness, etc ... That is why I sometimes despair of it.'[19] One such interruption was an invitation from John Cooper to contribute a chapter on early-seventeenth-century Spain to a volume in the *New Cambridge Modern History*.[20] This was a fitting subject for him, one on which he had hoped to give the Ford Lectures, and on which he had lectured to undergraduates;* but it was another distraction from his magnum opus. Though Hugh could not have known this at the time, the deadline was far from urgent; delays in obtaining some of the other chapters meant that the volume would not be published until 1970. Indeed another contributor, John Elliott, was so exasperated by the delays in publication that he insisted on the insertion of a footnote to the opening page of his chapter, explaining that he had submitted it eleven years before it eventually appeared in print. By this time, the *New Cambridge Modern History* had begun to appear a historical dinosaur, lying unread on library shelves.

While he was still struggling with his book on the Puritan Revolution, Hugh allowed himself to be diverted along a different path. In 1959 his article on 'The General Crisis of the Seventeenth Century' appeared in the left-leaning journal *Past and Present*. It was a belated response to an article by Eric Hobsbawm published in the same journal five years earlier. As one of the participants would later write, this article sparked 'one of the great historical debates of the twentieth century', a debate 'that shaped the approach of a whole generation of historians to seventeenth-century Europe, and indeed to early modern Europe as a whole'.[21] In the summer of 1957, in an attempt to capitalise on the interest provoked by Hobsbawm's article and to involve a wider group of historians, *Past and Present* had organised a one-day conference in London on the theme of the 'contemporaneous revolutions' of the seventeenth century in several different

---

* In one of these lectures Hugh described the relics brought back by the Spanish army from the Netherlands, among them 'the Virgin's nightie' – at which point some nuns in the audience walked out.

European countries. Hugh was to have opened the discussion, but he had chosen to go to Russia, and it was opened by Hobsbawm instead.[22] Hobsbawm had argued that the European economy had passed through a 'general crisis' in the mid-seventeenth century, which he interpreted in Marxist terms, as the last phase of the transition from a feudal to a capitalist economy. The Puritan Revolution in England was one manifestation of this wider general crisis. In Hugh's opinion, Hobsbawm's interpretation of the English Revolution was more sophisticated and more correct than those put forward by Hill, Tawney and others. He had criticised Hobsbawm's article in his essay 'Karl Marx and the Study of History', and afterwards there was an exchange of letters between him and Hobsbawm on the subject. The tone of this exchange was in striking contrast to that of the 'gentry' controversy: a respectful dialogue between scholars, debating what was perhaps the most contentious issue of the early modern period in European history.[23]

Hugh accepted the notion of a 'general crisis' throughout Europe in the mid-seventeenth century. Indeed, this was a phenomenon much commented on by contemporary observers. But while he acknowledged that it was more than a mere constitutional crisis, he rejected the hypothesis that it was a crisis of economic production. Rather, it was a crisis in the relations between society and the state. His essay developed the argument advanced in *The Gentry*, of conflict between 'Court' and 'Country'. The sixteenth century had seen the rise of the 'Renaissance State', the rule of the Christian Prince, a process by which the city-states of the Middle Ages surrendered their power to lavish, extravagant rulers. These princes operated through thousands of office-holders: an ever-expanding bureaucracy which drained the resources of society. The sixteenth century had been a period of boom, when the European economy was expanding; fuelling this expansion was the wealth generated by trade with Asia, and the bullion arriving from Africa and America. But by the end of the sixteenth century, cracks had begun to appear; even these stupendous riches were insufficient to 'the incredibly wasteful, ornamental, parasitic Renaissance courts and churches'. In 1618 a political crisis in Bohemia had set the European powers in motion, leading to a general war; meanwhile the European economy, ·strained to the limits by the habits of the peacetime boom, was suddenly struck by a great depression. Moreover, he argued, a new attitude of mind had come into being, 'created by disgust at that gilded merry-go-round which cost society so much more than it was willing to bear'. This was an attitude of hatred: 'hatred of the "Court" and its courtiers, hatred of princely follies and bureaucratic corruption, hatred of the Renaissance itself: in short, Puritanism'.

For Hugh, the general crisis of the seventeenth century was caused by the intolerable burden imposed on society by the apparatus of the Renaissance State, by the Court on the Country. The crisis became a catastrophe in England, where the last Renaissance court in Europe faced the ultimate disaster, when rational reformers were swept aside and more radical men seized power – 'amid the sacking of palaces, the shivering of statues and stained-glass windows, the screeching of saws in ruined organ-lofts, this last of the great Renaissance Courts was mopped up, the royal aesthete was murdered, his splendid pictures were knocked down and sold, even the soaring gothic cathedrals were offered up for scrap'. The disaster might have been avoided, had there not been, under the early Stuarts, a fatal lack of political skill; 'instead of the genius of Richelieu, the suppleness of Mazarin, there was the irresponsibility of Buckingham, the violence of Strafford, the undeviating pedantry of Laud. In England therefore the storm of the mid-century, which blew throughout Europe, struck the most brittle, most overgrown, most rigid court of all and brought it violently down.'

Written with tremendous verve and in a scintillating style, 'The General Crisis of the Seventeenth Century' showed Hugh as a master of the historical essay. It was also a forceful counterblast to Marxist historical interpretation, at a time when Cold War ideology influenced every intellectual debate. What prompted him to write the article at this moment, when he was struggling to write his book on the Puritan Revolution, is not clear. *Past and Present*, which had been founded as a Marxist journal in 1952, was undergoing its own revolution. Its editorial board, which had been dominated by Marxists such as Maurice Dobb, Christopher Hill and Rodney Hilton (Hobsbawm himself was one of three assistant editors), now admitted three non-Marxist historians, Lawrence Stone, Trevor Aston and John Elliott. Stone had written to Hugh in February 1959 encouraging him to contribute an essay on the subject to *Past and Present*, 'now genuinely free from ideological control'. He assured Hugh that *Past and Present* would in future no longer carry the subtitle 'A Journal of Scientific History'. Perhaps this invitation was simply irresistible. A further letter from Stone some six months later, responding to Hugh's 'General Crisis' essay, congratulated him on 'a brilliant synthesis, which carries conviction with me, though I would make some minor qualifications to your interpretation of the English situation'.[24]

Hugh's pioneering essay opened up the subject for further exploration. Following its publication, the Editors of *Past and Present* invited half a dozen historians, including Elliott, Stone, Hobsbawm and Jack Hexter, to contribute to a symposium on the ideas he had raised, with a last word coming from Hugh himself. Hugh later remarked to Elliott that they had let him off pretty lightly.[25] In due course some of these responses would be collected, together with subsequent writings on the subject published in *Past and Present*, in the volume *Crisis in Europe*.[26]

In July 1959, before 'The General Crisis of the Seventeenth Century' had gone to press, Hugh informed Elliott that he had returned to his book on the Puritan Revolution, and had reached 'page 280 of the second re-writing'.[27] In the meantime he had agreed with George Weidenfeld to write a book entitled *The Age of Christian Princes* for a series of illustrated historical works. Though it was clear that Hugh could not undertake the book until he had completed his magnum opus on the civil war, Weidenfeld was nevertheless keen to secure his signature to the contract. The book was therefore tentatively scheduled for publication in 1965. Weidenfeld offered an advance of £2,500, the equivalent of almost £50,000 today; even so, Hugh had instructed his agent to try for more.

The death of Lord Halifax in December 1959 left the Chancellorship of Oxford University vacant. Halifax had been Chancellor for twenty-six years. The role was largely ceremonial, since the executive function was carried out by the Vice-Chancellor. The relationship was analogous to that of the Monarch and the Prime Minister: the former reigned while the latter ruled. In December 1959 the Vice-Chancellor was the President of Magdalen, 'Tom' Boase, though as he was ill his duties devolved to his deputy, the Pro Vice-Chancellor, the recently knighted Maurice Bowra, a man accustomed to having his own way in University affairs. Bowra quickly called a meeting of the heads of colleges, at which a clear majority* of those present voted for his preferred candidate, Sir Oliver Franks, the former Provost of Queen's and the current Chairman of Lloyds Bank. So far as Bowra was concerned, that was the end of the matter. Theoretically all members of Convocation (i.e. holders of MA degrees)† were entitled to vote for a new Chancellor, but in practice there had not been a contested election since 1925. Unless another candidate entered the fray, Franks would take office unopposed.

Hugh would have none of this. A few days after the meeting of the heads of colleges, he wrote to the patronage secretary, David Stephens, asking whether the Prime Minister would consider standing. Franks, he argued, was an uncontroversial, apolitical, compromise candidate, the quint-essential administrator: worthy but dull. He was undoubtedly skilled in the conduct of official business; but this was not what the role required. What was needed was a person of real distinction, a great public figure from

---

* There were eighteen votes for Franks, seven for Lord Bridges, five for the Marquis of Salisbury, two for Lord Monckton and one for the Duke of Edinburgh.
† Any Oxford graduate was entitled to take an MA degree without further examination on or after the twenty-first term from matriculation, upon payment of a modest fee.

outside the academic world, an individual who would intervene only occasionally, and majestically, on the University's behalf, as Halifax had done when he diverted a noisome gasworks from Oxford to Reading – in short, Harold Macmillan. The heads of colleges had been wrongly led to believe that he was ineligible. To those who said that a sitting Prime Minister would be too busy, Hugh answered that this was to misunderstand the Chancellor's role, which was not an active one. Besides, the argument was historically unsound: within the past hundred years, two prime ministers had been Chancellors, Salisbury of Oxford, and Baldwin of Cambridge.

Stephens came down to Oxford the next day and took tea with Hugh. Macmillan was then halfway through a six-week tour of Africa, on which he would make his famous 'wind of change' speech to the South African parliament. Stephens thought it best to wait for the Prime Minister's return. A couple of days later, however, Hugh happened to meet Macmillan's son Maurice at a publishing lunch in London. Afterwards he took the opportunity for a private discussion with Maurice, who was immediately enthusiastic. Maurice was in daily private communication with his father and agreed to put the proposition to him once he had begun the long sea journey home.

Macmillan was 'profoundly flattered' when he received Hugh's invitation to stand, but equally reluctant. He had conflicting feelings about the University. He had spent two of the happiest years of his life up at Oxford before the First World War, but for years afterwards he would not go near it: 'everybody was dead. It was a terrible place, terrible atmosphere'. Also he knew how 'bitchy' some of the old dons could be.[28] After a few days' consideration he sent a message to Hugh via his son. 'Of course I would like to be Chancellor of Oxford University: who would not? It is the highest honour a University can give to any of its sons.' But he did not want his name to go forward until he could judge for himself the volume and character of his support when he returned to England in the middle of the month. If it was adequate, he would not shrink from the contest.[29]

Hugh launched a campaign on the Prime Minister's behalf, conducted with all the energy, skill and ruthlessness of which he was capable. Ably supported by his comrades-in-arms from the Party of Light, lieutenants Blake and Stuart, he lobbied hard for Macmillan, playing on the resentment felt by college Fellows that the heads of colleges had reached their choice without sufficient consultation. He made the analogy with the 'Country' party, in revolt against the tyranny of the Court. When it was all over, Hugh looked back on this period as one of frenetic activity: 'What efforts we made in that fortnight before the PM's return! What funerals I attended for the sole purpose of lobbying my fellow-mourners! What committees I attended, what long-lapsed friendships I revived, what obscure colleges I suddenly honoured by my visits to their high-tables and common-rooms! Of course all scholarship, all lectures, all pupils went by the board.'[30]

He issued a statement pointing out that Balliol, the Prime Minister's own college, had not been represented at the meeting of heads of colleges;* while 'dissenting non-collegiate bodies', such as Campion Hall and Regent's Park College, had been. He tried to canvass support from J.C. (now Sir John) Masterman (Provost of Worcester) and John Sparrow (Warden of All Souls), but neither would be drawn. Privately, Masterman advised Stephens that a contested election 'would do more harm than good'.[31] Nevertheless Hugh felt heartened by the many private messages of support his side had already received. 'Things are beginning to move our way,' Hugh reported to Stephens on 10 February, five days before the Prime Minister was due to arrive back in the country. 'My own view is that if the PM will accept nomination, his election is now certain.' He suggested that Franks might withdraw if the Prime Minister decided to stand. But he emphasised the need for Macmillan to give his decision soon after his return from Africa; otherwise there might be 'difficulties in holding an uncertain position stable for so long'.

Hugh sent Stephens several further dispatches over the following few days, reporting on the progress of the campaign. On the day before the Prime Minister's arrival, he was able to announce that 180 resident senior members of the University had agreed to nominate Macmillan, compared to 149 for Franks. It was true that twenty-eight of the thirty-six heads of colleges supported Franks, as opposed to only four for Macmillan; but Hugh adroitly turned this fact to his advantage. 'The university Establishment – those nameless, faceless, self-important Provosts of This, Masters of That, and Principals of The Other – are on the side of colourless, successful mediocrity,' he claimed. Ingeniously, he painted the Prime Minister as the candidate 'of those who oppose the Establishment': an outrageous contention, but one that Hugh made seem almost plausible. Macmillan, he asserted, appealed to 'the young and the gay' rather than 'the staid and the respectable'.[32]

Senior members of the Cabinet, including the Chancellor of the Exchequer, Derick Heathcoat-Amory, and the Lord Chancellor, Lord Kilmuir, were aghast when they learned that the Prime Minister was considering standing in the election. There was no guarantee that he would win, and considerable humiliation if he lost. In political terms, the gain was not worth the risk. There was an unfortunate precedent: in 1925 the former Prime Minister, Herbert Henry Asquith (by then Earl of Oxford

---

* The Master of Balliol was in Khartoum at the time.

and Asquith) had been nominated as Chancellor and defeated in a bitterly fought election. The Lord Chancellor made his way to Oxford for a secret meeting with Hugh, who tried to reassure him; but there was no concealing the fact that the Prime Minister might be defeated. For Macmillan, however, the danger was what made it fun.[33] When subsequently asked by one of his supporters at the 1922 Committee whether he wasn't exposing himself to an unnecessary hazard, the Prime Minister likened the election to fox-hunting: 'you chase something you don't really need at the risk of breaking your neck'. He was influenced, too, by a telegram of support from the Master of his old college, Balliol, reporting that in an informal canvass twenty-three out of the twenty-seven Fellows had declared themselves for the Prime Minister. On the evening after his arrival in England, Macmillan held a meeting with colleagues at Downing Street to discuss the subject. Present were the Lord Chancellor, the Minister of Labour Edward Heath, David Stephens, Macmillan's Private Secretary Philip de Zulueta, and his son Maurice. At 11.30 p.m. he telephoned Hugh to say that he was happy to allow his name to go forward.

Attention now switched to the estimated 30,000 former members of the University eligible to vote. 'A new period of desperate activity began,' Hugh wrote afterwards. He contacted hundreds of them personally: 'every pupil I can remember, and every parent whose son I have ever jobbed into Ch. Ch., has been written to,' he reported to Stephens.[34] He also wrote to friends. 'Will you come up on polling day (3 or 5 March) and vote for Anglicanism, orthodoxy and gaiety against dullness and dissent?' he asked in a typical letter (this one to Anthony Powell).[35] The election generated an unusual amount of press coverage, including editorials in *The Economist* and *The Times*, which came out strongly for Franks. Some pointed out sniffily that the Editor of *The Times*, Sir William Haley, had not been to university. Much of the coverage focused on the intrigue surrounding the contest: 'Even Tammany Hall was never like this!' ran a headline in the *Daily Express*, which speculated that Hugh's support for Macmillan was influencing some colleagues to vote for Franks. 'The Regius Professor is a man of strong views and has no false modesty in expressing them,' wrote the *Express* reporter Anthony Lejeune, himself an Oxford MA. 'In a long succession of controversies, he has shown an undoubted talent for making enemies.'[36] There were allusions to the fact that Macmillan had made Hugh Regius Professor, and suggestions that Hugh was attempting to act as kingmaker as a quid pro quo. A witty graffito alluded to the famous slogan from the 1938 Oxford City by-election: 'A Vote for Macmillan is a Vote for Trevor-Roper'. Granada Television devoted a special documentary to the election. The *Oxford Mail* reported that several American newspapers had sent reporters to cover the story. Even *Time* magazine ran a report. Public interest was heightened by the fact that so much was at stake for the Prime Minister. 'What a sporting character your master is, and how admirable!' Isaiah Berlin wrote to Stephens, announcing that, 'after much heart-searching', he had decided to support the Prime Minister.[37]

The election was held over two days, amidst unprecedented scenes. Both were beautifully sunny, 'such as might tempt any old Oxford man to revisit the place'.[38] Balliol provided free drinks to MAs, and laid on a luncheon for 150 guests. Her Majesty's Ambassador in Paris, Sir Gladwyn Jebb, flew over to England solely to record his vote, borrowing Hugh's gown to do so. The Chancellor of the Exchequer borrowed a gown from another Macmillan supporter, Sir Roy Harrod, who was reported to have locked two Franks supporters inside the Christ Church library to prevent them from voting. An 'election special' train from Paddington was packed with MAs. Those arriving by car filled the spare seats with like-minded voters. One Christ Church man who had come up from London to vote for the Prime Minister was horrified to discover that his sister had driven six friends from Bath to vote for Franks. He told anyone who would listen that he intended to disinherit her. Eight Manchester historians chartered a bus to vote for Franks; it was said that Hugh, who was due to lecture in Leeds, made it a condition of his attendance that Leeds University send eight voters to counter-balance the Manchester contingent. Several of those who had failed to take their degrees earlier took them on the day of polling, despite the extra expense.* It was estimated that as a result of the election, the University had reaped a windfall of £1,500. (One of those having to re-register his degree was the Minister for Education, Sir David Eccles.) A long queue snaked across quadrangles outside the Divinity School, where Bowra waited, resplendent in his Vice-Chancellor's robes. He examined each vote as it was cast, beaming at those who voted for Franks and glaring at those who voted for Macmillan. The historian Anne Whiteman unfurled a banner outside which read 'A Vote for Franks is a Vote for Haley'. Among those waiting to vote were Cabinet Ministers and peers, and MPs from all parties, including the newly elected Margaret Thatcher. Party affiliations were not a reliable indication of support: while the Leader of the Opposition, Hugh Gaitskell, voted for Franks, another prominent Labour figure, Richard Crossman (described by the *News of the World* as the 'leader of the opposition to the Leader of the Opposition'), voted for Macmillan. Hugh was convinced that the real division was not political:

> ... it was a battle between the Establishment and the Rebels, between, on the

---

* *The Observer* (20 February) reported these for one forty-year-old Wadham man as follows: readmission fee, £1 1s; nine terms' back dues, £6; BA degree fee, £12 10s; MA degree fee, £8; University fine, £3 3s; total; £30 14s.

one hand, the solemn, pompous, dreary, respectable *Times*-reading world which hates elections (indeed, hates life) and thinks that everything should be left to the experts, the professionals, themselves and, on the other hand, the gay, irreverent, genial, unpompous world which holds exactly opposite views, the world of the educated laity who do not see why they should be excluded from politics because they are not politicians, nor from intellectual matters because they are not scholars, nor from the university because they are not academics.[39]

On the second day of the election, a Saturday, the Trevor-Ropers gave a lunch party; among the guests were Dawyck Haig, the Bishop of Exeter, Gladwyn Jebb, Denys Page (now Regius Professor of Greek at Cambridge), and Randolph Churchill, who brought his son Winston, then an undergraduate at Christ Church. Randolph, who was in Oxford to report on the story for the *News of the World*, asked Hugh what he would do if the Prime Minister were defeated. 'Well,' he replied, 'for a start I would go and live in Scotland.'[40]

A quarter of an hour after polling closed on Saturday 5 March, it was Bowra's duty, as acting Vice-Chancellor, to announce the result to a waiting crowd, under the glare of television lights. As was customary, he spoke in Latin, his words incomprehensible to most of those present. Then the announcement of the result was repeated in English by the Senior Proctor, Robert Blake: the Prime Minister had won, with 1,976 votes, against 1,697 for Franks. Macmillan was at his country home in Sussex when he heard the news. That night he sent a telegram to Hugh, thanking him for his 'courage and perseverance'. Later the two men spoke on the telephone. The next day Macmillan wrote to Hugh at greater length. 'I feel I must once more record my great gratitude to you. Had it not been for your persistence and faith I do not think I would have been persuaded to take the risk. Now that it has been successful I realise how much I owe to your brilliant organisation of the campaign.'[41] Macmillan expressed his gratitude by inviting the Trevor-Ropers to a grand lunch at Chequers a couple of months later, where the other guests included the former Prime Minister, Sir Anthony Eden, and the Australian Prime Minister, Robert Menzies. Xandra was delighted.

Hugh went out of his way to act graciously towards the losing side. On the day after the election, Franks's campaign manager, the Master of Pembroke, R.B. McCallum, was his guest for dinner in Oriel; a few days afterwards Bowra came to dine at 8 St Aldates, together with the English don Lord David Cecil, younger brother of the Marquis of Salisbury, and his wife. Hugh had promised to serve Bowra the best bottle in his cellar.

On 19 March 1960, the *New Statesman* announced the result of competition no. 1,566. Competitors had been asked to provide an epigram in verse on the recent election of the Chancellor of Oxford University – an indication of the attention given to the contest. One of the winning entries was as follows:

> First come I, my name is Hugh,
> There's no voter I didn't pursue,
> I am Professor Regius,
> Whom I don't like won't rule us.*[42]

A week or so after the election the Trevor-Ropers left for a short holiday on the Continent. They flew to Paris, where they stayed a night at the Embassy, as guests of Gladwyn Jebb, and Hugh gave a lecture; then they took an overnight train to Rome, where they again stayed at the British Embassy, this time as guests of the Ashley Clarkes, and Hugh gave another talk. After attending a conference of historians in Perugia, they travelled on to Florence, for a final visit to I Tatti. Berenson had died the previous October, at the age of ninety-four. They lunched with Nicky Mariano, who presented them with a couple of books from Berenson's library as souvenirs. The house itself had been left to Harvard University. Hugh regretted its impending institutionalisation, which he regarded as 'little better than dissolution'.[43]

He disapproved of Sylvia Sprigge's biography of Berenson, which appeared around this time, especially deploring her emphasis on Berenson's financial affairs. These would come under further scrutiny in the January 1961 issue of *Encounter*, which featured a damaging attack by the American art historian Meyer Schapiro. In 'Mr Berenson's Values', Schapiro argued that Berenson's judgement had become corrupted by commercial considerations. Schapiro's censure extended beyond Berenson's business practices to his behaviour in general, and its effects on his personality. Schapiro was a man of the Left, offended by Berenson's contempt for the masses. Like Berenson, he was a Jew, whose family had migrated to America from Lithuania; he accused Berenson of having been a 'traitor' to his real identity, and argued that his character had suffered in consequence. 'The need to maintain an agreeable surface and various personal fictions made him a shallower thinker,' claimed Schapiro, 'too easily satisfied by gossip and wit.' Such comments were bound to irritate Hugh, who responded with a letter,[†] published in a subsequent issue of *Encounter*. 'In my recollection of him I simply do not recognize the extraordinary caricature which Mr Schapiro has constructed out of what seems to me an artful mixture of true facts and

---

* This style of comic verse is based on various rhymes composed by and current among members of Balliol in the late 1870s.

† Hugh consulted Isaiah Berlin about the text of this letter before sending it.

malevolent, unjustified inventions.' He insisted that there was nothing shameful in making money by issuing certificates of authenticity. Indeed, though he may not have made the association, it was akin to what he did himself, in authenticating Nazi documents. He acknowledged that Berenson was 'not always reconciled to his Jewishness'; but while there were some people 'who from the beginning are what they are and know what they are,' there were others 'who are, or who feel themselves to be, misfits in society, and who adjust themselves more or less painfully to it'.

> If some of the saints belong to the former category, most men of genius belong to the latter. It is thanks to their uncertainties and discomforts in it that they have become more acutely aware of the world around them, seen its iridescences and half-lights, looked behind the blunt, obvious data which other men, because they were born among them, have taken for granted. In such men the heightened awareness tends gradually to absorb the discomfort from which it may have been born, and it seems to me childish to make the discomfort, instead of the awareness, the basis of a final judgment of 'values'.[44]

He might almost have been writing about himself.

Hugh sometimes complained that he was the 'superfluous, expendable member of the family'.[45] If so, this was to some extent by choice. He never joined in family holidays. He was not at ease with children, and found them a nuisance, a distraction from his work. He virtually ignored Xandra's children while they were young, claiming not to want to play the father's role. To them he seemed irritable and distant. He refused to participate in family board games, and when a television arrived he sent it back. At meal-times they were required to sit silently, so as not to interrupt the adult conversation. They were discouraged from having other children to stay. Those few that did come reported that the atmosphere was tense and oppressive.

Xandra always found life a trial. Their two-centre existence, shuttling between Oxford and the Borders, created a host of minor practical problems. She detested housework, but her imperious ways ensured that domestic staff never stayed long. Like her husband, she did not encourage the children to bring their friends home, and complained loudly if required to prepare meals. (She was a notoriously poor cook.) She refused to entertain guests unless she could command the services of domestic staff to carry out the necessary chores. As a result Hugh was often compelled to apologise for their lack of hospitality. Xenia and James did what they could to help with the cooking, the carrying and the washing-up.

It seems likely that Xandra expected more from the marriage. Hugh was always absorbed in his work, and maintained the same routine he had set for himself as a bachelor. He seldom spoke at breakfast, and then retired to his study to work until lunchtime; after lunch he often took a walk, but Xandra did not enjoy walking, and did not accompany him. He would resume work in the afternoon and then break for tea, before returning to his study. At Chiefswood he was often to be found in the garden when not working, zestfully chopping down trees. Perforce she spent a lot of time alone.

By the early 1960s Xenia was growing into an intelligent and beautiful young woman, but she lacked confidence and found scant encouragement at home. Hugh was not fatherly. 'You look disgusting,' he told her on an occasion when she appeared wearing make-up. Xandra was too pre-occupied with her own feelings to notice those of her vulnerable daughter, and took little interest in either of her two eldest children, who were away at boarding school much of the time. In contrast, she doted on her youngest child, Peter, who became adept at manipulating his mother and irritating his stepfather, to the point when Hugh would explode with rage and storm out of the room.

He became more involved with the children as they approached adult-hood, especially Xandra's elder son, James, who came up to Christ Church to read classics in 1960. Hugh was familiar with undergraduates and com-fortable with boys of this age; besides, James was an intelligent young man who shared several of Hugh's interests. His last few years at school had been marred by depression. During his final term at Eton, James was so obviously unhappy that he was sent to see a psychoanalyst. As the eldest of the three children, he had been most exposed to the unpleasantness between his parents; at night he had heard them shouting at each other. It had been a bleak boyhood, and perhaps he had inherited the family gene which predisposed the possessor to depression. In a succession of letters Hugh tried to reach out to the unsure young man, to stimulate his intellectual interests, and to advise him about life. He was shocked when Xandra said that the boy was frightened of him. As he wrote in a letter to his stepson, James's shyness reminded him of how inhibited he himself had felt at a similar age.

> I admired people (generally for the wrong reasons) and felt that they despised me. How could they fail to do so when they were so successful, so good at games, so popular, or whatever it might be, while I was so unsuccessful, so unathletic, so awkward? It is true that I was quite clever at books, but I only felt that people despised me the more for that, and I tried to conceal it and show that I too, however unskilfully, did unintellectual things. But then I discovered that my whole view of the world was wrong, and really people don't go round looking for the same qualities which they have themselves and despising other people.

More often they despise themselves. What everyone in the world really wants, whether they are fully aware of it or not, is to be loved, and a character capable of inspiring or giving affection is <u>never</u> despised. That is one of the (many) reasons why I am very fond of you ... [46]

When doctors advised that James should go abroad, Hugh offered to take him to Greece. In mid-September they drove down from Scotland together, and then took a train from London to Venice. After lunch in Torcello they sailed to Piraeus, and then spent more than three weeks based in Athens, often getting up very early in the morning to set out on expeditions by boat or by bus, to islands or other parts of the mainland. They undertook some long walks and climbs, the older man setting a fast pace. On several occasions they shared a basic room together. 'We sometimes think that you would like to be with us,' Hugh wrote to Xandra; 'but generally, I must admit, we conclude that you would not. The early mornings, the crowded buses, the long waits, the walking, the bad, ill-cooked food, the smelling lavatories ... would <u>not</u> appeal to you.'

Their first expedition was to the island of Poros, in company with Freya Stark, whom Hugh had known vaguely since 1951: 'a terrible old tyrant', as he described her to Xandra. The famous traveller surrendered to hysterics when a hornet became entangled in her bonnet. One evening in the small Peloponnese town of Geraki, Hugh realised that he had lost his notecase, containing all their cash except some small change. That night he and James shared a tin of sardines and a tomato for dinner. But the next morning a priest interrupted a service to run out into the street and tell Hugh that his money had been found on a bus, and was waiting for him at the police station. Delighted, grateful and relieved, they decided to stay another night in Geraki before catching a 6.00 a.m. bus back to Sparta. James was startled to be woken out of deep sleep by an agitated Hugh, who told him that the bus was due in a few minutes' time. The two men dressed quickly and stuffed their possessions into rucksacks, emerging into the street to find it still not yet dawn. It was only when they reached the bus stop on the edge of town that Hugh checked his watch once more, straining to read the dial in the dark, and realised that he had confused the hands, mistaking 11.30 p.m. for 5.55 a.m.[47]

Though now plumper than he had been, Hugh still looked remarkably young for a man approaching fifty, so much so that the two Englishmen were sometimes mistaken for brothers. He was less pleased when they were mistaken for Germans. They returned to Oxford after almost four weeks away, three days into the Michaelmas term. Afterwards James reflected that though it had been kind of Hugh to take him away, it had been thoughtless not to have returned earlier, so that he could have started the term alongside the other 'freshers'. But this was a detail. In subsequent years James would record his 'huge gratitude' to his stepfather, 'since you rescued me from a circular, apparently infinite descent into greater gloom & greater apathy'.[48]

Hugh and his stepson began reading Homer together, an experience which reinforced the bond between them. At Chiefswood he instituted a practice of reading aloud after dinner. James, Xenia and Xandra would huddle around the fire to listen to him. In this way he read them Scott's *Old Mortality* and several of Jane Austen's novels. On one evening alone he read them two hundred pages of *Emma*.

The following spring Hugh took his stepson to see the Highlands. They set out for Skye in the Bentley, a tour marred by ever-present mist which obscured much of the scenery. Hugh's solicitude was not welcomed by the Admiral, who questioned his motives. James was certainly a strikingly good-looking young man, and perhaps Hugh was susceptible to male beauty. But his feelings for his stepson seem to have been emotional rather than sexual. He began to address his letters 'My dearest James', a form he used to no one else.

Alan Clark had telephoned Hugh during the summer of 1959, after a long silence, to reveal that he had written a book about the British Expeditionary Force in the First World War. This turned out to be a merciless attack on the competence of the generals, entitled *The Donkeys*: a reference to the saying that the British troops on the Western Front had been 'lions led by donkeys'. (Clark attributed this remark to a member of the German General Staff, though it seems that he may have invented it himself.[49]) Clark sent his old tutor a copy of the September issue of the magazine *History Today*, containing an article extracted from the book on the dismissal of Sir John French in 1915.* Hugh congratulated him on how well it was written, and confessed that when, during their telephone conversation, he had used the phrase 'the great man' in referring to Earl Haig, it had been 'a convenient, neutral, anonymous formula, in invisible inverted commas, inspired by the fact that the study-door was open and Xandra in the next room, and proper names are always overheard!' He confided to Clark that he was regarded as 'anti-Haig' by the family, though he considered himself to be only objective; which was why, for the sake of peace, he kept very quiet on the subject. The Haigs were understandably defensive about their father's reputation as 'the butcher of the Somme'; and as the eldest of his children, Xandra was particularly intolerant of any criticism of the Field Marshal. Before leaving for Greece, Hugh had shown the *History Today* article to James, who

* *History Today* mistakenly entitled the book *The Donkey*, possibly making matters worse.

thought it might seem 'too sharp' to his mother, so the two of them had decided not to mention it to her.

On their return Hugh found a letter from Clark written three weeks earlier, announcing that he was coming to Oxford and requesting a bed. He was due imminently. It was too late to stop him, and too late to explain 'the difficult matter of the book' to Xandra. Clark soon appeared on their doorstep. At Hugh's insistence nothing was said about the book during Clark's stay, though this proved awkward when Xandra cross-examined their guest about what he was doing. Before departing the next day, Clark explained to Hugh that he was going to lunch with the military theorist Captain Basil Liddell Hart, who had been helping him with the book. This exacerbated the offence: Liddell Hart had been very critical of Haig in the past and was regarded by the Haig family as an enemy.

Immediately after Clark had gone, Hugh went round to Christ Church to check on the arrangements for a dinner that evening with a visiting American historian, Samuel Eliot Morison of Harvard. He spoke with the butler, who showed him the seating plan. Hugh noticed to his horror that Liddell Hart had been invited; worse still, Xandra had been placed next to him. Convinced that Clark's book was bound to arise in conversation, he decided to tell her about it beforehand. Xandra was furious. 'I am <u>wild</u> with Hugh for making you conceal the fact that you are writing about World War I when you were staying here,' she fumed to Clark; 'I was bound to find out anyway & it is extraordinary to have stayed in our house & not told me what you were doing. But it is Hugh's fault and I am <u>extremely</u> angry.'[50]

The Donkeys proved to be an influential work, widely believed to have been a source for the show 'Oh What a Lovely War', later made into a successful film; though those responsible denied this, and the issue became subject to legal action. Its effect was to reinforce the negative stereotype of Haig as uncaring and incompetent, one only partly corrected by the appearance of John Terraine's sympathetic biography in 1963. The book cast a cloud over the affectionate relations between Hugh and his former pupil. Xandra regarded him evermore as 'The Enemy', and was suspicious of any contact between the two of them. The problem was compounded by the fact that Clark continued to snipe at Haig in book reviews for years afterwards, while always describing himself as a former Trevor-Roper pupil, in such a way as to suggest that his old tutor approved of what he had written. 'Can nothing be done to stop Alan Clark misusing your name?' demanded Blake.[51] Clark's second book, on the fall of Crete, put a further strain on their relations, when Clark took it into his head that Hugh had inspired critical reviews of the book by Michael Howard and C.M. ('Monty') Woodhouse, Conservative MP for Oxford City, a charge he strenuously denied. 'It is hard if I am to be accused by Xandra of inspiring your attacks on her father and by you of inspiring every critical review of your books!' protested Hugh. 'You are really too sensitive – and too insensitive at the same time!'[52]

Progress on his magnum opus was slow. Early in 1961 Hugh informed a German correspondent that its 'perpetual postponement' was 'getting on my nerves'; he was determined, he said, 'to use all the time I can to get on with it'.[53] In mid-February Hugh told Maurice Macmillan that he was 'just finishing' his book. He reported to Rex Allen that 'after a sudden, heroic effort', the book would 'soon (if that effort can be sustained) be finished'. He had decided that it should be a single, self-contained volume after all; 'otherwise it would be impossible to hold it together'. He asked whether, if it were in Macmillan's hands by the beginning of April, it could be published by Christmas.[54]

Hugh had already written to John Elliott in Cambridge, asking if he would be willing to read the typescript of a book which was 'almost finished'. Five chapters amounting to 450 foolscap pages were complete, and Hugh was working on the last, which he expected to be another sixty or seventy pages.

> This book has been the bane of my life for some years: I cannot find a satisfactory form or ending for it. But now I am ending it, *so oder so*,* as the late Führer would say. I would very much like someone to read it in typescript, bringing to it a fresh mind, to criticise not only possible gross errors of fact but also errors of shape and style – repetitions, obscurities, etc – of which I am sure that it is full ... the book attempts at one and the same time to analyse and narrate the breakdown of government in those years and, in the end, I fear, only makes confusion worse confounded.

The problems that Hugh encountered are obvious in the surviving versions of the typescript. 'It is time to turn from the narrative of events to the structure of politics,' reads a typical sentence, marking a change of direction; his prose, usually so effortless, is hobbled by such awkward 'signposting'. Phrases like 'as we have seen' or 'which we have described' betray the difficulties he was encountering with the form of the book. 'Our analysis of the last forty years has been long and tedious,' he admits at one point.

As an historian of Spain, Elliott was not the most obvious person from whom to seek an opinion, though he specialised in the same period, and useful comparisons could be drawn between the two countries; but anyway Hugh wanted advice on the shape as much as on the content. He admired

---

* 'One way or another.'

Elliott's prose, and the breadth of his historical vision. 'You are the only person I know whom I respect equally as a judge of substance and of form in such matters.'[55] In saying this Hugh was perhaps disingenuous, since he also asked his former pupil Michael Howard to read the typescript.* Howard had studied English history in the early modern period before specialising in military history, albeit from a sociological perspective. His highly regarded book on the Franco–Prussian War would appear later that year. He supplied his views on the typescript in a witty letter, in which he imagined the response to its publication. 'This won't do you any good,' he began:

> The idea of a historian in the mid-twentieth century, and a <u>professor</u> at that, daring to take a subject as wide as this, daring to combine economic, social and political history, daring to make jokes, daring not to give footnotes for every fact he mentions, daring above all to write so well that the shade of Macaulay will be sent howling down the corridors of Albany ... all this is so unthinkable, reactionary and hubristic that every mouse in the country will come scurrying up, sharpening his nasty little teeth, grinding his moth-eaten little axe, gibbering and squeaking malevolently before starting to gnaw and nibble at the bushes in the vast forest of your work. 'Professor Trevor-Roper seems unaware ... Professor Trevor-Roper seems to think – Has Professor Trevor-Roper never consulted ... Miss Grudge's masterly article conclusively proves ... Unfortunately Professor Trevor-Roper ...' Oh, the time they will have! The caperings and squealings at the Institute of Historical Research! 'It was of course a highly contentious appointment. It was a great pity that it did not go to Pennington,[†] as I strongly recommended ...'[56]

'Seriously, the book is magnificent,' Howard continued. 'I read it enthralled, and it really does set standards in historical writing – or rather, revive them – which will have a quite galvanising effect on mousedom.' Hugh's prose was certainly uninhibited, even at times skittish, with references to 'radical ninnies', 'Biblical gibberish', 'gaseous Welsh cant' and similar phrases scattered through his text. There were daring historical analogies, between the events of the 1620s and the 1930s, for example. Some of his comparisons were very entertaining. 'In quiet times, scholarly monks in their cloisters would amuse themselves by calculating the Number of the Beast or identifying the Locusts of the Bottomless Pit,' he wrote, 'with no more dangerous thoughts than animate modern beneficed clergymen as they solve *The Times* crossword puzzle in the library of the Athenaeum.'

---

* By a curious coincidence, Howard and Elliott would succeed him as the next two Regius Professors of Modern History at Oxford.
† Donald Pennington, a historian of the seventeenth century, then a lecturer at Manchester University, who in 1965 would succeed Christopher Hill as a Fellow of Balliol and college tutor.

There were also plenty of jibes at familiar targets: Catholic anthropologists or Communist scientists, for example, both cited as proof that the human mind was capable of dual allegiance. Though much of this was fun, Howard thought that the text was sometimes overwritten. He recommended 'very ruthless pruning and tightening up', to eliminate the occasional *longueurs*, repetitions and mannerisms.

Hugh elaborated to Elliott the questions that he was striving to answer. It was no longer satisfactory to explain the Revolution simply in political terms, as historians in previous generations had done. He acknowledged that structural defects within English society had contributed to the collapse of the monarchy in the 1640s. To understand the Puritan Revolution, therefore, it was necessary to trace these underlying problems back to the beginning of the seventeenth century. Yet he did not share the belief of Hill and other Marxist historians that an upheaval was inevitable, despite the existence of such fundamental problems. On the contrary, it was an essential part of his argument that reform could have prevented revolution right up to the very brink of war. Many years later he would identify 1641 as one of the 'Lost Moments of History', in which events might have taken a completely different course.[57] Furthermore, Hugh considered that there was a direct connection between the ideas of the country party of the 1630s, then in opposition, and the ruling party of the 1650s. There was a continuity of thought that had previously escaped the notice of historians, dazed by the crowded and dramatic events in between. This was an extension of his concept of an antithesis between Court and Country: the Revolution represented the victory of the Country over the Court.

Elliott found the typescript 'intensely readable, fast-moving, lucid and gripping'. He produced a sheaf of detailed notes. Most of these were easily dealt with. But he had a difficulty with the book's frame of reference. Its underlying theme, he decided, was 'The Unnecessary Revolution', a counterblast to the doctrine of inevitability preached by Marxists and neo-Marxists. What then did it add to the narrative histories already written by historians from Clarendon to Gardiner (and, one might add, Wedgwood)? If critics could say that he had not added anything substantial to these earlier accounts, they might argue that Hugh had written 'an unnecessary book'. Elliott found himself becoming 'increasingly Whiggish' as he read on. 'Surely liberty and property are crucial themes,' he insisted; 'as crucial as the hatred of an over-inflated court.' He urged Hugh to make an additional effort to present a rounded picture, a reassessment of the entire problem of the English Revolution in the light of modern knowledge. He recommended adding a chapter on the legal and constitutional questions at issue, when men strove to find a balance between the royal prerogative and the subjects' rights. This would serve to bring out more poignantly the drama of how a revolution at once unwanted and unnecessary had nonetheless occurred.[58]

Hugh replied that he had found Elliott's comments helpful.[59] He seems to have decided to accept Elliott's suggestions, though this meant considerably more work. He was still optimistic that the book could be finished without much further delay. A few days after receiving Elliott's letter he accepted an invitation to write a book on 'Hitler and National Socialism' for Anvil, an American paperback series. 'I am working on a book on a very different subject at present, and I want to finish it before I undertake anything else,' he explained. 'However, it is going fairly well and I now write to say that I will be free to undertake the book for you next year.'[60]

He remained outwardly confident. His two readers had given very positive reports on what he had written so far; and while some work remained to be done, the great bulk of it was behind him. But the momentum could not be sustained. Already he was being pulled in a different direction.

Controversialist

Early in April 1961 Hugh flew to Israel to cover the opening of the Eichmann trial for *The Sunday Times*. Adolf Eichmann had been a crucial figure in the administration of Nazi genocide, responsible for rounding up hundreds of thousands of Jews and transporting them to death camps. At the end of the war he had escaped capture and eventually fled to Argentina, where he had lived untroubled for ten years. But in 1960 he was kidnapped by Mossad agents and smuggled back to Israel to face trial. The proceedings would be conducted in Hebrew, with simultaneous translation into German for the benefit of the accused, and into English and French for the sake of the world's press. A bullet-proof glass screen protected Eichmann from assassination by the outraged relations of the dead.

This was a major international news event. Most of the British newspapers sent special correspondents to Jerusalem to cover the story. Lord Russell of Liverpool, whom Hugh had first met as one of the Judge-Advocates at the Nuremberg Trials, was employed by the *News of the World*; while *The Daily Telegraph* was represented by Hugh's old friend Freddie Birkenhead, who brought with him his wife and daughter (then in her first year as an Oxford undergraduate). Frank Giles, who had recently returned from Paris to become Foreign Editor of *The Sunday Times*, decided that Hugh should go; he was the obvious man for such a story. Though Hugh was reluctant to be diverted from his book, he persuaded himself that he must accept the commission or forfeit his lucrative contract with *The Sunday Times*.

On the flight out the man sitting in front of him turned around and said, 'You are Professor Trevor-Roper.' As Hugh wrote in a letter home to Xandra, this turned out to be 'a very cultivated rabbi', the Editor of the *Toronto Evening News*, who would prove to be 'an admirable source'; one of the strengths of Trevor-Roper's dispatches would be his sense of how the trial was seen by Jews outside Israel. The plane touched down at Rome, where Hugh mingled with the other passengers, who included Lord Russell and Brigadier Telford Taylor, the American chief prosecutor from Nuremberg, now present as a journalist. Hugh also spotted a young man whom he correctly identified as an Oxford undergraduate. 'I know who you must be,' Hugh said, surmising correctly that the boy, an undergraduate from

Balliol named Seltzman, was the special correspondent of *Isis*, the student magazine.[1]

Before the trial opened Hugh spent a day at the smart new Hebrew University of Jerusalem, as the guest of the remarkable Professor of Archaeology, Yigael Yadin. It was Yadin who had acquired the Dead Sea Scrolls after they had been discovered by wandering Bedouin, and who had subsequently found further scrolls in almost inaccessible caves, high up a sheer rock face. Before taking up archaeology Yadin had served as a soldier; in 1948 he had been head of operations in the war of independence, when the newly formed State of Israel had successfully defended itself against invading Arab armies. Hugh was fascinated to examine the scrolls, and to hear first-hand accounts of their discovery.

Together with the other most privileged foreign journalists, Hugh was staying at the King David Hotel in Jerusalem. Soon after his arrival he succumbed to his usual sinus trouble and took to his bed. Service was slow: the hotel was struggling to cope with the influx, coinciding with the start of the tourist season and the festival of Passover, when no bread was baked and all restaurants closed. Lady Birkenhead, exasperated by his constant demands for drinks and medicines, formed the view that he was a hypochondriac. It seems that he was feeling sorry for himself, and had been perhaps made neurotic by anxiety about Elliott's criticisms. 'I hate Israel & particularly Jerusalem,' he moaned in a letter to his brother; 'Climate horrible, food worse. Oh, to be able to slip over the frontier into civilized Arab lands!'[2] He became depressed at not having heard from his wife. 'What have I done? Why do you persecute me?' he asked plaintively, when an envelope arrived, addressed in her hand but containing only a letter from Robert Blake. 'Do you think that I am quite without feeling?' He was 'terribly shaken' by what he saw as her 'indifference'. He had lunched with the widow of Chaim Weizmann, the first President of Israel, but had felt no appetite or desire for conversation; and had taken tea with the Prime Minister, David Ben Gurion, where he had felt unable to say anything; 'fortunately he was quite happy to do all the talking'. He had cancelled all his other social arrangements. 'I simply cannot face society when I receive such blows from you.'[3]

Hugh recovered in time for the opening of the trial. Eichmann himself proved to be 'a miserable, dreary, empty, mean, rat-faced creature', sitting calmly in his bullet-proof dock, having apparently convinced himself that he should be acquitted, on the grounds that he had been 'only following orders'. Three days after the trial opened, Hugh attended the Holocaust Day ceremony, an open-air service on Mount Herzl where several thousand people gathered as the sun went down. Many of them were in tears during the service. This intense outpouring of human suffering contrasted pain-fully with Eichmann's bland, unapologetic indifference.

Hugh's 'masterly' introduction to the trial and his subsequent dispatches were the pick of those published in the British press, according to the *Jewish Observer and Middle Eastern Review*.[4] While acknowledging the misgivings felt by Jews outside Israel about the expediency of the trial, Hugh stressed its internal significance, and the personal role played by the Prime Minster in the decision to abduct Eichmann and bring him to trial. Hugh had argued from the start that the action was justified, uniting the Israeli public in their desire for justice, and reminding the world of the crimes committed against the Jewish people. Moreover it was a landmark in the Jewish story, an assertion of the right of Israel to speak for Jews everywhere, 'an essential stage in the triumph of Zionism'.[5] Later in the year Hugh would give the Herbert Samuel Lecture on 'Jewish and Other Nationalism' to the British Friends of the Hebrew University of Jerusalem, delivered at the Institute of Education in London. Viscount Samuel himself was in the chair.

Hugh was present for only the first ten days of the trial, which lasted until the late summer. Judgment was not delivered until mid-December, when Eichmann was found guilty and sentenced to death. He was executed by hanging on 31 May 1962. Hugh wrote several more pieces about Eich-mann, including a full-page review of Hannah Arendt's book *Eichmann in Jerusalem: a Report on the Banality of Evil.* He was repelled by Arendt's attempt to attenuate Eichmann's responsibility for his crimes, and to shift at least some of the blame onto his victims. He accused her of using 'half-truths and loaded language and double standards of evidence to set the old moral standards on their head'.[6]

A few weeks after his return from Israel Hugh flew to Ireland, to read a paper to a conference of historians in Galway. He had been invited there at the suggestion of Hugh Kearney, whose book *Strafford in Ireland* (1959) he had reviewed favourably in *The Sunday Times*, describing Kearney as 'a young Irish historian who writes with real understanding of Irish con-ditions, and yet with a clarity which has not always distinguished his countrymen'.[7] This remark gave rise to much unintended amusement, since though Kearney taught in Ireland and indeed spoke with an Irish lilt, he was English.

Hugh's paper was a by-product of his unfinished book on the Tawney–Weber thesis. It seems that he had originally intended to develop his thoughts on the subject in a lecture series on 'The Reformation and Social Change in Europe', to be delivered in Chicago in the autumn of 1957.[8] That American trip had been cancelled when Hugh had decided to concentrate on writing his big book on the Puritan Revolution. Instead, his critique of

Weber was condensed into a superb long essay, lucidly written and power-fully argued, 'Religion, the Reformation and Social Change'. Hugh read a draft of this essay at the conference in Galway. His audience, 'powerfully reinforced by local monks and nuns', gave it 'an unsympathetic but not, I felt, a very critical reception' – unsurprisingly, given the content of his talk.

In a letter to James he summarised the question he was trying to answer: 'Why did the economic and social and intellectual life of the Roman Catholic countries sink or stagnate, while that of the Protestant countries bounded forward, in the three centuries after the Reformation?'[9] Hugh acknowledged the significance of religious differences in the emergence of a capitalist economy. Surveying the whole period from 1500 to 1800, he agreed that there had been an unmistakable shift, economically and intel-lectually, from the Catholic countries of the Mediterranean to the Protestant countries of northern Europe. We must conclude, he said, that Protestant countries were, or became, more forward-looking than their Catholic counterparts. Hugh contemplated the issue faced by Marx and Weber from a different angle. Instead of asking why capitalism was created in Protestant countries in the sixteenth century, he asked why it was not created in Catholic countries. He argued that the Roman Catholic Church, in its medieval form, had been compatible with capitalist expansion. Eco-nomically, the Renaissance state had functioned adequately. But the Counter-Reformation had changed all that. The Counter-Reformation might be seen as a great spiritual revival; but sociologically it represented an enormous strengthening in the bureaucratic structure of society, a huge increase in the tax burden and in the controls which the Church imposed on economic activity. The bloated, rigid Church of the Counter-Reformation hindered and discouraged enterprise. Artisans as well as entrepreneurs fled to the less restrictive, more tolerant countries of the Protestant north.[10]

Hugh thought of this essay as one of his most significant, giving a new direction to Weber's formula. He received a number of congratulatory letters after it was published in a volume of conference proceedings. 'I regard the essay as the most important contribution in a generation to our know-ledge and understanding of the whole Reformation movement,' enthused the American scholar W.K. 'Kitch' Jordan.* 'It is enormously stimulating,' continued Jordan, 'should break upon a great deal of research, and is itself sufficiently sustained by research to stand in its present form.'[11]

The Dublin historian Desmond Williams described Hugh's Galway lecture as 'a remarkably brilliant tour de force, carefully conceived, well

---

* Author of *The Development of Religious Toleration in England* (four volumes, 1932–40), and two volumes on philanthropy in the early modern period, which Hugh had reviewed, favourably, for *Annales*.

delivered, though with a not unattractive hesitancy'. He remarked on the fact that Hugh was 'more obviously nervous prior to the delivery of the paper than any other lecturer I have ever observed'. During the conference Williams had seen quite a lot of Hugh in private, as he related in a letter to his mentor, the Cambridge historian Herbert Butterfield:

> His conversation was spicy, malicious and amusing. One listened to it without regard to the humanity of the speaker. He has a certain charming winsome school-boy freshness; and I suspect that the class-structure of his native Northumberland, Charterhouse and above all of an Oxford traditional High Table is largely responsible for this aspect of his developed personality. He has a remarkable eye for observation, psychological and physical. He allows his wit [to] run away with him; he enjoys the sound of his own words and the construction of his sentences. His audience also enjoys them; and he knows it. He does not enter into conversation; and delivers monologues, in response, however, to questions. I suspect his tongue is more unkind than his behaviour, except where an extraordinarily sensitive vanity is affected. There is another side to this complex character which I found sincere. He genuinely likes the countryside and solitary walks, flowers and the trees, etc. His accounts of Oxford politics will remain in the mind of those who heard him ... On the smaller but essential issues of social behaviour, he was surprisingly good, at least surprising to me who had judged him previously on his public performance ...[12]

Following the lecture Hugh was driven to Donegal, where Xandra was staying with Derek Hill. Some years before, Hill had bought a house there, encouraged by Henry McIlhenny and (so he imagined) Dawyck Haig. Hugh regarded Hill's social ambitions as absurd, but tolerated him for the sake of Xandra, who found him amusing company. Hill did not like to share his conquests, not even with friends. Sitting in the passenger seat of Hill's car, with a large dog on his lap, Hugh recognised the drive leading to McIlhenny's castle. His host accelerated past, implying without saying so directly that his neighbour was elsewhere. The Trevor-Ropers would discover, too late, that McIlhenny had been not only at home, but had invited them to dinner the night before.

A.J.P. Taylor's *The Origins of the Second World War* had appeared while Hugh was in Israel. Described as an 'historical shocker', this was a work of radical revisionism, the first substantial challenge to the consensus that Hitler had planned the European war which broke out in 1939. On the contrary, argued Taylor: the war had begun by accident. Hitler was a man of daring improvisation, who took lightning decisions and then presented them as the result of long-term policy. Insofar as Hitler had a foreign policy, argued Taylor, it was no different from that of his predecessors: to free

Germany from the restriction of the Treaty of Versailles, to restore a great German army and to make Germany the greatest power in Europe from her own natural weight. Taylor discounted Hitler's talk about remaking the world; in his view Hitler was a dreamer, and *Mein Kampf* was a work of propaganda. He dismissed the Hossbach memorandum, a junior officer's account of Hitler's address to his generals in 1937, which had been produced by the prosecution at Nuremberg in an attempt to prove a Nazi conspiracy to commit 'crimes against peace'. In Taylor's view this was evidence that Hitler was a violent and unscrupulous man, but it was not evidence that he had any concrete policies, and his prophecy of events bore little resemblance to what actually happened.[13] Taylor played down the significance of Hitler's table-talk, suggesting that Hitler had merely rationalised events that had already taken place.

As Hugh would point out, there was an element of *gaminerie* in Taylor's make-up that led him to enjoy provoking those who unthinkingly conformed to received opinions. *The Origins of the Second World War* was praised by some reviewers as a masterpiece; but condemned by others as perverse, disgraceful and intellectually deplorable. One enraged critic accused Taylor of writing an apologia for the Nazis. For a while Hugh kept his powder dry, except that he did write to *The Times Literary Supplement*, if only to question the logic of the anonymous reviewer, who had lauded *The Origins of the Second World War* as a 'startlingly brilliant performance'. However, it soon became known that Hugh was writing a long piece about the book. 'I look forward to reading it,' Taylor said in an interview with a tabloid newspaper. 'He knows as much about twentieth-century history as I do about seventeenth-century history – which is not to say nothing at all.'[14] (This last sentence has often been misquoted, omitting the word 'not'.)

Three months after the book's publication, Hugh launched a devastating polemic against it in the July issue of *Encounter*.[15] He accused Taylor of selecting, distorting, suppressing and arranging the evidence to support his thesis, and of ignoring the programme which Hitler had laid down for himself in *Mein Kampf* and elsewhere.

It was hardly surprising that Hugh should have disliked the book. Taylor had ironically described Munich as a 'triumph for all that was best and most enlightened in British life'. For Hugh, Munich had been a defining episode, the moment when he had 'boiled with indignation against the appeaser'. In the opening paragraphs of his piece he recalled the passions and doubts of the 1930s. After reading the German edition of *Mein Kampf*, he had become convinced that there could be no peace with Nazi Germany, and formed the resolve that Hitler must be stopped. To question that now was intolerable. But in addition, Taylor's portrayal of Hitler ran counter to much of what Hugh had written over the past decade. In 'The Mind of

Adolf Hitler', his introduction to *Hitler's Table-Talk*, he had argued that Hitler was a systematic thinker. And in 1959 Hugh had read a paper on 'Hitler's War Aims' to a conference in Munich, subsequently published in *Vierteljahrshefte für Zeitgeschichte*, in which he had stressed Hitler's consistency.[16] Taylor had written to him about this essay, warmly praising it as 'a masterly production – a beautiful exercise in intellectual composition', while disagreeing with some of his conclusions, maintaining that Hitler's acts were shaped much more by tactics than strategy. 'You believe ... you can read Hitler's mind,' Taylor continued. 'I hesitate: I can trace his acts (sometimes) & I'm not sure that his mind deep down was all that decisive in shaping these acts. But what you write is infinitely more interesting & stimulating than that written by others.'[17]

Taylor responded to Hugh's *Encounter* article in a subsequent issue, comparing what he had actually written with what Hugh had said he had written. Hugh had concluded his article by saying that the book 'will do harm, perhaps serious harm, to his reputation as a serious historian'; Taylor repudiated this allegation, and alongside it wrote: 'The Regius Professor's methods of quotation might also do harm to his reputation as a serious historian, if he had one.'[18]

The controversy between the two men attracted international attention, particularly in America, where both *The New York Times* and *The New York Herald Tribune* devoted several stories to the subject.[19] Newspapers relished the 'feud' between the 'fighting dons of Oxford', particularly when Hugh agreed to take part in a televised debate with Taylor. 'I hope that we shall have adequate time for a serious discussion,' he wrote to the BBC producer, Alasdair Milne. 'As the issue is important, I do not want to take part merely in a brief, jolly, public spectacle of two personalities momentarily in the public eye through a dispute on an academic topic.'[20] The debate was chaired by a former pupil of Taylor's, Robert Kee. Given the sharpness of the printed exchanges, it was curiously subdued – 'often lively but never bad-tempered', according to the *Oxford Mail*. Most commentators judged that Taylor won the contest, though some thought that Hugh had the better of the argument.[21] Taylor was the more experienced television performer, and by referring to his opponent as 'Hughie' while the latter addressed him as 'Taylor' he succeeded in making him seem stuffy. Afterwards Hugh feared that he had been 'steam-rollered'. He confessed to feeling 'a bit depressed about it'.[22]

The Trevor-Ropers were welcome at great houses. In the space of five weeks in the summer of 1961, for example, they spent a weekend at Boughton, as guests of the Duke and Duchess of Buccleuch; at Wilton, as guests of the Earl and Countess of Pembroke; and at Tyninghame, as guest of the

Haddingtons. This was the milieu in which Xandra had been raised, where she felt most comfortable. Hugh's feelings were more ambiguous. On the one hand he relished his success in penetrating the highest social circles in the land. On the other hand he found much of the social life tedious and the conversation banal. This ambiguity was manifest in a letter he wrote to James from Tyninghame one Saturday morning, after returning from a solitary walk along the seashore. He loved the juxtaposition of the ancient woods, silent except for the sound of fluttering wood pigeons, with the open, empty seashore, the crash of waves mingling with the cries of terns. The coast reminded him of his childhood, when he would explore the seashore, peering into rock pools and gazing out to sea.

But this entrée to a great house came at a cost, as he confided to James. Already the pleasantest part of the visit was over. Soon he would have to go down to lunch, and then motor to Edinburgh for a British Legion dinner, to commemorate the centenary of the birth of his late father-in-law, the Field Marshal. The Duke of Gloucester would be present, together with other dignitaries, and of course Xandra's brother and sisters. He felt 'social electricity' warming the air, as he became aware of the 'otherwise unemployed Sisterhood and Aunthood girding up their skirts and pre-paring, by a discreet thrust here or there, to outmanoeuvre each other and edge their way ahead of each other to the stifling, desiccating glow of boring royalty . . . God, how I hate it all! But I must keep my mouth shut and play my demure little part in the background. I wonder whom I shall have as a neighbour at this dreadful feast tonight. Some inarticulate Scottish warrior, I suppose, with no brains, no teeth, no conversation, and scores of medals.' At the end of his letter, Hugh revealed to James that Xandra had just made 'one of her prize remarks'. During conversation with Sarah Haddington the subject had arisen of a forthcoming lunch at the House of Lords, given by Frank Pakenham (Lord Longford since 1961), to which the Trevor-Ropers had been invited. 'Will Hugh mind?' enquired their hostess, aware that it would be a very Catholic occasion. 'Oh no,' replied Xandra carelessly; 'Hugh likes <u>intelligent</u> RCs.'[23]

In a letter from Madrid, Hugh informed James that they were staying 'in the luxury which Mummy persuades herself is her due'.[24] It was perhaps inevitable that the two of them should view Xandra satirically. She could not share their intellectual interests, while her devotion to formal society would seem increasingly dated as the 1960s progressed. She was prone to gaffes which provoked hilarity, all the more amusing because she often did not understand what was funny about what she had said. Speaking of one of her musical friends, she marvelled that he had 'the largest organ in England'. At an Oriel dinner, the conversation turned to the sorceress Circe.

'Hugh, wasn't she the woman who turned all her lovers to swine?' she asked across the table, before innocently continuing, 'Do you remember that we first met at a fancy dress ball, when I was dressed as Circe?' When a visiting young couple explained that they had spent the weekend with an aunt in Birmingham, Xandra looked blank. 'Birmingham?' she asked. 'Whose place is that?'

This alliance between her younger husband and eldest son provoked Xandra's jealousy, which occasionally erupted into the open. During a period when Hugh was away from home she became agitated at not hearing from him; and when a letter arrived in his familiar hand, addressed not to her but to her eldest son, she made a scene that lasted for hours. 'Mummy ... delivered attack after attack,' James wrote to his stepfather; 'I hated Peter, her, Chiefswood, if it were not for Peter she would die'. Xandra was jealous, too, of Hugh's developing friendship with the young historian Valerie Pearl, especially after she obtained a post at Somerville. She became a confidante, with whom he could exchange gossip and let off steam. It was not surprising that he should enjoy the company of this lively, clever and attractive woman, who inhabited the same professional world. They tended to meet *à deux*, in pubs in Oxford or near the British Museum.

Relations between the Trevor-Ropers became strained almost to break-ing-point. One morning Hugh called the two older children into his study. 'I nearly left last night,' he told them.

James continued to struggle with depression throughout his under-graduate years. It would be even worse for Xenia, who won a place at St Anne's College, Oxford, to read Modern Languages, starting in the Michaelmas term 1962. Her depressive illness was so serious that she was admitted to the Warneford psychiatric hospital in a kind of stupor, and for six days would neither eat nor speak. Xandra could not cope with this crisis. She refused to visit her daughter, and was hysterical when left alone; Hugh feared that she too might need admission to the Warneford. He had at first dismissed Xenia's depression as melancholia, but after the consultant physician convinced him that her condition was serious, he agreed that she should be given electroconvulsive therapy, and her condition speedily improved.

Xandra remained alarmingly thin. She was easily upset by food, and her health deteriorated. In the mid-1960s she had a breakdown, and was admitted to the Acland Nursing Home, where she stayed a month or so. After her discharge Hugh took her to the Loire Valley, in an attempt to restore her health. On her second day she was violently sick, and remained in bed at the hotel while her husband visited châteaux alone. After two days she was no better, so they cut short their holiday and returned to England. Xandra was readmitted to the Acland, under the care of the doctor who had looked after her before. She recovered quite quickly, but remained delicate and liable to further stomach upsets. The doctor advised her to eat plain English food and not to risk travelling abroad.

'When radicals scream that victory is indubitably theirs,' pronounced Hugh, 'sensible conservatives knock them on the nose.'[25] He was sharpening his pen for another attack. This time his target would be E.H. Carr, a Fellow of Trinity College, Cambridge, and author of the multi-volume *History of Soviet Russia*. Carr was a brilliant man, a subtle and witty writer, with a background in political journalism. He shared with Taylor a taste for paradox; inverting a phrase of Sir George Clark's, Carr had written of 'a hard core of interpretation surrounded by a pulp of disputable facts'. In 1961 he published *What is History?*, a book based on the Trevelyan Lectures he had given at Cambridge. Hugh used its publication as a jumping-off point for another long *Encounter* article, 'E.H. Carr's Success Story'.[26] His title referred to Carr's assertion that history 'is, by and large, a record of what people did, not of what they failed to do; to this extent it is inevitably a success-story'. Carr was a determinist, and Hugh a fierce opponent of determinism. Like Isaiah Berlin, who had reviewed the first volume of Carr's history of the Soviet Union in the *New Statesman*, Hugh was offended by Carr's 'realist' emphasis on the realities of power, to the exclusion of the 'dead-ends' and 'might-have-beens'. He objected to what he believed to be Carr's message: that what mattered about history was its relevance to the future, that history was the record of progress and that the historian should reflect this – what Berlin had labelled the 'Big Battalion' view.

Hugh had a personal motive for his attack on Carr. He had discovered from Berlin that Carr had been the *TLS* reviewer whose comments on his *Historical Essays* he had so much resented. Indeed he seemed to hint at this in his opening sketch of Carr, when he mentioned that 'many a lightly-envenomed dart, issuing with musical twang from the opaque forest of the *Times Literary Supplement*, has afterwards been identified – at least as long as one could rely on the affability of the forest-rangers – as shot from his blow-pipe'.

Carr had demolished the now discredited theory (beloved by medievalists in particular) that history derived from documents was somehow scientific. In fact, it was just as subjective as any other form of history. Documents had to be selected, and the selection process required a principle of selection; and then they had to be interpreted; the historian needed to consider the circumstances in which a document was written as well as its content. Moreover documents were written by individuals, often individuals from a narrow class, unrepresentative of the society which they inhabited. Hugh conceded that all this was true, that the documentary record of the past was two-dimensional; but he insisted that the historian could acquire 'stereoscopic vision', to see beyond the document to the three-dimensional reality of the time and the place in which it originated.

'Study the historian before you begin to study the facts,' urged Carr. He argued that all historians were confined within the limits of the society and class from which each of them had sprung. Hugh satirised this view. 'Is it not even conceivable that a historian may, by industry and genius, overcome these barriers? Might not even a slave-owning Athenian aristocrat, or a tithe-eating monk, or a securely endowed fellow of a rich Cambridge college, though obviously a product of his social situation, nevertheless observe and interpret at least the contemporary history whose three-dimensional form lies perceptible before him?'

Hugh analysed what Carr meant by 'objectivity': not, he decided, being 'objective' in the hitherto accepted sense of the word – i.e. uncommitted, dispassionate, fair – 'but the exact opposite, being committed to the side that is going to win: to the big battalions'. But what appeared to be the winning side in the present might not be the winning side of the future. One needed only to consider the example of Macaulay, who like Carr believed in progress, and saw all of human history as progressing towards an ideal, the Whig society of nineteenth-century England. Not even Macaulay, however, had carried 'the vulgar worship of success quite so far as Mr Carr'. In his book *The Twenty Years' Crisis*, published in 1939, Carr had argued that German power was a reality that had to be accepted, at the expense of the small nations of Europe; A.J.P. Taylor had described the book as 'a brilliant argument in favour of appeasement'. But the reality of German power seemed less impressive in 1962 than it had done in 1939; and few now defended the policy of appeasing Nazi Germany (except possibly Taylor).

Perhaps remembering Carr's patronising comments about essays that 'stray outside' his chosen period, Hugh questioned Carr's glib inter-pretation of the Cromwellian Revolution as essential to 'the overthrow of feudalism and the victory of bourgeois democracy'. 'I think that in respect of the Cromwellian revolution at least I may claim to have made a con-siderably deeper study of the subject than he,' asserted Hugh, and 'I am convinced that the overthrow of feudalism and the victory of "bourgeois democracy" could have been achieved in several other ways: so far from owing all, it may have owed nothing, nothing at all, to the "Cromwellian dictatorship", which may even have positively retarded it.'

An historian who skips over the alternative possibilities merely because they were not immediately realized (although they may have been realized in the long run), or who writes off all that is accidental or contingent by confusing it (as Mr Carr regularly does) with what is trivial, must seriously misjudge historical situations, human motives, and the course of events itself; and without these, what *is* history?

Pieter Geyl wrote to tell Hugh that he had read his *Encounter* article 'with joyous agreement – a feeling into which a slight disappointment obtruded to find that you had forestalled me!'[27] Carr himself claimed to have felt 'disappointed' by it, and even 'insulted' that Hugh had let him off so lightly. 'I thought I was at least as great a villain as Toynbee or Taylor,' he remarked cheerfully. Carr's comments were recorded in a series of interviews with British historians and philosophers – including Ayer, Hampshire, Taylor, Toynbee and Trevor-Roper – conducted for *The New Yorker* magazine by a young Indian, Ved Mehta. Hugh appeared in Mehta's interview as cold and haughty, almost disdainful – unlike Taylor, whom Mehta found 'beguiling', or Carr, who seemed almost avuncular. When he later read the article Hugh recognised that he was 'the villain of the piece'. He was sceptical about the value of the interview, and speculated that Mehta had prejudged him. Though Mehta was blind, he had provided a visual description of both Hugh and his 'study', which he portrayed as 'cold and bare', to support his picture of Hugh's personality. (In fact they had met in an office at the History Faculty.)

In preparing for the interview Mehta had read 'Arnold Toynbee's Millennium', and had been startled by 'the venom that shot out of Trevor-Roper's pen'. In Mehta's judgement Hugh was 'the cruellest and most lacerating' of Toynbee's critics, and his article on Taylor had been 'only a little less violent'. Afterwards Mehta reflected that Hugh had a gift for marshalling the faults of an historian 'without a grain of sympathy. . . . He put me in mind of a literary critic who has no love for writers, whose criticism is not an enhancement of our understanding, an invitation to read the book again in the light of his interpretation, but simply an instrument of destruction.' Though on further reflection, Mehta speculated that perhaps the explanation for the violence of this polemic lay not with Hugh's psychology, but with England itself:

> Going for the largest game, creating an intellectual sensation, striking a posture, sometimes at the expense of truth, stating the arguments against a book or its author in the most relentless, sometimes violent way, engaging the interest of practically the whole intelligentsia by using every nook and cranny of journalism, carrying on a bitter war of words in public but keeping friendships intact in private, generally enjoying the fun of going against the grain – all these features prominent in historical disputation were also part of the broader English mental scene.[28]

If Hugh was cruel in print, he was often kind in private. He would go out of his way to help scholars at an early stage in their careers. In 1961 he met

Piyo Rattansi, a young Kenyan-Asian working on science and religion; he was impressed by Rattansi, and encouraged him, supporting his job applications. Soon they were on first-name terms. Rattansi obtained a post at the Department of Philosophy at Leeds, which had a subsection specialising in the history of science. Afterwards, with Hugh's help, he was elected a Senior Research Fellow at Cambridge, and eventually gained a Chair in London. Hugh's sponsorship of Rattansi reflected his growing interest in the history of science. In 1966 he would lecture at Leeds, and there he met another young scholar working in this area, Charles Webster, whose work he similarly encouraged. Webster later became Oxford University's Reader in the History of Medicine and Director of the Wellcome Unit for the History of Medicine. Hugh would fight a long campaign on behalf of Margery Purver, an eccentric woman subject to paranoid delusions, whose history of the Royal Society* was initially resisted by other scholars and spurned by publishers. Hugh believed this to be an important and original work, combining fine scholarship with analytical power. Moreover he welcomed Purver's dismissal of the theory that the founders of scientific thought in England had been Puritans. Hugh helped to ensure that her book was eventually published by contributing an introduction to the volume.

Several of those young scholars whom he encouraged had second-class degrees, or even, in at least one case, a third: usually an insuperable obstacle to an academic career. Indeed his eventual successor as Regius Professor, Michael Howard, had a second-class degree, but over a long and distinguished career would triumphantly vindicate Hugh's faith in him. In a *Sunday Times* article Hugh protested, mildly, against 'the smug academic dogma' of the first-class degree. 'Even in the academic world it does not apply,' he insisted. 'Some of my best research students and most admired colleagues got seconds and went on thinking. Some of the most brilliant firsts were so satisfied that they stopped.'[29]

Hugh also went out of his way over many years to help Paul Winter, a naturalised Jew from the Sudetenland whose family had all perished at the hands of the Nazis. Winter lived in a bedsitter, and subsidised his research by working as a railway clerk. Hugh repeatedly supported his applications for research posts at All Souls, the Institute for Advanced Study and other prestigious academic institutions.

One of the duties of the Regius Professor was to supervise research students. The quality Hugh valued most in these was intellect; it did not so much matter to him who or what they were. Among his most favoured postgraduate pupils was a Jewish-American woman, a former broker on

---

* *The Royal Society: Concept and Creation* (1967).

the New York Stock Exchange; another was a long-haired Scotsman, then a left-wing firebrand. In both cases it was their ability that overcame any initial resistance Hugh may have felt towards them. He acknowledged as one of the ablest of his pupils a Canadian Catholic convert, James Mc-Conica, who had been an undergraduate at Exeter College. Having attended Hugh's lectures, McConica was well aware of his prejudice against Catholics. He was therefore perturbed when he learned that Hugh was to be his supervisor, especially when he observed how startled Lawrence Stone seemed at the prospect. He went to see his old tutor, Dacre Balsdon, in some distress. 'Dacre, Dacre, my supervisor is Hugh Trevor-Roper,' blurted McConica. 'Oh, how frightfully funny!' responded his old tutor. McConica faced his first interview with his supervisor with some trepidation. The Regius Professor was not especially welcoming, and strode up and down the room as he talked. 'I suspect that what you want to do is not what needs to be done,' he announced. 'The book I should like to see written is on the influence of Erasmus in England.'* Hugh then paused to ask whether McConica had read any of G.G. Coulton's works.† 'Coulton has been much persecuted by Roman Catholics. Are you by any chance RC?' McConica had to confess that he was. Hugh resumed his stride: '... much persecuted by <u>bigoted</u> Roman Catholics'. The relationship between supervisor and pupil proceeded satisfactorily, and they soon became friends, a friendship that survived even McConica's announcement that he had decided to study for the priesthood.

'There is no better way of learning about a subject than by supervising a sympathetic and stimulating research student,' Hugh observed in his foreword to a book by Felix Raab, whom he described as 'my pupil and my friend'. Raab was a graduate of Melbourne University, who had come to Oxford to work on Machiavelli: the son of Austrian Jews who had fled to Australia after the *Anschluss*. Hugh warmed to this exceptional young man, whom he described to Valerie Pearl as one of his best research students. 'Whenever he appeared at my door – a heavy, square frame, slightly stooping, black-bearded, with a genial glint in his large, bulging eyes – my spirits would rise.' Raab was similarly devoted to his supervisor. A voluble raconteur, he recounted with gusto an early encounter between the two of them, when they met to discuss an early draft Raab had submitted. They were seated facing one another across a table. Hugh extracted the draft from a folder and pushed it across the table with the nail of his middle

* McConica's book *English Humanists and Reformation Politics* was published by OUP in 1965.
† A pugnacious controversialist, Coulton attacked Catholic writers like Francis Gasquet and G.K. Chesterton for portraying the medieval period as an era in which religious devotion had bred social contentment. In return Coulton was attacked by Catholic writers, Hilaire Belloc in particular.

finger, commenting, 'My dear Raab, it won't do, you know.' Raab claimed that he pushed it back, declaring in his guttural Austrian-Australian accent, 'It bloody well will!'[30]

Though a very well-organised scholar Raab was also something of a free spirit, who had financed his study of history by what Hugh would later describe as 'an active, wandering, and enjoyable life as stage-electrician, bricklayer, odd-job man'. Every now and then Raab would escape to some remote region of Europe, to hike along wild and lonely trails. In September 1962 a letter Hugh had sent to Raab in Italy was returned as unclaimed. Raab had slipped and fallen into a ravine, while walking alone in the mountains of Calabria. It would be a month before his body was found. Raab had just submitted his thesis, for which he was posthumously awarded a D.Phil. Two years later it was published, with Hugh's elegiac foreword, as *The English Face of Machiavelli*.

In the bitterly cold winter of 1962/3, Hugh made a series of resolutions: 'to be more tolerant, better-tempered, etc'; to re-read the Greek tragedies; and to resume keeping a journal, a commitment he abandoned after less than a year, though afterwards he did keep journals of trips to exotic places overseas. He made no resolution to finish the magnum opus. Whenever this was mentioned he would become agitated, holding up a hand as if to ward off the question. 'Please don't talk about it,' he would beg.

The Trevor-Ropers spent the Hilary term 1963 in Paris, living in an apartment rented from a rich American woman. He had been invited there by Braudel, to lecture at the École Pratique des Hautes Études. Unfortunately the arrangements were haphazard, to the point of neglect. Hugh had prepared his talks on the assumption that he would be lecturing to students; on his arrival, he found that he would be lecturing only to professors. Since the lectures had never been advertised, the audiences were small, made smaller still by the fact that they had been scheduled at a time which clashed with others. 'Altogether I am feeling rather depressed,' he confided to James: 'Mummy finds so much to complain about!'[31]

With some difficulty he obtained a reading ticket for the Bibliothèque Nationale, where he would work most days. It was delightful to walk to the library each morning, from their flat on the Left Bank, past the Institut de France, across the footbridge of the Pont des Arts, through the courtyards of the Louvre and the colonnades of the Palais-Royal. On most days he would break for lunch with Xandra, and then go to the theatre or the cinema in the evening. The Trevor-Ropers attended plenty of lunches, dinners and parties. They saw Nancy Mitford several times, as well as Peter Ramsbotham, now Head of Chancery at the British Embassy. One afternoon they took tea with Violet Trefusis in her apartment. During the war Hugh had read her letters to her lesbian lover, Vita Sackville-West, who was married to Harold Nicolson, a junior Minister. She was under suspicion after an *Abwehr* intercept had revealed the recommendation of a Vichyite French aristocrat that she be recruited as a German spy. As a result her post was intercepted by the censors, steamed open and read by profane MI5 officers. Poor Miss Trefusis never knew that her privacy had been invaded.

There was a set of Voltaire's complete works in the Paris apartment where the Trevor-Ropers were staying. Hugh began to browse in these, suspecting that the volumes had been purchased solely for their bindings, and that he was the first person to read, or possibly even to open them. At the end of June he flew to Switzerland for a conference at the Institut et Musée Voltaire in Geneva, at which he presented a paper on 'The Historical Philosophy of the Enlightenment'. The Institut was the brainchild of Theodore Besterman, the editor of Voltaire's letters and founder of the journal *Studies on Voltaire and the Eighteenth Century*. Besterman had negotiated a deal with the city authorities in Geneva: he would donate his Voltaire collection, while in return they renovated Voltaire's former home and converted it into a museum and research centre for Voltaire scholars. This initiative was a great stimulus to Voltaire scholarship. Hugh was intrigued by Besterman, whom he regarded as a 'mystery man', while acknowledging that he was 'a great scholar and patron of scholarship'. He would later propose Besterman, successfully, for an honorary degree at Oxford.

Hugh's attendance at this conference marks the beginning of his interest in the origins of the Enlightenment. In particular, he was intrigued by the Scottish Enlightenment, a subject then ignored by Scots historians. Indeed the Keeper of the Public Records of Scotland, Sir James Fergusson of Kilkerran, had replied to an enquiry from Hugh that 'your phrase, "the Scottish Enlightenment", is unfamiliar to me'. Hugh thought this a rich topic for further study. 'What an extraordinary phenomenon it is!' he noted in his 1963 journal. 'How did it happen? What was the social, what the intellectual basis of this extraordinary efflorescence? What a problem to answer, or even to face!'[32]

Robert Blake concurred. 'It never ceases to surprise me that English historians (not to mention Scottish historians) so consistently neglect Scotland,' he observed to Hugh. 'Why, it might be as remote as Catalonia.'[33] One possible reason for this neglect was the view prevalent in Scotland that Scottish history should be written only by Scotsmen, born in Scotland and educated at Scottish universities. In a *New Statesman* piece some years earlier, Hugh had remarked that the sociology of Scottish history was quite untouched, and posed the question: 'What do they do in those torpid universities of the North?' The result was an outcry. Janet Adam Smith reported on the 'furious buzzing of Scotch professors'. This was the opening skirmish in a long war between Hugh and a section of the historical profession in Scotland; he regarded them as narrow and insular, while they regarded him as provocative and patronising. Henceforth Hugh always expected to be *persona non grata* in universities north of the Border. He took this as a challenge; and by exploiting the fact that Xandra's father had been Rector and Chancellor of St Andrews, succeeded in getting himself invited to lecture there, in the spring of 1962. His subject was 'Scotland and the Puritan Revolution': the period when first the Scots invaded England, and then the English invaded Scotland. His lecture was boycotted by the Reader in Scottish History, and he was told that those members of the Theology Faculty who attended had 'hated' it – unsurprisingly, because his tone was mocking towards Presbyterianism throughout. Hugh portrayed seventeenth-century Scotland as backward, primitive, bigoted, super-stitious and intolerant: a country where Calvinist clericalism (i.e. Presbyterianism) had succeeded in establishing 'a conservative tyranny', indeed a theocratic dictatorship. 'By an irony which seems also a law of history, the new religion of Calvinism, like Marxism today, had triumphed not in the mature society which bred it, but in the underdeveloped countries where the organs of resistance to it were also undeveloped.'

Later that year he gave the same lecture in Aberdeen, where, he was afterwards informed, some (though not all) of the 'divines' reacted with incoherent rage; and in Edinburgh, where his reception was, he felt, 'openly cold'; following the example of his colleague the Reader in Scottish History at St Andrews, the Edinburgh Professor of Scottish History ostentatiously stayed away. In due course the lecture was published, in a volume of essays presented to David Ogg. *The Scotsman* dismissed it as 'Professor Trevor-Roper's orgy of English nationalism'. In contrast, the Regius Professor of Divinity in Oxford, Henry Chadwick, congratulated Hugh on his 'witty, learned, and very illuminating' essay. 'Nothing I have read has so dis-entangled the extraordinary complexities of Anglo–Scottish relations in religion under Charles and Cromwell.' A letter from Christopher Hill was equally enthusiastic. 'You really do get better and better! I foresee a terrible time coming in the near future when I shall find no point of disagreement between us at all.' Hill thought it 'monstrous' that 'no Scot has even started to think like that'.[34]

A BBC internal memorandum from Donald Baverstock to Stuart Hood, the Controller of Programmes (Television), reported that Hugh was enthu-siastic about giving a series of televised lectures on 'grand historical subjects' such as 'The Fall of Rome', 'The Reformation', 'The Renaissance', and so on. 'No one is better than he at taking such huge subjects and making them absorbingly interesting,' the memo continued. Baverstock suggested that the lectures might be given at the new University of Sussex. Apparently Hugh had been 'excited' by this idea, making the point that Sussex's Pro Vice-Chancellor and Professor of History, Asa Briggs, was an ally. It was agreed to commission a first series, and that Hugh should be paid a fee of 200 guineas per programme. The series producer would be Alasdair Milne, who had produced the debate between Trevor-Roper and Taylor on the origins of the Second World War.[35] Hugh decided to take as his theme 'The Rise of Christian Europe'.

Television was still experimenting to find the best way to present complex ideas. A.J.P. Taylor had been a pioneer, with a series of lectures on the Russian Revolution which was broadcast on commercial television in 1957. His first series was such a success that it had been followed by others at regular intervals. In 1961 Taylor had transferred to the BBC. Taylor's lectures were unscripted, which made them compelling to watch; the viewer could see him thinking, as he searched for the next point in his argument.

No doubt Hugh was keen to show that he could do anything his rival could do. But Taylor had set a high standard. Hugh was incapable of working without a script. In any case Milne wanted to do something different, using stills and film to make the lecture come alive. Hugh's lectures were recorded on six successive evenings* in October 1963, before an audience consisting largely of students from the new university. Glancing around beforehand, he commented on the number of 'fashionable young ladies' present. He seemed nervous, and failed to engage with the audience. One reason was that he read the lectures rather than delivering them *extempore*, like Taylor. Late in the evening before the final recording, Milne was alarmed to discover that Hugh had not fully prepared the last lecture. He was willing to stay up all night to help, but Hugh declined the offer. The next morning his script was ready to record.

The lectures were broadcast weekly at 10.25 on Tuesday evenings, starting in the second week of November. Reactions to his performance were mixed. There was some criticism within the BBC about the way the series was produced, which perhaps did him no favours. The camera scanned the audience apparently at random, distracting attention from the lecturer. Several critics likened this technique to the one used on the pop music programme *Juke Box Jury*.

Hugh's lectures spanned a period more than eleven hundred years in duration: from 'the end of Antiquity', when the Roman Empire divided, until the middle of the fifteenth century – the dawn of the Italian Renaissance, and the time when Portuguese voyages of exploration signalled the European breakthrough towards domination of the rest of the world. He

---

* With one break, when a cold prevented Hugh from giving his fifth lecture.

remained unapologetic about his study being 'Europa-centric. ... It is European techniques, European examples, European ideas which have shaken the non-European world out of its past – out of barbarism in Africa, out of a far older, slower, more majestic civilization in Asia; and the history of the world, for the last five centuries, in so far as it has significance, has been European history.'

He began his opening lecture with an assertion that attracted much criticism:

> It is fashionable to speak today as if European history were devalued: as if historians, in the past, have paid too much attention to it; and as if, nowadays, we should pay less. Undergraduates, seduced, as always, by the changing breath of journalistic fashion, demand that they should be taught the history of black Africa. Perhaps, in the future, there will be some African history to teach. But at present there is none, or very little: there is only the history of the Europeans in Africa. The rest is largely darkness, like the history of pre-European, pre-Columbian America. And darkness is not a subject for history.

Hugh went on to make the point that the same could be said of the darkest eras of European history, and quoted Hume on 'the obscure and uninteresting period of the Saxon annals'. For him, as for the philosophic historians of the eighteenth century, the essence of history was movement and change; like Voltaire, he believed that there was little benefit to the public in chronicling that 'one barbarian succeeded another on the banks of the Oxus or the Jaxartes'. Hugh's remarks were logical enough. But witty asides about 'the unrewarding gyrations of barbarous tribes in picturesque but irrelevant corners of the globe' and other similar references sounded derogatory; and they were not tactful at a time of extreme sensitivity in relations between black and white, in Britain, in America, and in Africa itself. Nor was this opening likely to win over his audience in a new university that had made it a priority to attract African and Asian students. As the camera roamed the faces of the audience, it picked up expressions of puzzlement, irritation and outright hostility.

Six months after this broadcast, Britain's first Professor of African History delivered his inaugural oration to London University's School of Oriental and African Studies. Not surprisingly, he could not resist a few digs at Hugh's lectures. He drew a cheap laugh when he claimed that at Oxford, as at Cambridge, 'many historians have trouble seeing very far beyond the Channel'. Turning to the chairman, until recently a Fellow of an Oxford college, he asked her to assure the Regius Professor 'that both the Trevors and the Ropers are almost certainly of African descent, and that he had better give this matter some thought'.[36]

Almost two years later, a book based on Hugh's television lectures was published by Thames and Hudson, as the first in a new series edited by Geoffrey Barraclough. The publishers paid a generous advance of £1,500 – a handy sum, particularly given that the lectures were already written. The comparatively slight text (36,000 words) was bulked out with extensive illustration. In his foreword, Hugh referred to changes he had made since the transcripts of the lectures were published in *The Listener*, and his hope that these have 'left them less vulnerable to those professional medievalists who, I read, are "sharpening their knives" against me'. His hopes were vain. 'I am in the middle of tearing Trevor-Roper to pieces,' McFarlane told a friend, as he prepared his *New Statesman* review of *The Rise of Christian Europe*; 'it could hardly be more awful.'[37] In his review, McFarlane distinguished the historian 'Professor H.R. Trevor-Roper' from 'Hugh Trevor-Roper', the journalist. 'The Professor's journalistic *alter ego* seldom writes badly, even when he knows little and appears to have thought less,' he began ominously, before ridiculing some of the generalisations in the book. 'Can Mr Trevor-Roper have been sitting too long at the feet of Professor Toynbee?' asked McFarlane, in what must have been a painful stab. 'The truth is,' he concluded, 'that this hasty, shallow, somewhat philistine little book was not worth reprinting.'[38]

From time to time Hugh's editors enquired about progress on his magnum opus. Early in 1964, Harold Macmillan proposed a lunch. He had resigned as Prime Minister the previous October, after he had been diagnosed, incorrectly, as having inoperable prostate cancer. He withdrew from active involvement in politics and announced that he would not stand again for Parliament. 'I have just begun to do a little work at Macmillans,' he now told Hugh. After they lunched together on 19 February, Macmillan summarised his views about the Civil War book. 'While I agree with you that the scale of your book does present certain problems, I still feel that these are not insuperable,' he wrote. 'If you will forgive me for saying so, it is of some importance that a large and important work of this kind should be published without too much delay. After that it will be possible to follow it up with the publication of a collection of essays and so forth.'[39]

Xandra was dismayed at her husband's failure to finish his book. It had been her ambition to make a comfortable home, so as to enable him to write works of real substance; but in the ten years they had been married the only volume he had produced was one of recycled reviews. In January 1964 she confided her worries to Randolph Churchill. 'It is all most unfortunate about the book,' she wrote. 'I really don't know what is best to do.'

> Hugh finished the book about 2 years ago. Then, unfortunately, he sent a copy to a young historian called John Elliot [*sic*].

The latter returned it with suggestions that one subject should be longer & another shorter (I am <u>sure</u> he just wrote this to have something to say & had no idea of the dire consequences it would have), with the result that Hugh started to re-write the book. It is a very long & complicated subject & all historians are waiting for Hugh's book. I think he now feels that it must be perfection since he is taking so long to bring it out.

After all <u>no</u> real artist ever feels his work is perfect so Hugh will go on for ever tinkering with his book if he wants perfection. I am no historian so my arguments carry no weight. Two years ago he read most of the book to me & I thought it marvellous & was <u>horrified</u> when he started to re-write the whole thing.

I would gladly wring the neck of John Elliot who, I feel sure, has no idea of the havoc he has caused ...

I have not had a holiday for 2 years so that Hugh could spend all the vacations in Scotland writing his book.

He spent 2 months in Paris this time last year & the idea was that he would be away from commitments in Oxford & have time to finish his book. To my horror he spent all his time reading about something for another book (he said he needed to be near the libraries of Oxford for the Civil War book) & correcting some wretched book (Hitler's dispatches* I think it is called) that Andrew Dawnay (an ex-pupil) persuaded him to edit ...

Both his brother and sister have mentioned his book to him & he flew into a rage. As I am not a historian I feel I am not competent to advise him.

In fact I am made to feel that it is my fault he has not finished the book because he needs money all the time to help pay the housekeeping bills. This is really rather unfair ...

Anyway these attacks on Hugh are having a disastrous effect on him. The more people say he must finish the book, the more he turns his hand to other things!

Perhaps I should tell John Elliot what he has done & ask if he can now repair the damage.

I feel Hugh's book is like a picture that ... came off wonderfully in the first sketch but then, as he began to add & scrape out, became over-painted.

<u>Don't</u> say I told you all this.'[40]

In January 1964 Frank Giles asked Hugh to do 'one of your major pieces in depth' on the Auschwitz trials which had just opened in Frankfurt. In 1947 a trial had been held under Allied jurisdiction of the most senior officials responsible for the Auschwitz extermination camp, as a result of which twenty-three of the defendants had been sentenced to death. Now the smaller fry were being put on trial, under the jurisdiction of the Federal Republic.

---

* *Hitler's War Directives* (1964).

Hugh flew to Frankfurt at the end of February. This time the accused were not the bureaucrats or the commanders who had ordered murder, but the murderers themselves, those who had strangled, drowned, tortured and beaten their defenceless victims, who had pushed mothers and children alive into furnaces and perpetrated indescribable acts of sadism. At Nuremberg and at the trial of Eichmann in Jerusalem, the prisoners had been separated from the observers attending the trial, but here in Frankfurt no distinction was made. Hugh found himself sitting next to two SS dentists accused of selecting victims for the gas chambers, supervising their execution and removing the gold teeth from the corpses. Moreover, many of the defendants – those accused not of murder but of being accessories to murder – were free on bail, so that (as he reported to Xandra), you might encounter them sharing your table in the nearby restaurant, or standing alongside you in the gentlemen's lavatory. This was disconcerting, particularly after hearing the evidence of their horrible crimes. There was an especially dramatic moment when one of the defence lawyers challenged a witness to identify his client. As almost twenty years had passed since the camp had been liberated, and since the witness was frail as a result of his experiences at Auschwitz, Hugh feared that he might be unable to identify the accused among the mass of people present. The man walked slowly around the courtroom, peering through his thick spectacles; and then identified the defendant correctly. 'I think everybody in court (except the defendants) was as relieved as I was when he got him right,' Hugh told James.[41]

At the weekend he escaped to the Goethe museum, where he spent most of Saturday morning happily, forgetting about the horrors of Auschwitz. That same afternoon, as he was working in his hotel room, he suddenly remembered being told that Willi Johannmeyer, the German army officer whom he had interrogated about Hitler's will, now lived in Frankfurt. On a whim, Hugh looked up his name in a telephone directory and called the number. He was not at all sure that his call would be welcome, but thought that he would take a chance.

A woman answered. Hugh asked to speak to Herr Johannmeyer. 'What name shall I give?' the woman asked. 'Trevor-Roper,' Hugh replied, readying himself for lengthy expostulation, demands for repetition, spelling, etc. 'Ah, Herr Trevor-Roper', she answered smoothly, 'I will fetch him at once.' It was as if he were a familiar friend whom they met regularly, not an English officer who had last seen her husband nineteen years earlier, under somewhat strained circumstances. Johannmeyer came to the telephone and seemed absolutely delighted to hear from him. The next day Hugh called at the house and spent two hours with Johannmeyer and his wife. He found them both very civilised. Johannmeyer, who had never joined the Party, was strongly anti-Nazi; he said that the Auschwitz trials should have been held ten years before. Afterwards the two men kept in touch by letter.

'I do think that the Germans are improving,' Hugh wrote to his wife: 'the atmosphere is quite different from what it was a few years ago, and I can detect no sympathy at all for the old arguments which were still effective quite recently. For years, the Germans have pretended not to know about Auschwitz and have tried to defend everything else; now they – or rather a younger generation – admit all and repudiate all.'[42] In his *Sunday Times* article, 'Germany's Awakening Conscience', Hugh pinpointed the significance of the Auschwitz trial. The new Federal Republic had sought to reject the burden of the past by facing the terrible realities of the Nazi period. 'If the new society is to be free of guilt, the first necessity is that the guilt be seen.' This trial, however painful, was evidence of German success. 'When a society, conscious of past complicity, can nevertheless expose such public crimes to public justice and admit open enemies as advocates on both sides, and feel confident both of fair trial and public approval, then we may feel that totalitarian habits of mind are dead and a liberal system has arrived.'[43]

Nine months later the Trevor-Ropers were enjoying the Californian sunshine and dining with Hollywood movie stars. They had crossed by ocean liner from Greenock to Montreal, then made their way across Canada to Vancouver, and down the West Coast to California. At several stops en route Hugh had given a talk on 'Hitler's Place in History'; in Seattle he had lectured to a huge audience, estimated at 2,000-strong.

Hugh had been invited to spend the last three months of the year 1964 as a Senior Research Fellow attached to the William Andrews Clark Memorial Library in Los Angeles, which housed a fine collection of seventeenth-century English books (though not, of course, as good as the Bodleian's). It offered a substantial stipend, and a chance to give Xandra a holiday. The library, which had been endowed by a Montana copper king, was built in the style of an Italian palazzo, surrounded by handsome grounds. However, it was twelve miles from the university, in a district once fashionable but no longer so; the wealthy had long since fled the area, which was now distinctly down-at-heel. The library itself seemed moribund. No one else came there, except a few young women to catalogue the books. The librarian lived in Malibu and was seldom seen. Hugh soon realised that he had been hired merely as an expedient, so the trustees could certify that they had fulfilled their duties in their end-of-year report. In order to reach the library, Hugh was forced to leave the house early each morning and walk a mile and a half to catch a bus.* There was nowhere to eat nearby, so he was obliged to take a picnic lunch, which he ate in the garden. Xandra, who was not accustomed to rising early, complained volubly at being required to make his breakfast and a packed lunch by 7.30 each day. He had hoped to have some contact with the University, but since he was required to be at the library in working hours, and since the University shut down after five o'clock each evening, this proved difficult. It was only after they had been in the city almost two months that one of the history professors, who had been teaching a course on Hugh's ideas, discovered that he was there.

Fortunately Xandra had an introduction to George Cukor, the Academy Award-winning director of many successful films, including *The Philadelphia Story*, *A Star is Born* and *My Fair Lady*, which had been released earlier in the year and which was to win him an Academy Award. Cukor was a gregarious individual, whose famous soirées attracted the cream of Hollywood society. Hugh confessed to James that the Hollywood world was 'undoubtedly much gayer than the academic world here in Los Angeles' – an innocent remark, though Cukor was homosexual, and his guests included some startlingly handsome and muscular young men. Through Cukor the Trevor-Ropers met Merle Oberon and Olivia de Havilland. One evening they were invited to a dinner party at which several famous stars were present, including Tom Courtenay and Natalie Wood. 'You know,' Xandra told the assembled company, 'Hugh doesn't know who any of you are!'

At another dinner with Cukor and his friend Katharine Hepburn, who had starred in several of his films, the conversation turned to the newly published Warren Report. This was the Report of the Commission established by President Johnson to investigate his predecessor's assassination on 22 November 1963. It took its name from its chairman, Chief Justice Earl Warren; among the six other members was another future President, Gerald Ford, and the former CIA Director Allen Dulles (with whom Hugh had discussed the plot against Hitler). Hugh told his fellow diners of his belief that the primary purpose of the Commission was to calm the fears of a nation shocked by the violent death of their President. From the start there had been rumours of a right-wing plot to assassinate Kennedy, who was seen, rightly or wrongly, as the champion of progressive causes. The assassination had taken place in Texas, a notoriously reactionary state. The alleged assassin, Lee Harvey Oswald, seemed to have no clear motive. Considerable confusion about the circumstances of the assassination encouraged the proliferation of conspiracy theories. Oswald's murder while in police custody, by a local low-life criminal, suggested a cover-up.

---

* The Trevor-Ropers had bought a cheap car for use while they were in California, but Xandra wanted this during the day.

This was a subject in which Hugh was already interested. He was a member of a committee of prominent people in British public life, formed by Bertrand Russell to keep a watch on the activities of the Warren Commission, whose methods were thought to be unsatisfactory. Hugh was very much the odd man out on the 'Who Killed Kennedy?' committee, since all the other members were associated with the Left: the playwrights John Arden and J.B. Priestley; the critic Kenneth Tynan; the nutritionist Lord Boyd Orr; the sexologist Dr Alex Comfort; the publishers John Calder and Victor Gollancz; the former Editor of the *New Statesman* Kingsley Martin; the film director Tony Richardson; the Bevanite Labour MP Michael Foot; the poet and critic William Empson; the novelist Sir Compton Mackenzie; the art critic Sir Herbert Read; the radical Bishop of Southwark, Mervyn Stockwood; and Caroline Wedgwood Benn, the American wife of the Labour politician Anthony Wedgwood Benn (later known as Tony Benn). The committee never actually met, serving solely as a propaganda organisation for criticism of the Warren Commission. Benn confided to his diary his concern that his wife was being manipulated for ulterior leftist motives. To him, the committee appeared to be little more than an anti-American front.[44]

The Warren Commission's Report had been published a few days after the Trevor-Ropers' arrival in America; everywhere they went people had been talking about it. Informed American opinion, with very few exceptions, had accepted the main finding of the Commission: that Oswald had acted alone. There was a strong sense among the American intelligentsia that it would be irresponsible to encourage the wild theories circulating on the subject; to do so would be divisive, in a nation dangerously polarised. Hugh reported to Frank Giles that the American Left was 'almost hysterically anxious' that the Warren Report 'should be swallowed whole'.[45]

Hugh had read the Report, and was more sceptical, as he told Cukor and Hepburn. Some of the evidence appeared to suggest that Oswald had not been alone: in particular, evidence indicating that the President could not have been shot from the window where Oswald was positioned. In assessing the way that the Commission had conducted its investigation, Hugh could draw on his own experience in compiling his report into the death of Hitler. As an historian, he was interested in the process by which the Commission had collected and processed the evidence, and then reached its conclusions. He knew that it was essential, in assessing a document, to understand the circumstances in which it had been written, the pressures upon the writer, and the wider social and political context. He looked forward to the opportunity to make his own assessment of the 20,000 pages of evidence collected by the Warren Commission, which it was about to publish, two months after the Report itself had appeared.

Katharine Hepburn was fascinated by what Hugh had to say. Over the next few days word got around Los Angeles that the visiting English professor was a trenchant critic of the Report. A few evenings after the dinner, an obviously prosperous lady called at their apartment, followed by her obedient husband, bearing from the waiting car the first consignment of the twenty-six volumes of evidence. A day or two later a similar couple brought them another set. The Trevor-Ropers did not have the heart to tell the second couple that they had already been given one.

In the weeks that followed Hugh studied the evidence collected by the Commission, and found his suspicions confirmed. Why had the original notes for Kennedy's autopsy been destroyed? Why had the police disposed of the paper bag in which Oswald had concealed his rifle? Why were there no notes, stenographic records or tape recordings of Oswald's interrogation? How could the police have allowed Oswald to have been killed while in their custody? There was a lack of rigour in the Commission's uncritical acceptance of some, and rejection of other, evidence, and its seeming reluctance to ask essential questions. The Commission, he concluded, had shown culpable indifference in compiling its vast and slovenly report.

He was encouraged in these conclusions by Mark Lane, a New York attorney and political activist, who had won a reputation for supporting the underdog and championing progressive causes. In December 1963 Lane had published a notional defence brief for Oswald in a small-circulation, progressive newspaper, and in the spring of 1964 he had founded the Citizens' Commission of Inquiry into the Death of the President, an American equivalent to the British 'Who Killed Kennedy?' Committee. He formed a link with Russell's amanuensis Ralph Schoenman, and had visited Britain at the invitation of the Bertrand Russell Peace Foundation. On 29 November Lane dined with Hugh in Los Angeles.

Hugh contacted *The Sunday Times* in London, to suggest that he should write something on the subject. The paper had already printed a dispatch from its Washington correspondent, Henry Brandon, who had argued that the Warren Report had put a stop to all controversy. Despite this, Frank Giles agreed to Hugh's proposal. On 13 December Hugh's full-page article 'Kennedy Murder Inquiry is Suspect' appeared in *The Sunday Times*. 'Little did I think,' Hugh confessed afterwards in a letter to James, 'that it would cause such a stir.'[46] The very next day he received a telephone call from New York, asking whether he would fly there to debate the matter on television with Bernard Levin – a journalist who had become famous throughout Britain for his confrontational interviews on the satirical programme *That Was the Week That Was*. Hugh was still considering this request when Ralph Schoenman telephoned to inform him that Levin had written 'a violent diatribe' against him in the *Daily Mail*. Schoenman believed that Levin's article was actionable, but from the passages which he read over the phone it seemed to Hugh 'merely abusive'.[47] He refused the invitation to debate with Levin.

As he was completing his piece on the Warren Report, Hugh had received a telegram from home, with news that his mother had suffered a stroke and was obviously dying. His father wanted him to return. His brother Pat was somewhere in Africa; the family had been unable to contact him. Hugh hesitated, reluctant to curtail their trip. A few days later he received a telephone call from his sister, informing him that their mother was dead. He prepared to fly back to England, but delayed his departure when Xandra developed a throat infection. His ailing wife took precedence over his dead mother. Two days later he decided to stay, reasoning that there was no longer any point in returning now that he was too late to attend his mother's funeral. Bertie Trevor-Roper took it badly that neither of his sons was present.

On 20 December, the Sunday following publication of Hugh's article, *The Observer* devoted a full page to the questions he had raised about the Warren Commission. Each was scrutinised by the paper's Washington correspondent Godfrey Hodgson, and the results evaluated by its legal staff. 'The impressive quality of the Commission's report is not one whit impaired by Professor Trevor-Roper's assault,' the lawyers decided. The Report had established the central facts of the assassination 'beyond reasonable doubt'.[48] Hugh was accustomed to criticism in *The Observer*; but not in his own newspaper, especially not from a man he considered a friend. On that same Sunday, *The Sunday Times* carried a damning response to Hugh's article from the Warden of All Souls, John Sparrow. The absence of any serious debate on the Warren Report in America had the effect of high-lighting the public dispute between these two Oxford dons, who knew each other well.

Hugh enjoyed cordial relations with Sparrow; indeed, he had received a letter from him in California only a few weeks earlier. Sparrow was giving lectures on the Regius Professor's behalf while he was abroad. Nonetheless Hugh thought Sparrow 'ridiculous' as an intellectual figure – 'his mind goes unerringly to the periphery of any problem' – and 'a disaster' as a University figure. Sparrow's most recent contribution to scholarship had been an article in *Encounter* arguing that Lady Chatterley and her lover Mellors had practised anal sex.[49] 'He is very learned, but all his learning is concentrated on absurd trifles,' Hugh confided to Nicky Mariano.[50] And despite their cordial relations, there had been a recent tension between the two men, after Hugh learned that James had dined with the Warden and had formed the erroneous impression that James might be planning to stay with Sparrow while he and Xandra were away, instead of remaining alone at 8 St Aldates. 'I do think that John Sparrow, with his negative, atomising, trivialising mind, is a disastrous influence,' Hugh advised his stepson. Moreover (though he did not say this to James), Hugh was well aware that Sparrow was an enterprising homosexual, with a taste for young men. '<u>Please</u> do not stay with John Sparrow, as I hear you contemplate,' he urged. 'However unfairly, it will give you a Bad Name, which, in a centre of self-generating gossip like Oxford, will be an inconvenience.'[51]

Sparrow had been a successful barrister before being elected Warden of All Souls, a post for which his principal qualification had been that he was not A.L. Rowse. His brilliance was never in doubt, though he failed to fulfil his early promise. But when roused from his indolence by arguments he considered sloppy or sentimental, Sparrow became a polemicist as formidable as Hugh himself. He now employed his considerable skills as an advocate to destroy Hugh's case. According to Sparrow, Hugh's analysis of the Warren Report was a 'travesty': an account 'so marred by bias and blotted with inaccuracies that I find it hard to believe that it is written by the honest and intelligent man he is'. Sparrow showed that Hugh had misread or misinterpreted the evidence on which he founded his questions. He warned that such uninformed questioning was dangerously irresponsible. 'Nothing is easier than to create an atmosphere of suspicion, nothing – so long as the crackpots and credulous abound – more difficult to dispel.'

Hugh was staggered, but not yet floored. A fortnight later *The Sunday Times* printed his riposte to Sparrow. He conceded that he had made mistakes, and was ready to eat 'humble pie' in consequence, while insisting that 'vital questions' remained unanswered. Hugh denied that he had suggested the existence of a vast conspiracy: 'I explicitly stated that I distrust conspiratorial solutions.' But a week later Sparrow delivered another blow. 'Concerning his treatment of evidence, Professor Trevor-Roper says that he has had to "eat humble pie". I am afraid I have to offer him a second helping: his further article is as full of inaccuracies as his first.'[52]

By this time Hugh was back in England. On the day after his arrival he appeared on BBC Television's *Encounter*, in a special programme devoted to the subject of the Warren Report. He was questioned on air for half an hour, by a panel of three interrogators: the BBC correspondent Erskine Childers,* The *New York Times* reporter Anthony Lewis and the lawyer and *Observer* journalist Louis Blom-Cooper. The latter confided afterwards to a BBC executive that he thought 'HTR did distressingly well'.[53]

---

* Son of the politician, and grandson of the Irish nationalist and author of *The Riddle of the Sands*, both of whom bore the same name.

Afterwards Hugh flew up to Newcastle and then took a taxi to his parents' home in Alnwick. Together he and his father visited his mother's grave. The next day he was back in Oxford. It was only then that he saw for the first time Sparrow's second letter to *The Sunday Times*. Furious, Hugh told Frank Giles that he thought this response 'dishonest' – 'a series of shameless sophistries' – and wanted to fight another round; he wrote a further letter for publication, but Giles declined to publish it and called an end to the hostilities. 'We all feel that, splendidly worthwhile though the controversy has been, it has now spent itself,' wrote Giles, 'at least in terms of public interest.'[54] A review of the controversy in *The Washington Post* concluded that Hugh had 'started with a bang and ended with a whimper'.[55] Hugh wrote a formal note to Sparrow:

> Mr Trevor-Roper presents his compliments to the Warden of All Souls and begs leave to state that whereas the Warden, in his first article in the Sunday Times, expressed a hope that his personal relations with Mr Trevor-Roper would not be damaged thereby, and whereas nothing in that article did in fact cause any offence, nevertheless, Mr Sparrow's second article, in the issue of 10 January, which he has only just seen, so far transgresses the decencies of debate, and so combines offensive personal language with contemptible sophistries, that Mr Trevor-Roper presumes that the Warden is no longer interested in preserving such relations: which are accordingly severed.

After waiting a few days for Hugh's anger to cool, Sparrow sent him a calm and sensible reply. 'Surely we can agree to disagree,' he urged, 'and perhaps even to argue about this vexed question, and remain friends?'[56] Relations between the two men were soon restored. 'I never forgive but I often forget,' joked Hugh. Soon he resumed sending Sparrow indecent seaside postcards, addressed to 'Warden of All Soles Fishmarket' or 'Warden of Old Soules Prison', as if from ladies of loose morals. Another favourite pseudonym was the cabaret singer 'Maggie Bowra', based on a real *chanteuse* who performed in nightclubs in the Far East.

Most of Hugh's colleagues looked askance at his involvement in this issue. Though he received a letter of congratulation from Christopher Hill (itself an alarming endorsement), some of his usual allies (Raymond Carr, for example) considered his article unbalanced. Others were still more damning. John Archibald, an elderly Fellow of All Souls, wrote to the Warden congratulating him on his 'devastating' demolition of Hugh's arguments. Archibald was extremely critical of the Regius Professor himself: 'What were Trevor-Roper's "qualifications" for the Chair? What serious historical work has he done? My impression of him is of a vain, lightweight, journalistic type with a keen eye to the advertising value of any topic he chooses to write about; and a firm intention to make what he can of it. He produces agreeably written essays on miscellaneous diversified historical subjects but seems to fight shy of any serious historical study.'[57] He felt that Hugh had damaged both his own reputation and that of the Oxford History Faculty.

If Hugh was chastened by the response to his article about the Warren Report, he remained unrepentant. In 1966 he contributed an introduction to Mark Lane's book *Rush to Judgement*, which became an international bestseller. He continued to give interviews and to write on the subject,* though he eventually distanced himself from Lane, and severed relations altogether with Schoenman.

His involvement in the issue was to cause him further embarrassment, after Lane stated in a *Playboy* interview that Hugh had received a private message of encouragement from Robert Kennedy, the President's brother and Attorney-General in his administration. This was seized upon by those who believed in a cover-up, as evidence that the Kennedy family shared their doubts. In fact no such message had been received: the story originated from Xandra, who had indiscreetly repeated a private conversation and had muddled the facts. It was difficult for Hugh to put the record straight without exposing his wife to ridicule, so he kept silent.[58] As a result the *canard* circulates to this day.

Hugh continued to take an interest in the controversy, which showed no sign of abating as the years passed. As late as 1980, he was willing to lend his name to a book by the journalist Anthony Summers, who claimed that the President had been the victim of a right-wing conspiracy.† 'Some details may remain in doubt, but it is now clear that President Kennedy was the victim of a conspiracy,' began Hugh's endorsement: 'a conspiracy in which, it seems, uncontrolled U.S. intelligence agents were involved with embittered Cuban exiles and organised crime.' In maintaining this line, Hugh became increasingly isolated among his peers. Few serious commentators shared his view that there had been a conspiracy to kill the President. A large proportion of the American public, on the other hand, became convinced that there had been both a conspiracy and a cover-up. Books, films and articles on the subject, no matter how tendentious and contradictory, have undermined belief in the Warren Commission. The foreboding of those who tried to defend its findings has proved prescient. Until the attacks on the Twin Towers on 11 September 2001, no event has proved so fertile for conspiracy theorists as the assassination of President Kennedy.

---

* In 1966, for example, he contributed a long article on the subject to the French magazine *L'Express*, 'Qui a tué Kennedy?'
† *The Kennedy Conspiracy* (1980).

There is little doubt that Hugh was damaged by his article on the Warren Report. He was forced to retract a number of his criticisms afterwards. His continuing involvement in the controversy damaged him further. His support for murky conspiracy theories was deplorable, his reluctance to abandon the subject perverse. The episode demonstrated both the positive and the negative sides of Hugh as a controversialist: his independence of mind, his boldness and his determination; but also his rashness, poor judgement, obstinacy and, perhaps, arrogance – qualities which would prove disastrous.

Essayist

Within a week of his return from America in January 1965, Hugh took a train to Cambridge to give the first of his Trevelyan Lectures, collectively entitled 'Whig and Tory History'. The theme reflected his growing interest in historiography. He surveyed the rival arguments of Whig and Tory historians in the two centuries since the Puritan Revolution, from Claren-don to Macaulay. Hugh offered the Lectures to Macmillan. Apologising for the lack of progress with the book on the Puritan Revolution, he wrote: 'I fear the great work goes slowly.' A.D. Peters explained to Rex Allen that his client did not know when he would finish it, or how long it would be.[1]

'I am very busy writing up my Trevelyan lectures for publication,' Hugh reported to Valerie Pearl in the summer. 'As usual, they expand and expand in my hands and threaten to burst any framework I try to impose.'[2] But the Lectures were never published. Instead, shortened versions of three of the Lectures would be broadcast on BBC Radio and published in *The Listener*. The seven Lectures were given weekly, on consecutive Wednesdays. After-wards Hugh would stay overnight in Cambridge, and often his hosts gave a dinner party for him. Xandra joined him on several of these occasions. They stayed twice as guests of Herbert Butterfield in the Master's Lodge at Peterhouse. On another such evening their host was Michael Postan, the Professor of Economic History. Among those invited to the Postans' dinner party was E.H. Carr, whose review of his *Historical Essays* Hugh still strongly resented. Though there were only eight people present, Hugh contrived to avoid speaking to Carr for the whole evening.

At the end of the Hilary term the Trevor-Ropers drove up to the Borders in order to vote in the local by-election, caused by the death of the sitting Conservative MP. The new Conservative candidate, Robin McEwen, was a family friend. Indeed Xandra's brother had been out canvassing for him; 'I had no idea that there were so many slums in Galashiels,' Haig said afterwards. Nonetheless the constituency of Roxburgh, Selkirk and Peebles was regarded as a safe Conservative seat, especially as the Party leader, Sir Alec Douglas-Home, was a local man. Unfortunately McEwen was a dated figure, who wore shooting gloves while electioneering and seemed to exem-plify the 'grouse moor' image that the Tory leadership was trying to shed. He was also a Roman Catholic, which perhaps prejudiced Hugh against

him. McEwen's defeat by the young Liberal candidate, David Steel, precipitated a crisis in the Party, leading to the resignation of Douglas-Home
and his replacement by Edward Heath, a leader thought more suited to the
new age of meritocracy. Hugh thought Steel the best candidate by far.
Xandra voted for McEwen, and had assumed that her husband would do
the same. She was both amazed and horrified when she discovered that he
had voted for Steel. They had driven all the way to Scotland to vote, but
their votes cancelled each other out.

While in California, in the Huntington Library, Hugh had encountered
A.L. Rowse, who cut him dead. Relations with Rowse had never recovered
from Hugh's decision in 1943 not to write for his *Teach Yourself History*
series. More than twenty years later Rowse still begrudged this gesture of
independence from a man he had once considered his protégé. Moreover,
he resented the cracks in Hugh's reviews of his books. For his part, Hugh
admired Rowse's best work, while deploring his 'colossal egoism' and his
intense sensitivity to slights.[3]

Once both were back in Oxford, he wrote Rowse a polite letter of remon-
strance. In response, Rowse invited him to tea. He suggested that this
might provide an opportunity for an *éclaircissement*, to clear the air. Hugh
accepted the invitation, though, as he assured Rowse, he had no wish for
an *éclaircissement*.[4] The occasion does not seem to have been a success. 'You
need not have given so freely of your time yesterday,' Hugh wrote afterwards.

> I expressly wrote that I did <u>not</u> want 'an *éclaircissement*'. And alas, I fear it will
> do no good. The faults of my character, which you expressed with such an
> unsparing hand, are doubtless by now inveterate, past reform. It is a melancholy
> reflexion for me. However, I am glad to hear that your own state is so much
> better. It must be splendid to know that one is absolutely right, financially solid,
> popular in America, and quite independent of this country and its third-rate
> inhabitants. Thank you for portraying our respective characters so vividly. The
> contrast is certainly instructive.
>
> Look here upon this picture and on this, as someone (F. Bacon perhaps)
> somewhere says;* and I have looked at them with great interest. Since you told
> me, while giving me your unsolicited views, that my views were of absolutely
> no interest to you, you saw to it quite logically that I had no opportunity to
> express any of them. But you must allow me now to express one. It is relevant
> and I shall be brief.
>
> You said that the image of Oxford in America was damaged by the evidence
> of occasional intellectual differences here (you mentioned my difference, on the

---

* *Hamlet*, Act III, scene iv. Hugh was alluding to the controversy about the authorship of
Shakespeare's plays, in which both men participated.

origins of the war, with Alan Taylor). I am perhaps less attentive than you to the *nuances* of American opinion, or perhaps we move in different circles on that wide and varied continent; but my own view is that, if anything is likely to damage the image of Oxford, it is the spectacle of one Oxford scholar ostentatiously cutting another 8,000 miles from base. It was for this reason, and for no other, that I sought to establish normal outward civilities with you.[5]

Rowse did not reply for almost a month. When he did so, he reviewed their relations since he had praised Hugh's *Archbishop Laud* back in 1940. He accused Hugh of having written him an anonymous letter, correcting his style and grammar, during the war. Hugh was dismayed by this accusation. He apologised abjectly if he had written such a letter, but insisted that he had 'absolutely no recollection' of having done so. 'It must have been an error, the accidental omission of a signature, or a tipsy deviation. If you have evidence which convicts me, I must yield to the evidence, but I must confess that, short of such evidence, I simply cannot believe it.'

'I fear we shall never agree,' Hugh continued.

You demand total support, and I can only give partial support. I think I have always been quite consistent in my view of your work, both in my public and my private expression of it. I greatly admire the fineness of your scholarship and the vividness and sensitivity which you often achieve in your writing; but the speed and vigour with which you write, and the strength of the opinions which you hold, sometimes entail what seem to me crudities of thought and expression which I do not like. May I not say so? Do you like your flattery to be laid on with a trowel? Do you not appreciate it better – as Gibbon did – 'seasoned with a reasonable admixture of acid'?[6]

In 1965 an appeal was launched for funds to erect a statue of Sir Thomas More in Chelsea. A committee was convened to manage the appeal, including a general as chairman and an admiral as vice-chairman. Hugh was asked to write a 'brief but scholarly account of More's achievement' for the appeal brochure. He sought an assurance that the purpose of the appeal was to commemorate More 'as a national and not as a sectarian figure'.[7] This assurance was given, and Hugh duly produced his piece. At first it was accepted as uncontroversial. But concealed within it was a phrase that offended Father de Zulueta, the fashionable priest who tended the souls of the Chelsea Catholics. According to Hugh, More 'wished for the peaceful re-creation of an undivided, reformed, evangelical, Catholic Church'. This was too much for Zulueta and his Bishop, both of whom insisted on a change to the wording. Hugh refused. 'I am having a merry old time with the Chelsea papists,' he told Valerie Pearl. 'Now on all sides steam is being generated; the general and the admiral are at their wits' end; the bishop and the priest will not budge an inch; there are reports of pope-burnings in the King's Road, *auto-da-fés* in Cheyne Row; and in the end, I fear, Sir Thomas More will be forgotten and Fr. de Zulueta will set up a statue of Torquemada and my friends will set up a statue of Titus Oates ... Who can say that history is determined by purely economic motives?'[8] He did not attend the ceremony when the statue was eventually unveiled, four years later.

In 1960 Xandra had taken her husband to the first night of a play about More, Robert Bolt's *A Man for All Seasons*. Neither liked the Brechtian device of the Common Man,* and they left the theatre during the interval. When he later became friends with the playwright, Hugh was nervous that his wife might let this slip. There was a further twist to this story when the play was being filmed. The director, Fred Zinnemann, asked Hugh if he would be kind enough to intercede with the Duke of Northumberland to let him film a scene on the tidal Thames at Syon Park, the nearest place to London where the bank remained (and remains) undeveloped. Hugh complied, and the Duke consented to allow the filming; but in the event the technicians judged that the mud there was dangerously soft, and decided to seek another site.[9]

Hugh came to know Bolt in September 1965, when they visited the People's Republic of China together, as part of a small group sent by the Society for Anglo-Chinese Understanding (SACU). Hugh, like Bowra, Hill, and dozens of other luminaries, had been invited to become a sponsor of this new organisation by its chairman, the sinologist Joseph Needham.[10] Four years earlier Hugh had been approached by Needham to raise funds to support his multi-volume *Science and Civilization in China*, one of the monumental works of modern scholarship. Hugh venerated Needham as a scholar, though he thought him 'a complete ass' in practical affairs, and arranged for a charity with which he was involved, the Crompton Bequest, to donate £1,000 to the project.[11] Needham had been enormously appreciative.[12]

Hugh had few illusions about SACU. He suspected from the start that it was a Communist-controlled body, but he hoped to challenge that control from within, if not to upset it altogether. At Needham's invitation he joined the Society's Council of Management, together with the actress Vanessa Redgrave, the MPs Philip Noel-Baker, Dame Joan Vickers and Jeremy Thorpe, the physicist Nicholas Kurti, and others prominent in public life. In mid-September he was telephoned and asked if he would like to take

---

* Bolt used this character as a narrator, who at various points stood apart from the action to speak directly to the audience.

Bowra's place on a SACU party going to China at very short notice. (Bowra had been advised by his doctor not to undertake such a strenuous trip.) It was not convenient; but it was a unique opportunity, and Hugh had long been interested in China. He decided to go. Four days later he joined the other SACU 'delegates' at London Airport. Robert Bolt was another last-minute addition to the party, a substitute for Vanessa Redgrave.

In the early 1960s China was still mysterious, inaccessible to foreigners. Indeed, almost the only Britons permitted to visit China were those very few sent by SACU. Even sinologists were dependent on Chinese goodwill for a visa. There was little understanding of the nature of the Chinese regime. Despite the Chinese intervention in Korea in the 1950s, well-meaning Britons saw China as a victim rather than as an aggressor. Those dismayed by the Cold War with the Soviet Union hoped to avoid a similar confrontation with the Chinese.

They flew to Peking via Copenhagen and Moscow. To occupy him on the flights Hugh took *Middlemarch*, at James's suggestion. While changing planes at Copenhagen Hugh was called to the telephone. Denis Hamilton, Editor of *The Sunday Times*, was on the line, with a question: would he write something about China for them on his return? Hugh was non-committal. They were greeted in Peking by a delegation bearing flowers from the People's Association for Foreign Cultural Contacts. A representative delivered a speech setting the tone for the whole three-week stay, which was one of incessant propaganda. At factories, farms and schools they endured speech after speech in unvarying jargon from hand-picked workers, peasants and schoolchildren. Even museum curators parroted the Party line. This was mind-numbingly boring; Bolt, himself a former Communist, likened it to a constant waterfall of stale garbage pouring onto their heads. Escorted from place to place by 'guides', Hugh soon began to feel like a prisoner. No dialogue with their hosts was possible. Any dissent from the official line met with smug smiles, and the response: 'That is because of our different social systems', with the clear implication that the Chinese system was superior. Any questioning beyond the prearranged script was greeted warily, as their hosts weighed the hidden motive for the question and the possible consequences of an answer. Hugh soon realised that not a single statement made by any of their hosts could be taken at face value. He pressed to meet some fellow-historians. Eventually he was taken to the Institute of History, where three 'historians' were paraded before him; all three remained mute throughout, while a spokesman gave an irrelevant lecture on the situation in Formosa (Taiwan).

He and Bolt soon formed an alliance against the other two members of their group – the preening trade unionist Ernie Roberts and the complacent vice-chairman of the Society, Mary Adams – whose comments they found asinine and embarrassing. On several occasions Hugh and Bolt played truant, by getting up early and going out before their guides had arrived, earning frowns of disapproval from their minders. Their programme included a succession of choreographed rallies, parades and firework displays. 'Doesn't this remind you of Germany in the late 1930s?' Bolt murmured in Hugh's ear, at a tremendous performance of callisthenics in the huge stadium in Peking, where thousands of perfectly drilled human automata were nimbly turning themselves into slogans denouncing 'US aggression' and 'American imperialism'. The climax of their visit came on National Day, when they watched an endless procession past the Chinese leader, Mao Tse-tung, then in his early seventies and rumoured to be ailing. The half-million marchers waved wreaths of artificial flowers; in the parade were huge floats bearing gigantic mock-ups of Mao's writings, and models demonstrating Chinese industrial and agricultural triumphs. Afterwards they attended a mass banquet at which Chairman Mao was present. When he shuffled away from the table, assisted by two acolytes, the 5,000 guests broke into screams of hysterical adulation. The old totemic figure showed not a flicker of response.[13]

After three weeks of this Hugh and his new friend were longing to escape. To the rediscovered pleasure of truancy, they now added the euphoria of breaking up for the holidays. Leaving the other two members of their party behind, they flew back earlier than scheduled to London, via Moscow and Amsterdam. To them, the young woman on the KLM desk seemed like 'an angel': the first official they had encountered since leaving the West three weeks before who responded openly to their questions without calculating the consequences. Hugh ordered a bottle of Krug champagne to celebrate their release, before boarding the plane to Heathrow.

On his return he considered resigning from SACU. His experiences convinced him that the Chinese were not interested in understanding the British; they wanted trade and access to Western technical expertise, but no dialogue. He called on his contact at MI5, Richard Thistlethwaite, who provided interesting details about some of the individuals involved with SACU. Thistlethwaite encouraged him not to resign from the Society. Before a meeting of the Council of Management he had lunched with Dick White, who offered him a lift afterwards. Hugh reluctantly declined: to arrive at the headquarters of a Communist-front organisation in the limousine of the Chief of the Secret Service might be indulging his sense of irony too far.

Having considered the matter while he was away, Hugh agreed to the Editor's request to write an article for *The Sunday Times* about his visit. His report appeared on 31 October, three weeks after his return, occupying the whole front page of the 'Weekly Review' and much of the next page too. He described the frustrations experienced by a foreign visitor to China, above all the 'torrent' of self-satisfied propaganda in which the visitor was 'drenched'. But he was careful to say too that he found much to admire. Russian Communism had suppressed the nations of Eastern Europe, but Chinese Communism was a national movement, which could claim not merely to have changed the class structure, but to have restored national independence and pride after a century of foreign domination. He did not believe that the Chinese leaders wanted conflict with the West: 'the Chinese, though loud and threatening in their utterances, are cautious opportunists in their tactics'. He looked forward to a change in China:

> Fanaticism, Puritanism, the fruit of one heroic effort, rarely outlast one generation, and the doctrinaires of one generation are often the bores of the next. The Russians preached world revolution in the 1920s, but their revolution has now been digested. If capitalism in the rest of Asia is detached from 'colonialism' we may well find, in twenty years' time, that the Chinese revolution too will have been absorbed: that history will have reasserted its claims, and 'co-existence', from heresy, will have become orthodoxy in Asia too.[14]

John Sparrow wrote to congratulate Hugh on a 'brilliant, amusing, penetrating and powerful' article: 'I enjoyed every line of it.'[15] Unfortunately *The Sunday Times* headlined the piece 'The Sick Mind of China', a title against which Hugh protested, knowing that it would antagonise fellow members of the Society. 'They will SACU,' punned Bolt. At a public meeting of SACU in London two weeks later, where the four tourists were due to give an account of their visit to China, there were boos and hisses every time Hugh's name was mentioned. In an attempt at restraint he had placed before himself a card on which the words 'PRUDENCE!' and 'MODERATION!' were inscribed in large letters. Just before the meeting was due to close, SACU's deputy chairman Joan Robinson expressed her regret at Hugh's 'distressing lack of manners' in publishing such a 'discourteous' article about his Chinese hosts. The noise in the hall rose to a hubbub. Hugh felt a rush of blood and found himself on his feet, speaking without inhibition or restraint. Afterwards he could not recall much of what he had said. When a reporter from *The Guardian* asked if he planned to resign, Hugh retorted that he had no intention of doing so. Several people came up to congratulate him, including the rogue Communist Isaac Deutscher and the rogue Tory Stephen King-Hall: 'an enjoyable pair', as Hugh described them.

His experiences led him to investigate SACU's operations more closely. Papers were not circulated, votes wrongly recorded and actions taken without due authorisation. The real decisions, he soon found, were made not by the Council of Management but by the 'General Purposes Committee', a less eclectic body. Hugh concluded that the Society had neither proper bureaucratic responsibility in its government nor proper democratic methods in its functioning. Moreover, there was a mystery about where the money was coming from. The nominal treasurer had resigned six months earlier, and a substantial proportion of the funding seemed to originate from anonymous donations. The obvious implication was that the Society was being funded, directly or indirectly, by the Chinese government.

Hugh also took an interest in SACU's local branches, particularly its Oxford branch. With the help of Nicholas Kurti and others he was able to ensure its independence, though this was resented at the Society's headquarters. His continuing investigations put SACU's officers on the defensive. On 15 May 1966 an article appeared in *The Sunday Times* anticipating the climax of 'a bitter struggle' for control of the Society at the upcoming annual general meeting, when members of the Council of Management would be standing for re-election.[16] Just before the meeting, a letter was circulated referring to him by name and deploring 'the introduction of McCarthyism' into the Society's affairs. The letter was signed by Needham, Robinson and Adams, as chairman, deputy chairman and vice-chairman. Incensed by this slur, Hugh announced that he was considering an action for libel. This threat further heightened press interest. At the meeting itself Hugh failed by a few votes to be re-elected. These events, and his subsequent decision to quit SACU, were covered by most national newspapers, attracting much adverse publicity for the Society. Several other sponsors subsequently resigned, including Kurti, Freddie Ayer and the publisher Sir Stanley Unwin.

Events in China would soon overshadow the struggle within SACU. In the same month as Hugh's resignation, Mao launched the 'cultural revolution', initiating a disastrous decade of upheaval that would last until his death. The ensuing violence and chaos would do much to undermine the credibility of Chinese Communism in the West.

What made Hugh so interested in SACU? Why did he persist in its tedious and bruising internal struggle? He was not by nature a 'joiner', as he emphasised in a 1967 *Sunday Times* article, in which he deplored the habit of so many of his fellow-dons in signing pious round-robins condemning the activities of regimes at home and abroad. It was certainly true that he enjoyed combat. But was this a fight worth the time and energy he devoted to it? In his *Daily Mail* column, Bernard Levin marvelled at Hugh's naïveté. SACU, he said, had followed 'the classic pattern of the "front" organisation, in inviting as sponsors many people who were neither Communists nor fellow-travellers, and who indeed were in some cases staunch anti-Communists', while the real power remained in the hands of the true believers. 'I have seen too many of these "Friendship" societies, working indefatigably for a Cause, with a few unworldly figureheads on the notepaper to give them a respectable air, to have any doubts as to the nature of this one,' Levin continued. He expressed surprise that 'Professor Trevor-Roper should have taken so long to hear the yen drop'.[17]

A year after quitting SACU, Hugh accepted an invitation to visit Formosa, the large island off the coast of the Chinese mainland in which the Kuomintang regime had been entrenched since its defeat by the Communists in 1949. He had refused an earlier invitation in the mid-1950s, partly because of his dislike of air travel, and partly because he feared that visiting Taiwan would prevent him from ever visiting China itself. Now he was happy to accept, particularly as the invitation was extended to Xandra. On the flight he read *Wuthering Heights*, another of James's recommendations. The Trevor-Ropers spent almost a fortnight in Formosa, which impressed him as 'a society reformed in depth, confident and prosperous, investing in itself both materially and spiritually'. On the long journey home they spent a few days each in Thailand, Cambodia and Hong Kong. In the latter, Hugh was struck by 'the dreadful contrast between wealth and poverty', and 'felt a hatred of the British Empire'. The difference between what he saw in Hong Kong and what he had seen in Taiwan 'made me ashamed'.[18] After his return, he published an article in *The Sunday Times*, supportive of American policy in the region. 'When I see the beneficent revolution which America has patronised in Formosa, I look a little more sympathetically on its struggle in Vietnam,' he wrote. 'Barbarous in itself, that struggle is part of a wider whole: the rough, inflamed edge of a great social as well as military undertaking.' His article attracted an appreciative letter from his American friend, the conservative columnist Joseph Alsop.[19]

Around 6.00 p.m. one November evening, the telephone rang at No. 8 St Aldates. Xandra, who was alone and ill in bed, answered it. No one spoke at the other end, though she could hear heavy breathing. She replaced the receiver. A minute later it rang again, and again no one spoke when she answered the phone. These calls continued for around two hours, and only once did anyone speak, when a man said, 'This is Martin Bormann speaking. I have a message for Hugh Trevor-Roper.' Then another voice interposed, saying, 'Do not answer any questions, take no notice.' Xandra was confused and frightened, and relieved when her husband returned home around nine o'clock. He sent for the police.

Hugh believed that the calls came from a Nazi sympathiser called Peter Alphon, suspected of responsibility for the notorious 'A6 murders' in 1961; though another man, James Hanratty, had been convicted of this sordid crime and executed by hanging. The case became a *cause célèbre*, and a focus for those trying to abolish capital punishment. Hugh's review of two books on the A6 murders had just been published in *The Sunday Times*. One of these had been written by his old friend, the lawyer Lord Russell of Liverpool. Russell was also being pestered by Peter Alphon, who had called him hundreds of times from telephone boxes, to the point where Russell had felt obliged to take legal action to restrain him.

Through Russell, Hugh became involved in the campaign to clear Hanratty's name. In May 1966 a committee was formed to lobby for the A6 murder case to be reopened. As well as Trevor-Roper and Russell, the other members of the committee were the Labour peer Lord (Fenner) Brockway and Paul Foot, a young journalist who would make a career out of investigating miscarriages of justice. Foot came from a talented family: his father was British Ambassador to the United Nations and two of his uncles were Labour MPs; one of them, Michael Foot, rose to become leader of the Party in the early 1980s. Hugh warmed to Paul Foot, a witty left-winger who had been President of the Union in his last term at Oxford. While an undergraduate, Foot had edited the undergraduate magazine *Isis*, stepping into the shoes of Dennis Potter, later to become a playwright renowned for innovative television drama. Hugh had complained to the proctors, the officials responsible for undergraduate discipline, when Foot's *Isis* introduced critical reviews of University lectures. But he was impressed by Foot himself, whom he described to Russell as 'energetic, sensible and eager to be used'.[20]

Foot had great difficulty in interesting newspapers in the Hanratty case. Several of them turned him down flat when he proposed an article on the subject. Eventually he published a piece in the unlikeliest of places, the society magazine *Queen*. The campaign was successful in getting the case reopened, with inconclusive results until, much later, DNA evidence suggested that Hanratty had been the killer after all. Foot remained interested in the case, and in 1971 published a book on the subject, *Who Killed Hanratty?*

Hugh reviewed Christopher Hill's *Intellectual Origins of the English Revolution* for an American journal, *History and Theory*. 'I am somewhat surprised to find Hill, whose work can be so profound and illuminating, stuck, as it seems to me, in such old-fashioned attitudes,' he commented. Hill's equation, 'Puritan v. Royalist = Modern v. Ancient', seemed to him little more than a rehash of the arguments of the nineteenth-century Whig historians. John Elliott congratulated him on his 'devastating critique'.[21] Hill's book made a case for the Puritan origins of modern historiography, but Hugh demonstrated that Hill had selected only such evidence as supported his case; thus, 'scholarship is transformed into advocacy'.[22] In fact, every reference that Hugh checked should have led to conclusions opposite to those which Hill had drawn.[23] Hugh was offended by what he perceived as a betrayal of scholarly principles in support of a political line. 'Nothing in Christopher's book now surprises me,' he told Valerie Pearl. 'I'm afraid I am totally disillusioned by it and ask myself seriously what has happened to him. I believe he has simply galloped through a mass of often worthless secondary sources, picking out whatever snippets – unverified and often misquoted – seem to the eye of faith to support his predetermined conclusions. Does this seem too strong? It is not: I can document it again and again.' Hugh now put Hill in the same category as Stone: 'I can believe nothing that he says on trust.'[24]

His criticisms of Hill's argument led him to look afresh at Hill's assumptions. It had become a historical commonplace among twentieth-century historians that the intellectual revolution of modern Europe, no less than the commercial and industrial revolutions, had originated in the religious Reformation of the sixteenth century; that, directly or indirectly, Protestant reformers had opened the way to the new science and the new philosophy of the seventeenth century, and so prepared the way for the world to be transformed. Without the Protestant Reformation of the sixteenth century, there would have been no Enlightenment in the eighteenth; without Calvin there would have been no Voltaire. The Whig historians of the nineteenth century had seen the Protestants of the sixteenth and seventeenth centuries as the party of social, political and intellectual progress. The Marxists had grafted this earlier idea of progress onto their own philosophy of class struggle, asserting that the Puritan Revolution was not merely a constitutional revolution: it was also a 'bourgeois' revolution, and the bourgeois revolution was also an intellectual revolution. The new science, the new philosophy, the new historiography and the new economy were all the work of radical Protestants – and the more radical, the more progressive. Puritanism meant progress.

Hugh dissected this theory in another luminous essay, 'The Religious Origins of the Enlightenment'.[25] He readily conceded that the continuous intellectual tradition which led from the Renaissance to the Enlightenment had been watered by Calvinist Holland and Switzerland, and by Protestant England. Intellectual life was undeniably freer, heresy was undeniably safer, in Protestant than in Catholic countries. Yet the new philosophy had triumphed in Catholic France. Voltaire, the towering figure of the Enlightenment, had been French, not English, Dutch or Swiss – though he had fled to Calvinist Switzerland to escape persecution. It was therefore mistaken, argued Hugh, to conclude that the Enlightenment had been the child of Calvin. When we look into the religious origins of the Enlightenment, 'we do not discover them in any one Church or sect. They are to be found in both Churches and in several sects. What is common to the men who express such ideas is that all of them are, in some sense, heretical: that is, they either belong to dissident groups within their Churches or are themselves regarded as unorthodox. The orthodox churches – Catholic, Lutheran, Anglican, Calvinist – look askance at them.'

He rejected the prevalent opinion that the ideas of the Enlightenment had been hammered out in periods of ideological revolution and civil war; 'on the contrary, they had been worked out in periods of ideological peace and *rapprochement*, and were only interrupted and delayed, not furthered by the intervening periods of revolution'. Doctrinal strife resulted in shrivelling of the mind, narrowing of vision and severance of communication. Liberal, rational discussion required openness and tolerance. The three periods identified by Voltaire as pointing forward towards the Enlightenment had all been happily exempt from ideological conflict, and were all, for that reason, times of cosmopolitan intellectual correspondence. The early part of the seventeenth century had been one of the great ages of free exchange of ideas, the era when the phrase 'the Republic of Letters' (one of Hugh's favourites) first came into use.

It was perhaps ironical that such a secularly minded historian should stress the religious origins of the Enlightenment, the Promethean triumph, the moment when men first dared to interpret the world without deferring to God.

Early in 1966 Edmund Blunden was elected the Oxford Professor of Poetry.* Among the defeated candidates was the American poet Robert Lowell, who supported the Civil Rights Movement, and who was strongly opposed to his country's involvement in the Vietnam War. In a letter of commiseration, Hugh told Lowell (whom he had yet to meet) that he had voted for him – perhaps surprisingly, given that he had known the successful candidate thirty years. But Blunden, now seventy, had become a pathetic figure, who found it increasingly difficult to order his thoughts; he was a hopeless lecturer, and would surrender the Chair after only two years on the grounds of ill-health. Replying, Lowell thanked Hugh, both for his vote and for his letter. 'America is full of turmoil now,' Lowell reported; 'the thought of an Oxford vacation was alluring.' (A few years afterwards Lowell would come to Oxford as a Visiting Professor at All Souls.) 'I think I read almost all your pieces,' Lowell continued, 'and read them like poems. Your style cuts that way, and has the virtue of informing.'[26]

---

* The Professor of Poetry is elected by members of Convocation, i.e. Oxford MAs, just like the Chancellor.

Hugh was still reviewing regularly. A grateful friend, Charles Boxer*, thanked him for a review of his book *The Dutch Seaborne Empire*, 'which was certainly much more satisfactory to me than anything that could have been conferred on me in the Honours List'; he hoped that Hugh's recommendation would boost its circulation, 'as you have a following comparable (in numbers) to that of a major pop singer'.[27] However, Hugh had been writing less and less for the *New Statesman*. In 1966 Karl Miller, Janet Adam Smith's successor as Literary Editor, resigned after falling out with the new Editor, Paul Johnson. He soon found another position as Editor of *The Listener*, from which he wrote to Hugh, expressing the hope that he might persuade him to contribute from time to time.[28] Transcripts of Hugh's radio and television talks already appeared in *The Listener*, but after Miller's invitation he started to contribute book reviews as well, and the occasional article unconnected with a broadcast. He also began reviewing for *The New York Review of Books*, founded in 1962 when *The New York Times* (with its influential books section) was on strike. *The New York Review of Books* quickly built up a large circulation and was soon acknowledged as the leading intellectual magazine in the English-speaking world. Robert B. (Bob) Silvers, co-Editor of *The New York Review of Books*, was an Anglophile who gave generous space (too much, some Americans complained) to British intellectuals. Silvers hugely admired Hugh's work, and rated him among the best of his many fine contributors. After a slow start (three reviews in his first four years), Hugh began to write regularly for *The New York Review of Books*, and would continue to do so for the remainder of his working life. He had long argued that the distance between professional scholars and readers had become dangerously wide, and eagerly seized the opportunity Silvers offered him to write long and thoughtful articles, reaching out to a public beyond the confines of the citadels of academia.

Occasionally he could not help subverting his own high principles. In 1966 *The New York Review of Books* printed a letter from Miss Agnes Trollope, responding to a 'most interesting article' by Professor Lawrence Stone, 'in which he touches – alas, too briefly – on an important fact, *viz:* that in Puritan England, and nowhere else, "for reasons which are at present wholly obscure", there was a general practice of *coitus interruptus*'. Miss Trollope reported that she was engaged in a study of the English Civil War in Westmorland, 'in which my ancestors played an energetic part (on the Puritan

---

* A romantic figure, Boxer had been an Army officer before becoming an historian. Despite not having had a University education, he held two Chairs simultaneously: Professor of Portuguese at King's College, London, and Professor of Far Eastern History at the School of Oriental and African Studies (SOAS). Hugh was on friendly terms with Boxer, and sometimes consulted him about Portuguese history.

side), and I am anxious not to miss any of the penetrating and seminal ideas which Professor Stone so casually ejaculates, but which, if correctly received, have a fertilizing effect on my researches'. She solicited the Professor's help, explaining that 'I am not quite sure what *coitus interruptus* is, but it sounds like one of those things which foreigners do so much better than we'. She gave her address as 'The Quern, Buttocks, near Ambleside'.

Stone replied in the spirit of the joke, explaining that 'natural modesty and the Supreme Court forbid me to give detailed clinical answers in public to the intimate questions asked by Miss Trollope'. He recommended a course of reading to begin her 'historico-psychologico-demographico-sexual education'. This elicited a letter of protest from Miss Trollope, who complained that she was being fobbed off with twentieth-century psychological speculation. 'This will not do. I asked for Bread. I have been given a Stone.'[29]

Hugh derived much sport from Agnes Trollope. In two letters to Robert Silvers, he claimed to have met Miss Trollope in the British Museum, 'dressed from head-to-foot in moss-green checked tweed', and to have advised her to write the letter in response to Stone's article. He explained that she was an expert dog-breeder; 'if you ever need a review of a book on basset hounds I recommend that you get in touch with her'.[30] At an Oxford dinner party Hugh suffered a very boring monologue about basset-hound hunting from the wife of an agricultural don. After she had boasted of all the packs of basset-hounds she had followed, he enquired innocently whether she had ever been out with Agnes Trollope's pack in Westmorland. 'Oh, often!' she replied.

In due course the melancholy news was announced that Miss Trollope had passed away. Stone sent Hugh a postcard of condolence. 'So sorry to hear that Miss Agnes Trollope is dead,' he wrote. 'In her short life she brightened many lives – including mine.'[31]

Hugh's female alter ego provided a means for him to hit back at Stone, who in 1963 had crossed the Atlantic to become Dodge Professor of History at Princeton. The article to which Miss Trollope had responded had assessed Hugh's 'general crisis' theory of Court and Country, and found it wanting. 'The Trevor-Roper thesis won't do,' Stone had concluded; 'this ingenious and superficially attractive thesis does not stand up to close examination.'[32] In 1965 Stone published *The Crisis of the Aristocracy, 1558–1641*, a substantial work of the type that Hugh had conspicuously failed to produce. The widening gulf between the output of the two was often commented upon.*

* In 1983 Christopher Hill wrote a letter supporting Stone's claims for an honorary degree. 'Thirty years ago the former Regius Professor, Lord Dacre, launched a biting attack on Lawrence Stone which he has in one sense spent his life refuting. There can be no doubt now that Stone is the better historian. Trevor-Roper's output looks pitiful by comparison.'

Hugh's letters to Valerie Pearl were punctuated by disparaging remarks about the Dodge Professor. 'He is boasting all over England and America that the book is sold out and quite unobtainable,' Hugh told her sourly.[33]

Valerie Pearl, now at Somerville, was appalled to discover that Hugh had done nothing about his own book. 'I cannot think of your 800 pages on the Great Rebellion without writing to you and pressing you to publish it. You <u>must</u> do so,' she urged, offering to help by supplying material from the parliamentary diaries she had been reading in the British Museum.[34]

James tried to pull his stepfather out of the hole into which he had fallen. After reading classics as an undergraduate, he had chosen to specialise in Byzantine history, and following two years as a graduate student he had obtained a research post at Christ Church. During his time as a graduate student he continued to live in a self-contained annexe within 8 St Aldates, where he had witnessed Hugh's struggle to write his magnum opus. James now confronted his stepfather in his study. Nobody else dared to raise this sensitive subject with him. With difficulty James persuaded Hugh to show him what he had done, and to elaborate what work remained. He then proposed a plan, breaking the problem into parts and solving each one in turn. The first of the three volumes was virtually complete, and the second half-written. 'Topping and tailing' these two volumes, with lectures Hugh had already written, would make them publishable. Then he could tackle the third, much shorter volume. After these three volumes had been published, they could be edited down into a condensed, one-volume edition.

Hugh appeared to assent to this proposal. Soon afterwards, however, James was privately furious to find that he had moved on to write about an entirely new subject, the European 'witch-craze' of the sixteenth and seventeenth centuries. Hugh's excuse for striking out in this direction was that he needed something new to supplement a second collection of essays.

Some years later James tackled his stepfather again, urging him to return to the big book on the Puritan Revolution and finish it. 'It's too late now,' Hugh told him. The moment had passed. The explosion of research into the period – much of it sparked by the debate Hugh himself had initiated – meant that the book had become dated. It would have needed complete rewriting to have taken account of so much new material. Indeed, it was arguable that such a synthesis was no longer possible; the effort required to master the ever-increasing number of studies was beyond the capability of any one individual. It had certainly become too much for Hugh, demoralised as he was by his failure to produce a work that matched the standard to which he aspired. The book on the Puritan Revolution remained in manuscript, like an unfinished edifice open to the sky.

This failure cast a long shadow over his career. Though he tried to avoid the subject in conversation, he could not escape it in print. In 1967, for example, a reviewer in *The Times Literary Supplement* of his new volume of essays began by remarking that 'Professor Trevor-Roper's admirers will continue to be disappointed that he has not written a full-length book'.[35] This criticism would be made again and again – so much so that another reviewer suggested that Hugh must by now 'be heartily sick' of the advice that he should produce 'the great book so many people have been expecting from him for so long'.[36] His friends were no less unrelenting than his critics. In particular, Wallace Notestein regularly reminded him of his duty to scholarship. 'I believe that you are on your way to great eminence as an historian,' Notestein predicted early in 1968. In the same letter he identified one of the distractions that prevented Hugh from devoting sufficient time to books. 'I wish you did not have to spend energy on journalism. I cannot say that I find fault with you. But you cannot ride two horses indefinitely and you may be one of the greatest of English historians.' Notestein expressed the wish that 'some foundation would endow you for life'.[37] In the summer he reiterated his hopes 'that you may prove a great honor to the historical profession'. He wished that Hugh could devote all his time to history. 'I am not given to discovering geniuses on every bush,' he remarked, and then, in a PS, he pinpointed another of the distractions that kept Hugh from writing: 'The trouble with controversies is they will take your mind away from history. Historians need leisure and quiet almost as much as poets.' Notestein might have mentioned too the burden of administration; Hugh's letters from this period are peppered with complaints about the 'unending series of committees' which drained his leisure and his energy.[38] A few weeks after his last letter, Notestein again urged that 'the great book on Cromwell' should be done. It was understandable that Notestein, now ninety, should be contemplating futurity.* 'It will be a sin against the gods if you go down to the shades without four or five volumes in which you let yourself go about the whole Cromwellian crowd and the people in London and the country.' He warned: 'I shall haunt you from Hades.'[39]

Hugh replied that he was 'very touched by your kind remarks':

> The trouble is, I am too interested in too many things; and I write so slowly, so painfully slowly, that by the time I have written a chapter I have got interested in something else. And then, there are the delights of idleness: of walking in the country, of scratching the noses of horses, or the backs of pigs; of planting and lifting and cutting trees (I <u>love</u> trees) ... or the pleasures of convivial, social life: of slow monosyllabic conversation, over beer and cheese and pickled onions, in rural inns, or – alternatively – of gay, sparkling dinners in glittering palaces, where (like Rowse) I can listen, with guilty pleasure, to the inane but comforting

---

* Notestein died the following year.

flattery of jewelled duchesses. And then, perhaps most seductive of all, there is the pleasure of total vacancy ... It is all, I fear, very reprehensible. No doubt I should be proof against such worldly seduction. I ought to sit, night and day, in the Bodleian Library or the Public Record Office, 'with learned dust besprent' ... wearing an eye-shade over my nose, and munching a periodic dry bun, in order, by my copying of earlier copyists, to earn my place in some future *Dunciad*.[40]

Hugh never published his magnum opus on the Puritan Revolution. Indeed, for the rest of his lifetime he did not publish a 'big book' of any kind. He failed to live up to the high hopes that many of his admirers had placed in him. His ambition 'to write a book that someone, one day, will mention in the same breath as Gibbon' would never be fulfilled. He might have been a great historian, taking his place in the Pantheon alongside the great historians of the past, from Xenophon to Macaulay. But the mark of a great historian is that he writes great books, on the subject which he has made his own. By this exacting standard Hugh failed. Of the three 'proper' books (as opposed to collections of essays, or *pièces d'occasion*) which he published in his lifetime, only one – *Archbishop Laud* – was on an early modern subject, and that was a book that he later disowned. Another – *The Last Days of Hitler* – was a small masterpiece, but it bore no relation to his historical studies. The same could be said of his third full-length book – *Hermit of Peking*.

No one doubted that he had a brilliant mind; the breadth of his learning was dazzling; he was a superb writer. Such a combination approached genius: Notestein certainly thought so, and he was not alone in this opinion. For such a man to have squandered his marvellous gifts seemed to James, as it did to others, a tragic waste. Of course Hugh had many demands on his time; but he was wonderfully quick in dealing with business that might overwhelm others; and much of his time was occupied, not in duties, but in pursuits he chose himself. Indeed, it is hard to resist the conclusion that he veered into diversions to evade the tasks in his path. And yet, who was to say which route he should take? Life is short, and each of us is entitled to live it how we choose.

No doubt it was wearing to be constantly reminded of the books he had not written. But was he oppressed by a sense of failure? Less, perhaps, than another man might have been. More than most, Hugh lived within his own mind, and was content to do so. In some ways he resembled the scholars of the Renaissance and the early modern period, who loved learning for its own sake, not for the use that might be made of it. Much of the reading he undertook seems to have been for his own pleasure and stimulation, rather than for any practical or professional purpose. Writing, too, was its own reward. Publication was inessential to him.

What makes Hugh's case especially tantalising is the number of books he brought to the brink of completion and then abandoned. His career is littered with the hulks of unfinished works. But the effort was never entirely wasted. Many of his essays were quarried from unfinished manuscripts. This was the opposite of the process recommended by James, to build a book out of already written blocks.

Perhaps he was his own sternest critic, and would never be satisfied by a literary creation that was less than perfect. Perhaps his boldness deserted him when it came to finishing a book and presenting it to the public. Or perhaps he realised that his gifts were best employed, not in writing long books but in essays, suggesting ideas for others to explore at greater length.

Hugh had not intended to publish another volume of essays until he had completed the larger work; but he changed his mind, in response to the demand for certain pieces which were either out of print or hard to find. In February 1966 he set out the rationale for this new volume in a letter to Rex Allen. Most of the essays he wanted to include concerned the Puritan Revolution, but he planned to balance these English (or British) essays with several on European subjects. Indeed the essay most in demand was one such, 'Religion, the Reformation and Social Change', which would become the title essay in the new collection. There was also the related essay on 'The General Crisis of the Seventeenth Century'. He told Allen that he had two other essays on European subjects fit for inclusion: one on philo-Semitism, and another on the witch-craze in the sixteenth and seventeenth centuries.[41] Eventually he decided to omit the first of these two, and to include instead the essay on 'The Religious Origins of the Enlightenment'. This had been written originally for a *Festschrift* in honour of Theodore Besterman, but its natural relation to the other essays persuaded Hugh to include it in this volume. In the preface to the book, he expressed the hope that Besterman would nevertheless regard it as an offering.

When he looked at the essay on the witch-craze in detail, he decided to recast it completely, in response to comments by the French historian Roland Mousnier. Five months later he told Allen that it was 'giving me great trouble, partly because the subject is one of enormous complexity, partly because I have had very little time to work on it this term'.[42] It eventually grew to almost 30,000 words, more than twice the length of any of the others in the collection. He told Valerie Pearl that the witch-craze essay was consuming 'all my time'.[43]

He had a longstanding interest in this subject, perhaps stimulated by Wallace Notestein, who had published a *History of Witchcraft in England from 1558 to 1718* as long ago as 1911. For historians of a more enlightened age, the witch-craze of the sixteenth and seventeenth centuries presented a conundrum: how could one explain this great fear of witches sweeping across Europe, just as the continent trembled on the brink of modernity? How could intelligent and educated men, who seemed in so many ways similar to ourselves, have believed such pernicious nonsense? This extra-ordinary phenomenon was not, as one might imagine, a lingering ancient superstition, but an explosive new force which legitimised murderous per-secution and judicial torture. It was inextricably bound up with the idea of heresy; indeed, to disbelieve in witchcraft itself became a heresy, punishable by death. This was an inversion of the Christian orthodoxy of the Dark Ages, which held that belief in witches was pagan and a mark of the infidel. Hugh's witch-craze essay is permeated with a sense of disgust at the cruelty of the religious zealots towards their victims, their prurient fantasies and their appetite for blood. 'The springs of sanctimony and sadism are not far apart,' he remarked in a footnote. He described one learned divine, 'who would live to a ripe old age and could look back on a meritorious life in the course of which he had read the Bible from cover to cover fifty-three times, taken the sacrament every week, greatly intensified the methods and efficacy of torture, and procured the death of 20,000 persons'.

Hugh was fascinated by the work of the nineteenth-century American historian of the Inquisition H.C. Lea, whose unfinished *Materials Toward a History of Witchcraft* was not published until thirty years after his death. In 1959 Hugh had written a review article about Lea's work.[44] Like other nineteenth-century historians, Lea had interpreted the witch-craze as a last manifestation of ignorance and superstition. In his view, the more intelligent and educated men of the sixteenth and seventeenth centuries paid only lip service to the crude new demonology proclaimed by the Churches. Hugh came to feel that this explanation was insufficient. It was sobering to discover that even the most profound philosophers of the early modern period had subscribed to the witch-beliefs, in all their bizarre details. The witch-craze had to be seen in its social and intellectual context. It flourished in the ideological wars of the Reformation and Counter-Reformation. 'The frontal opposition of Catholics and Protestants, representing two forms of society incompatible with each other, sent men back to the old dualism of God and the Devil, and the hideous reservoir of hatred, which seemed to be drying up, was suddenly refilled.' Hugh drew a parallel between the witch-craze and the grotesque mythology of anti-Semitism in modern times, to illustrate how an apparently rational society can be convulsed by what appear from the outside to be the most primitive of superstitions. The Jew, no less than the witch, was a scapegoat, persecuted for social nonconformity, rather than for doctrinal or other given reasons.

He was pleased with this essay, which he believed to be one of his most important. 'It is a vast subject and I am rash to tackle it,' he admitted to Valerie Pearl; 'but it will annoy Keith Thomas, which (I suppose) is something.' Six weeks later he reported to her that he had finished the article and sent it in to Macmillans; 'if it (a) forestalls and (b) annoys Keith Thomas, I shall be satisfied'.[45]

Keith Thomas was then in his mid-thirties, and already recognised as an outstanding young historian. A pupil of Christopher Hill's, and a Prize Fellow of All Souls (two black marks against him in Hugh's book), he had been elected Fellow and Tutor of St John's College in 1957. As Editor of the *Oxford Magazine*, he had annoyed the Christ Church Mafia by penning an editorial, 'In My Father's House'; this satirised an article by Steven Watson, who had advocated a policy of accepting 'the future leaders of the country' as candidates for undergraduate degrees. The policy was one which had been followed by Christ Church for centuries, of course, but it was easily mocked as inappropriate and outmoded in modern, meritocratic Britain. Thomas had further annoyed Hugh's friends when he had spoken in Congregation against the proposed special decree to award a personal Chair to Dimitri Obolensky. Hugh tried to push through the decree; in the *Oxford Magazine* Thomas urged resistance to the Regius Professor's 'professorial dictatorship'. Hugh complained about Thomas to Valerie Pearl: 'He has lost no opportunity of attacking me in a disagreeable and positively contemptuous manner.'[46]

What seems to have irritated him most was the fact that Thomas appeared as spokesman for the historical avant-garde, disdainful of many of his elders in their reluctance to embrace the methods of the social sciences. This was the thrust of an article Thomas wrote for a special 'New Ways in History' issue of *The Times Literary Supplement* in 1966, 'The Tools and the Job', in which he argued that the time was long past when one could assume that 'common sense and good judgement' were sufficient 'to understand the workings of human beings'. Hugh was mentioned only in passing, as a misguided opponent of professionalism in historical study. According to Thomas, the appearance of Stone's *The Crisis of the Aristocracy* marked 'the transfer of the long-protracted "gentry" controversy to a different intellectual plane'. Stone's arguments were founded on voluminous statistics. While Thomas conceded that these might be challenged, 'the days when the introduction of impassioned rhetoric was thought to advance the understanding of social change are clearly over'.[47]

In fact, Hugh was not opposed to the drift of Thomas's argument, though he resented the terms in which it was made. Thomas's particular interest was anthropology, which he believed would offer new insights into historical studies. This Hugh agreed with. He too believed that history was enriched by the social sciences, by sociology in particular. For many years he had advocated that British historians should embrace other disciplines, as their French colleagues had done. It was not the argument that got up Hugh's nose, but the man making it.

Hugh's relations with Thomas were complicated by his friendly feelings for one of Thomas's graduate students, Alan Macfarlane, who in the mid-1960s was researching witchcraft prosecutions in Essex in the early modern period. Hugh offered himself as a mentor to this young man. Macfarlane was amazed to receive long, informal letters from the Regius Professor, who encouraged him, gave him dinner, invited him to Chiefswood, corrected his prose and helped him to find temporary teaching work. Hugh enlisted his protégé into his campaign against Stone, employing Macfarlane's services to post his 'Agnes Trollope' letters from the Lake District. Macfarlane was interested in anthropology, in which he would eventually make his career; before taking his D.Phil. in history he had already begun an M.Phil. in his new subject, on 'The regulation of marital and sexual relationships in 17th century England'. In their discussions of witchcraft, Hugh was slow to appreciate the fundamental differences between his own approach and that of Macfarlane. At the heart of these was a radically different attitude towards witch-beliefs. As a rationalist, Hugh regarded them as nonsense; as an anthropologist, Macfarlane treated them with respect. Their relations soured after Hugh belittled Macfarlane's criticisms of his witch-craze essay as 'those pernickety little arrows of yours which come whizzing out of your piddling little county of Essex', and dismissed the witch-beliefs of 'your pig-bound peasants'. As he subsequently explained, he had intended these remarks as genialities, but the misunderstanding exposed the deeper differences between them. He had hoped to examine Macfarlane's thesis, and was disappointed when the two examiners chosen were Christopher Hill and the Professor of Social Anthropology, E.E. Evans-Pritchard. Hugh believed that he had been excluded by Thomas, though in fact the choice had been Macfarlane's.[48]

'I don't know which side I am on in the alleged battle between Old and New Historians,' Hugh grumbled to Macfarlane.[49] He had reached his mid-fifties. For so long the *enfant terrible* of Oxford historians, he was now being portrayed as a stalwart of the old guard, a reactionary blocking the way forward. To undergraduates arriving in Oxford in the late 1960s, he seemed an outdated figure, still playing the old tunes that no one wanted to hear any longer. His personal style accentuated this impression: the precisely modulated voice, the tweed suits, the bow-ties, and his insistence on rules that others had discarded as anachronistic. During his lectures he often ordered those undergraduates not wearing gowns to leave.

Thomas reviewed Hugh's second volume of essays, *Religion, the Reformation and Social Change*, in *The Guardian*. 'This scintillating volume should give pleasure to anyone interested in the social and intellectual history of early modern Europe,' he began. He praised the essays as 'superbly digested, wide-ranging, and sometimes very funny'. The essay on the witch-craze was the least successful in the collection, in Thomas's view; 'its socio-logical analysis is distinctly lame'. He described Hugh as 'a master of belles-lettres'; but, 'like Gibbon himself, he is not interested in the doings of peasants'.[50]

Hugh was irritated at being portrayed as out of touch. In a letter to Geoffrey Elton he referred to Thomas as 'that silly young man'.[51] He was reviewing Elton's *The Practice of History*, and had written to say how much he was enjoying it. 'My delight at seeing certain of my – or your – colleagues tossed and gored is only <u>slightly</u> qualified by the glancing blow which I incur on p. 72.' In the review itself he argued that it was 'time a blow was struck for the claims of accurate, traditional scholarship against the smart-alecks of bogus "new ways in history"'. He took a swipe at those writers who

> ... seem to assume that their sociological, anthropological or psychological 'insight' in some way absolves them from the rules of scholarship in the use of 'hard' evidence. They brandish computerised statistics, gargle with sociological jargon, dogmatize about unverifiable sexual practices, and invoke the analogy of Congolese tribes in order to demonstrate theories about pre-industrial England; but they misunderstand their sources, misquote their texts and get their verifiable facts wrong. Mr J.P. Cooper, the late Miss Agnes Trollope, and other scholars have already exposed some of these fantasies ...[52]

No doubt Hugh was thinking particularly of Stone when he wrote these words, but Macfarlane took them to refer to himself. In the published version of his D.Phil. thesis he referred to Hugh's essay in patronising terms.[*][53] Hugh was hurt by this 'sudden, gratuitous attack'.[54] He retaliated in *The Sunday Times*, combining a review of Macfarlane's book with one of another book of essays on witchcraft which included a contribution by Thomas[†] – likening this strike to felling two birds with a double-barrelled shotgun.[55] He was stung by the criticism of his witch-craze article into composing a private memorandum on the subject, in which he argued that the 'furtive sniping' from Thomas and his pupils was misplaced. His witch-craze essay had been criticised for ignoring recent scholarship on

---

[*] Nine years later Macfarlane apologised for 'my rather shabby treatment of you in *Witchcraft*'.
[†] Alan Macfarlane, *Witchcraft in Tudor and Stuart England: a Regional and Comparative Study* and Mary Douglas (ed.), *Witchcraft Confessions and Accusations*.

witch-beliefs in other societies, but Hugh felt that these were irrelevant to the study of the witch-craze, which was a specific phenomenon, internal to the intellectual system of Western Europe; anthropological insights from other societies could shed no light on it.

There was no possibility of reconciling these two utterly different viewpoints. Hugh was encouraged by a letter from Professor Norman Cohn, author of the influential book *The Pursuit of the Millennium* (1957), who agreed that 'the great witch-hunt can be understood only in terms of a specific phase in the history of western Christianity'. He had found Hugh's witch-craze essay 'most illuminating and suggestive', so much so that after reading it he had given up the idea of writing a book on the subject himself.[56] (Cohn later reversed this decision, and published *Europe's Inner Demons* in 1975.)

Despite Hugh's resentment of Thomas's criticisms, their outward relations remained correct. Indeed, Hugh joined Thomas in setting up and running a fortnightly seminar for graduate students on problems in sixteenth- and seventeenth-century English history. Somebody would give a paper, leading on to a more general discussion. Among those who did so were John Elliott, his pupil Robert Evans, Hugh Kearney and a young graduate student who would become one of Hugh's most intimate confidants, Blair Worden.

Religion, the Reformation and Social Change was warmly received. The British edition sold well, and was reprinted regularly, being issued in a second edition in 1972 and a third, revised, edition in 1984. An American edition appeared under the title *The Crisis of the Seventeenth Century*, published by Harper & Row in 1968. A revised edition was published by the Liberty Fund, Inc., in 2001. The book was translated into German, French, Italian, Spanish, Portuguese and Japanese; and besides these, individual essays were translated into Polish, Swedish, Norwegian, Danish and Icelandic.

The European Witch-Craze of the Sixteenth and Seventeenth Centuries was published separately, with slight revisions, as a small book, by Pelican in Britain and by Harper & Row in the United States. A couple of years after it appeared in this form, *The New York Review of Books* printed a long essay by Lawrence Stone, reviewing several books about witchcraft. Its centrepiece was Keith Thomas's *Religion and the Decline of Magic*, which Stone praised as 'a major work of modern historical scholarship'. As for Hugh's slight volume, though written with 'his usual brilliant style and panache', and displaying to the full 'his capacity for bold intellectual synthesis', it now looked 'old-fashioned in its approach and wrong or at best overassertive in all of its main conclusions'.[57]

Hugh refused Robert Silvers's invitation to respond to this review. 'I simplify my life by not reading anything by certain writers, and Stone is one of the many names on this private index. I am afraid that I simply do not regard Stone as a scholar, and I see no point in reading dogmatism.' A young American sociologist, Toby E. Huff, wrote to *The New York Review of Books* to protest at Stone's 'virtually scurrilous attack on Trevor-Roper', which he described as 'untenable'. Thanking Huff, Hugh commented that Stone's work, whenever it was examined, was 'always found to rest on rotten foundations, which are concealed by a flamboyant superstructure'.[58]

Hugh's witchcraft essay had also been published in two parts in *Encounter*, in May and June 1967. *Encounter* was under pressure, after the revelation that it had been receiving secret funding from the CIA. Its co-Editor, Stephen Spender, felt obliged to resign, leaving Melvin Lasky in sole charge. Hugh sent him a letter of support.[59] 'The furore over *Encounter* and the CIA seemed to me farcical,' he wrote in his journal:

> I had always – ever since the Berlin Congress for Cultural Freedom in 1950 – taken it for granted that *Encounter* had funds from the CIA, but since it never refused to publish anything of mine,* and I did not write in the CIA interest, why should I object? The function of writers is to write, not to quibble at the source of their publisher's income. I cannot understand why Isaiah Berlin and Stuart Hampshire make such a fuss about the ideological and financial virginity of *Encounter*. Dick White, who shared my view, was equally puzzled when we discussed the matter ... [60]

---

* Not strictly true: Hugh had offered to write an exposé of SACU for *Encounter*, but Lasky declined.

Ghostwriter

One morning in December 1966 Hugh received a telephone call from Kenneth Tynan, Literary Manager of the recently established National Theatre.* Tynan wanted to consult him privately on 'a delicate matter'. He was hoping to stage an exciting new play by the young German playwright Rolf Hochhuth. The play, entitled *Soldiers*, was a critical examination of the ethics of Allied strategy in the Second World War, particularly the bombing of German cities. Tynan was keen for the National Theatre to show challenging and controversial work that would attract press coverage. But concern had been expressed about an episode in the play suggesting that the British Government had arranged the death of General Sikorski, the Polish Prime Minister-in-exile, in July 1943. Indeed, Hochhuth alleged that Churchill himself had been responsible.

Sikorski had been killed, together with his daughter, several of his staff and a British Member of Parliament, when the aircraft carrying them went down into the sea, soon after taking off from Gibraltar. The sole survivor was the Czech pilot, Edward Prchal. An RAF Court of Inquiry had found that the crash had been an accident. Tynan asked Hugh, as an historian who had worked in secret intelligence, whether he thought it possible that the aircraft had been sabotaged, in an operation authorised personally by the British Prime Minister. There was nothing new in this calumny: it had first been broadcast soon after the crash by Goebbels, to make trouble between Britain and the Poles, and was later taken up by Stalin, for the same reason. Churchill had died in 1965; his reputation was no longer protected by the laws of libel, which defend only the living. Hugh was startled that the National Theatre should consider putting on a play which recycled the smears of the Nazi Propaganda Minister, but he tried to keep an open mind on every issue. He told Tynan that he thought the story inherently improbable, and suggested that if he wanted to take it any further, he should speak to Bickham Sweet-Escott, who had been in the Special Operations Executive (SOE) and was in a better position to know if there was truth in the story. Tynan appeared to lose interest once he failed to obtain the answer for which he had hoped.

---

* The National Theatre Company had staged its first performance on 22 October 1963.

So far as Hugh was concerned, that ended the matter. A couple of months later, however, he heard from Robert Blake that Tynan was persisting in his attempt to stage *Soldiers* at the National Theatre. In his capacity as Lord Cherwell's executor, Blake had protested to the National Theatre's Chairman, Viscount Chandos – not about the alleged 'assassination' of Sikorski, but about the play's depiction of Cherwell as a pernicious influence on the British Prime Minister. According to Hochhuth, Cherwell's advocacy of area bombing had been motivated not by strategic considerations, but as a murderous policy of killing German civilians.[1] Hugh lost no time in adding his voice to Blake's, in protest against this 'outrageous and distorted' picture of their old friend 'the Prof'. Chandos, then Oliver Lyttelton, had been a member of the War Cabinet and a personal friend of both Cherwell and Churchill. He assured Blake that he would resign rather than allow the play to be staged at the National; and his determination ensured that the play was shelved, despite the support of the National's Director, Laurence Olivier. News of its contents caused a public furore. Randolph Churchill attacked the play on television. In Berlin, Hochhuth was booed when he appeared on stage after the first performance.[2] The Prime Minister, Harold Wilson, made a statement to the House of Commons condemning the play as anti-British. Wilson said that the allegations about Churchill's involvement in Sikorski's death should be 'dismissed and brushed aside with the contempt they deserve'.

Hugh deduced that Tynan had misrepresented his views to the National Theatre Board, and this was confirmed by a telephone conversation with Robert Bolt (a Board member), and subsequent correspondence with Viscount Chandos.[3] In a letter to *The Times*, Hugh declared that 'I myself will not believe any account of any private conversation which rests on the authority of Mr Tynan alone'.[4] Tynan demanded a retraction from Hugh, threatening a writ for libel if this was not forthcoming. Hugh sat tight, encouraged by a letter of support from the distinguished lawyer (Lord) Hartley Shawcross.[5] Tynan did not sue. A year later he was himself forced to pay £7,000 in damages after being found to have libelled Prchal.[6]

David Irving's book *Accident: the Death of General Sikorski* was published in the autumn of 1967, to coincide with the German premiere of Hochhuth's play. It was obvious that the two men had collaborated, though Irving was careful not to endorse Hochhuth's allegation of British involvement in Sikorski's death. Hugh praised the book in a *Sunday Times* review:

> In so thorny a subject there are few guides whom I would entirely trust, but one of them is certainly Mr David Irving. His book 'The Destruction of Dresden', published in 1963, showed him to be an ideal investigator: indefatigable in the pursuit of evidence, fearless in the face of it, sound in judgement, clear in

presentation. This new book is a worthy sequel. Mr Irving has used every available document, sought out every surviving witness, tested every statement. His narrative is both fascinating and moving. It conveys at once the mystery and the tragedy of the death of Poland's last independent statesman.[7]

Irving was then still in his twenties. He was a freelance writer rather than an academic historian. Indeed he was self-taught, having no degree and having never studied history at a higher level. Irving depicted himself as standing outside a corrupt Establishment, championing 'real history' against those who would suppress it. Though he made no secret of his extreme right-wing views, he had not yet become notorious. An assiduous researcher with a flair for discovering documents, Irving specialised in tendentious historical works about the Second World War. His *The Destruction of Convoy PQ-17* was found to be libellous of the escort commander, Captain Jack Broome, forcing Irving to pay £40,000 in damages and to withdraw the book from circulation. *The Destruction of Dresden* caused an international sensation, with its horrifying descriptions of carnage in the firestorm created by the Anglo-American bombing raids in February 1945. This book had been highly influential, playing on Allied feelings of guilt about the deaths of German civilians, and on German longing for Allied war crimes to set against those committed by the Nazis. Hochhuth's *Soldiers* exploited these same emotions. It has subsequently been shown that Irving's book hugely exaggerated German casualties.[8]

The text of *Accident* had been extensively revised on the advice of lawyers, blunting its edge. In a bizarre development, the author took out an advertisement in the personal columns of *The Times*, disassociating himself from interpolations provided by the publisher. The published version insinuated that there was more to the story than the author was able to tell. In a letter to *The Times* Irving expressed his 'fear' that the crash had not been an accident.[9] When confronted by David Frost on television, Irving appeared to lose his cool. He abandoned his ambiguous stance, and stated his belief that the British had sabotaged Sikorski's aircraft – a position he has maintained ever since. Hugh was puzzled that Irving should reach a conclusion so much at odds with the evidence. He could only deduce that Irving <u>wanted</u> to reach that conclusion, whatever his findings. He ascribed Irving's perversity to 'a strong political ideology, capable of distorting the evidence which, as a historian, he appeared to respect'.[10] In 1977 Hugh would deplore the fact that Irving had once again trotted out 'this stale and exploded libel'. Irving claimed that what he had written was 'incontestable', and cited as evidence the fact that he had not been sued, either by Prchal or the Churchill family.[11] Of course the Churchill family was in no position to sue, because Churchill was no longer alive.

Hugh corresponded with Irving, and gave him tea when he visited Oxford. Xandra took strongly against him from the start, but Hugh was more tolerant. He admired Irving's energy and his industry. Besides, he had a taste for mavericks and enjoyed the company of outrageous characters, even if he disagreed with their views: Michael Beaumont, for example, the right-wing, pro-German Master of the Bicester, with whom he had hunted before and after the war; or Kenneth de Courcy, the self-styled 'Duc de Grantmesnil', fantasist, convicted fraudster* and Editor of the 'Reds under the Bed' *Intelligence Digest*. Hugh lent Irving forty files of archival material he had collected in the course of his investigation into the death of Hitler – a decision he later regretted when he discovered that Irving was advertising microfilm copies for sale.

In a remarkably friendly letter he commiserated with Irving on his legal 'troubles':

> I must admit that I think you took a risk and perhaps made a mistake, but the consequences are disproportionate, and I greatly regret that a fellow-historian, whose energy and felicity of research I admire, should be involved in such difficulties. I hope that you will not be distracted by them from your serious work. I don't doubt that your courage will carry you through.[12]

Paul Foot, now working for the satirical magazine *Private Eye*, warned Hugh about Irving's connections with the far Right. He commented that the association between the 'trendy lefty' Tynan and the 'fascist' Irving 'must be one of the strangest alliances in British political (or artistic) history'. They were 'wonderfully ill-assorted bed-fellows', agreed Hugh – 'but the bed is provided by Hochhuth'.[13]

In two consecutive numbers of *Der Spiegel*, Hochhuth published a long article defending his claim that Sikorski had been assassinated by the British.[14] This allegation had been founded (at least in part) on evidence provided by Irving, who had identified a name in the diary of the Governor of Gibraltar as 'Sweet-Escott'. Inferring that Bickham Sweet-Escott had been in Gibraltar at the same time as General Sikorski, Irving speculated that he had been sent there to arrange for the General's assassination. But he had misread the name, as Hugh was able to demonstrate, and it was easily shown from other sources that Sweet-Escott could not have been in Gibraltar at the same time as Sikorski. Sweet-Escott successfully sued Hochhuth for libel, with supporting evidence provided by Hugh.

---

* De Courcy was convicted of fraud, forgery and perjury in 1963 and sentenced to seven years' imprisonment. He escaped from police custody by climbing through a lavatory window, but was later recaptured. At Wormwood Scrubs he shared a cell with George Blake. On his release he was picked up from prison by the family butler. Hugh received intermittent letters from De Courcy. In 1982 he and Xandra spent a disastrous holiday at De Courcy's Italian villa.

Hochhuth insisted that he possessed evidence for his allegation that could not be revealed for half a century, provided by a former SIS officer. Hugh responded to Hochhuth's article in a letter to *Der Spiegel*. He showed how Hochhuth had falsified known or ascertainable facts, and invited readers to draw their own conclusions about his further allegations based on undivulged material. Hochhuth responded with his own letter, in which he alleged that Hugh had been acting under the orders of the British Secret Service, that he had chosen to be 'a patriot rather than a scholar', that he had 'piled falsehood upon falsehood' on the instructions of his Whitehall masters, and that doubtless he would be rewarded with a knighthood for having 'sacrificed to his country his integrity as a historian'.*[15] Hugh sought reparation for these damaging statements from *Der Spiegel*, which eventually paid him £6,000 in damages and costs. He donated this money to a struggling postgraduate.

Tynan persisted in his attempts to mount a commercial production of *Soldiers* in London. On 12 December 1968, the play opened at the New Theatre (now known as the Noël Coward Theatre). Philip Toynbee reviewed it in *The Observer*, prompting a letter in response from Hochhuth. When this was published in the newspaper, Hugh pounced.[16] He sued for aggravated libel, linking the letter to *The Observer* to the letter to *Der Spiegel*. Though it was hard to see how the former could be regarded as libellous, *The Observer* quickly surrendered, publishing an apology and a retraction, and paying Hugh a settlement of £500 plus costs. Hochhuth was left alone to defend the action. In his affidavit to the High Court, Hugh admitted that he had not suffered much embarrassment or distress as a result of Hochhuth's words. 'I acted primarily because Hochhuth was seeking to taint the stream of historical evidence by attributing to Sir Winston Churchill a treacherous assassination and murder.' However, Hugh had a personal motive too: to defend his reputation as a serious historian against the charge that he was 'a hack of the British Secret Service, writing known falsehoods at its instigation'. The judge's comments made it obvious that his sympathies were wholly with Hugh, and he awarded the Regius Professor damages of £2,000 against the playwright.[17]

In 1969 a 'devastating' book appeared about the attempt to pin Sikorski's death on the British Prime Minister, *The Assassination of Winston Churchill* by Carlos Thompson. *The Sunday Times* published a favourable review. 'At the end of his long and complicated inquiry,' wrote the reviewer, 'not a shred of convincing evidence remains to support the allegations against Churchill.' The review appeared under Robert Blake's

---

* Irving often addressed his letters to 'Sir Hugh Trevor-Roper'.

name, but it was 'ghosted' by Hugh, because he was advised that his legal action might be compromised if it appeared under his own. The review ridiculed *Soldiers* as a 'drivelling farrago of nonsense', and condemned its 'cowardly posthumous charge' against a great man unable to defend his reputation.[18]

The journalist Susan Barnes (wife of the Labour politician Tony Crosland) interviewed Irving for *The Sunday Times Magazine*.[19] She consulted Hugh about him beforehand. In reply, he admitted that 'Irving does fascinate me – precisely because I cannot discover his motivation'. He was sure that Irving was not motivated solely by financial considerations. 'This is what makes his personality enigmatic, interesting, and perhaps dangerous.'[20]

In the long vacation of 1967 Hugh travelled north to St Andrews to give a paper to the second international congress on the Enlightenment, following the one held in Geneva and inaugurated by Theodore Besterman four years earlier. He had decided to speak on that phenomenon that so fascinated him, the Scottish Enlightenment. Predicting that this choice would not be welcomed by some Scottish historians, he told Valerie Pearl, 'I am insuring my life before the date of delivery'.[21]

He began by inviting his audience to appreciate the extraordinariness of the Scottish Enlightenment: that a country derided as one of the most backward corners of Europe should transform itself in a mere half-century or so into the intellectual capital of the world. Yet this was a problem from which modern Scottish historians 'turn impatiently away':

> Not for them, in this century, the sociological curiosity, the "philosophic history", which their predecessors may claim to have founded. They prefer to reiterate their atavistic war-cries: to remember Bannockburn, or to debate, for the thousandth time, the admittedly very debatable virtues of Mary Queen of Scots.

He described the primitive condition of pre-Enlightenment Scotland with relish: 'a by-word for irredeemable poverty, social backwardness, political faction'. A mere twelve miles from Glasgow, a simple cart could draw an admiring crowd, as if it were 'a satellite from the moon'. Scotland's universities were 'the unreformed seminaries of a fanatical clergy'. In the middle of the seventeenth century 'a brief flicker of Enlightenment had been reflected from the pikes and muskets of Cromwell's army', before Scottish learning 'relapsed into a dark age of its own'. Indeed, by 1700, the Church of Scotland was 'as obscurantist as the Church of Rome had ever been'. To 'those horrified Englishmen who visited it, Scotland was a mere desert, inhabited (if at all) by barbarous people whose whole way of life was at worst nasty, at best unintelligible. Returning travellers wrote of it as they might write of a visit to Arabia: those long treeless wastes; the squalid towns in the plains; the savage, unvisited tribes in the hills; the turbulent tribal chieftains; the rabble-rousing mullahs with their mysterious religious organisation.'

Hugh turned Weber's argument about the progressive influence of Calvinism on its head: in Scotland, Calvinism had been a force inhibiting progress and the free exchange of ideas. It was the heretics who had regenerated the structure and content of University teaching and enabled liberal ideas to spread, 'even inside the Kirk'. It was the outsiders, those exiled by historical events, who had returned to introduce new ideas into Scotland. In fact, claimed Hugh, almost every Scotsman of intellectual distinction at the opening of the eighteenth century 'was at least half a Jacobite'. This was an inversion of Whig (and Marxist) history, which portrayed the Jacobites as romantic reactionaries.

It was only to be expected that Hugh would stress the 'liberating effects' of the Union with England. 'It enriched Scotland materially; it enlarged its intellectual horizons; it transformed its society.' He contrasted the anglicised 'union dukes' of Argyll and Queensbury, living in princely splendour at Inverary and Drumlanrig, with the unreformed Lord Lovat at Castle Dounie, 'surrounded by 400 retainers gnawing mutton-bones and sleeping on straw'.

Hugh considered the principal figures of the Scottish Enlightenment – Francis Hutcheson, David Hume, Adam Ferguson, William Robertson, Adam Smith and John Millar – and asked himself what linked them: 'all these men were interested, above all, in the social behaviour of mankind'. What had sparked this interest, argued Hugh, was their discovery, 'in the full light and freedom of the eighteenth century', that their own society was archaic; this realisation, he believed, was as intellectually potent as had been the sixteenth-century European discovery of America: forcing the Scots to examine themselves afresh.

There was plenty in this argument to irritate patriotic Scotsmen; Hugh knew exactly where to touch their sorest spots. Indeed, it is hard to avoid the conclusion that he intended to provoke an angry reaction. 'I fear that the Europeans enjoyed it more than the Scots, who mumped furiously in the background,' he wrote afterwards to Wallace Notestein.[22] This lecture confirmed Hugh's reputation as a Hammer of the Scots, and equally the response to it confirmed his impression that historians in Scottish history departments were inward-looking and intolerant, clinging to a nationalist narrative. When another conference on the Scottish Enlightenment was convened in Edinburgh in 1970, Hugh was 'banned' from attending.[23] Yet the very fact that the conference was being held at all could be attributed to him. Over subsequent decades, historians from around the world became absorbed by the problem of the Scottish Enlightenment. While Hugh's interpretation was disputed, he was recognised (albeit grudgingly in some quarters) as having initiated the debate.[24] Hugh had found this problem in a dark, neglected corner and had dragged it into the open.

A few months after giving his lecture on the Scottish Enlightenment, Hugh first met a woman whose work he had admired for some years. Three years earlier he had written a laudatory review of Frances Yates's *Giordano Bruno and the Hermetic Tradition*; to read it, he said, was 'an intellectual adventure'.[25]

At the time of the book's publication, Frances Yates's name was barely known. Already sixty-five years old, she emerged only diffidently from the relative obscurity of the Warburg Institute, with which she had been associated since the war. She was unmarried, and lived quietly in Surrey with her sister. Her appearance was homely; but it belied her real intellectual power. 'She was so liberal in her communication, so eager and friendly in discussion, and spoke with such open charm, and with such a gleam in her eye,' Hugh wrote after her death in 1981, 'that I often saw her not as the formidably erudite scholar which she was, but as a benevolent, matronly lady, over-generous in her distribution, in a village sweet-shop.'[26] Idealistic and unworldly, she had pursued her own studies almost independent of others, and as a result her work was so original as to open up, for those who could follow her there, a new area of intellectual history. Hugh would be one of her earliest and most steadfast supporters. Some thought his enthusiasm for her work eccentric; others that it did him credit.

She wrote to thank him for his 'splendid' review, and a correspondence began. 'I read everything you write with the greatest interest,' he told her, and complained that her writings were sometimes hard to find. At his request, she sent him offprints.[27] Respectful comments peppered his letters. At his invitation she presented a paper to the graduate seminar in Oxford which he ran in conjunction with Keith Thomas. Soon afterwards he suggested they move on to first-name terms. She came to stay at 8 St Aldates, more than once, and he gave a dinner party in her honour. At Hugh's recommendation she became a client of his agent A.D. Peters. He worked hard to secure funding for her research, and to ensure that she was 'properly appreciated and properly rewarded'. Her fame spread: she was awarded a string of honorary degrees and honorary Fellowships, and in 1967 she was elected a Fellow of the British Academy. In 1970 she would be Ford's Special Lecturer; in 1972 she was appointed OBE, and in 1977 DBE. Hugh's unflagging admiration and encouragement had become essential to her, as she acknowledged on several occasions. 'You have been, and are being, a tremendous help to me, above all for your belief in the value of my work which encourages me more than I can say,' she told him.[28] In 1972 she would ask him to read the typescript of her book *The Rosicrucian Enlightenment*, which he described as 'splendid'. He referred more than once to the sense of excitement it gave him: 'reading your book I find myself quite breathless!'[29] To coincide with publication of *The Rosicrucian Enlightenment*, he wrote an appreciation of her career in *The Listener*:

> If I were asked whom, among living English historians, I most admire, I should have no difficulty in answering the question. There are many historians whose work I would always read for their insight, their power, their technical virtuosity or their style. But Frances Yates has a gift which transcends all these. It is the power not merely to answer old problems but to discover new, not merely to fill in details but to reveal a new dimension which alters the whole context in which those details must be seen. She does this by a technique which is very simple to state but very difficult to acquire: by recreating the mind of the past.[30]

In January 1963 Kim Philby had disappeared from his home in Beirut, aware that MI6 was closing in on him. The news of his defection became known, though the public remained unaware of his significance. Six months later he surfaced in Moscow, from which he sent a personal message to his nemesis Dick White. 'You have won this round,' it read, 'but I assure you that I will win the last.' What he meant by this became clear a few years later, when it was revealed that he had written an autobiography, soon to be published in the West. Philby would undermine confidence in the Secret Service by depicting its officers as privileged idiots, hopelessly out of touch with the modern world. It served Soviet interests to depict Britain as a morally bankrupt, class-ridden society. Though no longer useful as spies, Philby and his associates could still function as agents of Russian propaganda.

Responding to the imminent publication of Philby's memoirs, *The Sunday Times*, now edited by the dynamic Harold Evans, began an investigation. Evans assigned his 'Insight' investigative team to the story. One of their reporters, Phillip Knightley, made the startling discovery that Philby had been head of MI6's anti-Soviet section. Evidently he had been much more important than previously realised. Prompted by the fact that their rival newspaper, *The Observer*, was running a story with Philby's ex-wife Eleanor, *The Sunday Times* began to publish their findings on 1 October 1967. These were followed by an interview with Philby himself, conducted in Moscow by their reporter Murray Sayle. Meanwhile an arrangement was made with the publisher André Deutsch to publish the *Sunday Times*'s revelations in book form. Hugh was paid a special fee of £250 in appreciation of his assistance with the story. On request, he wrote an introduction of 4,000 words, but in the general atmosphere of excitement there seems to have been some confusion, since it turned out that the bestselling novelist John le Carré (another former 'spook') had also been asked to provide an introduction to the book, and that his would take precedence. Hugh accepted this as a *fait accompli* and withdrew his piece, only to find that *The Sunday Times* still wanted to publish it as a 'commentary' alongside le Carré's introduction. 'What a muddle!' Hugh exclaimed to his agent.[31]

At Dick White's request, Hugh lunched with him at a quiet French restaurant on Northumberland Avenue, just down from Trafalgar Square. Hugh made a record of their conversation soon afterwards. White was angry about the Russian tactic of encouraging defectors to publish memoirs designed to embarrass their former colleagues. On his side he was inhibited from publicising recent MI6 successes. The British policy of reticence played into the hands of the Russians. White was highly critical of le Carré, whose introduction mirrored the line taken by Philby. Le Carré's bestseller *The Spy Who Came in from the Cold* had suggested a moral equivalence between East and West; his introduction to the *Sunday Times* book depicted Philby's SIS colleagues as smug representatives of a fossilised Establishment. White was indignant about the 'present nihilistic attitude' of the press and the other media. He blamed much of this on the inept handling of the press by the Prime Minister, Harold Wilson. Unofficially White encouraged Hugh to publish something about Philby, as a corrective to Russian propaganda and ill-informed Western comment.

Of course, Hugh shared Philby's low view of their wartime SIS colleagues. He told White that nothing would persuade him to defend such people. On the other hand, he thought highly of White and his MI5 colleagues, and had been in a position to know that British Intelligence had outwitted the Germans time after time. Hugh admitted that he was fascinated by the Philby affair, partly because of his familiarity with the man himself, and partly because of the psychological difficulty of understanding his motives. Together they reviewed Philby's career in the light of his defection. Hugh questioned whether Philby had been in a position to do much harm – apart from the Volkov affair,* the event that had convinced White of his treachery. He offered his view that the prime function of important Communist agents in the West was not to supply information but merely to ensure their own survival and promotion, so that they might be in key positions when action was needed. White indicated that he had

---

* In 1945 Constantine Volkov, a Soviet intelligence officer serving in Istanbul, contacted the British, indicating that he wanted to defect. He offered to reveal the names of Soviet agents working for MI5 and MI6, including an un-named senior officer in counter-intelligence, afterwards assumed to have been Philby. Philby himself was asked to handle the matter, and betrayed the would-be defector to the Russians. As a result Volkov was forcibly returned to Moscow and executed. Le Carré used some details of the affair in his novel *Tinker Tailor Soldier Spy* (1974).

evidence supporting this view. His parting words were that it had been 'a pleasure to discuss the problems on a sophisticated level, after discussing them, at an abysmally low level, with the Prime Minister and Colonel Wigg'.*[32]

Hugh reached an agreement with the Associate Editor, Leonard Russell, to publish two long articles about Philby in *The Sunday Times Magazine*. He worked hard over the Christmas holidays to produce a text of almost 30,000 words. But in January Russell sent him a cringing letter, apologising abjectly for the fact that he had once again been displaced: the *Magazine* had commissioned a substantial piece from le Carré, which had already gone to press. 'This is really too mortifying,' Hugh complained to Russell; 'does not the editor co-ordinate these things?'[33] Evans agreed to raise his retainer, which had remained at the same level since it had been agreed in 1953, from £1,000 to £1,500 p.a.[34] Hugh was still keen to have the opportunity to express his own views on the subject, since he felt that le Carré's introduction was inaccurate and gave 'a grotesque slant to the book'. He wrote directly to Evans saying that he did not wish to be associated with le Carré 'under any circumstances'.[35] Instead he arranged to publish the article in *Encounter* – and later, with minor alterations and together with his essay on Admiral Canaris, as a short book, *The Philby Affair*, published by a small, independent firm, William Kimber, after it had been rejected by Macmillan.[36] He dedicated the book to 'D.P.R.': Patrick Reilly, the man responsible for blocking Philby's promotion after the war.[37]

In writing his article Hugh drew on his own experience of Philby. He placed his subject in the context of his generation – his own, since Philby was only two years older than him. To explain why Philby was attracted to Communism he recalled the time of the Spanish Civil War and the Popular Front against the mounting aggression of Hitler and Mussolini. 'In those days many of us believed that the communists were merely the most radical of our allies against fascism, the militants on the extreme left of an equal coalition in which men agreed to differ with mutual respect.' Hugh reviewed Philby's career within SIS, just as he had done over lunch with White. Acknowledging that Philby had been a pleasant and efficient colleague, he contrasted his own 'stormy' passage in the Secret Service with Philby's 'calm and steady course'. In considering the damage that Philby had done, Hugh made the point that White had felt unable to make officially: that Philby 'was but one passenger in a two-way traffic, and that while he was working for the Russians in Britain, some thirty Russian employees of the

---

* George Wigg, Labour MP for Dudley, had been a professional soldier before entering Parliament, rising to become a lieutenant-colonel in the Education Corps. As Paymaster-General in Harold Wilson's Government, he served as the Prime Minister's link with both MI5 and MI6.

KGB defected, with their secrets, to the West'. Hugh's *Encounter* article was a counterblast to 'the professional critics of all our institutions who have come out to make their hay on this occasion'. Prominent among these was le Carré, whose introduction Hugh condemned as 'a rich, flatulent puff'. Hugh argued against what he described as 'Mr Le Carré's general thesis, that the Secret Service is a microcosm of society – a rotten microcosm of a rotten society – and that each can thus be used to explain the other'. In a piece for *The New York Review of Books*, Hugh was still more critical of le Carré's 'vapid and vulgar' preface, which he described as 'an exercise in pretentious, rhetorical class-hatred which nowhere touches any point of fact'.*[38]

Philby's *My Secret War* was published too late to be available to Hugh in preparing his article. 'Philby's memoirs are deplorably good,' he reported to Harold Evans, when he eventually laid his hands on a copy of the American edition. 'He is <u>dead</u> right on certain characters (alas, his sketches of them are unpublishable in England): but of course he gives absolutely nothing away.'[39] Hugh was able to incorporate references to Philby's memoirs when his own piece was republished in book form. He drew particular attention to the fact that Philby had consistently depreciated White: 'the man whom, more than any other, he recognises as the author of his ruin and on whom he would fain be revenged'. Hugh believed that Philby's 'hatred and jealousy' of White was manifest.[40]

Hugh received several letters of congratulation on his Philby article, among them one from Dick White. 'I feel I must drop you a line to say how much I enjoyed and admired your piece about Kim,' wrote White, who had not seen it, and indeed had stipulated that he did not want to see it, before publication. George Kennan wrote to tell Hugh that he had read the article with 'intense admiration and satisfaction'. He thought it 'brilliantly perceptive' about the 'Western-intellectual captives of the communist movement', and that it contained 'the soundest and most perceptive comment on the role of secret intelligence that I have seen anywhere'. From another source he learned that copies of his article were being circulated within the CIA. Noel Annan was especially enthusiastic. 'It really was a most masterly article and exposes the maunderings of Muggeridge for what they are and the rubbish of le Carré, and all the other would-be experts on espionage,' enthused Annan. 'It contained splendid passages of irony about some of those extraordinary people who graced MI6 during the war; but what it really did – if anything can – is to put an end to those awful crude journalistic generalisations about the Establishment and the operations of Military Intelligence.'[41]

---

* In 1979, in a *Daily Mail* review of the television adaptation of le Carré's *Tinker Tailor Soldier Spy*, Hugh would describe him as 'a sensitive and thoughtful writer'.

On the other hand, Hugh's disdainful comments about his former SIS colleagues, in his article on Philby and elsewhere, made him deeply unpopular in those circles. One of these (a former Christ Church man) wrote to Hugh in response to an invitation to a college dinner, doubting that any former member of SIS would attend an occasion organised by him.[42] Despite this snub, Hugh failed to appreciate at the time how much offence he had caused.

Unexpected congratulations came from Philby himself, sent from a postbox address in Moscow. 'My dear T-R,' the letter began, 'I am delighted to see from your photograph in Le Figaro of April 1 that you seem to be growing younger with the passing years.' He explained that he was writing 'partly to offer you my greetings, partly to thank you for the many kind things you said about me, partly to comment on a few of your remarks'. Philby strongly denied that he nursed any special antagonism for White. 'The fact is that from 1951 I was quite sure that a whole string of security officers thought me deeply, if not wholly, suspect. I have never had reason to single out White as any more dangerous than the others.' Philby pooh-poohed any suggestion that he was psychologically abnormal. Malcolm Muggeridge (who had worked for Philby during the war) had written an article linking Philby's career as a Soviet agent with the fact that his father, the Arabist Harry St John Philby, had become a Muslim; Philby commented that 'such long-range psychiatry is fun and helps to fill a column, but it serves little else'.* Philby picked on Hugh's use of the word 'treason', and queried what was meant by the term. 'We could spend many days motoring around Iraq and discussing this without getting much nearer agreement,' he suggested. 'Of one thing I am certain: I should enjoy it immensely.' In closing, Philby referred to the fact that he was writing on the last day of April; 'Tomorrow I shall toast you, with deep sincerity, in one of my May Day glasses of champagne.' He signed himself 'Yours ever, Kim'. Afterwards he added a sentimental postscript: 'I am grateful for the chance that enabled us to fight together, for a time at least, on the same side.'

Hugh did not respond for some time. No doubt he consulted his former colleagues about whether it was right to do so. At last, almost five months later, he wrote a magnificent reply† which reciprocated Philby's cordiality (addressing him as 'My dear Kim'), while utterly repudiating what he had done:

> I always enjoyed your company, always look back on it with pleasure, and
> I appreciate your remark that you would enjoy a long discussion with me now.

---

* Hugh agreed with Philby on this point.
† There is no proof that he ever sent this letter, a copy of which he kept and which he appears to have typed himself.

But if we had few serious discussions in the past, how could we possibly have any in the future? Discussion needs common ground on which to stand, how deep down soever it may lie; and where could we find such ground now?

... You justify the treachery, the hypocrisy, the purges of the Stalinist period as a mere temporary phase, a necessary form of Caesarian surgery without which the next stage of progress cannot begin. I'm afraid I cannot accept such apocalyptic reasoning, nor could I find any basis for discussion with anyone who could seriously argue that Chamberlainism was an immutable, permanent 'evil', justifying total repudiation, while Stalinism was a temporary necessity, deserving permanent, unqualified support.

... To serve a foreign power, even to spy for a foreign power, does not seem to me necessarily treason. It depends on the foreign power, and the conditions of service. At most, it is mere political treason. But to serve unconditionally, to equate truth with the reason of state of any power, that to me is treason of the mind; and to make this surrender to a form of power that is cynical, inhuman, murderous, that to me is treason of the heart also.[43]

Hugh's propensity to express himself without inhibition exposed him to a charge of anti-Semitism, after his review of a book entitled *The French Enlightenment and the Jews* appeared in *The New York Times Book Review* under the provocative heading 'Some of My Best Friends are Philosophes'. In trying to explain the phenomenon, he had written that 'we must therefore face the possibility that there is an objective basis for anti-Semitism in the continuing Jewish way of life'. As he would explain, Hugh meant merely that the continuing distinctness of Jewish social life in the Dispersion was a cause of prejudice against Jews. For him, this was no more than a social fact, and certainly not a value judgement; but he failed to take into account the sensitivity of many of his readers. Angry complaints from the book's author, Arthur Hertzberg, forced the reviewer to defend himself. 'My own views,' he replied, 'are quite different from those which Mr Hertzberg unwarrantably attributes to me.' He did not want total assimilation.

The concept of 'one world,' whether it is the world of Western or Eastern uniformity, of capitalism or communism, of Catholicism or 'Reason,' or of that dreariest of abstractions, 'the common man', is repugnant to me. I prefer a complex, plural world of diverse and competing social organisms. This is not merely because I find emotional satisfaction in variety: it is also because I believe that such multiformity is the best guarantee of human liberty and the best basis for intellectual vitality. In political philosophy I am a Whig: I believe, with Montesquieu and Hume, in the equal validity of different social forms, and, with Burke and de Tocqueville, in the organic strength and corrective balance of a complex society nourished by living traditions. In intellectual matters I believe in the rivalry of co-existing schools and traditions of thought: in heresy and variety, not in unity and uniformity. On both counts I wish to see the Jews (and other minorities) retaining their distinct social character, in as many varieties as they like. I do not wish to see them, or any other non-conformists, reduced to the blank conformity of an identical, and therefore banal society. I agree with Mr Hertzberg that such a demand is arrogant. It also seems to me vulgar. It is precisely because I see positive value in variety that I am interested in the historical function of minority groups and their traditions, and have shown this interest by writing, from time to time, about English Catholics, French Huguenots, Quakers, Hutterites, and Jews. The general philosophy which I have just expressed is, I believe, implicit or explicit in everything that I have written.[44]

Hugh received a private letter of support on this issue from Moses Finley.[45]

The charge of anti-Semitism was made against him again the following year, this time by the journalist Henry Fairlie, in an article on the revival of anti-Semitism in America in the New York monthly *Interplay*. Fairlie had an old score to settle with Hugh, who had criticised his 'Establishment' article in *The Spectator*.* The charge was vigorously denied by Hugh's old friend and colleague Max Beloff, who described the accusation as 'absurd'.[46] In a letter to *Interplay* he testified that Hugh was known both as 'an untiring exposer of Nazism' and as 'an admirer and friend of the State of Israel'. He mentioned that Hugh's articles on Jewish themes had attracted admiring notices from Jewish scholars, and drew attention to the fact that Hugh had been the guest of honour and principal speaker at the 75th anniversary of the Jewish Historical Society of England. Beloff thought it 'improbable' that such a society would have chosen for such an event 'a non-Jewish historian against whom a charge of even the mildest kind of anti-Semitism could be brought'. He suggested that only a very forthright withdrawal and apology would satisfy 'Professor Trevor-Roper's many admirers, Jewish and gentile, in Britain, in Israel, and the rest of the civilised world'.[47]

After Beloff's letter was published, Melvin J. Lasky wrote to Hugh to say that he was pleased to see that in a subsequent issue of *Interplay* Fairlie had apologised for his 'ridiculous' accusation. He was less pleased by Fairlie's 'sly paraphrase' of his own private letter of reproof, which made it appear as if he had adopted 'some kind of middle-of-the-way position'. He wanted Hugh to know his sentiments were unambiguous, so that there could be no possible misunderstanding. Hugh was no anti-Semite.[48]

*

* See page 265.

Another of Hugh's pieces in *The New York Review of Books*, this time of a biography of Gibbon, provoked a letter of objection from A.L. Rowse. 'No doubt Trevor-Roper felt that he could have written the book better,' speculated Rowse; 'Then why does he not do it, instead of so much "smart-alec" journalism ...? We can all perceive, and enjoy, Trevor-Roper's self-identification with Gibbon. The only difference is that Gibbon wrote *The Decline and Fall*. And, what, pray, has Trevor-Roper to show for it at a comparable age?'

'I admire Gibbon and obviously know more about him than Dr Rowse,' replied Hugh, in a letter published below Rowse's; 'but it has never occurred to me to identify myself with him, any more than Dr Rowse (I presume) would identify himself with Shakespeare or Queen Elizabeth; so I shall charitably overlook the good doctor's concluding irrelevancies.'[49]

Hugh wrote privately to Rowse, to suggest that it might have been better for him to have addressed his letter from 'the Californian institution from which you wrote', rather than 'your summer cottage' at All Souls. This produced a predictable eruption. 'You must know by now how generally detested you have made yourself,' Rowse fulminated. He excoriated Hugh's letter as (a) impertinent, (b) offensive, and (c) incorrect. 'Why <u>are</u> you so <u>nasty</u> to people?'

'What a genius you have for what the lawyers call, in their specialised language, "vulgar abuse",' replied Hugh. 'It is hard work offering you peri-odical olive-branches, when they are invariably snatched up and swatted in one's face.'[50] To relieve his feelings he began to compose a satirical portrait of Rowse. In 1967 *The Spectator* had published, pseudonymously, his parody of John Aubrey, a 'brief life' of R.H. Dundas, described by Hugh Lloyd-Jones as 'a masterpiece'.*[51] Hugh disclaimed authorship, speculating that, if not a genuine Aubrey, it might have been written by his Christ Church colleague J.I.M. Stewart.†[52] The Editor of *The Spectator*, Nigel Lawson, who had become friendly with Hugh in his undergraduate days at Christ Church in the 1950s, protected his anonymity. Now Hugh began to circulate to a restricted number of close confidants another 'interesting document' which he claimed to have discovered in the Bodleian. Like the brief life of Dundas, this purported to be an unpublished Aubrey manuscript, a 'brief life' of 'Dr A.L.R. of Old-soules' college':

> He has a thin, exile voice, but harsh like a corncrake: no witt or warmth to soften it; and very shrill when at boasting or abuse (its usual office). But he can purr

---

* Hugh had been asked to review a biography of Dundas, and had refused. He had already given his copy to Oxfam, and was driving down from Scotland, when he had the idea to write a 'brief life' instead, which he composed behind the wheel, 'as the miles whizzed by'.

† James addressed a letter to his mother as to 'Lady Alexandra Aubrey'.

if stroked and wheedled. In his young days he had a lean hatchet face and a wild black forelock, very ferocious; when he screamed revolution, 'twould make a good subject's backbone curdle. But now that he is plump and pawky and does but cockadoodle about his genius, his ducats and his duchesses, and despise the rest of us as not worthy of him, none minds him.[53]

The year 1968 was one of upheaval. Protests against the Vietnam War served to radicalise students in Britain as in America, while French students challenged the authorities in Paris. There was much talk of revolution. The 'Prague Spring' promised liberalisation and reform in the Communist countries of Central and Eastern Europe. Meanwhile in Greece a coup by middle-ranking army officers had overturned a left-wing government. Everywhere, it seemed, battle-lines were being drawn.

In the early spring Hugh spent a fortnight walking in Greece. In Athens, he caught an early-morning bus for an eight-hour journey to reach the rugged and mountainous region of Epirus, in the north-west of the country bordering Albania, with a coastline on the Ionian Sea. He spent the next week walking, often rising very early in the morning and returning back to his room aching and weary. 'Alas, how few of my friends share my tastes,' he lamented to James, who had recently been skiing with his mother: 'I don't think I can imagine any, of those whose conversation I enjoy, enjoying my company on these occasions, any more than I would enjoy Portofino with Isaiah Berlin, or sliding down inert, lifeless snow with you.' He told James about the previous night's dream: 'I had rashly confessed, *inter pocula*,* to someone – perhaps you – that for the past 30 years I had been a Russian agent, and I was much exercised how to prevent this fact from coming out.'[54]

Following his return from Greece, Hugh was asked by Frank Giles to write an article for *The Sunday Times* about conditions there under the military junta. His piece appeared on 21 April, the first anniversary of the Colonels' coup. He reported that the only audible dissent came from a few émigrés in Paris and London; in the country itself 'all is peace'. He had been able to discover no sign of opposition, no suggestion of any practical alternative to the rule of the Colonels. Many people, in Britain and else-where, were saying that it was wrong to visit Greece under the current regime; but Hugh disagreed. He did not admire the current Greek gov-ernment, but then there were few governments that he did admire. 'The beginning of wisdom is to respect the reality of foreign countries. Instead of importing foreign ideological conceptions into Greece we should study what few of our crusaders will study – and no one can study if he virtuously

---

* 'In my cups'.

refuse to go there – the condition of modern Greece.' Hugh's article attracted a letter 'of sincere appreciation' from the Greek Ambassador, and an impassioned anonymous letter, deploring what he had written.[55]

After the 'Prague Spring', which raised hopes of internal reform within the Communist bloc, the experiment in 'socialism with a human face' ended on 21 August 1968, when Warsaw Pact forces entered Czechoslovakia and overthrew the reformist government of Alexander Dubček. 'The Czechoslovak affair is very depressing,' Hugh lamented to Valerie Pearl. 'I had hoped it would turn out better.'

> I hate the thought of being driven back into the mindless postures of the Cold War. Like Jacob Burckhardt, if I must die in the ditch, it will be for the civilization of old Europe, with its variety, its sophistication, its contradictions, its complexities, its hierarchies, its rich and varied cuisine, its wines; not for either of those two vast, blank, faceless, uniform continents, with their insipid viands and deplorable beverages.[56]

Some time later he responded to a moving appeal, sent at some personal risk, from Dr Bohumír Klípa, a Czech historian who had been published in *Past and Present* before the clampdown that followed the Soviet invasion. The historical profession had been purged and he, like many of his colleagues, was trying to survive as a manual worker. Nevertheless, he was appealing not on behalf of himself and others like him, but on behalf of two of their former colleagues who were threatened with long prison sentences. Klípa believed that their condition might be ameliorated if leading historians abroad raised objections to their trial and publicly displayed interest in their fate. He explained that he had written a similar letter to A.J.P. Taylor. Hugh joined with Taylor in writing a letter of protest which was published in *The Times*.[57]

During this period Hugh received regular letters from Air Chief Marshal Sir Theodore McEvoy, a former aide-de-camp to the Queen and a strong anti-Communist. McEvoy was active in 'Common Cause', an organisation set up to oppose Communist infiltration. Hugh was invited, together with Kingsley Amis and John Braine (both writers who had recently moved rightwards), to a dinner hosted by Common Cause.[58] The attempt to enlist Hugh seems to have come to nothing; perhaps he did not find the society of the retired brigadiers and major-generals, who formed a high proportion of the membership, congenial.

In the afternoon of 5 December 1968, Hugh arrived at the London School of Economics and Political Science to give the Oration, the School's one formal ceremonial occasion of the year. He was accompanied by his wife and stepdaughter, who was writing a thesis on Pushkin under the supervision of

Professor Leonard Schapiro. Recent Orators had included the art historian E.H. Gombrich, the astronomer Fred Hoyle and the poet Robert Graves. In the past year or so the LSE had suffered considerable student unrest, to the point where the governors had closed the School several times to allow passions to cool.[59] Hugh had been invited to give the Oration by the Director, Walter Adams, former Principal of the University College of Rhodesia, who was caricatured by some of the radical students as a 'lackey' of Ian Smith's minority-rule government. In the surging crowds of protesters objecting to Adams's appointment in 1967, an aged porter had suffered a heart attack and died.

Hugh agreed to speak on 'The Past and the Present' (with the subtitle 'History and Sociology'), a subject which the Director agreed could not possibly be regarded as inflammatory. Nevertheless, he warned of the risk that radical students might attempt to disrupt the occasion.[60] Hugh reacted by sharpening up the text of his speech, inserting a number of topical, even provocative, references.[61] In discussing the possible revival of Nazism, he mentioned several of its features that had recently been resumed: 'the arrogant cult of youth, the nihilism, the intolerance of dissent, the rejection of rational argument, the deliberate invocation of force to justify counterforce'.

Two nights before he was due to give the Oration, Xenia telephoned to say that the LSE was plastered with notices denouncing him. An article in *Beaver*, a students' union newspaper, no doubt responding to his article eight months earlier, described Hugh as 'a friend of the fascist colonels in Greece'.[62] As predicted, a group of radical students announced in advance that they intended to disrupt the meeting because they disapproved of Hugh's views. The LSE Academic Council posted a notice stating that it would regard such an action as a breach of academic freedom and treat it accordingly.

On Hugh's arrival at the LSE it was immediately obvious that there was going to be trouble: everyone seemed rattled. The Trevor-Ropers were hustled into a side room and given tea. Meanwhile Lord Robbins, Chairman of the LSE governors, was negotiating with the students. It seems that a meeting of the Socialist Society, convened in the Old Theatre where the Oration was due to be given, had over-run (as such meetings often did). The Society was unwilling to vacate the Old Theatre. Eventually Robbins struck a bargain with the protesters: they would allow Hugh to give his Oration, provided that he agreed to answer questions about his attitude to the Greek junta afterwards. Robbins fetched Hugh and led him into the Old Theatre, which was crowded with an estimated 800 students. There was no place for Xandra or Xenia, the remaining governors, or for the other distinguished guests: they were forced to listen as best they could from an adjoining room. Among those jostling for a place in the audience were Michael Howard and Melvin Lasky.

Robbins's speech of introduction was interrupted by a student leader, who presented a list of further demands. Eventually Hugh began to speak, flanked by several lounging students in place of stewards. The substance of his lecture was a powerful polemic for the continuing value of historical study, which he perceived to be under threat from shallow and 'trendy' thinkers – among them the Minister for Education, Edward Short, who had asserted that it was far more important for young people to know 'all the facts about Vietnam' than it was for them to know about the Wars of the Roses. In his lecture Hugh dissected this statement and left it in pieces. His Oration lasted the best part of an hour, and passed largely uninter-rupted. 'As I watched the faces of the more ostentatiously rude elements in the Old Theatre,' Adams wrote afterwards, 'I saw them change from an assumed indifference to a genuine intellectual interest as the force of the argument gripped them.'[63] Hugh himself described the effect of his Oration in more satirical terms to Noel Annan: 'like Orpheus, I strummed on, and in the end even the hairiest monsters subsided into a kind of stentorous drowsiness under the spell'.[64]

After he had finished speaking Hugh was escorted to the New Theatre across the road to face a cross-examination. Several hundred students filled all the steeply raked seating, and more perched on the steps leading up the aisles. Robbins chose to join those sitting on the steps, declining an offer from a young woman who volunteered to surrender her seat. At first Hugh dealt assuredly with the questioning – until, to general surprise, one of the porters stood up to speak. It emerged that he owned a holiday home in Greece, on an island which was being used by the regime to hold political prisoners. Though, according to *The Guardian*, he 'rambled on rather', his informed account of what was going on in Greece captivated the audience. Hugh grew visibly impatient with the speaker's repeated protestations of being 'only a humble working man', eventually snapping, 'Oh, shut up the cant and get on with it'. The hostile reaction from the student audience caused Hugh to wilt visibly, and soon afterwards Lord Robbins swept him off to dinner. The proceedings had lasted three-quarters of an hour. A report in *The Guardian* the next day suggested that Oration Day had proved a victory for the forces of moderation, and a letter to *The Spectator* argued that the radical students had been 'bitterly disappointed' by the outcome.[65]

The Director wrote to thank Hugh, not just for the Oration itself, which he described as 'brilliant and masterly', but also for 'the great service you rendered to the School'. He was sure that the occasion would prove a 'turning-point in our struggle against the anti-intellectualism of some of our students'. He apologised profusely for the discourtesies that accompanied the arrangements, and expressed further gratitude to Hugh for enduring them.[66] Lord Robbins also thanked Hugh for his 'splendid' lecture, 'and for the great help you gave to the sorely pressed authorities of the School in consenting to endure questions from that mob of rather rude and very excited students'. Robbins assured Hugh that he had turned 'what might have been a very ugly occasion into a triumphant success'.

This experience at the LSE sharpened Hugh's response to events taking place on his doorstep. Hitherto, as a professorial Fellow of Oriel, he had taken little or no part in Governing Body discussions with undergraduate representatives. Now, having witnessed the degrading spectacle of the LSE authorities being humiliated by student radicals, he was determined not to allow a similar situation to arise within Oriel. The proposals being advanced, within Oriel as elsewhere, were for enhanced undergraduate participation in the running of the college. Hitherto there had been little resistance to undergraduate pressure. A small group of radical dons was fomenting undergraduate unrest. The college, enfeebled by the absence of the Provost during his term as Vice-Chancellor, had been inclined to appease the student militants. Hugh thought this a disastrous policy. Though the proposed reforms appeared modest, he believed them to be the thin end of the wedge. Underlying these, and similar proposals at other colleges, was a radical programme of centralisation, by which Oxford's colleges would be transformed from independent, self-governing entities, each with its distinctive character and hierarchy, into uniform, democratically run 'communes', with no statutes or rules other than those agreed by the whole body. The new rules would be imposed on all members alike, dons as well as undergraduates. In these democratic communities there would be no deans responsible for discipline, no governing hierarchy and no college servants. There would be no separate common rooms or tables in hall, and no privileges to distinguish dons from undergraduates, or scholars from commoners. All were to be equal within these new democratic, egalitarian 'hostels'.

Hugh encouraged the college authorities to stand firm, stiffening the resistance of the Dean to the 'trendy' acting Provost, Christopher Seton-Watson, and those other members of the Governing Body who favoured appeasement of the student radicals. Hugh lobbied hard against such concessions. He rebutted arguments that the college should be run 'democratically'. Rhetoric about rights and principles was stolidly smothered. For example, he opposed the formation of an undergraduate 'welcome committee', funded by the college, to welcome schoolboy candidates for admission during the University vacation, because a similar committee at the LSE had proved to be a vehicle for radicalising the next generation of students. In Governing Body Hugh asked what function this committee would perform to justify the cost, and was told that some of the candidates had not known how to find the lavatory. He suggested that a notice giving directions would be just as effective and much less expensive.[67]

His prediction that the student revolt would be transient proved correct: within a couple of years the clamour for change within the college had died away. The most radical of the dons encouraging undergraduate unrest resigned his Fellowship.

Hugh was not opposed to change within the University. He regarded himself as a member of the Party of Moderation, standing between the radicals on one side and the reactionaries on the other. But he was resistant to pressure from below. Though in general he disparaged the practice of dons appending their names to circular letters, he did sign one, entitled 'Freedom in the Academic Community', condemning student 'sit-ins', intimidation and violence. Among the other signatories were Beloff, Blake and Sparrow. The letter was condemned by the President of the National Union of Students, Jack Straw, as 'a reactionary and unhelpful document', whose signatories were 'the Luddites of the academic world'.[68]

Hugh's most telling strikes against 'academic follies' were made under the shelter of a pseudonym. In November 1968 the first of a sequence of letters from 'Mercurius Oxoniensis' ('Messenger from Oxford') was published in *The Spectator*. These reported on events in Oxford to a notional London correspondent, 'Mercurius Londoniensis'. Though written in seventeenth-century prose – the same style* as the 'brief life' of Dundas – the letters referred to contemporary events and personalities, 'Master Sparrow' and 'the siege of All-soules coll.', for example. Humour proved a sharp weapon, puncturing the pretensions of the student radicals, whom Mercurius labelled 'fanatiques'. When a new struggle began between the undergraduates and the University authorities over access to confidential files, Mercurius ridiculed this demand: ''tis flattering themselves grossly to suppose that each or any of them has a file to himself, they being but *ephemera*, like may-flies or midges, whose nuisance is remembered no longer than their bite'.[69] Mercurius's letters appeared in *The Spectator* at regular intervals, interspersed with a letter from his sister 'Iris' (while Mercurius himself was described as being in hospital, after being 'hit plumb on the head' by a champagne bottle tossed casually out of a Lincoln College window while he was peering at the graffiti in Brasenose Lane), and another from a colleague in Scotland, 'Mercurius Edinensis'. They provided plenty

---

* John Aubrey and his friend Anthony Wood (author of *Athenae Oxonienses*) are sources for the style of Mercurius Oxoniensis. The name no doubt derives from the 'newsbooks' (partisan weeklies) that proliferated during the Puritan Revolution, under such titles as *Mercurius Civicus*, *Mercurius Rusticus*, *Mercurius Britannicus*, *Mercurius Pragmaticus* and *Mercurius Politicus*.

of scope for cracks at colleagues, as well as for an element of self-parody: for example, in reporting events at Oriel:

> ... some stirs are reported from Oriel coll., hitherto a quiet place, but lately infected (as it seems) from Balliol, whose fanatiques, being now strangled in their own nest, have with their dying breath spit the last dregs of their poison across the High-street. But this short flicker was soon snuff'd out. The fanatiques in Oriel did (as I am told) borrow courage from their masters to march in force into the Senior Common Room, where their governours were in session, debating the price of victuals in the beer-cellar, and, like Oliver his musqueteers, to turn 'em all out of doors; but afterwards being summoned by the Provost, and commanded to eat humble pie or risk the consequences of his wrath, their brave spirit quickly evaporated and now they have all returned quietly to their obedience.
>
> 'Tis thought that this outrage was not spontaneous by the young men, who here as elsewhere are civill enough when not misled, but instigated privily by one of their mentors ...
>
> I can tell you no more of the Oriel stirs, for that coll. is a very close place, and their feasts being frugall (and like to be attenuated by the new bursar, a strict oeconomist), I have not visited it these five years.[70]

'I don't know what you mean about Mercurius Oxoniensis,' Hugh wrote to Valerie Pearl, after she had hinted at his identity.[71] When Hugh Kearney raised the subject as they walked together down St Aldates, Hugh looked at him blankly. If challenged, Hugh denied that he was Mercurius, and speculated on who he might be: Hugh Lloyd-Jones, perhaps, or Robert Blake. He enjoyed misleading the curious by laying false trails. Mercurius's style was much imitated, which added to the confusion. The Somerville classicist Nan Dunbar composed a letter to Mercurius in seventeenth-century prose, and sent it c/o the Regius Professor, asking him to forward it to his *alter ego*; in due course she received a reply from Mercurius himself. When she mentioned this to Hugh, and enquired further about the whereabouts of her correspondent, he replied that 'M.O. is very elu-sive'.[72] He maintained his innocence, even after he was unmasked by the *Times* diarist 'PHS' in 1970.[*73] In this he was supported by Mercurius himself, who devoted one of his letters to 'this exquisite new piece of folly'. Indeed he claimed to have 'made merry together' with the Regius Professor over this case of mistaken identity.[74] The Editor of *The Spectator*, Nigel Lawson, kept up the pretence that Hugh was forwarding pieces on behalf of a friend, even in their private correspondence.

---

* The source was generally thought to have been Evelyn Waugh's son Auberon, who had been sacked by *The Spectator* and had found a niche at *The Times*; though he denied responsibility.

The publisher Jock Murray expressed his 'unbounded admiration' for the letters, and asked Hugh to convey his enthusiasm, 'if by any chance you know Mercurius Oxoniensis personally, and happen to bump into him'.[75] In due course Murray published a collection of the Mercurius letters.[76] The book's preface described its 'slightly crotchety' author as 'a college tutor in one of the colleges in Turl Street: a bachelor, of declining years and uncertain health, somewhat old-fashioned in his views, as in his language, fond of his glass of port or hock'. The book was reviewed (not uncritically) in *The Spectator* by Hugh himself, who pondered the question of Mercurius's identity. 'As one who has himself been suspected,' wrote Hugh, 'I am naturally as anxious as anyone to detect and neutralize the real culprit.' He considered, and reluctantly rejected, the Christ Church view that the letters were written by a syndicate. All the evidence, he concluded, pointed towards his colleague Dacre Balsdon.[77] As if returning the compliment, Balsdon reviewed the book in the *Oxford Mail.* He too speculated about Mercurius's identity. The author of the letters was obviously 'no abettor of student revolt, no friend of Papacy, no admirer at the moment of Balliol or of the Nuffield College of Psephology'. Clearly, too, he was a man 'resourceful in scholarship, caustic and scintillating in wit'. He noted that the first lines of letters V, VI, VII and IX contained the anagram 'TR WROTE THIS'. Weighing the evidence, and discounting the false trails laid to confuse the issue, Balsdon suggested that the likely author was 'a scholar, a historian for choice ... who perhaps started his career as a Fellow of Merton ... who then for a long period was a Student of Christ Church ... and who later (by elevation to a Professorship, it might be) emigrated to Oriel. Is there such a man?'[78]

John Sparrow informed Hugh of 'a trick that has been played at your expense'. A copy of the book, inscribed in a mock-seventeenth-century hand, had been left in his letter-box, by an unknown person. 'But mark what follows: he had procured an old envelope addressed to you, had put the book inside it, and directed it to me in a passable imitation of your hand.' Sparrow claimed not to be deceived by this 'ruse'.[79] Hugh pretended to have been sent an inscribed copy himself. Another copy, similarly inscribed, was delivered to Nan Dunbar. She was fascinated to find that the second half of a derogatory reference to her college – 'once of high repute, now in decline' – had been excised from the letter reprinted in the book. When the article had first appeared in *The Spectator*, she had complained to Hugh about Mercurius's 'gratuitous injury' to Somerville. Now she inferred that her intervention 'has had some good effect'.[80]

The Oriel Librarian wanted a copy of the *Letters of Mercurius*, and asked Hugh if he might 'use his influence' to secure him one. By 9.30 the same evening a copy of the book was resting in the Librarian's pigeon-hole.

The final Mercurius letter included in the book appeared just before Nigel Lawson stepped down as Editor of *The Spectator* in 1970, making way for George Gale. Mercurius referred to 'a dismall portent': the mutilation of 'the tutelary deity of all us lesser Mercuries', the statue of Mercury at the centre of Christ Church's Tom Quad. For a while no more was heard of Mercurius. The following February, however, a new letter was published, conveying the reassuring news that the repaired statue was being restored to its pedestal. Among the targets of the resurrected Mercurius was Christopher Seton-Watson. 'Behold!' mocked Mercurius; 'There heaves up from the floor of the House, like a porpoise from the deep, another of the Wykehamicall brethren, one Master Seton-Watson, the great patron of liberty in Oriel coll.' Seton-Watson attempted a response in the same spirit, in a letter published in the correspondence pages of *The Spectator* and signed 'Porcus-Piscis Orielensis'. When this proved ineffective in silencing his irritating critic, another, less good-humoured letter from 'Porcus-Piscis' appeared in *The Spectator*, referring to the 'grotesque fantasies and vulgar abuse' of Mercurius Oxoniensis.[81] Seton-Watson sent two private letters of complaint to Hugh, copying these to the Provost; Hugh urged him not to be upset 'by that silly old Mercurius', who was 'but an air-born insect, drifting like Thistledown, more buzz than sting, on the aimless breath of mere gossip: a swat, and behold! he is no more'.[82] Seton-Watson demanded a special meeting of the Oriel Governing Body to unmask Mercurius. The Provost summoned Hugh, citing a complaint that confidential college business was being publicised, and the allegation that Hugh was responsible.

'What an extraordinary suggestion!' exclaimed Hugh.

'Are you, or are you not, Mercurius Oxoniensis?' demanded Turpin.

After a pause, Hugh replied: 'You asked me for a straight answer, and the straight answer is no.'

Mercurius's letters continued to appear in *The Spectator* until 1973, with the occasional contribution from the mysterious 'Mercurius Cantabrigiensis'. Two of the last letters were addressed to 'Mercurius Californiensis'. In 1974 Hugh complained to a director of Sotheby's that an entry in an auction catalogue attributed the *Letters of Mercurius* to him. By doing so, he claimed, they were 'tainting the stream of bibliographical science'. Sotheby's apologised and issued a formal correction.[83]

Early in March 1969 the Trevor-Ropers flew to New York, for a stay in America lasting almost three weeks. The prime purpose of their visit was to see James, who had a Junior Fellowship at the Dumbarton Oaks Centre for Byzantine Studies in Georgetown, Washington. While in New York they had dinner one evening with Arthur Schlesinger Jr, Nicolas Nabokov and the Berlins, who were also in town, and another night with Bob Silvers. Hugh flew to Maine to give a lecture at Bowdoin College, and later they took a train, via Princeton, to Washington, where he lectured at the Folger Library. They stayed part of the time with the socialite Kay Hallé, whom they had come to know through her former beau Randolph Churchill. Hugh contributed an eloquent and amusing memoir of Randolph to a book she edited, *The Grand Original: Portraits of Randolph Churchill by his Friends* (1971). They dined one night with Hugh's old friend Joe Alsop; another with Evangeline Bruce (Virginia Clarke's sister), and her diplomat husband David, who had just left his post as Ambassador to the Court at St James's. Towards the end of their stay they took the train back to New York, and on their last night they dined with the Faculty of the City University of New York (CUNY), after Hugh had given a lecture. They were taken to a restaurant in Harlem, then regarded as a daring adventure; their hosts insisted that the whole party walk together in close formation, as though through an occupied city in wartime. Hugh noticed too that when they were given a lift to the opera, their host insisted on locking all the car doors once they were aboard. The previous year he had been shocked by the assassination of Martin Luther King, and now he was dismayed by the evident deterioration in relations between black and white.[84] 'The change since I was there last, four years ago, is extraordinary,' he reported to Valerie Pearl. 'The failure abroad, in Vietnam, the tension at home – in the cities, in the universities, between the races; these have unnerved Americans, and their sense of security, never very pronounced, has now collapsed.' He remarked that the insecurity of life in the great cities had become the staple of general conversation there.[85]

Hugh had been invited to Princeton by the early modern historian Theodore K. (Ted) Rabb. As Hugh's host, Rabb was in a sensitive position, since the outstanding figure in Princeton history was of course the Dodge Professor, Lawrence Stone. Rabb had been an undergraduate at Queen's College in the 1950s, and well remembered attending alternate lectures by both Stone and Trevor-Roper, in which each would attack what the other had said at the last lecture, while the young men looked on aghast. The passing of a decade had apparently not lessened the antagonism. For years, young historians at Princeton had gathered around their leader to hear stories of the Great Ogre of Oxford, Hugh Trevor-Roper. Now they were expecting a magisterial and annihilating counter-attack. But before the lecture Stone was nowhere to be seen. Rabb introduced the visiting speaker. At the very last moment, just as Hugh stood up to begin, Stone crept into the hall and found a seat in the back row. At the end of the lecture he slipped silently away.[86]

Spy

In 1969 Hugh was elected a Fellow of the British Academy (FBA), the highest honour that the academic world can bestow on an historian. New Fellows are elected by existing Fellows in the subject. Hugh's election, at the age of fifty-five, has been described as 'conspicuously late', though this is arguable.[1] Over the twenty-year period from 1960 to 1980 the average age of election to the Academy was fifty-three: Taylor was elected to the Academy at the age of fifty; Blake at fifty-one; Hill at fifty-three; Rowse at fifty-four; Hobsbawm at fifty-nine; Beloff at sixty. Elton had become a Fellow at the age of only forty-six; on the other hand Plumb had to wait until he was fifty-seven. What made the timing of Hugh's election to the Academy conspicuous was that it came twelve years after he had been appointed Regius Professor – but that had been a conspicuously early appointment.

Though Hugh's name had been discussed before 1969, he had not been nominated or balloted. As early as 1961 Taylor informed his sponsor, Sir George Clark (a former President of the Academy), that he had 'put up Trevor-Roper for the Academy but got no backer'. Hugh believed that he had been excluded from the Academy as a 'journalist'.[2] This was a criticism that could have been made too of Taylor, who wrote regularly for tabloid newspapers such as the *Sunday Express*. But alongside his newspaper articles Taylor had also produced several scholarly books, including a substantial volume of diplomatic history, *The Struggle for Mastery in Europe, 1848–1918*. Hugh's publication record, by contrast, was thin.

Until 1969 there was only one history section in the Academy, so that historians of all periods competed for places. There was a widespread perception that the medievalists got more than their fair share. For many years the profession was dominated by Galbraith's predecessor as Regius Professor, the medieval historian F.M. (later Sir Maurice) Powicke. Whenever elections to the British Academy were being considered, Powicke would plead that this time it should be the turn of the medievalists. If it was pointed out to him that the last five Fellows elected had been medievalists, Powicke would at once agree that the best man should be chosen; and in his view the best man would invariably turn out to be – a medievalist.[3] In 1968, in response to complaints that not enough historians were being elected, the history section was divided into three: medieval, early modern and modern (post-1800) historians; with the result that, from then on, candidates would be assessed by specialists in their own period. Hugh was one of the first group to be elected by the new Section XIII, for early modern historians. Plumb nominated him, and was supported by Charles Boxer and Geoffrey Elton. In the citation, Hugh was described as 'a scholar of quite exceptional learning with an outstanding capacity for historical analysis. He is a leading figure in seventeenth-century studies and, indeed, one of the most brilliant historians of his generation.'[4]

At the end of 1969 Robert Blake invited him to join a more informal society: 'The Club', a group of a dozen dons who dined together regularly. Hugh accepted, and remained a member of 'The Club' until his death. Members addressed each other as 'Brother', and referred to themselves collectively as 'The Brethren'. Masterman, Berlin and Sparrow were members; in the next few years they would be joined by Hugh's Christ Church colleagues David Pears and Charles Stuart, and the bookish politician Roy Jenkins, among others. Raymond Carr became a member at the same time as Hugh. 'There is a further vacancy,' Blake revealed; 'but although the Club found it easy to agree who should <u>not</u> be asked, there seemed considerable difficulty in agreeing on who should be.'

Hugh thanked Blake for proposing him. 'I shall enjoy those parties,' he wrote, 'at which I presume the conversation is about the Good, the True and the Beautiful and never descends to those frivolities and intrigues which, alas, are too frequently the subject of ordinary high table conversation.'[5]

Nan Dunbar's enthusiasm for Mercurius's letters led to a spirited correspondence with Hugh. 'When I see him – as I hope I shall when I am next in Oxford and if I should cross the High Street,' he promised her, 'I shall convey to him your kind and flattering remarks which I know will please him; for at heart he is a vain old curmudgeon and secretly relishes flattery, especially if it comes from scholars he respects, as I know that he respects you.'[6] Hugh enjoyed corresponding with this lively, formidable woman, then in her early forties, who shared his passion for classical literature. He could not resist the temptation to tease her, of course. Miss Dunbar was a proud Scot, born and educated in Glasgow, who retained a strong Glaswegian accent all her days. Hugh's essay on the Scottish Enlightenment had roused her to 'a frenzy of irritation'.[7] Their correspondence was conducted during brief lulls in their cross-Border sniping, which both obviously relished. Despite regarding Mercurius as 'an exceptionally nasty bit of work', she confessed to being 'unable to resist such delightful wit even when directed against people or bodies I hold dear'.[8] She relaxed her rule that the two of them should never meet, proposing that they should face each other and 'sign a non-aggression treaty'.[9] But before this could happen, a series of minor misunderstandings caused a rapid deterioration in their relations. She was upset when he brusquely rejected her recommendation to attend a conference in Edinburgh, having suggested that his attendance would brighten his 'tarnished image'; he retorted that he did not 'care twopence' for his 'image', and would not pay a penny to purchase a new one. When she regretted that he had not deigned to acknowledge an invitation to a party in Edinburgh Castle, he was clearly annoyed at the reprimand. 'I find the negative, pedantic, carping malevolence of the Edinburgh academic world, or some part of it, irritating,' he replied sharply. He had sought her advice about the pronunciation of the 'wretched Scotch title' Claverhouse, for a radio broadcast on 'Scott and the Study of History', an adaptation of the John Coffin Lecture he had given in London the year before, and then became impatient when the opinions she gathered failed to provide unambiguous guidance. The only responses to his broadcast that had reached him 'from the Scotch academic establishment' had consisted of 'pedantic quibbles', he complained; 'whether the word "Sassenach" may properly be rendered as "Saxon"; whether some irrelevant, incidental date cannot be questioned; whether my pronunciation of some 17th century Scotch name may not safely be faulted by those who cannot themselves agree on the correct form but who evidently have the right to condemn all dissenters to Eternal fire simply because they themselves have the supreme intellectual virtue of being Scotch.'

This letter elicited an arch rebuke from Miss Dunbar:

> I trust that for the benefit of a curious posterity you will set down as dispassionately as you can what appears to you to be the genesis of your hatred of my nation. It would be a pity to leave our successors, at any rate, in continuing ignorance of the causes of your malady. Hitherto I had inclined to the view that the trouble went back to the time before you could remember, and that most probably you'd been bitten in infancy by a Scotch terrier, and have consequently been biting back instinctively ever since at anything Scotch within sight. But since you mentioned some time back that you had been 'at school in Scotland', it has seemed to me more and more probable that your traumatic experience – for such there has clearly been, as all universally agree – took place at this mysterious school . . .

Hugh appeared oblivious to such psychoanalysing, but he did become tetchy when she criticised his radio talk. 'When people become abusive in correspondence it is generally a sign that they have lost confidence in their powers of reasoning,' he declared.[10] The correspondence ceased.

*

In the early 1960s Hugh had agreed to write a book on the first half of the seventeenth century for the *Fontana History of Europe*, a paperback series edited by J.H. Plumb and published by Collins. Among the other contributors to the series were John Elliott, Geoffrey Elton, the Renaissance historian John Hale and David Ogg; the first volume, Elton's *Reformation Europe, 1517–1559*, had appeared in 1963. The editor at Collins was Richard Ollard, himself the author of several good books of seventeenth-century history. Ollard had been a pupil of Ogg's, an undergraduate at New College in the late 1940s, when he had attended a seminar run by Hugh with Menna Prestwich. He was pleased to have secured Hugh as a contributor to his new series, though he soon became concerned about the apparent lack of progress. From time to time he tried to encourage Hugh; early in 1973, for example, he expressed his delight at the news that 'you feel stirring in you the book that we all want'.[11] But when there was still no sign of a manuscript a few years later, the contract was abandoned. 'I know I have wasted precious time for you; and for this I cannot forgive myself,' Hugh wrote to Ollard.[12] The volume was assigned to a pupil of Elliott's, the young historian Geoffrey Parker, whose *Europe in Crisis, 1598–1648* appeared in 1979.

Hugh entered into another commitment in 1970, when he agreed to be responsible for the seventeenth-century volume in the *History of the University of Oxford*. This ambitious project had been proposed by Alan Bullock back in 1966; a committee was set up to investigate the idea, and it was agreed to commission eight substantial volumes, covering the history of the University from its earliest times in the twelfth century until the present. The General Editor was Trevor Aston, a Fellow of Corpus and Editor of *Past and Present*; among the other editors of individual volumes would be Hugh's former graduate student, Jim McConica, and his Oriel colleague Jeremy Catto. The task of the volume editors was to organise the period into chapters and to commission contributors to write these. It was understood that the volume editors would themselves write an introduction and at least one chapter. Hugh made little progress, and in 1982 he was succeeded as editor by Nicholas Tyacke, who asked him to write a chapter. Four years later there was no sign of this either. The chapter was undertaken by Hugh's former pupil, Blair Worden, and the volume eventually published in 1997.[13]

In 1975 Hugh would give the Wiles Lectures in Belfast, on 'The Ecumenical Movement and the Church of England, 1598–1618'. These explored the period of relative peace and relaxation between the two phases of Europe's wars of religion, the first ending with the end of the French wars, the second starting with the outbreak of the Thirty Years' War. He portrayed the Church of England as an Erasmian 'middle way', with a broad, non-confrontational appeal, which had allowed England to enjoy peace and a measure of tolerance while the Continent had been torn between two extremes. Although he did not make any explicit references to the conflicts between Protestants and Catholics in modern Ulster, the parallel was implicit. As was often the case, his audiences were staggered by the range of his learning, and his capacity to see connections between episodes and developments that no previous historian had ever brought together.

One of the conditions was that the Lecturer should adapt his Lectures into book form; only then would the fee be paid. Yet even this inducement was insufficient to extract a finished text from Hugh.[14]

In March 1970 Hugh spent three weeks in America on a lecture tour. He had advertised his services via an agency which proudly proclaimed: 'there are educators by the score and historians aplenty, but there is only one Trevor-Roper'. Part of the purpose was to give Xandra a holiday. They flew to New York, and afterwards toured the Southern states. Their social schedule was hectic, with lunches, dinners and visits to the opera. In New York, for example, they lunched with Robert Silvers, the poet Robert Lowell and the daughter of Gladwyn Jebb, Vanessa, now married to the historian Hugh Thomas. In Philadelphia they stayed two nights as guests of Henry McIlhenny, before flying on to New Orleans, where Hugh met a penfriend from childhood, a Jewish doctor. In South Carolina they bumped into Steven Watson, also 'stumping across the continent to rattle his empty money-bags'.[15] At the end of the tour they relaxed with David and Evangeline Bruce at their ranch in Lynchburg, Virginia. Also staying there was Steven Runciman.

The lecture agency offered a choice of two startlingly different subjects for the Trevor-Roper lectures: Adolf Hitler or Sir Walter Scott. But in Columbia, South Carolina, Hugh rehashed a lecture he had first given at the University of London, 'The Plunder of the Arts in the Seventeenth Century'. This was the second* Walter Neurath Memorial Lecture, named after the founder of Thames and Hudson; and it would later be published by his firm as a short, beautifully produced and splendidly illustrated book. Hugh showed how several of the great European libraries and art collections assembled since the Renaissance – Heidelberg, Prague, Mantua and Whitehall – had been plundered, and their contents scattered, in the 'ideological strife' of the early seventeenth century; during such a struggle, with enemies fighting to destroy their opponents, the usual respect for rights and property had been suspended. The new collections reflected the New Order that had emerged from this period of strife, as well as the taste of the victors.

Some years later he returned to the same territory in a series of four

---

* The first, on Victorian architecture, was given by Professor Nikolaus Pevsner.

lectures delivered at the State University of New York, also published as a book by Thames and Hudson, under the title *Princes and Artists: Patronage and Ideology at Four Hapsburg Courts, 1517–1633*. He argued that the changing pattern of patronage illustrated distinct phases of the great ideological crisis of the time, reflecting different stages in the European *Weltanschauung*. The artists whom these rulers patronised reflected these changing attitudes. For Frances Yates, who reviewed the book in *The Times Higher Education Supplement*, this 'brilliantly original plan' of comparing the art of four Hapsburg courts opened 'new vistas of historical understanding'.[16] The historian John Kenyon,* reviewing the book in *The Observer*, was less convinced by the argument, though he too was dazzled by Hugh's virtuosity. 'His failure to produce a definitive major work of history irritates his admirers,' commented Kenyon, 'but some of his short essays have affected the way we think about the past more than other men's books. His range is prodigious – all the way from Constantine to Hitler – and his reading apparently limitless; no specialism is safe from his authoritative and disruptive intervention ... It is fascinating to see him seize a new subject in his powerful grasp, disembowel it in one swift, easy movement, skin it and cut it up, meanwhile offering a ceaseless commentary.'[17]

Princes and Artists appeared in French, Spanish and Italian editions, and was published separately in America by Harper & Row. John Russell praised the book in *The New York Times Book Review*, though he deplored its brevity. He detected the influence of Berenson (and through him, Burckhardt) on Hugh's thinking: Berenson had taught Hugh that art, like literature, was 'an inseparable part' of history, illuminating it and being illuminated by it.[18]

Hugh returned to America for another tour, this time alone, towards the end of 1970, beginning in Nova Scotia and continuing via Boston, Harvard, Philadelphia, Salt Lake City, San Francisco and Los Angeles. 'Never, never, never again will I come to Los Angeles,' he complained bitterly to Xandra, after a promise of five lectures at $1,000 each had shrunk to two. Californian universities were in upheaval, disrupted by student unrest on the one hand and budget cuts on the other. On his first morning in San Francisco Hugh was disconcerted to find that he was expected to give a press conference; the assembled journalists and photographers were anticipating a preview of his lecture on 'Youth's Revolt: Society's Cancer or Cure'. This subject, of which he had no foreknowledge, came as a surprise to him.[19]

Despite this discouraging experience Hugh would return to America to lecture again and again in the 1970s, often accompanied by Xandra. There

---

* A specialist in seventeenth-century English history and a regular reviewer, then Professor at Hull University.

'A vote for Macmillan is a vote for Trevor-Roper.' Hugh with scholar's hat and gown during the election for a new Chancellor of Oxford University, 1960, in which he orchestrated a successful campaign for the Prime Minister, Harold Macmillan.

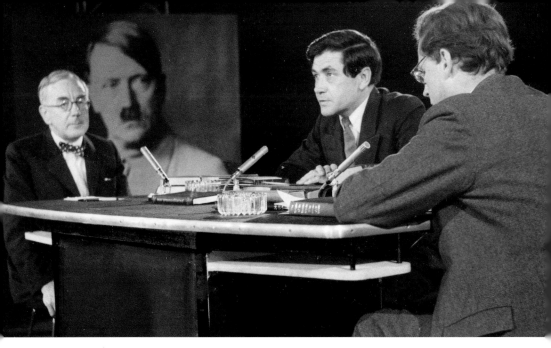

The 1961 televised debate with A.J.P. Taylor (facing camera) on the origins of the Second World War. The chairman was Robert Kee. Hugh referred to his opponent as 'Taylor'; Taylor called him 'Hughie'.

'Useful idiots.' A delegation to China organised by the Society for Anglo-Chinese Understanding (SACU), September 1965, only months before the 'cultural revolution'. Hugh stands on the right of the group; next to him is the playwright Robert Bolt.

LSE Oration Day, 5 December 1968. Hugh makes a defiant speech while flanked by student protestors. Seated beside him is Lord (Lionel) Robbins, Chairman of the LSE Governors.

The Trevor-Ropers in Pakistan, as guests of the Prime Minister, Zulfikar Ali Bhutto, in the spring of 1972. After Bhutto was deposed in a military coup and subsequently sentenced to death, Hugh lobbied hard to prevent his execution.

Partying with three prime ministers: Edward Heath, Harold Macmillan and Harold Wilson, 25 September 1973.

'We hear that you were, until recently, Master of Peterhouse.' An audience with Pope John Paul II, 14 January 1992.

The *éminence grise*. Maurice Cowling conducting a supervision.

'He likened his move from Oxford to becoming a colonial governor.' The Dacres aboard a Cambridge punt.

The 'Independent National Director' of Times Newspapers Limited.

Rupert Murdoch takes an unwelcome telephone call.

'Piece in Our Times', *Private Eye* cover, May 1983. In a parody of the scene when Chamberlain returned in triumph from Munich, Murdoch descends from an aircraft brandishing a 'Hitler diary', while Hugh and the editor of *The Times*, Charles Douglas-Home, stand in attendance.

'HITLER DIARIES: DACRE'S DOUBTS.' This *Evening Standard* headline greeted the harrassed historian on his arrival in England after the disastrous *Stern* press conference, 25 April 1983.

Overleaf
Reading became a struggle in old age.

were visits to the opera, and to high society friends like the Bruces, Kay Hallé and Brooke Astor. While in Washington they would often see Peter Ramsbotham, who was serving as British Ambassador there. One evening in January 1973 they dined at Kay Hallé's house in Washington with Henry Kissinger, National Security Advisor in President Nixon's administration. Kissinger, an admirer of Metternich, was a controversial figure, who would later be accused of war crimes. Nevertheless he was widely acknowledged to be the architect of America's disengagement from Vietnam. Hugh told Frances Yates afterwards that he had liked Kissinger very much: 'I found him far more attractive than those political academics of the Kennedy era: Schlesinger, Galbraith, Rostow.' He added, in parentheses, 'he is, of course, far more powerful'.[20]

The dinner took place on the very day that the Paris Peace Accords had been signed, ending direct American involvement in the Vietnam War. Hugh later recalled that he had been 'rather baffled' by Kissinger's apparent confidence in the ability of the South Vietnamese regime to withstand pressure from the North. 'He assured me, with apparent conviction, that the Thieu regime was internally far more solidly based than the regime in the North, and that there was no ground for apprehension at all. I was very surprised by this, but obviously could not dispute his information. In retrospect I often wondered whether he was deceiving me or deceiving himself.'[21]

In the summer of 1970 Hugh appeared on a BBC2 television documentary entitled 'Philby: A Ruthless Journey'. He admitted to an interviewer that his memories of Philby were friendly ones, and that if they were suddenly thrust together now, an enjoyable conversation would result. But he would prefer not to meet Philby again. 'There are things that stick in my throat.' Philby had 'sold his soul, not temporarily as many people did in the 1930s, but permanently to a form of society which has never ceased to be repressive and in many respects criminal. Moreover, he did this at the expense of every human contact. I mean, everyone he knew in the West, to whom he appeared so intimate, to whom he talked in so friendly a fashion, was in effect being betrayed.'

The documentary was discussed later that same evening on the live review *Late Night Line-Up*, which Hugh watched. Among those taking part was Lord Chalfont, formerly, as Alun Gwynne Jones, Defence Correspondent of *The Times* and subsequently Minister of State at the Foreign and Commonwealth Office in Harold Wilson's Labour Government, which had just come to an end after a Conservative victory in the general election of June 1970. As a junior Minister, Chalfont had tried to discourage *The Sunday Times* from investigating Philby in 1967. Still nominally a left-winger, he would later move sharply to the Right. Chalfont referred to the world of secret intelligence as 'sordid', 'squalid' and 'nasty': 'a rotten reflection of a rotten international system'. He described Hugh's contribution to the Philby documentary as 'gruesome'. It was 'rather curious', he felt, that Hugh should speak of not wanting to meet Philby again, 'as if there was something unclean about him', since (he said) Hugh himself had been a spy, 'and evidently a substantially less successful one'.

Hugh was irritated by Chalfont's gratuitous insults, and stung by the suggestion that there was a moral equivalence between himself and Philby. He wrote a letter of complaint about Chalfont's remarks to Charles Curran, the BBC Director-General. This was acknowledged, with a note that 'Mr Curran would be replying himself in due course'. When no reply arrived Hugh wrote again to Curran, demanding an apology. Instead he received a copy of a letter from Chalfont which compounded the offence. Chalfont alleged that Hugh had misquoted him: 'not a very good start from a professional historian!' In fact, it was Chalfont who had misquoted Hugh, in attributing to him the description of Philby as a 'moral leper'.[22]

A QC who happened to come to lunch with the Trevor-Ropers offered his opinion gratis that Chalfont had uttered three distinct libels, to an estimated value of £7,000. Hugh referred the matter to his lawyer, who demanded a full apology and a complete withdrawal. In due course the case against Chalfont and the BBC came to the High Court, where Hugh was victorious. He received numerous messages of congratulation on his victory, including a telegram from Harold Macmillan.[23]

Hugh was awarded damages of £2,500. He contemplated donating this windfall to the cost of redecorating Oriel College Library, until deterred by a struggle over window-boxes.[24] As acting Steward of Oriel, Hugh had employed the fashionable decorator, John Fowler, to choose a bold new colour scheme for the Senior Common Room. Xandra, a friend of Fowler's, had shown a keen interest in the process.* She scoured the antique shops of the southern counties of England to find lamps, grates and other items of furniture, and had even made alterations to the curtains herself. The effect of all this industry and talent was threatened, however, by the obstinacy of the college Treasurer. Fowler had recommended that the existing window-boxes outside the Senior Common Room should be discarded, as a Victorian addition which destroyed the beautiful proportions of the eighteenth-century windows. Moreover their colouring was incompatible with the new colour scheme. But the Treasurer would not allow the window-boxes to be moved. As a compromise Hugh arranged for them to be repainted. It simply remained to replace the 'hideous' red geraniums,

---

* In the early 1960s the Upper Library at Christ Church had been redecorated, under Fowler's supervision. Xandra had been closely involved throughout.

which now clashed with the red of the dining-room, by inoffensive white petunias. The Treasurer refused to countenance this unnecessary expense. One of the Fellows offered to pay for the new petunias himself, but this generous offer was ignored. Furious, Hugh denounced the Treasurer, in a letter to an Oriel colleague marked 'Private and Confidential', as a 'pig-headed vulgarian'. His 'extraordinary behaviour' had driven all the younger Fellows into active opposition, Hugh claimed. 'Left and Right are now united in hatred of the vulgar, petty despotism of the Treasurer,' whom Hugh described as 'an utter philistine, a tyrannical jack-in-office, and (what makes co-operation with him quite impossible) a double-crosser'. He questioned whether there was now any point in inviting Xandra to dine in a room 'in which our work is incomplete and, now, insulted'. The contest was fought in college committees and sub-committees, with lobbying for support in the intervals between meetings. Hugh threatened to divert the funds which he had been collecting to restore the Oriel Library.[25]

The controversy was resolved when, one morning, during a period when Hugh was conveniently away from Oxford, lecturing on witchcraft in Edinburgh, it was discovered that the window-boxes had been mysteriously (perhaps magically) abducted. The young Viscount Morpeth, then an undergraduate at Balliol – who happened to be a close friend of the Trevor-Ropers – later admitted responsibility.

Albert Speer had been released from Spandau prison in 1966, after serving the full twenty-year prison sentence he had received at Nuremberg. In 1970 Hugh assessed Speer's memoirs, *Inside the Third Reich*, for *The Sunday Times*. For him, Speer's character remained an enigma. It was the 'contrast between perception and blindness, between sensitivity and insensitivity, between moral standards and moral neutrality, and of his own admission of the contrast, and of his own inability to resolve it, which makes Speer psychologically so interesting, and gives to this book, so fascinating in its detail, so brilliant as narrative history, its disturbing human depth'.[26]

Back in 1945 Hugh had interrogated Speer as a prisoner awaiting trial. He had also been present during Speer's trial at Nuremberg. In 1971, following publication of the memoirs, he was able to spend another three and a half hours questioning Speer during a long interview for *Panorama*, conducted in a Munich hotel.* (Also taking part was the diplomat George Ball, another of those who, together with J.K. Galbraith, had interrogated Speer in 1945, on behalf of the US Strategic Bombing Survey.) Hugh was struck by the fact that nothing seemed to have changed for Speer during those years in Spandau: both in Speer's memoirs and in the interview he heard the same

---

* The interview was never broadcast.

voice, and sometimes the very same words, as he had heard in the interrogations twenty-six years before.[27] After the filming had finished he dined
with Speer. 'I spent a whole day with Speer and found him as fascinating,
and as mysterious, as ever,' he reported to Xandra afterwards.[28] He had
been impressed by Speer's lucidity and candour, and – just as in 1945 – had
found him agreeable and civilised in person. Nevertheless the interview left
him uneasy.

A couple of days later he read a transcript of two consecutive speeches
delivered to armaments workers in the Berlin Sportpalast in 1944, one by
Speer, the other by Goebbels. Speer's speech was unexceptionable: an appeal
to increase production for victory. But Goebbels's speech, which followed
immediately after from the same rostrum, was a loathsome anti-Semitic
tirade. How could Speer have sat through this? How could this educated,
urbane man – who by his own account already knew that the war was lost –
have tolerated this revolting demagoguery? And yet not only had Speer
done so, he had discussed oratorical style with Goebbels afterwards in
relaxed conversation, and indeed remained a friendly colleague of his until
the end. Hugh decided not to see Speer again.

Hugh continued to ponder this enigma after Speer's death in 1981. He
planned to write a biography of Speer, but never got around to it, and
encouraged the German historian Joachim Fest to write one instead. (Fest's
Speer: The Final Verdict would be published in 2001.) In 1995 Hugh reviewed
the remarkable biography *Albert Speer: His Battle with Truth* by the journalist Gitta Sereny, whose judgement was even more damning than his
own. He had concluded that Speer was immoral; 'she, after profounder and
more intimate study, found him not immoral, not amoral, but somehow
infinitely worse, morally extinguished':

> But in mitigation she shows – and this is what gives dignity to the story – that
> he recognised the fact and, in his long agony, sought to recover humanity, 'to
> become a different man.'[29]

The Trevor-Ropers had been tenants of 8 St Aldates since 1955. They counted
on staying there until 1981, when Hugh was due to retire from the Regius
Professorship, at the age of sixty-seven. In 1970, however, it had become
apparent that their lease might not be renewed when it elapsed in two years'
time. When Hugh had accepted the Chair in 1957, thereby ceasing to be a
working member of Christ Church, Charles Stuart had assured him that
nobody eligible was likely to want the house for a considerable period. But
more than a dozen years had passed since then, and the position had
changed. Stuart was no longer Censor, and was anyway not as close to
Hugh as he had been; Robert Blake had left Christ Church, to become
Provost of Queen's; and now there seemed to be someone else who wanted

the house. A vote was passed in the Governing Body that it should be returned to the college; the new Treasurer, Keith Batey, told Hugh that he would have to leave. Hugh mobilised support for a campaign to reverse this decision. He enlisted to the cause his old friends at Christ Church, Roy Harrod and Hugh Lloyd-Jones, and former members of the college whose opinion might carry influence, such as Denys Page. He also appealed personally to the Dean (Henry Chadwick), and was incensed by the Dean's non-committal response. After some argument the Trevor-Ropers were allowed a year-long extension to their lease, until September 1973. This was not enough to satisfy them, however.

In May 1972 Xandra sent a plaintive letter to John Sparrow, who was lunching with her husband and the Chancellor the following Sunday. 'I am sure he won't tell you that Christ Church is throwing us out of this house,' she told Sparrow. She thought it was 'perfectly monstrous' that they should 'literally be turned out into the streets' by her husband's old college. It was 'quite impossible' to find anywhere else to live in Oxford that they could afford. 'The result is that I am leaving Oxford,' she announced dramatically. All this derived from the way professors were treated in Oxford, she continued. Professors had 'no standing' in the University. 'I am really <u>seething</u> with rage.'

> From the moment he became Regius Professor I have been made to feel that we belong nowhere in Oxford.
>
> I have never been invited to any grand social occasion, such as the times when the Queen has come to Oxford. As you know, Professors come very low on the list of precedence in Oxford & therefore their wives are always excluded from any official gathering. And now we are being rendered homeless.

She argued that the plight of professors in Oxford, 'and particularly that of their wives', should be brought to the attention of the Chancellor.[30]

As Chancellor, Macmillan was in no position to meddle in an internal college matter. This did not prevent him from expressing his opinion privately. He was heard to say that he was shocked to hear of the college's 'Rachmanite behaviour'* towards his old friends. A Student of Christ Church, the economist Peter Oppenheimer, wrote to ask Hugh if what he had learned from the Chancellor was accurate, as the Governing Body had apparently been given a very different picture of the situation. At the Dean's request, Hugh prepared a statement of his case for remaining at 8 St Aldates, to be circulated to all members of the Governing Body. He gave it out that the Treasurer wanted the house for himself. Meanwhile he let it be known

---

* Peter Rachman was a slum landlord in 1950s London, whose name became synonymous with extortion and the intimidation of tenants.

that if the Governing Body would not reverse its decision, he would apply
to become a protected tenant under the Rent Act.* He outlined his strategy
to Roy Harrod. 'My main task must be to persuade members of the Governing Body, first, that it is just, second (failing that) that it is expedient to
leave things alone.'[31]

Faced with such determined resistance, the Governing Body reversed its
decision.[32]

If Oxford professors were not sufficiently appreciated at home, a different
view prevailed on the other side of the world – at least that was the implication of an anecdote Hugh told with relish, about the experience of his
secretary, Marion Hoey, after she returned from visiting her sister in Kuala
Lumpur. In Singapore she had to change planes. Her luggage was unloaded
late; it was heavy; and she was forced to lug it a long way. An airport official
showed no great eagerness to assist her, but he was willing to enter into
light conversation. What did she do back in England?

'I am secretary to an Oxford historian,' she answered loftily.

'That must be dull,' commented the official.

'Not at all,' she replied.

'Oh,' said he, 'I suppose you're going to say that you work for Hugh
Trevor-Roper.'

'That's precisely who I do work for,' she said smugly.

A look of incredulous veneration passed over his face. 'The greatest mind
in Europe!' he exclaimed, picked up her luggage, ran to the aeroplane,
saw her onto the best seat, and stood at attention as her plane rose into the
air.[33]

In the spring of 1972 the Trevor-Ropers spent ten days in Pakistan, as guests
of the Pakistani government. For years, the politician Zulfikar Ali Bhutto
had been urging Hugh to come to his country; now that he was President, he
could entertain them as official guests. Bhutto had been an undergraduate at
Christ Church in the early 1950s, reading law. At their first meeting Hugh,
in his capacity as Senior Censor, had rebuked the young Bhutto for not
wearing a gown. Despite this difficult start the two men were soon on good
terms. After leaving Oxford in 1952, Bhutto had kept in contact. In 1961
Hugh explained to the new Dean that Bhutto had 'greatly enjoyed being at
Christ Church, is devoted to it, and, he having broken the ice, has been
followed here by a swarm of other Bhuttos'.[34] In his regular communications

---

* A house of this size would not normally have been eligible, but 8 St Aldates was anomalous;
being contiguous with the college, it had a very low rateable value. As members of the Governing
Body assembled for their meeting, one commented sardonically that the Trevor-Ropers might
not have been the sort of people the Government had in mind when it introduced the Rent Act.

Bhutto often mentioned that he wanted his son and daughter to study at Oxford in due course.

A few years later the Pakistani High Commissioner in London came to see Hugh. He explained frankly that Bhutto would like an honorary degree. By this time Bhutto was Foreign Minister. He hoped to keep Pakistan close to the West, but other forces were pulling it eastwards. In particular, he had made an alliance with the Chinese, who were willing to supply weapons that Pakistan needed for protection against India. Bhutto was an able and ambitious man, who seemed destined to rise to the summit of Pakistani politics; like other Pakistanis who had been to Oxford, he had a sentimental attachment towards the place; an honour from his old University would please him greatly, and cement his attachment to Britain. Hugh had explained that an honorary degree was impossible at present, but did not rule out the possibility in the future. So the matter stood when the Trevor-Ropers flew out to Pakistan.

Over the intervening years much had happened in the country. Bhutto was out of office and in opposition; he had formed the Pakistan People's Party and made himself the most important politician in West Pakistan. In 1971 a political crisis had deteriorated into massacres and civil war, war with India, defeat, and the loss of East Pakistan, which became the new state of Bangladesh. Bhutto had assumed power as President of the rump of Pakistan, and in a surprisingly short time had restored the morale of his shattered country. When Hugh arrived in March 1972, he was amazed at the resilience of the people so soon after such a calamitous upheaval.

The Trevor-Ropers were treated as honoured guests. An elaborate programme was devised for them; they were escorted everywhere by military vehicles, with motorcycle outriders clearing citizens out of their path. Hugh was embarrassed by this privileged treatment, and secretly pleased when an obstinate bullock refused to give way to their cavalcade. They were taken by helicopter into the Swat Valley, in the tribal area on the border of Afghanistan. Wherever they went, the President would telephone to check that they were being properly entertained. Hugh had the impression that Bhutto ran the country as a personal fiefdom. Back in the capital, one of Bhutto's aides again hinted that the President should be given an Oxford degree. Nostalgia for the old University was universal in the elevated circles in which they moved: questions about The Trout, the Randolph and other familiar landmarks became a familiar refrain. The climax of their stay was a cruise with the President in a Pakistani (formerly British) destroyer. After lunch Bhutto invited Hugh to join him for a private discussion. Hugh spoke frankly about British perceptions of Pakistan. He learned that his host possessed the largest collection in Asia of books about Napoleon: perhaps an ominous sign. Afterwards he was disconcerted to hear from an aide that the President was an admirer of Stalin.[35]

On his return from Pakistan Hugh proposed that Bhutto should be awarded an honorary degree, but received a disappointing response from the Vice-Chancellor, Alan Bullock, who told him that the proposal had failed to attract support from the Hebdomadal Council, the University's 'Cabinet'.[36] The following April, Bhutto, who would become Prime Minister under the new constitution, thanked Hugh for 'all the assistance that made it possible for my daughter Benazir to gain admission to Lady Margaret Hall at Oxford'.[37] That summer Bhutto came to Britain on an official visit. The British Prime Minister, Edward Heath, gave a dinner for him at 10 Downing Street; the following night Bhutto reciprocated with a dinner for Heath at the Savoy Grill. The Trevor-Ropers were guests at both. Alec Douglas-Home, the Foreign Secretary (another Christ Church man), took the opportunity to ask Xandra whether it might not be possible for the University to give Bhutto an honorary degree. After the election of a new Vice-Chancellor, the economic historian John Habakkuk, Trevor-Roper tried again. He pointed out that the University had already awarded an honorary degree to the Prime Minister of India, Indira Gandhi, an Oxford woman.* It therefore seemed fitting that it should award such a degree to the Prime Minister of Pakistan, Zulfikar Ali Bhutto, an Oxford man.[38]

Habakkuk agreed, and this time the Council was unanimous in endorsing the proposal. The offer was made, and accepted. Arrangements were made for the Bhuttos to come to Oxford and stay with the Trevor-Ropers for the ceremony. But opposition emerged after the decree conferring the honorary degree was published in the *Oxford University Gazette*. An agitated Habakkuk telephoned Hugh to tell him that Richard Gombrich of Wolfson College, a lecturer in Sanskrit and son of the famous art historian Sir Ernst Gombrich, had announced his intention of opposing the degree when it came before Congregation (the University parliament). It was almost unprecedented for the award of an honorary degree to be challenged at this stage. The Vice-Chancellor wrote personally to the Pakistani Prime Minister to express his embarrassment at the situation.[39]

The day after receiving this news, Hugh travelled up to London by train. He later learned that Gombrich (whom he did not recognise) had shared his compartment, and reflected how lucky it was that he had been unaccompanied, because he shuddered to think what indiscretions might have been uttered had Xandra been with him. Hugh wrote to Gombrich offering to discuss the matter privately, but had received no reply by the time

---

* Mrs Gandhi had attended Somerville in the late 1930s.

Congregation met. Gombrich made a short speech in which he declared that Bhutto was guilty of atrocities. Then his supporters used a procedural device to adjourn the debate. At a second meeting of Congregation more than a fortnight later, the debate was resumed. Hugh spoke in defence of Bhutto's name. This meeting was much better attended, after considerable controversy within the University in the intervening weeks. The motion to award an honorary degree to Bhutto was lost by two votes. It was belatedly discovered that two of those who had voted had been ineligible to do so; the result should have been a tie, in which case the motion would have been carried on the casting vote of the Vice-Chancellor. At a third meeting, Congregation decided by a clear majority to deny Bhutto his degree. To Hugh, the decision was 'a shameful public affront' to a distinguished Oxford graduate.[40] A deliberate snub was much worse than careless neglect.[41] Moreover, this 'elaborate incivility' could damage relations between Britain and Pakistan. No one then mentioned (as someone surely would were a similar case to arise today) the effect on British people of Pakistani origin.

This was a precursor to a similar and even more controversial decision not to award a degree to Mrs Thatcher ten years later. It was unprecedented in recent times not to grant an honorary degree to an Oxford-educated British Prime Minister. Some saw this as Oxford displaying its independence of government; others as a damaging discourtesy, showing how detached dons had become from the rest of society. Both examples exposed the difficulty of awarding honorary degrees to serving politicians. The Bhutto decision was difficult to defend on logical grounds, especially once a degree had been awarded to Indira Gandhi. Later that same year Mrs Gandhi's government would declare a state of emergency and begin to rule by decree. The case against Bhutto was vague and unsubstantiated. Though Bhutto had practised an autocratic form of democracy, he had not suspended democratic institutions, as Mrs Gandhi had done. To Bhutto's supporters, it seemed a double standard: an insult not just to their leader, but to the Pakistani people as a whole. They muttered that Bhutto had been denied a degree not because of anything he might have done, but because he was leader of a Muslim country.

Immediately after the vote, Hugh blamed the defeat on 'the Left and the Jews', according to the reporter from the *New Statesman*, Christopher Hitchens. 'There was only one Jew on our side,' Hugh was reported as saying by *The Daily Telegraph*.[42] In protest at these comments, a group of about sixty students and a dozen dons, led by Dr Terry Eagleton of Wadham, turned up at the Examination Schools to picket one of Hugh's lectures, only to find that it had already been cancelled; the lecturer was then in Amsterdam. Reports of Hugh's remarks also elicited a number of anxious letters from several of his friends and supporters, including the medievalist Henry Mayr-Harting, a Jewish convert to Christianity. Isaiah Berlin asked for an assurance that he had been misquoted. 'I hope you can reassure me,' he wrote. 'I do not wish, after all these years of friendship, to contemplate the alternative.' Hugh replied that he had not meant to say anything contemptuous about Jews. 'I think you know that I would not do that.' But he repeated his observation that Jews had voted *en bloc* against the award of the degree. 'Having, as I so fondly believe, established my position as a philo-Semite, I claim the liberty to study the behaviour of Jews, as of other social groups, without humbug!' Berlin exonerated Hugh of any anti-Jewish feeling. 'But I wonder whether in some moods, you do not ("subliminally"* perhaps) divide men into gentlemen and the rest, and include Jews and leftists, with some clear exceptions, among "the rest": and that this has influenced your (I continue to think) unfortunate analysis, and conjures up the image of a "Jew-watcher".'[43]

Hugh's observations appeared less provocative in context. In a *Spectator* article (originally written for *The Sunday Times* but rejected by Frank Giles) he commented on the ironies of the vote. 'Those who voted for the radical socialist Mr Bhutto were, on the whole, the conservatives. Those who voted against him were the Leftists – and the Jews.' These last three words were removed from Hugh's draft before the article was printed.[44]

'If I'd sat for the damn thing I'd have got it easier,' joked Bhutto.[45] He assured Hugh that 'the bizarre happening in Oxford' would not, 'even in the slightest measure, influence my attitude towards the British people'.[46] A month later the Trevor-Ropers made another visit to Pakistan as his guests. Bhutto asked Hugh about Richard Gombrich, and expressed the hope that they might meet one day. Hugh replied nervously that they might not see eye to eye. 'Perhaps not,' said Bhutto, 'but I could shake him by the hand.' On their departure the Prime Minister presented Hugh with a signed photograph, framed in silver. In a letter of thanks after his return, Hugh issued an invitation to Bhutto and his wife to visit them at Chiefswood, which, he assured the Prime Minister, was far from the 'tribal areas' of Scotland.[47]

This was the last time Hugh saw Bhutto, who was deposed in a military coup in 1977. Bhutto was imprisoned and charged with ordering the murder of a political opponent. In October of that year Hugh received a letter from Bhutto's daughter, Benazir, then under house arrest: she appealed to him to find a British barrister willing to represent her father. Hugh identified a suitable person and engaged his services, pledging his own credit for the

---

* Hugh had tentatively suggested that Jews felt 'a subliminal fellow-feeling' with the Bengalis, as victims of racial persecution.

necessary fees. The barrister flew out to Pakistan, and returned a month later with a depressing conclusion: there was 'absolutely no hope of justice' for Bhutto. The trial was rigged; the evidence against him would have been inadmissible under English law; the case against him was so weak that in Britain it would not even have come to court. In due course Bhutto was found guilty and sentenced to death. Hugh appealed to the Pakistani Ambassador for clemency. He urged the Leader of the Opposition, Margaret Thatcher, to make representations to the Pakistani authorities. He wrote an article for *The New York Times*, predicting 'grave political consequences' if Bhutto was killed. 'His death could lead to the end of Pakistan and a further defeat for the West.'[48]

The campaign to save Bhutto's life was in vain: he was executed in 1979. Hugh's efforts on behalf of his friend had been noticed by Indira Gandhi, who, having no better means of contact, wrote asking him to pass on her condolences to the Bhutto family.[49] Five years later she too was dead, assassinated by two of her own security guards.

Hugh continued to try to assist the Bhutto family, whose freedom was restricted by the military regime. In 1982, for example, he appealed to Margaret Thatcher, now Prime Minister, to intervene with the Pakistani leader, General Zia, on behalf of Bhutto's wife, to allow her to seek medical treatment abroad.[50] Mrs Bhutto was given the necessary permission, and came to London, where her cancer was cured. Benazir Bhutto assumed the leadership of the Pakistan People's Party. In 1985 she visited Hugh to seek his advice on constitutional challenges to the continuing rule of General Zia. Democratic government was restored after the death of the General and several of his aides in a plane crash. Benazir served as Prime Minister of Pakistan from 1988 until 1990, and again from 1993 until 1996. She was assassinated after leaving a political rally in 2007.

In a letter to Frances Yates written in 1972, Hugh mentioned that he had just spent a few days in Paris working on Sir Theodore de Mayerne – then a largely forgotten figure, though in his time he had been the most famous physician in Europe. This was a subject that would occupy Hugh, on and off, for the remainder of his working life. His curiosity about Mayerne had been aroused when he read the *Conway Letters*, a volume of seventeenth-century correspondence recommended by Logan Pearsall Smith. Among these were some vigorous letters written by Mayerne, who had served as family doctor to the Conways. Hugh was attracted by the personality these letters revealed. In February 1971 he bought a portrait of Mayerne at Christie's. A few months later he gave a lecture about Mayerne to the Society of Apothecaries. 'I am now writing it up for publication,' he informed Frances Yates afterwards, 'and this, as always, forces me to face certain problems which, in the lecture, I could safely glide past.' He asked if she had come across Mayerne in the course of her studies: an indication of the obscurity into which this once-prominent figure had retreated.

Mayerne had been an alchemist, a disciple of the hermeticist Paracelsus and a practitioner of chemical medicine. The long-defunct ideas of Paracelsian philosophy had only recently been resurrected by Frances Yates and like-minded scholars such as Walter Pagel and Charles Webster, working outside the mainstream of medical history. Hugh was intensely interested in their discoveries. Six months later he mentioned to her that he was enjoying working on Mayerne, 'but feel <u>very</u> ignorant'. In another letter written about the same time he expressed his admiration for her energy, speed and punctuality, which he implicitly contrasted with his own sluggish performance. He reiterated that he was enjoying his work on Mayerne. 'It makes me read a great deal,' he told her. 'But the more I read, the less I write!'[51]

Why was Hugh drawn to Mayerne? One reason, no doubt, was his abiding interest in medicine, which might be traced back to his upbringing as the son of a family doctor.[52] But unlike his father or his brother, he was interested not in the practice of medicine so much as in the relationship of medicine to society. In his study of Hitler's last days, he had observed how quarrels among the *Führer's* doctors, ostensibly about the correct treatment of their all-powerful patient, were not really medical at all: they were an aspect of fierce infighting of the politicians. In a 1980 lecture, 'Medicine and Politics', he pointed out that these two activities, so separate in liberal, democratic societies, had interacted in Stalin's court much as they had done in Hitler's. For where absolute power is sustained and made terrible by ideology, the professional purity of medicine will be broken down and the Hippocratic rules corrupted. The same process could be observed during the early modern period, when power became concentrated into the hands of absolute monarchs, while grim systems of belief, competing with one another and growing fiercer by competition, claimed total loyalty. There too, medical controversy was inseparable from wider ideological debate. There too, medical careers were also political careers.[53]

Another attraction for Hugh was that Mayerne had been a Huguenot, a member of the 'Calvinist International' which Hugh had identified in his essay 'The Religious Origins of the Enlightenment'. Mayerne was a European figure, one whose operations and whose loyalties transcended national frontiers. Swiss by birth, Mayerne had studied in Montpellier, and had risen to become one of the most eminent physicians in France, thanks to his personal charm and adroit political sense as much as to the efficacy of his remedies. Among Mayerne's patients had been the

Protestant King of France, Henri IV. After Henri's assassination, Mayerne had fled to England, becoming once again the most fashionable and sought-after physician in the land, numbering James I and his sons among his patients.

As Hugh studied Mayerne, he uncovered a clandestine career. Alongside his overt practice of medicine, Mayerne had operated as a confidential diplomat, emissary and secret agent. His international practice, his private access to the powerful, his discretion and his political awareness combined to make him especially suited to such sensitive work – just as Hugh's unusual combination of linguistic and detective skills made him especially suited to be Mayerne's biographer, following Mayerne's trail through archives across Europe.

Hugh deplored the trend towards specialism in historical study. As it became deeper and deeper, scholarship could all too easily become narrower and narrower, of interest to fewer and fewer. One reason why Mayerne's significance had become obscured was that his activities had been so diverse. By the twentieth century his name was known only to specialists, and such specialists were blind to the breadth of his interests. For example, Mayerne mixed his own chemical remedies. It was but a short step from these to the paints and varnishes mixed by artists. Mayerne studied both topics; but since in modern times there is little or no dialogue between historians of medicine and art historians, neither had made the connection. Hugh recognised that Mayerne's overall significance had been overlooked because of this regrettable tendency towards specialisation. He saw an opportunity to reverse this process, to recapture the spirit and experience of a lost age in the life of one man. It was an ambitious task, but one suited to his manifold talents. His book would be subtitled 'The Various Life of Sir Theodore de Mayerne', in recognition of the variety which he so valued.

By March 1972 he had written four chapters, though the advent of term prevented further progress. He complained to Frances Yates about the demands on his time. 'These lectures, these committees, destroy my leisure and leave me unable to write anything! I have just been sitting on an electoral board whose session lasted three consecutive days; it is like a papal election. Also I have an absolute genius for losing paper.' He kept her regularly informed of his progress, even when he faltered. In July 1972 he reported that he had been going steadily through Mayerne's papers in the British Museum. 'It is very laborious but (I hope) rewarding; at least Mayerne emerges as a very different person from his current historical image (if he has one). But I sometimes doubt whether he is worth the trouble.'

Six months later he sent her another bulletin. 'I have not been idle,' he assured her. 'I have progressed with Mayerne. But how slowly! The subject is not very big but widens at the touch. It is that, I suppose, that makes him interesting to me.' He was about to go to Chicago for three weeks' lecturing on 'Historical Change and Historical Philosophy, 1750–1850', considering the philosophy of historians from Gibbon to Ranke. Afterwards he planned to pursue Mayerne through the archives of central Europe: Leiden, Sedan, Saarbrücken and Wolfenbüttel, and perhaps to Marburg and Stuttgart. But on his return from Chicago, he found himself trapped. 'Mayerne is at a standstill,' he lamented; 'my whole life is at a standstill: I seem totally buried in boring trivial academic and administrative problems.'[54] He made a similar complaint to Blair Worden. 'I feel that I shall never get out of this whirlpool and be master of my own time. My general philosophy, "the more you do, the more you do", is reaching the point of self-cancellation.'[55]

In December 1973 he complained that, on a recent trip to Germany, he had been able to devote only two days to research, 'owing to my endless duties at Oxford'.

By the following March he had to admit to Frances Yates that his work on Mayerne was 'in suspense'. He had undertaken 'a heavy dose' of lecturing in the current term in order to free himself for writing in the next. 'The only result is that I have been dragooned into examining next term,' he groaned; 'so farewell, peace of mind!'[56]

In January 1974 Hugh was appointed a 'National' Director of Times Newspapers Limited. This was the fulfilment of a long-held ambition. Back in 1964 Randolph Churchill had used his *Spectator* column on 'The Press' to attack Xandra's brother-in-law Gavin Astor – who by then had become the principal proprietor of *The Times* – for not making Hugh a director.[57] In 1967 the Astor family had sold a majority shareholding in *The Times* to the Canadian newspaper proprietor Roy Thomson (later Lord Thomson of Fleet), who already owned *The Sunday Times*, and who merged the two newspapers into one company, under the name Times Newspapers Limited. The Astor family retained a minority shareholding. Much anxiety was expressed about preserving the character of what was then seen as a uniquely precious national institution. Under the terms of the purchase the board would consist of the Editor-in-Chief and the Managing Director, plus four directors appointed by Thomson, and four by Astor, two of each of these groups being designated National Directors, charged with upholding *The Times*'s 'dignity and independence'. By the time Hugh was appointed to the board in 1974, the other National Directors were Lord Robens, Sir Eric Roll (later Lord Roll) and Lord Shawcross. Each received a fee of £1,000 per annum.

Harold Macmillan congratulated Hugh on this appointment. 'I hope you will be able to impart to it some of your own zest and strength,' he wrote. In reply, Hugh disclaimed any merit: it was 'pure nepotism', he said modestly. 'I have no doubt that I will soon find that there is no power either; who can argue with the owner of 85% of the shares?'[58]

Lord

At Basle Airport, one early August day in 1973, Hugh was ceremoniously handed a parcel by Professor Rudolf Geigy, Director of the Swiss Institute for Tropical Medicine, acting on the instructions of his late friend and colleague Professor Reinhard Hoeppli, who had died six months before. Neither of these two men was known to Hugh; though he had received a letter from Geigy earlier that summer, asking whether he would accept and, if he thought fit, transmit to the Bodleian Library a substantial work described as being 'of great literary and historical value'. In explanation of his request, Geigy enclosed a history of the document, and the written opinions of two distinguished scholars to whom it had been shown. Hugh had arranged to meet François Genoud in Freiburg, to discuss the publication in German of 'Hitler's last conversations', so it was not difficult for him to pass through Basle. As it turned out, Genoud did not show up; but when Hugh examined the contents of the parcel back in Oxford, he found that his journey had not been wasted. It also became obvious why the Swiss professors had been reluctant to entrust such an explosive package to the post.

Inside was 'one of the most fascinating (and outrageous) documents I have ever read', the beautifully written but obscene memoirs of an eccentric English baronet who had died in 1944, after living most of his adult life in China. Sir Edmund Backhouse had been a respected Sinologist, the co-author of two influential books, based largely on Chinese sources, which had provided a unique picture of the last days of imperial rule. Between 1913 and 1921 he had donated to the Bodleian Library a magnificent collection of Chinese books and manuscripts; in recognition, his name had been inscribed on a marble tablet honouring the Library's most generous benefactors. Backhouse's entry in the *Dictionary of National Biography* conveyed an impression of a shy scholar – but the memoirs revealed a hidden side to this reputable character. They showed that Backhouse had gone to Peking in the 1890s to enjoy the exquisite homosexual delights of Manchu decadence. Nor had he confined himself to these; at the age of thirty-one, he had become the lover of Tz'u-hsi, the Empress Dowager herself, she being then sixty-nine.

Backhouse had written these memoirs in the last year of his life, during the Second World War, encouraged by Professor Hoeppli, a physician on the staff of an American medical foundation who, as Swiss representative in Peking, looked after British, Dutch and American interests in Japanese-occupied China. Backhouse, by then an elderly recluse who lived and dressed as a Chinese, had gradually revealed to the curious Swiss doctor a past of remarkable lasciviousness. At preparatory school he had been taught by Paul Verlaine, whose protégé he became. In the holidays Verlaine had taken the young Backhouse to Paris, where he became the Ganymede of several eminent French writers. His six years as a schoolboy at Winchester had been 'a carnival of unbridled lust', during which he had sexual relations with at least thirty boys, maybe more – one of them being 'Bosie', Lord Alfred Douglas. At Oxford he had come under the influence of Walter Pater, and had been introduced into the society of Max Beerbohm, Aubrey Beardsley and Oscar Wilde, with whom, of course, he enjoyed carnal knowledge. His numerous adventures while travelling in Europe included an amorous night with an Ottoman princess; copulation with eunuchs in Constantinople; attending the coronation of Tsar Nicholas II; becoming 'intimate, too intimate' with a Russian prince; spending a month as Tolstoy's guest (a chaste interlude), holding extended conversations with the great man; and appearing on stage in Paris with Sarah Bernhardt, who afterwards introduced him to the Empress Eugénie. Back in London, he visited a homosexual brothel in Jermyn Street, where he met Henry James. He had returned to England to stay with Lord Rosebery at his seat Dalmeny House on the Firth of Forth, enjoying with him 'a long and protracted copulation which gave equal pleasure to both parties'; apparently the pace was set by the great man, for, as Backhouse diplomatically put it, 'my readers will agree that when a young man is privileged to have sexual intercourse with a Prime Minister, any proposal regarding the *modus operandi* must emanate from the latter'.

Backhouse's account 'leaves nothing, but nothing, to the imagination,' Hugh wrote excitedly to Valerie Pearl. He relished the thought of presenting this pornographic memoir to the prudish curators of the Bodleian and trying, with a grave face, to persuade them that it was their duty to publish it. The contrast with Backhouse's reputation as an unworldly, modest, bookish personality lent delicious piquancy to the story. Moreover, there was reason to hope that this valuable work might lead him to another even more so, the immense and detailed diaries of the Chief Eunuch of the Empress Dowager, believed to be lurking unnoticed among the records of a branch of Lloyds Bank.[1]

Hugh lent Backhouse's memoirs to his Oriel colleague, the historian Jeremy Catto, who promptly shared the news of their discovery with an editor at Macmillan, Caro Hobhouse. Alarmed, Hugh begged Catto not to tell anyone else, and instructed his publishers that the subject should be treated as confidential. He was anxious that gossip about this salacious memoir should not alarm the Backhouse family, who presumably controlled the copyright; nor did he want the curators of the Library to take up a posture against publication before he was ready to make the case for it. Besides, he was beginning to have doubts about Backhouse's veracity. His mind boggled at the discovery that such a character could have been appointed Professor of Chinese at King's College, London. 'Do you think that perhaps Sir E. Backhouse may have imagined it all?' he asked Catto. 'I am beginning to wonder.'[2] He made discreet enquiries about Backhouse; though 'the more one seeks to find out about him, the more elusive he appears'.[3] So far as Hugh could tell, there was no mention of Backhouse in the papers of any of the eminent writers or statesmen with whom he claimed to have consorted. Hugh resolved not to allow the memoirs out of his hands and into the public domain before checking the parts which were checkable. Within a few weeks his suspicions of the memoirs had hardened. 'I am now coming to suspect that they are, from start to finish, a malevolent tissue of ingenious fabrications designed to taint the stream of history,' he told Robert Blake.[4]

Hugh decided that nothing that Backhouse had written could be relied upon. He therefore decided to build up Backhouse's history, as far as possible, solely from external sources. In the process, what began as an exercise to test the reliability of the memoirs became an adventure in biography. The task would occupy him (on and off) for two years. In the quest for Backhouse, Hugh called upon many of the same detective skills he had employed in researching the last days of Hitler. His industry would earn him the sobriquet 'The Sleuth of Oxford'.[5]

He began by searching for anyone still living who might have known Backhouse in Peking. He traced several people who had glimpsed him, or met him over some necessary business. They described him as a charming, diffident old gentleman, with exquisite manners – but not one of them had any idea of his true personality, or why he had come to China, or what he did there. Seeking to penetrate behind such superficial impressions, Hugh hunted for documentary evidence. In the Bodleian he found two volumes of correspondence concerning the Backhouse collection, showing that Backhouse had been advanced substantial sums of money to purchase books or manuscripts on behalf of the Bodleian, which had never arrived. Hugh tracked down in Toronto the personal papers of *The Times*'s correspondent in Peking, J.O.P. Bland, the man who had written two books with Backhouse. These were supplemented by the papers of Bland's superior on *The Times*, Dr G.E. Morrison. A friend and former pupil of Hugh's, the Sinologist S.A.M. Adshead, made a search in Morrison's papers, deposited in the Mitchell Library in Sydney. Among these was a document summarising the remarkable entrepreneurial activities of Backhouse in the years 1914–1918. One source of information led to another, and so on. A chance allusion in a letter from an Oxford jeweller revealed that as an undergraduate Backhouse had been forced to flee England to avoid his creditors. A reluctant reference in a confidential note by the British Minister in Peking implied that Backhouse had been a secret agent of the British Government during the First World War, involved in a mysterious and protracted operation to purchase arms.

These archival sources strengthened Hugh's scepticism about the memoirs. But what they revealed was just as fascinating, and perhaps still more outrageous. Backhouse, the respected scholar, turned out to be a forger, a fraud, a charlatan of epic proportions, who had bamboozled distinguished scholars and librarians, cynical journalists, hard-headed Scottish and American businessmen, senior diplomats, generals and politicians. Hugh greeted each discovery with glee. Backhouse had convinced one of the largest shipbuilding firms in the world that he had brokered a deal for them to supply six battleships to the Chinese; persuaded the War Office that he could arrange for the supply of tens of thousands of light weapons for the Western Front; and duped an American printing company into believing that he had negotiated a contract to supply 650 million banknotes to the Chinese. None of these arrangements came to anything, of course; but somehow Backhouse's reputation remained unblemished. Those who had been taken in by him were either too stupid to realise what had happened, or too embarrassed to make an issue of it.

Gradually Hugh formed a picture of this elusive personality. He realised that Backhouse's behaviour could not be explained simply in terms of mercenary motives. Rather, he was a fantasist, for whom the line between reality and lies had become blurred. Hugh speculated that Backhouse may have convinced himself of his own fabrications. His irresistible air of sincerity, which overwhelmed his victims' resistance, suggests as much. Moreover there was often, if not always, a small seed of fact in the stories that sprouted from his imagination. Typically he would appropriate to himself dramatic roles played by others. This became the standard Backhousian technique: 'like the young cuckoo he extrudes the legitimate birds from the nest and swells to fill it alone'.

Backhouse's astounding career, as revealed by Hugh, invited comparison with another great fantasist, Frederick Rolfe, the self-styled 'Baron Corvo'.*

---

* A.J.A. Symons's *The Quest for Corvo* was a life of the eccentric author, artist, photographer and fraud Frederick Rolfe, who used the pseudonym 'Baron Corvo'. Subtitled 'An experiment in biography', the book told the story of the author's investigation of his subject, presenting aspects of Rolfe's life and character as they were revealed to him.

Inevitably, too, Hugh was reminded of the Reverend Robert Peters. The deceitfulness of such men was matched only by their cheek.

By the summer of 1975, two years after accepting the parcel at Basle Airport, Hugh was ready to resume discussions with Macmillan. 'Do you remember the Wicked Baronet about whose memoirs Caro Hobhouse most improperly told you just under two years ago?' he asked his editor, Alan Maclean. 'I panicked on hearing this and begged you to say nothing. Well, I have since made a study of him, and find him curiouser and curiouser, and have ended by writing a short* book on him.'[6] He told Blair Worden that what he had written was 'probably unpublishable', because vested interests would use the law to prevent its publication – 'but this may be all to the good, as it will probably, if published, destroy what shreds of reputation I may possess'.[7] In a later letter to Worden, he discussed the structure of the book:

> The difficulty throughout was the fact that I had not merely to discover my hero's life but to dispose of the two false lives – the life in the *DNB* and then (what Hoeppli added to and reconciled with that life) the life recounted in the *Memoirs*. Thus the process of reconstruction was inseparable from the process of demolition. Moreover, the interpretation had to be built up tentatively, leaving judgement on each episode in suspense, because each episode, taken singly, was inconclusive: it was only the general pattern, when that emerged, which ultimately destroyed the individual rationalisations of innocence.[8]

Hugh's solution to this problem was to dramatise the process, so that readers feel that they are taking part in the investigation, within the chronological structure of a biography. But the memoirs, which had been the starting-point of the trail, are discussed in detail only at the end of the life, when they were written; so that their sensational content is prevented from dominating the rest.

The result was a triumph. 'Entranced by the wicked Baronet,' read a telegram from Maclean. A contract was agreed, by which Macmillan paid an advance of £2,500. Hugh's former American publishers, Harper & Row, were slow to appreciate the potential for the new book, so A.D. Peters sold it instead to Knopf, for an advance of $7,500. Hugh wanted to call the book *Portrait of a Scholar*, but Macmillan thought that title too demure, so they settled on *A Hidden Life*; Knopf preferred *Hermit of Peking*.[9] He resisted pressure from both publishers to include at least some of Backhouse's memoir, because he was concerned that to do so might upset the Backhouse family, which could then create copyright problems, and because to print

---

* Not that short: 391 printed pages in the British edition.

the memoirs would undermine the argument of the book, that they were bogus.

The book was published in Britain at the end of October 1976, to almost universal acclaim. Among the reviewers who praised it were Rebecca West (*The Sunday Telegraph*), Peter Conrad (*The Spectator*), Dan Jacobson (*The Guardian*), Jack Lambert (*The Sunday Times*) and Michael Ratcliffe (*The Times*), who lauded it as 'the best and most original true story of the year'. Even his old enemy Philip Toynbee (*The Observer*) thought highly of it. The book was warmly received too by the panel on BBC Radio's *Critics' Forum*. According to Marina Warner, writing in the *New Statesman*, *A Hidden Life* was 'a model of the biographer's art'. American reviewers were equally enthusiastic. In *The New York Times Book Review*, Paul Theroux described Hugh's book as 'an absolute corker ... somewhere between *The Secret Life of Walter Mitty* and *The Quest for Corvo*, with an epilogue straight out of Frank Harris's *My Life and Loves*'.

An accident of history added to the timeliness of the book. In 1976 Mao Tse-tung died and his formidable widow, Chiang Ch'ing, leader of the notorious 'Gang of Four', established herself openly in the power which she had long exercised behind the scenes. She was said to have greatly admired the Empress Dowager, and to have consciously emulated her imperial ways. Her enemies readily accepted the parallel, and explicitly referred to her as 'the new Empress Dowager' in their propaganda against the regime. These events stimulated a revival of interest in the real Empress Dowager and the last days of imperial China, for which the volume edited by Bland and Backhouse constituted a principal source. Abroad, and especially in the United States, émigré Chinese scholars had already begun the process of historical revision. Hugh's exposure of Backhouse's unreliability meant that the history of the period needed to be written anew. This topicality helped to ensure that *Hermit of Peking* became a bestseller in America.[10]

As well as the public praise, Hugh received a number of private fan letters. Perhaps the most surprising of these came from the Cambridge historian Geoffrey Elton: a formidable character, known, indeed feared, for his exacting standards and pungent judgements. *A Hidden Life* was 'marvellous', enthused Elton, 'the sort of book that any sensible historian must wish he had written'.[11]

In the early 1970s cracks began to appear in the wall of reticence surrounding British Intelligence activities in the Second World War. Sir John Masterman's book about the 'XX' Committee, *The Double-Cross System in the War of 1939–1945*, appeared in 1972. This was based on a report written at the request of his superiors after the end of the war in Europe. A handful of copies had been distributed, but since then successive heads of MI5 had resisted Masterman's attempts at wider circulation. By the late 1960s Masterman felt strongly that no purpose was being served by continuing to keep the story secret; on the contrary, there were good reasons for making it public. The defections of the 'Cambridge ring' of spies had given the impression that British Intelligence was amateur, even inept; it was time to alert the public to one of its wartime successes. After the revelations about Philby early in 1968, several of Masterman's wartime colleagues urged him to publish. Herbert Hart, for example, argued that 'publication of the book would do much to counter the ill-effects of the Philby affair'. Masterman made one further attempt to persuade the authorities to allow him to proceed, but after this failed he decided to implement what he called 'Plan Diabolo', signing an arrangement with Yale University Press to publish the book in America, outside the reach of the British authorities. He presented this as a *fait accompli*, while expressing his willingness to make limited changes for security reasons. The Attorney-General advised the Prime Minister that there was a *prima facie* case for prosecuting Sir John Masterman under the Official Secrets Act. Masterman kept his nerve under pressure, maintaining that the official resistance to publication was emotional rather than logical. Eventually it crumbled, allowing simultaneous publication of the book in Britain and America. In considering the matter, the Foreign Secretary, Sir Alec Douglas-Home, had been briefed by Dick White, as head of MI6, and by his Permanent Under-Secretary, Denis Greenhill. All three had been pupils of Masterman's at Christ Church. 'If I can't trust my old tutor,' protested Douglas-Home, 'who can I trust?'[12]

Hugh encouraged Masterman to defy the ban. He was impatient with the cult of secrecy, which he felt no longer served any purpose. Bureaucratic inertia was preventing those with inside knowledge from publishing in this area, leaving it vulnerable to amateurs relying on poisoned documents, inaccurate gossip and the self-serving memories of vainglorious old men. Inevitably they produced accounts that were at best distorted, and sometimes utterly erroneous. Several of the books now appearing drew on information in captured German documents, available for scrutiny while the corresponding Allied documents were withheld. Modern researchers were being fooled by the wartime British deception operations, just as the Germans had been. The industrious American writer Ladislas Farago, for example, chronicled the exploits of German spies operating in Britain, without the slightest suspicion that these spies had been controlled by the 'XX' Committee.* The *Abwehr* had believed what the British wanted them to believe, and, based on his study of the German documents, Farago

---

* *The Game of the Foxes: The Untold Story of German Espionage in the United States and Great Britain During World War II* (1972).

believed it too. Having taken the bait, he now maintained that German intelligence had been much more successful in spying against the British than previously acknowledged. Farago, and others like him, tried to supplement what they found in the archives by interviews with those known to have been involved in secret intelligence during wartime. Hugh suggested to Farago that his assumptions might be mistaken, but he was too obtuse to take the hint.

By the mid-1970s the continuing activities of researchers and writers brought them close to the most jealously guarded secret of all: the breaking by British Intelligence of the German Enigma ciphers. In 1974 the authorities yielded to pressure and allowed Group Captain F.W. Winterbotham to publish his book *The Ultra Secret,* which revealed for the first time the source of Ultra intelligence. Over the next few years, almost every wartime operation would be reassessed in the light of this disclosure. One result was a boost to the publishing industry. In 1976 Hugh reviewed a huge book – almost 1,000 pages – entitled *Bodyguard of Lies,* a history of Allied deception. The author, the journalist Anthony Cave Brown, had interviewed Hugh some years earlier, after arriving in Oxford unannounced, armed with a letter from Harper & Row requesting his assistance. Hugh subsequently heard colourful stories of Cave Brown's peregrinations around the addresses of those formerly engaged in secret intelligence. Arriving at Winterbotham's house while the owner was out, he had climbed in through a window, found a bottle of whisky and helped himself, in the best traditions of Fleet Street.

Cave Brown had received a large advance from Harper & Row. Shocking revelations were promised. When the huge typescript dropped onto the desks of British publishers, several of them sought Hugh's advice. Hugh himself consulted old friends and former colleagues about Cave Brown's claims. He assessed the American edition in *The New York Review of Books,* poking fun at Cave Brown's passion for inessential detail, much of it wrong.[13] The book portrayed British Intelligence as a gentleman's game, an extension of country-house life. This thesis, remarked Hugh, 'seems to me worthy of a novelette'. His review was a masterly work of demolition, employing a succession of small detonations to bring the whole work crashing down in ruins. He showed how Cave Brown had absurdly magnified Menzies's role in intelligence operations, depicting the contest between MI6 and the *Abwehr* as a personal duel between Menzies and Canaris. Hugh suggested that Menzies (who had died in 1968) had been a principal source for the book. By his own admission Cave Brown had visited Menzies, then seventy-four, at his country house in Wiltshire. The elderly Menzies was proud of wartime achievements and distressed by subsequent failures – the last straw being the flight to Moscow of Philby, his most trusted officer, whom he had designated as his successor. Hugh diagnosed the distortion that ran through Cave Brown's book as a symptom of Menzies's senile vanity, aided by vague and weakened memory.

Hugh received compliments on this witty and judicious review from former intelligence colleagues such as Ewen Montagu, 'Tar' Robertson and Noel Annan. It elicited a furious response from Cave Brown himself, who insisted that Hugh had reneged on the good opinion of the typescript he had expressed to a British publisher.[14]

A few months after his piece on *Bodyguard of Lies* appeared in *The New York Review of Books*, Hugh was asked by Robert Silvers to write about another much-heralded American blockbuster, *A Man Called Intrepid: The Secret War*, by William Stevenson. This was a biography of Sir William Stephenson, the Canadian in charge of an organisation called British Security Co-ordination, responsible during the early part of the war for intelligence liaison with the Americans. Since author and subject had such similar names, and to avoid confusing them in his review, Hugh referred to Sir William as 'The Hero' and Mr William as 'The Biographer'. The latter had made some startling claims. 'Stripping away the veils of secrecy, abandoning all the checks of evidence, or probability, or decency, he has presented The Hero as the universal genius: the Midas who turned all that he touched into gold; the master of economic life; the prescient mastermind who directed all British and American intelligence; the secret manipulator of presidents, prime ministers, and kings.' Hugh ridiculed such claims as 'impertinent'. Far from having, as was boasted, 'overwhelming significance', the book was 'utterly worthless'. Hugh referred to his recent review of *Bodyguard of Lies*, and mentioned that Cave Brown had failed to understand the organisation of British Intelligence. 'To make such a charge against this biographer would be unfair. It would be like urging a jellyfish to grit its teeth and dig in its heels.'

Hugh ended his review by reflecting on the delusions common to both Menzies and Stephenson:

> During my own period in the secret service I was often astonished by the puerility of some of our grandees, which I ascribed to their insulation from real life, their absorption into a self-contained sub-culture. I now realise that the same quality, if events are magnified by war, can lead, in old age, to dangerous hallucinations. This is a sad fact, and we should draw the obvious conclusion. We should remember with affection our old clubland heroes, but publishers should flee from their approaches and friends should prevail upon them to be silent.[15]

Hugh had a longstanding interest in the Holocaust, the mass murder of Jews by the Nazis. He had reviewed books on the subject by Gerald Reitlinger and

Raul Hilberg, and considered the latter's *The Destruction of the European Jews* (1961) a masterly work, though almost unbearable to read because of its horrific subject-matter. In 1976 he indicated to the Board of Deputies of British Jews his willingness to give evidence in a forthcoming court case concerning a Holocaust-denying pamphlet entitled *Did Six Million Really Die?*, which he described as 'absurd, dishonest and pernicious'. The pamphlet, written by a member of the far-right National Front, had been widely distributed to schools in Britain and other countries. It had been banned in South Africa, and the distributors had appealed against the ban; in what was regarded as a test case, international Jewry campaigned for the ban to be upheld. Hugh said that he was 'happy to help the defence in any way that I can, including, if necessary, and if it is possible for me, giving evidence in South Africa'. He signed an affidavit testifying that he had studied the pamphlet and judged that, 'behind a simulated objectivity of expression, it is in fact an irresponsible and tendentious publication which avoids material evidence and presents selected half-truths and distortions for the sole purpose of serving anti-Semitic propaganda'.[16]

In the event his presence was not required. The publisher of the pamphlet was eventually put on trial in Canada, where Raul Hilberg gave evidence for the prosecution. He was convicted, but freed on appeal. Among those appearing in his defence was David Irving, whose *Hitler's War* was published with much fanfare in 1977.* The book was said to have been ten years in the making; or perhaps twelve. It was certainly a substantial work, drawing on a wide variety of original sources. Irving claimed to be offering a fresh view of his subject, untainted by the opinions of earlier historians. One aspect that was certainly original, and which attracted worldwide attention, was his claim that Hitler had been unaware of the mass extermination of the Jews.

Hugh had maintained cordial, if very cautious, relations with Irving for over ten years. Each lent the other documentary material. The two men were never on first-name terms. Irving had several times invited the Trevor-Ropers to dinner at his Mayfair flat, but each time Hugh had declined, expressing his regrets that other commitments made them unable to attend. Now Irving invited Hugh to a party to celebrate publication of *Hitler's War*. Hugh replied that he could not come, pleading another engagement – although his appointment diary was blank for the evening in question. He had begun a correspondence with Gerald Fleming, a scholarly writer determined to prove the flaws in Irving's arguments and whose tireless research matched Irving's own. 'I believe he has some scholarly qualities,'

---

* This was the date of first publication of the British and American editions; the book had already appeared in German.

Hugh told Fleming. 'But all Irving's virtues seem to me ruined by his prejudices and perversity: also by his obstinacy in perversity. He is not a historian but a propagandist, and he has never learned proper method. He writes like an autodidact – like Hitler.'[17]

The Sunday Times asked Hugh if he would like to review Irving's new book on Hitler. He had already seen an early copy. 'The book is exactly as I expected,' he told the Literary Editor, John Whitley;

> Irving is a man of great energy and some remarkable gifts which must be recognised. He has been very successful in digging out documents and he can be very exact in matters of scholarship. On the other hand he has some extraordinary blind spots and strong prejudices of which he seems to be unaware. He has been convicted before now of twisting the evidence in a scandalous manner, and I have already found instances of this in the new book. His method of documentation is such that the reader is bound to be impressed and cannot test. All this means that to review him effectively one needs space.

Whitley replied that he had put the case for more space to the Editor, Harold Evans, 'and I am happy to say that he is as keen as I am'.[18] Hugh's article filled the entire front page of *The Sunday Times* 'Weekly Review'. He praised Irving for his 'indefatigable scholarly industry', and for the 'many new details' he had uncovered. He found the book 'well organised and well written'. But he showed how Irving's 'consistent bias' had distorted the evidence throughout. Hugh examined the radical claim that Hitler had not authorised, and had not even known about, the extermination of the Jews. He showed how Irving had seized on a small and dubious particle of evidence, and built upon it a large general conclusion, overlooking or reinterpreting the more substantial evidence to the contrary.[19] Evans congratulated Hugh on 'an incisive and brilliant piece of work'.[20]

'Irving is a menace,' Hugh declared in a letter to Eberhard Jäckel, Professor of Modern History at the University of Stuttgart. 'He uses every controversy, which he initiates and prolongs, as a means of self-advertisement, and welcomes even adverse publicity for the same reason.'[21] Jäckel was a powerful critic of Irving's. He specialised in the history of the Third Reich, with a particular interest in Hitler. In the mid-1970s he and Hugh acted as joint editors for a three-volume edition of the Goebbels diaries, originated by the German publishers Hoffmann und Campe.[22] The two historians worked closely together to resolve difficult editorial issues, and developed a friendship based on mutual respect. They often exchanged views about Irving and about other topics in the murky sea of Nazi studies.

The Goebbels diaries appeared in German in 1977; a year later an English edition was published, by Secker & Warburg in Britain and by Putnam in

America. Copyright in the diaries was claimed by François Genoud, who sued Hamish Hamilton after they published some earlier Goebbels diaries in 1982. There was a further kerfuffle in 1992, when Genoud threatened to sue *The Sunday Times* for serialising a new version of the diaries obtained from Russian sources by Irving and purchased from him, while the *Daily Mail* was simultaneously serialising Goebbels' diaries purchased from Genoud.

In the summer of 1977 the Trevor-Ropers flew to Denver, Colorado, and travelled on to Boulder, where Hugh was due to give a series of lectures as part of a conference of teachers, organised by Professor Edward Rozek* of the University of Colorado. Hugh found that he was expected to lecture every day, five days a week, for three weeks. He had announced that he would speak on the great historians from Herodotus onwards, but he had not a single lecture ready on his arrival. 'I am congenitally incapable of preparing lectures, articles, anything, ahead of time,' he explained to Robert Blake; 'I always work best under the lash; and so I leave everything until it simply <u>has</u> to be done. Then my scholarly perfectionism comes into play: I hate doing anything badly; so I go through agonies of tumultuous industry at the last minute.' In Boulder he rose at five o'clock and started 'scribbling away like mad', contriving always to have a carefully prepared text – which was just as well, since he lectured at nine in the morning, following immediately after Hugh Lloyd-Jones, an excellent lecturer. Hugh was satisfied with the result, 'which may well make a book'.[23]

Despite the demanding programme, Hugh returned regularly to Boulder over the next few years. He seemed to enjoy the pressure. Xandra too enjoyed Colorado, and usually accompanied him. But in 1978 there was a last-minute complication. James had become engaged to Angela Huth, a novelist with one daughter from her previous marriage to the journalist and travel writer Quentin Crewe. Neither Hugh nor Xandra thought it an ideal match. Hugh remarked disdainfully that Angela wrote 'kitchen-sink' novels – which suggests that either he did not understand the term or, more likely, that he had not read any of her books. Practical considerations steered James and his fiancée to a date in late June for their wedding. Disgruntled, Hugh announced that he was committed to Colorado and could not delay his departure. In an impassioned letter James begged him to allow Xandra to remain behind for the wedding. This was grudgingly agreed: Hugh flew out to Colorado alone, and Xandra joined him there

---

* Rozek was an immigrant from Poland, who had shown outstanding gallantry in fighting the Nazis. He became a political scientist, notable for fierce anti-Communism. In the early 1980s he faced criminal charges for embezzlement following an acrimonious divorce. After a long struggle, he was eventually able to clear his name on all counts.

eight days later. He persuaded himself to send the couple a congratulatory telegram. 'I am <u>very</u> sorry that I was debarred from coming to your wedding,' Hugh wrote to his stepson afterwards.[24]

His own father had died in January that year, at the age of ninety-two. After Kathleen's death Hugh had visited Bertie occasionally, and discussed his welfare with Pat and Sheila. He admired his father's stoicism in his declining years. 'Although I hope that I shall not reach that age,* I hope that, if I do, I shall be able to imitate him, who never uttered a word of complaint but was invariably cheerful and wonderful good company.'[25]

In a lecture on the Scottish Enlightenment which Hugh gave in Edinburgh in 1977, and which was subsequently published in *Blackwood's Magazine*, he emphasised the benefits to Scotland of the Anglo–Scottish Union.[26] By the mid-1970s the Union was under more strain than at any time in its history. The clamour for Scottish independence was increasingly noisy. In the election of October 1974 the Scottish National Party (SNP) won eleven seats in Parliament, more than ever before; and these eleven MPs exerted a disproportionate influence on a weak Labour Government, internally divided and lacking an overall majority. In 1977 the Prime Minister, James Callaghan, was forced into a short-lived pact with the Liberals. His policy was to slake the thirst of Scottish voters for independence by granting a measure of self-government. In the same year a Scotland Bill, providing for a directly elected assembly if this were supported by a majority of Scottish voters in a referendum, was introduced to Parliament.

Hugh campaigned actively against the Bill. He lobbied MPs such as Maurice Macmillan, Tam Galbraith,[†] Hugh Fraser, Jonathan Aitken and Alan Clark. One evening he read a paper on 'The Unity of the Kingdom' to a group of Conservative MPs, journalists, bankers, industrialists and academics, gathered at Aitken's house in Phillimore Gardens. He took part in a BBC Television debate, 'We British'. For him, devolution was a disastrous policy, likely to exacerbate tribal resentment between the English and the Scots. There was evidence for this in the 'hate mail' he received from angry nationalists, though this was balanced by plenty of support, from Scotsmen as much as from Englishmen. Hugh opposed the Scotland Bill in two articles for *The Times*, and in an article for *The Scotsman*.[27] He argued that, far from satisfying the appetite for self-government, devolution would lead to the dismantling of Great Britain. Roy Jenkins told Hugh that he agreed with everything he had been saying, 'but it is too late'.

---

* Nor did he.
† Sir Thomas Galbraith, Conservative MP for Glasgow Hillhead 1948–82, a former Under-Secretary of State for Scotland.

Hugh's use of the term 'Scotch' antagonised Scots men and women who considered it archaic and possibly pejorative. It elicited a fierce rebuke from Nan Dunbar, breaking silence for the first time since her excommunication five years earlier.[28] Hugh replied crushingly to an OUP editor who had the temerity to question his use of 'Scotch' in the text of a lecture entitled 'Edward Hyde, Earl of Clarendon', delivered on the tercentenary of Clarendon's death.[29] '"Scotch" was good enough for David Hume,' insisted Hugh, 'and it's good enough for me.' In a letter published in *The Times* he defended his use of the term. He saw no reason to abandon correct English so lightly, he wrote, merely because it irritated some Scotsmen (and women). '"Scotch" is the form used by every good Scots writer – Hume, Robertson, Adam Smith, Scott, Carlyle, Cockburn, Stevenson – and I prefer their company to that of misleading academics or their docile and misled pupils.'[30]

The most 'misleading' of those academics, perhaps, was William Ferguson, whose *Scotland's Relations with England* Hugh reviewed unfavourably in *The Times Literary Supplement*. 'His book is simply the old nationalist thesis, illustrated with a mass of detailed but disorderly erudition, very little critical judgement, and a great deal of intemperate personal abuse,' he wrote. 'As one of the chief targets of this abuse,' he continued, 'I wondered, at first, if I was a proper person to review the book. However, as I read on, I soon discovered that such an objection would equally disqualify almost any other possible reviewer.'[31]

In his opposition to devolution, Hugh found himself in alliance with the Labour MP for West Lothian, Tam Dalyell. This might seem an unlikely partnership, but Dalyell was far from being a typical Labour MP. A Scots baronet, educated at Eton and Cambridge, he had been Chairman of the University Conservative Party before joining Labour at the time of the Suez crisis. Dalyell and Hugh contemplated writing a pamphlet together, though after some discussion Dalyell decided to press ahead on his own, and developed the proposed pamphlet into a short book.[32] Hugh contributed a foreword to Dalyell's *Devolution: The End of Britain?*, which was published in 1977.

The Scotland Act passed through Parliament and received the Royal Assent. A late amendment to the Bill had stipulated that the Act would be repealed if it failed to gain the support of 40 per cent of the Scottish electorate. Attention now turned to the referendum, held on 1 March 1979. Hugh kept up his opposition to the end, with a piece in *The Spectator* only days before the referendum, in which he urged Scottish voters to reject 'Labour's shabby project'.[33] In the event, they voted in favour, by a narrow majority (52 per cent to 48 per cent), but sufficient numbers abstained to prevent support from topping the stipulated threshold, and the Act was therefore repealed. The SNP withdrew its support from the Government, forcing an immediate general election on 3 May 1979. A swing to the right ensured victory for the Conservatives under their new leader, Margaret Thatcher. Labour was defeated, and the SNP was almost annihilated, losing nine of their eleven MPs. It would be almost two decades before a new Scotland Act established a Scottish assembly in 1998.

Even as he was battling against plans for Scottish devolution, Hugh was fighting a rearguard action closer to home. To their dismay, the Trevor-Ropers discovered that a site adjacent to Chiefswood had been earmarked for a new, 400-bed District General Hospital. This development threatened to end the arcadian isolation of their home, and incidentally to render it unsaleable. An article in *The Sunday Times* estimated Chiefswood's value at £75,000.[34] Hugh belatedly began to organise a protest, but the odds were stacked against him. Plans for the hospital were already well advanced: building was due to start in 1980. The Chairman of the Borders Health Board refused Hugh's request for an interview.

The local MP, David Steel, had been campaigning for a new hospital in the Borders since his election in 1965. As leader of the Liberal Party, then propping up the feeble Labour Government, Steel was in a position of influence. Hugh appealed to Steel as one of his constituents, one who had voted for him in the past. He argued that there was another, more suitable site for the hospital nearby. Steel agreed to a meeting at the House of Commons. While expressing sympathy for their personal circumstances, he told Hugh that it was too late to change the location of the new hospital. In any case, he said, only the drive and the view from the rear upstairs window of the house would be affected, because the greater part of the hospital would lie below the level of the walled garden. He suggested that the Trevor-Ropers might seek compensation for 'planning blight'. Hugh told him that he was not thinking in such terms: 'I want to save Chiefswood'.[35]

For him, the isolated setting was all-important. 'I like being here,' he told Blair Worden; 'I work uninterrupted, in my own world, in delicious solitude.' He often stayed there alone, seeing no one, and venturing out only to walk in the woods and along the stream. Indeed, as he told Worden on another occasion, 'the great advantage of living in Scotland is that one need have no truck with one's neighbours, and so can concentrate on literature. The great disadvantage is that sometimes one feels the need of intelligent society.'[36] Such remarks did not endear him to the locals.

He tried to muster support elsewhere. Tam Galbraith offered to help, though he was pessimistic about the possibility of generating political pressure against the new hospital. Support could not be expected from the

SNP, to whom Hugh was a *bête noire*: a letter to *The Scotsman* went so far as to urge that Hugh's 'castle' be sacked and the man himself be 'frog-marched to the Border'.[37] One local duchess is said to have described him as 'the most hated man in the Scottish Borders'.[38] Galbraith recommended Hugh to solicit support from bodies such as the National Trust for Scotland, the Georgian Society and, in particular, the Council for the Preservation of Rural Scotland.[39] If the proposed new hospital could be presented as a threat to Scotland's heritage, it might yet be stopped.

But all these efforts proved ineffective. Bureaucratic momentum proved unstoppable, and the hospital was built as planned. The Trevor-Ropers discovered that they were not entitled to compensation for planning blight, as the application to build the hospital had been lodged before the relevant law had come into force. To cap it all, Hugh was involved in a serious accident, while driving up the M6 motorway to Chiefswood: he skidded in the snow on Shap Fell and collided with 'a gigantic juggernaut'. He was unhurt, but his car (a Mercedes) was wrecked.*

After an absence of almost five years Hugh returned to work on Mayerne in the summer of 1978. At the suggestion of Robert Blake, he applied to spend a month during the following spring at the Rockefeller villa at Bellagio, which offered comfortable accommodation in the Italian lakes for scholars who needed a retreat from day-to-day concerns. His aim was to have the book finished in draft form beforehand, so that he could revise and polish it there. In September he told Blake that he had written five chapters in two months.[40] Four months later he reported on progress to Frances Yates. He had finished another chapter, he told her. Though, perhaps surprisingly, the Rockefeller Foundation had rejected his application, the prospect of a month in Italy had been an incentive to have the book complete by that time.[41] Yet he could not finish it. Even as he approached the end, gloomy thoughts arose in his mind. Once again he questioned whether the effort had been worthwhile; and again he put the book aside. 'I am always hoping to return to Mayerne,' he sighed in 1982.[42] He would work on it intermittently after his retirement in 1987, adding and revising passages, until illness compelled him to desist, when the work was almost complete. One reason for delay was his continuing hope that he might find Mayerne's personal papers, neglected in a remote corner of some obscure archive. By the time he had given up hope of them, the task of finishing the book was beyond him.

*

* The Bentley had been scrapped in the late 1960s, after breaking down on the M4 while Xandra was driving to London to collect her daughter. She was frightened of having to tell Hugh what had happened when they arrived at 8 St Aldates in a hired car; in fact he took the news well.

On 1 June 1979 Hugh received a letter from the new Prime Minister, Margaret Thatcher, offering him a life peerage. This was an unexpected honour. When Robert Blake had been ennobled in 1972, he boasted of being the first historian to be raised to the peerage since Lord Acton in 1869.* Blake had since been joined in the House of Lords by Alan Bullock and Asa Briggs, both of whom had played an important role in founding new academic institutions. Hugh could claim no such achievement. Moreover, he was aware that he was unpopular in high places. Noel Annan – himself a Lord – had recommended him for an honour, and had been told only recently that such a thing was 'impossible'.[43]

When Hugh made the tentative suggestion that he ought to refuse the peerage as inappropriate to a scholar, Xandra protested. 'Think of the people it will infuriate!' she exclaimed.[44] This argument persuaded him, if he needed persuading. In any case he planned to continue writing under the name Hugh Trevor-Roper. His peerage was announced in the Queen's Birthday Honours List on 16 June.

'Wouldn't the parents have been pleased!' wrote his sister Sheila. He received more than two hundred messages of congratulation on his peerage, including a telegram from Harold Macmillan, and letters from Lord Carrington and Ted Heath. Letters arrived, too, from 'Tar' Robertson and Dick White, who remarked that another RIS colleague, Stuart Hampshire, had received a knighthood in the same list. Among colleagues who sent felicitations were Noel Annan, Robert Blake, Christopher Hill, Eric Hobsbawm, Michael Howard, Dimitri Obolensky and Keith Thomas. 'I suppose Xandra now really will be Lady Trevor-Roper!' quipped her brother – though in fact, this new title offered the possibility of a new name.[45] Hugh was reluctant to be known as Lord Trevor-Roper. 'Double-barrelled titles are an invention, and a monopoly, of Wilsonian peers,[†] and I don't want to be in that *galère*,' he told Valerie Pearl.[46] There was already a Lord Trevor, and to adopt the title Lord Roper might seem something of a climbdown after so many years insisting on being addressed as 'Trevor-Roper'; and moreover carried the risk of confusion with the socialist cleric Lord Soper. In either case, some might assume that his first name had been Trevor all along. 'The Baron Mercurius?' suggested Nigel Lawson.

Hugh preferred to adopt a title that had been held by his family in the eighteenth century: 'the ancient, romantic and beautiful title of Dacre'. When he consulted Xandra, she was at once enchanted by it. But there was an obstacle, in the form of an existing Lady Dacre. The title, which passed

---

* Wrongly: see the footnote on page 104.
† He was wrong about this, as shown by the examples of Lords Baden-Powell (created 1929), Noel-Buxton (1930) and Courtauld-Thompson (1944).

through the female as well as the male line, had devolved onto Rachel, wife of the playwright William Douglas-Home. Indeed there was another Lord Dacre, Lord Carlisle (father of Hugh's friend George Morpeth), who held the title Dacre of Gillesland. To avoid confusion, Hugh proposed that he be known as Dacre of Glanton, the village where he had been born. (He had toyed with the idea of being Lord Dacre of Melrose, but thought better of it.) 'In the eternal game of one-upmanship,' Hugh boasted to Xandra, 'I think that Dacre of Glanton puts us one up on the Blakes, Briggs, Bullocks, etc; but I must not hint at this when I am dining with the Blakes tomorrow.'[47]

Hugh discussed the matter with Garter King of Arms, Sir Colin Cole. He pointed to other examples of peers with the same title, differentiated by place, such as the Lords Astor and Astor of Hever, or the Lords Russell and Russell of Liverpool. Garter saw no reason not to accept his proposed title, though he recommended that Hugh should inform Lord Carlisle and Lady Dacre, as a matter of courtesy. It was not clear whether their consent was required. Time being short before the summer recess, Hugh telephoned the Earl and the Baroness, and obtained the verbal agreement of both. Lord Carlisle subsequently confirmed his agreement in a friendly letter. His relative, the Duke of Norfolk, welcomed Hugh as another Dacre cousin. 'I think I have pulled it off,' Hugh wrote to his wife.[48]

He spoke too soon. On his next visit to the College of Arms, to sign the form for his patent, he learned that Lady Dacre had telephoned Garter to voice her objections. Her husband had apparently suggested that the similar titles would lead to misdirected correspondence. A series of tetchy exchanges followed. Lady Dacre's cousin, Lord Hampden, wrote to Hugh supporting her position, in his capacity as head of the family. But after almost two months of wrangling, Lady Dacre withdrew. Glanton Parish Council expressed its delight that he was taking its name. On 14 November Hugh was introduced to the House of Lords by his two sponsors, Lord Blake and his brother-in-law, Lord Astor of Hever (Gavin Astor). The ceremony involved the new peers bobbing and ducking, in unison with the heralds, three times, in deference to the doctrine of the Trinity. Almost five years later Hugh would write to the Leader of the House, Lord Wakeham, recommending that this 'ignominious, trivial and absurd' part of the ceremony be abandoned. In his view it was 'ridiculous, humiliating and lowering to the dignity of the House'. In reply, Wakeham strongly doubted whether there would be any support for a change. He pointed out that the mechanics of the ceremony made it difficult for any government to seek to 'pack' the House of Lords: its sheer prolixity meant that no more than three new peers could be introduced at any one sitting. Hugh accepted the force of this argument.[49]

The new Lord Dacre of Glanton accepted the Tory Whip, though he did not always support the Party line. In an interview with *The House Magazine* in 1986 he would describe himself as 'a wayward Conservative'.[50] He made his maiden speech in the House on 8 April 1981, in the debate on the Church of England's proposal to modernise the Prayer Book. The Church was insisting that this was an internal matter and no business of Parliament. Hugh argued that, on the contrary, the Church could not logically claim independence of Parliament, the representatives of the laity, while enjoying the benefits of establishment. In summing up as Lord Chancellor, Lord Hailsham (formerly Quintin Hogg)* welcomed the contribution to the debate made by his old friend, whose 'varied intellect and intellectual versatility' he had long admired, though he confessed that in the past he had considered him to be 'more of a flying buttress[†] than a pillar of the Church'.[51]

Nan Dunbar was another of those who wrote to congratulate Hugh on his peerage.[52] In January she had extended an olive branch in his direction, by seeking his permission to set a piece of his prose for translation into Latin by candidates reading classics at Glasgow University – which she described, pointedly, as 'the ultimate accolade'. In his reply Hugh addressed her as 'Nan' for the first time. He was delighted, he said, 'at any sign that my immortal prose is read'. He asked her to send him a copy of the paper 'so that I may purr with pleasure at the sight of it'. Later in the year she complied with his request. 'There are few pleasures so delicious as to re-read, and admire, one's own felicitous prose,' he responded.[53] Relations between the two of them thawed. She invited the Dacres to dine with her and her husband on Burns Night, and they accepted; Hugh ingratiated himself by having a second portion of haggis. Later in the year he dined as her guest at Somerville, and afterwards wrote conciliatingly, 'I always knew Mercurius was wrong about Somerville'. Their correspondence took on a teasing tone. On hearing that she was to preach in Glasgow Cathedral, he recommended her to consult a late-seventeenth-century work entitled *Scotch Presbyterian Eloquence Display'd*.[54] She sent him a home-made Valentine's Day card, illustrated with pictures of kilted Highlanders in defiant postures. He declared a *Pax Dacreana*.

Spy fever reached epidemic proportions towards the end of 1979, with the publication of *The Climate of Treason* by Andrew Boyle. The book alleged

---

* Hogg had inherited the title Viscount Hailsham from his father in 1950. In 1963 he disclaimed the title in a vain bid to succeed the ailing Harold Macmillan as leader of the Conservative Party and Prime Minister. He received a life peerage from the new Conservative Prime Minister, Edward Heath, in 1970.

† This was an allusion to a remark made by Winston Churchill, who once claimed that he supported the Church 'like a flying buttress – helpfully, but outside'.

that the traitors Burgess, Philby and Maclean had not acted alone in spying for the Soviet Union; there had been a 'fourth man', identified in the book as 'Maurice', and even a 'fifth man', 'Basil'. MI5 reacted to these claims by compiling a dossier of Boyle's errors. Dick White urged Hugh to blast the book in a review. 'I don't believe there ever was a climate of <u>treason</u>.'[55] Speculation was rife about the identities of the fourth and fifth men. It was reported that 'Maurice' had been a Cambridge don, whose surname contained five letters with a 'B'. *The Times* triumphantly identified Donald Beves, who had died in 1961. But this was the wrong don. In response to questioning from Labour MPs, the Prime Minister told an astonished House of Commons that Sir Anthony Blunt, Fellow of Trinity College, Cambridge, eminent art historian and former Surveyor of the Queen's Pictures, had been a spy. It was not clear whether he had supplied information to the Soviets since the war – when Russia had been an ally – though he had confessed to having tipped off Maclean in 1951, enabling him and Burgess to flee before they were apprehended. In return for Blunt's co-operation with his MI6 interrogators, he had been granted immunity from prosecution. News of this indulgent treatment provoked indignation. There was renewed talk of a 'cover-up' and a demand for Blunt to be punished in some way. It was announced that the Queen had stripped him of his knighthood.

Only a week before his exposure, the Dacres had attended a lecture given by Blunt and had talked to him at the reception afterwards. Blunt apologised for failing to recognise Hugh, pleading short sight – an explanation with which Hugh was sympathetic, though he had learned not to expect warmth from Blunt. Despite working alongside each other during the war, when Blunt had been an officer in Liddell's 'B' Division of MI5, they had not become friends. Hugh was repelled by Blunt's cold, aloof manner and supercilious drawl. 'I never dealt personally with Blunt,' he wrote later. 'He was simply a presence in the office and although we had occasional conversations, they never had any depth. I had a clear impression that he disliked me: that he looked down his nose at me and did not think me worth talking to: he was, after all, a Fellow of Trinity and I was a nobody.'*[56] In subsequent years, when they occasionally met, Blunt was always awkward, and seemed to want to avoid Hugh.

Hugh had already written his review of *The Climate of Treason* when news of Blunt's treachery became public. The following week Hugh wrote an article for *The Spectator*, arguing that nothing had been gained by Blunt's

---

* Some years after the war, at a dinner in County Donegal, Hugh was disconcerted to realise that his dinner companion, the Princess of Hesse-Darmstadt, had confused him with Blunt. He did not much like this.

exposure. The clamour was absurd, he felt, and quoted Macaulay, that there was no spectacle so ridiculous as that of the British people in one of its periodic fits of morality.[57] 'I hope that the Blunt mania will now die down,' he told Valerie Pearl. 'I despise Blunt – a sanctimonious Cambridge prig – but I hate witch-hunts.'[58]

Blunt resigned from his club, and surrendered his Fellowships of both Trinity and the Society of Antiquaries when it became obvious that he would otherwise be expelled. However, he was reluctant to resign from the British Academy.[59] The Council of the Academy considered the question and recommended his expulsion. A counter-motion deplored Blunt's conduct, but proposed that the Academy should not proceed further in the matter. It was argued that he had been elected a Fellow for his scholarly achievements; his political views and his personal conduct were irrelevant. Both these motions were on the agenda for the annual general meeting of the Academy on 3 July 1980. A.J.P. Taylor told *The Times* that he would resign if Blunt was deprived of his Fellowship; Plumb threatened to resign if Blunt was not. Eric Hobsbawm appealed confidentially to Hugh. 'If the Academy is to be stopped from making a fool of itself (and us),' wrote Hobsbawm, 'then it can be done only by people like yourself. I hesitate to say "by you", though I am sure your individual voice would carry a great and perhaps decisive weight, since you cannot be suspected of any sympathy for Blunt's past views, and you are on record as condemning his extra-curricular activities; not to mention your personal standing.' Hobsbawm felt that he could not speak up for Blunt himself. 'Quite apart from being counter-productive or dismissed as biased, people like myself cannot help but be seen as defending their past.'[60]

Hugh lunched with Blake before the annual general meeting, and found his companion strongly in favour of Blunt's expulsion, the more so as the lunch progressed and claret gave way to port. At the meeting itself Hugh was ready to speak on the other side, but found that it was unnecessary to do so. After forty minutes' tense discussion, a proposal that the Academy should 'pass on to the next item on the agenda' was carried by a large majority. Blake protested, and stalked out angrily. Fellows emerging from the Academy were nonplussed to find A.J.P. Taylor talking to reporters on the steps outside.

'I was personally against expelling Blunt,' Hugh was quoted as saying afterwards. 'I regard him with absolute contempt, but what is his crime? He betrayed his family, his colleagues, his friends. These are moral faults for which we despise people. They're not crimes for which we punish them. The Academy is not a tribunal of morals. If we say we'll expel so-and-so because he's a shit, we'll have to have a whole new set of rules.'[61]

*

Private Eye reported that Hugh wanted to become Provost of Oriel when Kenneth Turpin stepped down in 1979.[62] A group of his colleagues encouraged him to stand. Hugh was reluctant, as he reported in a series of letters to Xandra, who was recuperating in a nursing home after being knocked down by a car in London. 'The comedy about the Provostship goes on,' he told her early in December. 'It is becoming clear that none of the present external candidates is likely – on present form – to get a clear majority, and that if an internal candidate emerges, it is likely to be me (though I am not exactly a "candidate", since I am not at all eager to accept).' Xandra, on the other hand, was eager, especially as the post of Provost came with a fine house. Moreover, she liked the idea of her husband's being in command, as her father had been; she never grasped the academic concept of the 'Republic of Letters', which limits the powers of the head of college.

Hugh's disdain for Oriel had lessened over the years. He had become quite fond of the place, and dined there more frequently. But he had not courted popularity with his colleagues; indeed, he had deliberately offended some. On one occasion, for example, he invited his former pupil Peter Burke to dine at Oriel. As he was presiding that evening, he could instruct the butler where the diners would be placed at dessert. 'Whom do you want to sit next to?' he asked Burke loudly: 'I don't recommend anybody.' Thus even the suggestion that he might stand was enough to bring into being a party of those opposed to him, led by his old adversary Christopher Seton-Watson.[63] Nevertheless Hugh was tempted by the idea of becoming head of a college, if only to keep up with Blake. Eventually, at Xandra's urging, he allowed his name to go forward. He claimed to be relieved when it was rejected. 'The thought of being headman of that introverted village, with its peasant elders, did not attract me,' he told Worden.[64]

The college had difficulty in finding a new Provost. Several candidates were invited to stand, only to be rejected. In the end Turpin was persuaded to stay another year. Even then the problems were not over. The next Provost, the former BBC Chairman Lord Swann, resigned after serving only nine months. Hugh admitted to 'enjoying a certain *schadenfreude* on the matter'.[65] In any case, he was by this time head of another college, albeit in Cambridge. Late in 1979 he had received an invitation to become the next Master of Peterhouse. As he told his brother, this came as a complete surprise. He had no connection with the college. Research revealed that Peterhouse had last elected a Master who was not already a Fellow or an honorary Fellow in 1788. As a result, there was no procedure: candidates were not interviewed, but simply nominated and voted upon. 'But it is a pleasant surprise,' Hugh told Pat. 'Peterhouse has a fine Master's Lodge – said to be the best in Cambridge: an elegant Queen Anne house – as well as the best cuisine and a very fine cellar.' Of course, he explained, in accepting the sudden offer, 'I was not governed by such worldly considerations.'[66]

For Hugh, this new opportunity came as a lifeline. He had been due to retire as Regius Professor in 1981, at the age of sixty-seven, but he could continue as Master of Peterhouse until 1987. He had little hesitation in accepting. 'I have given up a year as Regius Professor for seven years as Master of Peterhouse,' he was quoted as saying.[67] Xandra was excited at the thought of a grand new house on which she could exercise her decorative skills. Soon after he had agreed to move to Cambridge, Hugh received the offer of a visiting professorship at the European University in Florence. This would have been a well-paid post, with few commitments, in pleasant surroundings. His life would certainly have been very different had he taken it. But by the time he received the offer he was already committed to Peterhouse.

Hugh tendered his resignation as Regius Professor to the Prime Minister. Interest now focused on the succession. After a survey of the History Faculty indicated its support for Keith Thomas, a representative committee met the patronage secretary. Each historian present gave his opinion that Thomas was the best man for the job – until the penultimate person asked, Professor Margaret Gowing, who dissented strongly and suggested Michael Howard instead. Jeremy Catto supported her nomination. The patronage secretary was therefore in a position to present two names to the Prime Minister. Unconfirmed rumours suggest that Hugh had used his influence against Thomas, and that Mrs Thatcher was given the impression that Thomas was extremely left-wing. In due course it was announced that the next Regius Professor was indeed to be Michael Howard. Since Howard already held the Chichele Chair in the History of War, this appointment could be presented as an economy, which perhaps appealed to the thrifty Prime Minister. It was also possible that Howard was the only eligible historian whose name was familiar to her. Hugh briefed his successor about his new duties over a bottle of champagne at the Ritz.[68]

Hugh had already been elected an honorary Student of Christ Church, and in the spring of 1980 he bagged another scalp he had long coveted for mischievous reasons, when the University of the South in Tennessee (generally known as 'Sewanee') awarded him a Doctorate of Divinity (DD). There was an agreeable irony about the title, which was guaranteed to annoy the clergy; he was delighted to hear that the canons of Christ Church were furious about it. At the Christ Church gaudy that year Hugh was due to make the speech proposing the toast. Their distinguished guest, the newly appointed Archbishop of Canterbury, Robert Runcie, had himself just been awarded an honorary DD, from Oxford University. Hugh welcomed him 'as the newest recruit to our devout fraternity'.[69]

On 20 May 1980 Hugh delivered his valedictory lecture as Regius Professor to a packed Examination Schools. Entitled 'History and Imagination', this was an assertion of the principle of free will, the choice of alternatives, as opposed to the determinist orthodoxies against which he had been arguing most of his career. Hugh reviewed the events of his own lifetime, and showed how much depended on accident, chance and the choices made by individuals. In conclusion, Hugh told a story against himself, recalling the words of Evelyn Waugh during one of their public spats in the *New Statesman* twenty-six years earlier.* 'One honourable course is open to Mr Trevor-Roper,' Waugh had written. 'He should change his name and seek a livelihood at Cambridge.'[70] The retiring Regius Professor expressed regret that Waugh was no longer alive to savour this little victory.

'I shall miss Oxford dreadfully,' Hugh confided to Worden. 'I hope you will visit me and lighten my exile in those remote fens.' He confessed to being 'still bewildered' by his appointment. 'What can be the meaning of it?' he wondered. 'What, a historian must ask, is the internal condition of a college which makes so strange an appointment?'[71]

As Master of a college he would have no formal role within the Cambridge History Faculty – which was perhaps just as well, since a confidant reported that 'your translation has caused consternation' among Cambridge historians. 'The Faculty is, and always has been, a delicately balanced, fractious body. It is feared that you may be an Ayatollah with little patience for their fractious politics.'[72]

Hugh received a heartening letter from Michael Postan, former Professor of Economic History at Cambridge, who had been a Fellow of Peterhouse from 1935 to 1965, and an honorary Fellow thereafter. (As co-Editor of the *Economic History Review*, Postan had published Hugh's 'gentry' articles in the 1950s.) 'I think I might, with my forty-five years' experience of the college, assure you,' wrote Postan encouragingly, 'that you will find its ambience more pleasant than that of any college I know.'[73]

---

* He had been reminded of this several weeks earlier by Arnaldo Momigliano, former Professor of Ancient History at University College, London, whom he met outside Blackwell's Bookshop.

Master

Peterhouse is the most ancient of the Cambridge colleges, founded in 1284. It occupies a site on the west side of Trumpington Street, next to the Fitzwilliam Museum. The Master's Lodge stands isolated on the east side. Beyond a neo-classical frontage lies Old Court, an imposing quadrangle, its façades presenting three different architectural styles. A narrow stone staircase on the south side curves up to the first-floor Parlour, where Fellows retire after lunch to drink coffee and read newspapers. Below is the panelled Combination Room, where Fellows in gowns gather in the evening before dinner, and then return for dessert. Strictly speaking, the Master can visit the Combination Room only as a guest, since he is not one of the Fellowship. At the sound of a gong, the Fellows and their guests arrange themselves in the order in which they will sit, guests being invited to take the place of honour next to the head. The Master, or, in his absence, the most senior Fellow present, leads the procession through a side entrance and onto a raised dais of the candle-lit Hall, where the undergraduates stand in anticipation of their arrival. A long table stretches before them. The Master takes his place at the far end, where the Butler stands behind him, and remains standing while the diners file down either side, filling up the table from the end. When all are in place, hands resting on the backs of their chairs, the gong sounds again and one of the scholars speaks the Latin grace. This marks the end of the ceremony, the signal for everyone present to be seated.

The Hall is the oldest college building in Cambridge,* its interior restored in the Pre-Raphaelite style. The Perne Library, built in the late sixteenth century, houses around 4,000 rare books, a collection as good as any in England. The chapel, constructed in the reign of Charles I, has been interpreted as a statement of the architectural ideals of Archbishop Laud and the High Church party. It is remarkably unaltered inside, with open balustraded stalls, and a special pew for the Master.[1] To the rear of the college is the deer park, the smallest in England, and beyond the college walls water-meadows lead down to the river. There have been no

---

* Jesus has incorporated some older buildings, originally forming part of a Benedictine nunnery, which pre-date the college's foundation in 1496.

deer in the park since 1934, when the last of the herd – a solitary doe – was destroyed. In a jaundiced moment Hugh would make an analogy with the Fellows: a small tribe, rarely venturing outside the college limits, gradually dwindling towards extinction from inactivity and inbreeding.

As well as being the oldest, Peterhouse is also the smallest Cambridge college. In 1980 the Fellowship numbered a mere two dozen. There was no procedure for finding and selecting new Fellows; they were elected on an *ad hoc* basis, almost always on the recommendation of an existing Fellow in the subject. The most junior of the Fellows had been elected to a full Fellowship and appointed a college lecturer while still an undergraduate. The new Master disapproved of this system of patronage. He felt that young scholars, however meritorious, should go out into the world and experience unfamiliar environments, rather than remaining in the same one throughout. He used the term 'test-tube babies' to indicate that new Peterhouse Fellows were cloned from the old. The fact that Peterhouse was one of the few remaining all-male colleges made it easier for Fellows to shape successors in their own image. By the 1980s almost all of those Cambridge colleges that had previously been reserved for men had begun to admit women and to recruit female Fellows, and pressure was mounting for Peterhouse to follow suit. The Governing Body had voted to admit women back in 1969, but the change in the college statutes had not been enacted by the deadline, and a second attempt to introduce the measure had failed by one vote to obtain the necessary two thirds majority. 'I know that it's probably inevitable,' Hugh's predecessor had said of admitting women to Peterhouse, 'but I hope we will vie with Trinity for the privilege of being the last.'

'I am discovering Peterhouse, which I like,' Hugh told Blair Worden, a couple of weeks into his first term. 'The Fellows are generally civilised and quite convivial, and I am generally learning to identify them.' Nevertheless, he was disappointed to discover that none of them was due to retire during his period of office, as he had hoped to inject some fresh blood into the narrowing arteries of the college. He asked Worden to pass on gossip about the Fellows, citing one of his favourite maxims: 'all information is useful'.[2]

Peterhouse was especially strong in engineering, and outstanding in the natural sciences, with no fewer than three Nobel Prize-winners among the Fellowship – though by the nature of their subject the scientists tended to be less of a presence in the college, working in often distant laboratories. They formed the 'silent majority', generally passive in college politics. Their colleagues referred to them disparagingly as 'commuters'. In fact the Department of Engineering was only just outside the deer park. As Hugh came to know the scientists better, he would appreciate that there were several highly cultivated individuals among them. 'In Oxford we assume that it is the scientists who are the philistines,' he observed in a letter to Worden. 'At Peterhouse the reverse is true.'[3]

History was another subject in which Peterhouse had a proud tradition. The best-known Master of recent times had been an historian, Sir Herbert Butterfield, who was head of the college from 1955 until 1968. Butterfield made his name by criticising the Whig interpretation of history; though in doing so he plunged his knife into a corpse already slain by Namier and his followers. Butterfield had been a Tory of a very different stamp from Namier, or indeed Hugh: Christian, pro-appeasement, illiberal. Noel Annan would describe him as 'a radical conservative'.[4] Some of Butterfield's ideas and attitudes had been adopted in a more extreme form by the next generation of Peterhouse historians. One displayed a poster of General Franco in his rooms, and was said to have worn a black armband on the anniversary of the Generalissimo's death.

Since Butterfield had retired in 1968 there had been two elderly Masters, neither of whom had succeeded in mastering the Fellowship. In such a small community an organised clique could exert a controlling influence. As elsewhere, the bachelor dons spent more time in college, especially in the evenings, when they dined together in Hall. This made it easier for them to co-ordinate their actions. For the decade before Hugh's arrival as Master, a small group of around half a dozen such dons in effect ran the business of the Governing Body, while the rest looked on or away.[5] Some of the other Fellows referred to them as 'vampires', because they emerged after dark; Hugh generally referred to them as the 'mafia'. Most were in early middle age when he took office as Master. They were not all of one mind: they included Catholics, Anglicans and atheists; historians and mathematicians; homosexuals and heterosexuals. One Fellow described them as being like overlapping spotlights focused on a single point. What united them, Hugh decided, was a hatred of liberalism.

The dominant figure in this group was an historian, Maurice Cowling, then in his mid-fifties and therefore almost a generation older than the others. A Fellow since 1963, he boasted that 'not a sparrow can fall to the ground within Peterhouse, but I know it'. It would be misleading to think of him as a typical leader. Rather, he saw himself as an *éminence grise*, one who operated in the shadows rather than in daylight. Cowling preferred to manipulate others rather than act himself. Hugh would refer to him 'leading from behind, like an old sheepdog'. His motives for his ceaseless intriguing were often unfathomable, and perhaps amounted to little more than a delight in making mischief. In this, of course, there was a superficial resemblance between Cowling and the new Master. Cowling's arched eyebrows contributed to his air of amused wickedness. Outwardly he adopted the role of a selfless elder statesman, exerting his influence for the benefit of the college. Occasionally he would deliver *ex cathedra* judgements which he circulated to the Fellowship.

Cowling's reputation as an operator was enhanced by his contacts in the press. Indeed Cowling had made a false start as a journalist before he found his *métier* as a don. In 1954 he had been appointed a junior leader-writer on *The Times*, succeeding Peregrine Worsthorne, a Peterhouse man and later a stalwart of *The Sunday Telegraph*, who became a lifelong friend. Another of his contacts in journalism was the bibulous former Editor of *The Spectator*, George Gale. Cowling built himself a wing onto George and Patricia Gale's large house on an Essex estuary. As Hugh would discover, Worsthorne had a weekend cottage nearby. 'There the co-owners gather at weekends, with like-minded guests, and walk along the sea-shore, like Walrus and Carpenter, exchanging melancholy reflections on the world,' he told Worden, 'and from this pool of collective wisdom Gale, Cowling, Worsthorne draw off buckets of sad sea-water to discharge, on their different levels, through their separate public fountains.'[6] Among the 'like-minded guests' to be found at Wivenhoe at weekends was Colin Welch, who created the *Daily Telegraph*'s 'Peter Simple' column, a Peterhouse man, a contemporary and close friend of Worsthorne's; and the *Daily Telegraph* columnist T.E. Utley. Yet another Cowling contact in the right-wing press and former undergraduate at Peterhouse was the political journalist Patrick Cosgrave, favoured for a short period by Mrs Thatcher. Cosgrave had been political columnist of *The Spectator* in the early 1970s, when Gale was Editor and Cowling Literary Editor. Two former Peterhouse dons, the philosopher Roger Scruton and the historian John Vincent, both wrote regularly for the newspapers. Within this fraternity there was plenty of talk about the 'Peterhouse Right' and its significance in 1980s Britain.

Hugh had known Cowling slightly for some years. As Literary Editor of *The Spectator* in the early 1970s, Cowling had overseen the second incarnation of Mercurius Oxoniensis. Even so, Hugh had always found him a close, mysterious person. Cowling's opaque utterances, so valued by his admirers as expressions of profound thought, appeared to Hugh deliberate obscurantism, an offence against clarity. His emphasis on the centrality of religion to British politics seemed wrong-headed, and his lack of interest in social forces obtuse, as if nothing had been learned about the study of history over the past two and a half centuries. Hugh was disinclined to sponsor Cowling for the British Academy when his name was mentioned in 1976.* 'I find Cowling's style rebarbative and his ideas sometimes perverse,' he had then told Blake; Cowling's was 'a strong mind trapped in its own glutinous frustrations'.[7]

---

* Cowling was never elected to the Academy. Possibly Hugh kept him out.

In his first term as Master, Hugh was asked by *The Listener* to review the first volume of Cowling's *Religion and Public Doctrine in Modern England*. This was a delicate assignment. Whole chapters were devoted to the thought of 'such Delphic prophets' as Butterfield, Oakeshott (a guru of the Cambridge Right) and the Peterhouse Dean, Edward Norman. Hugh would later describe it as 'a series of potted intellectual biographies of a miscellany of English worthies'.[8] It was alleged that the Dean, though himself one of the 'mafia', had sought (unsuccessfully) to compel Cowling to divulge what he had written about him before publication. Hugh contrived to find polite words about the book, though he admitted to finding it 'strangely organised'.[9] In private, however, he described it as 'a very rum work', most interesting for what it revealed of the thought patterns of Cowling and his ilk, which he outlined in ironic terms to Worden. 'The subject is the intellectual history of our time and the great spiritual crisis in which we have found ourselves. I find, on reading it, that this intellectual history has unfolded itself, and this crisis has been observed, and is to be resolved, almost entirely within the walls of Peterhouse.'[10] Hugh viewed the self-regarding dons of the Peterhouse Right with amused detachment. He commented on the introverted quality of Cowling's book in a letter to Hugh Lloyd-Jones. 'The outer world is occasionally mentioned *en passant*,' he remarked drily.[11]

Cowling's project was almost ludicrously reactionary: to roll back the advances of the Enlightenment, to substitute orthodoxy and doctrine for openness and debate. In the fight against 'liberal pieties', he considered rudeness ('reactionary bloodiness') to be a virtue, indeed a duty. 'Vile' was a term of commendation in Cowling's looking-glass lexicon. 'You are evil,' he told a young historian with obvious approval. 'We must have him,' he declared of a candidate for a Fellowship: 'he is horrible!' This kind of talk made Cowling an effective teacher: undergraduates found his cynicism both shocking and exhilarating.[12] No doubt his startling inversion of conventional morality stimulated young minds to fresh thought. But his ideas were essentially destructive. As a result of Cowling's influence Peterhouse gained an unenviable reputation for 'ill-mannered, xenophobic exclusiveness'. Discourtesy was not only tolerated, but encouraged. Guest nights frequently degenerated into protracted private parties, at which the bottle circulated until late into the night and the tone deteriorated accordingly. Such an atmosphere made it difficult to bring in guests. The lucky ones were ignored; others insulted. A Fellow who brought in a black South African clergyman was embarrassed when some of his colleagues refused to share the table with him. Distinguished Jewish visitors endured anti-Semitic sneers. On the first time she dined in college,* the wife of a newly-arrived Fellow found herself seated next to a drunken don, who proceeded to regale her with a detailed description of the sexual tastes of all those around her. A visitor from Merton attending a Peterhouse feast was placed beside Cowling, who said nothing for a long while, then broke his silence with the words, 'From the moment you sat down, I knew you were a shit'. The Reverend Lyle Dennen, husband of Hugh's stepdaughter Xenia, wrote a letter of complaint to the Master about comments made to him at dessert after he had dined in Hall as the Master's guest.

Cowling took the credit for Hugh's appointment. He claimed that he had pushed for Hugh as Master 'to serve everyone right'. It was he who had telephoned to ask if Hugh was willing to allow his name to go forward. There had been an attempt beforehand to run Brian Wormald, then the senior Fellow and on the brink of retirement, for Master, but this had failed, because Wormald was obviously incapable and the majority of the Fellows took the view that he would be a mere cipher of the ascendant group. Cowling had undertaken to find a more acceptable candidate. In doing so his principal objective had been to find a Master who would resist the pressure to admit women. While lunching at the Athenaeum, Cowling had posed a question to his cronies: 'Who on earth can we get as Master to keep women out?' At that moment Hugh happened to walk into the room. All eyes met in agreement: this was the man for the hour.

The informal process of selection rendered king-making easier.[13] 'Your election was, as you may guess, to a very great extent the result of effort on my part and on the part of those who have been working with me,' Cowling grandly informed Hugh, immediately after the result; though he explained that 'the final decision to invite you was made unanimously'. Because of this unanimity, Cowling assured him that there would be none of the resentment that sometimes accompanied such an election. 'There is a very general feeling that we have come not only to a good but even to a brilliant conclusion.'[14]

The first frame of reference for those unfamiliar with the college was Tom Sharpe's farcical novel *Porterhouse Blue* (1974). This depicted a modernising Master of a traditional college, thwarted in his attempts at reform by ultra-conservative college Fellows and even more reactionary college servants. The dons were all gluttons; the book's title referred to a special kind of stroke, known to afflict diners after excessive indulgence at the table. New-comers to Peterhouse were assured that the similarity in names was purely coincidental. Nevertheless, it was undeniable that the Fellows of the college

---

* Before the college admitted women, female guests were allowed to dine only on the annual 'Ladies' Nights'.

enjoyed a comfortable existence, as their predecessors had done over the centuries. In particular, the bachelor Fellows dined luxuriously every night, at tables lit by silver candlesticks, drinking fine wines from cut-glass decanters and waited on by college servants. They lived like the rich, and perhaps suffered *folie de grandeur*. The Dean, a Fellow since 1971, had been a leather-jacketed radical in jeans before his arrival at Peterhouse; since then he had moved sharply to the Right, and now deplored the liberalism of the Church of England. His reformed views were set out in his 1978 Reith Lectures *Christianity and the World Order*. Like the other bachelor Fellows, he took a strong interest in wine, and would sit waving a glass of claret over his stomach, sniffing it from afar.

Of the half-dozen or so regular dining bachelors, two were Catholic converts, recruited by Father Gilbey, Cambridge's version of Father D'Arcy. These were the architectural historian David Watkin and the mathematician Adrian Mathias. Both dressed in the newly fashionable fogeyish style: handmade pinstripes or three-piece tweed suits, polka dot ties and a selection of panamas. Both vigorously opposed the admission of women – as did the Dean, who was said to have talked of 'letting the scrubbers in'.

Even before he arrived at Peterhouse, Hugh had heard in Oxford that 'the hom. Party' gave its character to the college. Stories were told of cross-dressing, of undergraduates and dons being given girls' names. Within Cambridge, people spoke knowingly about 'Peterhouse tastes' and 'Peter-house inclinations'. There was an ever-present risk of scandal. Under-graduates visiting the rooms of one Peterhouse Fellow were greeted by a phallus-shaped candle; another Fellow was rumoured to have been thrown down the steps of the William Stone building by an undergraduate who found his advances unwelcome. Such unedifying tales made Peterhouse notorious.[15]

Two members of the 'mafia' founded the Grafton Club,* which met for a breakfast at the end of each term. Undergraduates wearing morning dress chomped their way through six meat courses, washed down with champagne, and lingered so long that they often had to be turned out by the college servants, to allow the Fellows to have their lunch. Afterwards they would roam drunkenly about the college, serenading below the windows of the Admissions Tutor as he conducted interviews, or dropping their trousers and 'mooning' to passers-by in Trumpington Street. Hugh's objections to the Grafton, as snobbish, gross and puerile, were dismissed by Mathias as 'middle-class moralising'.

---

* Named after the Duke of Grafton, a Peterhouse man who was Prime Minister from 1768 to 1770. Presumably the founders of the club were unaware that Grafton had been a Unitarian who wrote a tract against upper-class extravagance.

When Hugh referred jokingly to the bachelor dons as the 'Old Ladies', he was solemnly warned by an apprehensive Fellow that they were a caucus: that he could only rule through them, and must on no account quarrel with them. In particular, he was advised to keep in with Cowling if he did not want to become isolated within the college. The position of Master was a lonely one; after his arrival in Cambridge Hugh found that he lacked convivial company and intellectual stimulation. He had not appreciated how much he depended on contact with intelligent graduate students to provide both.

'Peterhouse is a very strange place,' he reported to Worden. 'I cannot help wondering, even more than before, why this college of papists, obscurantists, boring engineers,* lunatic mathematicians, and contorted historians ever even <u>thought</u> of me as its Head.'[16] At first he flattered himself that the Fellows had chosen him to reform Peterhouse, having woken from their slumber and observed how sunk and decayed the college had become. But he was soon disabused of this notion by Jean Floud, Principal of Newnham, who explained that they had chosen him because they believed him to be an extreme conservative, who would protect them from change of any kind – above all, from women.

Soon after his arrival at Peterhouse Hugh decided that the lethargic Domestic Bursar should be replaced. He had been shocked by the state of the college: by the lax procedures, the abuses, the neglect of college responsibilities, the declining academic standards (recent results in history were particularly low), the rare books defaced or missing from the library, the prevailing torpor. He imagined it as a small, unreformed Norman monastery in the twelfth century, on the Isle of Ely, surrounded by the web-toed peasantry of the Fens. There the monks dozed in the chapel or the warming-room, or exchanged gossip in the buttery, the more literate of them occasionally picking up a book to decorate the capital letters or ponder a new meaning in the Holy Writ. Only on saints' days would they be stirred to greater activity, by the prospect of thick soup and soused lampreys, roast teal and mulberry pie and great Fenland cheeses, all washed down with good red wine.

'I have so far found no one,' Hugh told Worden, 'whom I can regard as a real ally.'[17] He complained that he had been given no information about the college, or its procedures, by anybody. The Peterhouse Senior Tutor, a lawyer called Roderick Munday, seemed to Hugh reluctant to answer his questions, or to act on his suggestions. Cowling had retreated into his 'cave' in Fen Court. The new Master felt that he was left to find his way, unescorted by those whom he thought might reasonably have

---

* He later repented of this description.

been expected to act as guides. Very early on, however, he was told which direction he should follow, by an unannounced caller, Hallard Croft, a mathematician who had been a Fellow of the college almost twenty years. Though unused to Peterhouse procedures, Hugh was nonetheless surprised to receive what seemed to him a series of instructions: to remove a certain Fellow from a certain office; to appoint as a new Fellow a friend of Croft's, described as 'a great acquisition to the Combination Room'; to support another Fellow's candidature for the office of Wine Steward. Croft referred to decisions reached by 'Us'. As senior bachelor Fellow, Croft presided in Hall and in the Combination Room on most evenings. He announced a new rule: dinner jackets should be worn at dinner on Sunday nights. (His mathematical colleague Mathias already adhered to this convention.) When Hugh queried the authority for this innovation, he received no satisfactory reply. So he ignored it. On the following Sunday evening Croft and his friends entered, resplendent in their black ties, to find the Master dressed in a particularly scruffy tweed jacket. The new rule collapsed. 'Why did we elect him if he isn't going to do what we want?' Croft asked bitterly.

This was the first skirmish in what was to prove a war of attrition. The new Master had proclaimed his independence of the party which made him. Hugh had arrived with no agenda, but he was determined to be his own man and, having taken stock of Peterhouse, he was keen to raise standards and eliminate abuses. Somewhat to his own surprise, Hugh became a force for reform. He put it about that, if crossed, he might decide to vote for the admission of women: thus flaunting the spectre of an invading army of females to terrorise the Fellowship into submission. Shortly after this first clash Postan was overheard speaking contemptuously about the 'mafia'. 'They are such fools,' he declared; 'they thought that they were electing a Tory, and never realised that they were electing a Whig.'

It was a convention that incoming heads of colleges were invited to dine by their peers. While he made his tour of the high tables of Cambridge, Hugh expressed himself in uninhibited terms about the shortcomings of his colleagues. A series of more or less calculated indiscretions found their way back to those Fellows who had expected him to be their tool, heightening their suspicions of the new Master. Battle-lines were drawn. 'My reign', he told Worden at the end of his first year as Master, 'is now reaching that climacteric stage commonly known as "the end of the honeymoon period".'[18] Hugh expressed his determination to 'cleanse the Augean stables' of Peterhouse. Part of this process entailed substituting diligent college officers for those whom he believed to be dilatory or negligent in their duties. Hugh described to Worden his method for sprucing up the college:

'I have gone stealthily around with my secret flit-gun, squirting disinfectant liquid into neglected crannies; whereupon somnolent spluttering creatures tumble out and I hastily sweep them aside.'[19]

On his arrival at Peterhouse, Hugh had discovered that the Perne Library had been leaking rare books. One reason, no doubt, was because the undergraduates had been allowed to work there. Hugh concentrated his efforts on raising funds for a new undergraduate library, to be housed in the former Museum of Classical Archaeology, a handsome building belonging to the college and about to revert to its control through the expiry of the lease. The Governing Body had approved this decision in principle before Hugh's arrival, to mark the college's seventh centenary in 1984. All that remained was to find the necessary money: one and a half million pounds. Little had been done so far. Hugh scanned the lists of old Peterhouse men, searching for generous philanthropic tycoons; but discovered only retired schoolmasters, provincial solicitors, income tax inspectors, journalists and 'a few forgotten historians'. Dining in London, however, he pulled off what he regarded as a great coup, after he found himself seated next to the financial wizard Lord Weinstock. Though an undergraduate of the LSE, Weinstock had been evacuated during the war, so that he had actually studied at Peterhouse, to which he felt an as yet unrequited loyalty. He offered to help with fund-raising, expressing surprise at the modesty of the college's demands. Hugh lost little time in securing Weinstock's election as an honorary Fellow. Soon after, Weinstock became chairman of the Appeal.

Rather than welcoming this development, the Governing Body vetoed the architect's final plans as too expensive. One of the librarians suggested a solution: if they disposed of those rare books that had not already been stolen, the vacant shelves could be used to house an undergraduate library.

Hugh struggled to conceal his exasperation. He sent Worden a stanza, from an apparently unknown hand, found (so he said) loosely inserted in the undergraduate guide to Cambridge. 'I fear, from the evidence of the last line, that it may refer to my college,' he wrote. 'I hope not. What do you think?'[20]

> Are you fancy, popish, queer?
> We have room to put you here.
> A Library whose shelves are bare,
> A Garden with no flowers there,
> A deer-park with no deer.

*

At a specially arranged dinner in the autumn of 1981 Hugh was presented with a *Festschrift*, a volume of essays in his honour by pupils, colleagues and friends.* The volume was edited jointly by Hugh Lloyd-Jones, Valerie Pearl and Blair Worden – each of whom contributed an essay – and published by Duckworth. It had originally been meant to appear at the moment of his retirement from the Regius Chair, but his election as Master of Peterhouse had caused him to retire a year earlier than expected. The book opened with Hugh's inaugural and closed with his valedictory lecture, from which it took its title, *History and Imagination.*

The dinner was held in Oriel. Many of the contributors were present, as was the Chancellor, Harold Macmillan, who earlier in the year had spent a couple of nights as guest of the Trevor-Ropers at Peterhouse. 'I thoroughly enjoyed my days at Cambridge,' Macmillan had written afterwards. 'It was like a dream or rather a novel by C.P. Snow.'[21]

There was a disconcerting incident at the dinner, after the new Regius Professor, Michael Howard, made a speech, in which he explained that his essay included in the volume had not been his first choice. Originally he had written about the double-agent 'Garbo', a by-product of his work on the official history of deception in the Second World War. But since some of its content derived from secret sources, he had been obliged to apply for clearance to publish it, and this permission had been denied. The refusal seemed to him absurd, as Garbo's activities had already been revealed in print, with official approval, more than once. In his speech, Howard described the episode in a jocular manner, and then presented his predecessor with a copy of the banned essay, neatly bound, and entitled *History and Imagination, Confidential Annexe, Top Secret Ultra.* Hugh accepted this offering and made a light-hearted speech of thanks. Then the Chancellor rose to his feet. Macmillan began by saying that never in his life had he heard such a shocking speech as Professor Howard's. At first Hugh assumed that Macmillan was joking; only after he had been speaking for a few minutes did it become clear that he was serious. The Chancellor deplored the frivolous attitude towards security which Professor Howard had shown, and declared that 'we are living in a period of peril comparable with that of the 1930s'. This took him on to 'the crisis of our time', from which he continued by talking about Hugh. The last part of his speech had apparently been prepared as a conventional tribute, but the first part seemed to have been a spontaneous and indignant reaction to what he had just heard.

* As well as the three editors, the contributors were as follows: Toby Barnard (a former pupil), Robert Blake, Fernand Braudel, Jeremy J. Cater (another pupil), Jeremy Catto, John Clive (Professor of History at Harvard), Richard Cobb, John Elliott, Geoffrey Elton, Michael Howard, David S. Katz (lecturer in Early Modern History at the University of Tel Aviv), Robert S. Lopez (Professor Emeritus of History at Yale), Jim McConica, Arnaldo Momigliano, Dimitri Obolensky, Walter Pagel, Piyo Rattansi (Professor in the History and Philosophy of Science at University College, London), Kevin Sharpe (another former pupil), Charles Stuart, William Thomas (Hugh's successor at Christ Church) and Frances Yates.

Howard was stunned by this outburst, but he sat silent, and the occasion passed without further embarrassment. Afterwards, in private conversation with Hugh, he explained his belief that the Security Services had panicked after the Blunt affair, and were now strongly opposing disclosures of any kind. The Prime Minister had been won over by these 'new morons'; in a conversation with Howard she had expressed regret that the Ultra secret had ever been revealed. Such a view struck Hugh as lunatic, of no possible relevance now that the whole technology of intelligence had changed. Sadly, there was now nobody left in the Secret Services of the generation who had worked alongside the 'amateurs' recruited in the war years, independent thinkers who challenged orthodoxies and established procedures: as a result the Security Services had reverted to their pre-war ways, and were becoming increasingly clannish, introverted and obstinate. Dick White later confirmed this view, and expressed his disgust with the new policy of unthinking suppression. Howard revealed that there had been an explosion when he had told the authorities that he wanted to publish the Garbo essay in a volume honouring his former tutor, the retiring Regius. It had been made clear to Howard that he had aggravated his offence by his choice of recipient: Trevor-Roper was *persona non grata*, indeed *ingratissima*.[22]

Hugh had been aware for a long time of the resentment caused by his cracks about Cowgill, Vivian, Menzies and their kind in *The Philby Affair*, and in his other writings on intelligence matters. But until this moment he had not appreciated the depth of the dislike. 'My name is evidently a red rag to the intelligence services,' he told Noel Annan. These had come under the control of 'complete bone-heads', who resented, indeed hated him because he had escaped their power and was no longer, in Graham Greene's expression, 'torturable'.[23] Hugh had been taken aback by Annan's tantalising disclosure, when congratulating him on his peerage a couple of years earlier, of the entrenched opposition towards him and the hostility that his name aroused. Although, as he now told Annan, he had no great desire to please the Establishment, or to earn its favours,

> I was nevertheless surprised, even somewhat pained, to learn that I was regarded by it as such a monster of disrepute, not even to be named in the respectable company of (say) the Lord Kagan,* the late Sir Eric Miller,† Sir Anthony Blunt, etc etc; and I wondered how I had earned this disrepute. After all, though I have sometimes shown mild irreverence towards some sacred cows (without however shooting, maiming or worrying any of them), I have never been to prison, or declared bankrupt, or struck off the Register, or deprived of my Fellowship, or

---

* Joseph Kagan manufactured the Gannex raincoats favoured by Harold Wilson. In 1980 he was convicted of theft for stealing from his own companies, and served a ten-month prison sentence.
† Sir Eric Miller was a businessman who committed suicide while under investigation for fraud.

extruded from the British Academy. So how is it that my name arouses, in those influential breasts, such fierce, implacable emotions?

In reply, Annan amplified his earlier hint. He confirmed that he had recommended Hugh for an honour, more than once. All such recommendations went before the 'Maecenas Committee', composed of civil servants, the Presidents of the British Academy and Royal Society, and other eminent men in the fields of learning and the arts. Annan had been told that it was 'hopeless' to put forward the names of Trevor-Roper, Taylor or Plumb. 'Attempts have been made on behalf of all of them. All have failed and will continue to fail. Each has supporters: each has enemies. Abandon hope.' Annan had persisted, however, and in 1979 had convened an 'indignation committee' in favour of modern history, at a buffet lunch following a meeting of the British Museum trustees, chaired by Hugh's former pupil Edward Boyle, by now Lord Boyle. Those assembled included Robert Blake, now of course Lord Blake. These three peers had signed a round-robin letter in support of Hugh's claims. However, Annan took no credit for Hugh's peerage, which, he conjectured, had been a political appointment, not one arrived at by the procedures governing the Honours List. 'If I am right,' concluded Annan, 'this could explain why you succeeded in becoming a peer & failed to become a knight.'

Annan shared Hugh's belief that SIS had not been pleased by *The Philby Affair*, though obviously this could not explain the objections to Taylor or Plumb.* He believed that their 'blackballer' lay buried within the Civil Service and its files, his objections being passed on year after year.[24]

History and Imagination was reviewed by Taylor in the *London Review of Books*. In passing he praised Hugh as an historical essayist without rival. 'When I read one of Trevor-Roper's essays tears of envy stand in my eyes.' Taylor took the opportunity to make a personal remark. 'I often read that Trevor-Roper and I are rivals or even antagonists. On my side, and I can confidently say on Hugh's, this is totally untrue. We have always been good friends and no cross word has ever passed between us.'[25]

In February 1981, the Thomson Corporation† sold *The Times* and *The Sunday Times* to Rupert Murdoch's News International. For some years the Thomson management had been locked in battle with powerful print unions. In 1979 an industrial dispute had closed both papers for nearly a year. By the time this was resolved the Thomson Corporation had lost the will to continue the struggle. A search began for a buyer. On 29 October

---

* Plumb would receive a knighthood in 1982. He had been considered for a peerage in Harold Wilson's resignation Honours List in 1976.
† Its founder, Roy Thomson, had died in 1976.

1980 Sir Denis Hamilton, former Editor of *The Sunday Times* and now Editor-in-Chief of both newspapers, circulated to the directors a secret memorandum setting out the criteria for accepting a new owner. The buyer would have to be in a position to guarantee the survival of both titles, with the resources and the determination to introduce modern printing methods in the teeth of union opposition.

Several individuals and organisations expressed interest in purchasing Times Newspapers Holdings Limited (TNHL), including the newspaper proprietor Lord Rothermere, the tycoons Robert Maxwell and Tiny Rowland, and various consortia, including one led by the Editor of *The Times*, William Rees-Mogg. Hugh outlined his views in a letter to Robert Blake. 'I am in favour of a takeover by a Trust rather than by a millionaire, but the management seems to prefer the latter, if he can be found, and is not Maxwell,' he confided, adding that 'the National Directors are in an interesting position.'[26] In January 1981 Hamilton assessed the seven suitors who had come forward. He noted that 'Lord Robens and Lord Dacre were anxious that the traditional independence and the character of *The Times* should be guaranteed'.

Only one buyer, the Australian media mogul Rupert Murdoch, appeared able to meet the requirements set out by the Thomson management. Nevertheless there was considerable unease about entrusting *The Times* to him. In establishing his international newspaper empire he was said to have left a trail of broken promises. For this reason he was not thought to be an ideal proprietor for such an important national institution.

The board of Times Newspapers Limited stipulated that the sale should be subject to certain conditions, to guarantee the continued editorial independence and quality of the newspapers. One of these was that the system of National Directors, defined as 'independent national figures', should be 'preserved and enhanced', by increasing their number from four to six. The board was supposed to approve the choice of any new directors, and to give its assent before a new Editor of either paper could be appointed or dismissed. Editors had the right of appeal to the board against interference by the proprietor. Hugh saw it as his duty, and that of the other National Directors, to see that these promises were met. He successfully urged that the guarantees be submitted, as essential conditions, to the Secretary of State for Trade, John Biffen, as part of the application for exemption from the Monopolies Commission. Biffen explained in Parliament that these guarantees were enforceable in law and, if broken, entailed 'formidable sanctions'. Hugh doubted their real force; still, they had at least 'put a paper hook through the nose of Leviathan'. Towards the end of January Murdoch gave the required formal undertakings, and on the basis of these the board approved his purchase of the company.

It was therefore disconcerting when Murdoch announced that he had appointed two new National Directors without consulting the existing four. The proprietor argued that since both had experience of the newspaper world, they would 'strengthen' the board. One of these two was Denis Hamilton, whom Hugh liked, while being unconvinced that he was sufficiently independent for the role. Much more alarming, however, was the other proposed 'independent' director: Sir Edward Pickering, former Editor of the *Daily Express* and a mentor of the young Rupert Murdoch's in the early 1950s. When tackled, Murdoch played the *ingénu*, claiming not to have realised that his action had breached the undertakings he had given. The board acquiesced, admitting Pickering as the sixth director. Discussion then turned to the question of the replacement for Rees-Mogg, who was retiring as Editor of *The Times*. Murdoch proposed Harold Evans, Editor of *The Sunday Times* for the past fourteen years. Hugh expressed reservations about him, as too weak, too modish and too inconsistent. His fellow National Directors appeared to share his misgivings. Hugh was inclined to favour the more conservative Charles Douglas-Home, Foreign Editor of *The Times*, an Old Etonian and a former Army officer. The start of the board meeting at which this issue was being considered had been delayed, and Hugh was forced to leave before it finished for a longstanding appointment in Oxford. 'Then we must record Lord Dacre as voting against Harold Evans,' said Murdoch. Hugh agreed and left.

Given what had been said at the board meeting, Hugh was surprised to learn subsequently that Evans had been appointed. *The Guardian* reported that Lord Dacre alone had voted against him, giving the impression that he was isolated on the board and out of sympathy with the new Editor. Robens afterwards revealed what had happened after he had left: Murdoch admitted that he had already offered the job to Evans, who had accepted it. Douglas-Home was appointed Evans's deputy. Meanwhile Evans's former deputy, Frank Giles, became Editor of *The Sunday Times*. Giles was near retirement, and it was understood that this was a stopgap appointment.

The board was remodelled, with the addition of several more directors, including a new Managing Director, Gerald Long. It soon became clear that Murdoch expected it to rubber-stamp his decisions. No agenda was sent out in advance of meetings, so there was no opportunity to consider items beforehand. The dates of meetings were often changed at short notice, making it difficult for directors to attend. Hugh deplored Murdoch's casual attitude to the formal commitments he had undertaken. Nevertheless he liked Murdoch personally and admired his energy and ability, and the efficiency with which he conducted business. In personal relations Hugh found Murdoch agreeable and urbane, even charming when he wanted: very different from the caricature of the newspaper tycoon. One might have guessed that Lord Dacre of Glanton was the kind of effete Englishman that Murdoch despised; but if this was so, he did not make it obvious. In fact their personal relations were usually civil, though sometimes more coldly civil than others.

Hugh distrusted the proprietor's taste and his motives. Looking back from the perspective of the mid-1990s, he would argue that Murdoch had been 'a baleful influence on our public life'. The Australian was known to have expressed contempt for the stuffiness of the British Establishment. 'He aims to moronise and Americanise the population' and 'wants to destroy our institutions, to rot them with a daily corrosive acid'. Hugh speculated about the psychological reason for this attitude. As an undergraduate at Oxford Murdoch had been very left-wing, and had displayed a poster of Lenin on the wall of his room. Hugh recognised that Murdoch tended to appoint peers to the board of Times Newspapers Limited, as if to say, 'All these people are buyable, they're digging their own graves for me.'[27]

When one of the print unions threatened to 'withdraw co-operation' in October 1981, Murdoch lost patience and declared that he would shut down the papers. Claire Tomalin, who dealt with Hugh in her capacity as Literary Editor, asked him to speak to a group of anxious journalists about this worrying development. After consulting Frank Giles, Hugh agreed. Following the meeting Hugh received a peremptory letter from Murdoch, demanding to know whom he had seen, what had been discussed and what right Hugh thought he had to meet journalists at all. Hugh answered drily that he considered himself free to meet anyone he wished, provided that the confidentiality of the board was preserved.[28] Murdoch did not acknowledge this reply. Hugh told Worden that he was 'locked in battle with Murdoch, who seems to have taken a strong dislike to me'. He anticipated a letter asking for his resignation. 'Murdoch has for some time made it clear that he regards me as Public Enemy No. 1,' he observed afterwards.[29] Hugh spoke to Hamilton on the telephone, who said that Murdoch tended to over-react, and assured him that the matter could be forgotten.

Murdoch replaced Hamilton as Chairman of the board. Hugh's conference with the journalists was raised at its next meeting, in which he defended his behaviour. Afterwards Murdoch put his arm around Hugh's shoulder, in an apparent gesture of friendship and reconciliation. Hugh was reminded of the moment in William Roper's life of Thomas More, when Henry VIII had similarly put his arm around More's shoulder.

In January 1982 Murdoch summoned the directors to a lunch to discuss who should replace Hamilton as a director. He proposed John Gross, former Editor of *The Times Literary Supplement*. This choice came as a pleasant surprise to the other directors, who had been expecting Murdoch to propose someone more obviously compliant. Then Murdoch introduced another, quite unexpected subject: he had decided to replace Harold Evans as Editor of *The Times*. He expatiated on Evans's failings, just as Hugh had done before Evans had been appointed. Hugh felt that Evans was being unfairly treated, but having opposed Evans's appointment less than a year earlier, and having criticised him since, he found it awkward to defend him now. Murdoch then put forward his candidate as Evans's successor: Sir Edward Pickering. The National Directors were unhappy with this choice. Pickering was sixty-nine years old, and therefore unlikely to remain in the post long. In Pickering and Giles, both *The Times* and *The Sunday Times* would be under the command of short-term leaders. Hugh suspected that they would be induced to retire simultaneously, clearing the way for Murdoch to merge the two newspapers into a seven-day operation.

Early in February, Murdoch telephoned Hugh from New York. He wished, he said, to bring the directors up to date. He had written to all 2,700 employees, demanding that 600 of them should go, and threatening otherwise to liquidate both papers. Journalists on *The Sunday Times* discovered that ownership in the titles of the two newspapers had been quietly transferred to Murdoch's holding company, News International Limited, though the National Directors had not been consulted or informed. This raised the possibility that Murdoch might shut down the newspapers, and then restart them, free of any restrictions. When asked to explain the reasons, Long brazenly claimed that the transfer had been done to preserve the rights of the National Directors – the very opposite of what seems to have been the true purpose. As Hugh pointed out, it was a *prima facie* breach of the terms by which Murdoch had acquired the two newspapers. The revelation strained relations between Murdoch and the National Directors, who met privately to co-ordinate their response. 'Rupert Murdoch is a megalomaniac twister, surrounded by yes-men and hatchet-men,' fulminated Hugh.[30]

In the ensuing furore, News International Limited agreed to cancel the transfer. However, Hugh had no illusions that the National Directors would be able to restrain Murdoch in the long term. 'Of course I know perfectly well that it can't last,' he told Worden; 'whatever we think, we are courtiers in an oriental Sultanate, and there is a corps of janissaries, with bowstrings at the ready, at the palace door.'[31]

At the next board meeting, Murdoch announced that he now wanted to replace Harold Evans with Charles Douglas-Home. Hugh was amused to hear Murdoch repeat arguments which he himself had made less than a year before. Many of the staff were unhappy with Evans's leadership; Douglas-Home himself had been one of those who applied for redundancy, but had been persuaded to stay. The National Directors knew that *The*

Times was in turmoil. They refused to authorise the sacking of an Editor without due process; but they agreed to endorse the choice of Douglas-Home as his replacement if Evans were to resign voluntarily, in such a way that he could not later claim to have been forced out. This is essentially what happened. In March 1982 Murdoch asked for Evans's resignation. Evans refused to go quietly; for some days he remained in place, attempting to rally the staff behind him, announcing his determination to stay while simultaneously negotiating a settlement to leave. Each move was closely followed in the media. Hugh took refuge in the British Museum, the only place where he was not importuned by sheaves of messages from the press, radio or television. Evans telephoned him repeatedly, and during their long conversations Hugh became increasingly unsympathetic at what he saw as Evans's posturing, which threatened civil war within the newspaper. A group of *Times* journalists issued a statement calling on Evans to resign. Eventually he did so, with a substantial pay-off, and was replaced by Douglas-Home. Six months later Hugh was reappointed to the board for another two-year term.

'My life has been torture for three weeks owing to the battle over *The Times*,' Hugh had moaned to Worden at the height of the crisis. 'The telephone rings all day, nor can I ever escape the journalists.'[32]

The pressures on Hugh during this period made it difficult for him to find time to write. 'I am desperately behindhand in everything,' he complained in a typical letter from Peterhouse: 'past commitments unfulfilled, future commitments, rashly, heedlessly, or unavoidably accepted, and now pressing upon me.'[33] He had imagined that the duties of a Master of a Cambridge college would be less onerous than those of a Regius Professor; and he was disagreeably surprised to discover the reverse was true. After he had been at Peterhouse just over a year he complained that his migration to Cambridge had proved 'a terrible interruption' to his historical work.[34]

As a result yet another book was shelved, though it was nearly ready for publication. For almost two decades Hugh had been exploring the relationship between myth and history in Scotland, a subject which became urgent for him in the late 1970s, during the campaign for Scottish devolution. Hugh was repelled by Scottish nationalism's appeal to atavistic tribal loyalties. He knew that historical myth, however innocently concocted, could lead to unforeseen, even pernicious consequences, just as the romantic fantasies of Goethe and Wagner had fired the imagination of the Nazis. He believed that 'the whole history of Scotland has been coloured by myth': a harmless process in a nation at ease with itself, but dangerous once emotions had been roused by political ambition.

Hugh identified three overlapping myths that had shaped the self-image of that proud nation.* The first was the political myth of an ancient Scottish constitution: the claim that pre-medieval Scotland had been governed by a form of limited monarchy. Time after time this anachronistic notion had been torpedoed; but after a while it had always resurfaced. In the 1770s the Edinburgh advocate Lord Hailes, himself a learned historian of Scotland, had deplored the tendency of his fellow-countrymen to cling to myths, as if the honour of their nation depended on them. 'As fast as the cobwebs of fictitious history are brushed away,' he had sighed wearily, 'they will be replaced.'[35]

The second myth was that of Ossian, the Celtic Homer. Now largely forgotten, Ossian's *Fingal* caused a Europe-wide sensation after it was published in 1762. An epic poem in six books, it was purportedly the work of a blind, third-century bard, translated from the original Gaelic by James Macpherson, a young Scottish schoolmaster; in fact it was a modern production, cooked up to satisfy the new appetite for the sublime. Even more important, Ossian fed the Scots hunger for a literature they could call their own, and for a Scots genius to stand alongside Shakespeare. The Scots literati took the bait greedily – even the great sceptic David Hume, though he soon regretted his embarrassing mistake, and declared to Boswell that he would not believe *Fingal* an ancient poem 'though fifty bare-arsed Highlanders should swear it'. Hugh spent many years researching the Ossian fraud, developing a new theory to explain its origins. 'The important question,' he concluded, 'is not so much how *Fingal* came to be forged, but why the Scots continued for so long to insist that it was genuine.'[36]

The third myth was that of traditional Scots dress, which Hugh showed to have been got up, largely for commercial purposes, in the eighteenth and nineteenth centuries. The kilt had been devised by a Lancashire industrialist as a convenient uniform for his Scottish employees. By the late eighteenth century traditional Highland costume had become obsolete among the Scottish peasantry; but by an irony of history it was adopted by the Scots aristocracy, 'those whose ancestors regarded the Highland dress as the badge of barbarism, and shuddered at the squeal of the bagpipe'.[37] The apotheosis of this trend was the appearance of George IV in Edinburgh wearing a kilt of 'Stuart tartan' – disguising himself, scoffed Macaulay, 'in what, before the Union, was considered by nine Scotchmen out of ten as the dress of a thief'.[38] Hugh showed that the clan-based differentiation of the tartans was the invention of two brothers calling themselves the Sobieski Stuarts, who in 1842 published their *Vestiarium Scoticum*, an elaborate work of imagination which served as a pattern book for tartan manufacturers.

---

* He wondered what the 'next myth' might be, and tentatively proposed 'the myth of the Democratic Intellect'.

The Sobieski Stuarts claimed to be the only legitimate grandsons of Bonnie Prince Charlie (as well as the great-great-grandsons of John Sobieski, King of Poland); they demanded, and obtained, the deference due to those of royal birth, though these two 'engaging charlatans', as Hugh affectionately described them, had been born John and Charles Allen, in Egham, Surrey.[39]

Hugh outlined these ideas in a series of three lectures given at Emory University, Atlanta, Georgia, towards the end of March 1980. Afterwards he began working them up into a book, to which he gave a title suggested by Nan Dunbar, 'The Forging of a Nation'.[40] By the end of the year he had expanded the lectures into eight chapters. He intended to do some rethinking and further research before writing the final draft. But as soon as he paused, a wave of other commitments caught up with him and swept him off in another direction. In June 1982 he told Nan Dunbar, who had enquired about the book, that he could not, at present, realistically foresee its completion as a whole; but that in the meantime, he intended to make parts of it available separately.[41] The story of 'the Sartorial Myth' was published as a chapter in *The Invention of Tradition* (1983), a multi-author volume edited jointly by Eric Hobsbawm and a former pupil of Hugh's, Terence Ranger.

In 1983 Peterhouse voted to admit women, the last but one of the men's Cambridge colleges to do so.* By the early 1980s the undergraduate entry had collapsed: for some subjects there were fewer applicants than places. Two of the scientists, the molecular biologist Aaron Klug and the engineer Chris Calladine, plotted a linear curve showing the decline. It was obvious that some of the best potential undergraduates were avoiding those few colleges that remained single-sex. As a result the latter were fishing in a dwindling pool.

Klug presented the results to Cowling. 'What are we going to do about it?' he asked. 'Leave it to us,' Cowling responded. The 'mafia' opposed the admission of women on principle; in *The Times*, Roger Scruton urged Peterhouse to 'stick with the men'.[42] But Cowling was a trimmer: he knew better than to continue fighting a losing cause. Martin Golding, a Fellow in English and history who had been Hugh's choice as Admissions Tutor, discussed the matter with the Master. Hugh admitted that he was not enthusiastic about admitting women. He considered that the whole programme, in both Cambridge and Oxford, had been unnecessary, 'a costly and troublesome change from a bi-sexual confederation of colleges to a confederation of bi-sexual colleges'; but agreed that once the process had begun, there was no halting it. The evidence convinced him that Peterhouse

---

* The last to do so was Magdalene, in 1988. The last Oxford college to admit women was Oriel, in 1985.

was falling behind, shunned by some of the best state school students in particular. Though reluctant, he was willing to bow to the inevitable. In Governing Body, the Master proposed the necessary change to the statutes, in order, he said, to lift the issue above the rancorous partisan divisions in which it had been stuck in the past.[43] Cowling justified his *volte-face* with characteristic malice: he put it about that the Master had opposed the change, and that the Fellows had voted for it solely in order to spite him.

Expert

Early in 1983, the Dacres received an invitation to Windsor Castle. They would dine with the Queen and the Duke of Edinburgh, and stay the night afterwards. Princess Margaret and Queen Elizabeth the Queen Mother would also be present. The dress was black tie.

This was an exciting prospect for Xandra. The royal family meant much to her. Xandra's mother had been a Maid of Honour to both Queen Victoria and Queen Alexandra; two of her aunts had been Ladies in Waiting. Indeed her parents had met while Haig was staying at Windsor Castle in 1905, when they had been asked to make up a four at golf. He had proposed to her there two days later. The marriage ceremony had taken place in the private chapel at Buckingham Palace.

Xandra performed an extraordinarily low curtsey in the presence of royalty, lowering herself almost to her knees, her dress spreading wide like the uncurling feathers of a peacock. But from the time of her divorce, almost thirty years before, she had felt ostracised; and she remained sensitive to slights, real or imaginary. There had been an embarrassing scene during a dinner party for Princess Margaret at her sister Irene ('Rene') Astor's London house, to which Xandra was not invited – though she was a guest there and other friends of hers would be present. Xandra had spent the evening at the opera; she came back to find fur coats piled on her bed, and in her confusion she blundered into the drawing-room. Recognising the inevitable, Rene took her by the arm and led her forward. 'Ma'am, I am afraid this is my sister.' Xandra curtseyed and quickly withdrew into the background. In the early 1970s, when her husband, as Regius Professor, had been presented to the Queen on a royal visit to Oxford, she was excluded. This had been the root of her complaint that professors had 'no standing' in the University. Some years afterwards, the Trevor-Ropers were invited to a reception at the Palace for the Queen of Sweden, who had expressed a desire to meet some 'intellectuals'. For Xandra this was a breakthrough, a sign that she was readmitted to court, her sins forgiven. She cherished the Christmas cards that Peter received from his godfather, Prince Philip, which she preserved in an album. The invitation to Windsor Castle was the final mark of her acceptance. In a letter to his stepson James, Hugh referred ironically to the coming occasion as 'our social apotheosis'.[1]

The invitation was for the evening of 6 April. Early in March, towards the end of the Lent term,* the Trevor-Ropers spent twelve days cruising in the Caribbean aboard a luxurious, four-masted schooner, in the company of a party of Canadians, to whom Hugh had been asked to lecture. He hoped to find some millionaires whom he could persuade to contribute to the Peterhouse Appeal – but, as he wrote to Robert Blake beforehand, 'I am told that the Canadian rich, being in origin mean and philistine Scotsmen, not generous culture-loving Jews, are very difficult to land'.² The Trevor-Ropers returned to Chiefswood for the Easter vacation. There Hugh passed the time reading the philosophical works of Cicero and preparing, in a desultory manner, his essays for publication. He was disturbed from these academic activities by a telephone call from Colin Webb, Deputy Editor of *The Times*. Webb wanted to speak to him about a discovery which he described as being potentially of great historical importance. It was strictly confidential. The German magazine *Stern* claimed to have discovered the private diaries of Adolf Hitler.³

Hugh's first response was sceptical. No historian had ever hinted at the existence of such diaries. None of Hitler's associates or servants – not even Goebbels or Speer – had referred to him keeping a diary. Hitler himself was on record as saying that he found writing physically difficult, and it was generally supposed that he hardly ever wrote in his own hand once he was in a position to employ the services of a secretary. 'Besides, I said to myself, there are so many forgeries circulating profitably in the "grey market" of forged documents about Bormann, forged diaries of Eva Braun, falsified accounts of interviews with Hitler.'⁴ Hugh had considerable experience of this 'grey market', through his dealings with François Genoud and others. Ever since he made his name as a Hitler expert with the worldwide success of *The Last Days of Hitler*, Hugh had been called upon to judge the authenticity of documents from the Nazi period. It had become a profitable sideline. In 1979, for example, he had been asked by both *The Sunday Times* and Granada Books to authenticate the 'memoirs' of Eva Braun, and had pronounced them to be 'discredited forgeries'.⁵

On the other hand, *Hitler's Table-Talk* had emerged from this same 'grey' market, and had subsequently been accepted by historians as genuine. In considering such documents, therefore, Hugh had tried always to keep an open mind. It was conceivable that Hitler had kept a secret diary, which had remained undiscovered for almost forty years. Rumours of the existence of such diaries had circulated in the chaos of defeated Germany. Indeed there

---

* The first term of the calendar year, the Hilary term in Oxford, is known as the Lent term in Cambridge; followed by the Easter term (known in Oxford as the Trinity term), and finally the Michaelmas term, as in Oxford.

was corroborative evidence from Hitler's pilot, Hans Baur, that private papers of Hitler's had gone missing in the last weeks of the war. Hugh had interviewed Baur himself, after he had been released by the Russians in 1955. Baur had described how the *Führer* had been distraught when told that a plane carrying approximately ten large steel containers, packed personally by Martin Bormann, had been lost. 'In that plane,' Hitler had exclaimed, 'were all my private archives, what I had intended as a testimony for posterity! It is a catastrophe!'

Webb had seen one of the diaries himself. Some weeks earlier he and his fellow Deputy Editor, Charles Wilson, had been given a presentation by *Stern* executives who had come to London to sell syndication rights. The *Stern* sales team had first approached *The Sunday Times*, and shown the diary to Sir Edward Pickering and Webb's opposite number, Brian MacArthur. Since *Stern* usually published on a Thursday, MacArthur's first thought had been that other daily newspapers would have an opportunity to cover the story before *The Sunday Times* would be able to do so. He had therefore suggested that *Stern* should talk to *The Times*, reckoning that the two newspapers might make a joint purchase.

The presentations had been ceremonial. First, *The Sunday Times* team had been asked to swear an oath of secrecy. Then they had been permitted to read typed transcripts of selected passages. Finally, each had been instructed to don rubber gloves, before being allowed to examine a few pages of a single, leather-bound diary. This was a beguiling piece of theatre, but Webb and his colleagues were conscious of the need for caution. In 1968 *The Sunday Times* had paid a small fortune to purchase Mussolini's diaries, later shown to have been forged by two elderly Italian ladies. In considering such material, journalists had to strive for a difficult balance: staying cool, while in hot pursuit of what could be a sensational scoop. A further problem was the mistrust between *The Times* and *The Sunday Times*. Though now in offices next to each other in Gray's Inn Road, there was little communication between them. Indeed the aerial walkway between the two buildings was like a frontier between hostile states, nicknamed 'Checkpoint Charlie'. Each newspaper was proud of its traditions and jealous of its independence; both felt threatened by the Murdoch takeover and the possible move towards a 'seven-day operation', with the loss of overlapping jobs. Neither wanted to be the dumping-ground for stories rejected by the other; yet each was nervous of being scooped.

Stern's editors claimed to have carried out their own checks, which had convinced them that the diaries were genuine. They were confident that they had acquired a hugely valuable property. Hitler's name remained potent. Almost forty years after his death, there was enormous interest in his life and thought. Historians continued to debate vigorously his motives

and his intentions. The appetite for books, newspaper and magazine articles, radio and television programmes and feature films about Hitler
remained insatiable.

The Times Newspapers team was unwilling to rely on the word of *Stern*'s
salesmen that the diaries were authentic. They wanted their own expert
opinion before they were willing to bid. The *Stern* people were extremely
nervous about the story being leaked, and insistent on confining knowledge
of the discovery to the smallest possible number of individuals. Webb
proposed that Lord Dacre should be asked to authenticate the diaries:
not only was he a respected authority on the subject, with a worldwide
reputation, he was also a director of Times Newspapers, and thus a trusted
member of the 'family'. Employing him to verify the diaries was a means
to circumvent *Stern*'s security concerns.

Hugh outlined his doubts about the diaries over the telephone to Webb,
who took them cheerfully. 'The beauty of asking you to do this,' he
explained, 'is that if you find that they are fake and someone else buys
them, you can write a wonderful piece for us, exposing them as forgeries!'
Webb now came to the point. The diaries were being stored in a Swiss bank.
Would Lord Dacre be willing to fly to Zurich and examine them?

Hugh said that he would be so willing. He and Xandra were due to drive
south in a few days' time for the dinner at Windsor Castle on the evening
of 6 April – though he did not mention this to Webb, saying merely that he
would be free to fly to Zurich on the morning of 7 April. Webb explained
that he was about to leave for a week's holiday, but that before he left he
would brief the Editor, Charles Douglas-Home, who would contact him in
the next few days.

Webb's telephone rang only minutes after he had finished this conversation. It was the agent Pat Kavanagh from A.D. Peters, telephoning to
negotiate a sum for Lord Dacre's services. A startled Webb found himself
agreeing to a five-figure fee.

Around ten o'clock on the morning of Thursday 7 April, a hired car
dropped Hugh at Terminal 2 of Heathrow Airport. He was feeling irritable.
The car had already arrived to collect him from Windsor Castle, and he
had been packing his overnight bag, when a flunkey had tapped on the
bedroom door to say that he was wanted on the telephone. Hugh was
furious; their presence at the Castle was supposed to be confidential. The
call was from Charles Douglas-Home, announcing a change of plan. In
several telephone conversations over the past few days Hugh had repeatedly
warned that it would be impossible for him to provide an instant verdict
on the diaries' authenticity. Douglas-Home had assured Hugh that his
mission to Zurich was merely to gauge in general terms the look and feel

of the documents; Times Newspapers would not require him to pronounce on their authenticity until he had been given the opportunity to scrutinise a typed transcript of the diaries up to the end of 1941.[6] Hugh had therefore judged it unnecessary to do any preparation – which was just as well, since in Scotland he was isolated from sources of reference, far away from his books on the subject, which rested on the shelves of his study in Trumpington Street.

Besides, the excitement of the upcoming dinner at the Castle had made serious work difficult. Xandra had been almost hysterical with anxiety about being ready on time; because of this they had left the Borders a day early, and stayed the previous night with James and Angela. The evening at the Castle had passed smoothly, though Hugh found the conversation a little laboured at times. The other guests included the Thai Ambassador and the Ambassador for St Lucia, St Vincent and the Grenadines; several admirals, lieutenant-colonels, a squadron leader and the Marshal of the Royal Air Force; and Mrs Rosalind Goodfellow, Moderator of the General Assembly of the Church of Scotland. Fortunately Hugh's old friend Sir Oliver Millar, Surveyor of the Queen's Pictures, had been present also; as well as the playwright Alan Ayckbourn, a welcome if incongruous presence in such company. At dinner Xandra found herself seated next to Ayckbourn on one side and the Crown Equerry, Lieutenant-Colonel Sir John Miller, on the other. Hugh had been seated between the wife of the Admiral of the Fleet and the wife of the Thai Ambassador, Mom Luang Hiranyika Wannamethee.

Douglas-Home's telephone call had thrown him off-balance. Murdoch was now taking a personal interest in the project, and was determined to secure serialisation rights. Since several rival news organisations were sniffing around the diaries, he wanted to be in a position to bid quickly. If he waited for a verdict on the transcripts, he might lose the deal. Therefore it would be necessary for Lord Dacre to convey his interim impressions by telephone, as soon as he had seen the diaries. Hugh was embarrassed to be disturbed at the Castle (Xandra was still in bed, eating her breakfast), and surprised by the request, given what had been said in their previous conversations. His first response was to reiterate that it was impossible to provide an instant verdict. Douglas-Home said that it was essential, and assured him that he need give only an interim impression at this stage. Reluctantly Hugh acquiesced. As a director of *The Times*, with considerable experience in journalism, he understood the logic of Murdoch's demands.

Waiting for him at Heathrow Airport was *Stern*'s bureau chief in London, Peter Wickman, one of those who had made the presentation to Webb and his colleagues. Together the two men boarded the 11.15 a.m. flight for Zurich. They settled into their seats and chatted while the aircraft took off and the stewardesses served lunch. Afterwards Wickman handed Hugh a twenty-page, typewritten document, bound in a clear plastic folder and headed *Plan 3*. This offered an explanation of one of the strangest incidents in the Second World War: the solo flight to Britain in May 1941 by Hitler's deputy, Rudolf Hess, ostensibly on a mission of peace. It was generally believed that this initiative had been Hess's alone, and that Hitler had been unaware of it beforehand. Diary entries cited in this document, however, showed that Hitler had known of, and had approved, Hess's mission. Indeed, it had been part of an audacious plan to negotiate peace with Britain, sanctioned by the *Führer* himself. According to *Plan 3*, it had been settled in advance that if the mission proved a success, Hitler would acknowledge that Hess had acted with his consent; if not, he would declare that Hess had acted alone, in a fit of delusion.

Hugh made notes on an A4 lined pad. He formulated a series of questions to which he would require answers; and suspected that these answers would fortify, rather than dispel, his doubts. The contents of the Hess document reinforced his scepticism. It was difficult to reconcile the information contained in the diary entries with the fact that Hitler was known to have reacted angrily when told of Hess's flight. Hugh was well aware of this, having received a first-hand description. Albert Speer had been outside Hitler's study at the very moment when the *Führer* had been informed of Hess's flight; 'I suddenly heard an inarticulate, almost animal outcry,' he had told Hugh during his interrogation in 1945. Why should Hitler have reacted in this way if he had known of the flight in advance? Possibly his rage was simulated; but if so, it jeopardised the success of the mission at the outset. What had happened to his plan to wait and see if it was a success? Hitler had declared Hess insane; why should he have done so while the mission still hung in the balance? How could it be anything but a failure unless the British could be convinced that Hess had come with Hitler's approval? None of it made sense. Hugh told Wickman that he thought the Hess story was rubbish. He was now very doubtful about the diaries. It seemed likely that his journey had been wasted. On his notepad he scribbled a note to himself to remember some of the other 'finds' that had proved worthless: the diaries of Eva Braun, for example, or Ladislas Farago's 'discovery' of Bormann in South America.

From Zurich Airport, the two men took a taxi to the five-star Hotel Baur au Lac, where rooms had been reserved for them. Wickman telephoned ahead to the bank where the diaries were being kept, only a few hundred metres down Talstrasse. Everything was ready: in that case, he said, they would come over directly. A few minutes after three o'clock in the afternoon, Hugh was shown into a back room at the Handelsbank. Among the representatives from *Stern* waiting around a long table was one of the three

Editors-in-Chief, Peter Koch. On a side table stood several stacks of A4-sized exercise books, with stiff black covers. Notes pasted inside the covers stated that these were the personal property of the *Führer*, and gave instructions for their disposal in the event of his death. Hugh was told that there were some fifty in number, running from 1932, the year before Hitler's seizure of power, until just before his suicide in 1945. The volumes for 1944 were missing, but expected shortly. In addition, there were volumes on particular subjects – the Hess affair, the July Plot, etc. Also on the table was an album of copies made by *Stern*; a metal safety deposit box containing further documents, going back as far as 1908; a bound volume of Hitler's drawings and paintings; and a First World War helmet, said to have belonged to Hitler. Hugh was astounded by the sheer bulk of the archive, itself powerfully persuasive. 'Who, I asked myself, would forge 60 volumes when six would have served his purpose?'[7] Had he pursued this line of thought, he might have reached the obvious conclusion: a forger who was selling individual volumes on the 'grey' market had every interest in forging as many of them as possible.

Hugh was given the remainder of the afternoon to examine the material – just a few hours, in which he was able to do little more than sample the contents. He picked up a volume and began to turn the pages. It was difficult to read the cramped handwriting, particularly as it was written in an obsolescent Gothic script, but he recognised it as Hitler's, just as he had recognised the signature on the notes pasted inside the cover as Bormann's. Those entries he could decipher seemed banal – which seemed to argue their authenticity. He browsed diaries for various periods, observing that Hitler's hand deteriorated towards the end, a phenomenon known from other sources. There was the odd page pasted in, and the copy of an order. 'It all had a genuine <u>feel</u> about it,' he said later.

He was asked to sign a pledge of secrecy, written out in longhand by Koch. Hugh queried why this was necessary. 'In case *The Times* doesn't buy the diaries,' Koch explained. This seemed to Hugh a reasonable request, so without arguing any further, he signed. One reason for *Stern*'s secretiveness – though they seem to have said nothing about this at the time – was nervousness about copyright. It was by no means clear who owned the copyright in Hitler's works, and as a result they were vulnerable to piracy. This made *Stern* extremely reluctant to allow typed transcripts of the diaries out of their control.

As he was able to ascertain so little from the content of the diaries in the time available, Hugh questioned his hosts closely about the other checks they had made. The discussion continued over dinner that evening at one of Zurich's most expensive restaurants. He was assured that the paper had been tested and dated to the correct period, and shown reports from three independent experts authenticating the handwriting. 'That, it seemed to me, is as good as one can get.' He asked which German historians had examined the text of the diaries, and was told that none had, for fear of leakage. Though surprised, Hugh accepted this explanation. He concentrated his questions on the provenance of the diaries. He was told that they had been salvaged from the wrecked plane by a *Wehrmacht* officer – described as a general – in whose possession they had been kept until recently. This man had been traced by *Stern*'s reporter, Gerd Heidemann, working backwards from the site of the crash in East Germany, which he had been the first to identify. Hugh pressed Koch to reveal the identity of the officer, but Koch refused to divulge it, on the grounds that the man required the protection of absolute secrecy. This seemed plausible if, as he was told, the man was still living in East Germany. Hugh tried a different tack. 'Do you yourself know his identity?' he asked. 'Yes,' Koch replied. Hugh was told that *Stern* had possessed the material for three years and had thoroughly tested the story. He saw no reason not to believe any of this. As he wrote later, 'I took the *bona fides* of the editor as a *datum.*'

Given satisfactory answers to his questions, Hugh found his doubts gradually dissolving. From his hotel bedroom he telephoned Charles Douglas-Home, and told him that he believed the diaries to be genuine.[*] His only caveat was that he wanted to go to Hamburg to meet Gerd Heidemann, and to examine the other documents from the archive in Heidemann's possession. There seemed to be no hurry, because *Stern* was not planning to announce its scoop for another month, to coincide with the anniversary of Hess's flight to Scotland.[8] An excited Douglas-Home arranged to call back an hour later.

Hugh had brought with him to Zurich a note of Eberhard Jäckel's telephone number. He had intended to call Jäckel after examining the diaries. As co-editor of a volume of Hitler's early speeches and writings, Jäckel was one of the historians best qualified to assess any new Hitler material – though, as Hugh would learn later, even he had been taken in by material originating from the same source. Four years earlier Jäckel had examined one of the Hitler diaries, then in the possession of a secretive private collector, and had reprinted documents from the same archive, which were subsequently shown to have been forged. Had Hugh spoken to Jäckel, as

---

[*] According to Douglas-Home, Hugh urged him to 'Come at once! They're the real McCoy!' This terminology seems uncharacteristic. There are differing versions of what he did say. Hugh maintained that he gave a qualified opinion only, but Douglas-Home reported him as saying that he was '100 per cent certain' of their authenticity. According to an internal memorandum written by Brian MacArthur, Hugh told Douglas-Home that he was 'convinced' of the diaries' authenticity; asked if he had any shred of doubt, Hugh said 'none'. Presumably MacArthur was relying on Douglas-Home's account.

he intended, the disaster might have been avoided. 'I could have told Trevor-Roper immediately,' Jäckel lamented afterwards. But Hugh was inhibited by the pledge of secrecy he had signed at the Handelsbank, and he was punctilious in such matters. He decided not to call Jäckel.

An hour after their first telephone conversation, Douglas-Home rang back from Rupert Murdoch's office, to tell Hugh that they would be coming to Zurich the next day to examine the diaries, flying out in Murdoch's private jet. Hugh said that he could not wait for them; though there seems to have been no very strong reason why he should not have done, apart from the fact that Xandra was expecting him. In any case, he was assured that his presence was not required.

In retrospect, Hugh saw this as a moment when he should have made a stand. 'Although I had been asked for an immediate opinion, that opinion need not have been positive or final. Publication was not due until May 11 – more than a month ahead. Even if time had been pressing, I should have insisted on giving only a provisional answer.' But instead of doing so, he allowed himself to be swept forward on the wave of euphoria. He was aware that Murdoch regarded him as cautious and stuffy. Perhaps this made him reluctant to appear so. Whatever the reason, he was now committed. Henceforth events would be beyond his control.

Hugh flew back to England. He took a taxi from the airport to Oxford, where he collected Xandra, and the two of them drove up to Chiefswood. Meanwhile Murdoch flew to Zurich with Douglas-Home, Pickering, Long, and his Australian lawyer and long-term associate, Richard Searby. The party arrived at the Handelsbank and was presented with the material, just as Hugh had been the day before. Unlike him, they were not allowed to handle the diaries, though pages were held open for them to examine. Murdoch noticed that Douglas-Home was very excited. Searby asked if the paper and the ink had been tested. His questions were greeted with mild outrage. '<u>Of course</u> they have been tested!' He asked if they might see the results. They would be handed over once the contracts had been finalised, he was told. To Searby, this smelt fishy. Satisfactory test results would help to persuade a buyer to pay the price asked. To withhold them was against reason. Once outside the bank Searby told Murdoch that he suspected the diaries were forgeries. But Murdoch was not listening.

Over the next ten days, while Hugh busied himself with other work, he received several telephone calls from Webb. In the first of these Webb told him that News International had bought the British rights, and was hoping to add the American rights. It had been decided to serialise the diaries in *The Times*, with the possibility that *The Sunday Times* might run a second serialisation subsequently. Hugh agreed to write an article for *The Times*, to be published when the news was announced. It was arranged that he should fly to Hamburg to attend a *Stern* press conference on publication of the diaries. He would also go there in advance of publication, to record a television programme for *Stern* confirming the authenticity of the documents. *Stern* had been willing to send a television crew to Cambridge, but Hugh resisted this because he wanted to use the opportunity to meet and question Heidemann.

Peter Wickman telephoned to ask for a quotation that *Stern* could use to launch the diaries. Peter Koch had already drafted three quotes, none of which Hugh liked. Reluctantly he assented to the statement that the diaries represented 'the most important historical discovery of the decade', 'a scoop of Watergate proportions'.

On 17 April the Dacres motored from Chiefswood to Cambridge. Webb telephoned again the next day, twenty-four hours before Hugh was due to fly to Hamburg. The whole deal had collapsed in ruins. It had been agreed that Times Newspapers would have British rights and *Newsweek* American rights. The two news organisations had made a joint bid, at the asking price. But at the last moment *Stern* had asked for more money, and imposed new, unacceptable conditions. Murdoch and his *Newsweek* counterparts had withdrawn. Nevertheless Hugh's arrangement with *Stern* was to stand, and *The Times* still wanted him to write his article reporting the discovery.

While Hugh had been in Scotland, another historian had examined the diaries in the Handelsbank. *Newsweek* had employed the services of Gerhard L. Weinberg, a German-born professor at the University of North Carolina at Chapel Hill, who specialised in the study of Nazi Germany.* Initially reluctant, Weinberg had been persuaded to cross the Atlantic for just a few hours to examine the diaries. During the flight he had been shown the reports from the handwriting experts. Weinberg had brought with him a copy of the unpublished diary of Hitler's valet, covering the latter part of 1943, reckoning that, if the Hitler diaries were forgeries, it should be possible to spot discrepancies between them. Unfortunately, he found that the entries in the *Stern* diaries were too sketchy to make an adequate comparison. Like Hugh, Weinberg was impressed by the bulk of the material. He too had difficulty in reading the handwriting, but noted that almost every page of the diaries carried Hitler's signature, and thought it unlikely that any forger would take the risk of repeating the signature so many times. Afterwards he had written a three-page memorandum on his findings. 'On balance I am inclined to consider the material authentic,' he

---

* Weinberg was well qualified for the task: in 1958 he had discovered among captured German files Hitler's so-called 'Second Book', an unpublished sequel to *Mein Kampf.*

concluded. 'Assuming the material is authentic, it is doubtless of enormous importance.'[9]

In fact, neither Weinberg nor Trevor-Roper had been able to employ his historical expertise in evaluating the authenticity of the documents. Both had made deductions based on the outward appearance of the diaries and what they had been told about them, rather than on their content. Their opinions were therefore worth no more than that of any other intelligent observer. This point eluded their paymasters.

On Tuesday 19 April Hugh flew to Hamburg as arranged. He was met at the airport by Heidemann, the reporter who had found the diaries. There was a moment of confusion as Hugh took this fat, balding man in his early fifties to be a chauffeur sent by *Stern*. Heidemann drove Hugh directly to his 'museum', a flat in Milchstrasse which he used solely to display his collection of Nazi and other memorabilia. Hugh was staggered by its scale: hundreds of folders of documents, plus some 400 drawings and water-colours, apparently rescued from the wrecked plane. An oil painting of a battle in Flanders in which Hitler had fought was hanging over the man-telpiece, with his signature on the back. Other 'Hitler' paintings showed Frederick the Great and Kaiser Wilhem I. There were also lesser collections devoted to Hitler's models and imitators: Mussolini, for example. Heidemann pointed out a pair of Idi Amin's underpants.

The fastidious British historian began to feel uneasy. He was all too familiar with the mentality of those obsessed by Hitler and the Nazi period, but he had not previously encountered it in a member of the press. He began to wonder how a journalist could afford to maintain a 'museum' like this, and to stock it with such a lavish collection.

In front of his treasures, Heidemann became voluble. The more he boasted, the less his guest liked him, but Heidemann seemed not to notice. He laughingly confided that Hitler had kept a file on Himmler's Jewish ancestry – but not only that: Himmler had a file on Heydrich's Jewish ancestry, and Heydrich had a file on Hitler's Jewish ancestry! Most astonishing of all was what Heidemann said about Martin Bormann. Apparently Bormann had escaped from Berlin and was still alive. 'Where is he now?' asked Hugh. 'Not far from here,' Heidemann replied, adding that Bormann was willing to emerge from hiding, and that the story would break soon, probably two months after that of the Hitler diaries.

When Hugh cross-examined Heidemann about the provenance of the diaries, he heard much the same story as he had heard from Koch, with a few more details. A German general had retrieved them from the wrecked plane and secreted them in a hayloft, where they had remained for thirty-five years. Like Koch, Heidemann would not reveal the identity of this general. However, he did say that the man was now living in Switzerland,

and wished to remain anonymous to avoid tax. Hugh noted the discrepancy between this account and the one he had been given in Zurich, that the officer was living in East Germany.

Heidemann drove Hugh to the Atlantic Hotel, where a room had been reserved for him. There he met the television crew and recorded a short interview. Heidemann watched the recording, and afterwards insisted that they dine together, ignoring Hugh's protest that he would prefer to have a quiet meal alone and an early night. During the meal, Hugh noticed that his companion was drinking heavily. He began to experience the sequence of emotions familiar to those who found themselves trapped in a conversation with Heidemann: bewilderment, incredulity, distaste and claustrophobia.[10] The reporter began talking about his friend 'Martin'. In 1938, he said, 'Martin' had arranged for secret Party archives to be sent to Madrid for safety. Hugh ridiculed this, pointing out that Madrid was still in Communist hands in 1938. Heidemann was unruffled: in his adaptable narrative, Madrid gradually changed to a villa outside Madrid, and 1938 to 1939. He produced a photograph of 'Martin', purportedly taken recently. It showed a man in his mid-sixties: evidently not Bormann, who would have been then eighty-two. Hugh began to have doubts about Heidemann.

When at last he was able to escape to his room, Hugh reviewed what he had learned in the last few hours about *Stern*'s star reporter. Heidemann was clearly a fantasist, naïve and gullible, disturbingly obsessed by Hitler. But Hugh reasoned that these qualities must have been obvious to his colleagues, who would therefore have been all the more vigilant in checking his stories. Just as Hugh had assumed that Philby's Communist past was known to SIS, so he assumed that Heidemann's lack of judgement must have been apparent to *Stern*. Hugh's doubts about Heidemann did not shake his confidence in the diaries themselves. Heidemann reminded him of Ladislas Farago, a dogged researcher even if he was absurdly credulous. There was no reason to doubt that he was capable of tracking down the diaries. Heidemann was only the channel through which the documents had passed. There was solid evidence for their authenticity, independent of the unreliable reporter who had found them: the tests on the paper; the reports from the handwriting experts; the checks carried out by *Stern*; and the fact that Koch knew the identity of the *Wehrmacht* officer who had retrieved them from the plane.

The next day was Wednesday, 20 April. Hugh returned to London and spent the afternoon at the House of Lords. He arrived back in Cambridge late. Around midnight he received a telephone call from New York. It was Rupert Murdoch. Negotiations with *Stern* had reopened. News International had secured the syndication rights, in America as well as in Britain.

Anxious that *Newsweek* might pre-empt them, using the material they had been shown, *Stern* had brought forward their publication date to Monday, barely four days ahead.* They planned to announce on Friday morning that the diaries had been found. Murdoch told Hugh that he wanted to begin serialising the diaries in the coming weekend's *Sunday Times*. Douglas-Home now cut in. 'We want a big piece from you for Saturday's *Times*,' he said; 'Can you do it?' Hugh said that he could, if he worked 'flat out'.

All through Thursday he laboured over the 3,000-word article. As always, he wrote in longhand, using a fountain pen. Though fluent, Hugh rarely found writing easy: he liked to write a first draft, and then return to it after a night's sleep. On the morning of Friday 22 April he rose at 5.00 a.m. and continued working on the piece until it was collected by motorcycle messenger at 9.00 a.m.

At 11.00 a.m. German time, *Stern* announced that it had acquired the diaries of Adolf Hitler, and would begin publishing them on Monday. News organisations scrambled to find experts willing to comment. Eberhard Jäckel, for example, though 'shaken by Trevor-Roper's position', expressed extreme scepticism. In London, David Irving found himself inundated by enquiries from around the world. He told everyone that the diaries were fakes and the same day wrote to *The Sunday Times*, pointing out that he had given them 'an exclusive lead to these documents' the previous December and demanding a commission on the purchase price.[11]

Frank Giles asked two of his senior journalists, the Features Editor Magnus Linklater and the Political Editor (and joint Deputy Editor) Hugo Young, to join him in his office. There he explained that the *Sunday Times* would begin serialising the Hitler diaries that weekend. Both men were alarmed at this development, aware of the damage that could be done to the newspaper's reputation if the diaries turned out not to be genuine. They implored Giles to allow them to make their own checks on the diaries before publication. But their boss covered his ears with his hands, indicating that he could not listen to such pleas. 'We are required to publish it,' he insisted. The other deputy editor, Brian MacArthur, was already in Germany trying to extract material from *Stern* for the approaching weekend's serialisation. He had arrived home from the theatre on Thursday night to find a message from Murdoch, ordering him to fly out to Hamburg the next morning.

In the offices of *The Times* in Gray's Inn Road, Charles Wilson scrutinised Hugh's text. Wilson was a tough Scot, not excessively scrupulous: a

---

* Another version has it that *Stern* brought forward the date because of fears that it would be pre-empted by its arch-rival *Der Spiegel*.

journalist of the kind appreciated by Murdoch, whose priority was to make the most of the story. He scored out qualifications in Hugh's text to sharpen it up. Thus, for example, the sentence 'Taken together, this seems to me to constitute clear proof of their authenticity' became 'I am now satisfied that the documents are authentic.' The final version, as printed on the 'Comment' page of Saturday's *Times*, read confidently. An 'archive of great historical significance' had recently come to light in Germany, Hugh's article began. 'It is Hitler's private diary, kept by him, in his own hand, throughout almost the whole of his reign ... '.

Meanwhile the Bonn correspondent of *The Times*, Michael Binyon, was sitting in the same offices, working on the story of the find for the next day's front page. His colleague Peter Hennessy peered over his shoulder and scanned the first paragraph. He whistled. It was Hennessy who a few years earlier had written the story wrongly identifying Donald Beves as the 'Fifth Man'; he was therefore alert to the dangers of rushing into print. In fact Wilson had originally asked him to write the article, and had been furious when Hennessy declined. 'If I were you,' advised Hennessy, 'I'd describe them as the "alleged" diaries of Adolf Hitler.' He also suggested that the second paragraph should begin: 'If true, they show that ... ' Binyon followed this sensible advice and inserted these qualifications, but Wilson took them out. 'We haven't bought fucking <u>alleged</u> diaries,' he growled.

At 3.00 p.m. that Friday afternoon Hugh was telephoned by Phillip Knightley, whom he had known since 1967, when Knightley had been part of the *Sunday Times* 'Insight' team investigating Philby. Four months earlier, Knightley had received a telephone call from David Irving, alerting him to the existence of diaries supposedly written by Adolf Hitler. Since he was just about to leave for a long visit to his native Australia, Knightley had passed the contact on to his colleague Magnus Linklater. This lead had fizzled out when *The Sunday Times* declined to pay Irving's expenses. Knightley's first day back in the office had been Tuesday 19 April, the same day that Hugh had flown to Hamburg to meet Heidemann. That evening he had been told that *The Sunday Times* might be running extracts from the Hitler diaries. Knightley was sufficiently concerned to write a memorandum on the subject to his Editor, Frank Giles. He summarised the lessons of the fiasco of the Mussolini diaries, emphasising that one could not rely on expert authentication. Five experts of various types had been asked to give an opinion on the Mussolini diaries: not one of them had said that the diaries were fake. 'Secrecy and speed work for the conman,' warned Knightley. He urged that *The Sunday Times* should insist on carrying out its own tests. Knightley's memorandum asked all the right questions, the questions that nobody else had been asking. Giles forwarded his memorandum to Pickering. 'I would like to emphasise that this is written in the utmost good faith, without any idea of spoiling a fair prospect or messing up arrangements already entered into,' Giles wrote in his covering note. He did not comment on the substance of Knightley's memorandum.

Knightley's telephone call caught Hugh as he was getting ready to leave, along with a party of his colleagues, for a performance of Verdi's *Don Carlos* at Covent Garden. Knightley explained his concerns and elaborated the history of the forged Mussolini diaries, as he had done in the memorandum to Giles. They discussed the differences and the similarities between the two cases. Knightley questioned Hugh closely about his reasons for authenticating the material. Several times in the conversation Hugh mentioned how he had been impressed by the sheer volume of the material. 'He went a long way towards reassuring me,' Knightley admitted afterwards. Ironically, the telephone conversation had the opposite effect on Hugh. Writing the article had allayed the doubts that had been troubling him; now these had been reawakened.

The party for Covent Garden was collected from Peterhouse by coach. His fellow-passengers noticed that something was bothering him. Xandra told the clergyman sitting next to her that Hugh was 'very worried' about something, but she wasn't allowed to say what it was. On the approach to central London, *Evening Standard* billboards announced the discovery of the Hitler diaries. Outside the Opera House the press were waiting. Hugh pushed past them without making a comment.

Sitting in the audience of the Royal Opera House, Hugh reflected on his experiences in the past few days. This was the first moment when he was able to stop and think. One thing in particular was bothering him: a letter Heidemann had shown him, written to a girl by the young Hitler in 1908. If this letter was genuine, why did it form part of Hitler's archive? Surely it should have been with the recipient, not the sender? In any case, this newly discovered document seemed to Hugh too convenient. One of the few details known about Hitler's young manhood was that he had sent just such a letter, to a girl known only as 'Stephanie'. This had been recorded in a memoir by August Kubizek, with whom Hitler had shared rooms in Vienna. It seemed too strong a coincidence that the only letter known about from this period should be the only one to survive. Could it have been forged to fit Kubizek's story? But Heidemann had insisted that the letter was one of the documents salvaged from the crashed plane. So if this was a forgery, then the whole archive was suspect. Hugh began to consider the archive from the point of view of a forger.

> How would a forger of Hitler's diaries proceed? I decided that he would concentrate on a period when Hitler's movements were well documented, and, outside that period, select only detached episodes for which public evidence

was accessible. He would also, since his main material was derivative or trivial, vary it where he safely could with interesting deviations. The diaries, I noted, had a discomforting correspondence with this model.

The fact that there was almost nothing else in the archive dating from before 1932 was in itself suspicious: after that date, Hitler's life was well documented. Hugh had been doubtful of the Hess story ever since he was handed the plastic folder by Peter Wickman on the flight out to Zurich. His doubts about it had been allayed by the evidence presented at the Handelsbank. Now he realised that the whole story could be one of those interesting variations that a forger might adopt. Hugh again asked himself why *Stern* had not consulted a German expert. The answers he had received before now seemed to him unsatisfactory.

He retraced the chain of reasoning that had led him to believe the diaries authentic. *Stern* had claimed to have conducted a thorough inquiry, and to have independently established the link to the wrecked aircraft. Had they? Or had they relied on Heidemann? This was a chilling possibility. During their evening together, only three nights before, Heidemann had not struck him as 'a critical spirit'.

'If at that moment I could have stopped the course of events, I would have done so,' Hugh wrote later. In the darkened auditorium of the Royal Opera House, he briefly considered going in search of a public telephone, to call *The Times*. But he realised that it was too late to stop the press. Before retiring that night, Hugh recorded his anxieties in a notebook, beginning 'I am now overcome by doubt ...'

A copy of Saturday's *Times* was delivered to the Master's Lodge early the next morning. Soon after seven o'clock Hugh retrieved it from the doormat. Dominating the front page was the headline, 'Hitler's secret diaries to be published', above a story by Michael Binyon. Bullet points advertised some of the 'revelations' to come. Binyon reported that Lord Dacre was 'among those convinced' that the diaries were genuine. Below a picture of the *Führer*, an emboldened headline announced that the diaries themselves were being serialised in tomorrow's *Sunday Times*. Hugh's own article, 'Secrets that survived the Bunker', occupied the whole 'Comment' page.

Minutes later, he received a telephone called from Magnus Linklater, who apologised for disturbing him so early in the morning, and told him that he had been working all night on the story. "I know that we've been through this a thousand times,' said Linklater, 'but are you sure of the authenticity of the diaries?'

According to Linklater, Hugh replied that he was '100 per cent convinced' that they were genuine, and then qualified his opinion. 'Put it this way. I'm

99 per cent convinced.' The conversation ended. Though Hugh was now far from convinced of the diaries' authenticity, he could hardly say so to a journalist he had never met before. Unable to reach Douglas-Home at his London house, he called Webb at home in Dulwich, and explained that he had been awake most of the night, worrying.

'I can no longer stand by the judgement I made in that piece,' he told Webb.

'Do you mean that you're not satisfied that they're genuine?'

'That's what I'm saying.'

Webb said that he would try to reach Douglas-Home, who would call him back. He instructed Hugh not to take any calls on the subject from anyone else, took a note of his direct line number and asked him to wait by the telephone.

It took an hour or so before Douglas-Home called back from his weekend house in Gloucestershire. He seemed unperturbed by the revelation that his expert adviser was now in retreat. 'Are you <u>convinced</u> that they are forgeries?' he asked, apparently satisfied so long as the possibility remained that they were genuine. On the previous evening, while Hugh had been at the opera, Douglas-Home had taken part in a live television discussion with David Irving on BBC Television. He was at a disadvantage with Irving, not least because he was not a German speaker. But he was confident nonetheless. 'I've <u>seen</u> these documents,' Douglas-Home insisted; 'they smell of history.' He now reassured Hugh that there was a provision in the contract with *Stern* stipulating that the money paid by Times Newspapers would be returned if within ninety days the diaries were found to be forged. Douglas-Home added that *Stern* had made unacceptable, even insulting conditions, no doubt due to fear of piracy. Hugh asked if he should keep to his plan to fly to Hamburg on Sunday and face the press conference on Monday morning. Douglas-Home thought that he should. After hanging up, Hugh called Peter Wickman. He would keep his promise to attend the press conference in Hamburg, he said, but only if Heidemann came to his hotel on Sunday evening ready to answer questions, and bringing with him a typed transcript of the Hess file.

Webb and Douglas-Home discussed their expert's change of heart on the telephone. 'You might like the pleasure of telling Frank Giles,' Webb remarked ironically. He was left with the impression that Douglas-Home would do so. It would have been a difficult call. At that very moment *Sunday Times* journalists were hard at work on the next day's edition, trying to construct a front-page story around a few quotations from the diaries grudgingly extracted at the last moment from *Stern*. Later Giles and his colleagues would feel bitter that they had been made to look ridiculous. 'Had either Trevor-Roper himself or Douglas-Home or Webb informed me in the course of Saturday the 23rd, of Trevor-Roper's growing doubts,' Giles wrote later, 'we at *The Sunday Times* would have presented the whole affair differently.' It would have been almost impossible to have discarded the story at that late stage, of course. But they could have used more guarded language, toned down the headlines and avoided some of the more embarrassing claims which would prompt so much gloating from their critics and rivals.[12]

But Douglas-Home did not contact Giles. Later he would offer what Giles described as 'a fairly handsome apology' for not having done so. His excuse was that Hugh had been 'in such a condition of doubt and perturbation that it was very difficult at any moment during the day to gauge his exact state of mind', so that he had thought it better to say nothing.[13] This may have been a rationalisation. Webb believed that the breakdown in communication was a simple confusion: he thought that Douglas-Home would contact Giles, while Douglas-Home thought that he would. A further reason for Douglas-Home's failure to act may have been that he was resting, following a dose of the powerful drugs he had been given for the cancer which would kill him two years later, at the age of only forty-eight.

As the day wore on, Hugh was a little surprised not to hear from Frank Giles. He had understood that either Douglas-Home or Webb would communicate with his *Sunday Times* colleague.[14] It did not occur to him to contact Giles himself. He had been employed by *The Times* to examine the diaries, and all his dealings had been with *The Times*. Except for the telephone calls from Knightley and Linklater, he had heard nothing from *The Sunday Times* throughout. In retrospect, it seems a little odd that Giles had not been in touch with his old friend earlier. But he had never been enthusiastic about the diaries. They had been imposed on him by Murdoch, and he had not felt able to challenge the proprietor's will.

Innocent of Hugh's doubts, the staff of *The Sunday Times* had made an extraordinary effort to produce an issue worthy of such a story. By the end of the day they were justifiably satisfied with what they had achieved. The front page was dominated by a huge close-up of Hitler's face, on top of which was superimposed a photograph of Heidemann holding some of the diaries. Beneath the masthead ran a banner headline: 'WORLD EXCLU-SIVE: How the diaries of the *Führer* were found in an East German hayloft'; and below that an even bigger headline, 'The secrets of Hitler's war'. A standfast promised 'sensational disclosures'. A bullet point announced that a special pull-out section of the *Colour Magazine* was being prepared 'for this major publishing event'. On the right-hand side of the front page, nuggets from the diaries were picked out in bold type. 'Look at that,' said Brian MacArthur proudly, brandishing the proofs when they arrived in the newsroom. 'You will never see a front page like that as long as you live.'

In the centre of the paper was a three-page treatment by Phillip Knightley, telling 'the full story' of the find. 'Hitler's diaries, which *The Sunday Times* is to serialize, have been submitted to the most rigorous tests to ensure their authenticity,' he wrote. 'One of the world's leading experts on Hitler and the Nazi period, Hugh Trevor-Roper, Lord Dacre of Glanton, has staked his academic reputation on his conclusion.' Hugh later protested that he would never have used such a journalistic expression.

Around seven o'clock on Saturday evening, as the presses began to roll, senior members of the *Sunday Times* editorial staff congregated in the Editor's office for a glass of wine. They did so every week; but this issue was special. The editorial team of *The Sunday Times*, one of the world's great newspapers, was celebrating an exercise in their professional skills under extreme pressure. As always, they scrutinised the first editions of rival newspapers, which had just arrived in the office. Predictably, these led with stories intended to devalue the *Sunday Times*'s scoop. 'Serious doubts cast on Hitler's secret diaries', ran *The Observer*'s headline. This much was to be expected; it was part of the game. None of the rival papers then had any inkling that the *Sunday Times*'s expert witness shared some of those doubts.

Talk turned to the next week's issue. Giles proposed to invite Hugh to write another article, demolishing 'all these carping criticisms' of the diaries. He picked up the telephone, dialled, and began talking. After a few opening pleasantries his tone abruptly changed. 'Well, naturally, Hugh, one has doubts, but I take it these doubts aren't strong enough to make you do a 180-degree turn on that?' he asked. The buzz of conversation subsided as the assembled journalists strained to catch what was being said. 'Oh,' Giles said flatly, 'Oh, I see. You <u>are</u> doing a 180-degree turn.' The euphoria in the room vanished like air escaping from a balloon. Knightley pounded the table; Linklater sat on the floor with his head between his knees; MacArthur, who had been leaning back against the wall, slid slowly down, his glass still upright in his hand.

Giles later described Hugh's manner during this telephone conversation as resembling that of a Victorian divine, assaulted by doubts induced by Darwin and his fellow rationalists. The tormented historian described himself as under siege in the Master's Lodge by telephone enquiries from the world's press.

Once the call had ended, the editorial team had to decide what to do next. The first decision was whether to stop the press. This could not be done without the proprietor's authorisation. Somebody was sent to track down Murdoch. Giles asked MacArthur and another member of his editorial team, Paul Eddy, to meet Hugh at Heathrow tomorrow and escort him to Hamburg for the *Stern* press conference. He despatched a telex to

Peter Koch, emphasising the urgency of the situation and warning of the 'grave danger' that everyone involved in publishing the diaries would be 'disastrously compromised' unless *Stern* released more information about their provenance. 'It is imperative, repeat imperative, that you provide evidence which will withstand the attacks now being made upon us.' Giles would try to persuade Hugh to keep quiet about his doubts for the time being; if they persisted, he could write about them exclusively for the next issue of *The Sunday Times*. The office emptied to allow Giles to call him back. Meanwhile Murdoch had been located in America. MacArthur was speaking to him on the telephone. He explained their dilemma. Given that Lord Dacre was now expressing doubts, should they halt the press and recast the paper?

Murdoch's instruction was brief and explicit. 'Fuck Dacre,' he said. 'Publish.'

Around two o'clock on Sunday afternoon, Hugh arrived at Heathrow's Terminal 1, prepared to catch the 3.15 British Airways flight to Hamburg. The press was waiting for him as he stepped out of the car. There was a clamour of questions, as microphones and television cameras were shoved into his path. 'I do believe that the Hitler diaries are genuine,' he said, 'but there are complications. I will not put a percentage figure on my belief. I admit that there are problems ...' He conceded the possibility that the diaries might be forged.[15] Hugh tried to escape into the men's lavatory, but they followed him even there. Soon after he emerged, MacArthur and Eddy caught up with him. Flanking the elderly historian on either side, they led him to the gate, clearing a path through a gaggle of shouting reporters and camera-men. 'At least we made them walk backwards,' Hugh remarked grimly, once they had passed beyond reach of their pursuers.

Another television crew was waiting for them in Hamburg. The *Sunday Times* party was met by Antony Terry, the paper's veteran correspondent in Bonn, who had a taxi waiting. Hugh was driven to the Hotel Atlantic, where a room had again been booked for him. After a long delay Heidemann arrived, much later than arranged. Hugh had prepared a list of questions for him. Almost forty years earlier, as an SIS intelligence officer, he had acquired considerable skill in cross-examination while interrogating captured Nazis. His use of these techniques riled Heidemann. Old antagonisms would surface in this confrontation between the British interrogator and the German collector of Nazi relics, a former member of the Hitler Youth.

Hugh began by asking Heidemann to clarify how the diaries had come into *Stern*'s possession. Heidemann said that peasants from East Germany had supplied some of the material. Hugh pounced. This was the third version of the story he had been told, he said. Peter Koch had said the *Wehrmacht* officer who had supplied the documents was living in East Germany; last week Heidemann had said that he was living in Switzerland; now he was saying that some of the documents had been supplied by un-named peasants. Which was correct? Heidemann blustered. Hugh tried again. Koch had told him that the reason why this man did not want his name disclosed was that he feared reprisals from the East German authorities; Heidemann had told him that he was worried about tax. Which was correct, please? Hugh pressed Heidemann to reveal the identity of the *Wehrmacht* officer who had retrieved the documents from the plane. Since he had told Koch who he was, why not tell Hugh? Heidemann denied that he had revealed the man's identity to Koch. 'Herr Koch knows only what I tell him,' he said irritably, and protested that he was being grilled like a prisoner of MI6. 'We are no longer in 1945,' he burst out angrily.

'Either the diaries are genuine or they are not,' Heidemann continued, 'and either way it has nothing to do with the *Wehrmacht* officer.'

'Can you tell me any reason why I should believe in the existence of this officer?' asked Hugh.

'No, why should I?' said Heidemann.

'Well,' replied his interrogator, 'then why should I believe?'

Heidemann buckled under the relentless pressure. After an hour he left, declaring that he had endured enough.

Hugh studied the Hess file that Heidemann had brought with him. It consisted partly of correspondence, supposedly between Hitler and Hess, typed on unheaded paper. This seemed to him suspiciously amateur.

That evening Hugh and his *Sunday Times* minders dined with the 'Stern Gang': Koch, his fellow-Editor Felix Schmidt, and Gerd Schulte-Hillen, the Managing Director of the publishing company that owned the magazine. Heidemann had been supposed to join them, but he had stalked off. This dinner had been intended as a pre-launch celebration, in honour of the distinguished historian who had authenticated the diaries. Over the weekend more than two million copies of a special issue of the magazine had been printed, ready to go on sale the next morning. *Hitlers Tagebücher entdeckt* ('Hitler's Diaries Discovered') was printed in bright red letters on the cover, which showed a stack of blue exercise books engraved with what appeared to be Hitler's monogram. Inside, thirty-eight pages were given over to the story.

Hugh had prepared another list of questions for *Stern*, which he read out of the same pocket-diary from which he had earlier directed questions at Heidemann. This was not at all what the *Stern* team had expected. Hugh taxed Koch about the identity of the *Wehrmacht* officer. Koch now denied that he had ever claimed to know the man's name; he said that, as an Editor, he would never press one of his journalists to reveal his sources. Hugh was astonished by this *volte-face*. He threatened not to attend the next morning's press conference. There was an icy atmosphere around the table as the dinner ended.

After the Germans had left, Hugh remained at the table with Eddy, MacArthur and Terry, while they discussed what he should do. MacArthur urged him to 'be more confident'. At midnight the three *Sunday Times* men, who were staying in a different hotel, departed. Hugh was passing through the Hotel Atlantic lobby on his way up to bed, when he happened upon an old friend, the diplomat Sir Nicholas Henderson, former British Ambassador in Bonn and later in Washington. The pair made for the bar, where, over a succession of beers, Hugh explained his difficulties. 'What's on my mind is that I must make up my mind tonight,' he said. To Henderson, the story strongly suggested that the diaries were forged. He recommended Hugh to boycott the next morning's press conference. But Hugh's sense of personal honour intervened; he felt bound to keep his side of his bargain with *Stern*. After all, Heidemann had come to the hotel, bringing the Hess file, and he had been willing – for a while – to answer questions. In that case, Henderson's advice was that he should express his scepticism publicly and firmly. But Hugh felt he must consider the interests of *The Times*: Douglas-Home had asked him to leave the question of authenticity open, if possible. He decided to sleep on the matter. Unexpectedly they were joined in the bar by the economist Peter Oppenheimer, a don at Christ Church. The three continued talking until 2.00 a.m.

The next morning, Michael Binyon encountered a panicky Brian MacArthur in the foyer of the Atlantic. Their expert adviser had locked himself in his room and was refusing to come out, MacArthur told him. Douglas-Home telephoned Hugh from London. How was he feeling this morning? Hugh reported on his unsatisfactory interview with Heidemann. Far from allaying his doubts, it had increased them. He was still uncertain what he should do. Assuring him that no money had yet been paid to *Stern*, Douglas-Home urged Hugh to attend the press conference as arranged, and not to 'burn his boats'. So long as any chance remained that the diaries might be genuine, he should not formally denounce them as forgeries. At the end of the conversation Hugh promised to go, and said that he would do his best.

The conference was held in *Stern's* canteen. The dining-hall was packed with more than 200 journalists, including twenty-seven television crews. Each was issued with a press kit, comprising photographs and twenty pages of information on the diaries. A set of tables had been laid out at the far end of the hall, and equipped with microphones. At eleven o'clock Hugh filed in, together with Koch and several of his *Stern* colleagues. Heidemann was one of them, this morning as taciturn as he had been voluble the previous Tuesday. Hugh was startled by the size of the audience, the rowdy atmosphere and the heat of the dazzling arc-lights. They took their seats behind the tables; then Koch delivered an aggressive and confident opening speech, criticising historians like Jäckel who had pronounced judgement on the diaries without having seen them. He dismissed David Irving – who was sitting in the hall as a representative of *Bild Zeitung*, a mass-circulation German newspaper, often described as the German equivalent of *The Sun* – as an historian 'with no reputation to lose'. Once Koch had finished his introduction, the *Stern* documentary film *The Find* was shown. Hugh held his head in his hands as he watched the footage of his own interview confidently proclaiming the diaries' authenticity, recorded here in Hamburg only six days before. As the film finished and the lights came up again, a smartly dressed young woman stepped forward to the tables and spread out a dozen volumes of the diaries. There was a scramble for photographs. Guards tried to prevent anyone from approaching too close. Koch persuaded a reluctant Heidemann to pose for photographs with the diaries. Then he invited questions from the floor. Most of them were fired at the elderly British historian, whose halting manner contrasted with that of Koch's upbeat introduction.

Taking a deep breath, and gazing into the middle distance, Hugh began to speak. He tried to keep the matter open, while admitting the grounds for doubt. 'The question of the authenticity of the diaries is inseparable from the history of the diaries. The question is: are these documents linked necessarily to that aeroplane? When I saw the documents in Munich I understood – or misunderstood – that the link had been established ...' Koch stared at him in dismay. Under pressure, Hugh conceded that the diaries could be fakes. The burden of proof must now be assumed by *Stern*, he insisted. He regretted that 'the normal method of historical verification' had, 'perhaps necessarily', been 'sacrificed to the requirements of a journalistic scoop'.

Hugh was asked about the potential damage to his reputation if the diaries turned out to be forgeries. He paused before answering. 'I suppose my personal reputation is linked to anything I say,' he said eventually. 'I am prepared to express my opinion and if I am wrong I am wrong, and if I am right I am right.' He emphasised the point with his fist. 'I don't worry about these things.' Hugh's indecision undermined his authority. For those sympathetic to him, the conference was an excruciating experience. A former pupil of Hugh's, covering the story for *The New Republic*, described it as 'rather like watching a Victorian gentleman trying to back pedal a penny farthing'.

Suddenly David Irving leapt up and grabbed the microphone available
for questioners. He had been provoked by Koch's description of him as
having no reputation to lose. 'I may not have a doctorate,' he declared, 'or
a professorship, or even the title "Lord", but I believe I have a reputation in
Germany nevertheless.' Koch tried to stop him, demanding that he pose
questions, not make speeches; but Irving raised his voice above Koch's
protests. He waved aloft some papers. 'I know the collection from which
the diaries come,' he said. 'It is an old collection, full of forgeries. I have
some here.' The television cameras swivelled around towards Irving, who
stood with both arms held high, documents in both hands. Reporters
stampeded towards him, scattering chairs and knocking over lights and
microphones.

A scuffle broke out. Now shouting, Irving challenged *Stern* to confirm
whether the ink used to write the diaries had been tested. As Koch equivo-
cated, the audience began to chant: 'Ink! Ink!' Irving sat down in triumph,
beaming. 'Torpedo running!' he whispered to a journalist sitting next to
him. The hubbub took some while to die down. Soon afterwards Irving
left the hall, after a burly reporter invited him to come outside. Some
supposed that he had been evicted. In fact, he had been invited to take part
in a live discussion on the NBC *Today* show.

The conference had been going almost two hours when Gerhard Weinberg, the historian hired by *Newsweek*, arrived, flown in by helicopter from
Bonn. He had agreed to attend in response to pleas from Peter Koch. But
Weinberg was to disappoint his hosts as much as Trevor-Roper had done.
He told the conference of his discovery that none of the samples sent to the
handwriting experts for identification had come from the diaries themselves. Thus the twin pillars of evidence on which their authentication
rested – the provenance and the handwriting – were both tottering. Weinberg went on to demand that the diaries be made available for experts to
study. Koch broke in to say that of course experts would be given an
opportunity to study the diaries.

'When?' he was asked.

'When the journalistic evaluation has been completed,' Koch replied
lamely.

The press conference, which had begun so triumphantly, ended in
humiliation. The elaborate orchestration had deteriorated into chaos. The
two experts flown in to support *Stern*'s story had instead both undermined
it. This was a public relations fiasco.

Afterwards Hugh accompanied his *Sunday Times* minders to their hotel
for a snack lunch. He glanced at the menu and then passed it to one of the
journalists. 'I can't decipher this,' he said. 'You'll have to read it for me.'
Perhaps he meant that his eyesight was not good enough to read the menu,

but the journalists understood that he could not translate the German text. MacArthur looked at his colleagues in dismay. Was this the expert on whom they had founded their claims of 'the biggest story since Watergate'?

Hugh flew back to England, dodging the press. He had been pursued to Hamburg Airport by Barbara Dickmann, presenter of the film shown at the press conference. She tried to persuade him to stay, to participate in a live televised discussion the next evening with German historians in Wiesbaden; or if he would not stay, to return. *Stern* promised a very high fee. Hugh refused, though he later relented when told he could take part via a link from London.

A huge headline in the *Evening Standard* greeted him on his arrival at Heathrow: 'HITLER DIARIES: DACRE'S DOUBTS'. Above was the tag-line: 'Eminent historian has second thoughts'. His spirits drooped. On his return to Cambridge, he found the press camped outside the Master's Lodge. Xandra had been having a 'dreadful' time, besieged in her home while reporters tried the doorbell and the telephone rang constantly. One of the calls had been from Colin Webb, with more bad news: the first payment had already been made to *Stern*. Hugh instructed the Porters' Lodge not to put through any more calls, though it was impossible to block the direct line.

The next day's headlines focused on his change of mind: 'I'M NOT SURE NOW CONFESSES HITLER DIARIES PROFESSOR'; 'HITLER: THE GREAT RETREAT'; 'BOFFINS BATTLE ON NAZI DIARIES'; 'I'M NOT QUITE SO SURE, SAYS DACRE'. Later that day, Hugh travelled down to London to participate in the discussion on German television, in a live link from London. Among those present in the Wiesbaden studio were Peter Koch, David Irving and Eberhard Jäckel. Weinberg also took part, in a link from Bonn. Hugh alone spoke in English, to ensure, he said, that he expressed himself precisely. This made a poor impression on the German television audience. Jäckel spoke to him privately on the telephone afterwards, regretting that he had not been able to warn his old friend of the danger.

A curious interlude followed, lasting almost a fortnight, while nobody knew for certain whether or not the dairies were authentic. *The Sunday Times* was in the most awkward position, having to straddle two irreconcilable positions: investigating a possible hoax, while protecting its scoop in case the diaries turned out to be genuine. Frank Giles left for a holiday in Greece, leaving MacArthur at the helm of a ship that appeared in danger of foundering. Eventually, after Murdoch had given his personal guarantee, the newspaper was allowed to borrow two volumes of diaries to make its own detailed checks. Meanwhile speculation was rife about their origin. *The New York Times* conjectured that they were the product of Communist agents in East Germany, aiming to undermine West Germany's relations with its allies, a view echoed by the American Ambassador to the United Nations, Jeane Kirkpatrick. In contrast, the Soviet news agency Tass claimed that they were right-wing propaganda, a Western attempt to distract the young generation from 'the fight for peace'. Radio Moscow alleged that the whole thing was a CIA plot. Others suggested that the diaries originated from a Nazi cell in South America, intent on rehabilitating Hitler.[16] *Stern* stated that Hugh had changed his opinion about the authenticity of the diaries on the orders of the British Secret Service. The Chief Rabbi sent a letter to *The Times*, arguing vehemently that, genuine or not, the diaries should not be published. 'Hailing this find as "the biggest discovery since the Dead Sea Scrolls" is a sacrilege which only compounds the insult to the millions who perished and suffered under this tyranny.'

In the absence of any definite verdict on the diaries, Hugh was an obvious target. His last-minute change of mind had made him look foolish: he had shown poor judgement in coming forward to authenticate the diaries without adequate proof, and then had retreated when it was too late. He appeared weak and indecisive. He was condemned by Conor Cruise O'Brien in an *Observer* editorial, and by Bernard Crick in the *New Statesman*, for sacrificing standards of historical accuracy to commercial pressure.[17] A.L. Rowse was unable to resist the opportunity to insert the knife into his former 'protégé' in the *Daily Mail*. His article, headed 'The Trial of Lord Dacre', described the Master of Peterhouse (then aged sixty-nine) as 'a young man in a hurry'.

Hugh's policy was to say nothing in response to any of these criticisms, 'to make no statements, give no interviews, evade the media altogether, and let them do their worst, rather than say anything that might embarrass *The Times*, in which alone I will, I hope, ultimately be able to express my case, rather than let it go by default'.

'For days after my return, my life was torture,' he noted in his diary. He could elude the crowd of camera crews and reporters only by shinning over a wall into a car park, crossing Trumpington Street well away from the college and entering Peterhouse through the rear. Then he would steal into the College Secretary's office behind the backs of the waiting pressmen. On one occasion he begged a lift from Aaron Klug, whose car was in the car park. While the Master of Peterhouse crouched on the floor, the Nobel Prize-winning scientist drove out past the besiegers, dropping his furtive passenger near the entrance to the deer park.

Hugh's enemies at Peterhouse made no effort to conceal their glee at his discomfort. It was said that the newsagent on the corner opposite the college had been bribed to keep a placard outside for several weeks, inscribed 'HITLER DIARIES HOAX'. A limerick began to circulate around Cambridge:

> There once was a fellow called Dacre,
> Who was God in his own little acre,
> But in the matter of diaries,
> He was quite *ultra vires*,*
> And unable to spot an old faker.

Later his detractors would inaugurate an undergraduate dining society, 'The Authenticators'.

Nevertheless Hugh was determined to face the wider world. He would not be a prisoner in his own home. Two days after the discussion on German television, he again travelled down to London, this time for a memorial service and a session of the House of Lords, and afterwards took a train to Oxford for a meeting of 'The Club'. The next day several distinguished guests arrived at Peterhouse for the annual Perne Feast. Among those staying at the Master's Lodge were the statistician Sir Claus Moser and his wife, and the Lord Chancellor, Lord Hailsham, known for his theatrical gestures. Assuming that the crisis was past, Hugh instructed the Porters' Lodge to resume putting through calls. At once the telephone started ringing. Hailsham offered to answer the telephone on behalf of his hosts. To a bemused David Leigh of *The Observer*, the Lord Chancellor posed as an old family butler.

At the end of the following week tests confirmed what everyone had been suspecting, that the diaries were faked. Chemical tests proved the paper to be of post-war manufacture. It turned out that the claim made by *Stern's* representatives that the paper had been tested was, at the very least, disingenuous: the paper had been sent for testing, but the results had not yet been received. It was soon shown that the handwriting tests were based on a comparison between two sets of documents, both supplied from the same archive.

Confirmation that the diaries were forgeries sounded the bell for a fresh round of mockery. *Private Eye* devoted several pages to the story, with spoof extracts from the diaries themselves ('translated from the original Belgian'), an account of 'My Days of Agony by Lord Lucre of Glenlivet (better known as Sir Hugh Very-Ropey)', gloating from historians such as 'Lord Bollock', 'A.J. P. Tharg' and 'A.L. Raus', and 'sensational proof' of the authenticity of the diaries, provided to Times Newspapers 'by Goebbels's gardener's great-niece'. The cartoon on the cover must have been especially painful to Hugh. Headed 'PIECE IN OUR TIMES', a reference to Neville Chamberlain's

---

* Literally, 'beyond strength', exceeding the authority of a person; out of his depth.

notorious statement on his return from meeting Hitler at Munich, it depicted a triumphant Murdoch descending from the steps of his private plane, brandishing a diary, and inside a speech bubble the statement, 'I have in my hand a worthless piece of paper bearing the faked signature of Hitler himself'. Standing to attention at the bottom of the steps were the cartoon figures of Douglas-Home and Hugh on one side, and a uniformed flunkey on the other.

Once it was clear the diaries were forgeries, Hugh wrote an article for *The Times*, taking responsibility for the newspaper's mistake.[18] 'Whether misled or not, I blame no one but myself for giving wrong advice to *The Times* and *The Sunday Times*,' he concluded. He made a public apology to the Editors of both newspapers. In a private letter to Douglas-Home, Hugh said that he was 'deeply penitent for all the trouble and expense I have caused by allowing myself to be so hurried. I should have insisted on time for a proper evaluation.'[19] He wrote a similar letter to Murdoch, expressing 'my sincere apologies for the trouble and damage that I have caused to you and *The Times*'. He offered to resign as an independent director and to forgo the fee. Murdoch refused his offer of resignation, but accepted his decision not to take a fee. 'As you say, we have all taken a hell of a caning over this affair,' Murdoch agreed. 'We all made mistakes, not least myself.'[20] In fact Murdoch had good reason to feel relaxed about the outcome. His money had been repaid by *Stern*, while *The Sunday Times* had retained 20,000 of the large increase in circulation stimulated by the diaries. The ethos of the paper had been damaged; but then Murdoch had never been very keen on its ethos.

Hugh had asked Douglas-Home to pass on his apologies to Giles, but it seems that this was another message that did not get through. When Hugh encountered Giles's wife at a party some weeks after, Lady Kitty gave him 'a formidable drubbing' for not having apologised to her husband personally. Hugh tried to set this right in a seven-page letter.[21] Soon afterwards Giles was replaced as Editor by Andrew Neil.

Hugh's *mea culpa* was greeted with 'whoops of sanctimonious glee' by his enemies in the press. The *Daily Mail* asked if he would resign as Master of Peterhouse. Auberon Waugh, rephrasing his father's famous denunciation, suggested that the only honourable course remaining to the disgraced historian would be to change his sex and move to Essex.[22] In particular, Peter Hillmore, who wrote the 'Pendennis' column in *The Observer*, tormented him for week after week. 'From the volleys of stones which have assailed me from almost every window in Fleet Street I realize that no one else in that populous and well-informed thoroughfare would have been so foolish as to err or so feeble as to recant,' he had commented drily in his piece for *The Times*. Meanwhile, Hugh received many private letters, most expressing sympathy and support. 'It is at times like this when you discover who your real friends are,' he commented to one correspondent; though many of the letters came from strangers. On the other hand, some letters were hostile. A particularly unkind barb came from Lady Dacre, who instructed her solicitor to write to him, referring to the embarrassment caused to her 'in the light of publicity given widely to recent events', and requesting him to ensure that, when referred to or reported in the media, he was described by his full name as Lord Dacre of Glanton, to avoid 'unfortunate confusion'.[23] Through the medium of the *Sunday Telegraph* columnist Kenneth Rose ('Albany'), Hugh expressed his regret that anyone felt damaged by accidental association with him; but pointed out that the only public statements he had made on the matter had appeared in *The Times*, edited by her nephew Charles; and that only a fortnight earlier her own husband William Douglas-Home had referred to him as 'Lord Dacre' in a whimsical letter to that newspaper. 'By now, I suppose,' Rose suggested, 'he will have received a solicitor's letter from his wife.'[24]

A vicious postcard arrived from George Morpeth's father, Lord Carlisle, who signed himself 'Dacre of Gillesland'. He addressed the card to 'Life Peer Ld. Dacre of <u>Glanton</u> (Trevor-Roper)':

> You are a disgrace to the Dacre title which you have no right to use. Your knowledge of German is non-existent & you & yr. wife are a ludicrous pair of social climbers. How much does The Times pay you, you old fraud.[25]

Hugh bore the weight of criticism, mockery and abuse without complaint; only rarely did his anguish show. A week after his public apology appeared, the Dacres spent a weekend in the country with their friends Charles and Kitty Farrell. 'I can't understand how I came to make that mistake,' Hugh wailed to his host. James and Angela Howard-Johnston had been invited to lunch; when they arrived, Hugh did not appear. James went in search of his stepfather, whom he found lying in the foetal position on a bed in a spare room, his face turned to the wall. But even then, Hugh was resilient. The Farrells had arranged a dinner party for that evening; among the guests were the former Foreign Secretary, Lord Carrington, and his wife Iona, and the Australian lawyer Sir Zelman Cowen, who had succeeded Lord Swann as Provost of Oriel. By the time they arrived Hugh had recovered his ironic persona. Over dinner he explained that in his *Times* article he had tried to wear his 'white sheet of penitence' with a suitable combination of gravity and elegance – 'with panache', insisted Carrington.

Hugh expected the others responsible for the fiasco of the Hitler diaries to take their share of the blame. In this he was disappointed. He was not the only one to succumb to the fraud, but he was the one to whom most of the odium attached. As the historian of *The Times* has commented, he proved a useful scapegoat, deflecting criticism from the newspaper's own decision-making.[26] The damage to his reputation was substantial and long-lasting. For him, if not for Times Newspapers, the Hitler diaries proved a disaster.

There has been much speculation about the reasons for his mistake. It has often been said that his German was inadequate for the job. 'I do not read German with ease or pleasure,' he had confessed, in an article about *Mein Kampf*. It has even been suggested that he did not read German at all,* and that his interrogations of captured Nazis in 1945 must have been made through interpreters. This is nonsense. He was not fluent in German, but he could speak it well enough to hold a conversation, as has been testified by German friends such as Eberhard Jäckel and the Oxford historian Hartmut Pogge von Strandmann. In 1982, the year before the Hitler diaries scandal, he delivered a lecture in German at a conference in Düsseldorf.[27] He read German books and documents, and often received letters written in German, though he usually chose to reply in English. His German was certainly adequate to the rudimentary task of reading diary entries. The problem he encountered in this case was twofold: firstly, that the handwriting was so spidery as to be largely illegible, and secondly, that the diaries were written in an antiquated script, which most Germans cannot read. Gerhard Weinberg, who was born in Germany, had similar difficulty in deciphering the diaries.

The two diaries borrowed by *The Sunday Times* were shown to Norman Stone, a Cambridge historian whose biography of Hitler had appeared in 1980. After examining them, he had no doubt that they were forged. The cumulative effect was of 'a Charlie Chaplin Hitler', he reported. But they were written 'in a sometimes difficult to read old-German handwriting which has been obsolete for at least a generation'. It had taken Stone ten hours to transcribe and read enough of the text to appreciate and be sure of its defects.[28] Hugh had been given much less time to form a judgement.

His mistake was to have allowed himself to be hustled into giving an opinion before he was ready, and to have relied on what he was told, rather than on what he had personally ascertained. He was too trusting. This was naïve, but not venal. Weinberg – a sober, respected and careful scholar – reached the same conclusion, using similar reasoning.

Some commentators have suggested that Hugh should have refused to accept the commission to examine the diaries because of his association with Times Newspapers. According to them, a 'conflict of interest' should

---

* The founder and publisher of *Stern*, Henri Nannen, made this allegation in the *Süddeutsche Zeitung*, a national newspaper. He wrote to Hugh afterwards, apologising for the reference to him as 'Der Hitler Lord'. Hugh replied in German.

have inhibited him. It is hard to follow this line of argument. Hugh had no personal interest in declaring the diaries genuine, and much to lose if he were mistaken. Nor did Times Newspapers have a commercial interest in the diaries at that stage. On the contrary, Times Newspapers had strong commercial reasons for scepticism. The fact that Rupert Murdoch did not in the end lose money on the deal does not mean that he might not have done had things worked out differently. Far from being a conflict of interest, there was an identity of interest between Times Newspapers and the expert they had employed to examine the diaries. It would have been a different matter, of course, if he had been hired by *Stern* to authenticate the diaries.

The charge of hubris has been made against him. It was certainly true that he was arrogant. His brilliance made him impatient with the ponderous progress typical of historical study. He often cut corners. So much work had come his way as a result of the worldwide success of *The Last Days of Hitler* that he had perhaps become careless about it. 'Trevor-Roper thought that he had taken out a patent on Hitler,' complained A.J.P. Taylor in the 1960s. Yet far from being over-confident, there was a sense in which he had begun to feel marginalised. At an historical congress in Berlin in January 1983, Pogge von Strandmann had noticed that Hugh was on the sidelines, treated with respect for past achievements but not as an historian who was participating in the modern debates on the Nazi period. Perhaps Hugh was pained by this, and hoped that his involvement with the Hitler diaries would restore him to the central position he had once occupied in Hitler studies. Of course, it had the opposite effect.

The forger was soon revealed to be a low-life conman called Konrad Kujau. Heidemann, who had purchased the diaries from Kujau over a period of years, refused to believe that such a man could have been responsible for their manufacture: 'he's far too primitive'. But Kujau's guilt was soon beyond dispute. A flamboyant character, he cheerfully accepted his prison sentence, perhaps realising that he had enjoyed a good run. Heidemann was shown to have siphoned off into his own accounts a large proportion of the sums *Stern* had paid for the diaries. He too served a prison sentence. The executives of *Stern* and its parent company were stunned at the revelation that they had been so easily duped. Koch left the company with a large severance fee.

It was ironic that Hugh, of all people, should have been deceived by such a crude forgery. Not long after the story broke, Hugh was due to give an address to the Perne Club, a Peterhouse society at which speakers presented papers on politics, culture and literature. Xandra came along to support her husband. Some were bemused that his chosen topic was Ossian, the most notorious fraud of the eighteenth century. There was therefore an uncomfortable, nervous atmosphere when Hugh began. In the course of his talk Hugh mentioned the aged country surgeon of Lochaber, who, according to Macpherson, could recite the entire Gaelic epic from memory. He described the vain search for this valuable individual. 'But where was the surgeon?' Hugh asked rhetorically – before answering his own question: 'Mysteriously, he seemed to have vanished into thin air, like Scotch mist.'

'Oh dear,' Xandra's wavering voice rang out: 'just like the *Wehrmacht* officer!'

This remark relieved the tension; the room erupted in laughter.

Stoic

Amidst the worldwide hullabaloo over the diaries, Hugh was faced with a domestic spat. The local problem was not Adolf Hitler, but Hallard Croft.

As Director of Studies in mathematics, Croft had been remarkably successful; in one year Peterhouse had gained more firsts than Trinity, generally regarded as the top college in the subject. Recently, however, he had shown signs of restlessness. It soon became clear that he was smouldering with resentment. In early May 1983, shortly before a Governing Body meeting, he circulated a paper on the teaching of mathematics, in which he implied that he lacked 'the support of the regime', and threatened to resign as Director of Studies. Hugh advised Croft that the tone of his paper lowered the dignity of public business, inviting Croft to withdraw it and submit another. Croft did not reply, but at the meeting itself he suddenly produced a short memorandum headed 'Censored Version'. It stated that he was unwilling to continue as Director of Studies, 'for personal reasons, which I am not allowed to communicate to the GB'. Hugh declined to accept this document. He considered that Croft's manner towards him became increasingly surly thereafter. A month later, Croft responded with a curt refusal to a routine request that he continue serving on a college committee. Hugh requested him to reconsider, in a formal but civil letter. This elicited a furious response from Croft: he declared the Master's letter 'damned impertinent'; he refused to be 'exploited' or involve himself any longer in 'college trivia'; and ended by stating his determination to do no more than his basic teaching (a few hours each week) 'under the headship of such an evil personality as yourself'.

If ever there was a right moment to make such a declaration, this was not it. Croft's Fellowship was due for renewal at the Governing Body meeting on 4 July, only a few days hence. Had he waited one more week before sending his offensive letter, he would have been safe, for renewal (which fell due every five years) was usually a formality. No doubt Croft never considered that his Fellowship might be in danger. But his letter could be interpreted as a breach of the college statutes, in refusing to obey the instructions of the Master.* Hugh felt that it was impossible to allow

* On admission, every Fellow reads aloud the declaration 'I will obey the Master thereof in all things lawful and proper', and then signs the Admissions Register.

such defiance to go unpunished and retain his authority. Moreover, he suspected that Croft was being used by the caucus to intimidate him. There was a recent precedent. From confidential papers discovered in the Master's Lodge, Hugh learned that one of his predecessors had received a succession of sneering, insulting and offensive letters over a period of a years, from a former member of the 'mafia' who had since left the college to take up a post at another university. Just as these attacks had been intended to break his predecessor's will, so Croft's insolence, Hugh felt, was meant to bring him to heel.

After careful scrutiny of the college statutes, and consultation with the college's solicitors, the Master withdrew Croft's name from the list of those whose Fellowships were to be renewed; and since no Fellow present at the meeting was prepared to propose its renewal – both Cowling and Norman were abroad – Croft's Fellowship lapsed. Realising the danger he was in, Croft wrote an abject letter of apology, but it was too late. In the next few days Hugh received letters from several of the Fellows supporting the non-renewal of Croft's Fellowship. Ten days after the meeting, he formally notified Croft that his Fellowship would cease at the beginning of the Michaelmas term, unless the Governing Body chose to reverse its decision at its next meeting.

The Croft affair convulsed the college. When Cowling heard the news, he circulated a letter to the Fellows, protesting that the decision not to renew Croft's Fellowship had shown 'injustice, precipitancy and rancour', and demanding a special Governing Body meeting to reconsider the matter. Hugh resisted this demand. Cowling tried to make an issue of Croft's homosexuality, but this was a red herring. Croft had broken his oath to obey the Master: deliberately, defiantly and repeatedly. He was further accused of gross incivility towards college guests. His private inclinations were irrelevant in either case.

As so often, Cowling's opposition was expressed in genial, even admiring terms. 'Even when I am least reconciled to what you are doing, as at present,' he told Hugh, 'I can but yield to your description of what you conceive, and not least to your description of the bed of "bent, rusty and poisoned nails" on which you suppose yourself to be lying.' Cowling recalled with relish what he had apparently said to the bachelor Fellows at the outset: 'I told them that you were horrible and you that you would hate them.' He still believed, he continued, 'that the marriage was just and may even turn out to be profitable and enjoyable'.[1]

Norman had no such ambiguous feelings. It was 'unforgivable' of Hugh to allow such matters to be determined in his absence, and that of others such as Cowling. A succession of clashes had turned the Dean into an implacable enemy of the Master. Hugh had refused to allow the appointment of a curate as college chaplain, which would have allowed Norman to take over the direction of historical study in the college. 'I want neither one thing nor the other,' he told Hugh Lloyd-Jones; 'and I think that now I have blocked both.'[2] Norman had interpreted this, with some justification, as reneging on a commitment. In Governing Body meetings he attacked the Master, but when this proved counter-productive he lapsed into silence. It seemed to Hugh that Norman had adopted a policy of refusing to recognise him, to speak to him, or to return his salutations. 'I fear that our Dean is going mad,' Hugh observed facetiously to one of the senior Fellows.

Despite the difficulties with the Dean, Hugh was regular in his attendance in the Peterhouse chapel, dressed as a Doctor of Divinity. In the stall reserved for the Master he kept a volume of Horace, to ease the *longueurs*. He referred to this as 'a work of devotion'.

Another clash followed the conflict over the chaplain, after Norman sent a casual note regretting that he could not attend the annual audit meeting of the Governing Body, as he had an appointment in London. Exasperated, Hugh pointed out that he could not give him leave of absence: unless the Governing Body voted that he had 'just cause', he must be fined £10 for breaching the statute requiring attendance. Norman wrote curtly that he would be at the BBC, seeing a producer. Hugh answered that he could not regard this as 'just cause', since the date of the meeting had been set five months earlier. Norman insisted that it had been customary to assume that any Fellow who sent apologies for absence would not do so unless he had 'just cause'. Hugh pointed out that this was indeed the case for ordinary meetings, but in respect of this one there was a special statute explicitly denying such a usage. Norman replied that he would consider the matter. When he did not appear for the meeting, Hugh drew attention to his absence, and the Governing Body spent forty minutes discussing the consequences. At length the Fellows voted that the Dean had not 'just cause' for his absence, and that he should therefore pay a fine. 'Now for item 1,' said Hugh, relieved – and just then Norman slid into the room. His timely appearance was greeted with a burst of laughter from his colleagues, who assumed that he had been listening at the keyhole.

Though Hugh had the fine remitted, Norman was not mollified. He complained that the Master had made a practice of 'resurrecting medieval statutes' in order to persecute the Fellows. (In fact, the statutes had been overhauled as recently as 1972.) This new provocation – the disciplining of Croft – roused Norman to an even higher level of hostility. The Master received a report that the Dean had declared 'total war' against him.

Hugh's uneasy relations with his colleagues had been jeopardised by unguarded comments over lunch at the Beefsteak Club. In a *Sunday*

Telegraph article, Peregrine Worsthorne reported that the Master had described Cowling and Norman as 'bigots'. Hugh was furious about this breach of protocol, and tried to have Worsthorne censured. The essence of the Beefsteak was that all conversation was privileged, since all members sat at the same table. He was infuriated too by Worsthorne's statement that the Master 'detests all religions in general, and Christianity in particular'.[3] He insisted that Worsthorne had no authority for this statement, which, in the opinion of solicitors, was defamatory – especially given that Hugh was at the time serving on a parliamentary committee negotiating with the Archbishop of Canterbury about the Prayer Book. *The Sunday Telegraph* paid Hugh's costs, and Worsthorne issued an apology, couched in ambiguous terms. He wrote that he had gained this 'false impression' of Hugh's hostility to religion 'by reading his published works, and other public statements'. Worsthorne claimed to have 'always thought of him as a latter-day Edward Gibbon – a comparison which was in no way intended to be anything but complimentary'.

Such press coverage was damaging to the Master's relations with the Fellows. They were left with the impression that Hugh talked down the college, to friends and strangers alike, not only in Cambridge, but in London and Oxford too. Most felt loyal to Peterhouse, even if they disliked the 'ruling' caucus. The previous Master expressed anxiety about the recent publicity. The Dean resumed his verbal attacks on the Master. Hugh eventually decided that Norman was an asset to him, highlighting the intemperance of the opposition, and made an analogy with Dennis Skinner (the MP nicknamed 'The Beast of Bolsover') as an asset to Mrs Thatcher.

Word reached Hugh that the Dean was denouncing him to anyone who would listen: in particular, he was complaining that the Master had described him as 'a shit'. Hugh wrote to the Dean, denying that he had ever used 'such an indelicate and injurious metaphor'.[4] Within minutes of this letter being delivered, the telephone rang in the Master's Lodge. Xandra answered the call. It was the Dean, demanding to know the Master's whereabouts. Xandra explained that he was in the college. Norman found Hugh in the College Secretary's office. 'Just the man I want!' he exclaimed. The Master said that he would be free shortly. 'No, now!' the Dean insisted. He brandished the letter. 'Let us take a stroll in the court,' Hugh suggested. 'No, here,' the Dean declared, 'here, before witnesses!' The Master replied that if he wanted to discuss a private matter, it must be done in private, and walked out into the court. Norman followed: he had put up with this long enough, he announced, and now he demanded a public apology. Retreating across the road, pursued by the Dean, Hugh explained that his letter had been intended to correct a misunderstanding, not to create one; he expressed his regret that his olive branch had been snatched from his hand and used as a stick to beat him. He urged the Dean to accept it in the spirit of Christian amity ... By this time he had reached the front door of the Master's Lodge, through which he speedily slipped. He shut the door behind him, remembering an incident in his boyhood, when he had fled across a field from an angry bull and escaped only just in time over a gate.

In mid-July Hugh left Cambridge for the Borders. Most of the other Fellows had already departed for the summer. Reporters began to appear unheralded at Chiefswood. Hugh received several letters from a former Fellow of Peterhouse associated with the 'mafia'. At first the writer purported to be seeking the Master's permission to write a piece about the history of the college in the twentieth century. He claimed to have proof that Butterfield's behaviour during the war had put him at risk of internment under rule 18B of the Emergency Powers Act. Hugh knew of Butterfield's pro-German sympathies, and he was aware too that another distinguished Peterhouse historian had compromised himself in the 1930s by his extravagant praise for Hitler. As he read these letters, Hugh gradually realised that he was being threatened: if he did not relent and allow the renewal of Croft's Fellowship, Peterhouse would be submerged in scandal. This was a delicate moment, while the Appeal to raise funds for the new library was still in its infancy. It would be embarrassing for Lord Weinstock to be heading an Appeal on behalf of a college with a Nazi past.

Hugh defied his correspondent to publish. The threatened article never appeared. Later that summer, however, several pieces did appear in the press about the 'Croft affair'.[5] They stated confidently that a majority of the Fellows was opposed to the Master's actions, and predicted that Croft would be reinstated. There was even talk that the Master might be deposed. It was obvious that at least one of Croft's supporters had spoken to journalists. The newspapers concerned were silenced by legal letters sent on Hugh's instructions. Complicated discussions followed. The pressure on the Master increased in the run-up to the next Governing Body meeting in October. Cowling circulated several 'encyclicals' to the Fellowship, arguing that this was a mere personal dispute in which the college should not be involved, and calling for Croft to be retained. By this time the issue had become a trial of strength. Hugh contemplated giving up the struggle and resigning if he were unsuccessful in winning the support of the Fellows in Governing Body.[6] He did not believe the bluster about there being a majority for Croft's reinstatement; but he was concerned that the 'jellies' in the Fellowship might be intimidated by threats of serious legal repercussions.

On the Friday before the Monday meeting of the Governing Body, the Senior Tutor, the sole law Fellow in the college, intervened. In a detailed letter, which was circulated to every Peterhouse Fellow, he advised that the college had been 'in a state of illegality' for the past few months; that Croft had every right to take his 'just grievance' to the Visitor (the Bishop of Ely); that the Master was in breach of college statute; that there could be no possible outcome from the affair except public humiliation, vast expense and a peremptory order to restore Croft's Fellowship. He further advised the Master that the college had no alternative but to reinstate Croft immediately and unconditionally.

Barely had Hugh received this letter when Cowling came to see him, followed almost immediately by another of the Fellows. Both begged him to accept a compromise. They told him that the Senior Tutor was in a state of exaltation, confident that he would defeat the Master. His legal expertise would terrorise the Fellowship into submission. The only way out, both suggested, was to settle on whatever terms Croft would accept.

Hugh was unimpressed. He found both the tone and the content of the Senior Tutor's letter impertinent, and sought independent advice from a QC, who worked over the weekend to provide an opinion. This arrived by motorcycle messenger on Monday afternoon, only minutes before the Governing Body meeting was due to start. The document was immediately copied and distributed to the Fellows, while the Master declared a recess to enable them to read and digest it. Counsel's opinion proved to be a devastating document, an Exocet missile which blew the Senior Tutor's arguments out of the water.

The Governing Body meeting lasted much longer than usual. In the debate about Croft's Fellowship, the Dean made a series of spirited attacks on the Master, while Cowling vainly tried to restrain him ('Remember, Edward, we are here to discuss the case of Dr Croft, not to impeach the Master!'). A proposal to reinstate Croft immediately and unconditionally was defeated by eighteen votes to seven. Cowling had tried to tack a qualifying amendment onto it, which the Master disallowed on procedural grounds. Norman next proposed that Croft be reinstated, provided that he was debarred from presiding at high table or in the Combination Room. This was defeated by the same majority. Finally a compromise proposal was put forward: that Croft be elected a Fellow on a new basis, from the following February. The attraction of this proposal was that Croft would retain his Fellowship but have to be readmitted: which would mean that he would again have to take the oath of obedience to the Master, and would lose his twenty-two years' seniority, thereby forfeiting any chance of becoming senior Fellow. Indeed, as the newest of the Fellowship, he would suffer the humiliation of being obliged to serve port and coffee to the junior Fellows. This proposal was passed by fourteen votes to eleven. Hugh would have been happy to see the back of Croft, but he was satisfied with this solution.

He was reminded of Perkin Warbeck, the pretender who tried to dethrone Henry VII, and was punished, not by execution, but by being made a scullion in the royal kitchen.*

Always skilful at playing a losing hand, Cowling claimed to have supported the Master all along. Norman was enraged at the outcome, and vented his fury on an innocent television crew filming a cello recital in the chapel. His frustration was obvious in the opening words of an article he wrote around this time for *The Times Higher Education Supplement*: 'Herbert Butterfield was the last distinguished historian to become Master of Peterhouse'.[7]

Croft had been restrained, though not reformed. More than two years after his reinstatement, there was an incident at dessert, which Hugh subsequently described as 'damaging to the interest or good name of the college'. It was a guest night, and the Master was trying, through the Fellow presiding in the Combination Room, to make seating arrangements for the guests, one of whom was a candidate for a Fellowship. When asked to move down one place, Croft appeared to explode, raging that the Master had 'no authority in the Combination Room', and continued shouting for some while, to general embarrassment. Hugh, though evidently shaken, responded quietly and firmly. In a letter written afterwards he formally warned Croft of the consequences of any repetition; and reminded him of the undertakings he had given when seeking the renewal of his Fellowship.[8] Unsurprisingly, the candidate Fellow decided that this was not a community that he wished to enter.

Hugh has been criticised by some of his Cambridge colleagues for his handling of Croft. It has been suggested that he was impolitic, or petty. Yet it is hard to see how he could have ignored such an overt challenge. His private letters show that he felt his Mastership was at stake. It is noteworthy that more than two-thirds of the Fellowship supported his disciplining of Croft, despite the threat of legal complications.

Harold Macmillan was by no means the only observer to liken the drama at Peterhouse to the plot of a novel by C.P. Snow: the comparison was obvious. Early in 1984, a young man who had been an undergraduate at Peterhouse, now working for the BBC, exercised his right to dine in college. The Master, who was presiding that evening, seated his guest on his right, with his habitual formal courtesy. He enquired what had brought the young man back to Cambridge. 'A bit of historical *re*search,' replied the young man, oblivious to the reddening of the cheeks and twitching of the eyebrows induced by his emphasis on the first syllable. 'And for what purpose?' the Master enquired. 'We're making films of C.P. Snow's sequence of

---

* Though in fact his memory played him false, as it was Lambert Simnel, not Perkin Warbeck, who received this humiliating punishment.

novels,'* the young man boldly explained, 'and I thought I'd like to get the authentic feel of high table conversation.' He sipped his claret. 'Perhaps,' he suggested, 'you watched the first episode?'

Hugh shook his head. 'No,' he responded. 'In the first place, I don't own a television set;[†] in the second, I can't stand Snow's writing; third, there's far too much of that sort of thing that goes on here in reality.' A long silence ensued, brought to an end by one of Hugh's colleagues, sitting on the other side of the young guest. He quoted a friend, who had described Snow as 'rising between two stools: the chemists admiring him as a novelist, and the novelists as a chemist'.

'A German phenomenon, I think,' interpolated Hugh, 'if I may say so: as in the case of the so-called gentleman scholar whom scholars respect because they are snobs while gentlemen, being gentlemen, respect anyone with pretensions to scholarship.'

'But surely, Master,' the young man rashly protested, 'one can be both a gentleman and a scholar?'

'Indeed so,' Hugh replied; 'and' (giving his interlocutor a pitying look), 'I think, neither.'[9]

The Master had been embarrassed by the poor response from Fellows to the college Appeal. He had written to each of them personally, by hand, and received in return grudging contributions, excuses and a few outright refusals, some barely civil. Only a few had made the kind of financial contribution he thought appropriate. In a letter to Cowling, Hugh described this fund-raising as 'the most uncongenial task I have ever undertaken'.[10] It was difficult to ask strangers to contribute generously to the college when Fellows themselves seemed so reluctant.

As Peregrine Worsthorne had reported after their conversation at the Beefsteak, Hugh was concerned that the progress of the Appeal might be impeded 'by the college's reputation for political and even religious oddity'. This concern seemed justified when Lord Weinstock sent him a cutting from *Private Eye*, reporting that a Peterhouse Fellow had been observed parading in a swastika armband at a Boat Club dinner, while his acolytes gave Nazi salutes and volunteered anti-Semitic remarks to the astonished audience. 'Can the enclosed cutting possibly be true?' asked Weinstock.[11] Though he did not of course mention this to Weinstock, Hugh learned that another Peterhouse Fellow had been spotted in a disreputable London club, dressed as an SS officer.

---

* *Strangers and Brothers*, a thirteen-part series, first broadcast in 1984.
† In fact there was a television in Xandra's sitting-room, where Hugh watched a natural history programme narrated by David Attenborough, and was inspired to draw a parallel between the creatures he saw depicted on screen and some of his colleagues across the road.

The seventh centenary in 1984 was marked by a series of junkets. On one Saturday, for example, there was a lunch for 250 old members, to whom the Master had to make an uplifting speech, followed by a lunch for Princess Margaret and more than a dozen other guests on the Sunday. Hugh tried to prod his colleagues into including some form of academic or intellectual element in the celebrations. 'Must we have only dinners, garden-parties, drinking bouts?' he asked. He had tried to elevate the intellectual level of the college by encouraging the election of Visiting Fellows such as Henry Mayr-Harting, Arnaldo Momigliano, Hugh Kearney and the Australian John Morgan, the former Oriel chaplain. The presence of such scholars was, he felt, a civilising influence. 'What I find most depressing at Peterhouse is the total absence of intelligent conversation,' he told Noel Annan. 'It is like a private school (not unlike that private school in *Decline and Fall*) – or a private hotel with regular boarders who hate each other but depend on each other. I made Arnaldo Momigliano a Visiting Fellow in order to have someone to talk to; but he, not unnaturally, prefers Turin.'*[12]

Xandra organised a special concert to mark the seventh centenary, assisted by the broadcaster Richard Baker, himself a Peterhouse man. In Governing Body, the Master proposed a commemorative lecture – perhaps even a series of lectures – on the history of the college, but was greeted with complete silence. 'Perhaps,' he suggested, 'the historians ... the famous Peterhouse history school?' Cowling's response emerged from the Stygian darkness at the far end of the Combination Room: 'Do it yourself.' Afterwards, one of the scientists quietly urged him to persevere.[13] Thus encouraged, Hugh planned a course of five commemorative 'Peterhouse Lectures', under the overall title 'Aspects of University Culture in Seven Centuries, 1284–1984'. He would give two of them himself; another was given by a former Visiting Fellow from Oxford, Henry Mayr-Harting; and a fourth by an art historian who had no connection with the college. Only one other Peterhouse Fellow, Aaron Klug, contributed a lecture. The lectures were open to the public, and were delivered in the Michaelmas term, in the elegant lecture theatre of the new library. By his own admission, Hugh's lectures contained several 'pointed, not to say malicious' references to the recent history of the college. Indeed the title of one of his lectures referred to the 'New Right' in Oxford and Cambridge – albeit the New Right of the seventeenth century.

Hugh had been an Oxford man too long not to feel some prejudice against Cambridge. He once likened his move there from Oxford to becoming a colonial governor. He never went native. References to Cambridge as

---

* Dismissed on racial grounds (he was Jewish) in 1938 from his post as Professor of Roman History in the University of Turin, he was reinstated as a supernumerary professor in 1945.

a 'torpid, introverted village' situated among 'dreary Fens' punctuated his letters. When Hugh sat for a portrait by Lawrence Gowing commissioned by the college to hang in the new undergraduate Library, he wore his Christ Church tie. Such details did not go unnoticed.

At the end of the first week of the Michaelmas term 1984, the Dacres celebrated their thirtieth wedding anniversary with a buffet lunch party for their friends at the Master's Lodge. No one from Peterhouse was invited. 'I fear there will be a lot of flibbertigibbets,' Hugh warned Charles Stuart beforehand: adding, in parentheses, 'five Duchesses have accepted: surely this is indecent: it makes me feel like J. Plumb*'.[14] In a letter to Noel Annan Hugh professed to be 'deeply ashamed' by this aristocratic predominance. 'I must scrape the highways and hedges for commoners – perhaps I shall even let some of the F. of P. in.' Earlier Hugh had claimed to Annan that he had been opposed to Xandra's plan for a party, on the grounds that no one would come to Cambridge; 'you might as well, I protested, invite the *beau monde* to a party in Biggleswade'.[15] This bon mot was soon in general circulation, as no doubt Hugh had intended.

Hugh allowed himself to be renominated as a director of Times Newspapers Limited in September 1984. He reasoned that it was important for him to remain on the board, as he was the only independent National Director left who had been in place at the time of the Murdoch takeover, the others having recently retired. He did not reflect that it suited Murdoch to retain a director whose moral authority had been weakened by the disaster of the Hitler diaries. In 1985 the directors' fees were raised to £4,000 p.a.

The Times had suffered much less from the trauma of the Hitler diaries than its Sunday stable-mate. Douglas-Home had proved an effective Editor, calming the nervous mood of the staff after the upset of Evans's departure. He had less difficulty with Murdoch than his predecessor, perhaps because he was more in sympathy with his proprietor's views. Under Douglas-Home's leadership *The Times* became more populist, adopting a pro-Thatcher line, and sniping at institutions which Murdoch resented, such as the BBC. In May 1985 Hugh wrote to his old friend Alasdair Milne, by now Director-General of the BBC and under siege from the Thatcher Government, to complain about insinuations that attacks on the BBC in *The Times* were motivated by Murdoch's television interests.[16]

Douglas-Home died in the autumn of 1985, after a long struggle with bone cancer. Previously Murdoch had consulted the directors about editorial appointments, but now he simply informed them of his intentions by fax from New York. The directors agreed with the proprietor that his

---

* Plumb was a notorious social climber.

nominee, Charles Wilson, was the best internal candidate, but still doubted that Wilson had sufficient moral or intellectual weight for the task. Since they were given no opportunity to discuss their doubts with Murdoch in person, they reluctantly gave their assent, but added a rider expressing their reservations about his choice. Hugh read this aloud to Murdoch on the transatlantic telephone. The proprietor noted their assent and ignored their reservations.

Early in 1986 negotiations between News International and the print unions over the introduction of new technology broke down, precipitating an all-out strike. Murdoch switched production to a purpose-built plant in Wapping. This was besieged by angry print workers, who organised mass demonstrations outside. The plant, protected by large numbers of policemen, was often likened to a fortress. Many of the journalists felt uncomfortable crossing picket lines and decided to accept redundancy, including the Literary Editor, Claire Tomalin, the journalist with whom Hugh was most often in contact as a contributor. Hugh crossed the picket line himself, when he visited Wapping at the proprietor's suggestion. Murdoch conducted him personally around the whole plant. Hugh was impressed by the high morale of the workers; the atmosphere within the plant reminded him of wartime. He admired Murdoch for his courage in taking on the unions. But when he saw *The Sun* rolling off the presses he was sad to reflect that so much effort and struggle had gone into producing such 'corrupting poison'. The strike lasted more than twelve months before collapsing. The power of the print unions had been broken, and other newspapers soon followed News International in modernising their print-ing practices.

In the summer of 1986 *The Sunday Times* carried a front-page story – 'Queen dismayed by "Uncaring" Thatcher' – alleging that there was a rift between the Queen and the Prime Minister. Several of the independent National Directors were angered by what seemed to them an unacceptable debasement of the standard of responsible journalism. Four of them arranged to meet privately at the offices of *The Economist*. During the meeting a letter to Murdoch was drafted, and its text approved by the two absentees over the telephone. The letter, signed on behalf of all six of them by Hugh as the senior director, condemned the article. It further questioned the way that Andrew Neil had handled the aftermath of the story's pub-lication, and criticised the 'rough and authoritarian' manner in which he had expressed himself when interviewed about it on television. Hugh was also critical of Neil's refusal to publish the Palace's response to the story. He raised the matter at the next board meeting, but the united front of the independent directors was broken when one of them, the newsreader Sir Alastair Burnet, disassociated himself from the letter, even though he had been present when it was drafted. This enabled Murdoch to brush the matter aside. Afterwards he wrote courteously to Hugh, recognising the right of the independent directors to express concerns on matters affecting the reputation of the newspapers. 'But having taken into account all you have to say and considered the editorial safeguards laid down in the undertakings that govern your duties and my powers and responsibilities, I have come to the conclusion that this is not a matter in which I can properly exercise proprietorial intervention.' Hugh recognised that by this argument Murdoch had turned the tables on them.[17]

In recent years Hugh had contributed fewer and fewer reviews to *The Sunday Times*. The rapid turnover of editorial staff did not foster long-term relations with contributors. Early in 1986 he protested that a short review of his had been printed with no fewer than twenty-four typographical errors. Since Claire Tomalin's departure he no longer knew who occupied her chair; so he was forced to address his protest 'Dear Literary Editor'. He complained that no proof had been sent to him, 'nor <u>can</u> the proof have been read by anyone, since it is a mass of grotesque errors, and these errors are errors of substance as well as of printing, so that any reader who thinks that the Sunday Times is a serious paper must think that I am not a serious historian'.[18] This would be his last piece for *The Sunday Times*, after an association which went back thirty-five years. He began to review instead for *The Sunday Telegraph* and, more occasionally, for *The Daily Telegraph*.

In December 1987 Murdoch asked Hugh to consent to withholding his name from the list of those going forward for re-election to the board. 'I now have to envisage a managerial and directorial structure capable of carrying us through to the nineties and beyond,' wrote Murdoch. 'I am deeply aware of the contribution you made in those often hectic and exciting years, and I am particularly grateful for your support in often difficult circumstances.'

'You put me in a difficult position,' Hugh replied. 'I have enjoyed being a National Director and would be happy to continue, but of course I would not wish to do so against your wishes. On the other hand, for an "independent" director to be asked by the chairman to resign with only a weekend's notice, and without time to consult those whom he ought to consult, does look rather peremptory.' Murdoch showed that he was not pleased by this resistance. A few days later Hugh received a visit from Murdoch's lawyer, with whom he had enjoyed friendly relations until this point. When Hugh was asked to give a guarantee that he would resign, he responded that he had no desire to stay, especially if he was not acceptable to the proprietor, but insisted on leaving in his own way. Then, having made his gesture of defiance, he resigned from the board before the next meeting.[19]

*

Renaissance Essays appeared in 1985, the first in a projected set. For some years Blair Worden had been encouraging Hugh to republish his essays, many of which were hard to find. Back in 1983 Hugh had met the energetic publisher Tom Rosenthal, Chairman of Secker & Warburg, to discuss adapting his review of the *Lisle Letters* into an introduction to a condensed, one-volume edition. From these limited conversations a more ambitious plan was hatched for Secker & Warburg to become Hugh's principal publisher. Hugh was unhappy that Macmillan had allowed the second edition of *Religion, the Reformation and Social Change* to go out of print. Moreover there had been various staff changes at Macmillan, with the result that almost all of those with whom he had dealt in the past had left. Rosenthal offered to reissue *Religion, the Reformation and Social Change* in a revised, third edition, as part of a plan to collect Hugh's essays in a set of five volumes, loosely gathered in chronological order. Secker & Warburg would also publish the Mayerne biography. Rosenthal offered an overall advance of £20,000 for all six books, payable in instalments on delivery and publication of each volume. A contract was agreed with Michael Sissons of A.D. Peters, who had taken over as Hugh's agent following Peters's retirement. Richard Ollard, now retired from Collins, acted as a freelance editorial consultant. After some discussion it was agreed that the University of Chicago Press would co-publish the essays in America, paying an advance of $2,000 per volume.

The critical reception of *Renaissance Essays* was mixed. In *The Times Literary Supplement*, Robin Briggs welcomed the book as 'a distinguished and very entertaining volume'; but in *The London Review of Books*, Conrad Russell described Hugh's method as 'a little old-fashioned', and suggested that the Master of Peterhouse, now in his seventies, had not kept abreast of a changing body of knowledge.[20] Nevertheless, the effect of this collection, and those that followed, would enhance Hugh's reputation as an historian of ideas. Paradoxically, his standing within the profession steadily rose, at the very time when the public could hardly esteem him less.

Robert Silvers congratulated Xandra on the index: 'the friskiest, wittiest, and most enjoyable one I've seen for years'. He told her that he was advising people to '<u>start with the index</u>'[21] In fact, of course, it was not Xandra but her husband who enlivened the index; she did the hard graft, while he added the final flourishes – entries such as 'Aristotle: not exempt from universal folly'; 'Botolf, alias Sir Gregory Sweetlips: a plotting priest'; 'Anne Boleyn, Queen, 76; dislikes monkeys, 82; to be beheaded with sword, not axe, 86, 88'; and 'Aquinas: his Whig views'.

Silvers asked Hugh to review the second volume of Cowling's *Religion and Public Doctrine*. There was a curious pre-history to this review. Before receiving a copy of the book Hugh had been telephoned by Cowling, who informed him that the publishers, Cambridge University Press, were 'making trouble' over a certain passage in the foreword. Cowling asked Hugh to approve a long sentence, which he read out over the telephone. 'It was about myself,' Hugh explained in a letter to Worden. 'I didn't think it very civil, but it was also unintelligible; so I simply said that I did not presume to censure or authorise the writings of my colleagues, and declined to comment.'[22] The passage, written in typically convoluted prose, was a form of backhanded acknowledgement:

> The Master and Fellows of Peterhouse have contrived to provide conditions in which work can be done, the Master, Lord Dacre, in particular, by reasons of the brilliance of his enmities, the Enlightened nature of his sympathies and the chronologically locatable character of his distaste for intellectual Toryism and ecclesiastical Christianity, provided goads and spurs of which he has almost certainly been unaware.[23]

Afterwards Hugh learned that this was a substitute for a more offensive passage, which so alarmed the officers of the Press that they had cancelled the original page, even though it had by then been printed. He was delighted to hear that this process was immensely expensive.[24] Hugh wrote to Cowling to say that he had read the book 'with close attention, from cover to cover, including the Foreword', and that he had found the last sentence very mysterious. 'What is the reader meant to infer?' he asked.

> What he must infer, I think, is that the subject of your work has been vigorously, and acrimoniously ('with brilliant enmity') discussed between us and that this dialogue has in some way, and to some extent, affected the argument, or the form, of your book. But not only have we never had any discussion on the subject: we have never (to my great loss) had any discussion on any intellectual or historical subject, since you live withdrawn in your inaccessible cave of Adullam* in Fen Court, emerging only for dinner, at which, if I should attend it, you take care to sit at the opposite end of the table, and thereafter beat a hurried retreat back into the Cave.[25]

Hugh reviewed the book itself in satirical terms. Though the case was 'vigorously presented' in 'forceful language', there was no engaging with it, since Cowling rejected rational argument and sneered at those whom he despised. In any case, there was some difficulty in understanding the

---

* The stronghold, mentioned in the Old Testament, in which David sought refuge from Saul. The term 'Adullamites' is used to refer to groups of political outsiders plotting their comeback or the overthrow of the status quo, especially after recent defeat. Cowling would have been familiar with the term, since it was coined to describe a dissident faction within the Liberal Party during the Victorian period.

substance of Cowling's beliefs. 'Perhaps if we strain our eyes and become accustomed to the opacity by which they are protected, we shall discern something of them,' Hugh suggested.

Cowling responded in a letter to *The New York Review of Books*, in which he insisted that the opacity of his prose was 'deliberate'.[26]

Mrs Thatcher's respect for Hugh was shown by the fact that she had made him a peer within weeks of taking office. In the eleven years that she was Prime Minister he would be her guest on several occasions. They did not always see eye to eye, however. In March 1985 Hugh attended a dinner party at 10 Downing Street, hosted by Hugh Thomas* and his wife Vanessa, for the Prime Minister to meet writers and scholars, among them Noel Annan, Anthony Powell, Raymond Carr, V.S. Naipaul, Iris Murdoch, Anthony Quinton and Hugh's former pupil, Theodore Zeldin. Afterwards Hugh wrote to tell Blake that he had been 'rather shaken' by some of the things Mrs Thatcher had said. 'She has no friends, listens to no-one, and never relaxes,' he told Blake.

'Do you think that our dear P.M. has gone bananas?' Hugh asked Annan. Her impatience of obstruction by the organs of society – committees of inquiry, parliamentary procedure, courts of law and the House of Lords – had been depressingly evident at 'that curious dinner party'. He was dismayed to hear her boasting of having 'seen off' the miners. 'Her Toryism seems rather that of Charles I than of Edmund Burke.'[27]

In the summer of 1982, Hugh had been invited to 10 Downing Street, together with Michael Howard, to discuss the text of a speech the Prime Minister was due to deliver to the United Nations General Assembly after the victory over Argentina in the Falklands War (according to *Private Eye*, Hugh wittily dubbed her 'Margarita Antarctica'). There were about ten people present, all civil servants apart from these two. Mrs Thatcher was apparently in a vile temper. 'Her manner of conducting the conversation was to go round the table clockwise and bully each guest in turn,' Michael Howard recollected later. Eventually she reached Hugh.

'So, Lord Dacre,' she began ominously, 'and when can we expect another book from you?'

'Well, Prime Minister,' Hugh replied, 'I have one on the stocks.'

'On the stocks? *On the stocks?* A fat lot of good that is! In the shops, that is where we need it!'[28]

'A tory in the Chamber,† now that I am back in Cambridge, faced with the

---

* An ally of Mrs Thatcher's, he was made a life peer in 1981.
† i.e. the House of Lords.

squalid toryism of Peterhouse, I naturally become very whiggish again,'
Hugh told Blair Worden.[29] In Oxford he had resisted change; in Cambridge
he found himself becoming a radical reformer. The effects of changes he
had initiated or encouraged gradually became apparent. His appointee
Martin Golding proved a success as Admissions Tutor, for example. 'I am
greatly cheered by the very marked change in the character of the undergraduates,' Hugh reported to the sociologist Ed Shils, a former Fellow of
Peterhouse, who became a confidant on college matters. 'I have seen a great
deal of them recently and I find them very different from, and superior to,
those who dominated the place when I came here: more cultivated, more
humane, altogether more attractive.' Hugh kept notes on index cards about
each undergraduate, not always favourable.

Shils was a member of the Committee on Social Thought, the inter-
disciplinary graduate program in Chicago, founded by Hugh's old friend
John Nef. Arnaldo Momigliano was also a member. In March 1985 Hugh
visited Chicago and lectured to a Committee audience, a welcome contrast
to 'a grim lunch' with the Chicago History Faculty. He particularly took to
another Committee member, the novelist Saul Bellow.[30]

The longer that Hugh was Master of Peterhouse, the more effective he
became, largely because he had been able to dislodge from their positions
those college officers who had attempted to thwart him. Towards the end
of 1985 he ensured that Roderick Munday ceased to be Senior Tutor. Hugh
argued that after serving ten years Munday's time was up, though in fact
there was nothing in the statutes to limit the term. Two other college offices
had become vacant, so the Master proposed a 'slate' of three candidates,
including Philip Pattenden, a young classics don who seemed to him efficient and practical, as Senior Tutor. Munday was keen to continue in the
role, and was backed by Cowling and Norman, who argued that the Master
had not followed the 'correct procedure' in proposing his slate of candidates. Norman forced a vote in Governing Body, but failed to secure
significant support. It was obvious that the power of the once-dominant
caucus had been broken. The Dean complained that 'Dacre's Dirty Dozen'*
had supplanted them. Hugh phrased it differently: 'The Fellows of Peterhouse have been brought to order, if not to life.'

As he approached the end of his term as Master, he was better able to
implement reforms. In particular he instituted a policy by which new
Fellows were chosen by advertisement and interview, rather than by the
old informal system of patronage and blackballing, which had lent itself to

---

* Possibly an allusion to the 1967 film *The Dirty Dozen*, set in the Second World War, in which
an Allied force of twelve hardened criminals, led by an American army major with an attitude
problem, are sent on a suicide mission behind enemy lines.

favouritism and abuse. He would have liked his Mastership to be prolonged so that he could continue the good work that he had begun, but this hope proved vain. Towards the end of 1986 the Fellows began considering the choice of his successor. Characteristically, Cowling circulated one of his 'encyclicals' on the subject. 'We've had a bumpy ride during the last six years,' he wrote; 'Now we need somebody who will make us happy.' Once reconciled to the inevitability of his departure, Hugh covertly pushed the candidacy of first John Hale and then Hugh Thomas; but after months of consideration the Fellowship chose instead Henry Chadwick, former Regius Professor of Divinity at both Oxford and Cambridge and Dean of Christ Church. Chadwick thus became the first person in four centuries to be head of a college at both universities. As Dean, Chadwick had not always been a decisive leader. His emollient personality contrasted with that of his wife Peggy, whom he had met when he was a schoolmaster and she a matron in a boarding school; the boys nicknamed them 'Oil' and 'Vinegar'. To Hugh, this was 'a lunatic, bizarre choice'.[31] He feared that the college would 'revert to its old condition of mouldering anarchy permeated by destructive intrigue'.*[32]

The death of Harold Macmillan (who had become Earl of Stockton in 1984) at the very end of the year 1986 created a vacancy for a new Chancellor of Oxford University. Soon afterwards, Hugh was approached by a don at Pembroke, who claimed to speak for a number of Oxford colleagues wanting to nominate him. Hugh indicated that he might stand if no more suitable candidate came forward, but he argued that Macmillan's successor ought to be another lively political figure: perhaps Lord Hailsham, who had the advantage of being a Christ Church man, though it had to be admitted against him that he was now seventy-nine. In reality, Hugh was tempted by the possibility. He failed to recognise that the stain of the Hitler diaries had made it impossible for him to be elected, even if he had been a strong candidate before, which was by no means certain. Nor did Xandra; and, as often happens, husband and wife reinforced each other's illusions. This proved awkward when James was expected to agree that his stepfather should stand. Hugh asked his supporters to take soundings, in particular of Robert Blake, his oldest friend among the senior figures of Oxford.

A few days later he received a letter from Blake, who had evidently not yet been sounded at the time of writing. The letter ran through the various

---

* Intrigue within Peterhouse persisted for some years. In 2001, workmen redecorating the Small Parlour, a room to which two to three Fellows at a time would retire from the Combination Room below to discuss college business in private, discovered a bugging device hidden behind a bookcase. By the end of the first decade of the twenty-first century, however, Peterhouse intrigue had subsided to the level of that of any other college.

categories of candidate, and gradually reduced the list to four academics, of whom, he suggested, only two were suitable: Hugh and himself. If Hugh decided to stand, Blake offered to withdraw in his favour, but if not ... Hugh replied that he wished to wait and see if Hailsham would stand; but if it should come down to the academics, he would remember Blake's civil offer.

At a dinner of 'The Club', Hugh's suggestion that Hailsham should be the next Chancellor was shouted down, despite the presence of several other Christ Church men. Afterwards he wrote to Blake, proposing that they should meet to discuss the matter. Blake's reaction was instantaneous. First, he announced to the press that he was a candidate; next, he replied to Hugh that he was unable to meet that week.

Hugh was very surprised. He had assumed that Blake would not think of standing, since Ted Heath, who had made him a peer, was known to be considering whether to throw his hat into the ring. Hugh consulted Charles Stuart, who replied that he very much hoped Hugh would restrain his young champions, 'because I don't think you can possibly win'. Stuart pleaded with Hugh to 'keep out of the battle in dignified silence', warning that 'the Philistines' were 'numerous and hostile – don't let them have the pleasure of doing you down'. No doubt this was sound advice, even if it was unwelcome. 'I shall not compete with Robert,' Hugh replied; 'our natural constituencies overlap and I would not wish to drain away any votes: so I have asked my supporters to proceed no further.' He informed Blake of his decision, and said that he wished him well.[33]

Heath did stand, and so did another political heavyweight, Roy Jenkins. Hugh did not vote in the election that followed, being in Australia at the time. The Conservative vote was split evenly between the two Tory candidates, allowing Jenkins to triumph with less than 40 per cent of the vote. Blake came second, with 32 per cent, to Heath's 29 per cent. Heath was said to be 'very cross', and Blake 'seething with resentment' at the result. 'Nobody loves a bad loser,' Hugh commented to Worden.[34]

On the first Sunday of his last term at Peterhouse, Hugh decided to go into the Combination Room after dinner, as a friendly gesture. When he arrived the 'mafia' was ensconced, and there was no attempt to make room for him. Picking up a chair, he asked brightly, 'May I join you?' The Dean muttered something which he did not catch. Hugh asked him to repeat what he had said. 'It was private,' Norman snapped. 'But this is the Combination Room – our Common Table ...' Hugh protested. 'Not when you are here,' declared the Dean. He rose to his feet and stalked out of the room, leaving a full glass of claret behind him, followed by Watkin and Croft. Hugh was left alone in the Combination Room with Cowling. 'I hope you're not going to leave too!' said the mortified Master. 'Oh no,' replied Cowling, and they held an agreeable conversation *à deux* before retiring.

After this unpleasant experience, Hugh decided never again to enter the Combination Room in the evening. But soon after the end of term, he went into the Parlour around ten o'clock one evening to read the papers. 'Talk of the devil!' Mathias exclaimed loudly as Hugh entered. Hugh was surprised to find members of the 'mafia' there, with some others; he subsequently discovered that they had been excluded from the Combination Room by a conference. Watkin had brought in a guest. Despite Mathias's welcome, the Master decided it would not be civil to sit there alone reading the papers, so he joined the group. A junior Fellow offered him coffee, admitting that by this hour it would be cold. Hugh politely declined the offer. He was then offered wine, which he also refused. 'Then what <u>do</u> you want, coming in here?' Watkin asked defiantly. Appreciating that he was unwanted, Hugh left.

Their impending departure from Peterhouse made it necessary for the Dacres to find a new house. Xandra was adamant that she did not want to live at Chiefswood, which they decided to sell. The sale proved difficult: largely, in the opinion of the agent, due to the presence of the hospital. Eventually they sold it to a doctor who worked there, for £160,000 – £20,000 less than the asking price. Hugh was melancholy when the moment came to leave Chiefswood for ever. Meanwhile they had been looking for a house within easy reach of London, Oxford and Cambridge. Eventually they found an early Victorian rectory, described by the agents as 'a magnificent period home of delightful proportions with a self-contained family annexe', surrounded by almost an acre of gardens. It offered an easy rail connection to both Oxford and London, being only a few minutes' walk from Didcot station. The Old Rectory was a dignified house, with high ceilings and well-proportioned rooms. But it was surrounded by an unlovely modern estate, in a town dominated by a huge power station, with little character and few amenities, and no access by foot to open country. Hugh would refer mockingly to Didcot as 'the Thebes of the Thames Valley'. Nevertheless the Dacres decided that this was the house for them, and early in 1987 they completed the purchase for £180,000. Visitors often described the Old Rectory as 'the only nice house in Didcot'.

Moving was a considerable upheaval for a couple in their seventies, especially as it meant squeezing the contents of two houses into one. The Dacres resisted pressure from the Chadwicks to move out of the Master's Lodge before they were ready. Perhaps Hugh remembered Chadwick's lack of support when the Christ Church Treasurer had been trying to evict the Trevor-Ropers from No. 8 St Aldates. Chadwick was especially impatient to move into the Master's Lodge as he wanted his daughter to be married during the summer from his elegant new home. As a result there was a certain amount of strain between the new Master and the old, attracting the attention of the gossip columnist Nigel Dempster. According to him, callers to the Porters' Lodge asking for the Master were answered: 'Which one?'[35]

As he left Peterhouse, rather more hurriedly than he might have wished, Hugh looked back on 'seven wasted years'. He was grateful to the four-fifths of the Fellows who had always – 'if rather silently' – given him their support. 'But that other fifth, that caucus, that <u>mafia</u> . . .'[36]

In what Hugh described as 'a last gesture of paranoid hatred' his enemies tried to prevent the college from electing him as an Honorary Fellow. Such an act would be an unprecedented snub to a former Master. Nevertheless it was not impossible: the election of an Honorary Fellow required the approval of two-thirds of the whole Governing Body. Cowling circulated a memorandum on the subject, suggesting that the vote would divide 'the Fellows with whom he has quarrelled from those who [sic], corporately, he despises'.

> My relations with Lord Dacre are so peculiar that I do not mind whether he is elected or not. I do urge the Governing Body, however, to ask what it is going to do if Lord Dacre makes even more public than he has so far the contempt which he has been making pretty public ever since he arrived here seven years ago.[37]

Cowling warned of the danger that Hugh might be 'going public, so to speak, in the newspapers or in a book'. He suggested that any invitation should be accompanied by a homily on the virtues of silence. This was rich, coming from such an inveterate manipulator of the press. Indeed an article by Cowling on the subject appeared in *The Sunday Telegraph* on the day before the election. Fortunately the 'Men of Sense' prevailed, as Hugh reported to Worden. On the principle that 'when beleaguered, show the flag', he planned to attend the forthcoming Commemoration of the Bene-factors Feast, 'and exude hypocritical geniality to those whom I know to have voted against me'.[38]

As if in compensation for the enmity of the 'mafia', Hugh developed a new friendship with the eminent molecular biologist Max Perutz, whose association with Peterhouse stretched back as far as 1936. There was only a few months' difference in age between the two of them, but their early experiences had been very different. Perutz came from a Jewish back-ground, and had been born and educated in Austria. He was a very dis-tinguished scientist, with wide-ranging interests. In 1962 he was a joint winner of the Nobel Prize for chemistry; in 1975 he was made Companion of Honour, and in 1988 he was awarded the Order of Merit.* 'I was very sorry that you had to retire just as I was beginning to get to know you better,' Perutz wrote to Hugh soon after he left Cambridge.[39] They began to correspond regularly on a wide range of topics, and tried to meet on those occasions when Hugh came to Cambridge or Perutz came to Oxford. On several occasions Perutz visited Hugh at Didcot.

The letters between these two often compared perspectives on the events of the twentieth century. Both remained intellectually curious into their ninth decades, and both obviously enjoyed their exchanges. 'How literate and wide-ranging the best scientists are!' Hugh exclaimed, after reading a book Perutz had sent him. 'I always felt somewhat ashamed of the Arts teaching at Peterhouse: the historians are so blinkered, so monoglot, so parochial, while you and Aaron and Jacques Heyman[†] preserve the old ideal of a humanist culture. I could never persuade any of the historians to discuss any subject of general, even historical, interest: indeed, they generally resented the suggestion. I sometimes think that most dons read only each other's footnotes (to see if they are mentioned in them).'[40]

In preparing volumes of his essays for publication, Hugh was invariably behind schedule, exasperating his agent Michael Sissons. His letters to Ollard and to his in-house editor Barley Alison were peppered with apologies for his tardiness. On one such letter he drew a cartoon of himself on his knees, his hands clasped in prayer. 'I have behaved monstrously,' he confessed to Ollard, 'not answering your letters, not sending in any texts, hiding from human view and human contact. <u>Peccavi</u>.[‡] I am a miserable sinner: behold me in a white sheet, sackcloth and ashes, praying for indulgence.'[41] Part of the problem was that he made work for himself. In preparing his volume of Renaissance essays he had found that several of them overlapped, or otherwise did not satisfy him, so he conflated or enlarged them and, in doing so, rewrote them. Similarly, he had intended the second volume to consist of essays on seventeenth-century England and Ireland which he had already published. However, in the course of re-reading and collating these, he was inspired to write five new essays, substantial enough when taken together to form a book; and they supplanted what he had written before. Averaging 25,000 words each, the new essays were very different in scale from the book reviews and occasional pieces that had

---

* During Hugh's time at Peterhouse, a complaint was made that the Master associated with the Jewish Fellows of the college. Hugh pleaded guilty to the charge. 'I tend to prefer the company of the Jewish Fellows because they are the most intellectually distinguished,' he explained.
† Professor Jacques Heyman, head of the University Department of Engineering, 1983–92.
‡ 'I have sinned.'

constituted his first collection in 1957, some of which had been only a few hundred words long.

Though the essays in this new volume were sufficiently distinct to stand alone, there was an underlying theme linking them, like the movements in a symphony. Hugh rejected as unhistorical the dichotomy between Puritanism and Laudianism, the one progressive and the other reactionary. 'It is only if we dissolve the imaginary spectrum stretching from Right to Left that the ideas which have been artificially fitted into it recover their individuality and can be studied in their true context,' he wrote. He was suspicious of using the concept of linear progress as a means of distinguishing between political groupings.[42] His distaste for Puritan fanaticism, and for religious intolerance generally, is evident throughout. In considering the Revolutionary period, his heroes were not the men at the centre of the conflict but the intellectuals of Great Tew, the country house which Clarendon likened to 'a college situated in a purer air' than Oxford, 'a university bound in a lesser volume'. Hugh admired their moderation, their resistance to religious interference, their rejection of bigotry and their adherence to rational thought and humanist scholarship. Indeed his description (in an earlier lecture) of the philosophy of the Great Tew circle seemed to echo his own beliefs: 'the conviction that intellectual advance was entirely compatible with existing social institutions and existing orthodoxy, provided that neither the one nor the other was too rigid, that tradition was admitted to be variable, and that reason was accepted as the means of change'.[43]

Hugh's irreverence showed in his essay on James Ussher, Archbishop of Armagh, whose precise calculations enabled him to state not merely that the world had begun in 4004 BC, but that Creation had taken place on Sunday 23 October, 'and that the machinery was set in preliminary motion on the previous day, at about 6.00 p.m.' Hugh recalled his own boyhood, when he had passed the time in such calculations himself, working from the dates of events such as the Deluge and the Exodus confidently printed in the margins of the Bibles supplied in the pews of his local church at Alnwick. 'This information, which gradually became, for me, the main pleasure of church-going, gave to my knowledge of the Old Testament a valuable sense of historical continuity.'[44]

Catholics, Anglicans and Puritans appeared within months of Hugh's retirement from Peterhouse, to wide acclaim. Reviewers praised him as a master of the long essay; in this form, perhaps, he had found the ideal means to express ideas that he had struggled to incorporate within a longer narrative. The book's opening paragraph stated Hugh's belief that 'intellectual history can never be pursued in isolation'; it was always 'conditioned by its social and political context', albeit 'quickened and distorted by events'.

This was a very different notion of history from Cowling's concentration on 'high politics'. The most substantial essay in this new collection, 'Laudianism and Political Power', derived from one of the lectures Hugh had given to commemorate the seventh centenary of Peterhouse in 1984, in which he had depicted the college as 'a citadel of ultra-Laudianism'. Those who looked up 'Peterhouse' in the index found subheadings such as 'high-table conversation not very agreeable', 'its new chapel ... shocking goings-on there', 'four revolting Fellows of' and 'main source of perverts'. These entries bore only a tangential relationship to the text.

Hugh continued to exchange pot-shots with his old enemies. In 1989 Cowling's new preface to the second edition of his book *Mill and Liberalism* was adapted as an article in *Encounter*. In this he made large claims for the influence on Thatcherism of the 'New Right', which he identified as 'five overlapping movements, conducted by about fifty people' (one of these movements being the 'Peterhouse Right'). There was a sideswipe against Hugh, who had become 'an Ancient Mariner', imposing his complaints about Peterhouse on anyone who would listen – 'though clubmen in London, journalists on the Isle of Dogs, colleagues in the House of Lords, hosts in American universities, and innocent Fellows of Oxford and Cambridge colleges, must wonder why it is necessary to slay the birds that made his breeze to blow'.[45] Hugh published an article in *The Independent Magazine*, pouring doubt on Cowling's grandiose claims for the importance of the Peterhouse Right. The magazine subsequently published Cowling's letter of protest, Hugh's response to this, and Cowling's response to Hugh's response. The sniping continued.[46]

In 1988 Hugh submitted a 'discovery' to the *Cambridge Review*: a letter from Odysseus, newly restored to power in Ithaca, to Menelaus, by then resettled in Sparta. This valuable find, Hugh claimed, had emerged from the sand of Egypt, where it had lain preserved for millennia. He submitted the letter in the form of a 'literal translation' from the archaic Greek. It was written in a reassuringly informal style. 'Your family has certainly had bad luck in matrimonial matters,' Odysseus observed, commenting that his own wife, Penelope, 'has been a brick' throughout. Odysseus advised Menelaus to look out for an itinerant bard – 'blind as a bat but a jolly good poet' – who had entertained them 'with some fine rhapsodies on that Trojan business'.

The submission was returned by the *Cambridge Review*, accompanied by a note saying that the editors could make neither head nor tail of it. A careful reading might lead the reader to deduce that Odysseus was Hugh himself, returned to Ithaca (Didcot) and the arms of Penelope (Xandra) after several years swimming in the sea of Academe (Cambridge). His most memorable adventures had been in the island of the one-eyed Cyclopes (Peterhouse), where could be found the cave of the ogre Polyphemus (Cowling). 'As I contrived to escape alive,' wrote Odysseus, 'I can look back indulgently on the old monster, whom I last saw impotently, but very publicly, denouncing me from a cliff after I had got away.' For the benefit of unwary travellers, and to aid identification, Odysseus had obligingly provided a cartoon of the lair of Polyphemus.[47]

A third volume of essays, *From Counter-Reformation to Glorious Revolution*, followed five years after *Catholics, Anglicans and Puritans*. Reviewing the volume for *The Times Literary Supplement*, Lawrence Stone praised Hugh as 'the most witty, perceptive, thoughtful and brilliant historical essayist of our time'. He described his 'sense of exhilaration at coming into contact with a man capable of writing such lucid prose, imbued with such a strong sense of the supreme value of moderation and toleration in fanatical times, and so deeply marked both by his classical upbringing and his international cultural interests'. Yet it was hard not to feel a sense of regret, he continued, 'that not for half a century has Trevor-Roper written a major work of history'. In this collection of essays, Stone saw sketches of 'what might have been'.[48]

Hugh thanked him for this magnanimous review. 'It was kind of you to write,' replied Stone. 'I wrote the review since: (1) I have always admired you as an essayist, and wanted to make that very clear; (2) On reading the book I found that our views about 17th century historiography in particular, and our general attitude, were in fact so extremely close; (3) The TLS made it clear that they hoped for a really nasty review, a request which I found repugnant.' John Elliott had told him, he said, that the Mayerne book was 'finished', and Stone expressed the hope that Hugh would now publish it.[49] Stone commented on his relations with Hugh in a letter to an unidentified friend. 'Our quarrels are so old now that I thought it was high time they were buried and forgotten. Anyway we now have many more dangerous enemies in common.'[50]

Hugh was asked by Oxford's Vice-Chancellor, the barrister Sir Patrick Neill, to give the 1988 Romanes Lecture. This was a prestigious appointment. The Romanes Lectures had been founded late in the nineteenth century, and were wide-ranging in scope: the first lecture had been given by Gladstone, and subsequent lecturers had included several prime ministers and former prime ministers, and one American President, Theodore Roosevelt. Recent lecturers had included Sir Lewis Namier, Sir Karl Popper, Sir Isaiah Berlin, Sir Ernst Gombrich, Sir Peter Medawar, Lord Zuckerman, Iris Murdoch and A.J.P. Taylor.

The lecture was delivered in the Sheldonian Theatre in February.

Admission was free of charge and open to the public, so the lecturer needed to allow for listeners who might have little or no historical knowledge. Hugh chose as his subject 'The Lost Moments of History', a title deriving from Dame Frances Yates, who had died in 1981. Yates had identified a lost moment in the late sixteenth century when the Netherlands might have been unified. Hugh speculated that the division between the two Germanies might prove as permanent as the division between Holland and Belgium. In fact, by the time his lecture appeared in print,* German reunification was less than two years away. But this unexpected development was itself an illustration of the unpredictability of history, a theme on which Hugh had often dwelt. A condition of rejecting notions of historical inevitability was an acceptance that one could not foresee the future. Hugh's lecture was permeated with philosophical wisdom, and delightfully written, enlivened by vivid metaphors and deft asides. Afterwards he received several appreciative letters, including one from Isaiah Berlin, who praised the lecture as 'beautifully shaped, every word in place, a work of art'.[51]

A chain of events across central Europe in 1989 led to the crumbling of the Berlin Wall, and began a process that seemed likely to lead to German reunification, after forty years of division between East and West. In a letter to Max Perutz, Hugh described the changes taking place as 'the most exciting and moving in a generation'.[52] In the following March he was one of a group of academics invited to lunch at Chequers, to discuss with the Prime Minister problems that might be posed by a reunited Germany.[53] The discussion was off the record. Before the meeting, those invited were sent a discussion paper in the form of a list of questions, which suggested certain generalisations about 'the German character'. Hugh thought these rather naïve, though he suspected that they represented Mrs Thatcher's own views. Another of the participants, George Urban, Director of the Centre for Policy Studies, would later write that she believed in an 'Alf Garnett version of history'.[54] Apart from Urban, the others invited to participate were all historians specialising in modern Germany: two British, Timothy Garton Ash and Norman Stone; and two Americans, Gordon Craig and Fritz Stern. Also present were the Prime Minister's husband Denis, her private secretary, Charles Powell, and the Foreign Secretary, Douglas Hurd.

The seminar continued all afternoon, until 6.30 in the evening. All the invited participants agreed that the presuppositions of the discussion paper were wrong. Urban would later say that most of those present were surprised and appalled by the Prime Minister's opposition to German reuni-

---

* It was printed in *The New York Review of Books*, 27 October 1988.

fication and her resistance to the 'Great European Project'. Hugh's presence in Germany at the end of the war gave added authority to his contributions. At one point he suddenly said, 'Prime Minister, if anyone had told us in 1945 that there was a chance of a Germany united in freedom, a solid member of the west, we could not have believed our luck – and so we should welcome it, not resist it.' Another of the participants has described this as 'an electrifying moment'.[55] The Prime Minister did not speak much at the meeting, though she acted as chairman. Her attitude was one of a leader who had summoned a group of wise men to hear their views. In her public statements afterwards Hugh felt that she was noticeably less anti-German.[56]

The fact of the meeting was reported in *The Sunday Telegraph*, though not the content. Almost four months later, however, *The Independent on Sunday* published verbatim a summary of the discussion drawn up for the Prime Minister by Charles Powell. The participants were upset for two reasons: first, because they had understood that the discussion would be confidential; and second, because Powell's summary emphasised the views put forward in the preliminary discussion paper, as if these had represented the consensus of those attending, when in fact the opposite was the case. Garton Ash remarked to Hugh that in spite of what each of them had written, it was now 'firmly established that we had participated in an anti-German cabal'. Gordon Craig was particularly angry, as he felt that his reputation in Germany had been affected. Both he and Fritz Stern wrote articles in the German press disowning Powell's leaked minute.

In a *Sunday Telegraph* article, Hugh welcomed the changes taking place in Europe as 'a great step forward'. He rejected the concept of heritable national characteristics: the notion implicit in the discussion paper that the Germans were more prone to 'aggression, angst, sentimentality, etc'.

> What we simplify as 'national character' is in fact, I believe, the product of environment, of social structure, of 'culture': that is, of continuous education within a consistent tradition. Change that, and the supposed 'national character' changes with it.

Hugh no longer feared the revival of the old aggressive militarism in Germany. 'Nazism was its last expression, or perversion; the defeat of Nazism its dead end.' Indeed, he believed that Germany, 'having caught the disease in its most virulent form, may now be immune'.[57]

At 8.20 p.m. on a Monday evening, early in October 1990, Hugh found himself sitting in a train, speeding westwards through darkened country-side. This in itself was not unusual. But he was bruised and bleeding, from wounds to his forehead and his right wrist. With growing alarm he realised that he could not recall how he came to be there. He had been to a Cabinet Office party, to celebrate the completion of the official history of British Intelligence during the Second World War. Around 7.45 he had left and begun walking down Whitehall, hoping to find a cruising taxi to take him to Paddington station; or, failing that, to take the tube from Charing Cross. The last thing that he remembered was checking his watch. Of how he had reached the station, and how he had sustained his injuries, he had no memory.

He began to seek external evidence. He discovered that he was on the correct train, the 8.15 for Didcot. He still had with him his briefcase and his notecase (though he had lost his address book), so he assumed that he had not been mugged – at least, not successfully. As he still had the same money in his notecase as before, he deduced that he had not taken a taxi to Paddington, and concluded that he must have walked to the Underground station, boarded a train, emerged at Paddington, studied the departures board, identified and boarded the correct train and found a seat, all in a somnambulist trance. At some point he had sustained these injuries. Perhaps he had fallen down the escalator, but he had no memory of a fall. He did not know if anyone had helped him up, or guided him towards the train. In the next few days he underwent a series of hospital tests, which failed to solve the mystery. Then his brother mentioned that their father had suffered similar blackouts – once in the casino at Monte Carlo. Hugh remembered another occasion, about a year earlier. While descending the steep steps of the Savoy Hotel on the riverside exit, he had suddenly plunged headlong down them. There had been no warning, and no sensation of falling; he merely found himself sprawled in an undignified posture at their foot. At the time he assumed that he had tripped, but now he realised that this too had been a blackout. He suffered further blackouts when going down a flight of stairs in the House of Lords, and on the stone steps outside Didcot railway station.

In January 1992 Hugh was invited to a Colloquium at the Vatican to discuss the collapse of communism, and granted a private audience with Pope John Paul II. This was an occasion rich in comic possibilities.

The conversation began conventionally enough, with a review of recent events in international affairs, particularly developments in Eastern Europe, the problems caused by the collapse of Communism and the danger that a 'consumer society' might replace it. Then they discussed Cambridge. The Pope was a personal friend of Ed Shils, who had visited him at the papal summer palace of Castel Gandolfo, and no doubt kept him informed of the bizarre goings-on in his former college.

'We hear that you were, till recently, Master of Peterhouse,' the Pope began.

'Yes, indeed: seven years did I labour in the tents of Jethro,' Hugh replied. 'But I am now released ...'

'They tell Us that there is an active group of Catholics in that respectable society. Is that so?'

Hugh acknowledged that this was indeed true. The Pope asked for news of the Peterhouse Catholics, and pressed the former Master for his views on this group. When Hugh showed reluctance to speak, the Pope expressed his concern about a recent scandal. 'It has been whispered to Us that it gives Our religion a bad name in your country.'

'It is Your Holiness that has said the word,' replied Hugh: 'and what can I do but defer to Your Holiness?'

'I feared as much,' the Pope said. Turning to the Cardinal in attendance, he instructed him to make a note of this point, and was assured that the Cardinal had already done so.[58]

On his retirement from Peterhouse, Hugh had been offered £100,000 for his memoirs by George Weidenfeld – a huge sum in 1987, a level reached then only by pop stars and sporting legends. He hesitated, uncertain whether he could tell the truth about Peterhouse. The rules forbidding those who had served in secret intelligence from writing about their war service was a further obstacle. Mrs Thatcher's Government was then engaged in an international struggle to prevent another former MI6 agent, Peter Wright, from publishing his memoirs. The Cabinet Secretary, Sir Robert Armstrong (son of Sir Thomas Armstrong, the former Christ Church Organist), flew out to Australia in a vain attempt to prevent the book's publication there. Hugh disliked what Wright had done, but felt that the whole episode was an unnecessary embarrassment, caused by the Government's obsession with secrecy.

'Write your memoirs and write them now,' Annan urged Hugh:

> They cannot stop you. Submit nothing to them. To incarcerate an emeritus Regius Professor and Peer of the Realm is beyond them ... Press on. Don't be deflected. Deny me, if necessary, the pleasure of seeing you in the House. But write and publish. My own feeble memoir* (handed to the publisher on 24 December) will vanish: yours will be a landmark – and vastly entertaining.[59]

Hugh began drafting his memoirs, but his failing eyesight made writing more and more difficult. His hand, once so clear, became cramped as he

---

* *Changing Enemies: The Defeat and Regeneration of Germany* (London, 1995).

could no longer follow what he had written. Eventually Weidenfeld suggested that he might write 'an assisted autobiography'. The publisher seems to have envisaged that someone might act as a scribe, or perhaps ghostwriter. The journalist Frank Johnson was recruited to help. Hugh liked Johnson, who was an amusing companion; they held plenty of convivial conversations on a wide range of topics, recorded on tape. In the process the book was transformed from a memoir into a dialogue: Johnson putting questions and Hugh providing answers. This was not a satisfactory form, as Hugh eventually realised. Nor did he find Johnson a penetrating interrogator: time after time, he allowed Hugh to escape with bland or perfunctory replies. The historian, who had been anticipating a tricky follow-up question, would discover that Johnson had moved on to a new topic. This was not the way to get the best from him. 'I'm like a tube of toothpaste,' Hugh would say: 'I need to be <u>squeezed</u>.' Moreover, the two men had little in common intellectually. Johnson had a quick but untrained mind; he had not been educated at a higher level, a lack that he felt keenly. He was aligned politically with the Peterhouse Right. Belatedly, Hugh insisted that the contract should be cancelled.

In old age Hugh mellowed. He became more approachable, more tolerant and more open. The kindness had always been there, but hidden behind a sometimes forbidding mask. Now the mask slipped, or perhaps it was no longer needed. Perhaps the searing experience of the Hitler diaries had humbled him. It must have been a relief, too, to escape from the daily hostility he encountered at Peterhouse – though he remained determined to brave it on visits to Cambridge.

In the early 1990s Xandra began to succumb to Alzheimer's disease, and suffered a series of small strokes. Her manner remained intact, but her mind slipped away. Hugh was obliged to take on more and more of the everyday chores. 'I have been having a very difficult time,' he wrote to his old friend Patrick Reilly in 1995. 'I have to be permanently here in case of mishap, which is a great restraint of liberty. I also have to be cook, housekeeper, chauffeur, shopper, etc etc.'[60] A further problem was that failing eyesight made it impossible for him to continue driving. The now-retired Butler from Peterhouse, Tom Moffett, made several excursions from his home in Cambridge to Didcot to help. Hugh cared for Xandra tenderly, without resentment, though the drudgery left him little time for intellectual activity. Her son James tried to exercise her failing memory by talking to her about the past. He asked her when Hugh had come into her life. She could not remember. He tried a different question: had Hugh been in her life while she had been at Cambridge? 'Yes,' she said, after much thought; '*But that was another Hugh.*'[61]

It seemed to James too that his stepfather had changed beyond recognition. This became even plainer when he and his sister organised a conference with three professionals to decide how their mother should continue. When it was clear that she must go into a nursing home, their stepfather, usually so cool and in command of himself, burst into tears. Both James and Xenia were amazed; this was a side of Hugh previously unfamiliar to them. When he visited Xandra in the home, she received him politely, though it was evident that she had no idea who he was. She died in 1997, at the age of ninety.

He missed Xandra 'dreadfully'. His was not a lonely existence, however. His old friends died, in a depressing cortège; but new friends took their place. He had always enjoyed the company of younger people, and this characteristic was especially noticeable now. Contact with the young seemed to enliven him. He was willing to forgive ignorance, or gaucherie; he enjoyed their vigour and irreverence. He wrote long, carefully constructed letters to younger friends, who were amazed by the trouble he took over them. He insisted on cooking for visitors, though it was alarming to watch him peer over the gas cooker, a piece of lighted newspaper in hand, and then leap back as the burner burst into flame. He suffered several further blackouts. As his eyesight deteriorated, he found travelling alone more and more difficult. Worst of all, he could not read; and because he could not read, he could not write. His stepson James, his former pupil Blair Worden and others took turns to come and read aloud to him. Notwithstanding these difficulties he accepted invitations to lecture, learning his speeches so that he could deliver them from memory. He arranged the points he wanted to make in his mind, envisaging them, while he spoke, as 'coat-hangers on a rail'. Using this method he successfully lectured in Italy in 1997 and in Portugal in 1998. Memory became more significant to him once he could no longer consult notes. He trained his memory by reciting poetry to himself – especially 'The Walrus and the Carpenter', which took up just the length of time needed to walk between his house and the station.

Hugh was diagnosed with glaucoma and then a cataract. A consultant eye surgeon recommended an operation, but warned that it carried the risk of blindness. Not wanting to take the risk, he chose to struggle on. He began to suffer hallucinations: at first simply geometrical shapes superimposed upon reality, like a very poor television image, but then scenes of events which seemed real but which his logical mind knew could not be: bicycle or horse races, for example. He would look up from his desk and see the trees in leaf in mid-winter, or the landscape whizzing past as if he were aboard a train. While being driven through ordinary urban streets, he saw fantastic architectural constructions like Piranesi drawings. Once, as he went to put out the dustbins, he found himself lost in a cemetery of dead machines, surrounded by rusting combine harvesters, lorries, cranes and derricks. Inside, the house grew an extra staircase. He suffered these hallucinations with resignation. On another occasion, when he felt that he must clear his mind of the images that he knew could not be real, he groped his way out into the garden, to find his path blocked by giant trees. He felt his way forward with his stick, seeing the trees dissolve before him, until he crashed into something solid. One of his worst moments came on a platform of Didcot station. He arrived to find the Oxford train already standing there. It looked a little odd, like a tube train, but otherwise real enough. He was about to board it when he had a sudden doubt as to whether it was standing on his side of the track or the other. He paused, not daring to get on, but not wanting to miss it either. So he asked the stationmaster, who told him that 'the Oxford train will be here any minute'.

'What about this train?' Hugh asked.

'What train?' the man said. 'There is no train.' Hugh felt irritated with the man for being so obtuse, but as he stared at the train carriages, they melted into nothingness.

One night he caught a very late train back from London, after giving a talk at Charterhouse earlier in the evening. Xenia had seen him onto a train at Paddington, after trying vainly to persuade him to stay the night with her. He descended onto the platform at Didcot around two o'clock in the morning. Outside the station he saw what appeared to him to be piles of Hepplewhite chairs. The walk to the Old Rectory was only a few hundred yards, but he became disoriented and then lost, imagining himself in an endless tunnel. Every now and then he would pass what looked to him like heaps of old machinery. He blundered about the empty streets of the town for an hour or more, falling several times, until at last, in near-despair, he sat down on the pavement, where a police car, alerted by an anxious Xenia, eventually found him.

Hugh was eventually diagnosed with Charles Bonnet Syndrome: a neurological condition in which the unconscious mind dredges up images from the memory to compensate for failing eyesight. Finding a rational explanation was a comfort to him. Hugh decided to risk the eye operation. He described the moment when the bandages were removed as 'like the first day of creation', light flooding in to replace the darkness. He turned to his stepdaughter, who was standing by the bed. 'Xenia,' he exclaimed in wonder, 'I can see your face!'

The operation was a success. He lost his fear of venturing out. He could read again, with the aid of a machine which magnified and illuminated the text, though reading was a struggle. He resumed writing. In the spring of 2002, aged eighty-eight, he delivered a substantial article on Thomas Sutton to the new *Oxford Dictionary of National Biography*, drawing on pencilled notes he had made more than half a century earlier. In acknowledging the piece, the editor, Brian Harrison, described it as having 'all the touches of the master: its style is as clear as a bell, lapidary and concise, and yet has a nice irony about it'.[62]

The hallucinations did not disappear immediately, however. Nine months or so after the operation, he woke at three o'clock in the morning to find a woman beside his bed, statuesque and immobile. He tried to question her, but she did not reply, and slowly dissolved into the air. 'Now I know all about ghosts,' he said. 'I've seen one now and solved one of life's mysteries – and the rational world is restored.'[63]

As well as the problems with his eyes, Hugh suffered from a growing list of other ailments: irritable skin, a swollen hand, a cyst in his kidney and an enlarged prostate. He was diagnosed with cancer. As James witnessed, he bore all these burdens with fortitude and resilience. Like his father, Hugh never uttered a word of complaint, but was invariably cheerful and good company. Towards the end of 2002, the cancer accelerated, and he was admitted to a hospice on the outskirts of Oxford. Even then, he did not succumb to self-pity. 'Let's not talk about me,' he said to a visitor who saw him only days before his death; 'I'm boring. Tell me about you.'

Hugh died on Sunday 26 January 2003, at the age of eighty-nine. His wealth was assessed for probate purposes at £1,638,119. A funeral service was held at the Church of St Thomas the Martyr, Oxford, on 4 February. Among the speakers were his stepson James and his stepdaughter Xenia, and his friend Jeremy Catto. His body was cremated, and his ashes scattered in the grounds of Dryburgh Abbey, on the banks of the Tweed. A month later a memorial service was held in Christ Church Cathedral. The address was given by Blair Worden, who paid eloquent tribute to his mentor and friend.

> The aspect of Hugh's life that must have earned most widespread gratitude is the achievement of his writing in making sophisticated historical thinking accessible and enjoyable to a lay audience. He always respected his readers' intelligence: his concessions to journalism were ones only of form, not of substance; and so he produced, in ephemeral publications, enduring thought in enduring language. The musicality of Hugh's prose, its elegance and grace and wit, its subtlety and delicacy, its precision of nuance and of irony, will make their claim to lasting recognition. His avowed aim, and his certain achievement, was to make history live.

'Hitler Diaries Hoax Victim Lord Dacre dies at 89', *The Times* reported on the day after his death. It printed a shrewd but malicious obituary by his old adversary, Maurice Cowling. This was an unkind way for a serious newspaper to remember one of its own directors, especially as the paper itself bore some responsibility for the gaffe. Other obituaries suggested that Hugh's reputation as an historian had been 'damaged', 'tarnished', or 'besmirched'. A 1992 piece in *The Daily Telegraph* had described him as 'once eminent but now discredited'.*[64]

As Worden rightly remarked, this was absurd. Hugh had 'suffered a humiliating lapse of judgement which gave legitimate pleasure to people who had felt the sometimes merciless force of his pen or tongue. But it was at most a chapter in a richly varied life.'[65] The list of learned men who have been fooled by forgeries is a long one: Johnson was deceived by Lauder; Hume by Macpherson; and so on. In the long run, such embarrassing errors are generally reckoned to be no more than blemishes.

Hugh's misfortune was to have made such an error in the age of the mass media, when his mistake became front-page news across the world. Many men would have been crushed by the weight of ridicule that descended upon him. But he withstood it; and soon returned to the lists, his armour dented but his lance still strong. The essays he wrote after the debacle of the Hitler diaries, while he was in his seventies, are among his very best work. By the time of his death in 2003, the publication of these essays had done much to restore his standing as an early modern historian. The publication of two posthumous works in 2006 continued the process of his rehabilitation. Hugh's letters to his mentor Bernard Berenson, published as *Letters from Oxford*, were a reminder of Trevor-Roper in his confident prime; the volume's editor, Richard Davenport-Hines, made a strong case for him as 'the greatest letter-writer of his generation', one 'whose irony, grace and knowledge make him the twentieth-century equivalent of Madame de Sévigné or Horace Walpole'. Later that year Hugh's biography of Mayerne at last appeared, rescued from the unfinished typescript by Blair Worden and skilfully nurtured to publication. *Europe's Physician: The Various Life of Sir Theodore de Mayerne* was praised as the work of a master historian, drawing on sources in six countries and eight languages. 'No young scholar would want to write this book, and perhaps no younger scholar could,' wrote *The Times Literary Supplement* reviewer, David Wootton; 'But if you want to understand the age of the religious wars, or if you want to be reminded that the purpose of a great history book, as of a great play or a great novel, is to transform how you see the world around you, then you should read this last relic of a lost age. Great history books are few and far between. This is one.'[66] In a major piece reviewing both

---

* Hugh had received letters of apology from the Editor, Max Hastings, and the author of the piece, Geoffrey Wheatcroft. Apparently the phrase had been inserted by an underling, identified by *Private Eye* as Claudia Fitzherbert, granddaughter of Evelyn Waugh.

works in *The New York Review of Books*, Keith Thomas praised Hugh as 'almost certainly the most gifted of a remarkable generation of British historians'. This was a generous tribute from a colleague who had sometimes suffered from Hugh's lack of charity.

Another long-abandoned book appeared in 2008, resuscitated by Jeremy J. Cater, with help from Worden, after it had lain in hibernation since the early 1980s. The response to *The Invention of Scotland: Myth and History** showed that, even from the grave, Hugh remained able both to delight and infuriate.

The appearance of so many posthumous works inevitably caused some to quip that Trevor-Roper had been much more productive since his death than he ever was in his lifetime. Other more or less complete manuscripts survive in his archive, including the carefully crafted notebooks he kept during the war, and memoirs of his early years. At least three more volumes of essays are envisaged; one appeared after this book was set up in type.[67] Further volumes of letters must surely follow, when it is safe for them to be published. Meanwhile the works he published in his lifetime continue to give pleasure and instruction. In particular, *The Last Days of Hitler*, unlike most works of contemporary history, is a classic that can never date. It is probably too early to say how posterity will rate Hugh. But there can be now nobody alive under the age of forty who remembers the Hitler diaries fiasco. It seems certain that his work will continue to be read long after his blunder has diminished into a mere footnote.

---

* The title was changed on the advice of the publishers.

Books by Hugh Trevor-Roper

This is a list of some of Trevor-Roper's principal works. It is not comprehensive, and for example does not include editions of edited works such as *Hitler's Table-Talk*. The date of publication is of the first edition only; the place of publication is London unless otherwise stated. The last four books were published posthumously.

Archbishop Laud (1940)

The Last Days of Hitler (1947)

The Gentry, 1540–1640 (1953)

Historical Essays (1957); published in the USA as *Men and Events*

The Rise of Christian Europe (1965)

Religion, the Reformation and Social Change, and Other Essays (1967); published in the USA as *The Crisis of the Seventeenth Century*

The Philby Affair, Espionage, Treason and Secret Services (1968)

The European Witch-Craze of the Sixteenth and Seventeenth Centuries (1969)

The Letters of Mercurius (1970)*

The Plunder of the Arts in the Seventeenth Century (1970)

Princes and Artists: Patronage and Ideology at Four Habsburg Courts, 1517–1633 (1976)

A Hidden Life: the Enigma of Sir Edmund Backhouse (1976); published in the USA and reissued in paperback in the UK as *Hermit of Peking: The Hidden Life of Sir Edmund Backhouse*

Renaissance Essays (1985)

Catholics, Anglicans, and Puritans: Seventeenth Century Essays (1987)

From Counter-Reformation to Glorious Revolution (1992)

Europe's Physician: The Various Life of Sir Theodore de Mayerne (2006)

Letters from Oxford: Hugh Trevor-Roper to Bernard Berenson (2006)

The Invention of Scotland: Myth and History (2008)

History and the Enlightenment: Eighteenth Century Essays (2010)

* published pseudonymously

Notes

CHAPTER 1: Boy (pp. 1–16)

1   There are several variations on this anecdote. In another version, a neighbour who was dining with the Trevor-Ropers repeatedly called his host 'Roper'. The eminent historian was not amused. 'My name is Trevor-Roper,' he insisted. 'Well,' replied his guest, 'my name is Montagu-Douglas-Scott, but Scott has always been good enough for me.' Letter from Lady Emma Tennant, 'High Table hauteur', *The Spectator*, 17 March 2007.
2   Aymers Vallance, 'Roper Memorials', *Archaeologia Cantiana* (1932), Vol. XLIV; Hugh Trevor-Roper, *The Gentry, 1540–1640* (Economic History Society/Cambridge University Press, 1953), pp. 10–11.

3 *Country Life*, 19 July 1962 and 21 February 2008.
4 HT-R to Dr John K. Rowlands, 20 December 1995; DP 6/26/2.
5 Dr Alex Turnbull, 'B.W.E. Trevor-Roper', *British Medical Journal* (1978), 1, pp. 247–9.
6 'Stancliffe Hall (November 1942)', wartime notebooks, II, p. 146; DP 13/29.
7 Ibid., pp. 143–6; DP 13/29.
8 HT-R to Blair Worden, 29 August 1975.
9 HT-R to KT-R, 20 June and 9 May 1926; DP 17/6.
10 'Stancliffe Hall (November 1942)', wartime notebooks, II, pp. 143–6; DP 13/29.

CHAPTER 2: Carthusian (pp. 17–24)

1 Anthony Quick, *Charterhouse: A History of the School* (London, 1990), p. 107.
2 Ibid., p. 108.
3 Frederick Raphael, *Cuts and Bruises* (Manchester, 2006), pp. 193–4.
4 'Moments', wartime notebooks, I, pp. 19–21; DP 13/29.

CHAPTER 3: Undergraduate (pp. 25–42)

1 M.I. Ogilvy-Stuart to Brian Harrison, 20 August 1990 (Christ Church Archives).
2 Hugh Trevor-Roper, *Christ Church, Oxford: The Portrait of a College* (privately published, 1950), p. 1.
3 Ibid., p. 3.
4 Ann Thwaite (ed.), *My Oxford* (London, 1977), p. 68.
5 Anthony Sampson, *Anatomy of Britain Today* (London, 1965), p. 225. See also Keith Thomas, 'College Life 1945–1970', in Brian Harrison (ed.), *The History of the University of Oxford, VIII: The Twentieth Century* (Oxford, 1994), p. 214.
6 Hugh Trevor-Roper, *Christ Church, Oxford: The Portrait of a College*, p. 9.
7 Roy Harrod, *The Prof: A Personal Memoir of Lord Cherwell* (London, 1959), p. 151.
8 A.L. Rowse, *A Cornishman at Oxford* (London, 1965), p. 124.
9 Ibid., pp. 313, 309–12.
10 Ibid., p. 23.
11 A.J. Ayer, *Part of My Life* (London, 1977), p. 91.
12 HT-R to PT-R, 21 November 1932; DP 1/3/17.
13 A.J. Ayer, *Part of My Life*, p. 87ff.
14 HT-R to PT-R, 21 November 1932; DP 1/3/17.
15 HT-R to PT-R, 24 January 1932; DP 1/3/17.
16 HT-R to PT-R, 17 July 1933; DP 1/3/17.
17 Martin Ceadel, 'The "King and Country" Debate 1933: Student Politics, Pacifism and the Dictators', *Historical Journal*, 22, 2 (1979), pp. 397–422.
18 *Oxford Magazine*, 16 February 1933, LI (1932–3), pp. 426–7.
19 *Oxford Magazine*, 9 November 1933, LII (1933–4), p. 174; 8 November 1934, LIII (1934–5), p. 114; and 4 June 1936, LIV (1935–6), p. 663.
20 HT-R to KT-R, undated (1936); DP 17/6.
21 HT-R to PT-R, 12 November 1933; DP 1/3/17.
22 'History and Imagination', in Hugh Lloyd-Jones, Valerie Pearl and Blair Worden (eds), *History and Imagination: Essays in Honour of H.R. Trevor-Roper* (London, 1981), p. 358.
23 HT-R to PT-R, 19 May 1934; DP 1/3/17.
24 *Oxford Magazine*, late spring 1933, LI (1932–3), p. 724.
25 *Oxford Magazine*, 21 November 1935, LIV (1935–6), p. 207.
26 *Oxford Magazine*, 22 November 1934, LIII (1934–5), pp. 173–4.
27 J.C. Masterman, *On the Chariot Wheel: An Autobiography* (Oxford, 1975), pp. 146–53.
28 A.L. Rowse, *A Cornishman at Oxford*, p. 192.

29 A.J. Ayer, *Part of My Life*, pp. 142–3.
30 *History and Imagination: Essays in Honour of H.R. Trevor-Roper*, p. 358.
31 HT-R to PT-R, 14 June 1934; DP 1/3/17.
32 A.J. Ayer, *Part of My Life*, p. 99.
33 *To Keep the Ball Rolling: the Memoirs of Anthony Powell, I, Infants of the Spring* (London, 1976), p. 179.
34 Leslie Mitchell, *Maurice Bowra: A Life* (Oxford, 2009), p. 163.
35 HT-R to Blair Worden, 19 September 1987.
36 'Self-appreciation' (November 1941), wartime notebooks, I, pp. 42–6.
37 HT-R to PT-R, 6 June 1935; DP 1/3/17.
38 *Oxford Magazine*, 5 December 1935, LIV (1935–6), p. 255.
39 HT-R to PT-R, 26 April 1936; DP 1/3/17.

CHAPTER 4: Researcher (pp. 43–65)

1 Entry for 1 April, 1937 diary; DP 13/29.
2 [A]ll [S]ouls [C]ollege, uncat. Ts., 'Fellowship Examination, 1936: Examiners' Report'. I am grateful to Dr Simon Green for allowing me to see extracts from this report.
3 Entry for 28 January, 1937 diary; DP 13/29.
4 HT-R to John Field, 16 May 1939; Macmillan Archives.
5 Entry for 13 December, 1937 diary; DP 13/29.
6 *My Father's Son: The Memoirs of Major the Earl Haig* (Barnsley, 2000), p. 48.
7 HT-R to PT-R, 7 May 1937; DP 1/3/17.
8 Entry for 5 March, 1937 diary; DP 13/29.
9 Entry for 5 December, 1938 diary; DP 13/29.
10 Selina Hastings, *Evelyn Waugh: A Biography* (London, 1994), p. 227.
11 Entry for 8 July 1930, Michael Davie (ed.), *The Diaries of Evelyn Waugh* (London, 1976), p. 320.
12 Elizabeth Longford, *The Pebbled Shore* (London, 1986), p. 54.
13 Entries for 27 January, 1 and 9 February, 1937 diary; DP 13/29.
14 Leslie Mitchell, *Maurice Bowra: A Life*, pp. 317 and 314.
15 Entry for 7 February, 1937 diary; DP 13/29.
16 Freddie Birkenhead to HT-R, 29 April 1973; DP 1/2/17.
17 'My pleasures' and 'Moments', wartime notebooks, I, pp. 15–16 and 19–20; DP 13/29. HT-R dates this moment to the summer of 1936, but the evidence of his 1937 diary suggests that it happened then.
18 Entries for 18 April, 2 and 23 May, 27 January, 4 July, 8 December, 28 July, 15 August, 1937 diary; DP 13/29.
19 Wartime notebooks, I, p. 16; DP 13/29.
20 Entry for 15 November, 1937 diary; DP 13/29.
21 HT-R to PT-R, 22 April and undated June 1937; entries for 30 May, 1 and 4 June, 1937 diary; DP 1/3/17 and 13/29.
22 Introduction to *Archbishop Laud*, pp. 5–6.
23 HT-R to John Field, 16 May 1939; Macmillan Archives.
24 Entry for 11 March, 1937 diary; DP 13/29.
25 Entries for 28 February, 1 July, 1937 diary; DP 13/29.
26 Entry for 4 July, 1937 diary; DP 13/29.
27 Entries for 23 and 25 August, 7 September, 1937 diary; 11 January, 9 and 13 February, 1938 diary; DP 13/29.
28 Entries for 4 April and 4 September, 1937 diary; DP 13/29.
29 Claude Jenkins to J.N.L. Myres, 29 June 1938; DP 1/2/1.
30 Entries for 28 September, 8, 10, 11, 18 and 29 October, 7 and 29 November, 1937 diary; DP 13/29.

31 Entry for 23 October, 1937 diary; DP 13/29.

32 Entry for 10 November, 1937 diary; DP 13/29.

33 Entries for 6 and 8 November, 1937 diary; DP 13/29.

34 Cited in Ben Rogers, *A.J. Ayer: A Life* (London, 1999), p. 66.

35 Entry for 19 January, 1938 diary; DP 13/29. A.J. Ayer, *Part of My Life*, p. 192.

36 Entries for 4 and 5 February, 1938 diary; DP 13/29.

37 Entries for 16 and 10 February, 18 March, 1938 diary; DP 13/29.

38 Entries for 13 January, 12 December and 20 February, 1937 and 1938 diaries; DP 13/29.

39 'William Somerville: The Poet of the Chase', *Country Life*, 10 June 1939, pp. 614–15. Entry for 15 July, 1938 diary; DP 13/29.

40 *Oxford Magazine*, 20 January 1938, LVI (1938–9), pp. 288–9.

41 Entries for 27 March, and 1, 4, 7, 11 and 13 April, 1938 diary; DP 13/29.

42 Entries for 14 June, 22 and 28 April, 1938 diary; DP 13/29.

43 Entries for 14, 8 and 11 June, 1938 diary; DP 13/29.

44 'The Authorship of Prometheus Bound' (June 1938 and Maurice Bowra to HT-R, 15 June 1938); DP 6/38. Entry for 27 October, 1938 diary; DP 13/29.

45 For example, Mark Griffith, in *The Authenticity of 'Prometheus Bound'* (Cambridge, 1977), and M.L. West, *Studies in Aeschylus* (Stuttgart, 1990).

46 Unheaded entry, wartime notebooks, I, p. 10; DP 13/29.

47 I am grateful to the late David Pears for drawing my attention to this rift, and to Cliff Davies for supplying confirmatory material from the Wadham Archives.

48 Entries for 10 June, 5 and 23 May, 1938 diary; 'Ἁλιέυτίκά (October 1942)', wartime notebooks, II, pp. 124–8; DP 13/29.

49 HT-R to PT-R, 6 May 1938; DP 1/3/17.

50 HT-R to PT-R, 13 July 1938; entries for 27 and 28 July, 1 August, 2 March, 1938 diary; DP 1/3/17 and 13/29.

51 'Retrospect', wartime notebooks, II, p. 156; DP 13/29.

CHAPTER 5: Cadet (pp. 66–76)

1 HT-R to PT-R, 28 September 1938; DP 1/3/17.

2 'Moments', wartime notebooks, I, pp. 19–21; DP 13/29.

3 'Hitler's Mein Kampf', *The Listener*, 25 January 1973.

4 'A Prediction of the Crisis', *The Spectator*, 7 October 1938, pp. 551–2; also 'Hitler's Next Move', 14 October 1938, p. 602.

5 Entries for 18 and 21 November, 1938 diary; DP 13/29.

6 I.C.B. Dear, *Oxford Companion to the Second World War* (Oxford, 1995), p. 1136.

7 *History and Imagination: Essays in Honour of H.R. Trevor-Roper*, pp. 358–60.

8 A.L. Rowse, *A Cornishman at Oxford*, pp. 32–3.

9 Entries for 17 August, 1 February, 27 October, 1938 diary; DP 13/29.

10 Entries for 3 November, 8 October, 1938 diary; DP 13/29.

11 'Archbishop Laud' (Historical Revision No. CVIII), *History*, XXX, No. 112 (September 1945), p. 183.

12 'Preface to the Second Edition', *Archbishop Laud* (Basingstoke, 1962), p. x.

13 *The Gentry, 1540–1640*, p. 1.

14 *Archbishop Laud* (London, 1940), p. 6, pp. 2–3.

15 Lovat Dickson report dated 13 February; HT-R to Harold Macmillan, 25 February and 2 June 1939; Harold Macmillan internal report to Daniel Macmillan, 14 May 1939; Macmillan Archives.

16 H. Maurice Relton, 'Archbishop Laud', 6 May 1939; Macmillan readers' reports, Vol. 2H (1940), pp. 326–7 (British Library). I am especially grateful to Dr Arnold Hunt for his help in locating this report.

17 HT-R to John Field, 16 May 1939; Macmillan Archives.

18 Daniel Macmillan to HT-R, 12 May, and Harold Macmillan to HT-R, 1 June 1939; Macmillan letterbooks, British Library collection.

19 Keith Feiling to Messrs Macmillan, 29 May 1939; Macmillan letterbooks, British Library collection. I am obliged to Dr Arnold Hunt for deducing correctly that this report had been misfiled and thereby locating it.

20 HT-R to PT-R, 7 July 1939; DP 1/3/17

21 'My horse', wartime notebooks, I, p. 40; DP 13/29.

22 HT-R to BB, 6 July 1951, Richard Davenport-Hines (ed.), *Letters from Oxford: Hugh Trevor-Roper to Bernard Berenson* (London, 2006), p. 66.

23 HT-R to PT-R, 7 July 1939; DP 1/3/17.

24 David Ogg to HT-R, 21 July and 5 August 1939; DP A74/1.

CHAPTER 6: Soldier (pp. 77–91)

1 HT-R to PT-R, I November 1939; DP 1/3/17. H.W. Garrod, 'Memoirs of a visit to Merton', 21 October 1939; Merton Archives.

2 HT-R to PT-R, I November, 3 and 11 December 1939; DP 1/3/17.

3 HT-R to PT-R, 20 December 1939; DP 1/3/17.

4 J.C. Masterman, *The Double-Cross System in the War of 1939 to 1945* (New Haven and London, 1972), p. 3, *passim.*

5 Andrew Roberts, 'The Last Refuge of Arthur Bryant', *Eminent Churchillians* (London, 1994). Nicholas O'Shaughnessy, letter to *The Times Literary Supplement*, 24 May 2006.

6 F.H. Hinsley and C.A.G. Simpkins, *British Intelligence in the Second World War, IV: Security and Counter-Intelligence* (London, 1990), p. 72.

7 'Interception Work of RSS', 19 November 1940; National Archives WO 208/5097.

8 J.C. Masterman, *The Double-Cross System in the War of 1939 to 1945*, pp. 41–2.

9 'Interception Work of RSS', 19 November 1940; National Archives WO 208/5097.

10 'RSS and MI6', 15 September 1942; National Archives KV 4/170. My attention was drawn to this source by Edward (E.D.R.) Harrison, who was kind enough to allow me to read an early draft of his 'British Radio Security and Intelligence, 1939–43', *English Historical Review*, CXXIV (February 2009), pp. 53–93. This pioneering article has informed my understanding of RSS and has been an important source for this chapter and the next. Another useful article is P.R.J. Winter, 'A Higher Form of Intelligence; Hugh Trevor-Roper and Wartime British Secret Service', *Intelligence and National Security*, Vol. 22, No. 6 (December 2007), pp. 847–80.

11 *British Intelligence in the Second World War, IV*, p. 72; 'Radio Security Intelligence Conference', 17 May 1945; National Archives HW 36/6.

12 Trevor-Roper wrote two accounts of these events, from which much of the above is drawn: an article 'Sideways into SIS', published in Hayden B. Peake and Samuel Halpern (eds), *In the Name of Intelligence: Essays in Honour of Walter Pforzheimer* (Washington, 1994); and 'Penetrating the Enemy Secret Service', a lecture given to the 'Spies, Lies and Intelligence' conference at Christ Church in September 2002. Both accounts, while full of amusing detail, were written more than half a century after the events they describe, and when I have found discrepancies between what he wrote and contemporary documents I have relied on the latter.

13 'My book', wartime notebooks, I, p. 9; DP 13/29.

14 H.W. Garrod, 'Memoirs of a visit to Merton', 21 October 1939; Merton Archives.

15 HT-R to Lovat Dickson, undated (early 1940); Macmillan Archives.

16 HT-R to Harold Macmillan, 10 February, and to Lovat Dickson, 31 March 1940; Macmillan Archives and Lovat Dickson to HT-R, 27 March and 9 April 1940; Macmillan out-letter book 464 (14 March to 11 April 1940), pp. 233, 541 (British Library).

17 Robert Gathorne-Hardy, *Recollections of Logan Pearsall Smith: The Story of a Friendship* (London, 1949), p. 174.

18 Ibid., p. 2.
19 *British Intelligence in the Second World War, IV*, p. 44.
20 'Interception Work of RSS', 19 November 1940; National Archives WO 208/5097. 'British Radio Security and Intelligence, 1939–43', *English Historical Review*, CXXIV (February 2009), pp. 53–93.
21 HT-R to Blair Worden, 15 August 1974.
22 HT-R to KT-R, 28 February 1943 and 9 August 1942; DP 17/6.
23 '1940' and 'Illness is a great thing … ', wartime notebooks, I, pp. 108–110 and 6; DP 13/29.
24 H.W. Garrod to Norman Gibbs, 17 June 1940, & to John (Hill?), 19 July 1940; Merton Archives.
25 H.W. Garrod to John Hill, 20 September 1940; Merton Archives.
26 '1940', wartime notebooks, I, p. 111; DP 13/29.
27 Ibid.
28 'British Radio Security and Intelligence, 1939–43', *English Historical Review*, CXXIV (February 2009), pp. 53–93.
29 Ibid.
30 'The Ostrich' (January 1945), wartime notebooks, III, p. 269; DP 13/29. Hugh Trevor-Roper, *The Philby Affair: Espionage, Treason and Secret Services* (London, 1968), p. 37.

CHAPTER 7: Major (pp. 92–121)

1 Liddell Diaries, 5 February 1945; National Archives KV 4/196.
2 *The Philby Affair*, p. 26.
3 'Diary, Nov–Dec 1967'; DP 13/5.
4 *The Philby Affair*, pp. 26, 32 and 28–9.
5 'German Espionage in the Union & Portuguese East Africa', National Archives KV 2/757. 'British Radio Security and Intelligence, 1939–45', *English Historical Review*, CXXIV (February 2009), pp. 53–93.
6 Liddell Diaries, 26 August and 9 September 1941; National Archives KV 4/188.
7 *British Intelligence in the Second World War, IV*, pp. 183 and 132.
8 Ibid., p. 132.
9 Liddell Diaries, 19 and 12 June 1941; National Archives KV 4/188.
10 *The Philby Affair*, p. 32.
11 Logan Pearsall Smith to HT-R, 29 September 1942, 22 March 1943 and 29 August 1941. Liddell Diaries, 1 September 1941; National Archives KV 4/188.
12 'Self-appreciation (November 1941)', wartime notebooks, I, pp. 42–6; 'Autopsy'; DP 13/29.
13 Kim Philby, *My Silent War* (1968), p. 33. 'British Radio Security and Intelligence, 1939–43', *English Historical Review*, CXXIV (February 2009), pp. 53–93.
14 Wartime notebooks, I, p. 48; DP 13/29.
15 Logan Pearsall Smith to HT-R, 29 September 1942, 22 March 1943 and 29 August 1941; DP 1/3/18.
16 Logan Pearsall Smith to HT-R, 1 September 1942; DP 1/3/18.
17 Logan Pearsall Smith to HT-R, 20 October 1944; DP 1/3/18.
18 Logan Pearsall Smith to HT-R, 17 October 1944; DP 1/3/18.
19 'Things that Repel me (July 1942)', 'Women (April 1942)', 'Self-Revelation: Stuart Hampshire (April 1942)', wartime notebooks, I, pp. 106, 69–70, 64–7; DP 13/29.
20 'Vera Historia: or the True History of Logan Pearsall Smith, Bob Gathorne Hardy & John Russell'; DP 1/3/18.
21 Logan Pearsall Smith to HT-R, 2 October 1942 and 14 January 1943; DP 1/3/18. Smith's sister Alys would receive a life interest in the bulk of his estate, which would pass to Trevor-Roper and the other beneficiaries upon her death. In the event this will was superseded.
22 Logan Pearsall Smith to HT-R, 16 August 1941; DP 1/3/18.
23 Logan Pearsall Smith to HT-R, 20 October 1942; DP 1/3/18.
24 HT-R to Alasdair Palmer, 14 September 1989.

25 Logan Pearsall Smith to HT-R, 31 August 1943; DP 1/3/18.
26 'September 1942', wartime notebooks, II, pp. 123–4; DP 13/29.
27 HT-R to A.L. Rowse, 28 March 1943; Exeter University. 'Geoffrey Baskerville' (October 1942), 'Logan & A.L. Rowse', 'A.L. Rowse', wartime notebooks, II, pp. 190–1; DP 13/29.
28 'The Old Age of Logan Pearsall Smith'; DP 1/3/18.
29 Logan Pearsall Smith to HT-R, 26 June 1941; DP 1/3/18. Cyril Connolly, 'Logan Pearsall Smith', *New Statesman and Nation*, 9 March 1946.
30 'Logan Pearsall Smith', wartime notebooks, IV, pp. 362–4; DP 13/29.
31 Logan Pearsall Smith to HT-R, 5 September 1944; DP 1/3/18.
32 Logan Pearsall Smith to HT-R, 14 January 1943; DP 1/3/18.
33 Logan Pearsall Smith to HT-R, 5 September, and HT-R to Logan Pearsall Smith, 11 September 1944; DP 1/3/18.
34 Logan Pearsall Smith to Edward Weeks, 14 December 1945; DP 1/3/18.
35 'The Secret Service (March 1942)', wartime notebooks, I, p. 58; DP 13/29.
36 Wartime notebooks, I, p. 7; DP 13/29.
37 HT-R to Lord Cherwell, 22 February 1942; Cherwell Papers K295/1.
38 HT-R to Lord Cherwell, 15 April and 10 May 1942; Cherwell Papers K295/6 & 7.
39 Guy Liddell to DS (Petrie), 21 December 1942; National Archives KV 4/97.
40 Hugh Sebag-Montefiore, *Enigma: the Battle for the Code* (London, 2000), pp. 181–3.
41 Edward Travis to CSS (Menzies), 21 April, HT-R to CSS, 27 April, de Grey to DD (GC and CS) (Edward Travis), 28 April 1942; National Archives HW 14/35.
42 Edward Travis to CSS (Menzies), 14 May 1942; National Archives HW 14/37.
43 'SIS (May 1942)', wartime notebooks, I, p. 75; DP 13/29.
44 HT-R to PT-R, 25 February 1942; DP 1/3/17.
45 Liddell Diaries, 6 and 18 November 1941; National Archives KV 4/188.
46 Lord Dacre to Ralph Erskine, 9 December 1996; DP 10/44.
47 Liddell to Petrie, 15 May 1942; National Archives KV 4/120.
48 Liddell Diaries, 1 and 11 December 1941; National Archives KV 4/191.
49 HT-R to Lord Cherwell, 17 December 1942; Cherwell Papers K295/11.
50 'Woods and Streams (12 December 1942)', wartime notebooks, II, pp. 149–51; DP 13/29.
51 Kim Philby, *My Silent War*, p. 61.
52 *The Philby Affair*, pp. 77–9.
53 'A Higher Form of Intelligence: Hugh Trevor-Roper and Wartime British Secret Service', *Intelligence and National Security*, Vol. 22, No. 6 (December 2007), pp. 867–9.
54 Liddell Diaries, 12 April 1943; National Archives KV 4/191.
55 'British Radio Security and Intelligence, 1939–43', *English Historical Review*, CXXIV (February 2009), pp. 53–93.
56 Ibid.
57 'Abwehr Incompetence', 4 August 1943; National Archives HW 19/347.
58 'Decline of the Abwehr', 18 March 1944; 'German Strategic Deception', 5 June 1944; National Archives HW 19/333 and 347.
59 DGW (White) to DB (Liddell), 14 March 1943; National Archives KV 4/217.
60 Wartime notebooks, III, pp. 246–51; DP 13/29.
61 'Remorse (April 1943)', wartime notebooks, II, pp. 185–6; 'J.L.F. (March 1942)', I, pp. 62–4; 'Nebulones (July 1943)', II, pp. 211–12; III, p. 261; DP 13/29.
62 Logan Pearsall Smith to HT-R, undated but annotated 'spring or summer 1943' in T-R's hand, and 31 August 1943; DP 1/3/18.
63 'Nel mezzo del cammin di nostra vita … (June 1943)', wartime notebooks, II, pp. 203–6; DP 1/3/18.

CHAPTER 8: Sleuth (pp. 122–142)

1 'The Solution (May 1944)', wartime notebooks, III, pp. 251–2; DP 13/29.

2 'Agenda (March 1945)', wartime notebooks, III, pp. 274–5; DP 13/29.

3 Wartime notebooks, III, pp. 256–9; DP 13/29.

4 'Accidie (March 1945)', wartime notebooks, III, pp. 272–3; DP 13/29.

5 Logan Pearsall Smith to HT-R, 17 October 1944; DP 1/3/18.

6 'Image (August 1943)', wartime notebooks, II, p. 212; DP 13/29.

7 Liddell Diaries, 16 October 1944; National Archives KV 4/195.

8 National Archives KV 2/275 and 276.

9 Edward (E.D.R.) Harrison, 'Hugh Trevor-Roper and *Hitlers letzte Tage*', *Vierteljahrshefte für Zeitgeschichte*, 57 (2009). I am grateful to Edward Harrison for allowing me to read this article before publication, and I am indebted to it as an overall source for this chapter and the next. See also Harrison's 'The Last Days of Hitler Revisited', *The Spectator*, 17 March 2007.

10 'The German Intelligence Service and the War'; National Archives CAB 154/105.

11 The evidence of Trevor-Roper's notebooks indicates that this may not have been true, however, since they appear to suggest that the report on the German Intelligence Service was incomplete when White asked Trevor-Roper to undertake an investigation of Hitler's fate. See 'The Death of Hitler', wartime notebooks, III, p. 339; DP 13/29.

12 'Roman Catholic historians, (April 1945)' and 'Kent, (May 1945)', wartime notebooks, III, pp. 280–6 and 290–2; DP 13/29.

13 Untitled (March 1945?) and untitled (July 1945), wartime notebooks, III, pp. 271–2 and 309–10; DP 13/29. John Bright-Holmes (ed.), *Like It Was: The Diaries of Malcolm Muggeridge* (London, 1981), 5 May and 9 July 1945.

14 HT-R to Richard Ingrams, 7 June 1976; DP 1/2/20.

15 A.J. Ayer, *Part of My Life*, pp. 290, 217–18.

16 H.W. Garrod to HT-R, 6 June 1945; DP 1/2/1.

17 '*Götterdämmerung*', wartime notebooks, III, pp. 312–19; DP 13/29.

18 'Reelkirchen', wartime notebooks, III, pp. 343–9; DP 13/29.

19 The account that follows is compiled from several sources: HT-R's introduction to the Third Edition of *The Last Days of Hitler* (1956); 'The Death of Hitler', wartime notebooks, III, p. 339, DP 13/29; 'Solved: Hitler's Final Riddle', *The Sunday Telegraph*, 30 April 1995; report on 'The Death of Hitler', in 'Investigation into the Whereabouts of Hitler'; National Archives, 208/3787.

20 'Hugh Trevor-Roper and *Hitlers letzte Tage*', *Vierteljahrshefte für Zeitgeschichte*, 57 (2009).

21 White to Robertson, 10 September, Robertson to White, 19 September 1945; 'Investigation into the Whereabouts of Hitler'; National Archives, 208/3787.

22 HT-R to Leslie Randall, 6 February 1946; DP 10/20.

23 HT-R to Noel Annan, 9 May 1992; Annan Papers.

24 Wartime notebooks, III, pp. 350–3; DP 13/29.

25 The principal source for the following account is 'Hitler's Will', wartime notebooks, III and IV, pp. 353–61; DP 13/29. There is also the account given in the introduction to *The Last Days of Hitler*.

26 'Hitler's Will', wartime notebooks, III, pp. 353–6 and IV, pp. 357–62; DP 13/29.

27 HT-R to Mrs Keith Price (Sheila Trevor-Roper), 1 April 1946.

CHAPTER 9: Student (pp. 143–163)

1 'Logan Pearsall Smith', wartime notebooks, IV, pp. 362–4; DP 13/29.

2 'Vera Historia: or the True History of Logan Pearsall Smith, Bob Gathorne Hardy & John Russell'; Robert Gathorne-Hardy to HT-R, 24 February, and Alys Russell to HT-R, 10 March 1950; DP 1/3/28.

3 HT-R to Charles Stuart, 21 January 1946; DP 1/3/28.

4 HT-R to A.H. Gurney, 9 November 1947; DP 6/5/1947.

5 This paragraph draws on the memoir of Lawrence Stone by Cliff Davies in the *Oxford Dictionary of National Biography*.

6 'Lawrence Stone – As Seen by Himself', in A.L. Beier, David Cannadine and James M. Rosenheim (eds), *The First Modern Society: Essays in English History in Honour of Lawrence Stone* (Cambridge, 1989), p. 579.

7 Much information in the following few paragraphs is taken from Richard Shannon's British Academy memoir of Lord Blake, which he kindly allowed me to see before publication. The quotations from Blake himself come from drafts for his unpublished memoirs. I have also drawn on Kenneth O. Morgan's affectionate obituary published in *The Independent* (25 September 2003).

8 HT-R to Charles Stuart, 14 March 1946; DP 1/3/28.

9 Robert Blake to HT-R, 12 January 1958; DP 1/2/3.

10 *Captain Professor: The Memoirs of Sir Michael Howard* (London, 2006), p. 127.

11 HT-R to Solly Zuckerman, 26 October 1946; Zuckerman Archive, UEA.

12 *Captain Professor*, p. 126.

13 HT-R to Charles Stuart, 14 March 1946; DP 1/3/28.

14 In composing this passage I have drawn particularly on the memories of a former under-graduate pupil of HT-R's from this period, Roger Pemberton, and have drawn too on the vivid description provided by a postgraduate pupil of a later generation, Jeremy J. Cater, in his Editor's foreword to Trevor-Roper's posthumous work, *The Invention of Scotland: Myth and History* (New Haven and London, 2008), p. vii.

15 Graham Turner, 'I liked the elegant, frivolous life ... ', *The Daily Telegraph*, 28 January 2003; interview with the author.

16 Michael Banton to HT-R, 22 August 1988; DP 2/1/70.

17 HT-R to Lady Alexandra Howard-Johnston, 18 February 1954; DP 17/1/2.

18 I am grateful to Sir Ilay Campbell for this anecdote.

19 Interviews with Piers Mackesy and Richard Rhodes.

20 Ion Trewin, *Alan Clark: The Biography* (London, 2009), p. 70, HT-R to XH-J, 12 October 1953; DP 17/1/1.

21 HT-R to 'Nim' (Mrs J.C. Church), 5 May 1948.

22 HT-R to Bernard Berenson, 22 May 1949, quoted in *Letters from Oxford*, p. 35.

23 HT-R to PT-R, 6 June 1946; DP 1/3/17.

24 HT-R to XJ-H, 27 February 1954; DP 17/1/1.

25 Hamish Hamilton to Bernard Berenson, 3 December 1951, quoted in *Letters from Oxford*, p. xxxvii. Sibyl Colefax to HT-R, 15 May 1950; DP 1/2/1.

26 'A Dialogue on Fox-Hunting'; DP 9/13.

27 Preface to the Seventh Edition of *The Last Days of Hitler* (London, 1995).

28 'Dick' White to HT-R, undated but 11 or 12 June, HT-R to White, 10 and 14 June 1985; DP 10/20.

29 HT-R to Roger Pemberton, 23 April 1998.

30 A.J. Ayer, *Part of My Life*, p. 312.

31 HT-R to 'Nim' (Mrs J.C. Church), 30 March 1946.

32 'The Last Days of Hitler', wartime notebooks, IV, pp. 367–9; 'Publication of The Last Days of Hitler by Mr Trevor Roper' (extract from JIC sub-committee minutes); DP 13/29 and 10/30.

33 HT-R to 'Dick' White, 10 May; HT-R to Hamish Hamilton, 21 May and 2 June; Hamish Hamilton to HT-R, 22 May and 4 June 1946; DP 10/30.

34 HT-R to Lovat Dickson, 3 June 1946; Macmillan Archives.

35 HT-R to Lovat Dickson, 2 and 4 July 1946; ibid.

36 'Dick' White to HT-R, 4 July 1946; DP 10/30.

37 HT-R to Charles Stuart, 14 July 1946; DP 1/3/28.

38 Wartime notebooks, IV, pp. 364–7; DP 13/29.

39 HT-R to Lovat Dickson, 18 September 1946; Macmillan Archives.

40 Gilbert Ryle to HT-R, 9 August, Lord Cherwell to HT-R, 30 August 1946; DP 10/30.

41 HT-R to Lord Cherwell, 19 September 1946; Cherwell Papers K295/15.

42 HT-R to Lovat Dickson, 31 October, 14 November and 24 December 1946; Macmillan Archives.

43 HT-R to Lovat Dickson, 12 December; Macmillan Archives. Dickson to HT-R, 13 December 1946; DP 10/30. HT-R to Guy Liddell, 12 December 1946; DP 6/5/1946.

44 'Dick' White to HT-R, 20 March; DP 10/30. HT-R to Peter Ramsbotham, 19 March 1947; DP 1/3/12.

45 'Jesuits and Nazis', *The Tablet*, 21 June 1947.

46 'Nim' (Mrs J.C. Church) to HT-R, 23 March 1947.

47 HT-R to Charles Stuart, 26 March 1947; DP 1/3/28.

48 Rex Allen to HT-R, 28 October 1947; Macmillan letterbook 499–500, British Library.

49 'Hugh Trevor-Roper and *Hitlers letzte Tage*', *Vierteljahrshefte für Zeitgeschichte*, 57 (2009).

CHAPTER 10: Traveller (pp. 164–182)

1 'A Theme for Gibbon', *The Spectator*, 21 March. 'Sic Semper Tyrannis', *New Statesman*, 29 March 1947.

2 L.B. Namier to HT-R, 28 April, HT-R to LBN, 30 April 1947; DP 10/29/3.

3 Robert Gathorne-Hardy to HT-R, 28 June 1948; DP 1/2/1. Lawrence Stone to HT-R, undated 1947; DP 6/5/1947.

4 Earl Haig to HT-R, 26 March and undated 1947; DP 6/5 and 1/2/1.

5 John Bright-Holmes (ed.), *Like It Was: The Diaries of Malcolm Muggeridge*, 5 July 1948, HT-R to Muggeridge, 6 July 1948; Wheaton College (IL) Special Collections.

6 J.K. Galbraith to HT-R, 15 July, HT-R to Galbraith, 29 August 1947; DP 10/29/3.

7 'Death in the Bunker', *Church Times*, 28 March 1947.

8 Dr Johann Neuhäuser to HT-R, 7 January and HT-R to Neuhäuser, 18 January 1950; DP 10/29.

9 'Jesuits and Nazis', *The Tablet*, 21 June 1947.

10 Fr Bernard Basset to HT-R, 3 April, 30 May and 5 June (July) 1947; HT-R to Basset, 30 April and 5 June 1947; DP 10/29/3.

11 Evelyn Waugh to HT-R, 12 April 1947; DP 1/3/29.

12 Evelyn Waugh to Maurice Bowra, 1 July 1947; DP 1/3/29. Noel Annan, *The Dons: Mentors, Eccentrics and Geniuses* (London, 1999), p. 155.

13 *The Tablet*, 28 June 1947.

14 'Backhouse notebook'; DP 6/1/2.

15 George P. Brett Jr to HT-R (with enclosures), 2 October, HT-R to Brett, 9 October, Lovat Dickson to HT-R, 30 October and HT-R to Dickson, 31 October and 2 November, Harold Macmillan to HT-R, 3 (twice) and 5 November; DP 6/12.

16 'The Bunker Revisited', *New Statesman*, 8 July 1950.

17 Trevor-Roper Contributor file I, BBC Written Archives.

18 Memoranda by R.E. Kean and Anna Kallin, *c.* 15 February 1961; Trevor-Roper File II, BBC Written Archives.

19 HT-R to Stuart Hampshire, 2 October, HT-R to Guy Liddell, 29 September 1946; DP 9/1.

20 'The Plot against Hitler', transmitted on the BBC Home Service on 20 July 1947; Liddell Hart Centre for Military Archives, King's College, London; LH 15/15/57.

21 Harold Macmillan to HT-R, 6 June 1947; Macmillan letterbook 497–8, British Library.

22 J.R.M. Butler to HT-R, 11 October 1947; DP 1/2/1.

23 HT-R to Professor G. Leibholz, 10 March 1948, HT-R to Professor Dr Gerhard Ritter, 18 January 1950; DP 9/1.

24 'The Story of a Plot that Failed', *The New York Times Magazine*, 15 January 1956.

25 'The German Opposition, 1937–1944' and 'The Open Society', *Polemic* 8 (undated, 1947) and 3 (May 1946).

26 See, for example, Orwell's 'Notes on Nationalism' or 'The Prevention of Literature'.

27 'Communism in Europe', 'Communism in France', 'Has Fascism a Future?' and 'Challenge of De Gaulle', *The Observer*, 14 and 21 September, 10 and 31 August 1947. See also 'The Politburo Tries a New Tack', *The New York Times Magazine*, 19 October 1947.

28 HT-R to George Pinney, 7 November 1947; DP 1/2/1.

29 Alys Russell to HT-R, 3 July 1947; DP 1/2/1.

30 The following passage draws deeply on two sources: the description of the household at I Tatti in Kenneth Clark's memoir *Another Part of the Wood: A Self-Portrait* (London, 1972), pp. 133–65; and Richard Davenport-Hines's introduction to *Letters from Oxford*, pp. xiii-xxxix.

31 HT-R to Nicky Mariano, 25 April 1951, *Letters from Oxford*, p. 62.

32 HT-R to Berenson, 25 October 1947, ibid., p. 5.

33 HT-R to Charles Stuart, 31 December 1947; DP 1/3/28.

34 HT-R to Berenson, 22 January and 29 February 1947, *Letters from Oxford*, pp. 9–12. See also 'Policies in Prague', *The Observer*, 22 February 1948.

35 James Stourton, *Great Collectors of Our Time: Art Collecting since 1945* (London, 2007), pp. 89–91.

36 Sir Ilay Campbell, personal communication.

37 'Dick' White to HT-R, 3 December 1948; DP 1/2/1.

38 HT-R to 'Dick' White, 22 January 1947; DP 9/1.

39 HT-R to Charles Stuart, 24 March 1949; DP 1/3/28.

40 HT-R to Berenson, 7 May 1949, *Letters from Oxford*, pp. 33–4.

41 'The Lost Moment in History', *The New York Review of Books*, 27 October 1988.

42 HT-R to Charles Stuart, 3 August 1949; DP 1/3/28.

43 HT-R to Berenson, 12 January 1950 and Berenson to Clotilde Marghieri (transcribed by Richard Davenport-Hines from the originals at I Tatti); HT-R to Nicholas Gage, 22 June 1956.

44 Solly Zuckerman to Air Commodore C.B.R. Pelly, 27 March and 14 June, Zuckerman to Tedder, 27 March and 9 May 1947, Zuckerman to HT-R, 11 and 15 September 1948; Zuckerman Archive, UEA. 'Summary Report of BBSU Report by H.R. Trevor-Roper'; National Archives AIR 20/6393.

45 HT-R to Lovat Dickson, 5 May 1950; Macmillan Archives.

46 HT-R to Dr Othmar Ziegler, 12 July 1948; DP 6/5/1948.

CHAPTER 11: Historian (pp. 183–201)

1 'Thomas Sutton', *The Carthusian* (October 1948), pp. 2–8.

2 HT-R to Berenson, 8 November 1948, *Letters from Oxford*, pp. 26–7.

3 'Archbishop Laud' (Historical Revision No. CVIII), *History*, XXX, No. 112 (September 1945), pp. 183 and 185.

4 'The Bishopric of Durham and the Capitalist Reformation', *Durham University Journal*, March 1946.

5 Oxford University Archives, Bodleian Library FAG/1/311.

6 Geoffrey Cumberlege to HT-R, 8 November, HT-R to Cumberlege, 30 November 1946; Oxford University Press Archives.

7 HT-R to Berenson, 8 November 1953, *Letters from Oxford*, pp. 130–31.

8 Lawrence Stone to R.H. Tawney, 10 December 1947; Tawney II, box 27, LSE Archive.

9 HT-R to Berenson, 8 November 1953, *Letters from Oxford*, p. 131.

10 HT-R to Lawrence Stone, 2 August, and Stone to HT-R, 10 August 1948; DP 9/6/1. Charles Stuart, 3 August and 1 September 1948; DP 1/3/28.

11 Menna Prestwich to HT-R, 22 August 1948; DP 9/6/1.

12 'The Anatomy of the Elizabethan Aristocracy', *Economic History Review*, Vol. XVIII, Nos 1 and 2 (1948), pp. 22 and 20.

13 Robert Blake to HT-R, 11 September 1952; DP 1/2/2.

14 HT-R to Berenson, 25 September 1951, *Letters from Oxford*, pp. 73–4.

15 Harold Macmillan to HT-R, 4 February and 12 May 1948; Macmillan letterbooks 501–2 and 503–4, British Library.

16 'The Bishopric of Durham and the Capitalist Reformation', *Durham University Journal*, March 1946, p. 53.

17 HT-R to Berenson, 8 November 1953, *Letters from Oxford*, p. 130. HT-R to Wallace Notestein, 4 January 1951.

18 HT-R to Earl Haig, 9 September 1950.

19 HT-R to M.M. Postan, 19 September and 1 November 1950; Economic History Society Q/3. HT-R to J.E. Neale, 19 September, Neale to HT-R, 20 September; HT-R to A.L. Rowse, 28 October, John Prestwich to HT-R, 11 December 1950; DP 9/6/1.

20 H.J. Habakkuk to M.M. Postan, 12 November 1950; Economic History Society Q/3.

21 HT-R to M.M. Postan, 4 November and 6 December 1950, Postan to HT-R, 2 November, Postan to Stone, 2 November, and Stone to Postan, 3 November 1950; Economic History Society Q/3, LSE Archives.

22 Lawrence Stone to HT-R (Monday), HT-R to Stone, 28 November 1950; DP 9/6/1.

23 HT-R to Wallace Notestein, 4 January 1951.

24 HT-R to M.M. Postan, 8 March and 11 April 1951; Economic History Society Q/3.

25 J.H. Hexter, 'Storm over the Gentry', first published in *Encounter*, reprinted in *Reappraisals in History* (London, 1961), p. 138, John Kenyon: *The History Men: The Historical Profession in England since the Renaissance* (London, 1983), p. 247.

26 'Lawrence Stone – As Seen by Himself', in A.L. Beier, David Cannadine and James M. Rosenheim (eds), *The First Modern Society: Essays in English History in Honour of Lawrence Stone*, p. 582.

27 'The Elizabethan Aristocracy: An Anatomy Anatomised', *Economic History Review*, Second Series, Vol. III, Nos 1, 2 and 3 (1950–1), pp. 279, 289, 297, 294 and 294–5n.

28 'The Elizabethan Aristocracy – A Restatement', *Economic History Review*, Second Series, Vol. IV, Nos 1, 2 and 3 (1951–2), pp. 313 and 320–1.

29 M.M. Postan to HT-R, 16 May 1952; DP 9/6/1.

30 Lawrence Stone to R.H. Tawney, 17 April (1952); Tawney II, box 40, LSE Archives.

31 Robert Blake to HT-R, 17 March 1951; DP 1/2/2.

32 Speech on accepting an honorary doctorate of letters from the University, printed in *Wadham College Gazette*, January 1995, p. 61.

33 Charles Stuart to HT-R, 4 April 1951; DP 1/2/2.

34 E.T. Williams to HT-R, 14 April 1951, J.E. Neale to HT-R, 23 April and 6 July 1951; DP 6/12.

35 L.B. Namier to HT-R, 17 July 1951; DP 6/12.

36 HT-R to Berenson, 22 March 1957, *Letters from Oxford*, pp. 220–1.

37 HT-R to Earl Haig, 12 July 1951, Robert Blake to HT-R, 5 July 1951; DP 1/2/2.

38 Trevor-Roper's undelivered paper has been printed as an appendix to a paper by Irene Gaddo, 'Cold War Warriors: Hugh Trevor-Roper e il Congresso per la Libertà della Cultura', *Annali della Fondazione Luigi Einaudi XL* (Florence, 2006).

39 HT-R to Berenson, 28 July 1950, *Letters from Oxford*, p. 47.

40 Hugh Trevor-Roper, 'Ex-Communist v Communist: The Congress for Cultural Freedom', *Manchester Guardian*, 10 July 1950. Peter de Mendelssohn, 'Berlin Congress', *New Statesman and Nation*, 15 July, and 'For Cultural Freedom' (unsigned); *The Economist*, 8 July 1950.

41 Hamish Hamilton to Berenson, 8 July and 25 October 1953, Berenson to Hamilton, 1 March 1952.

42 Hamish Hamilton to HT-R, 10 January 1950 and 12 September 1951, HT-R to Hamilton, 4 June, 22 and 26 November 1950; Hamish Hamilton Archive.

CHAPTER 12: Destroyer (pp. 202–222)

1 Wallace Notestein to HT-R and HT-R to Notestein, 22 and 28 January 1951, *Letters from Oxford*, pp. 281 and 287.

2 'The Puritan Class War', *New Statesman and Nation*, 4 March 1950.

3 HT-R to Berenson, 6 January 1951, *Letters from Oxford*, p. 58.

4 R.H. Tawney to HT-R, 21 February 1951; DP 1/2/2.
5 HT-R to Earl Haig, 12 July 1951.
6 HT-R to Frank Newcomb, 7 February 1955; DP 6/37/1.
7 *The Gentry, 1540–1640.*
8 M.M. Postan to H.A. Habakkuk, 24 July, Habakkuk to Postan, 28 July; Economic History Society G2 and G3.
9 HT-R to Berenson, 30 August 1952, *Letters from Oxford*, p. 96.
10 Habakkuk to HT-R, 27 August 1952; Economic History Society G2 and G3.
11 HT-R to Sir Richard Rees, 4 October 1952; University College, London collection.
12 Sir Richard Rees to HT-R, 12 October, R.H. Tawney to HT-R, 14 October 1952; DP 9/6/1.
13 HT-R to Lovat Dickson, 12 and 18 November 1952; Macmillan Archives. H.J. Habakkuk to HT-R, 23 October 1952; Economic History Society G2 and G3.
14 M.M. Postan to HT-R, 20 January and HT-R to Postan, 24 January 1953; Economic History Society G2 and G3.
15 Sir Lewis Namier to HT-R, 24 April and J.E. Neale to HT-R, 27 April 1953, J.H. Hexter to HT-R, 6 February 1954; DP 9/6/1.
16 'The Rise of the Gentry – A Postscript', *Economic History Review*, New Series, Vol. VII, No. 1 (1954), pp. 97 and 95.
17 HT-R to Roy Harrod, undated but early October 1954 and 28 March 1955, Professor E.A. Robinson to Harrod, 2 April 1955; RES (Royal Economic Society)/6/1/481, LSE Archives.
18 Unpublished letter, May 1955; DP 9/6/1.
19 J.P. Cooper to HT-R, 12 December 1952; Trinity Archive.
20 Wallace Notestein to HT-R, 22 January 1951, *Letters from Oxford*, p. 281.
21 J.P. Cooper, 'The Counting of Manors', *Economic History Review*, New Series, Vol. VIII, No. 3 (1956), p. 388.
22 J.H. Hexter, 'Storm over the Gentry: The Tawney–Trevor-Roper Controversy', *Encounter*, May 1958; letters in response to the article, July, August and November 1958.
23 HT-R to Earl Haig, 25 November 1950 and 28 January 1951.
24 'The Copyright in Clarendon's Works', *The Times Literary Supplement*, 17 February and 9 July 1950.
25 Arthur Norrington to B.J.L. Kingsford, 20 February, Kingsford to Norrington, 21 February, Norrington to G.N. Clark, 2 March, Norrington to W.D. Hogarth, 9 March 1950; Oxford University Press Archives.
26 D.M. Davin to Geoffrey Cumberlege, Cumberlege to Davin, 24 and 29 January 1951; Oxford University Press Archives.
27 HT-R to Nicky Mariano, 14 January, and to Berenson, 28 January 1952, *Letters from Oxford*, pp. 81 and 85.
28 HT-R to Lord Cherwell (13 November 1952), Cherwell to HT-R (15 July 1952); Cherwell Papers K295/17 and 18. These dates cannot be correct, since the reply is dated before the original. My best guess is that both date from July 1951, when Hugh seems to have been in Iceland.
29 HT-R to A.D. Peters, 5 May 1952; A.D. Peters Archive. Memorandum dated 24 March 1953; ST/MAN/3/43, News International Archive.
30 HT-R to XH-J, 22 May 1953; DP 17/1/1.
31 HT-R to Earl Haig, 2 April 1951.
32 HT-R to Valerie Pearl, 7 August 1973.
33 HT-R to Berenson, 4 May 1951, *Letters from Oxford*, p. 64.
34 HT-R to Berenson, 25 September 1951, ibid., p. 73.
35 HT-R to Berenson, 25 September 1951, ibid., p. 73.
36 HT-R to Earl Haig, 20 October 1951.
37 J. H. Elliott, 'Learning from the Enemy: Early Modern Britain and Spain' (2007 Dacre Lecture), in *Spain, Europe and the Wider World, 1500–1800* (New Haven and London, 2009), p. 26.
38 HT-R to Berenson, 9 August 1953, *Letters from Oxford*, p. 122.
39 A.J.P. Taylor to HT-R, 7 June 1953; DP 5/1.

40 HT-R to Berenson, 25 September 1951 and 17 February 1954, *Letters from Oxford*, pp. 72–3 and 141–2.

41 HT-R to Gerald Brenan, 11 March 1968 and 23 November 1952.

42 HT-R to XJ-H, 17 December 1954 and 10 April 1956; DP 17/1/1.

43 HT-R to Berenson, 24 July 1952 and 25 September 1951, *Letters from Oxford*, pp. 93 and 74. HT-R to Hamish Hamilton, 23 September 1951; Hamish Hamilton Archive.

44 HT-R to Rex Allen, 25 February 1953; Macmillan Archives. HT-R to Berenson, 2 September 1953, *Letters from Oxford*, p. 124.

45 George Weidenfeld, *Remembering My Good Friends: An Autobiography* (London, 1995), pp. 289–91.

46 'Thus Spake Hitler', *The Observer*, 3 May 1953. 'Hitler Speaks Again: Steel and Concrete as God', *Manchester Guardian*, 24 April 1953.

47 George Weidenfeld to HT-R, 2 February 1953; DP 6/6/1.

48 HT-R to Berenson, 22 September 1953, *Letters from Oxford*, p. 129.

49 George Weidenfeld to HT-R, 20 May 1953; DP 3/8/1 and 2.

50 George Weidenfeld, *Remembering My Good Friends: An Autobiography*, p. 291.

51 The figures have been confirmed by Holocaust scholars, though it remains unclear who deserves credit for their release. See Yehuda Bauer, *Jews for Sale? Nazi–Jewish Negotiations, 1933–1945* (New Haven and London, 1994), pp. 102–5 and 243–8.

52 This account draws on several files in the Trevor-Roper Archive, DP 10/52/1–11.

53 Ralph Hewins, *Count Folke Bernadotte: His Life and Work* (London, 1950), pp. 242–4. HT-R to Lovat Dickson, 14 and 23 February 1950; Macmillan Archives.

54 'Kersten, Himmler, and Count Bernadotte', *The Atlantic Monthly*, February 1953. In 1974 the Dutch historian Louis de Jong published *Hat Felix Kersten das Niederländische Volke gerettet?*, a devastating critique of Kersten's claim to have saved the Dutch people from deportation to the East.

55 HT-R to Berenson, 9 December 1952, *Letters from Oxford*, p. 99.

56 HT-R to Nicky Mariano, 18 January 1953, ibid., p. 108.

57 National Archives FO 371.

58 'Swedes defend Bernadotte: Reply to Mr Trevor-Roper', *Manchester Guardian*, 26 April 1956.

59 Francis Hackett, 'Brimstone and Silver', *The New Republic*, 28 May 1956.

60 Barbara Amiel, 'A Death in Jerusalem', *The National Interest* (Summer, 1995). HT-R to Barbara Amiel, undated 1995; DP 10/51/3.

61 E.g. HT-R to Gerald Fleming, 2 May 1977. Fleming had written a meticulous report on the provenance of the Bernadotte letter.

62 'Folke Bernadotte and the White Buses', in David Cesarani and Paul Levine (eds), *Bystanders to the Holocaust: A Re-evaluation* (London, 2002), p. 264.

CHAPTER 13: Lover (pp. 223–256)

1 HT-R to Earl Haig, 13 April 1950.

2 Maurice Bowra to Justice Felix Frankfurter, 1 March 1953; Frankfurter papers, Library of Congress.

3 See Richard Ollard (ed.), *The Diaries of A.L. Rowse* (London, 2003), p. 287. Rowse's diaries are perhaps not a wholly reliable source.

4 HT-R to Earl Haig, 24 February 1954.

5 *My Father's Son: The Memoirs of the Earl Haig*.

6 HT-R to Earl Haig, 13 April 1950.

7 HT-R to Berenson, 11 December 1948, *Letters from Oxford*, pp. 28–9.

8 HT-R to Earl Haig, 24 February 1954.

9 HT-R to Earl Haig, 12 July and 20 October 1951.

10 XH-J to HT-R, 7 and 12 May 1953; DP 17/2/1.

11 HT-R to XH-J, 14 and 22 May 1953; DP 17/1/1.

12 XH-J to HT-R, 19 May, HT-R to XH-J, 22 May 1953; DP 17/2/1 and 17/1/1.

13 XH-J to HT-R, 25 and 30 May 1953; DP 17/2/1.

14 HT-R to XH-J, 3 June 1953; DP 17/1/1.

15 XH-J to HT-R, 4 and 6 June 1953; DP 17/2/1.

16 HT-R to Sheila Price, 26 March 1954.

17 HT-R to XH-J, 8 June (twice), telegram from XH-J to HT-R, 8 June 1953; DP 17/1/1 and 17/2/1.

18 XH-J to HT-R, 8 and 9 June, HT-R to XH-J, 31 May 1953; DP 17/2/1 and 17/1/1.

19 XH-J to HT-R, 11 and undated June 1953; DP 17/2/1.

20 HT-R to XH-J, 18 June 1953; DP 17/1/1.

21 XH-J to HT-R, 18 and 28 June 1953; DP 17/2/1.

22 HT-R to XH-J, 23 June, XH-J to HT-R, 5 October 1953; DP 17/1/1 and 17/2/2.

23 XH-J to HT-R, 30 June 1953, Earl Haig to HT-R, 30 May 1953; DP 17/2/1.

24 XH-J to HT-R, 3 (twice) and 4 July; HT-R to XH-J, 5 July 1953; DP 17/2/1 and 17/1/1.

25 HT-R to XH-J, 7 July 1953; DP 17/1/1.

26 Berenson's diary of 24 and 25 July 1953; quoted in *Letters from Oxford*, p. 118.

27 HT-R to Nicky Mariano, 1 August 1953.

28 HT-R to Berenson, 9 August and 17 June 1953, *Letters from Oxford*, pp. 115 and 121, HT-R to XH-J, 6 and 2 August 1953; DP 17/1/1.

29 HT-R to XH-J, 12 August 1953; DP 17/1/1.

30 All the quotations above are taken from the manuscript 'English Roman Catholics'; DP 9/8.

31 HT-R to XH-J, 17 and 28 August 1953; DP 17/1/1.

32 XH-J to HT-R, 2 August 1953, Earl Haig to HT-R, dated 'Bank Holiday' (1 August?) 1953; DP 17/2/1. HT-R to XH-J, 11 August 1953; DP 17/11.

33 HT-R to XH-J, 4 August 1953; DP 17/1/1.

34 XH-J to HT-R, 5 August 1953; DP 17/2/1.

35 HT-R to XH-J, 8 August 1953; DP 17/1/1.

36 HT-R to XH-J, 8 August 1953; DP 17/1/1.

37 XH-J to HT-R, 9 August 1953; DP 17/2/1.

38 HT-R to XH-J, 11 August 1953; DP 17/1/1.

39 XH-J to HT-R 15, 16, 17 and 24 August, HT-R to XH-J, 27 and 28 August 1953; DP 17/2/1 and 17/2/1.

40 Robert Blake to XH-J, 12 August, Blake to HT-R, 1 September 1953; DP 17/2/1 and 1/2/2.

41 Brian Harrison (ed.), *History of the University of Oxford, VIII: The Twentieth Century*, p. 92.

42 HT-R to Berenson, 2 September 1953, *Letters from Oxford*, p. 125.

43 HT-R to XH-J, 19 and 21 September 1953; DP 17/1/1.

44 HT-R to Berenson, 5 February 1953, *Letters from Oxford*, p. 110–11.

45 XH-J to HT-R, 18 October 1953; DP 17/2/2.

46 XH-J to HT-R, 19 October 1953; DP 17/2/2.

47 XH-J to HT-R, 21 and 22 October, HT-R to XH-J, 21 October 1953; DP 17/2/2 and 17/1/1.

48 HT-R to XH-J, 23 and 24 October 1953; DP 17/1/1.

49 XH-J to HT-R, 2 and 13 November 1953; DP 17/2/2.

50 HT-R to XH-J, 6, 7 and 13 November 1953; DP 17/1/1.

51 HT-R to XH-J, 22 November 1953; DP 17/1/1. HT-R to Berenson, 17 June 1953, *Letters from Oxford*, p. 115.

52 XH-J to HT-R, 3 December 1953; DP 17/2/2.

53 XH-J to HT-R, 25 November, HT-R to XH-J, 20 November 1953; DP 17/2/2 and 17/1/1.

54 HT-R to XH-J, 29 November, XH-J to HT-R, 29 November 1953; DP 17/1/1 and 17/2/2.

55 HT-R to Berenson, 8 November 1953, *Letters from Oxford*, pp. 132–3.

56 HT-R to XH-J, 5 November 1953 and 17 January 1954; DP 17/1/1 and 17/1/2.

57 HT-R to Sheila Price, 17 July 1962.

58 XH-J to HT-R, 25 and 29 November, 3, 21, 22 and 26 December, HT-R to XH-J, 20 and 29 November 1953; DP 17/2/2 and 17/1/1.

59 HT-R to XH-J, 20, 21, 22, 24 and 26 December 1953; DP 17/1/1.

60 HT-R to Nicky Mariano, 23 December, Berenson to Hamish Hamilton, 31 December 1953; quoted in *Letters from Oxford*, p. 134.

61 HT-R to XH-J, 4 January 1954; DP 17/1/2.

62 HT-R to Professor Carol Kyle, 25 February 1973; DP 3/8/1 and 2.

63 Berenson diary, 13 January 1954; quoted in *Letters from Oxford*, p. 134.

64 HT-R to XH-J, 7 January 1954; DP 17/1/2.

65 HT-R to XH-J, 6 January 1954; DP 17/1/2. 'Sir Thomas More and the English Lay Recusants', and subsequent correspondence, *New Statesman and Nation*, December 1953 and January 1954.

66 XH-J to HT-R, 5 and 13 January 1954; DP 17/2/3.

67 HT-R to XH-J, 17 January 1954; DP 17/1/2.

68 XH-J to HT-R, 13 January, HT-R to XH-J, 6 May 1954; DP 17/2/3 and 17/1/2.

69 HT-R to XH-J, 3 February 1954; DP 17/1/2.

70 XH-J to HT-R, 12 and 9 February 1954; DP 17/2/3.

71 HT-R to XH-J, 10 February, XH-J to HT-R, 12 and 18 February 1954; DP 17/1/2 and DP 17/2/3.

72 XH-J to HT-R, 27 February 1954; DP 17/2/3. Hamish Hamilton to Berenson, 17 March, Berenson to Hamilton, 20 March 1954.

73 HT-R to XH-J, 10 February, XH-J to HT-R, undated (c. 19 March and 10 February 1954), Earl Haig to HT-R, 17 February 1954; DP 17/1/2 and 17/2/3. Hamish Hamilton to Berenson, 24 April 1954.

74 HT-R to XH-J, 5, 6 and 17 March 1954; DP 17/1/2

75 XH-J to HT-R, 19 and 23 March 1954; DP 17/2/3.

76 HT-R to XH-J, 19 March (dated 1953, but in reality 1954), 3 and 6 April 1954; DP 17/1/2. HT-R to Alan Clark, 7 April 1954; DP 1/3/4.

77 XH-J to HT-R, 14 March, 9 and 10 April; DP 17/2/3. Esmée Fitzgibbon to XH-J, 7 February 1954; DP 17/3/1.

78 HT-R to XH-J, 15 and 16, 17 April 1954; DP 17/1/2.

79 XH-J to HT-R, 17, 18 and 20 April 1954; DP 17/2/3.

80 HT-R to XH-J, 20, 21 and 27 April, XH-J to HT-R, 21 and 27 April 1954; DP 17/1/2 and 17/2/3.

81 HT-R to XH-J, 28 April, XH-J to HT-R, 30 April (three letters) 1954; DP 17/1/2 and 17/2/3.

82 HT-R to XH-J, 1 May, XH-J to HT-R, 1 May (two letters) 1954; DP 17/1/2 and 17/2/3.

83 HT-R to XH-J, 5 February and 24 April, XH-J to HT-R, 22 April 1954; DP 17/1/2 and 17/2/3.

84 XH-J to HT-R, 24 and 27 June, HT-R to XH-J, 24 May 1954; DP 17/2/3 and 17/1/2. Geoffrey Norris to XH-J, 2 July 1954; DP 17/3/2. HT-R to Mrs J.C. Church, 13 July 1954. C.M. Bowra to Billa Harrod, 17 July 1954; Harrod Mss, British Library. I am grateful to Leslie Mitchell for this last reference.

85 XH-J to Billa Harrod, 23 May and 22 June 1954; British Library Add Mss 72804.

86 HT-R to XH-J, 30 June, XH-J to HT-R, 1 July 1954; DP 17/1/2 and 17/2/3.

87 XH-J to HT-R, 5, 29 and 17 July, HT-R to XH-J, 16 July (2 letters) 1954; DP 17/2/3 and 17/1/3.

88 HT-R to Berenson, 8 September 1954, *Letters from Oxford*, p. 151. HT-R to XH-J, 11, 2 and 9 September 1954; DP 17/1/3.

89 HT-R to Sheila Price, 1 August 1954.

90 HT-R to XH-J, 3 and 30 June, XH-J to HT-R, 27 June 1954; DP 17/1/2 and 17/2/3.

91 HT-R to XH-J, 4 and 6 September 1954; DP 17/1/3. HT-R to Berenson, 8 September 1954, *Letters from Oxford*, p. 153.

92 HT-R to XH-J, 6 May and 4 September, XH-J to HT-R, 7 September 1954; DP 17/1/2, 17/1/3 and 17/2/3.

93 HT-R to XH-J, 11 and 13 September, XH-J to HT-R, 13 and 11 September 1954; DP 17/1/3 and 17/2/3.

94 HT-R to Berenson, 24 October 1954, *Letters from Oxford*, p. 154.

95 HT-R to Berenson, 5 February 1955, Hamilton to Berenson, 12 October 1954, ibid., pp. 166 and 156n.

96 Noel Annan to HT-R, 21 October 1954; DP 1/2/2.

97 HT-R to Michael Stephens, 13 October 1954, with annotations by Anna Kallin; Trevor-Roper
    Talks file I/ BBC Written Archives.

CHAPTER 14: Husband (pp. 257–277)

1   HT-R to XT-R, 2 and (undated) November, 'No-Popery Day', 6, 27 and 28 November, 2 (two
    letters) and 8 December, Billa Harrod to XT-R, 6 December 1954; DP 17/1/3. XT-R to HT-R,
    8 and 30 November, 1, 5 and 6 December 1954; DP 17/2/4.

2   HT-R to XT-R, 4 December 1954; DP 17/1/3.

3   XT-R to HT-R, 26 December 1954; DP 17/2/4. HT-R to Berenson, 11 December 1954, *Letters
    from Oxford*, p. 158; HT-R to XT-R, 9 and 17 December 1954; DP 17/1/3.

4   HT-R to XT-R, 8 December 1954; DP 17/1/3.

5   XT-R to HT-R, 9 and 26 December 1954; DP 17/2/4.

6   Sir Ian Gilmour to HT-R, 12 August 1955; DP 4/2.

7   Janet Adam Smith to HT-R, 20 and 26 April, HT-R to Adam Smith, 20 and 23 April 1955;
    DP 12/24. 'Not So Secret Service', *The Spectator*, 29 April 1955.

8   Earl Haig to HT-R, several undated letters and 19 January 1955; DP 1/2/2 and 3. HT-R to Earl
    Haig, 18 January, 6 and 8 February 1955.

9   HT-R to Berenson, 5 February 1955, *Letters from Oxford*, p. 164.

10 HT-R to Berenson, 17 June 1953, ibid., p. 115.

11 D.M. Davin to Jack Bennett, 9 April 1947, 'Richard Corbett Poems'; Oxford University Press
    Archives.

12 Frances Stonor Saunders, 'How the CIA Plotted Against Us', *New Statesman*, 12 July 1999.

13 HT-R to Mr Miller, 18 March 1999; 'Desiderius Erasmus', *Encounter* IV (May 1955), reprinted
    in *Historical Essays* (London, 1957), pp. 35–66.

14 HT-R to Berenson, 28 May 1955, *Letters from Oxford*, p. 171. 'The Faustian Historian' and
    subsequent correspondence, *New Statesman and Nation*, 6, 20 and 27 August, 10 and 24
    September, 1, 8, 15, 22 and 29 October 1955. HT-R to Isaiah Berlin, 24 August 1955; Berlin
    Papers. See also *History and Imagination: Essays in Honour of H.R. Trevor-Roper*, p. 368.

15 'Karl Marx and the Study of History', *Problems of Communism*, reprinted in *Historical Essays*,
    (London, 1957), pp. 285–98.

16 HT-R to Isaiah Berlin, 18 February 1955; Berlin Papers.

17 'Huguenots and Papists', *New Statesman and Nation*, 5 November 1955.

18 HT-R to Berenson, 27 August 1955, *Letters from Oxford*, pp. 180–1.

19 HT-R to XT-R, 25 and 27 May 1955; DP 17/1/3. HT-R to Berenson, 10 June 1956, *Letters from
    Oxford*, pp. 198–9.

20 'The Establishment', *The Spectator*, 21 October 1955.

21 HT-R to Joseph Alsop, 30 September and 29 October 1955; DP 4/2. 'The Oppenheimer Case',
    The Spectator, 21 October 1955.

22 Eric Hobsbawm to HT-R, 3 February, HT-R to Hobsbawm, 8 February 1960; DP 1/1/H.

23 Thomas Wilson to HT-R, 1 October 1953; DP 1/2/2.

24 'A Case of Co-Existence: Christendom and the Turks', *New Statesman and Nation*, 14 May
    1955.

25 *Letters from Oxford*, pp. 163–4n.

26 'Fernand Braudel, the *Annales*, and the Mediterranean', *Journal of Modern History*, Vol. 44,
    No. 4 (December 1972). HT-R to Berenson, 18 February 1951, 23 March, 28 May and 20 July
    1955, *Letters from Oxford*, pp. 60, 168, 171 and 175. 'Capitalism and Material Life', *The New York
    Times Book Review*, 1 November 1974. HT-R to Frank Spooner, 7 December 1956 and 10
    August 1958, and to C.M Bowra, 16 April 1955; DP 1/1/Spooner.

27 HT-R to XT-R, 22 October 1953 and 10 September 1955; DP 17/1/1 and 17/1/3.

28 HT-R to KT-R, 12 October 1955; DP 17/6.

29 'Hitler's Fate, I & II', *The Sunday Times*, 18 and 25 March 1956.

30 HT-R to Nicky Mariano, 3 December 1955, *Letters from Oxford*, pp. 183–4.

31 Berenson to Hamilton, 14 December 1955, ibid., p. 185.

32 HT-R to Berenson, 13 April 1956, ibid., p. 194.

33 HT-R to A.D. Peters, 26 September, 25 October and 8 November, Cass Canfield to Peters, 8 October, Simon Michael Bessie to Peters, 29 November 1954; A.D. Peters Archive.

34 Wallace Notestein to HT-R, 23 January, 5 February, 26 May and 1 June 1956; DP 1/1/N.

35 HT-R to Wallace Notestein, 27 June 1956; Yale University Library.

36 HT-R to Berenson, 10 June 1956, *Letters from Oxford*, p. 199.

37 HT-R to Stuart Schram, 24 July 1956; DP 1/1/S.

38 HT-R to Peters, 22 April, 30 May and 2 June, Jason Epstein to HT-R, 2 April, Barbara Noble to Peters, 7 May 1956; A.D. Peters Archive.

39 HT-R to Berenson, 18 August 1956, *Letters from Oxford*, pp. 200–1.

40 HT-R to Berenson, 26 September 1956, ibid., p. 204.

41 'Twice Martyred', *New Statesman and Nation*, 25 August 1956; reprinted in *Historical Essays* (London, 1957), pp. 113–18.

42 Correspondence about 'Twice Martyred', *New Statesman and Nation*, 1, 8, 15, 22 and 29 September and 6 October 1956. HT-R to Geoffrey Elton, 8 September 1956; Elton Papers.

43 HT-R's report on Hill's *Economic Problems of the Church: From Archbishop Whitgift to the Long Parliament*, HT-R to Hill, 15 August, Hill to HT-R, 6 September and 20 August 1956; DP 9/14/2, 4/1 and 1/1/H. 'Church Mice', *New Statesman and Nation*, 8 September 1956.

44 HT-R to Isaiah Berlin, 1 May 1956; Berlin Papers.

45 HT-R to Berenson, 18 August 1956, *Letters from Oxford*, p. 201. HT-R to XT-R, 17 September 1956; DP 17/1/3.

46 Berenson diary, 29 October 1956, *Letters from Oxford*, p. 205.

47 HT-R to Berenson, 13 November 1956, ibid., pp. 207–8.

48 HT-R to Boyle, 8 November and 2 December 1956; University of Leeds Special Collections.

49 HT-R to Berenson, 25 November 1956, *Letters from Oxford*, pp. 208–12. Gilmour to HT-R, 19 November 1956; DP 1/2/3.

CHAPTER 15: Professor (pp. 278–297)

1 HT-R to John Elliott, 29 December 1956.

2 Oxford University Archives, Bodleian Library J26/EH/1, files 2–6. HT-R to PT-R, 29 March 1957; DP 1/3/17.

3 C.R. Boxer to HT-R, 25 July, Steven Runciman to HT-R, 21 July 1956; DP 1/2/3.

4 A.J.P. Taylor to HT-R, 3 July 1955. 'Hysteria before Hitler', *The Sunday Times*, 3 July 1955, and 5 November 1955; DP A74/2.

5 HT-R to XT-R, 17 September 1956; DP 17/1/3.

6 HT-R to Nicky Gage, 28 October 1956.

7 HT-R to Charles Stuart, 23 December 1956.

8 HT-R to J.C. Masterman, 13 December 1956; DP 1/2/3.

9 Charles Stuart to HT-R, 15 January 1957; DP 1/2/3.

10 Robert Blake to HT-R, 10 January 1957; DP 1/2/3.

11 *The Observer*, 20 January; *Oxford Mail*, 29 January 1957.

12 Isaiah Berlin to Charles Webster, 28 January and 2 February 1957; LSE Archives.

13 K.B. McFarlane to Gerald Harriss, 6 March 1957; Gerald Harriss (ed.), *K.B. McFarlane: Letters to Friends, 1940–1966* (Magdalen College, Oxford, 1997), p. 147.

14 HT-R to Donald Baverstock, 16 March 1957; Trevor-Roper Television file I, BBC Written Archives.

15 *The Philby Affair*, pp. 56–7.

16 HT-R to XT-R, 26, 30 and 31 March, 4 April 1957; DP 17/1/4.

17 *History and Imagination: Essays in Honour of H.R. Trevor-Roper*, pp. 366–7.

18 HT-R to XT-R, 9 and 19 April 1957; DP 17/1/4.
19 Isaiah Berlin, 'L.B. Namier', in Henry Hardy (ed.), *Personal Impressions* (London, 1980), pp. 77–80.
20 HT-R to Sir Lewis Namier, 19 January, Namier to Trevor-Roper, 25 January 1957; DP 1/2/3.
21 J.C. Masterman, *On the Chariot Wheel: an Autobiography*, pp. 295–6; Anne Whiteman, 'Lucy Stuart Sutherland, 1903–1980', *Proceedings of the British Academy*, 119, pp. 611–30.
22 A.J.P. Taylor to HT-R, 4 June 1957; DP 11/1/2.
23 Sir Lewis Namier to HT-R, 6 June, HT-R to Namier, 8 June 1957; Adam Sisman, *A.J.P. Taylor: A Biography* (London, 1994), pp. 248–9.
24 Various including Hill to HT-R, 6 June 1957; DP 1/3/22 and 6/13/2.
25 Lawrence Stone to HT-R, 6 June 1957; DP 6/13/2.
26 Maurice Bowra to Justice Felix Frankfurter, 22 July 1957; Frankfurter Papers, Library of Congress.
27 A.J.P. Taylor to Sir George Clark, 11 June 1957; Adam Sisman, *A.J.P. Taylor: A Biography*, p. 249.
28 Taylor to HT-R, 11 June 1957; DP 6/13/2.
29 Evelyn Waugh to Ann Fleming, 18 July 1963, in Mark Amory (ed.), *The Letters of Evelyn Waugh*, p. 610. Evelyn Waugh, 'Aspirations of a Mugwump', *The Spectator*, 2 October 1959.
30 'Hugh Trevor-Roper', *The Sunday Times*, 9 June 1957.
31 'Heat, Light and Sound', *The Times Education Supplement*, 14 June 1957. Martin Seymour-Smith, 'The Biggest Little Magazine', *Birmingham Post*, 7 January 1964.
32 'Arnold Toynbee's Millennium', *Encounter*, June 1957. HT-R renewed his criticism of Toynbee more than three decades later in 'The Prophet', a review of *Arnold J. Toynbee: A Life* by William H. McNeill, *The New York Review of Books*, 12 October 1989.
33 'Two Big Brains Quarrel … ', *Daily Express*, 1 July. 'Literary Letter from England', *The New York Times*, 4 August 1957.
34 'Table Talk', *The Observer*, 9 June 1957.
35 AJP Taylor to HT-R, 4 June 1957; DP 11/1/2.
36 'London Diary', *New Statesman and Nation*, 6 July 1957.
37 'The Protector', *The Observer*, 1 September 1957.
38 HT-R to Mark Bonham Carter, 30 August, and to A.D. Peters, 30 August, 4 September and 28 October, Peters to HT-R, 13 October 1952; A.D. Peters Archive.
39 HT-R to Hamilton, 4 October 1956 and 6 February 1957; Penguin Archive. Adam Sisman, *A.J.P. Taylor: A Biography*, p. 245. Peters to W.A. Evill, 19 July 1957; A.D. Peters Archive.
40 The surviving manuscript of the book on the Weber–Tawney thesis is in the Trevor-Roper Archive; DP 9/7/1.
41 HT-R to Berenson, 10 July and 17 October 1957, *Letters from Oxford*, pp. 236–41.
42 HT-R to PT-R, 23 August 1957; DP 1/3/17.
43 'Mirror of a Contemporary Mind', *The Sunday Times*, 3 November. 'The Regius Professor', *The Observer*, 20 October 1957.
44 XT-R to HT-R, 22 August 1958; DP 17/2/4.
45 A.J.P. Taylor to HT-R, 18 October 1957; DP 11/1/2. 'A Corner in Rationality', a review of HT-R's *Historical Essays, New Statesman and Nation*, 19 October 1957. I have assumed that HT-R was able to see A.J.P. Taylor's review before the official publication date, as copies of the *New Statesman*, like those of other subscription magazines, were dispatched a few days early.
46 'A Professor in the House', 'Historical Essays' and 'The Disembodied Voice' (letters from HT-R), and 'Anonymity Again' (editorial), *The Times Literary Supplement*, 1 and 8 November 1957, 3 and 10 January 1958. 'Behind the Lines', *The Bookseller*, 30 November 1957. HT-R to F.W. Bateson, 13 November 1957, and to Gavin Astor, 8 January 1959; DP 6/12.
47 Lawrence Stone to HT-R, 1, 10, and 27 December 1957 and undated (1958), HT-R to Stone, 9 December 1957; DP 6/12 and 1/1/N. 'Puritanism and Revolution', *The Times Literary Supplement*, 23 December 1958.
48 HT-R to Professor C.H. Dobinson, 21 March 1959; DP 1/1/D.

49 HT-R to Sheila Price, 13 December 1959.

50 A.J. Ayer, *More of My Life* (London, 1984), pp. 135–9.

51 HT-R to Berenson, undated, mid-December 1957, *Letters from Oxford*, pp. 244–6. I am particularly grateful to Jeff Walden of the BBC Written Archives Centre for investigating this complaint on my behalf.

52 Isaiah Berlin to Rowland Burdon-Muller, 13 December 1957; Isaiah Berlin, *Enlightening: Letters 1946–1960*, ed. Henry Hardy and Jennifer Holmes (London, 2009), pp. 601–2. This letter is copyright © The Isaiah Berlin Literary Trust 2009, and is quoted with the Trustees' permission.

CHAPTER 16: Scholar (pp. 298–327)

1 HT-R to Berenson, undated, mid-December 1957, *Letters from Oxford*, pp. 244–6.

2 Harold Macmillan to HT-R, 1 June 1949; Macmillan Archives.

3 HT-R to Berenson, 5 February 1955 and 17 October 1957, *Letters from Oxford*, pp. 244–6, 163 and 241. HT-R to Jamie Hamilton, 6 September 1957; Penguin Archive. HT-R to A.D. Peters, 6 and 10 September, Hamilton to Peters, 7 September, and Peters to HT-R, 9 September 1957, and Peters to Lovat Dickson, 3 January 1958; A.D. Peters Archive.

4 Hamilton to Berenson, 2 and 22 December 1957, *Letters from Oxford*, p. 244n. Peters to Hamilton, 16 December 1957; A.D. Peters Archive.

5 HT-R to Rex Allen, 27 December 1957, and Allen to HT-R, 8 January 1958; Macmillan Archives. A.D. Peters to Cass Canfield, 25 March 1958; A.D. Peters Archive.

6 HT-R to Berenson, 10 July 1957, *Letters from Oxford*, p. 234.

7 Memorandum on the Oriel 'revolution'; DP 11/8.

8 *House and Garden*, September 1957.

9 Isaiah Berlin to R.B. Muller, 28 June 1958; Michael Ignatieff, *Isaiah Berlin: A Life* (London, 1998), pp. 232–3; unpublished memoir by Lady Dacre.

10 HT-R to XT-R, 12 August 1958; DP 17/1/4.

11 HT-R to Nicky Mariano, 3 December 1958, *Letters from Oxford*, p. 260.

12 HT-R's 'The Case of Robert Peters' and 'Robert Peters: Curriculum Vitae', plus associated correspondence; DP 1162.

13 HT-R to Alan Bell, 27 March 1983.

14 HT-R to XT-R, 11 August 1958, 21 October 1959, and 11 August 1958, XT-R to HT-R, 10 February 1959 and 10 August 1958; DP 17/1/4 and 17/2/4.

15 HT-R to XT-R, 6 and 3 September, 13 April 1958; DP 17/1/4.

16 HT-R to Nicky Mariano, 6 July 1959, *Letters from Oxford*, pp. 272–3.

17 HT-R to Nicky Mariano, 3 December 1958, ibid., pp. 262–3.

18 HT-R to John Elliott, 9 July 1959. HT-R to Nicky Mariano, 6 July 1959, *Letters from Oxford*, p. 273. HT-R to Rex Allen, 21 July 1959; Macmillan Archives.

19 HT-R to Berenson, undated, *Letters from Oxford*, pp. 249–50. The editor places this letter, obviously written early in the year, in 1958; I suspect, though, that it was written a year later.

20 'Spain and Europe 1598–1621' in J.P. Cooper (ed.), *The Decline of Spain and the Thirty Years War, 1609–48/59*, New Cambridge Modern History, IV (Cambridge, 1970).

21 J.H. Elliott, 'The General Crisis in Retrospect: A Debate without End', *Spain, Europe and the Wider World, 1500–1800*, p. 52.

22 'Seventeenth Century Revolutions'. *Past and Present*, No. 13 (April 1958). J.H. Elliott, 'The General Crisis in Retrospect: A Debate without End', *Spain, Europe and the Wider World, 1500–1800*, pp. 54–7.

23 'Karl Marx and the Study of History', *Problems of Communism*, reprinted in *Historical Essays* (London, 1957), pp. 294–5. Eric Hobsbawm to HT-R, 1 November, HT-R to Hobsbawm, 9 November 1956; DP 1/1/H.

24 Lawrence Stone to HT-R, 6 February and 17 July 1959; DP A74/3.

25 J.H. Elliott, 'The General Crisis in Retrospect: A Debate without End', *Spain, Europe and the*

Wider World, 1500–1800, pp. 57–8.

26 Trevor Aston (ed.), *Crisis in Europe 1560–1660: Essays from Past and Present* (London, 1965).

27 HT-R to J.H. Elliott, 9 July 1959.

28 Alastair Horne, *Macmillan 1957–1986* (London, 1989), pp. 268–72.

29 Maurice Macmillan to HT-R, 8 February 1960; DP6/16.

30 HT-R to Wallace Notestein, 23 March 1960, *Letters from Oxford,* p. 300.

31 J.C. Masterman to David Stephens, 12 February 1960; Macmillan Papers.

32 HT-R to David Stephens, 8, 10, 11, 14, and 21 February 1960, ibid.

33 Alastair Horne, *Macmillan 1957–1986,* pp. 269–70.

34 HT-R to David Stephens, 28 February 1960; Macmillan Papers.

35 HT-R to Anthony Powell, 21 February 1960; DP 1/1/P.

36 Anthony Lejeune, 'Even Tammany Hall was never like this!', *Daily Express,* 22 February 1960.

37 Isaiah Berlin to David Stephens, 21 February 1960; Macmillan Papers.

38 HT-R to Wallace Notestein, 23 March 1960, *Letters from Oxford,* p. 305.

39 HT-R to Wallace Notestein, 23 March 1960, ibid., p. 307.

40 Randolph Churchill, 'It's Haroldus', *News of the World,* 6 March 1960.

41 Harold Macmillan to HT-R, 7 March 1960; DP6/16.

42 'Weekend Competition', *New Statesman and Nation,* 19 March 1960.

43 HT-R to Wallace Notestein, 7 March 1959.

44 *Encounter,* January and April 1961.

45 HT-R to JH-J, 20 July 1966.

46 HT-R to JH-J, 19 June 1960.

47 HT-R to XT-R, 21 September and 7 October 1960; DP 17/1/4.

48 JH-J to HT-R, 18 July 1966 and 10 April (1964?); DP 17/5.

49 Ion Trewin, *Alan Clark: The Biography,* pp. 180–2 and 188–9.

50 HT-R to Alan Clark, 31 August and 18 October, XT-R to Clark, 21 October 1960; DP 1/3/4.

51 Robert Blake to HT-R, 16 September 1961; DP 1/2/5.

52 HT-R to Alan Clark, undated (1962?), 22 February and 7 December 1963; DP 1/3/4.

53 HT-R to Peter de Mendelssohn, 1 February 1961; DP 1/1/M.

54 HT-R to Rex Allen, 22 February 1961; Macmillan Archives.

55 HT-R to John Elliott, 4 February 1961; DP 1/3/4.

56 Michael Howard to HT-R, 19 March 1961; DP 9/4/4.

57 'The Lost Moments of History' (1988 Romanes Lecture), published in *The New York Review of Books,* 27 October 1988.

58 John Elliott to HT-R, 3 March 1961; DP 9/4/4.

59 John Elliott to HT-R, 11 April 1961; DP 9/4/4.

60 HT-R to Professor Louis L. Snyder, 16 March 1961; DP 1/1/S.

CHAPTER 17: Controversialist (pp. 328–358)

1 HT-R to XT-R, 4 and 5 April 1961; DP 17/1/4.

2 HT-R to PT-R, 12 April 1961; DP 1/3/17.

3 HT-R to XT-R, 17 April 1961; DP 17/1/4.

4 *Jewish Observer and Middle Eastern Review,* 14 and 21 April 1961.

5 'Behind the Eichmann Trial', 'The Nuremberg of the Jewish People', 'What Eichmann's Trial Means to World Jewry', 'The Eichmann Trial : A Landmark in the Jewish Story', *The Sunday Times,* 9, 16 and 23 April and 17 December 1961.

6 'Eichmann: The Tidy-Minded Executive', 'Eichmann as a Pawn of Fate', *The Sunday Times,* 26 February and 11 June 1961. 'Eichmann is Not Unique', *The New York Times Magazine,* 17 September 1961. 'Time to Move On' and 'How Innocent was Eichmann?', *The Sunday Times,* 3 June 1962 and 13 October 1963.

7 'A Tyrant in Ireland', *The Sunday Times,* 15 November 1959.

8 HT-R to Frank Spooner, 4 August 1956; DP 1/1/Spooner.

9 From the preface to the First Edition of *Religion, the Reformation and Social Change, and Other Essays* (London, 1967), p. xii; HT-R to JH-J, 28 May 1961.

10 'Religion, the Reformation and Social Change', in G.A. Hayes-McCoy (ed.), *Historical Studies IV: Papers read before the Fifth Irish Conference of Historians* (Bowes and Bowes, 1963), reprinted in Hugh Trevor-Roper, *Religion, the Reformation and Social Change, and Other Essays*.

11 W.K. Jordan to HT-R, 9 April 1964; DP 1/1/J.

12 T.D. Williams to Herbert Butterfield, 6 and 15 June 1961; Butterfield Papers, Cambridge University Library. I am indebted to Professor Hugh Kearney for drawing these letters to my attention.

13 Adam Sisman, *A.J.P. Taylor: A Biography*, pp. 182, 287ff.

14 *Evening Standard*, 1 June 1961.

15 'A.J.P. Taylor, Hitler, and the War', *Encounter*, July 1961.

16 'Hitlers Kriegsziele', *Vierteljahrshefte für Zeitgeschichte*, April 1960, published as 'Hitler's War Aims' in H.W. Koch (ed.), *Aspects of the Third Reich* (London, 1985).

17 A.J.P. Taylor to HT-R, 17 June 1960; DP 12/23.

18 'How to Quote: Exercises for Beginners', *Encounter*, September 1961.

19 'A.J.P. Taylor vs. Hugh Trevor-Roper', 'Book on World War II Starts Scholars' Feud', *The New York Herald Tribune*, 23 July and 3 August. 'Historian's [*sic*] Feud Delights Britons', *The New York Times*, 30 August 1961.

20 HT-R to Alasdair Milne, 15 June 1961; BBC Written Archives.

21 Ved Mehta, *Fly and the Fly-Bottle* (London, 1963), p. 103.

22 HT-R to Alasdair Milne, 30 June 1961; BBC Written Archives.

23 HT-R to JH-J, 17 June 1961.

24 JH-J to HT-R, 7 October 1961.

25 Ved Mehta, *Fly and the Fly-Bottle*, p. 111.

26 'E.H. Carr's Success Story', *Encounter*, May 1962.

27 Geyl to HT-R, 30 June 1962; DP 1/1/G.

28 Ved Mehta, *Fly and the Fly-Bottle*, pp. 113–15, 95, 97, 99, 117, 118–19. '1963 Notebook'; DP 13/29.

29 'Questions of Degree' and 'A Degree of Judgment', *The Sunday Times*, 2 and 9 August 1964. F.R. Leavis to HT-R, 12 August 1964.

30 I am grateful to Barry Smith of the Australian National University for this anecdote.

31 HT-R to JH-J, undated (early 1963).

32 '1963 Notebook'; DP 13/29.

33 Robert Blake to HT-R, 3 May 1963; DP 1/2/7.

34 *The Scotsman*, 1 June 1963, Henry Chadwick to HT-R, 12 May, and Christopher Hill to HT-R, 25 March 1963; DP 1/2/7.

35 Donald Baverstock to C.P. Tel (Stuart Hood), 15 May 1963; TV Art 3, BBC Written Archives.

36 'Forgotten Relatives', *The Observer*, 24 May 1964.

37 K.B. McFarlane to Rees Davies, 25 January 1966; *K.B. McFarlane: Letters to Friends, 1940–1966* p. 236.

38 'Turning-Points', *New Statesman*, 18 February 1966.

39 Harold Macmillan to HT-R, 23 January and 26 February 1964; Macmillan Archives.

40 XT-R to Randolph Churchill, 23 January 1964; Churchill Archives, Churchill College, Cambridge. I am grateful to Sir Martin Gilbert for drawing my attention to this letter.

41 HT-R to JH-J, 29 February 1964.

42 HT-R to XT-R, 27 February and 3 March, HT-R to JH-J, 29 February 1964; DP 17/1/4 and 17/5.

43 'Germany's Awakening Conscience', *The Sunday Times*, 8 March 1964.

44 Colin Kidd, 'The Warren Commission and the Dons: An Anglo-American Microhistory', *Modern Intellectual History* (forthcoming). I acknowledge Professor Kidd's article as a general source for much of what follows.

45 HT-R to Frank Giles, 26 December 1964; News International Archive, ST/DepED/FG/1/42.

46 HT-R to JH-J, 6 January 1965.

47 HT-R to Robert Blake, 17 December 1964; DP 1/2/8.
48 'Trevor-Roper and the Warren Commission: Who is Right?', *The Observer*, 20 December 1964.
49 'Regina v. Penguin Books, Limited', *Encounter*, February 1962.
50 HT-R to Nicky Mariano, 23 March 1962, *Letters from Oxford*, p. 204n.
51 HT-R to JH-J, 23 October 1964.
52 HT-R, 'Kennedy Murder Inquiry is Suspect' and 'The Warren Commission: Vital Questions still Unanswered', *The Sunday Times*, 13 December 1964 and 3 January 1965. John Sparrow, 'John Sparrow on the Warren Report' and 'Making Mysteries about Oswald', *The Sunday Times*, 20 December 1964 and 10 January 1965.
53 Louis Blom-Cooper to Paul Hodgson (Head of Public Affairs Programmes, BBC2), 29 January 1965; TV Talks T58/59, BBC Written Archives.
54 HT-R to Frank Giles, 18 January, and Giles to HT-R, 20 January 1965; News International Archive, ST/DepED/FG/1/42.
55 'The Warren Report Stands as Written', *The Washington Post*, 17 January 1965.
56 HT-R to John Sparrow, 18 January, Sparrow to HT-R, 25 January 1965; Sparrow Papers.
57 Christopher Hill to HT-R, 24 January 1965; DP 1/2/9. John Archibald to John Sparrow, 21 December 1964; Sparrow Papers.
58 HT-R to John Sparrow, 30 October 1967; Sparrow Papers.

CHAPTER 18: Essayist (pp. 359–382)

1 HT-R to Rex Allen, 25 January, A.D. Peters to Alan Maclean, 29 January 1965; Macmillan Archives.
2 HT-R to Valerie Pearl, 20 July 1965.
3 Undated 'A.L. Rowse' memorandum (1954?); DP 1/3/13.
4 HT-R to A.L. Rowse, 19 and 23 May, Rowse to HT-R, 21 May 1965; DP 1/2/ 9.
5 HT-R to A.L. Rowse, 26 May 1965; DP 1/2/9.
6 A.L. Rowse to HT-R, 21 June, HT-R to Rowse, 22 June 1965; DP 1/2/9.
7 Sir Arthur Richmond to HT-R, 18 May, HT-R to Richmond, 24 May 1965; DP 6/12.
8 HT-R to Valerie Pearl, 13 August 1965.
9 Robert Bolt to HT-R, 28 February 1966; DP 1/2/10.
10 Simon Winchester, *Bomb Book and Compass: Joseph Needham and the Great Secrets of China* (London, 2008), p. 243.
11 HT-R to Valerie Pearl, 6 December 1965.
12 Joseph Needham to HT-R, 27 December 1961; DP 6/27.
13 'Understanding Mao; or, Look Back to Stalin', *The New York Times Magazine*, 12 February 1967.
14 *The Sunday Times*, 31 October 1965.
15 John Sparrow to HT-R, 1 November 1965; DP 6/14.
16 'Battle to control China society', *The Sunday Times*, 15 May 1966.
17 'Waiting for the Yen to drop', *Daily Mail*, 23 May 1966.
18 'Diary, Nov.–Dec. 1967'; DP 13/5.
19 'The Two Asias: Give America a Chance', *The Sunday Times*, 4 February 1968. Joseph Alsop to HT-R, 28 February 1968; DP 5/2.
20 HT-R to Lord Russell, 6 October 1966; DP 1/1/R.
21 J.H. Elliott to HT-R, 12 January 1966; DP 1/1/E.
22 *History and Theory: Studies in the Philosophy of History*, V, No. 1 (1966), p. 73.
23 HT-R to Jimmy Phillips, 22 August 1965; DP 1/2/9.
24 HT-R to Valerie Pearl, 12 September 1965.
25 See John Robertson, 'Hugh Trevor-Roper, intellectual history and "The Religious Origins of the Enlightenment"', *English Historical Review*, forthcoming. I am grateful to Dr Robertson for allowing me to read this essay in advance of publication.
26 Robert Lowell to HT-R, 8 March 1966; DP 1/2/10.

27 Charles Boxer to HT-R, 2 January 1966; DP 1/2/1.

28 Karl Miller to HT-R, 27 March 1967; DP 1/2/11.

29 'Communication from Buttocks', *The New York Review of Books*, 28 April 1966, further undated letter from 'Agnes Trollope' (May 1966?); DP 1/2/10.

30 HT-R to Robert Silvers, 25 March and 26 May 1966; DP 1/2/10.

31 Lawrence Stone to HT-R, undated (1966?); DP 1/1/N.

32 Lawrence Stone, 'The Century of Crisis', *The New York Review of Books*, 3 March 1966.

33 HT-R to Valerie Pearl, 31 July 1966.

34 Valerie Pearl to HT-R, 3 February 1966; DP 1/2/10.

35 'Historian of crisis', *The Times Literary Supplement*, 19 October 1967. The recently compiled database of *TLS* reviewers does not reveal the reviewer's identity. John Robertson has speculated that it may have been J.P. Cooper.

36 F.S.L. Lyons, 'The Grand Manner', *Irish Times*, 3 February 1968.

37 Wallace Notestein to HT-R, 8 March 1968; DP 1/2/12.

38 See, for example, Nigel Lawson's response to HT-R, 27 June 1968; DP 1/2/12.

39 Wallace Notestein to HT-R, 17 July and 7 August 1968; DP 1/2/12.

40 HT-R to Wallace Notestein, 21 July 1968; Notestein Papers, Yale University Library.

41 HT-R to Rex Allen, 4 February 1966; Macmillan Archives. The two articles had both been published in *Horizon*: 'The Persecution of Witches' on 2 November 1959 and 'Philosemitism' on 4 March 1960.

42 HT-R to Rex Allen, 1 July 1966; Macmillan Archives.

43 HT-R to Valerie Pearl, 25 July 1966.

44 'The Pincer and the Book', *New Statesman and Nation*, 4 June 1959.

45 HT-R to Valerie Pearl, 25 July and 11 September 1966.

46 HT-R to Valerie Pearl, undated (September 1967?).

47 Keith Thomas, 'The Tools and the Job', *The Times Literary Supplement*, 7 April 1966.

48 HT-R to Alan Macfarlane, 29 March, 19 April and 15 June 1967; Macfarlane to HT-R, 16 April 1967.

49 HT-R to Alan Macfarlane, 16 January 1968.

50 'Tilting at apple-carts', *The Guardian*, 1 September 1967.

51 HT-R to Geoffrey Elton, 12 September 1967; 'Books (1)', Elton Papers.

52 'Historian's Credo', *The Sunday Times*, 15 October 1967.

53 Alan Macfarlane to HT-R, 19 November 1967; *Witchcraft in Tudor and Stuart England* (London, 1970), p. 9.

54 HT-R to JH-J, 5 August 1970.

55 'Witching hour', *The Sunday Times*, 8 November 1970.

56 Norman Cohn to HT-R, 16 November 1970; DP 1/1/C.

57 'The Disenchantment of the World', *The New York Review of Books*, 2 December 1971.

58 HT-R to Robert Silvers, 8 May, and to Toby E. Huff, 8 May 1972; DP 3/6. 'Witches & Beggars', *The New York Review of Books*, 4 May 1972.

59 Melvin J. Lasky to HT-R, 10 October 1967; DP 1/2/9.

60 'Diary, Nov.–Dec. 1967'; DP 13/5.

CHAPTER 19: Ghostwriter (pp. 383–408)

1 Robert Blake to HT-R (enclosing correspondence with Viscount Chandos), 8 February 1967; DP 1/2/11.

2 'Author of Churchill play booed', *The Times*, 10 October 1967.

3 HT-R to Viscount Chandos, 9 February 1969; DP 6/7.

4 *The Times*, 17 January 1969.

5 Kenneth Tynan to HT-R, 17 January, HT-R to Lord Shawcross, 20 February 1969; DP 6/7.

6 Kathleen Tynan, *The Life of Kenneth Tynan* (London, 1987), pp. 275, 315.

7 'A Liberator crashes', *The Sunday Times*, 8 October 1967.

8 Richard J. Evans, *Telling Lies about Hitler: the Holocaust, History and The David Irving Trial* (London, 2002), p. 170.

9 *The Times*, 6 January 1968.

10 HT-R to Susan Barnes, 5 April 1970; DP 6/21.

11 'Hitler: does history offer a defence?', *The Sunday Times*, 12 June 1977. David Irving to HT-R, 20 June 1977; DP 6/19.

12 HT-R to David Irving, 6 March 1971; DP 6/19.

13 Paul Foot to HT-R, 3 March, HT-R to Foot, 29 March 1969; DP 6/21.

14 *Der Spiegel*, 2 and 9 October 1967.

15 *Der Spiegel*, 20 November and 4 December 1967.

16 'Was Sikorski assassinated?', *The Observer*, 8 December 1968.

17 'Churchill play man to pay libel damages', *Evening News*, 17 June 1971.

18 'The Sikorski case', *The Sunday Times*, 11 May 1969.

19 Susan Barnes, 'David Irving: An English gentleman who knows how to lose', *The Sunday Times Magazine*, 6 September 1970.

20 HT-R to Susan Barnes, 5 April 1970; DP 6/21.

21 HT-R to Valerie Pearl, 28 July 1967.

22 HT-R to Wallace Notestein, 18 September 1967; DP 1/3/7.

23 HT-R to Janet Adam Smith, 6 September 1969; Folder 65, National Library of Scotland Acc 12342. HT-R to Blair Worden, 8 September 1969.

24 See Colin Kidd, 'Lord Dacre and the Politics of the Scottish Enlightenment', *Scottish Historical Review*, LXXXIV, 2, No. 218 (October 2005), pp. 202–20; also John Robertson's introduction to Trevor-Roper's eighteenth-century essays, *History and the Enlightenment* (New Haven and London, 2010). I am grateful to Professor Robertson for allowing me to see this introduction before publication. Trevor-Roper's 1967 lecture on the Scottish Enlightenment appears in this collection.

25 'The Last Magician', *New Statesman*, 5 June 1964.

26 'Dame Frances Yates', *The Sunday Times*, 11 October 1981.

27 Frances Yates to HT-R, 8 and 19 June, HT-R to Yates, 15 June 1964; W1A Frances Yates Papers.

28 Frances Yates to HT-R, undated (1970?); W1A Frances Yates Papers. See also Marjorie G. Jones, *Frances Yates and the Hermetic Tradition* (Lake Worth, Florida, 2008), especially pp. 145–6.

29 HT-R to Frances Yates, undated (1972); W1A Frances Yates Papers.

30 'Frances Yates, Historian', *The Listener*, 18 January 1973.

31 HT-R to Leonard Russell, 30 October and 2 November, Russell to HT-R, 6 November, HT-R to Margaret Stephens (A.D. Peters), 7 November 1967; DP 12/24.

32 'Diary, Nov.–Dec. 1967'; DP 13/5.

33 Leonard Russell to HT-R, 18 January, HT-R to Leonard Russell, 26 January 1968; DP 12/24.

34 ST MAN/3/243; News International Archives.

35 Leonard Russell to HT-R, 18 January, HT-R to Russell, 20 January 1968, HT-R to Harold Evans, 29 January 1968; DP 12/24.

36 A.D. Peters to Tim Farmiloe, 13 February, Farmiloe to Peters, 21 February 1968; Macmillan Archives.

37 D.P. Reilly to HT-R, 2 January and 14 April 1968; DP 1/2/43.

38 'The Ideal Husband', *The New York Review of Books*, 9 May 1968.

39 HT-R to Harold Evans, 11 April 1968; ST/ED/HME/1/40, News International Archives.

40 Hugh Trevor-Roper, *The Philby Affair*, pp. 55–6.

41 'Dick' White to HT-R, 27 March, Noel Annan to HT-R, 29 March 1968; DP 1/2/12. George Kennan to HT-R, 5 May, Howard M. Smyth to HT-R, 23 August 1968; DP 1/2/43.

42 Sir Humphrey Clarke to HT-R, 29 April 1968; DP 1/2/12. HT-R to Viscount Morpeth, 1 November 1970.

43 'Kim' Philby to HT-R, 30 April, HT-R to Philby, 21 September 1968; DP 1/3/10.

44 'Some of My Best Friends are Philosophes' and 'The Chosen People', *The New York Review of Books*, 22 August and 24 October 1968.

45 M.I. Finley to HT-R, 22 October 1968; DP 1/2/12.

46 Max Beloff to HT-R, 13 June 1969; DP 1/1/B.

47 Henry Fairlie, 'Guilty Whites, Angry Blacks, Threatened Jews', *Interplay*, June/July 1969. Letter from Max Beloff, *Interplay*, August/ September 1969; DP 1/1/B.

48 Melvin. J. Lasky to HT-R, 11 September 1969; DP 1/2/13.

49 'Nullum esse librum tam malum . . .' *The New York Review of Books*, 25 April 1968.

50 HT-R to A.L. Rowse, 6 April and Good Friday, Rowse to HT-R, 10 April 1968; DP 1/3/13.

51 'John Aubrey', 'A brief life: R.H. Dundas', *The Spectator*, 9 June 1967. Hugh Lloyd-Jones to HT-R, 10 June 1967; DP 4/2.

52 HT-R to Wallace Notestein, 18 September 1967; DP 1/3/7.

53 'Bodl. Ms Aubrey (unnumbered)', sent (for example) to John Sparrow, 2 April 1974; Sparrow Papers.

54 HT-R to JH-J, 4 April 1968.

55 'Greece: The Colonels' coup may not have been in vain', *The Sunday Times*, 21 April 1968. P.A. Verykios and 'One of 8,000,510 Greeks' to HT-R, both 24 April 1968; DP 5/2.

56 HT-R to Valerie Pearl, 29 August 1968.

57 'Predicament of Czech historians', *The Times*, 21 May 1971.

58 Frank Tehern to HT-R, 2 May 1969; DP 1/2/13.

59 'Governors threaten LSE closure', *The Daily Telegraph*, 6 December 1968.

60 Walter Adams to HTR, 30 October and 2 December 1968; DP 9/13/1.

61 HT-R to Valerie Pearl, 13 December 1968.

62 'Who is Trevor-Roper?', *Beaver*, 5 December 1968; DP 9/13/1.

63 Walter Adams to HT-R, 20 December 1968; DP 9/13/1.

64 HT-R to Noel Annan, 21 February 1969; Annan Papers.

65 'LSE doves leave the hawks pecking', *The Guardian*, 6 December 1968. Letter from D.C. Watt, *The Spectator*, 20 December 1968.

66 Walter Adams to HT-R, 20 December 1968; DP 9/13/1.

67 'Oriel awakes'; DP 11/8.

68 'NUS chief attacks academics' letter', *The Times*, 23 November 1970.

69 'On Student Strikes & Pasquills' and 'On Fantiques & Files', *The Spectator*, 25 April and 7 March 1970.

70 'The Battle of the Philosophers', *The Spectator*, 14 February 1970.

71 HT-R to Valerie Pearl, 13 December 1968.

72 Nan Dunbar to Mercurius (date illegible) April, Mercurius to Dunbar, 24 April, Dunbar to HT-R, 28 April, HT-R to Dunbar, 6 May 1970; DP 1/3/27.

73 'Wherein Master PHS unmasks Mercurius Oxoniensis', *The Times*, 9 March 1970.

74 'On a Professor and a Novelist', *The Spectator*, 21 March 1970.

75 'Jock' Murray to HT-R, 3 April 1970; DP 6/20.

76 *The Letters of Mercurius* (London, 1970).

77 'Of our own correspondent', *The Spectator*, 14 November 1970.

78 'Whose is the hand behind the phantom quill of Oxford?', *Oxford Mail*, 19 November 1970.

79 John Sparrow to HT-R, 8 November 1970; DP 6/20.

80 Nan Dunbar to HT-R, 24 April and 18 November 1970; DP 1/2/14.

81 *The Spectator*, 13 and 20 February and 13 March 1971.

82 Christopher Seton-Watson to HT-R, 16 and 28 March, HT-R to Seton-Watson, 17 March and 9 April 1971; DP 6/20.

83 HT-R to Lord John Kerr, 31 January 1974; DP 6/20.

84 HT-R to XT-R, 5 April 1968; DP 17/2/4.

85 HT-R to Valerie Pearl, 4 April 1969.

86 HT-R to Valerie Pearl, 4 April and 3 November 1969. Personal communication from Professor Christopher R. Friedrichs.

CHAPTER 20: Spy (pp. 409–429)

1 Blair Worden, 'Hugh Redwald Trevor-Roper', *Proceedings of the British Academy, 150*, p. 269.
2 HT-R to Valerie Pearl, 27 August 1965.
3 Noel Annan, *Our Age: Portrait of a Generation* (London, 1990), p. 269.
4 For information on Trevor-Roper's election to the British Academy, and on elections generally, I am grateful to Peter Brown, formerly Secretary to the Academy.
5 Robert Blake to HT-R, 19 December 1969; DP 1/2/13. HT-R to Blake, 28 December 1969; DP 1/3/16.
6 HT-R to Nan Dunbar, 25 August 1970; DP 1/3/27.
7 Nan Dunbar to HT-R, 9 June 1970; DP 1/2/14.
8 Nan Dunbar to HT-R, 18 November 1970; DP 1/2/14.
9 Nan Dunbar to HT-R, 9 June and 18 November 1970; DP 1/2/14.
10 HT-R to Nan Dunbar, 13 June, 9, 11 and 23 September, 18, 24 and 29 November, Nan Dunbar to HT-R, 7 October; DP 1/3/27.
11 Richard Ollard to HT-R, 9 January 1973; DP 1/2/16.
12 HT-R to Richard Ollard, 26 May 1975.
13 DP 6/19 and A235.
14 Blair Worden, 'Hugh Redwald Trevor-Roper', *Proceedings of the British Academy, 150*, p. 269.
15 HT-R to Robert Blake, 19 April 1970; DP 1/3/16.
16 'Artists and the spirit of their age', *The Times Higher Education Supplement*, 5 November 1976.
17 'Imperial art collectors', *The Observer*, 14 November 1976.
18 'Princes and Artists', *The New York Times Book Review*, 30 January 1977 HT-R to John Russell, 4 February 1977; DP 18/8.
19 HT-R to XT-R, 2 and 3 December 1970; DP 17/1/4.
20 HT-R to Frances Yates, 9 February 1973; Frances Yates Papers.
21 HT-R to E. Badian, 26 May 1975; DP 1/1/B.
22 HT-R to Charles Curran, 30 July and 19 August, acknowledgement to HT-R, 5 August, forwarded letter from Lord Chalfont, 18 August 1970; DP 6/35/1.
23 'Professor receives libel damages', *The Times*, 27 March 1973.
24 HT-R to Blair Worden, 18 September 1970.
25 HT-R to 'Graham' (Alexander Graham McDonell Weddell, Vice-Provost), 27 May 1971; DP 11/8.
26 'The Emperor's new clothes', *The Sunday Times*, 18 October 1970.
27 Transcript of the *Panorama* interview; DP 10/4.
28 HT-R to XT-R, 28 March 1971; DP 17/1/4.
29 'The lie that saved Albert Speer's life', *The Sunday Telegraph*, 10 September 1995.
30 XT-R to John Sparrow, 17 May 1972; Box 81, Sparrow Papers.
31 HT-R to Roy Harrod, 5 July 1972; British Library Add. Mss 71620.
32 '8 St Aldates'; DP 11/7.
33 HT-R to Blair Worden, 5 January 1973.
34 HT-R to the Dean of Christ Church (C.A. Simpson), 20 November 1961; DP 6/39/1.
35 'Pakistan Diary'; DP 6/39/2.
36 Alan Bullock (Vice-Chancellor) to HT-R, 15 November 1972; DP 1/2/16
37 Zulfikar Ali Bhutto to HT-R, 7 April 1973; DP 1/2/16.
38 HT-R to John Habakkuk, 25 October 1974; DP 6/39/1.
39 John Habakkuk to Zulfikar Ali Bhutto, 21 January 1975; DP 6/39/1.
40 'A Shameful Public Affront', *The Spectator*, 15 March 1975.
41 Draft letter to 'Tom' (Dr Thomas Braun?), April 1975; DP 6/39/1.
42 'Mr Bhutto's Lost Cause', *New Statesman*, 28 February. 'Oxford Rejects Bhutto', *The Daily Telegraph*, 25 February 1975.
43 Henry Mayr-Harting to HT-R, 26 February; Isaiah Berlin to HT-R, 28 February and 4 March, HT-R to Berlin, 28 February 1975; DP 6/39/1.

44 'A Shameful Public Affront', *The Spectator*, 15 March 1975.

45 George Hutchinson, 'That Oxford degree is the least of Mr Bhutto's troubles', *The Times*, 8 March 1975.

46 Zulfikar Ali Bhutto to HT-R, 5 March 1975; DP 6/39/1.

47 Zulfikar Ali Bhutto to HT-R, 30 April 1975; DP 6/39/1.

48 'Bhutto's Fate', *The New York Times*, 24 June 1978.

49 Indira Gandhi to HT-R, 9 April 1979; DP 6/39/1.

50 HT-R to Margaret Thatcher, 11 November 1982; DP 6/39/1.

51 HT-R to Frances Yates, undated 1972, 8 May, 9 and 19 November 1971; WIA Frances Yates Papers.

52 The passage that follows draws deeply on Blair Worden's 'Editor's Foreword' to Trevor-Roper's biography, *Europe's Physician: The Various Life of Sir Theodore de Mayerne* (New Haven and London, 2006), and also Worden's memoir, 'Hugh Redwald Trevor-Roper', *Proceedings of the British Academy, 150*, pp. 270–1.

53 'Medicine in Politics', *The American Scholar*, Winter 1981/2, pp. 23–41.

54 HT-R to Frances Yates, 21 March, undated and 21 July 1972, 3 January and 24 February 1973; WIA Frances Yates Papers.

55 HT-R to Blair Worden, 7 March 1973.

56 HT-R to Frances Yates, 7 December 1973 and 11 March 1974; WIA Frances Yates Papers.

57 'The Press', *The Spectator*, 10 January 1964.

58 Harold Macmillan to HT-R, 31 January, HT-R to Macmillan, 5 February 1974; Macmillan Papers.

CHAPTER 21: Lord (pp. 430–453)

1 HT-R to Valerie Pearl, 7 August 1973.

2 HT-R to Jeremy Catto, 7 and 27 August 1973.

3 HT-R to Professor J.R. de Salis, 21 September 1973; DP 1/1/D.

4 HT-R to Robert Blake, 28 September 1973; DP 1/3/16.

5 'The Sleuth of Oxford: A Conversation with Hugh Trevor-Roper', 11 June 1979; DP 4/9/2.

6 HT-R to Alan Maclean, 4 August 1975; Macmillan Archives.

7 HT-R to Blair Worden, 29 August 1975.

8 HT-R to Blair Worden, 30 September 1976.

9 HT-R to Robert Blake, 19 August 1976; DP 1/3/16.

10 'Afterword' to the Eland Press reissue of *Hermit of Peking* (1993).

11 Geoffrey Elton to HT-R, 31 October 1976; DP 6/1.

12 This paragraph draws on E.D.R Harrison's article 'J.C. Masterman and the Security Service, 1940–72', *Intelligence and National Security*, December 2009.

13 'The Ultra Ultra Secret', *The New York Review of Books*, 19 February 1976.

14 Letter from Anthony Cave Brown and HT-R's reply, *The New York Review of Books*, 14 October 1976.

15 'Superagent', *The New York Review of Books*, 13 May 1976.

16 HT-R to Dr Jacob Gewirtz, 21 October 1976; DP 6/8.

17 HT-R to Gerald Fleming, 14 June 1977; DP 6/21.

18 John Whitley to HT-R, 9 and 25 March, HT-R to Whitley, 15 March 1977; DP 6/21.

19 'Hitler: does history offer a defence?', *The Sunday Times*, 12 June 1977.

20 Harold Evans to HT-R, 2 June 1977; DP 6/21.

21 HT-R to Eberhard Jäckel, 20 July 1978; DP 6/21.

22 'Goebbels Diaries'; DP 6/23.

23 HT-R to Robert Blake and Jeremy Cater, 1 and 9 August 1977; DP 1/3/16 and 1/3/32.

24 HT-R to JH-J, 15 July 1978.

25 HT-R to Jeremy Cater, 16 February 1978; DP 1/3/32.

26 'The Scottish Enlightenment' (XVth International Congress on the History of Science, August 1977), *Blackwood's Magazine*, November 1977.

27 'Scotching the myths of devolution' and 'This time there will be no musketeers to hold Great Britain together', *The Times*, 28 April and 23 September 1976, 'Fief in our time', *The Scotsman*, 23 August 1976.

28 Nan Dunbar to HT-R, 14, 17 and 21 May 1976; DP 11/19.

29 *Edward Hyde, Earl of Clarendon* (Oxford, 1975).

30 *The Times*, 28 April, 23 September and 15 October 1976.

31 'Covenant and Union', *The Times Literary Supplement*, 9 September 1977.

32 HT-R to Alan Maclean, 25 August 1976; Macmillan Archives.

33 'Labour's shabby project', *The Spectator*, 24 February 1979.

34 'Historian fights for his "castle"', *The Sunday Times*, 30 October 1977.

35 HT-R to David Steel, 6, 20 and 29 September, Steel to HT-R, 19 and 26 September and 26 October, HT-R's memorandum on a meeting with Steel, 20 October 1977; DP 11/5.

36 HT-R to Blair Worden, 29 August 1975 and March 1978.

37 HT-R to Blair Worden, 27 November 1977.

38 'Great Dons of the World', *Private Eye*, 21 September 1984.

39 HT-R to Tam Galbraith, 5 September, Galbraith to HT-R, 13 and 24 September 1977; DP 11/5.

40 HT-R to Robert Blake, 21 September 1978; DP 1/3/16.

41 HT-R to Frances Yates, January, no year give but almost certainly 1979; WIA Frances Yates Papers.

42 HT-R to Blair Worden, 20 February 1982.

43 Noel Annan to HT-R, undated (June 1979); DP 6/13/1.

44 HT-R to Anthony Powell, 26 June 1979, (from John Powell).

45 'Praeterita 2'; DP 6/13/1.

46 HT-R to Valerie Pearl, 2 July 1979.

47 HT-R to XT-R, 23 July 1979; DP 1/3/35.

48 HT-R to XT-R, 23 July 1979; DP 1/3/35.

49 HT-R to Lord Wakeham, 27 January, 7 and 8 February, Wakeham to HT-R, 1 February 1984; DP 12/1.

50 'Profile: Lord Dacre of Glanton', *The House Magazine*, 16 May 1986.

51 *Parliamentary Debates* (Hansard), Fifth Series, CDXIX (House of Lords), 1980–1, pp. 638–9.

52 Nan Dunbar to HT-R, undated, HT-R to Nan Dunbar, 23 July 1979; DP 1/3/27.

53 Nan Dunbar to HT-R, 19 January and 5 June, HT-R to Nan Dunbar, 22 January and 6 June 1979; DP 1/1/D and 1/3/27. The piece was extracted from the text of a lecture Hugh had delivered to a seminar in Venice in April 1971, under the title, 'What is Historical Knowledge for us Today?'

54 HT-R to Nan Dunbar, 29 December 1979; DP 1/3/27.

55 'Dick' White to HT-R, 10 February 1980; DP 10/48.

56 Memorandum for Miranda Carter; DP 10/46.

57 'The Unholy Trinity' and 'Blunt censured, nothing gained', *The Spectator*, 17 and 24 November 1979.

58 HT-R to Valerie Pearl, 3 December 1979.

59 For a fuller account of this affair, see Adam Sisman, *A.J.P. Taylor: A Biography*, pp. 389–93.

60 Eric Hobsbawm to HT-R, undated (March 1980); DP 12/4.

61 'Daggers drawn among the dons', *The Observer*, 24 August 1980.

62 'Groves of Academe', *Private Eye*, 4 November 1978.

63 HT-R to XT-R, 3, 6 and 12 December 1978; DP 17/1/4.

64 HT-R to Blair Worden, 27 February 1979.

65 HT-R to Blair Worden, 27 July 1981.

66 HT-R to PT-R, 3 January 1980; DP 1/3/17.

67 Oliver Pritchett, 'The last (Oxford) days of Hugh Trevor-Roper', *The Daily Telegraph*, 6 January 1980.

68 Michael Howard, *Captain Professor*, pp. 206–7.
69 HT-R to Blair Worden, 29 May 1980, HT-R to Hugh Lloyd-Jones, 27 July 1980; DP 1/3/30.
70 Evelyn Waugh, 'Sir Thomas More', *New Statesman and Nation*, 2 January 1954.
71 HT-R to Blair Worden, 4 June and 11 January 1980.
72 Nicholas Phillipson to HT-R, 15 May 1980; DP 1/2/24.
73 M.M. Postan to HT-R, 15 December 1979; DP 1/3/23.

CHAPTER 22: Master (pp. 454–474)

1 A.F. Kersting and David Watkin, *Peterhouse: an Architectural Record, 1284–1984* (privately published, 1984).
2 HT-R to Blair Worden, 16 October 1980.
3 HT-R to Blair Worden, 3 September 1983.
4 Noel Annan, *The Dons: Mentors, Eccentrics and Geniuses*, p. 264
5 Philip Pattenden, 'Master of Peterhouse', *Peterhouse Annual Record 2002/2003*, p. 207.
6 HT-R to Blair Worden, 15 January 1981.
7 HT-R to Robert Blake, 30 December 1976; DP 1/3/16.
8 'The Moral Minority', *The New York Review of Books*, 13 March 1986.
9 'Is it really necessary to be a Christian to oppose liberal cant?', *The Listener*, 5 February 1981.
10 HT-R to Blair Worden, 15 January 1981 and 29 November 1980.
11 HT-R to Hugh Lloyd-Jones, 29 November 1980; DP 1/3/30.
12 Michael Portillo, 'Maurice John Cowling' (address given at a memorial service on 29 October 2005), *Peterhouse Annual Record, 2004/2005*, pp. 119–20.
13 Philip Pattenden, 'Master of Peterhouse', *Peterhouse Annual Record, 2002/2003*. This affectionate and amusing obituary has provided a general source for my account of HT-R's term as Master of Peterhouse.
14 Maurice Cowling to HT-R, 5 December 1979; DP 11/ 9.
15 'College Guide', *Varsity Handbook* (*c.* 1984), p. 43.
16 HT-R to Blair Worden, 29 November 1980.
17 HT-R to Blair Worden, 29 November 1980.
18 HT-R to Blair Worden, 7 December 1981.
19 HT-R to Blair Worden, 15 June 1982.
20 HT-R to Blair Worden, 7 December 1981.
21 Harold Macmillan to HT-R, 18 June 1981; DP 1/2/25.
22 HT-R to Isaiah Berlin, 9 October 1981; DP 1/3/1. HT-R to Michael Howard and to William (?), 18 November 1981; DP 1/2/25.
23 HT-R to Noel Annan, 17 November 1981; Annan Papers. Sir David Spedding to HT-R, 10 August 2000; DP 1/2/40.
24 HT-R to Noel Annan, 17 November, Annan to HT-R, 23 November 1981; DP 1/2/25.
25 'Tribute to Trevor-Roper', *London Review of Books*, 5 November 1981.
26 HT-R to Robert Blake, 23 October 1980; DP 1/3/16.
27 Graham Turner, 'I liked the elegant, frivolous life ...' *The Daily Telegraph*, 28 January 2003.
28 Rupert Murdoch to HT-R, 16 October, HT-R to Murdoch, 19 October 1981; DP 5/6.
29 HT-R to Blair Worden, 7 December 1981 and 17 January 1982.
30 HT-R to Blair Worden, 20 February 1982.
31 HT-R to Blair Worden, 17 January 1982.
32 HT-R to Blair Worden, 20 February 1982.
33 HT-R to Blair Worden, 7 December 1981.
34 HT-R to Robert Blake, 5 November 1981; DP 1/3/16.
35 Jeremy J. Cater (ed.), *The Invention of Scotland: Myth and History* (New Haven and London, 2008), p. 31.
36 Ibid., p. 187.
37 Ibid., p. 191.

38 Ibid., p. 217.
39 Ibid., p. 232.
40 HT-R to Jeremy Cater, 17 January 1981; DP 1/3/32. Cater has carefully traced the genesis of the book in his 'Editor's Foreword' to *The Invention of Scotland: Myth and History*.
41 HT-R to Nan Dunbar, 20 June 1982; DP 1/3/27.
42 Roger Scruton, 'Stick with the Men, Peterhouse', *The Times*, 22 March 1983.
43 HT-R to Philip Pattenden, 30 November 1993; DP 11/16.

CHAPTER 23: Expert (pp. 475–506)

1   HT-R to JH-J, 8 March 1983.
2   HT-R to Robert Blake, 3 February 1983; DP 1/3/16.
3   Robert Harris, *Selling Hitler* (London, 1986), p. 15. In writing this chapter I have drawn extensively on Harris's authoritative account; Graham Stewart's *History of The Times, VII, 1981–2002: The Murdoch Years* (London, 2005); contemporary coverage of the story in *The Times* and *The Sunday Times*, especially Trevor-Roper's own articles; interviews with participants; files in the News International Archives; and the two boxes of papers in the Trevor-Roper Archive, including his own diary of the episode. Where possible, I have relied on primary sources. For example, both Harris and Stewart state that Trevor-Roper saw the diaries in Zurich on 8 April, drawing on the story in *The Sunday Times* of 1 May. In fact, it is clear from Trevor-Roper's own records that he saw them the day before, 7 April. There are a number of minor discrepancies between these sources. For example, Harris says that Trevor-Roper saw the diaries in 'a ground floor room' of the Handelsbank; Stewart describes him descending 'into the vaults'. Trevor-Roper's documents show that Harris is correct.
4   'Secrets that survived the Bunker', *The Times*, 23 April 1983.
5   'Myths'; DP 10/20.
6   Graham Stewart, *History of The Times, VII, 1981–2002: The Murdoch Years*, pp. 169–70.
7   'Hitler: a catalogue of errors', *The Times*, 14 May 1983.
8   'Anatomy of a Scoop', *The Sunday Times*, 1 May 1983.
9   Robert Harris, *Selling Hitler*, pp. 270–2; News International Archive, A489/5024.
10 Robert Harris, *Selling Hitler*, p. 286.
11 Ibid., pp. 305–6.
12 Frank Giles, 'Note for file', News International Archive, A809/9829; also the same author's *Sundry Times* (London, 1986), pp. 243–4.
13 Frank Giles, *Sundry Times*, p. 244.
14 HT-R to Frank Giles, 10 July 1983; DP 6/25.
15 'Hitler Diaries: Dacre's Doubts', *Evening Standard*, 25 April 1983.
16 Robert Harris, *Selling Hitler*, pp. 331–3.
17 Conor Cruise O'Brien, 'The Tragic History of Double Dacre', *The Observer*, 1 May. Bernard Crick, 'Chequebook History', *New Statesman*, 29 April 1983.
18 'Hitler: a catalogue of errors', *The Times*, 14 May 1983.
19 Undated letter to Charles Douglas-Home, News International Archive, A489/5024.
20 Rupert Murdoch to HT-R, 24 May 1983; DP 6/25.
21 HT-R to Frank Giles, 10 July 1983.
22 Auberon Waugh, 'Joke of the Decade', *The Spectator*, 30 April 1983.
23 John Rubinstein to HT-R, 9 May 1983; DP 6/25.
24 'Albany at Large', *The Sunday Telegraph*, 5 June 1983.
25 Lord Carlisle to HT-R, undated but postmarked 26 May 1983; DP 6/25.
26 Graham Stewart, *History of The Times, VII, 1981–2002: The Murdoch Years*, pp. 178–9.
27 'War der Nationalsozialismus ohne Beispiel?' ('Was National Socialism Unique?'), given on 25 May 1982; DP 4/1.
28 News International Archive, ST/ED/Amalg/12/1.

CHAPTER 24: Stoic (pp. 507–540)

1 Maurice Cowling to HT-R, 25 July 1983; DP 11/12.
2 HT-R to Hugh Lloyd-Jones, 8 November 1981; DP 1/3/30.
3 'Mammon & Eve defy tradition', *The Sunday Telegraph*, 27 February 1983.
4 HT-R to Edward Norman, 17 July 1983; DP 11/9.
5 'Cambridge don axed in clash with Lord Dacre', *The Sunday Telegraph*, 21 August. 'Future of Cambridge don in doubt after letter to Lord Dacre', *The Guardian*, 22 August; 'Lord Dacre in row with Peterhouse Fellows', *The Daily Telegraph*, 23 August 1983.
6 HT-R to Charles Stuart, 20 August and 4 September 1983. HT-R to Blair Worden, 3 September 1983.
7 'Christian and Sceptic', *The Times Higher Education Supplement*, 9 December 1983.
8 HT-R to Hallard Croft, 12 March 1986; DP 11/12.
9 I am indebted to Professor John A. Davis for this anecdote.
10 HT-R to Maurice Cowling, 31 December 1982; DP 11/11.
11 Lord Weinstock to HT-R, 26 April 1984; DP 11/11.
12 HT-R to Noel Annan, 10 April 1985; Annan Papers.
13 HT-R to Blair Worden, 31 January 1984.
14 HT-R to Charles Stuart, 26 September 1984; DP 1/3/28.
15 HT-R to Noel Annan, 30 August and 26 September 1984; Annan Papers.
16 HT-R to Alasdair Milne, 16 May 1985; DP 5/5.
17 HT-R to Rupert Murdoch, 31 July and undated (August?), Murdoch to HT-R, 6 August 1986; DP 5/6.
18 HT-R to 'The Literary Editor, Sunday Times', 12 February 1986; DP 5/4.
19 Rupert Murdoch to HT-R, 2 December 1987, HT-R to Murdoch, 4 December 1987 and 25 February 1988; DP 5/6.
20 Robin Briggs, 'Figures and Fissures', *The Times Literary Supplement*, 22 November 1985. Conrad Russell, 'Christendom', *London Review of Books*, 7 November 1985.
21 Robert Silvers to XT-R, 10 July 1985; DP 18/3.
22 HT-R to Blair Worden, 18 December 1985.
23 'Foreword', *Religion and Public Doctrine in Modern England, II: Assaults* (Cambridge, 1985).
24 HT-R to Blair Worden, 18 December 1985.
25 HT-R to Maurice Cowling, 30 December 1985; DP 11/9.
26 'The Moral Minority' and 'The Peterhouse School', *The New York Review of Books*, 13 March and 10 April 1986.
27 HT-R to Noel Annan, 10 April 1985; Annan Papers.
28 Michael Howard, *Captain Professor*, p. 193.
29 HT-R to Blair Worden, 19 June 1984.
30 HT-R to Ed Shils, 8 June 1985; HT-R to Hugh Lloyd-Jones, 2 March 1985; DP 1/3/30.
31 HT-R to Hugh Thomas, 4 February 1987.
32 HT-R to Lord Blake, 29 May 1987; DP 1/3/16.
33 Charles Stuart to HT-R, 28 January; DP 1/1/S. HT-R to Charles Stuart and Robert Blake, both 30 January 1987; DP Soc Dacre. 'Queries'.
34 HT-R to Blair Worden, 12 April 1987.
35 'Peterhouse blues as Dacre stays on', *Daily Mail*, 29 July 1987.
36 HT-R to Blair Worden, 19 September 1987.
37 'Honorary Fellowship: Lord Dacre', 23 November 1987.
38 HT-R to Blair Worden, 1 January 1988.
39 Max Perutz to HT-R, 1 October 1987; DP 1/3/8.
40 HT-R to Max Perutz, 1 May 1988; DP 1/3/8.
41 HT-R to Richard Ollard, 4 February 1987.
42 'Introduction', *Catholics, Anglicans and Puritans: Seventeenth Century Essays* (London, 1987), pp. xii – xiii.

43 'Three Historians. I: the Earl of Clarendon', *The Listener*, 30 September 1965.

44 *Catholics, Anglicans and Puritans: Seventeenth Century Essays*, p. 159.

45 'The Sources of the New Right', *Encounter*, November 1989.

46 'Hugh Trevor-Roper on the Peterhouse Effect', *The Independent Magazine*, 9 December, response from Maurice Cowling, 23 December 1989, 'Cowling Assumptions', 6 January, 'Advice from Peterhouse', 20 January 1990.

47 'Phaecia and the Cyclops: A New Document'; DP 4/9/2.

48 'The undaunted Whig', *The Times Literary Supplement*, 5 June 1992.

49 Lawrence Stone to HT-R, 8 June 1992; DP 1/1/S.

50 Lawrence Stone to Edward Chaney, 17 June 1992; DP 18/2/1.

51 Isaiah Berlin to HT-R, 26 February 1988[9]; DP 4/4/1.

52 HT-R to Max Perutz, 7 December 1989; DP 1/3/8.

53 'Chequers meeting'; DP 6/18.

54 George Urban, *Diplomacy and Disillusion: At the Court of Margaret Thatcher* (London, 1996), pp. 118–59.

55 Timothy Garton Ash, 'Britain fluffed the German question', *The Guardian*, 22 October 2009.

56 HT-R to Max Perutz, 15 August 1990; DP 1/3/8.

57 'How nations can change their spots', *The Sunday Telegraph*, 29 July 1990.

58 'A note of my conversation with the Pope', 14 January 1992; DP 13/48.

59 Noel Annan to HT-R, 29 December 1994; DP 6/4.

60 HT-R to Patrick Reilly, 19 September 1995; Reilly Papers, Bodleian Library MsEng c 6888.

61 James Howard-Johnston, 'Memories of Hugh', *Peterhouse Annual Record*, 2002–3, p. 214.

62 Brian Harrison to HT-R, 24 June 2002; DP 6/37/4.

63 Candida Crewe, 'Now I know all about ghosts', *The Daily Telegraph*, 8 April 2002.

64 'A.J.P. Taylor', *The Daily Telegraph*, 8 September 1990.

65 Blair Worden, *The Sunday Telegraph*, 2 February 2003.

66 See, for example, David Wootton's review 'Painted Black', *The Times Literary Supplement*, 16 February 2007.

67 John Robertson (ed.), *History and the Enlightenment* (New Haven and London, 2010).

Index

NOTE: Works by Hugh Trevor-Roper (HT-R) appear directly under title; works by others under author's name

A6 murders (1961), 367–8

Abercrombie, Lascelles, 71

Abwehr: signals intercepted by RSS, 81–2, 85, 88, 90; analysed by RAB, 94; Enigma ciphers broken, 97; HT-R's proposals for deception of, 105, 116; conflict with SD, 113, 116; organisation and internal differences, 117–18; and British deception, 436–7

Acton, Sir Harold, 27, 275

Adams, Mary, 364, 366

Adams, Walter, 401–2

Adshead, S.A.M., 432

Adullam, cave of: Cowling's refuge, 520

Aeschylus: *Prometheus Bound*, 62

Age of Christian Princes, The (HT-R; projected), 312

Aitken, Jonathan, 270, 442

Alison, Barley, 527

All Souls College, Oxford: HT-R fails to gain election to, 35, 43–5

Allen, John and Charles *see* Sobieski Stuarts

Allen, Lancelot, 18, 20

Allen, Rex, 299, 324, 359, 376

Alnwick: Castle, xvii; HT-R's father settles in, 4–5; HT-R revisits, 64, 67, 124, 160, 356

Alphon, Peter, 367–8

Alsop, Joseph, 265, 267, 408

Alsop, Stewart, 265

Amalekite: Tawney protests that an erring colleague is not an, to be smitten hip and thigh, 206 & n

Amis, Sir Kingsley, 400

Amos, Miss (governess), 9–10, 13–14

Annales school (of history), France, 267

Annan, Noël (*later* Baron): and Bowra, 37–8, 146, 167; accompanies HT-R to post-war Berlin, 135; praises HT-R's *Last Days of Hitler*, 164; misses HT-R's wedding, 255; praises HT-R's review of Toynbee's *Study of History*, 256; praises HT-R's article on Philby, 394; and HT-R's LSE Oration, 402; congratulates HT-R on review of Cave Brown, 438; recommends HT-R for honour, 446, 466; on Butterfield, 456; and security services' hostility to HT-R, 465; and HT-R's low opinion of Peterhouse conversation, 515;

and guests at HT-R's wedding anniversary lunch, 516; at Thomases' Downing Street party, 521; advises HT-R to write memoirs, 534; *Changing Enemies*, 534n

anti-Semitism, 377, 396–7

Archbishop Laud (HT-R), 73–6, 83–4, 161n, 247, 261, 361, 375

Archibald, John, 356

Arendt, Hannah: *Eichmann in Jerusalem*, 330

aristocracy: conflict with gentry, 203–4; *see also* Court and Country antithesis

Armstrong, Sir Robert (*later* Baron), 534

Armstrong, (Sir) Thomas, 104, 269

'Arnold Toynbee's Millennium' (HT-R), 339

Ashley, Maurice, 295

Ashley Clarke, Virginia *see* Clarke, Virginia (Ashley), Lady

Aston, Trevor, 311, 412

Astor, Brooke, 415

Astor of Hever, Gavin, Baron, 63, 294, 428, 447

Astor, Lady Irene (*née* Haig), 225n, 475

Astor, Michael, 260, 266

Atlantic Monthly, The, 102, 218–20

Attlee, Clement (*later* 1st Earl), 162

Aubrey, John, 398, 404n

Auschwitz: HT-R reports on trials, 348–50

Austria: HT-R visits with Xandra, 253–4

'Autopsy' (HT-R), 96

Ayckbourn, Alan, 479

Ayer, Sir Alfred Jules ('Freddie'): at Christ Church, 29; on Masterman, 36–7; Pakenham fails to convert to Catholicism, 48; friendship with HT-R, 56–8, 61, 154; character, 57; denies taking Lindemann's bicycle, 59; and HT-R's protest against Munich Agreement, 68; cuckolded by Hampshire, 238–9; on clarity of expression, 101; returns to Oxford after war, 130; HT-R congratulates on appointment to Chair of philosophy, 157; and *Polemic* (magazine), 171; speaks at 1950 Congress for Cultural Freedom, 198–9; on TV 'Brains Trust', 295; resigns from Society for Anglo-Chinese Understanding, 366; *Language, Truth and Logic*, 57

Ayer, Renée, 239

Backhouse, Sir Edmund, 430–5
Baden-Baden, 40
Baden-Powell, Lieut.-General Robert, 1st Baron, 17
Baker, Richard, 515
Ball, George, 417
'Ballad of Sir Pakenham' (HT-R), 108
Balliol College, Oxford: HT-R teaches at, 53
Balsdon, Dacre, 341, 406
Banton, Michael, 149
Baring, Thomas, 179
Barnes, Susan, 388
Barraclough, Geoffrey, 256, 293, 347
Barrington-Ward, J.D., 31
Barrington-Ward, Robert, 31n
Basset, Father Bernard, SJ, 166
Bataillon, Marcel: *Érasme et L'Espagne*, 262
Bateson, F.W., 294
Batey, Keith, 419
Bathos (HT-R's juvenile magazine), 15
Baur, Hans, 477
Baverstock, Donald, 283, 344
Beadle, Gerald, 296
Beaulieu-sur-Mer, French Riviera, 307
Beaumont, Michael, 179, 386
Beaumont, Robert, 32, 71
Beaumont, Timothy (*later* Baron), 59, 179
Beaver (student newspaper), 401
Bedford-Franklin, Colonel (headmaster), 11
Beefsteak Club, 509–10
Belhaven Hill (school), Dunbar, 12–15
Bellagio (Italy): Rockefeller villa, 445
Bellarmine, Cardinal Robert, 166
Bellow, Saul, 522
Beloff, Max (*later* Baron), 44, 397, 404, 409
Bemersyde (estate), Scottish Borders, 224, 226, 237, 249, 254, 259
Beneš, Edvard, 177–8, 196
Benn, Tony and Caroline, 352
Bennett, J.A.W. ('Jack'): co-edits *The Poems of Richard Corbett* with HT-R, 261
Berenson, Bernard: marriage, 84; co-edits *The Golden Urn*, 96n; and David Hopkins, 153; background and career, 174–7; HT-R visits, 174, 176, 212; letters from HT-R, 176–7, 184, 189, 204, 212, 214, 255, 260, 272–3, 296, 298, 309, 539; and HT-R's travels, 177–80; HT-R praises Namier to, 195n; and HT-R's attendance at Congress for Cultural Freedom, 199; friendship with Hamish Hamilton, 200; gives HT-R letter of introduction to King of Sweden, 219; HT-R visits with Xandra, 232–3, 242, 270, 275; and HT-R's high morale, 239; and HT-R's attachment to

Xandra, 246–7; on HT-R's sexual inexperience, 247; and Xandra's divorce, 252; and HT-R's married life, 258; HT-R tells of lecturing in Paris, 267; and HT-R's visits to Germany to question released POWs, 270; describes HT-R, 275; HT-R criticises Eden's Suez policy to, 276–7; urges HT-R to write on Cromwell, 291; death, 318; HT-R defends against attack by Schapiro, 318–19; Sylvia Sprigge writes biography, 318; influence on HT-R, 414; HT-R's letters to published, 539
Berger, General Gottlob, 129, 131, 155, 220
Berlin: HT-R examines Hitler's bunker, 135–6; Wall collapses, 531
Berlin, Sir Isaiah: friendship with HT-R, 58; and HT-R's application for chair of Modern History, 195; introduces HT-R to Weidenfeld, 214; suggests HT-R publish article in *Atlantic Monthly*, 219n; on HT-R's lack of human intimacy, 223; meets Xandra with HT-R, 227; and HT-R's affair with Xandra, 247; supports HT-R against Marxist critics, 263; HT-R enquires about Finley, 264; and HT-R's differences with Hill, 275; appointed Chichele Professor of Social and Political Theory, 282; on contest for Regius Chair of Modern History, 282; Namier praises Taylor to, 286; praises HT-R's Inaugural Lecture, 297; entertains Shostakovich in Oxford, 300–1; HT-R consults over response to attack on Berenson, 318n; reviews first volume of Carr's history of Soviet Russia, 337; and funding of *Encounter*, 382; HT-R imagines holiday with, 399; HT-R meets in USA (1969), 408; in 'The Club', 410; and HT-R's accusation of Jewish opposition to Bhutto's honorary degree, 424; praises HT-R's Romanes Lecture, 531
Bernac, Pierre, 225, 300
Bernadotte, Count Folke, 216–22
Bernstein, Sidney (*later* Baron), 158
Berry, (Mary) Pamela *see* Huntly, Marchioness of
Bessie, Michael, 271
Besterman, Theodore, 343, 376, 388
Betjeman, (Sir) John: in wartime Ireland, 110
Beveridge, Sir William (*later* Baron), 75
Beves, Donald, 449, 488
Bhutto, Benazir, 422, 424–5
Bhutto, Zulfikar Ali, 420–5
Bible of Ghosts (HT-R; juvenile book), 12
Bielenberg, Peter, 170n
Binyon, Michael, 488, 490, 496

Birchfield (house), near Melrose, 226, 239, 259–60, 268, 307

Birkenhead, Frederick Smith, 2nd Earl of, 48, 50, 328

Birkenhead, Sheila, Countess of, 329

Blair, Tony, 179n

Blake, George, 386n

Blake, Robert, Baron: at Gridiron Club, 46; tutorship at Christ Church, 145–7; biography of Disraeli, 168; accompanies HT-R on continental tour, 173; teases HT-R over wealth, 189; opposes Stone's promotion, 194; supports HT-R's application for chair of Modern History, 195; edits Field Marshal Haig's diaries, 223; marriage, 238; and HT-R's marriage, 252; meets Waugh, 256; opposes Finley's appointment to Christ Church, 264; supports Macmillan for Oxford Chancellor, 313, 317; on Alan Clark, 323; on Scottish Enlightenment, 343; and Tynan's staging of *Soldiers*, 383; as supposed author of review of Carlos Thompson's Churchill book, 387–8; signs letter on academic freedom, 404; as supposed 'Mercurius Oxoniensis', 405; elected Fellow of British Academy, 409; invites HT-R to join 'The Club', 410; as Provost of Queen's, 418; and HT-R's scepticism over Backhouse, 432; and HT-R's unpreparedness for lectures, 441; suggests HT-R spend time at Bellagio, 445; life peerage, 446; introduces HT-R to Lords, 447; favours Blunt's expulsion from British Academy, 450; contributes to *Festschrift* for HT-R, 464n; supports proposed honour for HT-R, 466; and takeover of *The Times*, 467; and HT-R's view of Mrs Thatcher, 521; as candidate for Oxford Chancellorship, 523–4

Bland, J.O.P., 432, 435

Bletchley Park: Government Code and Cipher School, 80–2, 88, 93–5; Whaddon Hunt enters, 103–4; personal relations and tensions at, 106–7

Bloch, Marc, 267

Blom-Cooper, Louis, 355

Blunden, Edmund, 56, 370

Blunt, Anthony, 95, 449–50, 465

Boase, T.S.R. ('Tom'), 303–4, 312

Bodley, Sir Thomas, 184n

Bolt, Robert, 362–5, 384; *A Man for All Seasons*, 362

Bonham Carter, Mark (*later* Baron), 291

Bonhoeffer, Dietrich, 171

Bookseller, The (magazine), 294

Borkenau, Franz, 199

Bormann, Martin: speculations on whereabouts and fate, 133, 135, 244, 485; signs Hitler's will, 139; Genoud controls literary estate, 214, 216; death confirmed, 245; records Hitler's Table-talk, 302; forged documents on, 476; and Hitler's 'archive', 477

Boswell, James, 472

Boughton, Northamptonshire, 153

Boulder, Colorado, 441

Bowes (Charterhouse schoolboy), 20, 23

Bowle, John, 293

Bowra, Sir Maurice: circle, 37–8, 61–2; absence at Harvard, 49; supports Lindsay in pre-war election campaign, 69; politics and ideals, 146; disparages HT-R to Waugh, 166–7; on HT-R's inhumanity, 223; on HT-R's attachment to Xandra, 251–2; at HT-R's wedding, 255; and HT-R's proposed postgraduate seminar, 267; and HT-R's candidacy for Regius Professorship, 280, 286n, 288; as Pro-Vice Chancellor of Oxford University, 312; and Macmillan's election to Oxford Chancellor, 316–17; HT-R entertains after Chancellorship election, 317; and SACU, 362–3

Boxer, Charles R., 279, 371 & n, 410

Boyle, Andrew: *The Climate of Treason*, 448–9

Boyle, Sir Edward (*later* Baron), 249, 276, 466

Braine, John, 400

'Brains Trust' (television programme), 295

Brandon, Henry, 353

Braudel, Fernand, 188, 267, 342, 464n

Braun, Eva, 133, 137, 165, 270, 476, 480

Brenan, Gerald: friendship with HT-R, 213, 271; *The Spanish Labyrinth*, 212–13

Brett, George P., Jnr, 167–8

Briggs, Asa (*later* Baron), 280, 345, 446

Briggs, Robin, 519

Brinton, Crane, 294

British Academy: HT-R elected Fellow, 409–10; Blunt's Fellowship, 450

British Bombing Survey Unit, 157, 181, 182n

British Broadcasting Corporation (BBC): HT-R broadcasts for, 168–9, 195–6, 211, 242, 250, 270, 289, 334, 344, 355, 411, 415

British Security Co-ordination, 438

British Union of Fascists, 34

Britten, Benjamin (*later* Baron), 300

Brodrick, Father James, 166–7

Brooke, John, 286

Broome, Captain Jack, 385

Bruce, Evangeline and David, 408, 413, 415

Bruern Abbey, Oxfordshire, 260

Bruno, Giordano, 166n

Bryan, Colonel Dan, 275

Bryant, (Sir) Arthur, 79, 104n

Buccleuch, Vreda Esther Mary, Duchess of, 239, 247, 255, 334

Buccleuch, Walter John Francis, 8th Duke of, 92, 239, 247, 252, 255, 334; *see also* Dalkeith, Earl of

Buchman, Frank, 48

Bueno de Mesquita, D.M., 145

Bullock, Alan (*later* Baron), 164, 215, 279, 412, 422, 446; *Hitler: A Study in Tyranny*, 215n

Burckhardt, Jacob, 263

Burgdorf, General Wilhelm, 139, 142

Burgess, Guy, 265–6, 449

Burke, Peter, 451

Burnet, Sir Alastair, 517

Burnham, James, 198–9

Butler, J.R.M., 171

Butler, Samuel, 38–9, 55, 102, 120, 128

Butterfield, Sir Herbert, 256, 332, 359, 456, 458, 511, 513

Caccia, Harold (*later* Baron), 158–9

Calladine, Chris, 473

Callaghan, James (*later* Baron), 442

Calvinism, 369, 389

Cambridge: HT-R lectures in, 359; HT-R's prejudice against, 515–16; *see also* Peterhouse

Cambridge Review, 529

Cambridge University Press, 520

Campion Hall, Oxford, 48–50

Canaris, Admiral Wilhelm, 113–14, 117–18, 126, 138, 180, 393, 437

Canfield, Cass, 271

Canterbury Club, Oxford, 58, 63

Caribbean: HT-R and Xandra cruise in, 476

Carlisle, Charles James Ruthven Howard, 12th Earl of (Lord Dacre of Gillesland), 447, 503

Carr, Edward Hallett, 256, 337–9, 359

Carr, (Sir) Raymond, 410, 521

Carrington, Peter Carington, 6th Baron, 446, 503

Carthusian, The (school magazine), 22, 190

Carver, John, 61

Cater, Jeremy J., 464n, 540

Catholics, Anglicans and Puritans (HT-R; essays), 528

Catto, Jeremy, 412, 431–2, 452, 464n, 538

Cave Brown, Anthony: *Bodyguard of Lies*, 437–8

Cecil, Lord David, 317

Cecil, Robert *see* Salisbury, 1st Earl of

Chadwick, Henry, 344, 419, 523, 525–6

Chadwick, Peggy, 523

Chalfont, Alun Gwynne Jones, Baron, 415

Chamberlain, Neville: appeasement policy, 66–8, 76; Feiling writes life of, 138

Chandos, Oliver Lyttelton, 1st Viscount, 384

Channon, Paul, 297

Charterhouse (school), Godalming, Surrey: HT-R wins scholarship, 15; HT-R attends, 17–23; Pat attends, 20, 28

Cherwell, Frederick Lindemann, Viscount ('the Prof'): at Christ Church, 33, 54; Churchill favours, 54; bicycle misappropriated, 58–9; recommends HT-R to Swinton, 97; and HT-R's dissatisfaction with SIS colleagues, 104–6, 112; peerage, 105; HT-R gives intelligence paper to, 114–15; praises *The Last Days of Hitler*, 160; HT-R shifts car, 210; watches Coronation on TV with HT-R, 228; at HT-R's wedding, 255; and *Soldiers* play, 384

Chicago: proposed lecture series (1957), 330; HT-R lectures in (1972), 428

Chiefswood (house), near Melrose, 307–8, 320, 444–5, 525

Childers, Erskine, 355 & n

China: HT-R visits with Bolt, 362–4; HT-R writes article on, 364–5; Mao's 'cultural revolution', 366

Christ Church, Oxford: HT-R wins scholarship to, 23, 27–8, 36; character and life at, 25–30; HT-R writes guide to, 25n; HT-R invited to apply for Studentship, 123; HT-R appointed to research lectureship, 130, 137–8; post-war changes, 144; HT-R's machinations at, 146–7; HT-R's studentship ratified, 146; HT-R leaves for Oriel, 299; HT-R's honorary Studentship, 452

Christie, Agatha, 285

Church of England: HT-R's view of, 124

Churchill, Randolph, 33, 317, 347, 384, 408, 428

Churchill, Sir Winston: Feiling helps, 36; friendship with Lindemann, 54; denounces Munich Agreement, 68; and Oxford by-election (1939), 69; and Bletchley Park intelligence, 88, 106; and conspiracies against Hitler, 114; 'Iron Curtain' speech (Fulton, Missouri), 178n; accused of having Sikorski killed, 383, 387; on supporting Church of England, 448n

Churchill, Winston, Jr, 317

Civil War (English): and gentry, 185; *see also* English Revolution

Clarendon, Edward Hyde, 1st Earl of: *History of the Rebellion*, 185, 208–9, 326, 528

Clark, Alan, 152, 177–8, 248, 288, 322–3, 442; *The Donkeys*, 322–3

Clark, Sir George Norman, 209, 288, 337, 409

Clark, Sir Kenneth (*later* Baron), 102, 152, 174–5, 201

Clark, William, 280

Clarke, Colonel Dudley, 118

Clarke, Virginia (Ashley), Lady (*later* Virginia Surtees), 239, 243, 249, 318

Clive, John, 464n

'Club, The', 410, 501, 524

Cobb, Richard, 464n

Coghill, Nevill, 84, 108

Cohn, Norman, 381

Coldstream, Sir William, 223

Cole, Sir Colin, 447

Colefax, Sibyl, Lady, 125, 154

Collier's (magazine), 275

Collins (publishers), 291, 412

Collinson, Patrick, 207

Committee on Social Thought, Chicago, 522

Common Cause (organisation), 400

Communism: and rise of fascism, 70, 172; and intellectual life, 171–2; HT-R mistrusts, 173, 202, 263–4; attacked at Congress for Cultural Freedom, 197–200; *The God that Failed*, 198; repressed in USA, 265; opposed by Common Cause organisation, 400; collapse, 533

Congress for Cultural Freedom, Berlin (1950), 196–200, 263, 382

Congress of the Intellectuals, Wroclaw (1948), 197, 263

Connolly, Cyril, 85, 98–9, 102, 154, 293

Conrad, Peter, 435

Conway Letters, 425

Cooper, Alfred Duff (*later* 1st Viscount Norwich), 54, 68

Cooper, Lady Diana (*née* Manners), 266

Cooper, Douglas, 307

Cooper, John P., 207, 271, 309

Corbett, Richard, Bishop of Norwich: *Poems* (ed. HT-R and J.A.W. Bennett), 261

Corbishley, Monsignor Charles, 127

Cork, Richard Boyle, 1st Earl of, 184n

Cornhill (magazine), 190

Cosgrave, Patrick, 457

Coulton, G.G., 72, 341

Counter-Reformation, 331

Country Life (magazine), 60

Court and Country antithesis, 203–4, 261, 310–11, 326, 372

Courtenay, Tom, 351

Cowen, Sir Zelman, 503

Cowgill, Major Felix, 81–2, 89–90, 93–7, 104, 107–8, 110–13, 115–16, 125

Cowling, Maurice: likens HT-R to Waugh, 167n; heads faction at Peterhouse, 456–61, 522, 529; views and principles, 458; takes credit for HT-R's election, 459; on admission of women to college, 473–4; and renewal of Croft's Fellowship, 508, 510–14; and HT-R's proposed commemorative lecture at Peterhouse, 515; inhabits cave of Adullam, 520; prose style, 521; and appointment of successor to HT-R as Master of Peterhouse, 523; and Peterhouse Fellows' snubbing of HT-R, 524–5; and election of HT-R to honorary Fellowship of Peterhouse, 526; HT-R satirises, 530; writes obituary of HT-R, 538; *Mill and Liberalism*, 529; *Religion and Public Doctrine in Modern England*, 458, 519–21

Cox, A.D.M. (David), 75

Craig, Gordon, 215, 531–2

Crick, (Sir) Bernard, 500

Croft, Hallard: calls on HT-R unannounced, 462; confrontation with HT-R, 507–8; Fellowship in jeopardy, 508, 511–13; snubs HT-R, 524

Crompton Bequest (charity), 362

Cromwell, Oliver, 254, 260, 272, 291, 298–9

Crossman, Richard, 316

Crumbling of the Monarchy, The (HT-R), 299, 301; *see also Great Rebellion, The*

Cukor, George, 351–2

Cumberlege, Geoffrey, 209

Curran, Charles, 416

Czechoslovakia: pre-war political situation, 66, 68, 70; HT-R visits, 177–8; Warsaw Pact forces invade (1968), 400

D-Day *see* Normandy landings

Dacre family, 2

Dacre, Rachel Douglas-Home, Baroness, 446–7, 503

Dacre of Glanton, Baron *see* Trevor-Roper, Hugh

Daily Mail, 441, 502

Daily Telegraph, The: HT-R reviews for, 518; obituary of HT-R, 539

Dalkeith, John Montagu Douglas Scott, Earl of (*later* 9th Duke of Buccleuch), 152–3

Dalyell, Tam: *Devolution: The End of Britain?*, 443

Dansey, Claude, 93

D'Arcy, Father Martin, 48–50, 57, 63, 167, 294

Dashwood, (Sir) Francis, 150–1, 179

Davenport-Hines, Richard, 539

Davies, G.S., 18; *Charterhouse in London*, 184

Davin, Dan, 209

Davison, Jim (HT-R's uncle), 31

Dawson, Dickie, 108–9

Dawson, Geoffrey, 31n

Deakin, (Sir) William ('Bill'), 44n, 188

Deane-Jones, Idris, 56

'Death of Hitler, The' (HT-R; report), 137

de Courcy, Kenneth, 386 & n

de Grey, Nigel, 107

de Grunne, Father Dominic, 255

de Havilland, Olivia, 351

Dell, Edmund, 208 & n

Dempster, Nigel, 526

Dennen, Revd Lyle, 459

Dennen, Xenia (*née* Howard-Johnston; Xandra's daughter): HT-R first meets, 239; Peters makes advances to, 306; helps mother in house, 319; HT-R disparages, 320; clinical depression, 336; writes thesis on Pushkin, 400; attends HT-R's LSE Oration, 401; marriage, 459; sees HT-R onto train, 537; HT-R able to see her face after eye operation, 537; speaks at HT-R's funeral service, 538

Denniston, Commander Alistair, 80, 82, 93, 106

Denniston, J.D., 30

Deutscher, Isaac, 365

de Zulueta, Father Philip, 315, 361–2

Dickens, Charles, 2, 16

Dickmann, Barbara, 499

Dickson, Lovat, 74, 79, 83, 159–60, 167, 182, 217

Did Six Million Really Die? (pamphlet), 439

Didcot: Old Rectory, 525

Disraeli, Benjamin, 168, 308

divorce: conventions in 1950s, 239

Don at Arms, A (HT-R; projected), 83

Dönitz, Admiral Karl, 132, 136, 138

'Double Cross' system (MI5), 117

Doubleday (US publishers), 272

Doughty, C.M.: *Arabia Deserta*, 212

Douglas, Lord Alfred ('Bosie'), 431

Douglas, Mary (ed.): *Witchcraft Confessions and Accusations*, 380n

Douglas, Norman, 180

Douglas-Home, Sir Alec (*later* Baron Home of the Hirsel), 359–60, 422, 436

Douglas-Home, Charles: succeeds Evans as editor of *The Times*, 468, 470–1, 516; and serialisation of 'Hitler diaries', 478–9, 482–3, 487; and HT-R's doubts over authenticity of Hitler diaries, 491–2, 496; caricatured in *Private Eye*, 502

Douglas-Home, William, 503

Dubček, Alexander, 400

Dublin: HT-R visits in wartime, 108–9; HT-R interrogated in, 109–11; HT-R lectures in, 275

Dulles, Allen W.: relations with HT-R, 171; and Warren Report, 351; *Day of the Whirlwind*, 170–1

Dumbarton Oaks Center for Byzantine Studies, 407

Dunbar, Nan, 405–6, 410–11, 443, 448

Dundas, R.H. ('Robin'), 34, 150, 252, 398

Durham University Journal, 185

Eagleton, Terry, 423

Eccles, Sir David, 316

Economic History Review, 187–8, 192–3, 195, 204–7

Economic History Society, 204–5

Economic Journal, 265

'Ecumenical Movement and the Church of England, The' (HT-R; Wiles Lectures), 412–13

Eddy, Paul, 493–4, 496

Eden, Sir Anthony (*later* 1st Earl of Avon), 276, 279, 281, 317

Eichmann, Adolf: trial and execution, 328–30

Einstein, Albert, 33

Elizabeth II, Queen: entertains HT-R, 475; reported rift with Margaret Thatcher, 517

Elizabeth, Queen of George VI (*later* Queen Mother), 147, 475

'Elizabethan Aristocracy, The: An Anatomy Anatomised' (HT-R), 193, 205, 207

Elliott, John, 271, 309, 311–12, 324–7, 347–8, 368, 381, 412, 530

Elphinstone, Andrew, 129

Elphinstone, John, 129

Elton, Geoffrey, 274, 380, 409, 410, 435; *Reformation Europe, 1517–1559*, 412

Elton, Godfrey (*later* Baron), 104 & n

Emory University, Atlanta, Georgia, 473

Encounter (magazine), 207, 262, 269, 318, 333–4, 339, 382, 393, 529

Engels, Friedrich, 185

England's Grievance Discovered (tract), 183

Engle, George, 191n

English Revolution (Puritan): Tawney on social changes in, 184–5, 207; Marxist historians on, 274, 310; HT-R's unpublished book on, 298, 309, 325–6, 359, 373–5; HT-R criticises Hill on, 368–9

Enigma ciphers, 81; broken by Bletchley, 97, 437

Enlightenment, 343, 369–70, 388; *see also* Scottish Enlightenment

Ensor, Sir Robert C.K., 68–9, 279

Epstein, Jason, 272

Erasmus, Desiderius, 261–3

European Witch-Craze of the Sixteenth and Seventeenth Centuries, The (HT-R), 381

Europe's Physician (HT-R), 539; *see also* Mayerne, Sir Theodore de

Evans Brothers (publishers), 170–1

Evans, Harold, 391, 393–4, 440, 468, 470–1, 516

Evans, Robert, 381

Evans-Pritchard, E.E., 379

Evening Standard, 499

Fairlie, Henry, 397

Falklands War (1982), 521

Farago, Ladislas, 480, 486; *The Game of the Foxes*, 436 & n, 437

Farrell, Charles and Kitty, 503

fascism: Marxist view of, 70; *see also* Nazism

Fath, Jacques, 225, 241

Fawtier, Robert, 186

Febvre, Lucien, 267

Feiling, (Sir) Keith, 36–7, 42, 45, 69, 104, 124, 138, 195

Ferguson, William: *Scotland's Relations with England*, 443

Fergusson, Sir James, 343

Fest, Joachim: *Speer: The Final Verdict*, 418

Finley, Sir Moses I., 264–5, 397

Firth, C.H., 150

Fischer, Fritz, 68n

Fisher, Geoffrey, Archbishop of Canterbury, 296

Fisher, H.A.L., 124

Fitzgibbon, Constantine, 171

Fitzgibbon, Esmée (*earlier* Howard-Johnston), 249

Fitzherbert, Claudia, 539n

Fleming, Ann (*formerly* Viscountess Rothermere), 37, 154

Fleming, Gerald, 439–40

Fletcher, Frank, 17–18, 21–2

Flodden, battle of (1513), 8

Florence: European University, 452

Floud, Jean, 461

Fontana History of Europe (series), 412

Foot, Paul, 368, 386

Ford, Gerald, 351

Ford Lectures (1957), 278, 286

'Forging of a Nation, The' (HT-R; unpublished lectures), 473; *see also Invention of Scotland, The*

Formosa (Taiwan), 367

Fortitude, Operation, 117

Foster, Michael, 58–9, 138

Fowler, John, 297n, 416

Fraenkel, Eduard, 39n

France: HT-R in, 61, 266–7, 301, 307, 318, 342–3; guarantees support for Poland, 70; surrenders (1940), 86; *see also* Paris

Franco, General Francisco, 53, 212, 456

Frankland, Noble, 182n

Franks, Sir Oliver, 312, 314–17

Fraser, Hugh, 442

Freiburg-in-Breisgau, 39–40

Freud, Sigmund, 61

From Counter-Reformation to Glorious Revolution (HT-R; essays), 530

Furneaux, Robin Smith, Viscount (*later* 3rd Earl of Birkenhead), 297

Gage, Nicholas (*later* 8th Viscount), 270

Gaitskell, Hugh, 316

Galbraith, John Kenneth, 165, 417

Galbraith, Sir Thomas ('Tam'), 442, 444–5

Galbraith, V.H., 194–6, 268, 278, 280, 286

Gale, George, 407, 457

Gale, Patricia, 457

Gallagher, Frank, 109–10

Galway, Ireland, 330–2

Gambier-Parry, Colonel Richard, 88–9, 105–6, 108

Gandhi, Indira, 422–3, 425

Gardiner, S.R., 150, 326

Garrod, H.W., 124, 130

Garton Ash, Timothy, 531–2

Gash, Norman, 134n

Gathorne-Hardy, Robert, 85, 98–9, 144, 164; *Recollections of Logan Pearsall Smith*, 144

Gaulle, Charles de, 173

Gebhardt, Karl, 157

Geigy, Rudolf, 430

'General Crisis of the Seventeenth Century, The' (HT-R), 309, 311–12, 376

Genoud, François, 214–16, 239, 302, 430, 441, 476

Gentry, 1540–1640, The (HT-R), 205, 207, 260–1, 310

Gentry controversy: 185–94, 202–8; *see also* Court and Country antithesis

George IV, King, 472

George VI, King, 147

'German Intelligence Service and the War, The' (HT-R; unpublished report), 126–7

Germany: rise of Nazism, 32; HT-R visits (1935), 39–41; as threat, 54; aggressiveness, 66–7, 70; responsibility for First World War, 68; advance in west (1940), 85–6; wartime power struggles, 113–14, 116; retreat (1944–5),

Germany—*contd*
125; administration under Nazis, 126; intelligence services' weaknesses, 126; surrenders
(May 1945), 129; HT-R visits after war, 131–2,
134–7, 270; under Allied military occupation,
131; *The Last Days of Hitler* not published
in, 162; opposition to Hitler and Nazism,
169–71; strategic bombing of, 181–2; divided,
197; and origins of Second World War, 332;
HT-R detects improvements in attitudes,
350; Chequers seminar to discuss reunification, 531–2

Geyl, Pieter, 240, 256, 339

Gibbon, Edward, 120, 122, 157, 164, 202, 212, 398

Gilbey, Father Alfred, 460

Giles, Frank: HT-R meets in Italy, 180; marriage, 266; in Paris, 266; asks HT-R to write
on Auschwitz trials, 348; and HT-R's scepticism on Warren Report, 352–3, 356; invites
HT-R to write on Greek political situation,
399; and HT-R's support for Bhutto, 424; as
editor of *Sunday Times*, 468–70; and Hitler
'diaries', 487–9, 491–4, 499

Giles, Lady Kitty, 502

Gill, Walter, 77–8, 80–2, 85, 88, 94, 116, 159

Gilmour, Lady Caroline, 259

Gilmour, Sir Ian (*later* Baron), 259, 276–7

Glanton, Northumberland, 3–4, 6

Glenveagh Castle, County Donegal, 178–9

Gloucester, Princess Alice, Duchess of, 252

God that Failed, The (Louis Fischer and others),
198

Goebbels, Joseph, 132–3, 135, 137, 139, 166, 168,
214, 383, 418; diaries, 440–1

Golden Urn, The (magazine), 96n

Golding, Martin, 473, 522

Gombrich, E.H., 401

Gombrich, Richard, 422–4

Goode (HT-R's schoolfellow), 15, 23

Goodfellow, Rosalind, 479

Goodhart, Arthur L., 252

Gordon Walker, Patrick (*later* Baron): at
Oxford, 33, 37, 53, 56; and 1939 Oxford by-
election, 69; elected MP (1945), 130

Göring, Hermann, 130, 138, 155, 158, 160

Gowing, Lawrence, 223, 516

Gowing, Margaret, 452

Grafton Club, Cambridge, 460

Granada Books (publishers), 476

Graves, Robert, 17, 401

Great Rebellion, The (HT-R): writing, 299, 308,
312, 324, 347–8, 373–4; Michael Howard and
Elliott read typescript, 325–7; argument, 326;
remains unpublished, 375

Great Tew, 528

Greece: HT-R holidays in, 211–12, 399; HT-R
visits with stepson James, 321; military coup
(1968), 399–400

Greene, Graham, 465

Greenhill, Denis, 436

Gregorovius, Ferdinand: *History of the City of
Rome in the Middle Ages*, 31

Greyfriar (school magazine), 23–4

Gridiron Club, Oxford, 46, 53, 56, 58–9

Gross, John, 469

Gunpowder Plot (1605), 187

Habakkuk, Hrothgar (John), 188, 192–3, 204–5,
422

Haddington, Sarah, Countess of, 252, 294, 307,
335

Haig, Field Marshal Douglas, 1st Earl, 47–8,
322–3, 335

Haig, George Alexander Eugene Douglas
('Dawyck'), 2nd Earl: friendship with HT-
R, 47, 63, 165, 224, 227, 236–7; mocked at
school for father's military leadership, 48; as
prisoner of war in Colditz, 129; congratulates
HT-R on *The Last Days of Hitler*, 164; and
HT-R's writing against Stone, 192; and HT-
R's failure to gain Modern History Chair,
195; and HT-R's writing on Sutton, 203; and
HT-R's relish for bellicosity, 208; and HT-
R's walking holiday in Greece, 212; HT-R
confesses depression to, 223; returns to
Bemersyde, 224; and Xandra's divorce plans
and relations with HT-R, 231–2, 235–8, 248,
249; 'attractive to pansies', 242; invited on
HT-R trip abroad with Xandra, 253; gives
away Xandra at wedding, 255; criticises Xandra's reluctance for domestic duties, 259–60;
at HT-R's Oxford Chancellorship party, 317;
and Derek Hill's house in Donegal, 332

Hailes, Sir David Dalrymple, Lord, 472

Hailsham, Quintin Hogg, Baron, 33, 69–70,
448, 501, 523

Hale, John, 412

Haley, Sir William, 315

Halifax, Edward Frederick Lindley Wood, 1st
Earl of, 66, 280, 312–13; *see also* Wood, Peter

Hallé, Kay, 408, 415

Hamilton, Sir Denis, 363, 467, 469

Hamilton, Hamish (publisher): aims to
publish HT-R, 158–9, 200–1; on HT-R's lack
of charity, 200; instructs HT-R never to
mention missed opportunity to publish *Last
Days of Hitler*, 201; on HT-R's sexual inexperience, 247; invited to HT-R's wedding,

255; and Xandra's devotion to Berenson, 270; asks HT-R to write on Cromwell, 291; HT-R cancels Cromwell contract with, 298–9

Hamilton, Yvonne, 200–1, 247, 255

Hampden, Anthony David Brand, 6th Viscount, 447

Hampshire, Sir Stuart: elected Fellow of All Souls, 43; friendship with HT-R, 58; relations with Renée Ayer, 238–9; wartime intelligence work, 96, 113, 125; on women, 98; interrogates Schellenberg, 126; and HT-R's proposed book on German opposition to Hitler, 169; and *Polemic* (magazine), 171; suggests broadcast talks on 'Human Nature in Politics', 242; and funding of *Encounter*, 382; knighthood, 446

Hancock, (Sir) William Keith, 188

Hanratty, James, 367–8

Hanslope Park, Buckinghamshire, 88

Hardie, Frank, 33

Harewood, George Henry Hubert Lascelles, 7th Earl of, 129

Harker, Oswald ('Jasper'), 78, 106

Harper and Row (US publishers), 271, 434, 437

Harrison, (Sir) Brian, 538

Harrod, (Sir) Roy, 33, 69, 206, 227, 252, 255, 269, 316, 419–20

Harrod, Wilhelmina (*later* Lady; 'Billa'), 33, 227, 244, 251, 255, 257, 269

Hart, Basil Liddell, 170, 323

Hart, Herbert Lionel Adolphus, 111, 132–3, 160–1, 436

Hastings, (Sir) Max, 539n

Healey, Denis (*later* Baron), 70

Heath (Sir) Edward: and Oxford by-election (1939), 69; and Macmillan's candidacy for Oxford Chancellorship, 315; succeeds Douglas-Home as Party leader, 360; entertains Bhutto, 422; congratulates HT-R on peerage, 446; as candidate for Oxford Chancellorship, 524

Heathcoat-Amory, Derick (*later* 1st Viscount Amory), 314

Heathcoat-Amory, Edward Fitzgerald ('Gerald'), 58–9, 119

Heaton, Eric, Canon of Salisbury, 296

Heidelberg, 40

Heidemann, Gerd, 482, 484–6, 488–9, 491–2, 494–7, 505

Henderson, Sir Nicholas, 496

Hennessy, Peter, 488

Henri IV, King of France, 427

Henry VIII, King, 25–6, 469

Henson, Herbert Henry, Bishop of Durham, 83

Hepburn, Katharine, 351–3

Herbert Samuel Lecture (1961), 330

Hermit of Peking (HT-R) *see Hidden Life, A*

Hertzberg, Arthur, 396

Hess, Rudolf, 480, 490, 495

Hesse-Darmstadt, Princess of, 449n

Hewins, Ralph, 217–18

Hexter, J.H. (Jack), 205, 207, 311

Heyman, Jacques, 527

'Hickey, William' (*Daily Express* columnist), 290

Hidden Life, A (HT-R; in US as *Hermit of Peking*), 375, 434–5

Highlight (TV programme), 283

Hilberg, Raul: *The Destruction of the European Jews*, 439

Hill, Christopher: supports Lindsay in 1939 election campaign, 70; in controversy over Tawney, 207; supports Hobsbawm in attack on HT-R, 263; suggests HT-R support Hobsbawm's application for US visa, 265; praises HT-R's 'Twice Martyred' review, 274; supervises Valerie Pearl, 274–5; congratulates HT-R on appointment to Regius Chair, 287; reviews HT-R's *Historical Essays*, 293; on editorial board of *Past and Present*, 311; on Puritan Revolution, 326; praises HT-R's views on Scottish history, 344; supports HT-R in Warren Report controversy, 356; and Society for Anglo-Chinese Understanding, 362; examines Macfarlane's thesis, 379; elected Fellow of British Academy, 409; congratulates HT-R on peerage, 446; *Economic Problems of the Church from Archbishop Whitgift to the Long Parliament*, 274; *The Good Old Cause* (ed. with Edmund Dell), 208; *Intellectual Origins of the English Revolution*, 368–9; *Puritanism and Revolution*, 294

Hill, Derek, 242, 332

Hillary, Richard, 120

Hillmore, Peter, 502

Hilton, Rodney, 53, 311

Himmler, Heinrich, 113–14, 118, 130–1, 138–9, 166, 216–18, 220, 263, 485

Historical Essays (HT-R; *Men and Events* in USA), 293–4, 337

'History of the English Ruling Classes, A' (HT-R; projected), 122

'History and Imagination' (HT-R; lecture), 452, 464

History of the University of Oxford (ed. Trevor Aston), 412

Hitchcock, Alfred, 158

Hitchens, Christopher, 423

'Hitler: New Light on a Dark Career' (HT-R), 142

Hitler, Adolf: rise to power, 32, 39, 54; and Chamberlain's peace efforts, 66–8, 76; as threat, 66–7; British view of, 69; occupies Czechoslovakia, 70; supposed conspiracy against, 113; deceived over Allied invasion of Europe, 117; orders execution of prominent British prisoners, 129; inner circle and gossip, 130; refuge and death in Berlin Bunker, 131, 155–6; HT-R investigates fate, 132–7, 155, 270; will found, 138–42; HT-R writes on last days, 155–6; July plot against, 156, 159, 169–71; sexual experiences, 165; German opposition to, 169; new table-talk found, 302; A.J.P. Taylor on, 332–3; HT-R's view of, 333–4; and doctors, 426; and extermination of Jews, 439; *Mein Kampf*, 68, 214, 333; *Table-Talk*, 213–16, 334, 476

Hitler 'diaries': HT-R asked to authenticate, 467–8; his initial scepticism, 476, 480; examines and believes to be genuine, 482–3; Murdoch buys, 483–4, 486–7; examined by Weinberg, 484–5; HT-R meets Heidemann, 485–6, 494–5; doubts, 489–91; Murdoch decides to publish, 494; disastrous *Stern* press conference, 494–8; HT-R under siege, 500–1; shown to be forgeries, 501; HT-R mocked and derided, 501–3; damage to HT-R's reputation, 503–4, 538–40

'Hitler's Place in History' (HT-R; lecture), 350

Hobhouse, Caro, 431, 434

Hobsbawm, Eric, 263, 265–6, 309–11, 409, 446, 450; ed. (with Terence Range): *The Invention of Tradition*, 473

Hochhuth, Rolf: *Soldiers* (play), 383–8

Hodgson, Godfrey, 354

Hoeppli, Reinhard, 430–1, 434

Hoey, Marion, 420

Hogg, Quintin *see* Hailsham, Baron

Hollywood, 351

Holocaust, 438–9

Homosexuality: early 1950s press campaign against, 243

Hood, Stuart, 344

Hooker, Sir Joseph, 206n

Hopkins, David, 149, 151, 153

Hopkins, Harry, 133

Horizon (magazine), 154

Hossbach memorandum (1937), 333

Hourani, Albert, 44

House and Garden (magazine), 300

House Magazine, The (House of Lords), 448

Howard, Sir Michael: on HT-R's return from war service, 147; reviews Alan Clark's book on Crete, 323; reads and praises typescript of HT-R's *Great Rebellion*, 325–6; succeeds HT-R as Regius Professor, 340, 452; attends HT-R's Oration at LSE, 402; congratulates HT-R on peerage, 446; contributes to *Festschrift* for HT-R, 464; Macmillan attacks for supposed security breach, 464–5; Thatcher invites to Downing Street, 521

Howard-Johnston, Lady Alexandra *see* Trevor-Roper, Lady Alexandra Henrietta Louisa

Howard-Johnston, Angela (*formerly* Huth; James's wife), 441, 479, 503

Howard-Johnston, Rear-Admiral Clarence Dinsmore ('Johnny'): marriage to Xandra, 225, 229; serves in NATO, 226; character, 229; and Xandra's relations with HT-R, 231–2, 235, 238–41; divorce from Xandra, 246–9, 252; extra-marital affair, 252; conflict with Xandra over ownership of Birchfield, 259–60; suspects HT-R's feelings for James, 322

Howard-Johnston, James (Xandra's son): HT-R first meets, 239; told of parents' separation, 247; helps mother in domestic work, 319; education, 320; HT-R's relations with, 320, 335–6, 342; holiday in Greece with HT-R, 321–2; and HT-R's article on Warren Report, 353; dines with Sparrow, 354–5; recommends books to HT-R, 367; academic career, 373; advises HT-R on magnum opus, 373; letter to mother as 'Aubrey', 398n; HT-R relates dream to, 399; Junior Fellowship at Dumbarton Oaks, 407; engagement and marriage to Angela Huth, 441, 479; and HT-R's reaction to mockery over Hitler diaries hoax, 503; attends ailing mother, 535; and HT-R's health decline and death, 536, 538

Howard-Johnston, Peter *see* Howard-Johnston, Philip

Howard-Johnston, Philip ('Peter'; Xandra's son), 239, 260, 320, 475

Howard-Johnston, Xenia (Xandra's daughter) *see* Dennen, Xenia

Huff, Toby E., 382

Hughes, R.L., 115

Hume, David, 346, 389, 472

Humphreys, Christmas, 296

Huntly, (Mary) Pamela, Marchioness of (*née* Berry), 154, 167, 247

Hurd, Douglas (*later* Baron), 531
Hurstfield, Joel, 304
Hutchinson (publishers), 217
Huth, Angela *see* Howard-Johnston, Angela

Iceland: HT-R visits, 159–60, 169, 180, 209
Independent Magazine, The, 529
Independent Revolution, The (HT-R), 299; *see also Great Rebellion, The*
Independent on Sunday, The, 532
Ingham, Wilfrid, 13–15
Interception and Intercepted Intelligence (HT-R report), 105
Interplay (US magazine), 397
Invention of Scotland, The: Myth and History (HT-R; posthumous), 471–3, 540
Ionides, Michael, 283
Ireland: HT-R visits in wartime, 108–10, 116; HT-R revisits, 178–9; HT-R reads paper in, 330
Irvine, A.L., 22–3
Irving, David: HT-R's relations with, 386, 388, 439–40; and Goebbels diaries, 441; declares Hitler 'diaries' fake, 487–8, 491, 497–9; Koch disparages, 497; *Accident: the Death of General Sikorski,* 384–6; *The Destruction of Dresden,* 385; *Hitler's War,* 439
Isis (Oxford undergraduate magazine), 368
Israel: HT-R visits, 243–4, 328–30
Italy: HT-R reports on for *Observer,* 173; HT-R visits, 178, 180, 232, 242, 245, 275, 318, 445; *see also* Berenson, Bernard

Jäckel, Eberhard, 440, 482, 487, 497, 499, 504
Jacob, Ernest, 64
Jacob, Sir Ian, 296
James I, King of England (James VI of Scotland), 427
Jebb, Sir Gladwyn (*later* Baron Gladwyn), 266, 316–18
Jenkins, Canon Claude, 45, 53, 56
Jenkins, Roy (*later* Baron), 410, 442; elected Chancellor of Oxford University, 524
Jesuits: HT-R attacks in *Last Days of Hitler,* 166; HT-R criticises martyr books, 273–4
Jewish Historical Society of England, 397
Jews: HT-R's view of, 396–7, 423–4; and Holocaust, 438–9
Johannmeyer, Major Willi, 139, 141–2, 349–50
John Paul II, Pope, 533
Johnson, Frank, 535
Johnson, Paul, 371
Jordan, W.K. ('Kitch'), 331
July Plot (20 July 1944), 156, 169–71

Kallin, Anna, 169, 256
Kannenberg, Artur, 137
Katz, David S., 464n
Kavanagh, Pat, 478
Kearney, Hugh, 330, 381, 405, 515
Kee, Robert, 334
Kell, Sir Vernon, 78
Kennan, George, 292, 394
Kennedy, John Fitzgerald: assassination, 347, 351–2
Kennedy, Robert, 357
Kenyon, John, 414
Kerensky, Alexander, 180
Kersten, Felix, 216–22, 240
Kilmuir, David Patrick Maxwell Fyfe, Earl of, 314–15
Kimber, William (publisher), 393
King, Martin Luther, 408
King-Hall, Stephen, 365
Kingsford, B.J.L., 209
Kingsmill, Hugh, 128
Kirkpatrick, Jeane, 500
Kissinger, Henry, 415
Klípa, Bohumír, 400
Klug, (Sir) Aaron, 473, 500, 515, 527
Knightley, Phillip, 391, 488–9, 492–3
Koch, Peter, 481–2, 484–6, 494–8, 505
Koestler, Arthur, 198
Korean War (1950–53), 197, 199
Kristol, Irving, 262
Kubizek, August, 489
Kujau, Konrad, 505
Kurti, Nicholas, 362, 366

Lambert, J.W. (Jack), 435
Lancaster, Nancy (*formerly* Tree), 297
Lancaster, Pat, 19
Lane, Mark, 353; *Rush to Judgement,* 357
Lasky, Melvyn J., 196, 199n, 262, 382, 397, 402
Last Days of Hitler, The (HT-R): influenced by Tacitus, 22; writing, 155–8, 183, 185; publication and success, 158–62, 164–5, 182, 186, 189, 375, 476, 505, 540; serialised in *Daily Telegraph,* 161; Catholics protest at anti-clericalism in, 165–7, 210; modified in second edition, 168; and Bernadotte, 216–17; third edition (1956), 270
'Last Days of Stalin, The' (HT-R; unpublished article), 275
Late Night Line-Up (TV programme), 415
Latimer, Geoffrey, 42
Laud, William, Archbishop of Canterbury, 52–3, 55–6, 64, 73–4, 101, 185, 528

'Laudianism and Political Power' (HT-R; essay), 529

Law, Richard, 152

Lawson, Nigel (*later* Baron), 398, 405, 407

Lea, H.C.: *Materials Toward a History of Witch-craft*, 377

le Carré, John, 392–4

Leigh, David, 501

Letters from Oxford (HT-R), 539

Levin, Bernard, 353–4, 366–7

Lewin, Ronald, 168

Lewis, Anthony, 355

Lewis, Clive Staples, 75n, 138

Liddell, Cecil, 110

Liddell, Guy, 78, 93, 95–6, 106, 111–12, 114, 118, 161

Life Guards: HT-R joins Territorial unit, 70, 76

Lindemann, Frederick *see* Cherwell, Viscount

Lindsay, Alexander Dunlop (*later* 1st Baron), 69–70

Linge, Heinz, 270

Linklater, Magnus, 487–8, 490, 493

Lisle Letters, 519

Listener, The (journal), 347, 359, 371, 391, 458

Lloyd-Jones, Hugh, 398, 405, 419, 441, 458, 509; (ed.): *History and Imagination* (HT-R's *Festschrift*), 464, 466

Lockhart, John Gibson, 308

Lockhart, Sophia (*née* Scott), 308

Loder's Club, Oxford, 46

logical positivism, 57

London Review of Books, 519

London School of Economics and Political Science: HT-R gives Oration (1968), 400–2

Long Crichel House, Dorset, 243

Long, Gerald, 468, 470, 483

Longden, 'Bobbie', 34

Longford, Elizabeth, Countess of (*née* Harman), 49, 255

Longford, Francis Aungier Pakenham, 7th Earl of: at Oxford, 33–4; conversion to Catholicism, 48; prepares for war, 76; on HT-R's *Archbishop Laud*, 83; HT-R satirises, 108; and HT-R's wartime visit to Ireland, 108–11; as Labour Minister, 145; attends HT-R's wedding, 255; invites HT-R to lunch at House of Lords, 335

Lopez, Robert S., 464n

Lorenz, Heinz, 139, 141

Los Angeles, 350–1, 353, 414

'Lost Moments of History, The' (HT-R; Romanes Lecture), 531

Lowe, John, Dean of Christ Church, 130, 147, 186n, 251, 305

Lowell, Robert, 370, 413

Lutyens, Sir Edwin, 50

Lynstead (house), Kent, 127–8

MacArthur, Brian, 477, 482n, 487, 492–4, 496, 499

Macaulay, Thomas Babington, Baron, 52, 338, 450, 472

McCallum, R.B., 317

MacCarthy, (Sir) Desmond, 99

McCarthy, Senator Joseph, 264–5

McConica, James, 341, 412, 464n

McCreary, Michael, 212

McEvoy, Air Chief Marshal Sir Theodore, 400

McEwen, Robin, 359–60

Macfarlane, Alan, 379–80; *Witchcraft in Tudor and Stuart England*, 380n

McFarlane, Kenneth Bruce, 207, 280, 282, 347

McIlhenny, Henry P., 178, 332, 413

McLachlan, Donald, 170

Maclean, Alan, 434

Maclean, Donald, 265, 449

Maclean, Melinda, 265

Macmillan, Daniel, 74

Macmillan, Harold (*later* 1st Earl of Stockton): and Oxford by-election (1939), 69; publishes HT-R, 74–5, 160–2, 190; publishes Arthur Bryant's *Unfinished Victory*, 79; supports HT-R in dispute over *The Last Days of Hitler*, 167–8; and Evans Brothers' proposal to HT-R, 170; as Prime Minister at time of HT-R's candidacy for Regius Professorship, 281, 286–9; Parliamentary statement on Kim Philby, 284; elected Chancellor of Oxford University, 313–17; on HT-R's Civil War book, 347; resigns as Prime Minister, 347; and HT-R's successful libel suit against Chalfont, 416; and proposed termination of lease on St Aldates house, 419; congratulates HT-R on appointment to Times Newspapers directorship, 428; congratulates HT-R on peerage, 446; attends celebratory dinner for HT-R at Oriel, 464; criticises Howard for supposed security breach, 464–5; and Croft affair at Peterhouse, 513; death, 523

Macmillan, Maurice, 313, 315, 324, 442

Macmillan (publishers), 74, 83, 158–9, 204–5, 210, 272, 298–9, 434, 519

Macpherson, James, 472, 506

'Maecenas Committee', 466

Magdalen College, Oxford, 63–4, 303–4

Magdalene College, Cambridge, 473n

Mallowan, Sir Max, 285

Maltby, Ted, 88, 95, 105–6, 108, 112

Manchester Guardian, 199

Manning, Cardinal Henry Edward, 234

Mao Tse-tung, 364, 366; death, 435

Margaret, Princess, 154, 475, 515

Mariano, Nicky, 174, 176, 219, 233, 244, 301, 307–8, 318, 354

Marlborough, John Churchill, 1st Duke of, 36, 100

Marshall Plan (for European Economic recovery), 177

Marx, Karl: Popper attacks, 172; HT-R's disenchantment with, 242, 263; and rise of capitalism, 331

Marxism: view of history, 37, 51, 172, 202–3, 263, 274, 310–11; HT-R's disillusionment with, 70; economic strategy, 173; *see also* Communism

Masaryk, Jan, 178

Masterman, Sir John C.: tutors HT-R at Christ Church, 36–7, 42; and HT-R's early academic career, 53, 64; and HT-R's teaching at Uppingham, 63; recommends Stuart for wartime intelligence work, 95; MI5 work in war, 117; takes sabbatical in India, 145; returns to university teaching after war, 147; as elector for Chair of Modern History, 195; and HT-R's marriage, 252; supports HT-R for Regius Professorship of Modern History, 280–1; as University Vice Chancellor, 281; and HT-R's philosophy of history, 293; attends HT-R's Inaugural Lecture, 296; opposes contested election for Oxford Chancellorship, 314; in 'The Club', 410; *The Double-Cross System in the War of 1939–1945*, 435–6

Masur, Norbert, 218, 220

Mathias, Adrian, 460, 462, 525

Maxwell, Robert, 139, 142, 467

Mayerne, Sir Theodore de, 425–8, 445, 519, 530, 539

Mayr-Harting, Henry, 424, 515

Maze, Paul, 63

'Medicine and Politics' (HT-R; lecture), 426

Mehta, Ved, 339

Melland, Brian, 94, 222

Menuhin, Yehudi and Diana, 225, 300

Menzies, Sir Robert, 317

Menzies, Major-General Sir Stewart ('C'), 92–3, 105–7, 112, 114–16, 158, 437–8

'Mercurius Oxoniensis', 404–7, 410, 457

Merton College, Oxford: HT-R's Junior Research Fellowship, 53, 55–6, 58

Mexico: HT-R visits, 301

MI5: in wartime, 78–80, 82, 87–9, 125; efficiency, 92; forms joint wireless committee with SIS, 95; differences with sister services, 96, 111–12; estimate of Vivian, 116; HT-R cooperates with, 116; 'Double Cross' system, 117; HT-R informs of Communist sympathisers, 266; on Boyle's *Climate of Treason*, 449

MI6 *see* Secret Intelligence Service

MI8 *see* Radio Security Service

Millar, Sir Oliver, 479

Miller, Sir Hubert, 96n

Miller, Karl, 371

Milne, Alasdair, 334, 345, 516

Milne, Ian ('Tim'), 93, 158

Milner, John, Bishop of Castabala, 234

Mincemeat, Operation, 116

'Mind of Adolf Hitler, The' (HT-R), 333–4

Mitford, Nancy, 342

'Modest Proposal, A' (HT-R), 60, 83

Moffett, Tom, 535

Momigliano, Arnaldo, 453n, 464n, 515

Monroe, Elizabeth, 284

Montagu Douglas Scott, Lady Victoria (*née* Haig; 'Doria'), 225n

Montagu, Ewen, 95, 438

Montgomery, Field Marshal Bernard Law, 1st Viscount, 133, 158

Moral Rearmament (Oxford Group; Buchmanites), 48

More, Sir Thomas, 1, 361–2, 469

Morell, Dr Theodor, 135

Morgan, John, 515

Morison, Samuel Eliot, 323

Morocco, 258, 271

Morrison, Dr G.E., 432

Mortimer, Raymond, 85, 243

Morton, A.L.: *A People's History of England*, 71

Morton, Desmond, 105–6

Moser, Sir Claus, 501

Mosley, Sir Oswald, 32, 34

Mountbatten, Admiral of the Fleet Louis, 1st Earl, 249

Mousnier, Roland, 376

Muggeridge, Kitty, 128, 165

Muggeridge, Malcolm, 128, 165, 394–5

Munday, Roderick, 461, 522

Munich Agreement (1938), 67–9, 276, 333

Murdoch, Rupert: acquires Times Newspapers Limited, 466–9; and Hitler 'diaries', 477, 479, 483–4, 486–7, 492–4, 502, 505; and appointment of editor to succeed Douglas-Home, 516–17; and HT-R's renomination as director of Times Newspapers Ltd, 516; defies print union and moves production to Wapping, 517; *Times* directors protest at report of

Murdoch, Rupert—*contd*
  Queen's rift with Margaret Thatcher, 517–18;
  requests HT-R's resignation, 518
Murray, John ('Jock'), 406
Mussolini, Benito: as threat, 54; overthrown,
  117; death, 160; HT-R declines to write on,
  200; forged diaries, 477, 488–9
Myres, John Nowell Linton, 35, 252

Namier, Sir Lewis B., 44, 64, 104n, 164, 195, 205,
  254, 286–8, 456
Nannen, Henri, 504n
National Theatre, 383–4
Nazi-Soviet Pact (1939), 93
Nazism: rise in Germany, 32, 39–41, 172; oppos-
  ition to, 169–70
Neale, John E., 192, 195, 205, 304
Needham, Joseph, 362, 366
Nef, John U., 522; *History of the British Coal
  Industry*, 73, 183
Neil, Andrew, 502, 517
Neill, Sir Patrick, 530
New Cambridge Modern History (series), 309
New Republic (journal), 221
New Statesman (journal), 68, 210–11, 245, 259,
  262, 264, 273, 317–18, 371
New York, 407, 413
New York Herald Tribune, 334
New York Review of Books, The, 371, 381–2, 394,
  398, 437–8, 521
New York Times: HT-R writes for, 142; funds
  HT-R's trip to Germany, 169; on A.J.P. Tay-
  lor–HT-R controversy, 334; on forged Hitler
  diaries, 500
New Yorker (magazine), 339
Newby, P.H., 144 & n
Newman, Cardinal John Henry, 234
News International Limited, 466–8, 470, 483,
  486, 517
Newsweek (US magazine), 484
Nicolson, Sir Harold, 293, 343
Nicolson, Nigel, 214
'No Popery and Wooden Shoes' (HT-R), 279
Noel-Baker, Philip (*later* Baron), 362
Norman, Edward, Dean of Peterhouse:
  Cowling devotes chapter to, 458; as former
  radical, 460; clashes with HT-R, 508–11;
  Cowling attempts to restrain, 512; frus-
  tration obvious, 513; opposes HT-R's can-
  didates for college office, 522; snubs HT-R,
  524
Normandy landings (1944): deception plan, 117
Norrington, Arthur, 209

Northumberland: Dukes of, 4; character and
  history, 8–10
Northumberland, Hugh Algernon Percy, 10th
  Duke of (1955), 251, 362
Northumberland, John Dudley, Duke of, 184n
Notestein, Wallace, 191, 193, 202, 207, 271–2, 374,
  389; *History of Witchcraft in England from
  1558 to 1718*, 376–7
Nuremberg: HT-R attends war crimes trials,
  157

Oakeshott, Michael, 458
Oberon, Merle, 351
Obolensky, Dimitri, 301, 378, 446, 464n
O'Brien, Conor Cruise, 500
Observer: HT-R writes on Europe for, 173, 177;
  HT-R reviews for, 210; HT-R disparages,
  266; on HT-R's criticism of Warren Report,
  354; and Hochhuth's Sikorski play con-
  troversy, 387; on Philby, 391; scepticism over
  Hitler 'diaries', 493
Odysseus: HT-R's 'letter' from, 529–30
Ogg, David, 45, 75–6, 344, 412
Old Rectory *see* Didcot
'Oliver Cromwell and his Parliaments' (HT-R),
  254, 260, 272
Ollard, Richard, 412, 519, 527
Oppenheimer, Peter, 419, 496
Oriel College, Oxford: character, 299–300; HT-
  R relocates to, 299; HT-R acts against
  student and academic unrest, 403–5; and
  'Mercurius Oxoniensis' letters, 407; redec-
  oration of Library, 416; dispute over
  window-boxes, 416–17; Provostship, 451;
  celebratory dinner for HT-R, 464; admits
  women, 473n
Orwell, George, 128, 173, 196, 204, 213
Ossian, 472, 505
Oswald, Lee Harvey, 351–3
Oxford: political activities in 1930s, 33–4; by-
  election (1939), 69–70; and impending war,
  69; Xandra and HT-R occupy house in (No.
  8 St Aldates), 269–70, 281–2, 300, 307, 419–20
Oxford Dictionary of National Biography: HT-
  R contributes to, 537
Oxford Magazine, 42, 60, 378
Oxford Mail, 282, 334, 406
Oxford Movement, 52, 299
Oxford University: HT-R studies at, 23; under-
  graduate life at, 28–9; King and Country
  debate (1933), 33; HT-R's disenchantment
  with, 124; HT-R returns to after war, 137, 144;
  Regius Professorship of Modern History,
  278–83, 286; Chancellorship election (1959),

312–17; student unrest and demands, 403–5; history of, 412; denies honorary degree to Bhutto, 421–3, 424; Chancellorship election to succeed Macmillan (1986), 523–4; *see also* individual colleges

Oxford University Press: holds perpetual copyright of Clarendon's *History of the Rebellion*, 208–9; publishes Christopher Hill, 274

Page, Denys, 30–1, 32n, 34, 36, 95, 112, 161, 265, 317, 419

Pagel, Walter, 426, 464n

Pakenham, Frank *see* Longford, 7th Earl of

Pakistan: HT-R and Xandra visit, 420–2, 424

Panorama (TV programme), 417

Pares, Richard, 282; ed. (with A.J.P. Taylor): *Essays Presented to Sir Lewis Namier*, 254n, 286

Paris: HT-R in, 266–7, 301, 318, 342–3; May events (1968), 399; *see also* France

Parker, Alastair, 191

Parker, Geoffrey, 412

Parkins, Robert *see* Peters, Revd Robert

Pasmore, Victor, 223

Past and Present (magazine), 309, 311–12

'Past and the Present, The' (HT-R; Oration at LSE), 401

Pattenden, Philip, 522

Paul, Prince of Yugoslavia, 275

Pearl, Valerie: thesis on City of London in Puritan Revolution, 274; HT-R praises Raab to, 341; and HT-R's Trevelyan lectures, 359; and Thomas More statue, 361; letters from HT-R, 373, 431; and HT-R's essay on witchcraze, 378; and HT-R's criticism of Scottish history, 388; and 'Prague Spring', 400; and 'Mercurius Oxoniensis', 405; and HT-R's experience of New York, 408; and HT-R's interest in Backhouse, 431; and HT-R's peerage, 446; and HT-R's view of Blunt, 450

Pears, David, 410

Pears, (Sir) Peter, 300

Pearson, Hesketh, 128

Pembroke, Sidney Charles Herbert, 16th Earl and Mary Dorothea, Countess of, 334

Pennington, Donald, 325 & n

Percy family *see* Northumberland: Dukes of

Perne Club (Peterhouse), 505

Perne Library, Peterhouse, 454, 463

Persson, Sune, 221

Perugia, 318

Perutz, Max, 526–7, 531

Peterhouse College, Cambridge: HT-R elected Master, xvii, 451–3, 461; character, 454–6,

458–61; HT-R's Mastership and reforms, 462–3, 471, 522; fund-raising Appeal, 463, 514; admits women, 473–4; and HT-R's misjudgment over Hitler diaries, 500–1; Croft affair and HT-R's disputes with colleagues, 507–13; seventh centenary celebrations, 515, 529; Chadwick succeeds HT-R as Master, 523, 525–6; HT-R snubbed in Combination Room and Parlour, 524–5; HT-R elected Honorary Fellow, 526; Pope John Paul II discusses with HT-R, 533–4

Peters, A.D. (literary agent), 210, 258, 272, 291, 298–9, 359, 390, 519

Peters, Revd Robert (i.e. Parkins), 302–6, 434

Petrie, Sir David, 106, 111–12, 259

'Philby: A Ruthless Journey' (BBC television documentary), 415–16

Philby Affair, The (HT-R), 393, 465–6

Philby, Harry St John, 395

Philby, Kim: wartime intelligence work, 93, 96, 125, 146; dismisses 'Canaris and Himmler' report, 113–14, 118; Blake works for, 146; resigns from intelligence service, 265; accused of being spy, 284, 436; HT-R in Iraq with, 283–4; defects to Moscow, 391–2, 437; HT-R writes on, 393–5, 465–6; TV documentary on, 415; and 'fourth man', 449; *My Secret War*, 96, 113, 394

Philip, Prince, Duke of Edinburgh, 475

Picasso, Pablo: 'Guernica' (painting), 70

Pickering, Sir Edward, 468, 470, 477, 489

Pirenne, Henri, 184

Plas Teg, North Wales, 2–3

Plumb, Sir John H., 409, 410, 412, 450, 466 & n, 516

Plunder of the Arts in the Seventeenth Century, The (HT-R; lecture and published book), 413

Pocock, J.G.A., 207

Pogge von Strandmann, Hartmut, 504–5

Polemic (journal), 171–3

Pope-Hennessy, (Sir) John, 94

Popper, Sir Karl: *The Open Society and its Enemies*, 138, 172, 483

Portugal, 212, 268

Postan, Michael, 192–4, 204–7, 359, 453, 462

Potter, Dennis, 368

Poulenc, Francis, 300–1

Powell, Anthony, 37, 128, 315, 521

Powell, Charles, 531–2

Powicke, Sir E. Maurice, 286, 409

'Prague Spring' (1968), 399–400

Prchal, Edward, 383–5

Prescott, Orville, 294

Prestwich, John, 145, 188, 192

Prestwich, Menna, 188–9, 412

Princes and Artists: Patronage and Ideology at Four Hapsburg Courts, 1517–1633 (HT-R), 414

Pritchett, (Sir) Victor S., 290

Private Eye (magazine), 386, 451, 501, 514, 521, 539n

Problems of Communism (US publication), 263

Protectorate of Oliver Cromwell, The (HT-R), 299; *see also Great Rebellion, The*

Protestantism: ethic, 72–3, 297; and capitalism, 272, 331; economic and social advancement, 331

Pryce-Jones, Alan, 247 & n, 294

Puritanism, 274, 294, 368–70, 528

Purver, Margery, 340

Queen (magazine), 368

Question Time (radio programme), 211

Quinton, Anthony, Baron, 521

Raab, Felix, 341–2

Rabb, Theodore K. ('Ted'), 408

Radio Analysis Bureau (RAB; *later* Radio Intelligence Service, RIS), 89, 94, 112–13, 115, 117–18, 125

Radio Intelligence Service (RIS) *see* Radio Analysis Bureau

Radio Security Service (RSS), 78–82, 85, 87–9, 95, 105–6, 113, 117

Ramsbotham, Major Peter, 132, 135, 139–41, 161, 170, 342, 415

Ratcliffe, Michael, 435

Rattansi, Piyo, 339–40, 464n

Read, Conyers: *Mr Secretary Cecil and Queen Elizabeth*, 259n

Reay, Aeneas Alexander Mackay, 13th Baron, 240

'Recall to Religion, The' (HT-R), 52

Recognizances for Debt (documents), 183–4, 186–7, 189, 193

Red Brick Cottage, Bruern Abbey, 260, 266

Rees, Sir Richard, 204–5

Rees-Mogg, William, Baron, 467–8

Reformation: as political movement, 71–2; HT-R's view of, 123, 272

Reilly, Sir Patrick, 96, 125, 292, 393, 535

Reitlinger, Gerald, 438

Reitsch, Hanna, 168

Religion, the Reformation and Social Change (HT-R; collection; *The Crisis of the Seventeenth Century* in USA), 376, 380–1, 519

'Religion, the Reformation and Social Change' (HT-R; essay), 331, 376

'Religious Origins of the Enlightenment, The' (HT-R), 369, 376, 426

Relton, H. Maurice, 74–5

Renaissance Essays (HT-R), 519

Ribbentrop, Joachim von, 158

Richardson, John, 307

'Rise of Christian Europe, The' (HT-R: TV lectures), 345–6; published as book, 346–7

Robbins, Lionel Charles, Baron, 401–3

Robens, Alfred, Baron, 428, 467–8

Roberts, Ernie, 363

Robertson, T.A. ('Tar'), 79–80, 125, 134, 438, 446

Robinson, Joan, 365–6

Rockefeller Foundation, 445

Rolfe, Frederick ('Baron Corvo'), 433

Roll, Sir Eric (*later* Baron), 428

Roman Catholicism: conversions to, 48–9; HT-R attracted to, 49–50, 127; and anti-clericalism in *Last Days of Hitler*, 166–7; HT-R's mistrust of, 169, 173; HT-R writes on 19th-century revival in England, 233–4, 251, 254, 261; similarity to Communism, 264; economic and social stagnation, 331; and Thomas More statue, 361–2

Romanes Lecture (1988), 530

Roper family, 1–2

Roper, Cadwallader Blayney (HT-R's great-grandfather), 2

Roper, Sir John *see* Teynham, Baron

Roper, William (16th century), 1, 469

Roper-Dixon family, 127

Roper-Lumley-Holland family, 127

Rose, Kenneth, 503

Rosebery, Archibald Philip Primrose, 5th Earl of, 431

Rosenthal, Tom, 519

Rothermere, Esmond Cecil Harmsworth, 2nd Viscount, 154

Rothschild, Jacob (*later* 4th Baron), 153, 270

Routh, Dennis, 43–4

Routh, Martin Joseph, 43n

Rowse, A.L.: at Christ Church, 27; criticises Masterman, 36; elected Fellow of All Souls, 44; on deaths of contemporaries, 70–1; reviews Morton's *People's History of England*, 71–2; and HT-R's *Archbishop Laud*, 75, 83, 361; character and qualities, 100; suggests HT-R write on Marlborough, 100; on writing history, 185; reads HT-R's article attacking Stone, 192; HT-R suggests for book on Elizabeth I, 271; and All Souls Wardenship, 355; relations with HT-R, 360–1, 398; objects to HT-R's review of Gibbon biography, 398; elected Fellow of British

Academy, 409; attacks HT-R over Hitler diaries misjudgment, 500; *A Cornish Childhood*, 100

Rozek, Edward, 441 & n

Runciman, Sir Steven, 279–81, 413

Russell, Alys (*née* Smith), 143–4, 174, 206n

Russell, Bertrand, 3rd Earl, 84, 96n, 352

Russell, Conrad, 5th Earl, 519

Russell, John, 102, 144, 414

Russell, Leonard, 265, 393

Russell of Liverpool, Edward Frederick Langley Russell, 2nd Baron, 328, 368

Russia *see* Soviet Union

Rutherford, Miss (school matron), 13–14

Ryle, Gilbert: friendship with HT-R, 56–7, 64, 67; in Newcastle, 64, 76; endorses Lindsay's by-election manifesto, 69; sees Picasso's 'Guernica', 70; reads proofs of HT-R's *Archbishop Laud*, 76; intelligence war work, 95, 106; reads 'self-appreciations' from Pearsall Smith, 96; on HT-R's meeting with Swinton, 97; on clarity of expression, 101; attends War Cabinet office meetings, 117; report on *Abwehr* sabotage department, 118; character and temperament, 121; appointed Waynflete Professor of Metaphysical Philosophy, 125; debates against hunting, 154; reads proofs of *The Last Days of Hitler*, 160; *The Concept of Mind*, 125

St Aldates, Oxford (No. 8): Xandra and HT-R occupy, 269–70, 281–2, 300, 307; proposal to end HT-R's lease thwarted, 419–20

St Andrews University, Scotland, 344, 388

St Margaret's, Westminster: HT-R denounced from pulpit (1940), 83; (1949), 83n

Salisbury, Robert Cecil, 1st Earl of, 260–1

Samuel, Herbert, Viscount, 330

Sayle, Murray, 391

Schacht, Hjalmar, 214

Schapiro, Leonard, 401

Schapiro, Meyer, 318

Scharffenburg, Johan, 221

Schellenberg, Walther, 126

Schlesinger, Arthur, Jr, 293, 407

Schmidt, Felix, 495

Schoenman, Ralph, 353–4

Schörner, Field Marshal Ferdinand, 139, 142

Schulte-Hillen, Gerd, 495

Scotland: HT-R's interest in Enlightenment history, 343–4, 388–9, 442; HT-R's hostility to, 411; HT-R opposes devolution, 442–3, 471; myth and history in, 471–2, 540

Scotland Act (1998), 444

Scotland Bill (and Act, 1977), 442; repealed (1979), 443–4

Scotsman, The (newspaper), 442, 445

'Scott and the Study of History' (HT-R; radio broadcast), 411

Scott, Sir Walter, 16, 308

Scottish Enlightenment: neglected by Scottish historians, 343; HT-R decides to speak on in St Andrews, 388–90; HT-R's essay arouses Nan Dunbar to a frenzy of irritation, 410; Edinburgh lecture, 442

Scruton, Roger, 457, 473

Searby, Richard, 483

Secker & Warburg (publishers), 519

Secret Intelligence Service (SIS; MI6): in wartime, 81, 87–90, 92, 437; organisation and direction, 92–3; HT-R criticises, 103–4, 127; and tensions at Bletchley Park, 106–7, 111–12; role, 114; and Philby's defection, 391–5; hostility to HT-R, 465–6

Sereny, Gitta: *Albert Speer: His Battle with Truth*, 418

Seton-Watson, Christopher, 403, 407, 451

Sharpe, Kevin, 464n

Sharpe, Tom: *Porterhouse Blue*, 459

Shawcross, Hartley, Baron, 384, 428

Shils, Ed, 522, 533

Short, Edward (*later* Baron Glenamara), 402

Shostakovich, Dimitri, 300–1

Sicherheitsdienst (SD), 113, 118

Sicily: invasion deception plans, 116–17

Sikorski, General Wladyslaw, 383–7

Sillitoe, Sir Percy, 259

Silone, Ignazio, 198–200

Silvers, Robert B. ('Bob'), 371–2, 382, 408, 413, 438, 519

Simms, Brian, 13–14

Simnel, Lambert, 513n

Simpson, Cuthbert, 305

Sinclair, Sir Archibald (*later* Viscount Thurso), 69

Sissons, Michael, 519, 527

Sitwell, Ann, 34

Sitwell, Sir Osbert, 99

Skinner, Dennis: Peterhouse Dean compared to, 510

Slater, Humphrey, 171

Smith, Alic, 279–81

Smith, Major Burrows, 170

Smith, Janet Adam, 210, 259, 343, 371

Smith, Logan Pearsall: HT-R confesses to on being propositioned in Avignon, 35; experiences supernatural vision, 51n; admires

Smith, Logan Pearsall—*contd*
HT-R's *Archbishop Laud*, 84; friendship with HT-R, 84, 98; background and interests, 94–5; introduces John Pope-Hennessy and HT-R, 95; capricious behaviour, 97–8, 103; changes will, 97, 99; letters to HT-R, 97, 119; sends books to HT-R, 99–101; HT-R writes portrait of, 101; teases HT-R for fox-hunting, 104; advises HT-R on future career, 119–20; mocks HT-R's beliefs, 124; death and new will, 143–4; HT-R writes Hitler book for, 157, 164; recommends the *Conway Letters* to HT-R, 425; *Trivia*, 84, 101–2, 120, 232; *Unforgotten Years*, 85

Smyth, Canon Charles: denounces HT-R, 83n

Snow, C.P., Baron, 513–14

Sobieski Stuarts (John and Charles Allen): *Vestiarium Scoticum*, 472–3

Society for Anglo-Chinese Understanding (SACU), 362–7

Somerville, William, 60

Southern, Richard, 280–2

Soviet Union: blockades Berlin (1948), 197; releases German POWs, 270; and Stalin's death, 275; HT-R visits, 292

Spain: HT-R visits, 212–13, 258, 268–71, 335

Spanish Civil War, 53, 212–13

Sparrow, John Hanbury Angus, 38, 314, 354–6, 365, 404, 406, 410, 419

Spectator, The (journal), 68, 71, 73, 259, 265, 276, 398, 402, 443, 449, 457; 'Mercurius Oxoniensis' letters, 404–7

Speer, Albert, 136, 165, 417–18, 480; *Inside the Third Reich*, 417

Spencer, Albert Edward John, 7th Earl, 151

Spender, Sir Stephen, 32, 58, 262, 382

Spiegel, Der (German magazine), 386–7, 487n

Sprigge, Sylvia, 180, 318

Stalin, Joseph, 113–14, 133, 177, 314; death, 270, 275; and Sikorski's death, 383

Stancliffe Hall (school), near Matlock, Derbyshire, 10–12

Stannard, Martin, 167n

Stark, Freya, 321

Stauffenberg, Count Claus von, 169–70

Steel, David (*later* Baron), 360, 444

Stephens, David, 280, 312–15

Stephenson, Sir William, 438

Stern, Fritz, 531–2

Stern (German magazine): and Hitler 'diaries', 476–8, 480–2, 484–7, 490–1, 493–500, 502, 505

Stevens, Sir Roger, 219

Stevenson, Revd Colin, 305

Stevenson, William: *A Man Called Intrepid*, 438

Stewart, J.I.M., 398

Stone, Lawrence: relations with HT-R, xvii, 186, 188–90; studies history at Oxford, 145; praises HT-R's *Last Days of Hitler*, 164; character and career, 186–8; conflict with HT-R, 191–3, 202, 372, 379–80, 382; congratulates HT-R on appointment to Regius Professorship, 287–8; campaign against *TLS* anonymous reviews, 294–5; on editorial board of *Past and Present*, 311; and HT-R's supervision of McConica, 341; article in *New York Review of Books*, 371–6; Princeton Chair, 372, 408; reviews HT-R's witchcraft book, 381; praises HT-R's *From Counter-Revolution to Glorious Revolution*, 530; 'The Anatomy of the Elizabethan Aristocracy', 187–8, 190–2, 202, 206; *The Crisis of the Aristocracy, 1558–1641*, 372, 378; 'The Elizabethan Aristocracy – A Restatement', 193, 205

Stone, Norman, 504, 531

Storch, Hillel, 220

Stoye, John, 39

Strachey, Oliver, 82, 95

Straw, Jack, 404

Stuart, Charles: with HT-R in wartime intelligence, 95, 125; hunting, 95; and HT-R's post-war return to Oxford, 144; replaces Masterman at Christ Church, 146; and HT-R's completion of *The Last Days of Hitler*, 159, 161–2; and HT-R's journey to Czechoslovakia, 177; and HT-R's reminiscence on Canaris, 180; HT-R comments on Stone to, 188; supports HT-R's application for chair of Modern History, 195, 281; marriage, 238; and Ford Lectures (1957), 278; supports Macmillan for Oxford Chancellorship, 313; in 'The Club', 410; and lease on St Aldates house, 418; and HT-R's thirtieth wedding anniversary lunch, 516; and HT-R's proposed candidacy for Oxford Chancellorship, 524

Stubbs Society, Oxford, 185–6, 189

Stumpfegger, Dr Ludwig, 135

Suez crisis (1956), 276–7

Summers, Anthony, 357

Sun, The (newspaper), 517

Sunday Express, 283

Sunday Telegraph, The: HT-R reviews for, 518; on German reunification, 532

Sunday Times, The: HT-R writes and reviews for, 210–12, 243–4, 256, 258, 268, 270–1, 283,

285, 301, 328, 349–50, 363–5, 367–8, 379, 399, 440; declines HT-R's review of Alsop book, 265; on HT-R's appointment to Regius Professorship, 289; and HT-R's investigation into Kennedy's death, 353–6; on Society for Anglo-Chinese Understanding, 366; investigates Philby, 391–3; serialises Goebbels diaries, 441; sold to News International, 466, 470; and forged Eva Braun diaries, 476; and Hitler 'diaries', 477, 483, 487–8, 490–4, 498, 502; reports rift between Queen and Margaret Thatcher, 517; HT-R discontinues reviews, 518; printing errors, 518

Surtees, Robert S., 47, 60

Sussex, University of, 344–5

Sutherland, Lucy (*later* Dame), 287

Sutton, Thomas, 183–7, 190–1, 203, 537

Swann, Kenneth, 54, 119

Swann, Michael, Baron, 451, 503

Sweden: and Bernadotte's role in war, 216–19, 221

Sweet-Escott, Bickham, 383, 386

Swinton, Philip Cunliffe-Lister, Viscount (*later* 1st Earl), 87, 96–7, 115

Sykes, Norman, 278

Symons, A.J.A.: *The Quest for Corvo*, 433n

Syon Park, 251, 362

Tacitus, 22, 169

Tate, Nicolas, 151

Tatti, I (house) *see* Berenson, Bernard

Tawney, Richard Henry: promotes Weber's work, 72; qualities and influence, 72–3, 185; Stone and, 145, 187, 191, 194; on economic pressures and social change, 184–5, 191; HT-R criticises, 202–8, 272; protests against personal censure, 206; 'Rise of the Gentry', 202–3

Taylor, A.J.P.: teaching Fellowship at Magdalen, 64; praises HT-R's *Last Days of Hitler*, 168; applies for chair of Modern History, 195–6; character and qualities, 196, 279–80; attends 1948 Congress of the Intellectuals, 197; congratulates HT-R on Franco article, 212; praises HT-R's introduction to *Hitler's Table-Talk*, 215–16; retains college post after divorce, 239; declines invitation to HT-R's wedding, 255; delivers Ford Lectures (1955–6), 278; disappointed in contest for Regius Professorship of Modern History at Oxford, 279–83, 286–8; rift with Namier, 288; congratulates HT-R for attack on Toynbee, 291; suggests HT-R write on Cromwell, 291; reviews HT-R's *Historical Essays*, 294; on

Hitler, 332–4; television debate with HT-R, 334; television lectures, 345; on Carr's *The Twenty Years' Crisis*, 338; Ved Mehta describes, 339; Klípa appeals to, 400; elected Fellow of British Academy, 409; and Blunt's Fellowship of British Academy, 450; denied honour, 466; reviews HT-R *Festschrift* (*History and Imagination*), 466; on HT-R's expertise on Hitler, 505; *The Hapsburg Monarchy*, 75n; *The Origins of the Second World War*, 332–3; *The Struggle for Mastery in Europe, 1848–1918*, 409

Taylor, Brigadier Telford, 328

'Teach Yourself History' series, 100

Tedder, Marshal of the RAF Arthur William, 1st Baron, 158, 181

Terry, Anthony, 494, 496

Teynham barony, 1–2

Teynham, John Roper, Baron, 1, 204

Teynham, Kent, 127

Thames and Hudson (publishers), 346–7

Thatcher, (Sir) Denis, 531

Thatcher, Margaret (*later* Baroness): votes for Macmillan as Chancellor, 316; not awarded honorary degree, 423; HT-R's representations on Bhutto's behalf, 425; elected Prime Minster, 444; offers HT-R peerage, 446; given the impression that Keith Thomas was extremely left-wing, 452; HT-R dubs her 'Margarita Antarctica', 521; HT-R shaken by what she says at dinner party, 521; presides over Chequers seminar to discuss German reunification, 531–2

Thistlethwaite, Richard, 364

Thomas, Hugh (*later* Baron), 413, 521, 523

Thomas, Keith, 378–81, 390, 446, 452, 539; *Religion and the Decline of Magic*, 381

Thomas the Rhymer (Thomas of Ercildoune), 24

Thomas, William, 464n

Thomas, Vanessa, Lady (*née* Jebb), 413, 521

Thompson, Carlos: *The Assassination of Winston Churchill*, 387

Thomson Corporation, 466

Thomson, Roy (*later* Baron), 428, 466n

Times The: supports Franks for Oxford Chancellorship, 315; HT-R opposes Scottish devolution in, 442; sold to Murdoch's News International, 466–71; and Hitler 'diaries', 477, 483, 488, 490, 492, 496, 502, 516; moves to Wapping, 517; obituary of HT-R, 538

Times Literary Supplement, The, 206, 208, 294, 374, 519, 530

Times Newspapers Limited: HT-R appointed 'National' Director, 428; sold to Murdoch, 466–8; and Hitler 'diaries', 478–9, 484, 504–5; HT-R reappointed as director, 516

Tomalin, Claire, 469, 517–18

Tonight (TV programme), 283

Toynbee, Arnold Joseph, 172, 240, 339; *Study of History*, 206, 255–6, 289–91

Toynbee, Philip, 397, 435

Travis, Commander Edward, 106–7

Trefusis, Violet, 342–3

Trevelyan Lectures (Cambridge, 1965), 359

Trevor family, 2

Trevor, Sir John, 2

Trevor-Roper family: social status, 6

Trevor-Roper, Lady Alexandra Henrietta Louisa (*née* Haig; *then* Howard-Johnston; 'Xandra'): pre-marriage affair with HT-R, xvi, 230–7, 239–43, 250; meets HT-R, 108, 226–7; background, 225; first marriage and children, 225–6, 229; correspondence with HT-R, 227–31, 247, 268, 284–5; divorce from Johnny, 231–2, 246–50, 252–3; visits I Tatti, 232, 242, 270, 275; pregnancies by HT-R and miscarriages, 234, 236, 240–1; questioned by Howard-Johnston, 240–1; doubts over marriage to HT-R, 249–50; invited to royal garden party, 250–1; introduced into Oxford society, 251; meets HT-R's parents, 253; trip to Austria with HT-R, 253–4; church marriage to HT-R, 254–5; stays with Harrods, 255, 269; house – hunting, 257–8, 269; investment income, 258; marriage relations, 258–9, 284–6, 306, 319–20, 336; brother Dawyck criticises, 259–60; occupies Red Brick Cottage, 260, 266; spends time with children at Birchfield, 268; occupies No. 8 St Aldates, Oxford, 269–70, 281–2, 300, 307, 419–20; visits Russia with HT-R, 292; on HT-R's *Historical Essays*, 294; at HT-R's Inaugural Lecture, 297; entertains musicians in Oxford, 300–1; in Paris, 302, 342; loses weight, 306, 336; money disputes with HT-R, 306; acquires Chiefswood (house), 308; family and home life, 319–20; and Alan Clark's *The Donkeys*, 322–4; neglects to write to HT-R in Israel, 329; in Donegal, 332; social life, 334–5; innocence and gaffes, 335–6; in Spain with HT-R, 335; health deterioration and breakdown, 336–7; resents HT-R's relations with son James, 336; on HT-R's slowness in finishing book on Civil War, 347; in USA with HT-R, 350–1, 407, 413; votes for McEwen in by-election, 360; receives anonymous phone-call, 367; dislikes David Irving, 386; and redecoration of Oriel College Library, 416–17; complains against termination of lease on St Aldates house, 419; visits Pakistan with HT-R, 420–1, 424; in Boulder, Colorado, 441; and HT-R's life peerage, 446; and HT-R's proposed Provostship of Oriel, 451; knocked down by car, 451; at Peterhouse, Cambridge, 452; invited to Windsor Castle, 475, 479; on Caribbean cruise, 476; and press demands on HT-R over Hitler diaries, 499; attends HT-R's Perne Club lecture, 505–6; organises concert for Peterhouse seventh centenary, 515; thirtieth wedding anniversary, 516; compiles index to HT-R's *Renaissance Essays*, 519; and HT-R's proposed candidacy for Oxford Chancellorship, 523; moves to Old Rectory, Didcot, 525; suffers Alzheimer's disease and strokes, 535; death, 536

Trevor-Roper, Bertie (HT-R's father): social status, xvii, 6; birth, 2; medical career, 3–5; qualities and interests, 5–6; relations with children, 5; burned as Father Christmas, 7; religious indifference, 9; meets Xandra, 253; and wife's death and funeral, 354; death, 442; suffers blackouts, 533

Trevor-Roper, Charles (HT-R's great-uncle), 2

Trevor-Roper, Charles (Richard's son), 3

Trevor-Roper, Claude (HT-R's uncle), 31

Trevor-Roper, George (HT-R's great-uncle), 2

Trevor-Roper, Hugh (Baron Dacre):

ACADEMIC/PROFESSIONAL LIFE: classical studies and learning, 21–3, 31, 34–6, 62; wins scholarship to and studies at Christ Church, Oxford, 23, 30, 34–6; fails election to All Souls Fellowship, 35, 43–5; historical studies as undergraduate, 36–7; awarded first-class honours degree, 42; accepts University Senior Scholarship, 45; writes thesis, 45, 52–3; and Marxist view of history, 51, 172, 202; researches and writes on Archbishop Laud, 52–3, 55–6, 64, 73–6, 83, 101; Junior Research Fellowship at Merton, 53, 55–6, 58; part-time teaching at Uppingham, 63; supports Rowse's view of Reformation, 72; war work in RSS intelligence, 77–82, 85, 89–97, 104–6, 111–12; relations with SIS and Bletchley colleagues, 92–5; role at Bletchley Park, 105–7; treason 'trial', 114–16; transferred to Menzies' supervision and promoted to Major, 115; wartime deception plans, 116–17; proposes writing history of English ruling classes, 122–3; interrogates German prisoners, 125–6, 129, 157; runs research branch of SHAEF's War Room, 125, 130; report on German intelligence services, 126–7; appointed to research lectureship at Christ Church, 130, 137–8; investigates Hitler's fate and will, 133–42, 155, 270; teaches Lawrence Stone, 145; Christ Church Studentship ratified, 146; teaching and tutoring, 147–50; earnings, 161–2 & n, 189, 216, 258; interest in July Plot against Hitler, 169–71; reports on European affairs for *Observer*, 173–4, 177; withdraws from British Bombing Survey Unit report, 181–2; appointed University lecturer, 185; as Censor, 186; attacks Lawrence Stone's article on Elizabethan aristocracy, 188, 190–4, 202, 207, 372n; proposes book on *The Army in Politics, 1649–1660*, 190; spoof lecture series, 190n; fails to be appointed to chair of Modern History, 195; criticises Tawney's thesis on gentry, 202–8; reviewing and journalism, 210–11, 243–4, 256, 258, 268, 273, 371, 518; writes introduction to *Hitler's Table-Talk*, 215; as authority on Third Reich, 222; pamphlet on Roman Catholic revival in England, 233–4, 251, 254; appointed Special Lecturer in modern history, 239; defers sabbatical year, 241, 250; on Cromwell, 254, 260, 272, 291, 298; co-edits *The Poems of Richard Corbett*, 261; writes on Erasmus, 261–3; lectures at École Pratique des Hautes Études, Paris, 266–7, 342–3; proposes historical reforms on lines of *Annales* school, 267–8; takes sabbatical year (1956), 271; study of Weber's thesis of capitalism and rise of Protestantism, 272, 291–2; applies to be Ford's Lecturer (1957), 278; successful candidacy for Regius Professorship of Modern History, 279–83, 286–7; attack on Toynbee, 289–91; philosophy of history, 293; Inaugural Lecture, 296–7; withdraws from Hamilton contract for Cromwell book, 298–9; moves to Oriel College, 299; authenticates new Hitler material, 302, 476; difficulties and delays in writing *The Great Rebellion*, 308–9, 312, 359, 373–5; proposes Macmillan for Oxford Chancellorship, 312–17; reports on Eichmann trial, 328–30; delivers Galway lecture (1961), 330–2; criticises Taylor's *Origins of the Second World War*, 333–4; critique of E.H. Carr, 337–9; encourages younger scholars and supervises research students, 339–41; interest in Scottish Enlightenment, 343, 388, 442; reports on Auschwitz trials, 348–50; criticises Warren Report on

Kennedy assassination, 351–8; delivers Trevelyan Lectures (Cambridge, 1965), 359; failure to write great book, 374–6, 414; and Sikorski conspiracy controversy, 383–7; on Philby and SIS, 390–6; delivers LSE Oration, 400–3; acts against student unrest, 403–5; elected Fellow of British Academy, 409–10; studies Sir Theodore de Mayerne, 425–8, 445, 519, 530, 539; appointed 'National' Director of Times Newspapers Ltd, 428; investigates and writes on Backhouse, 430–5; reviews books on British wartime intelligence, 437–8; lectures at University of Colorado, 441; speeches in Lords, 448; elected Master of Peterhouse, Cambridge, 451–2, 461, 522; retires as Regius Professor, 452–3; conflicts with Peterhouse colleagues, 462–3, 471, 507–11, 522; duties as Master of Peterhouse, 462, 471; receives *Festschrift* (1981), 463–4; security services' hostility to, 465; in dispute over Murdoch's acquisition of *The Times*, 466–71; on myth and history in Scotland, 471–2; agrees to admission of women at Peterhouse, 474; examines and accepts Hitler 'diaries', 478–86, 488–90, 504–5, 539–40; doubts over Hitler 'diaries', 491–500; attacked and ridiculed for misjudgment over Hitler 'diaries', 500–4; resigns from *Times* board, 518; publication of essays in five volumes, 519, 527–8; retires from Peterhouse, 522–3; considers standing for Oxford Chancellorship, 523; delivers 1988 Romanes Lecture, 530–1; invited to write memoirs for Weidenfeld, 534–5; posthumous publications, 539–40

HEALTH: eyesight, 8, 535–6; childhood illnesses, 12, 20; recurrent sinus problems and treatment, 85–7, 95, 209, 223, 242, 248, 329; depression, 96, 223, 269, 324; appendectomy, 124; breaks back in hunting accident, 179; suffers blackouts and injuries, 532–3, 536; hallucinations (Charles Bonnet Syndrome), 536–8; successful operation on eyesight, 537; decline, cancer and death, 538

INTERESTS & ACTIVITIES: juvenile writing, 12, 15, 23–4; early reading, 14–15; golfing and beagling, 20–1, 28; love of nature and countryside, 21, 64, 332; sketching and caricatures, 21, 24; drinking, 28, 46–7, 58–9, 61, 65; gambling, 28, 40–1; hunting and riding, 28, 59–60, 75, 77, 87, 103–4, 108, 112, 154, 179; political indifference, 32–3; club activities in Oxford, 35–6; keeps journal, 47, 342; loses belief in metaphysics and theology,

Trevor-Roper, Hugh:
INTERESTS & ACTIVITIES—*contd*
50–1; freemasonry, 51; lost work (?novel), 55; motor cars and motoring, 55, 57, 153, 163, 445 & n; buys and keeps horse (Rubberneck), 75, 103; keeps record of books read, 99–100; keeps notebooks, 102–3; attends War Cabinet office meetings, 117; investigates Roper family history, 127; buys Bentley, 163; radio broadcasts, 168–9, 211, 242, 250, 411; attends 1950 Congress for Cultural Freedom, 196–9; television appearances, 270, 283, 295–6, 334, 344, 355, 415; differences with Society for Anglo-Chinese Understanding, 362–7; campaigns to clear Hanratty of murder conviction, 368; attends Chequers seminar on German reunification, 531–2; letter-writing, 539

PERSONAL LIFE: pre-marriage affair with Xandra, xvi, 230–3, 235–7, 239, 241–3, 250; as sexual enigma, xviii, 35, 154; family background and name, 1–2; birth, 4; relations with parents, 5, 55, 237; childhood and home life, 7–10, 16; home education, 9–10; schooling, 10–15, 17, 19–23; religious scepticism, 11–12, 51–2, 71; wins scholarship to Charterhouse, 15; knowledge of German language, 31–2, 35, 41, 182, 504; undergraduate life, 36–9, 42; rejects orthodox morality, 38; sexual inexperience, 46–7, 247; attracted to Catholicism, 48–51; fined for careless driving, 59; and war threat, 66–7; on death of friends and contemporaries, 70–1; pre-war military training, 70, 76; relations with Logan Pearsall Smith, 84–5, 97–102, 119–20; apprehended as suspected spy, 86–7; loses possessions in bombing, 87; writes 'self-appreciation', 96, 98; attitude to women, 98; literary style, 101–3, 173, 212, 272, 324; Irish police visit and interrogate, 109–10, 116; considers future, 29, 120–2; views on religion and clerics, 123–4; social life and entertaining, 150–3, 334–5; feud with Waugh, 167, 244; opposition to Communism, 173, 202, 263–4; Oxford colleagues' opinion of, 189; combativeness, 208–9; damages Cherwell's car, 210; meets Xandra, 226–7; correspondence with Xandra, 227–31, 247, 268, 284–6; confesses to earlier love, 235; Xandra suspects of 'liking men', 236; partiality for undergraduates, 236; tolerance of homosexuality, 243; and Xandra's divorce, 246–7, 249–52; attends royal garden party, 251; church marriage to Xandra, 254–5; marriage

relations, 258–9, 284–6, 306, 319–20, 336; temporary stay at Red Brick Cottage, 260, 266; opposes aggressive policy towards Communist bloc, 266; linguistic skills and cosmopolitanism, 267; Berenson describes, 275; sets up trust, 291; money disputes with Xandra, 306; acquires Chiefswood (house), 308; attitude to stepchildren, 319–22; relations with stepson James, 319–22, 335–6, 342; appearance, 321; misses mother's funeral, 354; denies accusation of anti-Semitism, 396–7; meets and supports Bhutto, 421–5; on father's death, 442; opposes Scottish devolution and nationalism, 442–3, 471; in motor accident, 445; denied honour, 446, 466; life peerage (as Baron Dacre of Glanton), 446–7; denies owning television set, 514 & n; Gowing portrait, 516; thirtieth wedding anniversary, 516; buys and occupies Old Rectory, Didcot, 525–6; audience with Pope John Paul II, 533; life in old age, 535–6; weeps at Xandra's entering nursing home, 536; death, 538; cremation and memorial service, 538

TRAVELS: in France, 20, 61, 266–7, 301, 307, 318, 342–3; visit to Germany (1935), 39–41; visits to Ireland, 108–10, 116, 178–9, 330; wartime tour abroad, 118; visits occupied Germany, 131–2, 270; holidays in Iceland, 159–60, 169, 180, 209; in Italy, 174–8, 180, 212, 232–3, 242, 270, 275, 318, 445; to Czechoslovakia with Alan Clark, 177–8; first visit to USA (1949), 179–80; walking holiday in Greece, 211–12; in Spain, 212–13, 258, 268–71, 335; visit to Israel, 243–4, 328–30; visits Austria with Xandra, 253–4; in Morocco, 258, 271; abroad without Xandra, 268–9, 284–5; tour of Middle East, 283–5; visit to Soviet Russia, 292; in Mexico, 301; returns to USA, 350–1, 407–8, 413–14, 428, 441; visits China with Bolt, 362–4; visits Formosa, 367; lecture tours in USA, 412–14; to Pakistan, 420–2, 424; on Caribbean cruise, 476

Trevor-Roper, Hugh (HT-R's grandmother's second husband), 2

Trevor-Roper, Kathleen (*née* Davison; HT-R's mother): marriage, 3; relations with children, 5–6, 55; character, 6; gambling, 6; social status and concerns, 6–7; religious conformity, 9; meets Xandra, 253; suffers stroke, 354; HT-R visits grave, 356

Trevor-Roper, Patrick (HT-R's brother; 'Pat'): birth, 4; schooling, 14, 20, 28; letters from HT-R at Oxford, 28, 37–8, 42, 47; medical studies at Cambridge, 37; HT-R warns of Nazism in Germany, 41; and HT-R's anti-clericalism, 52; and HT-R's war work, 77; and condemnation of HT-R's *Archbishop Laud*, 83; flat bombed in war, 87; wartime letters from HT-R, 108; offers HT-R and Xandra use of rooms, 239; at Long Crichel House, 243; provides evidence to Wolfenden inquiry, 243; no 'threat' to nephews, 243; as best man at HT-R's wedding, 252, 255; letter from HT-R in Israel, 329; in Africa during mother's final illness, 354

Trevor-Roper, Richard (HT-R's grandfather), 2

Trevor-Roper, Richard Dacre (HT-R's cousin), 2–3

Trevor-Roper, Sheila (HT-R's sister): birth, 4; home life, 7; character, 8; on HT-R's life peerage, 446

Trollope, Agnes (imaginary figure), 371–2, 379–80

Truscott, General Lucian K., 141

Turner, Graham, 147–8

Turpin, Kenneth, 300, 451

'Twice Martyred' (HT-R; review), 273–4

Tyacke, Nicholas, 412

Tynan, Kenneth, 147, 383–4, 386

Tyninghame (house), 252, 307, 334–5

Tz'u-hsi, Dowager Empress of China, 430, 435

'Ultra' intelligence, 80, 105, 116, 126–7, 437, 465

United States of America: HT-R first visits (1949), 179–80; anti-Communism in, 265; HT-R visits with Xandra (1964), 350; (1969), 407–8; and Warren Commission report, 351–2; HT-R's lecture tours in, 413–14

University College, Oxford, 75

University of South in Tennessee ('Sewanee'), 452

Uppingham school, 63

Urban, George, 531

Ushaw College, Durham, 127

Ussher, James, Archbishop of Armagh, 528

Utley, T.E., 457

Vanderbilt, Cornelius, Jr, 179

Vanderbilt, Mrs Cornelius, 179

Vatican: colloquium on collapse of Communism, 533

VE-Day (8 May 1945), 129

Venlo incident (1939), 88, 114

Vienna: HT-R visits as undergraduate, 32; *see also* Austria

Vietnam War, 367, 370, 399, 408; ends, 415

Vincent, John, 457

'Vision of Judgment, A' (HT-R; lost), 102

Vivian, Valentine, 93, 105–7, 110–12, 115–16, 125

Volkov, Constantine, 392 & n

Voltaire, François Marie Arouet, 343, 346, 369

Wakeham, John, Baron, 447

Wannamethee, Mom Luang Hiranyika, 479

'War Room' (SHAEF), 125, 130

Warbeck, Perkin, 413

Warren, Earl: Commission Report (on assassination of J.F. Kennedy), 351–8

Watkin, David, 460, 524–5

Watson, Steven, 130, 304, 378, 413

Waugh, Auberon, 405n, 502

Waugh, Evelyn: Catholicism, 49; D'Arcy criticises Ayer to, 57; criticises HT-R's *Last Days of Hitler*, 166–7; feud with HT-R, 167, 245, 256, 273–4; A.D. Peters acts for, 210; and HT-R's book on Catholic revival in England, 233; denounces HT-R's appointment to Regius Professorship, 288; suggests HT-R transfer to Cambridge, 453

Webb, Colin, 476–9, 483, 491–2, 499

Weber, Max, 190, 272, 291–2, 330–1, 389; *The Protestant Ethic and the Spirit of Capitalism*, 72–3, 297

Webster, Charles (medical historian), 340, 426

Webster, Sir Charles Kingsley, 182n, 278

Wedgwood, (Dame) Cecily Veronica, 76, 83, 298–9, 326

Weeks, Edward A., 102

Weidenfeld, George (*later* Baron): publishes *Hitler's Table-Talk*, 214–16; publishes *The Bormann Letters*, 216, 244; HT-R visits, 239; invited to HT-R's wedding, 255; commissions *The Age of Christian Princes* from HT-R, 312; offers fee to HT-R for memoirs, 534

Weidenfeld, Jane (*née* Sieff), 215, 255

Weinberg, Gerhard L., 484–5, 498, 504

Weinstock, Arnold, Baron, 463, 511, 514

Welch, Colin, 457

Wernham, R.B. (Bruce), 195

West, Dame Rebecca, 435

Westminster, Loelia, Duchess of, 300

Weymouth, Alexander Thynne, Viscount (*later* 7th Marquis of Bath), 270

Whaddon Hall (and Hunt), 89, 103, 154

Wheatcroft, Geoffrey, 539n

Wheeler-Bennett, Sir John, 78, 159, 170, 195

'Whig and Tory History' (HT-R; lectures), 359

White, 'Dick' (Richard Goldsmith): as head of MI5, 79, 259; as head of MI6, 79, 284; in wartime MI5, 79, 95, 111; on Vivian, 116;

White, 'Dick'—*contd*
recommends HT-R be sent to Middle East, 118; praises HT-R's report on German intelligence services, 127; heads Counter-intelligence in British Zone of occupied Germany, 131–2; and HT-R's study of Hitler's fate, 132–3, 155–6, 158–9, 161; and HT-R's hunting accident, 179; and HT-R's visit to China, 364; and funding of *Encounter*, 382; and Philby's defection to Moscow, 391–5; briefs Prime Minister on Masterman's 'Double Cross' book, 436; congratulates HT-R on peerage, 446; on Boyle's *Climate of Treason*, 449; opposes suppression of security information, 465

White, Henry Julian, Dean of Christ Church, 27, 31

Whiteman, Anne, 316

Whitley, John, 440

'Who Killed Kennedy?' committee (British), 352–3

Why I Oppose Communism (composite publication), 263

Wickman, Peter, 479–80, 484, 490–1

Wigg, George (*later* Baron), 393

Wilamowitz-Moellendorff, Ulrich von, 31, 41–2

Wiles Lectures (Belfast, 1975), 412–13

William Andrews Clark Memorial Library, Los Angeles, 350

Williams, Alwyn Terrell Petre, Bishop of Durham, 130

Williams, Desmond, 331–2

Williams, E.T. ('Bill'), 55n, 195

Wilmot, Chester, 170

Wilson, Charles, 477, 487, 517

Wilson, Harold (*later* Baron), 384, 392

Wilson, Thomas, 266

Windsor Castle, 475–6, 478

Winter, Paul, 340

Winterbotham, F.W.: *The Ultra Secret*, 437

Wiseman, Cardinal Nicholas Patrick Stephen, Archbishop of Westminster, 234

witch-craze and witchcraft, 373, 376–82

Wodehouse, (Sir) P.G., 80

Wood, Anthony, 404n

Wood, Natalie, 351

Wood, Peter, 46, 49–50, 56, 60, 63

Woodham-Smith, Cecil, 249

Woodhouse, Christopher Montague (*later* 5th Baron Terrington; 'Monty'), 323

Woodward, Sir E. Llewellyn, 43, 64, 195, 278

Wootton, David, 539

Worden, Blair: HT-R confesses early marriage prospect to, 235n; attends HT-R's graduate seminars, 381; writes chapter for *History of the University of Oxford*, 412; and HT-R's complaint of overwork, 428; and HT-R's writing on Backhouse, 434; and HT-R's life at Chiefswood, 444; and HT-R's Mastership of Peterhouse, 452, 455–8, 461–3, 522; and HT-R's leaving Oxford, 453; and HT-R's dispute with Murdoch, 469–70; encourages HT-R to republish essays, 519; and Cowling's convoluted passage on HT-R, 520; and Blake's rejection as Oxford Chancellor, 524; reads to HT-R in old age, 536; gives address at HT-R's memorial service, 538; defends HT-R's reputation, 539; edits HT-R's life of Mayerne, 539

Wordsworth, William, 15, 120

World War II (1939–45): outbreak, 77; HT-R's friends killed in, 119; victory, 125; A.J.P. Taylor on origins, 332–3; British Intelligence and deception in, 435–7; *see also* Radio Analysis Bureau; Secret Intelligence Service

Worlledge, Colonel J.P.G., 82, 88, 109, 116

Wormald, Brian, 459

Worsthorne, Sir Peregrine, 457, 509–10, 514

Wotton (house), near Aylesbury, 179n

Wright, Peter, 534

XX Club, Oxford, 154

Yadin, Yigael, 329

Yates, Dame Frances, 390–1, 414–15, 425–8, 445, 464n, 531

Young, Hugo, 487

Zander, Colonel Wilhelm, 139–40

Zeldin, Theodore, 149, 521

Zhukov, Marshal Georgi Konstantinovich, 132

Zia ul-Haq, General Mohammed, 425

Zinnemann, Fred, 362

Zionism, 244, 330

Zuckerman, Solly (*later* Baron), 147, 157–8, 161, 181, 255

/1240.

MERTON COLLEGE,
OXFORD.

20-12-39

Pat

Thank you for the p.c.

a use such a vulgar form)

a !). Since I last wrote,

has been complicated by two

ule. First, I have ~~been~~ heard

My dearest Xandra

How awful

filled w

ch an em

es.   The

mai

inst ofte

(sha

CHRI

o

My darling

I hav

at

The

Easter Vacation

Oxford. Lunch Merton.
To Windsor castle to stay.
Queen's dinner: Thai amb:
HC of E Caribbean; Ld + Lady
Lewin; Sir J. Miller;

Windsor castle. Motor to
Heathrow. Fly Zurich.
(X returns to Oxford)
meet Stern directors at
Handelsbank. Dine with them.
Stay Hotel Baur au Lac.
Zurich. Fly to London. Taxi

APRIL 1983

W
6

6.45
lorry's suit   12.15

Th
7